Sigrid Estrada

About the Author

MARTIN GILBERT has written more than sixty books and is one of the foremost historians of the twentieth century. In 1968, he was appointed official biographer of Sir Winston Churchill. He wrote six of the eight volumes of the landmark biographical series and also compiled eleven volumes of Churchill documents. In addition, he is the author of a definitive history of the Holocaust, a series of twelve historical atlases, and comprehensive studies of both World War I and World War II. Since 1962, he has been a Fellow of Merton College, Oxford (an Honorary Fellow since 1994). He was knighted in 1995. He lives in London.

A HISTORY OF
THE TWENTIETH
CENTURY

GREAT READING WHEN YOU HAVE
THE TIME —

BEST OF EVERYTHING IN THE NEW
MOVE —

ALL MY LOVE,
DAD

1/11/03

Hope that this will be
a useful reference —
Good luck, and fun,
with your new work.
Lots of love,
Mom

BOOKS BY MARTIN GILBERT

THE CHURCHILL BIOGRAPHY

Volume III: 1914–1916
Document Volume III: (in two parts)
Volume IV: 1917–1922
Document Volume IV: (in two parts)
Volume V: 1922–1939
Document Volume V: 'The Exchequer
 Years' 1922–1929
Document Volume V: 'The Wilderness
 Years' 1929–1935
Document Volume V: 'The Coming of
 War' 1936–1939

Volume VI: 'Finest Hour' 1939–1941
Document Volume VI: 'At the Admiralty'
 September 1939–May 1940
Document Volume VI: 'Never Surrender'
 May–December 1940
Document Volume VI: '1941: The
 Ever-Widening War'
Volume VII: 'Road to Victory' 1941–1945
Volume VIII: 'Never Despair' 1945–1965

Churchill: A Photographic Portrait
Churchill: A Life

OTHER BOOKS

The Appeasers (with Richard Gott)
The European Powers 1900–1945
The Roots of Appeasement
Children's Illustrated Bible Atlas
Atlas of British Charities
Atlas of American History
Atlas of the Arab–Israeli Conflict
Atlas of British History
Atlas of the First World War
Atlas of the Holocaust
The Holocaust: Maps and Photographs
Atlas of Jewish History
Atlas of Russian History
The Jews of Arab Lands: Their History
 in Maps
In Search of Churchill
The Jews of Russia: Their History in Maps
Jerusalem Illustrated History Atlas
Sir Horace Rumbold: Portrait of a
 Diplomat

Jerusalem: Rebirth of a City
Jerusalem in the Twentieth Century
Exile and Return: The Struggle for Jewish
 Statehood
Auschwitz and the Allies
The Jews of Hope: The Plight of Soviet Jewry
 Today
Shcharansky: Hero of Our Time
The Holocaust: The Jewish Tragedy
The Boys: Triumph over Adversity
First World War
Second World War
The Day the War Ended
Empires in Conflict: A History of the
 Twentieth Century 1900–1933
Descent into Barbarism: A History of the
 Twentieth Century 1934–1951
Challenge to Civilization: A History of the
 Twentieth Century 1952–1999

EDITIONS OF DOCUMENTS

Britain and Germany Between the Wars
Plough My Own Furrow: The Life of Lord Allen of Hurtwood
Servant of India: Diaries of the Viceroy's Private Secretary 1905–1910

A HISTORY OF
THE TWENTIETH
CENTURY

The Concise Edition of the

Acclaimed World History

MARTIN GILBERT

Perennial

An Imprint of HarperCollins*Publishers*

The Library of Congress has catalogued the hardcover edition as follows:
Gilbert, Martin.
History of the twentieth century, concise edition /
by Martin Gilbert—Concise ed.
p.   cm.
Includes bibliographical references and index.
Contents: v. 1 1900–1933 — v. 2. 1933–1951 —
v. 3. 1952–1999.
ISBN 0-688-10067-8
1. History, Modern—20th century. I. Title.
D421.G55 2001
909.82—dc21   2001032612

ISBN 0-06-050594-X (pbk.)
02 03 04 05 06 RRD 10 9 8 7 6 5 4 3 2 1

CONTENTS

ILLUSTRATIONS

LIST OF MAPS

INTRODUCTION

Some of humanity's greatest achievements took place in the twentieth century, and some of its worst excesses. It was a century of improvement in quality of life for millions of people, yet also a century of decline in many parts of the globe.

When the century began, some of its future tyrants were already embarked upon their destructive careers. At the same time, science and medicine were taking enormous strides forward. The motor car was in its infancy, and within a decade, aircraft would take to the skies. As in previous centuries, the high value placed on human life by religion and custom was in almost constant conflict with the savageries of war. Patriotism and imperialism were at a high point. And expectations of better things to come were rising.

The clash of nations and their alliances, the strivings of Empires and their collapse, and the struggles of nationalities and national groups, were central to the century. No year passed without human beings being killed in war, or struggling to recover from the ravages of war. 'It is called the century of the common man,' wrote Winston Churchill, 'because in it the common man has suffered most.' The often tragic fate of the 'common man', and woman and child, runs like a dark thread through these pages. There are also golden threads among them – the courage and perseverance of innumerable individuals, and the assertion of the equal rights of all nations, and of the rights of the individual, against the frequently crushing burdens of State oppression and military tyranny.

There were many national and international efforts by which the human race sought to control its own destiny and regulate its conflicts. Treaties and agreements, promises and armistices, seemed in almost every year to be the pointers of hope for the future. The century began with imperialism in the ascendant, and yet already under daily threat. As Empires tried to overcome that threat, national movements devised means of subverting them. The First World War was fought predominantly by the European Empires, each of which had established during the second half of the nineteenth century commercial dominance and territorial control over much of the globe. The rivalries between the great industrialized and militarized nations were to pit their peoples against each other.

The Empires which dominated the world when the century began had all dissolved by the time it ended. The Soviet Union, successor to the Russian Empire of the Tsars, survived longest, into the final decade of the century. Other national groupings, such as Yugoslavia, came into being as the century moved forward, but also broke up. On 19 December 1996, *The Times* listed the diplomats who had attended a memorial service in London on the previous day. They included the Ambassadors of Macedonia, Croatia, Albania, Lithuania and Ukraine, and the Chargé d'Affaires of the Slovak Republic. None of these six countries had existed as an independent entity in 1900.

Revolutions and revolutionaries everywhere strove to change the old order, and in the process often did not respect the rights which even the worst of the old orders had established. Indeed, the secret police regimes of the old order were not necessarily any worse, and were often more benign, than those by which they were replaced in the hope of a better tomorrow. Everywhere mankind strove for that better tomorrow, while not always preserving what had been achieved for today. The 'common man', the ordinary citizen, the soldier, the prisoner and the refugee are seldom named in the history books, yet it remains the century in which their lives have been transformed the most, sometimes for the good, sometimes for the very much worse.

This history explores the way in which the twentieth century, the culmination of many centuries of political and social evolution, was not the inevitable progress towards perfection that so many fighters for truth had assumed it would be. The twentieth century began, and ended, with war being fought somewhere or other on the globe, with troops in mortal combat, and with death and injury reported daily in the newspapers.

Much of the century was dominated by the struggle between the rule of law and lawlessness; between the rights of the individual and the destruction of those rights. In 1937 President Roosevelt asked, of the people of the world: 'Surely the 90 per cent who want to live in peace under law and in accordance with moral standards that have received almost universal acceptance through the centuries, can and must find some way to make their will prevail.' Roosevelt added: 'It seems to be unfortunately true that the epidemic of world lawlessness is spreading.'

The scale of the loss of human life in wars, civil wars and natural disasters did not diminish after Roosevelt's warning, indeed it escalated. There were the daily death tolls of the Sino-Japanese War, the Italian-Abyssinian War, the Spanish Civil War, the Second World War in all its component parts, and then the daily death tolls of the post-war conflicts, including the civil war in China, the Korean War, and the French wars in Vietnam and Algeria. More secret, but no less terrible, were the killings perpetrated by totalitarian regimes: the fate of millions of defenceless Russians, Chinese, Jews, Cambodians and Rwandans killed in cold blood is an almost unimaginable horror of these years.

The motor car also made its contribution to the suffering of the human species, as, on the roads, each year saw slaughter that would be shocking, even unacceptable, if it occurred in war. In the twenty-eight years between 1933 and 1961 almost a million United States citizens were killed in road accidents. These statistics relate to individual human beings, each of whom has a name, family, a career cut short, a life unfulfilled. Road deaths have been a persistent aspect of life in the twentieth century since before the Second World War.

There have been many victors in the twentieth century, but even for those countries that were victorious, suffering and loss, and the memory of harsh times and bitter lessons, have never been far from the surface. The struggles that emerged after both the First and Second World Wars were the struggles to prevent future war, to create a mechanism and state of mind conducive to the peaceful settlement of disputes. But the struggles, whether of nationalism in its extreme forms, or between the Communist and non-Communist world, or between the colonial rulers and those whom they ruled, repeatedly lurched towards violence, and the threat of violence. Ethnic hatreds also pulsated through the decades; in 1935 the British historian H.A.L. Fisher commented, almost in despair: 'An insane racialism threatens to rupture the seamless garment of civilization.'

The most forceful threat of destruction, which also proved the most powerful deterrent to destruction – emerging from the Second World War, and created during the war as a means of victory – was atomic power. This was a threat that led to intense anguish within democratic societies, where the anti-nuclear debate brought moral and medical arguments to bear upon the strategic arguments. It was the development of the Hydrogen bomb that led seven Nobel Prize winners, among them Albert Einstein, to call in 1955 for the renunciation of nuclear weapons by all governments possessing nuclear weapons, and for those governments 'to find peaceful means for the settlement of all matters of disputes between them'. The Nobel laureates stressed that 'a war with H-bombs might possibly put an end to the human race'.

In the last three decades of the twentieth century, television images brought every element of the global struggle to the homes and sitting rooms of hundreds of millions of people. The Vietnam War was the first, the Gulf War one of the last. Famine and civil war also came almost simultaneously to the screens of people thousands of miles away from the suffering, thrust, as it were, into their living rooms.

Every historian has his own perspective, derived from personal experiences and interest over many years, in my case over thirty-eight years of research and writing. Some events are central to any presentation of a historical period, and only a rash writer would omit them. This is true of many episodes in this volume, such as man's first airborne flight, the Russian Revolution of 1917, Hitler's coming to power, the rule and demise of Stalin or Mao Tse-tung, the dropping of the atom bombs on Hiroshima and Nagasaki, the assassination of President Kennedy, the Vietnam War, or man's landing on the moon. Hundreds more episodes are part of this narrative because they illustrate some aspect of the unfolding years. Events that made an impact at any given time may subsequently have faded from the public mind, but I have tried, in view of their importance when they took place, to include them, and also to include the names of those – now largely forgotten – who once bestrode the pages of the newspapers or whose images filled the television screens for their brief period of achievement or notoriety. Recurring anniversaries also present the historian with new material uncovered as a result of the upsurge in public interest and the testimony of those who were alive at the time, providing a bridge between those who witnessed events and subsequent generations whose lives have been unconsciously influenced by them.

General history can be as sharply focused as detailed studies. Over many years I have tried to interweave the wider sweep of events with the stories and names of those who made their contribution often in small corners or without fanfare. 'Lest we forget', the cry of pain that lies behind so many memorials and memorial meetings, is a testimony to the desire of the human spirit not to turn away from the individual, not to overlook the stories of individual heroism, suffering, achievement and hope. During my work on the history of the twentieth century it is the part of the individual on which I have tried to focus: not only individual actions, but the struggle for the rights of the individual, for civil rights and human rights, in every land. By the end of the century those rights were better understood, and more widely respected, than in earlier decades, but not universally. Every decade since the century began saw a diminution of human rights somewhere on the globe, as well as their advancement elsewhere. Real progress is not a law of nature; setbacks as well as progress can be found in each year covered by these pages. Gradually, human beings see their lives and livelihoods enhanced, even in countries such as the Soviet Union – now itself a thing of the past – where they had long been at the margin of national policy or ideology; and gradually the achievements of the century, including those in technology and medical science, become more and more widely available; but despite that, the struggles for a better life with which the century began do not end as the century ends, and, although the nature of those struggles has often changed, the search for a better life – for human fulfilment – will certainly challenge, frustrate and inspire the twenty-first century as well.

Martin Gilbert
Merton College
Oxford

15 February 2001

Author's Note

This single-volume history is a condensation of my three-volume history of the twentieth century, *Empires in Conflict* (spanning the years 1900–1933, and published in 1997); *Descent into Barbarism* (1933–1951, published in 1998) and *Challenge to Civilization* (1952–1999, published in 1999). In all, the three volumes amounted to 2,700 pages of text. In reducing this to 800 pages I have tried to be faithful to my original portrayal and perspective. Each volume contains its own acknowledgements, bibliography, maps and itemized index, which readers of this volume may wish to consult.

CHAPTER ONE

The First Decade
1900—09

As the twentieth century opened, wars were being fought on two continents: in Africa and in Asia. In South Africa, the Boer War was entering its eleventh week, the Boers, in their two independent republics, the Transvaal and the Orange Free State, having taken on the might of the British Empire in neighbouring Cape Colony and Natal. The first battle of 1900 in South Africa took place on January 6, when Boer forces tried to drive the British from their positions inside the town of Ladysmith, where 20,000 British troops had defended the besieged town for more than two months. Within a month Ladysmith was relieved, 500 British cavalrymen breaking through the Boer ring and galloping through the main street shouting, 'We are here!'

Another besieged town, Mafeking, was relieved in May. The rejoicing in London when this news reached the capital was so vociferous and enthusiastic that the verb 'to Maffick' – to celebrate without inhibition – entered the language and remained there for several decades. A month later, Pretoria, the capital of the Transvaal, was occupied. Britain had asserted its imperial power.

In China, 'Boxer' rebels, their full name meaning 'Righteous harmonious fists', acting in defiance of the Chinese imperial Government, were attacking foreigners and Christian missions wherever they could. In May 1900 they marched towards Peking under the slogan, 'Death and destruction to the foreigner and all his works'. On the last day of that month an international force of 365 marines reached Peking, with troops from the United States, Britain, Russia, Italy, France and Japan. Two weeks later the Boxers entered the city, destroying most of the foreign-owned buildings that were not within the protective zone of the foreign Legations. The city's Roman Catholic Church was burnt to the ground and Chinese Christians living near it were massacred. Austrians at their Legation managed to rescue a Chinese Christian woman who was being burned to death near their Legation wall. After the Third Secretary of the Japanese Legation was set upon and murdered, Japan announced that she could have 'no more communication with China – except war'.

Foreigners who could reach the security of their respective Legations were protected by the marines, and an international naval force was on its way. On July 28 the German Kaiser, William II, was present at the North Sea port of Bremerhaven when 4,000 German soldiers set sail for China. Wishing them good fortune, he declared: 'When you meet the foe you will defeat him. No quarter will be given, no prisoners will be taken. Let all who fall into your hands be at your mercy. Just as the Huns, a thousand years ago, under the leadership of Attila, gained a reputation in virtue in which they will live in historical tradition, so may the name of Germany become known in such a manner in China that no Chinaman will ever again even dare to look askance at a German.'

In the European Legations, under siege for three weeks, sixty-two Europeans were killed. Brought to China by sea, a combined force of 36,000 British, Russian, German, French and Japanese troops advanced on Peking. American troops also took part. On August 14, Russian and American troops attacked the central gates of Peking. British Indian troops were the first to reach the besieged Legations. Fighting continued around the Legations for another two days, when Japanese troops entered the Forbidden City. The siege of the Legations was over. In the subsequent savage battle for the nearby Roman Catholic Cathedral and the compound around it 400 Europeans were killed, 200 of them children from the orphanage inside the compound.

News of the scale of the killings in China took time to reach those who had despatched the expeditionary force. It was not until late in September that it was learned that at one Catholic mission far from Peking, four priests and seven nuns had been killed, and 1,000 Chinese Christians beheaded.

The twentieth century opened with working men in all industrialized countries determined to improve their situation by direct participation in the political process. In London on February 27, representatives of all the British working-class organizations founded the Labour Representation Committee. Its aim was to bring about 'the independent representation of working people in Parliament'. A quarter of a century later, the secretary of the committee, Ramsay MacDonald, became Britain's first Labour Prime Minister. At the end of the century, a sixth Labour government was in power, and with a substantial parliamentary majority.

In Austria-Hungary in 1900, the internal divisions of the Habsburg Empire – with its mixture of Germans, Czechs, Slovaks, Ruthenes, Poles, Hungarians, Roumanians, Serbs, Croats and Italians – were much in evidence. During a meeting of the Austrian Parliament that summer the Czech opposition members disrupted the proceedings by blowing penny trumpets, beating cymbals, and producing an array of catcalls. After seven hours of disruption the Prime Minister closed the session. In December 1900, after a ten-year absence, the Italian deputies resumed their seats in the Austrian regional Parliament in the Tyrol, having boycotted the assembly on the grounds that they could always be outvoted by the German-speaking deputies. On their return they insisted that their speeches and interjections, which they would only make in Italian, should be translated into German, and read out in full.

Not only in his Austrian dominions, but also in his Hungarian kingdom – the twin pillars of his Dual Monarchy – the Emperor Franz-Josef faced disaffection. Speaking in the Hungarian Parliament in Budapest, the Hungarian Prime Minister said he was prepared to take the necessary measures 'to assert the rights of Hungary and its independence'. Until the time came to do so, he added, 'let us husband our strength and keep our powder dry'.

The Russian Empire also faced internal strife. On April 23 a secret meeting was held in the Empire's Georgian province to celebrate May Day, and with it the hopes of the workers for an end to autocracy.

In the previous year's gathering, seventy workers had attended. In 1900 the number was 200. One of the speakers that day was Josef Dzhugashvili, a Georgian who had just been expelled from the Tiflis Theological Seminary, after five years studying to be a priest. He was in charge that year of Marxist propaganda among the Tiflis railway workers, and had indeed already made contact with them while at the seminary. Later he took the name Stalin – Man of Steel.

The leaders of the small, largely exiled, Russian Social Democratic Labour Party, which had been founded in 1898, were convinced that the nineteenth-century Marxist analysis, whereby the collapse of the hated capitalist system could only come about through class conflict, made revolution inevitable in the highly industrialized States. The Party's leader, Vladimir Ulyanov, known by his underground name of Lenin, had left Russia in 1900 after three years in exile in Siberia. From his exile in Switzerland, he built a centralized Party structure, determined to see the day when the Tsarist Empire would be no more.

In July the Senate of Finland, a Russian province since 1808, rejected an imperial manifesto making Russian the official language of Finland, a country in which only 8,000 out of 2,700,000 people spoke Russian as their native tongue. Only two years had passed since the suppression of a measure of Finnish autonomy and the exile of many Finnish national leaders. Despite this rebuff by the Finnish Senate, the power of St Petersburg seemed unchallengeable.

The Ottoman Empire was likewise troubled by political agitation and civil war among its non-Turkish and non-Muslim nationalities. In the province of Macedonia, whose ethnic mix of peoples gave its name to the French salad *Macédoine de fruits*, more than a hundred ethnic Bulgarians were murdered by local Greeks during 1900. The small, landlocked province was home to Turks, Serbs, Bulgarian Christians, Bulgarian Muslims (known as Pomaks), Roumanians (known as Vlachs, some of them Greek Orthodox, others Muslim), Greeks, Albanians (Christian and Muslim), and Albanianized Serbs (known as Arnauts).

Within Turkish Macedonia, the Bulgarian Christians actively resorted to the forcible conversion of the Muslim Pomaks to Christianity. In the neighbouring Turkish province of Albania, a local

Muslim chief ordered the murder of more than 200 Christians. A Christian village was set on fire and several Christians who had been taken hostage were murdered because no ransom was paid for them. In the distant eastern regions of the Ottoman Empire, Kurdish villagers attacked and murdered at least sixty Armenians, and possibly as many as 400, in 1900. Britain, one of its consular representatives in the region having been assaulted, protested vigorously. Nor was Britain itself untroubled by dissent. In September, Phoenix Park in Dublin saw a large Irish nationalist demonstration demanding Home Rule for Ireland, the abolition of 'landlordism' and the withdrawal of Irish political representation in the Westminster Parliament. But far more than political unrest, disease cursed the British Empire in 1900. In Hong Kong a hundred people a week were dying of bubonic plague that spring and summer. In India, during the course of a two-year famine, two million people died.

The year 1900 saw national rivalries in the realms of both sport and invention. The first modern Olympic Games to be held outside Athens was held that year in Paris. The table of gold medal winners was headed by France with twenty-nine, the United States with twenty, and Britain with seventeen. Austria-Hungary won four, Germany three and Russia none.

Inventions could both inspire enthusiasm and foreshadow conflict. In Britain, William Crookes found the means of separating uranium. In the United States, the revolver was invented. In Germany, on the evening of July 2, the first airship, the creation of Count Zeppelin, made its trial flight, travelling a distance of thirty-five miles. Man had found a means of powered travel through the air.

On 22 January 1901 Queen Victoria died. She had reigned for sixty-one years. At her funeral procession in London, five sovereigns, nine crown princes or heirs apparent, and forty other princes and grand dukes rode on horseback to pay their respects. In southern Africa the British conquest of the two Boer republics was almost complete, but Boer guerrilla fighters continued to evade capture, fought on, and refused to surrender. In an attempt to force the guerrillas to give up, the British military authorities seized thousands of Boer women and children, whose menfolk were still fighting, and detained them in seventeen special camps, known as 'concentration camps'. Conditions in the camps were bad, with almost no medical facilities, and little food. A further thirty-five camps were set up for black Africans who worked on the farms of the absent fighters, so they too would be unable to plant or harvest crops, or look after livestock. The death toll in the camps was high, and was denounced in Britain by the Liberal Party leader, Henry Campbell-Bannerman. 'When is a war not a war?' he asked, and gave the answer: 'When it is carried on by methods of barbarism in South Africa.' The government instituted improvements and the death rate fell, but 28,000 Boer women and children died in the camps, as did 50,000 Africans.

Britain clashed with Turkey in 1901, when the Turkish Sultan tried to extend his control to the small sheikhdom of Kuwait, in the Persian Gulf. When he tried to land a Turkish military force, the Sheikh of Kuwait, who had made a treaty with Britain two years earlier, appealed for help to his new ally. A British warship arrived in the Persian Gulf and announced it would open fire if the Turkish forces tried to land. This naval threat was effective; and the Sultan abandoned his claim to sovereignty over Kuwait. Ninety years later, Britain was among a coalition of powers which made war on Iraq for having overrun the small, and by then oil-rich, sheikhdom.

In Europe, the rivalries of the great Empires were still in embryo, as were some of the weapons of war. In 1901 Britain launched its first submarine: within ten years, fifty-six had been built. The motor car, also in its infancy, was likewise to transform war, with the evolution within fifteen years of the armoured car and the tank. Another development with significance for the whole century, both in peace and war, took place on 11 December 1901 when, in Newfoundland, the electronics engineer and inventor Guglielmo Marconi received by wireless telegraphy what he called 'faint but conclusive' signals from his transmission station in Cornwall. It was henceforth possible, *The Times* reported, to solve 'the problem of telegraphing across the Atlantic without wires'.

On 6 September 1901 the President of the United States, William McKinley, who was visiting a Pan-American Exhibition at Buffalo, was shot by an anarchist with whom he was shaking hands. McKinley, who died eight days later, was a veteran of the American Civil War. Under his administration America had defeated Spain and acquired the Philippines. It was he who had agreed to the annexation of Hawaii by the United States, and the effective control of the United States over Cuba.

McKinley was succeeded as President by Theodore Roosevelt, his forty-three-year-old Vice-President, who three years earlier had raised and commanded a volunteer cavalry regiment of cowboys and college graduates, the Rough Riders, in the Spanish-American War. 'Great privileges and great powers are ours,' the new President declared on taking the oath of office, 'and heavy are the responsibilities that go with these privileges and these powers. According as we do well or ill, so shall mankind in the future be raised or cast down.'

In the Philippines, the United States was hunting down the leaders of the national movement which was fighting in the hills. On March 23 the rebel leader and his staff were captured, but fighting continued, forcing the Americans to maintain an army of 50,000 men in the Philippines. As in South Africa it was the tactics of guerrilla fighting that proved impossible for even the most disciplined army to master. The guerrilla forces could melt away into the undergrowth, forest and jungle as soon as they made their strike, and then regroup whenever they decided to strike again. During one such attack, three American officers and forty-eight of their men were killed.

On January 10, oil was discovered in Texas, a historic moment for the future wealth and power of the United States. That same year, also in the United States, the mass production of motor cars began. American industrial power was becoming as great as that of all the industrial nations combined. When the United States Steel Corporation was formed in 1901 it was popularly known as the Billion-Dollar Corporation. Its capital was in fact even larger: $1.3 billion. America's wide-ranging overseas possessions included the Philippines, the home of seven million Filipinos – almost ten per cent of the population of the continental United States. Puerto Rico, acquired from Spain in 1898, had almost a million inhabitants. But the great demographic change in the United States was taking place not through acquisition but through immigration. During one year, 1901, almost 500,000 immigrants arrived from Europe, a figure which was to be maintained year after year for the next decade. The largest single group that year were Italians, 135,996 in all. Russian Jews made up more than 80,000.

The Russia from which so many immigrants came was in constant turmoil. During a student protest in St Petersburg proclamations were distributed with revolutionary slogans, among them 'Down with the Tsar', and the red flag of revolution was flown on the steps of the cathedral. During riots in the Georgian capital, Tiflis, fourteen demonstrators were injured and fifty arrested. 'This day marks the beginning', wrote Lenin from his exile in Switzerland, 'of an open revolutionary movement in the Caucasus.' Among those who took part in this confrontation was Josef Stalin.

Count Leo Tolstoy, the Russian writer and thinker, then aged seventy-three, was an active supporter of the student protests in Moscow. His sympathy with the demonstrators led to his excommunication by the Russian Orthodox Church. In an appeal to the Tsar to protect civil liberties in Russia, he wrote: 'Thousands of the best Russians, sincerely religious people, and therefore such as constitute the chief strength of every nation, have already been ruined, or are being ruined, in prison and in banishment.' Dissent should not be punished as a crime. It was quite wrong to believe that the salvation of Russia could only be found 'in a brutal and antiquated form of government'.

Neither the internal nor the imperial policies of Russia were to change. Throughout 1901 the Russification of Finland continued with vigour, and Finnish citizens were forced to serve against their will in Russian regiments. Local resistance to Russian policy was constant. In Helsinki, in 1902, of 857 men summoned to the army only fifty-six obeyed. When a vast crowd demonstrated against army service, the Tsar's Cossack troops used their knotted whips to disperse the demonstrators. Across the Gulf of Finland, other subjects of the Tsar, the people of Estonia, were also seeking some means of national expression. In 1901 a group of young Estonians started a newspaper aimed at raising national consciousness.

In the German province of Alsace-Lorraine, acquired by conquest from France thirty years earlier, there was discontent when a new German Secretary of State was appointed for the province. He had hitherto ruled the Danish majority in North Schleswig, another German imperial conquest of the nineteenth century, and had been hated for his hostility to the Danes under his control, where he had placed restrictions on the use of the Danish language on all those living in the province. The swift growth of the Polish population in those parts of East Prussia which at the end of the eighteenth century had been part of the Polish sovereign lands partitioned by Germany, Austria and Russia, was also a cause of internal dissent. In December 1901 twenty Polish schoolchildren who refused to say their prayers in German, a language they did not understand, were flogged. When the mother of one of the children was asked by the president of the court what language she supposed Christ to have spoken, she replied without hesitation, 'In Polish.' The German Government bought considerable tracts of land in the predominantly Polish region and settled Germans on it, further exacerbating Polish hostility.

The German Government was determined to suppress Polish national sentiment. The Polish language was not allowed to be taught in schools – though it could not be forbidden in homes – and Poles were excluded from the civil service, which included the teaching professions. During a raid on several Polish-language newspaper offices, documents were found which confirmed the desire of the Poles inside the German Empire for a national future for Poland. Several editors, and thirteen Polish students, were arrested and imprisoned. The crisis was exacerbated when the German Chancellor, Count von Bülow, characterized Germans as hares and Poles as rabbits, telling a journalist: 'If in this park I were to put ten hares and five rabbits, next year I should have fifteen hares and a hundred rabbits. It is against such a phenomenon that we mean to defend German national unity in the Polish provinces.'

A peace agreement between the Great Powers and China was signed on 7 September 1901. In the first peace treaty of the new century the Chinese Government recognized the right of eleven foreign Powers to establish garrisons along the land and river communications between

Peking and the sea. China also agreed to pay a cash indemnity for the loss of European life and property. In South Africa, despite overwhelming British numerical strength, the Boers refused to give up their struggle, and in a raid on Christmas Day 1901 attacked a British army camp, killing six officers and fifty men. The British army erected 8,000 blockhouses throughout the countryside, linked by 3,700 miles of barbed wire, to prevent the Boers from sending arms and reinforcements to their respective units. Slowly the Boer detachments were isolated and worn down. But the war created a backlash of strong anti-war feeling in Britain, which brought together anti-war representatives from many lands, and at a Universal Peace Conference in Glasgow the words 'pacifism' and 'pacifist' were officially adopted to describe the gathering and its participants.

Music saw the introduction of the gramophone record in 1901. Made of shellac, with a spiral groove, it was compact, accessible and relatively hardy. The first Nobel Prizes were also awarded that year, as the result of a benefaction left by the Swedish inventor of dynamite, Alfred Nobel, who had died five years earlier. The first prizes were awarded for physics, chemistry and medicine. Ill-health and disease were to dominate the twentieth century. More than a quarter of a million Indians died of plague in 1901. In China drought and famine led that same year, in a single month, to an estimated two and a half million deaths.

In February 1902 the last of the heavy guns in Boer hands were captured. A Boer delegation crossed the Atlantic to seek help in continuing their struggle, and was received by Theodore Roosevelt, but he told them, to their bitter disappointment, that the United States 'could not and would not interfere' in the struggle. The Boers had reached the end of their powers of resistance, and agreed to lay down their arms. When news of the end of the war reached London on the afternoon of June 1, rejoicing began in the streets and continued through the night. There was also mourning in many homes. More than 6,000 British soldiers had been killed in South Africa. A further 16,000 had died from fever.

That year the United States took direct action to assert its influence in the Western hemisphere when, after a revolutionary outbreak in Colombia, President Roosevelt ordered a battleship and a cruiser to the area, and a battalion of United States marines was landed. Only when the Colombian Government crushed the revolutionaries were the marines withdrawn.

Off the coast of Haiti it was not the United States, but Germany, that took action against revolutionary activity, when a German gun-boat sank the flagship of the Haitian revolutionary leader. The resent-ment in the United States was not so much that Germany had taken this action, which was beneficial to the United States, but that it had been carried out in a way characterized by one American newspaper as 'unnecessarily brutal, wanton, and uncalled for'. Within the German Empire relations between the Germans and their Polish subjects remained tense. In March 1902 more than twenty Polish students who were studying in Berlin were accused of political agitation and expelled from Prussia. A month later the Prussian Government issued a decree limiting Polish immigration. Steps were also taken to prevent Germans, who had bought land cheaply from the Prussian authorities in an effort by the authorities to increase the German population in Polish areas, from selling that land to the Poles. Model German farms were established, to encourage German farmers to move to the predominantly Polish regions. To the distress of the Polish minority in Germany, the Kaiser declared that what he called 'Polish aggress-iveness' was 'resolved to encroach upon Germanism'. The law forbid-ding the use of the Polish language at public meetings where Poles were gathered was strictly enforced.

Within Austria-Hungary labour unrest led to troop intervention in February 1902 in the Austrian port of Trieste. During a mass demonstration in support of an eight-hour working day, troops opened fire and twelve rioters were killed. In the Spanish city of Barcelona that month, several rioters demanding higher wages and better working conditions were shot dead and a state of siege declared for the second time within a year. In the Belgian city of Louvain eight workers were killed when troops opened fire on demonstrators demanding universal suffrage. In the United States a coal strike which threatened to create a winter coal famine was only called off by the personal intervention of President Roosevelt, who first threatened to sent Federal troops to work the mines if the miners did not return to work, and then persuaded both mine owners and miners to accept the verdict of a commission of enquiry.

In Russia, revolutionaries were encouraged during 1902 by the reluctance of the Tsar's soldiers to open fire on demonstrators who refused to disperse when ordered to do so. One regiment was removed from Moscow when it was discovered that it could not be relied on to open fire on demonstrators when ordered by its officers to do so. In the city of Tula, less than a hundred miles to the south, a sergeant refused to order his men to open fire on strikers. When the officer in charge struck the sergeant with his sword, the soldiers mutinied.

The annual intake of soldiers into the Russian army was coming more and more from groups influenced by anti-Tsarist propaganda. Young university teachers, doctors and lawyers were likewise influenced by the anti-monarchical, anti-aristocratic and anti-capitalist emphasis of the revolutionaries. The Jewish Socialist Workers' Party, the Bund, created a year before the Social Democratic Labour Party, was particularly strong in western Russia and the Polish and Lithuanian provinces of the empire. It too favoured a revolutionary solution to redress the widespread peasant poverty and the harsh conditions in so many factories. A third Russian revolutionary party, founded in 1902, was the Socialist Revolutionary Party, whose 'fighting section' concentrated on the assassination of politicians, soldiers, policemen and police spies.

In April, the Russian Minister of the Interior was assassinated in St Petersburg by one of the students expelled the previous year from Kiev university after anti-government demonstrations. During a student uprising in Moscow university, 400 students, some armed, seized the main academic buildings, flew the red flag, and built barricades against the troops sent to evict them. They were all eventually captured and imprisoned. In an attempt to curb unrest in the Caucasus, the Tsarist police arrested a number of Social Democratic agitators, among them Josef Stalin. After eighteen months in jail he was sentenced to three years' exile in Siberia, from which he later escaped. The conditions under which he was exiled were far more lenient than those which he himself was to impose on so many others – numbering in their millions – within three decades.

*   *   *

A Serb-Croat conflict erupted in 1902. That September, in Zagreb, capital of the Hungarian province of Croatia-Slavonia, groups of Serbs and Croats fought each other in the streets. The clashes began after a Serb-edited Belgrade journal, whose article was reproduced in the Zagreb Croat newspapers, denied that the Croats were a separate nationality; they were no more, it asserted, than 'a nation of lackeys'. The destiny of the Slavs of Croatia, the article insisted, was to be absorbed in Serbia; they spoke the same language as the Serbs, and differed only in their Catholicism from the Greek Orthodox Serbs; they were one people. The riots began when a large group of Croats, angered by Serb assertions, attacked a Serbian bank, newspaper offices, businesses and shops, most of which were wrecked. More than a hundred people were injured, some seriously. Violence only ended after martial law was declared, a curfew imposed, and Austro-Hungarian troops sent in to keep order.

In the Balkans, in the areas still under Ottoman rule, armed Bulgarians crossed the border into Macedonia, attacked Turkish army posts, and declared a provisional government. Serb and Greek villages that refused to provide the insurgents with arms and supplies were looted and burnt down. The Sultan ordered an immediate restoration of Ottoman authority. Several Christian villages were then destroyed by his troops, and some villagers massacred.

Natural disasters worldwide were no respectors of imperial boundaries. In February 1902 an earthquake in the Caucasus, where a century of Russian rule continued to be resented, killed 2,000 people. Three months later, 30,000 people were killed when the town of St Pierre, on the French West Indian island of Martinique, was totally destroyed in May by the volcanic eruption of Mont Pelée. A further 2,000 were killed within twenty-four hours on the nearby British island of St Vincent, when the Soufrière volcano erupted. In Egypt, 20,000 people died of cholera; when the British authorities began to put disinfectants in the water supply, in the hope of curbing the disease, they were accused by the local population of poisoning the water.

In British India, more than half a million people died of plague in 1902. But the efforts of the Indian Medical Services to combat the diseases that periodically ravaged the sub-continent were persistent. That year, the Nobel Prize for Medicine was awarded to a British medical officer, Major Ronald Ross, who had served in India for eighteen years, for his discovery of the malaria parasite, and for his pioneering studies in combating the disease.

War between the Powers was still, by most contemporary calculations, unthinkable in 1903, yet the prospect of such a war could grip the public mind: the most popular thriller published in Britain that year was Erskine Childers' *Riddle of the Sands*, a spy story about a German invasion. The means whereby war could be waged more effectively were continually being developed. In January 1903 the headquarters of the British First Army Corps, based at Aldershot, south-west of London, made successful contact by wireless telegraphy with the ships of the Channel Squadron, while the building of a new naval base at Rosyth, in Scotland, was in part designed to keep an eye on Russia's naval exit from the Baltic.

Inside Russia, heightened political unrest led the Tsar to issue a manifesto offering to improve the condition of village life. Two weeks later he abolished the system under which peasant communities were held collectively responsible for the taxes of their members. In the same manifesto, however, the local self-governing bodies were made even more subservient to officials appointed by St Petersburg. Both urban and rural workers in Russia were turning to violence. In March there was a strike of 500 workers in the State-run ironworks at Zlatoust, in the Ufa province; only a charge by sabre-wielding mounted troops was able to disperse the strikers. In May the Governor of Ufa was assassinated. In June, there were demonstrations by workers in the port cities of Batum on the Black Sea and at Baku on the Caspian. In Baku, 45,000 strikers took to the streets, troops were sent in, and several hundred workers were killed. In July and August disturbances spread to every industrial and manufacturing town in southern Russia. Men known to be police spies were assassinated in Pinsk and Nizhni-Novgorod.

Fifty-three of the leading figures in the Russian Social Democratic Party, most of them exiles, met in the summer of 1903, first in Brussels and then in London. There was a conflict between those who wanted a broadly-based Party with a large membership, and those who wanted a small, disciplined, professional centre. Lenin, who led the call for a small, tightly-knit central authority 'of people whose profession is that of revolutionist', lost by a narrow margin, twenty-eight votes to twenty-three. At the end of the meetings, however, his faction won by a majority of two the vote on who should control the Party newspaper. Because they were a majority on that occasion, albeit only just, Lenin's faction called themselves henceforth *Bolsheviki* – Majority-ites. But the rival faction, the *Mensheviki*, the Minority-ites, later won control of the newspaper. Bolsheviks and Mensheviks held together as a single party for another nine years; then they went their separate revolutionary ways.

Inside Russia the Social Democrat Party met secretly in November 1903, with delegates, including those from the Jewish Bund, calling for the abolition of autocracy and the establishment of a democratic republic. In Baku several thousand army recruits marched in procession through the town with a red flag inscribed 'Down with the autocracy! Long live the Republic!' Students in Kiev tore down the portrait of the Tsar, and replaced it with one of the man who had assassinated the Russian Minister of the Interior the previous year.

The Russian Government decided to introduce a traditional scapegoat: the Jews, of whom there were more than five million in Russia. On April 20, during a day of deliberately unchecked violence in Kishinev, forty-three Jews were killed and several hundred Jewish women were raped. When Jewish leaders went to St Petersburg to ask for justice, the Minister, Vyacheslav Plehve, told them that the existence of a Jewish revolutionary movement forced the government to take action. If the Jewish labour movement continued to grow, he warned, he would miss no opportunity 'of rendering the lives of the Jews intolerable'.

The pogrom at Kishinev was followed by another at Gomel, which was also officially condoned. Police and soldiers formed protective lines for the rioters, who once again looted, raped and murdered with impunity. When a group of Jews took up arms in an attempt to break through to some of those who were being attacked, they were fired on by the police. The killings in Kishinev and Gomel intensified the emigration of Russian Jews, many of whom made their way to the United States, Canada, Britain and, in small but steady numbers, to Turkish-ruled Palestine.

The Russian Empire, in turmoil within, continued to act as an imperial power overseas. At Port Arthur, in Manchuria, the building of thirty-five miles of coastal fortifications, docks and a new town on what had earlier been Chinese territory was continuous. By the end of 1903 the port could accommodate eight warships and a fleet of torpedo boats. Russia was becoming a Pacific naval power, only 600 miles from Japan. The Japanese public, incensed by Russia's forward moves in China and its occupation of the Chinese province of Manchuria, called for Japan to reassert control over the Korean peninsula. Russia responded by sending troop reinforcements to the Far East along the recently completed Trans-Siberian Railway. Britain and France called on both sides to negotiate rather than fight. The United States announced it would remain neutral in any conflict.

As war in the Far East was averted, for the time being at least, the focus of international attention turned to the Balkans. On the night of 10 April 1903, King Alexander and Queen Draga of Serbia were murdered in their palace in Belgrade, and their naked, mutilated bodies were thrown from the palace window. Also murdered that night were the Prime Minister and the Minister of War. The murdered King was twenty-six years old. A week earlier he had suspended Serbia's liberal constitution – which he himself had promulgated two years previously – revoked the law introducing secret ballots at the elections, and abolished freedom of the press. He had also excluded the Radical deputies from both the Senate and Council of State. After the murders it was reported from Belgrade that the capital wore a 'festive aspect' and that 'intense joy' prevailed. Soldiers, horses and guns were decorated with flowers. A tyrant had been overthrown, and a new King, Peter Karageorgevitch, then living in Geneva, was elected in his place by the parliament.

Contrasting events in Serbia with those of her eastern neighbour, Roumania, a British commentator noted that during 1903 Roumania was 'in the happy position of a country which has no history. The only noteworthy (and a very discreditable) incident in her home politics was an extensive emigration of Jews to America, in consequence of their being denied the rights of Roumanian subjects.' In Macedonia, the Turkish suppression of unrest among the Serb, Greek and Bulgar populations continued on its harsh course, with burnings and executions. Church leaders in Britain, France and the United States denounced Muslim 'savagery'. A mass meeting in London demanded an end to Turkish rule in Macedonia. The Emperor Franz-Joseph and Tsar Nicholas II, meeting at Mürzsteg, south-west of Vienna, agreed to put joint pressure on the Sultan to institute substantial reforms for the peoples of Macedonia. The British Government agreed to use its influence in Constantinople to put pressure on Turkey to comply. On 24 October 1903 Austria and Russia issued 'Instructions' to Turkey, known as the Mürzsteg Programme. Reforms in Macedonia were essential, the instructions read, and would be supervised by representatives of the Powers.

The Turkish Government hesitated to submit to the demands of two foreign powers. On December 16 Austria-Hungary issued a stern warning from Vienna: Turkey 'must change if she wished to live'. Three weeks after this warning Turkey agreed to carry out the Austro-Russian demands. An Italian officer was to reorganize the Macedonian police. Austrian and Russian civilian officials were to question the local inhabitants about their grievances. Race and religion were no longer to be a barrier to official employment. Administrative borders were to be redrawn to take account of ethnic groupings.

Although Austria-Hungary had been so keen on forcing the Turks to institute reforms in Macedonia, her own internal situation was far from reformist. Throughout the Hungarian province of Croatia there were protests in May 1903 by Croats at the unfair distribution of revenue raised by taxation, and at the exclusive use of Hungarian names and the Hungarian language on the local railways. The Hungarians, too, had cause for grievance: it was only after angry scenes in the Hungarian Parliament in Budapest that Franz-Josef allowed Hungary's national flag to be flown alongside the imperial flag on military establishments inside Hungary, and gave Hungarian officers the right to transfer to regiments within Hungary.

In the Austrian provinces of the Habsburg Empire, Czechs were demanding their own university and the adoption of the Czech language in all official proceedings relating to Bohemia in the Vienna parliament. In November 1903, Czech deputies put forward a pro-gramme of national demands, including special lessons in primary schools in the Austrian province of Silesia, where there was a Czech minority, 'to assist the development of the Czech national spirit'. The Czech demands were parallelled by demands from the Italian minority in the Tyrol, who wanted a university in Innsbruck. There followed a German protest demonstration against the Italian demands. These manifestations of national discontent within the Habsburg Empire caused many outside observers to wonder how long the Dual Monarchy could survive the tensions within it.

In foreign policy, the growing closeness of Germany and Austria-Hungary, and their association with Italy, raised the possibility of a strong new naval power in the Mediterranean. To counter this, Britain and France were drawing closer together, and in October 1903 they signed an agreement referring disputes between them to the Perma-nent Court of Arbitration at The Hague, and in April 1904 signed the Entente Cordiale, whereby France recognized Britain's predominant position in Egypt, and Britain recognized France's predominant pos-ition in Morocco. In the Sudan, where five years earlier Britain and France had clashed over who was to control the upper regions of the Nile, a British force marched, with French approval, against a Muslim opponent of British rule, captured him and hanged him.

In northern Nigeria, British forces moved against the Muslim ruler who had defied the coming of British control over the region. Three hundred of his men were killed in the fighting. During the final battle of the campaign a European eyewitness wrote of how 'hordes of horsemen and footmen armed with spears, swords, old guns and bows and arrows appeared, charging the square over and over again, only to be mown down by machine-gun and carbine fire'. With that victory there was relief among the British administrators in West Africa that, as one contemporary wrote, 'the fear of a Maho-medan movement which would sweep the whites back into the Delta need no longer be entertained'.

The German colonial administrators in German South-West Africa faced local unrest when the Hottentot tribe rose in revolt. A punitive expedition was ordered by the Kaiser, to protect the 4,600

German residents in German South-West Africa and the 1,500 Boers who had emigrated there from South Africa. Thousands of the native Hottentots were killed.

President Roosevelt spoke in the summer of 1903 of the 'destiny' of the United States as a Pacific Power. A few weeks after his speech an 'All-American cable' was opened, linking San Francisco to the Philippines. An extension to Shanghai created telegraphic communication between the American and Asian continents. The new cable, linked with the existing Indo-European system, enabled Roosevelt, on July 4, American Independence Day, to send a message from Washington DC around the globe.

Unimpressed by the power of Washington, the Government of Colombia refused to allow the United States to build a canal across the Panama Isthmus at its narrowest point – the Colombian province of Panama. The people of Panama, despite being subjected to Colombian rule, were as keen as the United States to benefit from the wealth which would be created by building and working the canal. On November 3, in a bloodless revolution, the Panamanians declared independence from Colombia. An American gunboat watched over the scene, threatening to intervene if Colombian troops attacked the Panamanians. The Colombian troops withdrew and the Republic of Panama came into being, negotiating a treaty with the United States under which, in return for a guarantee by Washington to safeguard the independence of the new republic, Panama ceded in perpetuity a strip of land ten miles wide, extending from the Atlantic to the Pacific Ocean, on which the United States could not only build and control the canal, but maintain military garrisons, and exercise all the rights of sovereignty.

The year 1903 had its share of natural and unnatural disasters. In August, eighty-four Parisians were killed when fire broke out in the Paris metro. In December, during a theatre matinée in Chicago, fire killed more than 600 people, mainly women and children. In India the number of deaths from plague totalled 842,264. A policy of mass inoculation was embarked upon, but with local superstitions leading to resistance, the government had to promise to abstain from any attempt to carry out preventative measures by force. By the end of the year the total number of plague deaths during the previous three years reached 1,673,000.

Among the wealthier nations of the world, the search for a life of comfort, health and leisure was ever present. In 1903 the first 'garden city' was founded, at Letchworth in England, aimed at combining urban living with pastoral and even agricultural pursuits. That same year President Roosevelt established the first national wildlife refuge in the United States, Pelican Island, off the east coast of Florida. Nature was to be protected by Federal law and maintained by Federal money.

The welfare of human beings was enhanced in Germany, where the principle of sickness benefits for workers was confirmed and extended. In France, Pierre and Marie Curie discovered the properties of radium. That radium would have a dramatic influence in the treatment of cancer was not yet known, but the nature of its properties was clearly of medical significance. As *The Times* reported, 'radium emanations act powerfully upon the nerve substance, and cause the death of living things whose nerve centres do not lie deep enough to be shielded from their influence.'

Architecture and commerce combined in 1903 with the opening of the New York Chamber of Commerce and Stock Exchange. Also in New York, that year saw the opening night of the musical *The Wizard of Oz*, and one of the earliest feature films, *The Great Train Robbery*. The first motor taxicab was introduced to the streets of London that year, threatening the horse-drawn cab with extinction. Most dramatically for the future of the century, on 17 December 1903, at Kitty Hawk, North Carolina, two American brothers, Orville and Wilbur Wright, fitted a twelve horse-power petrol engine to one of their gliders. Thus powered it flew in the air for forty yards. This was the first successful aeroplane flight.

On 5 February 1904 negotiations being conducted between Russia and Japan over Russian claims for some influence in Korea, and Japanese claims for a similar influence in Manchuria, were broken off. Three nights later, Japanese torpedo boats attacked the Russian naval squadron at Port Arthur. Two Russian battleships and a cruiser were damaged. Russia and Japan were at war. Russian troops stationed in Manchuria marched into Korea. Two months later they were driven back, and Japanese forces entered Manchuria. At the same time Japanese troops, helped by gunboats and torpedo boats, besieged Port Arthur. This left Japan free to land an army in Korea without fear of Russian naval opposition.

Russia's position at sea was further weakened when, in April, the Russian flagship struck a Japanese mine off Port Arthur and sank; the Russian naval commander-in-chief, forty officers and 750 men were drowned. The Japanese fleet suffered no losses until May, when two Japanese cruisers rammed each other in dense fog off Port Arthur, with the loss of 235 lives, and a Japanese battleship struck two Russian mines and sank. Four hundred officers and men were drowned.

Eight months after the outbreak of the war, using the Trans-Siberian Railway, the strength of the Russian force in Manchuria reached 320,000, three times what it had been at the outset, but losses in battle were heavy. To augment the numbers, 7,000 convicts doing hard labour in the remote and desolate camps of Sakhalin island, nearly 3,000 of whom were convicted murderers, were offered a year off their sentences for every two months they were in action. An additional 15,000 ex-convicts, including 5,000 murderers who had served their sentences, but who had been forced after their release to live in settlements near the labour camps, were offered the right to return to Russia, if they agreed to fight. They were not, however, given the right to live in any provincial capital, or to own property.

In the main the convicts made poor soldiers, and the Russian army remained mostly on the defensive. Such clashes as did take place led to heavy Russian loss of life. In August the Russian fleet, bottled up in Port Arthur, decided to try to seek battle with the Japanese in the open water, and was defeated. To redress the balance the powerful Russian Baltic Fleet set sail for the Far East, a journey half way around the world. As it made its way eastward, 6,000 Japanese soldiers were killed in a failed attempt to break into Port Arthur.

*   *   *

Since May 1903 news of a reign of terror in the Belgian Congo had been reaching Europe as a result of the efforts of Edmund Morel, a shipping clerk in Liverpool, who published graphic accounts of atrocities which had come to his notice during the system of forced labour which was imposed by the Belgian authorities – under the direct rule of King Leopold – on the local inhabitants. Morel wrote of women chained to posts as hostages until their menfolk returned with rubber; and of Belgian punitive expeditions which, on their return to base, brought baskets of human hands as proof of their ruthlessness. Morel estimated that by such methods King Leopold, for whom the Congo was a personal domain, drew £360,000 annually from rubber alone.

In February 1904, nine months after Morel's first foray into print, Roger Casement, the British Consul in the Belgian Congo, sent a report of Leopold's activities to the Foreign Office in London. He had seen Congolese women and children chained in sheds as hostages, and men beaten up for failure to produce sufficient rubber at collection points. He reported that the Belgian authorities kept some 10,000 men under arms to police the Congo, and wrote of mass executions, and of terrible mutilations inflicted on the natives by white officials. Casement estimated that as many as three million native Congolese had died of disease, torture or shooting during the previous fifteen years.

As news of the Congolese atrocities spread there was widespread outcry at King Leopold's sanction of such hideous practices, and against the enormous financial profit he had made. Critics included President Roosevelt and King Edward VII among heads of State, and Mark Twain and Joseph Conrad among writers. But it was only after two years of international protests that the Belgian Parliament began to debate the situation in the Congo, and only after two more years that Leopold agreed to hand over his personal control to the Belgian Parliament. Roger Casement was knighted by the British King for his skill in exposing the Congo atrocities. Later he was active in the struggle to liberate Ireland from British rule. During the First World War he attempted to recruit Irish prisoners-of-war in Berlin to fight against Britain, was caught by the British after landing on the coast of Ireland, tried as a traitor, and shot.

The British Empire was continually exerting its strength. During 1904, a senior political officer of the Government of India, Colonel Younghusband, advanced into Tibet accompanied by 3,000 British and Indian soldiers, commanded by a senior British officer, General Macdonald. At the village of Guru, inside Tibet, the Tibetans blocked Macdonald's way. 'I did my level best to prevent fighting, and twice refused Macdonald's request to begin,' Younghusband wrote to a friend. 'But when the Tibetan general refused to carry out Macdonald's order to the Tibetans to lay down their weapons, began struggling with an Indian soldier, and loosed off his revolver, the fat was in the fire. I was miserable at the time, for of course it was a loathsome sight, and, however much I felt even then it would probably work out well in the end, I could not but be disgusted at the sight of those poor wretched peasants mowed down by our rifles and Maxims.'

In the fighting around Guru 600 Tibetans were killed. There were no British or Indian deaths. Younghusband and Macdonald pressed on toward the Tibetan capital, Lhasa. In subsequent skirmishes a further 2,100 Tibetans were killed, for the loss in action of thirty-seven British and Indian troops. Younghusband reached Lhasa, and the British flag was raised over the Himalayan kingdom. 'The Tibetans', he was surprised to find, 'were excellent people, quite polished and polite and genial and well-mannered, but absolutely impossible on business matters.' They accepted all Britain's demands, agreeing that their southern frontier would be the line defined by Britain fourteen years earlier. They would destroy all fortifications between Lhasa and the frontier. They would open markets in two towns in which traders from British India would be permitted to trade. They would also pay Britain the massive sum (for them) of £500,000, in seventy-five annual instalments. Until the Tibetan indemnity was paid, that is, until 1979, Britain would occupy the Chumbi Valley in southern Tibet.

General Macdonald's return journey was made more difficult by a sudden drop in temperature as he and his men made their way through steep ravines at 18,000 feet. Less than forty British and Indian soldiers had been killed in the fighting. More than 200 died of cold and exposure on their way home.

*   *   *

In Africa, as in Asia, the imperial powers continued to assert their authority. In Morocco the French Government began strenuous efforts to control the warring Muslim factions. In Angola, where Portugal had been the colonial power for more than 300 years, one of the native peoples, the Cuanhamas, had attacked an isolated column of Portuguese-officered troops, killing 254 of them. The Portuguese, who prided themselves on the enlightened nature of their administration, took punitive action. Five thousand soldiers set off to punish the Cuanhamas. The result was what a British report described as 'a massacre'.

In German South-West Africa the Herero people had risen in revolt, seizing German-owned houses and cattle, and surrounded several German garrisons. When a small German military detachment was attacked, and twenty-six German soldiers killed, a punitive expedition was despatched. Shortly after the expedition arrived the other large tribe in the colony, the Witbois, who had hitherto been armed by the Germans as allies in the struggle, joined the Hereros. In the months that followed, thousands of Hereros and Witbois were killed. When news of the severity of the punitive measures reached Europe, there was widespread indignation that destruction on such a scale had been inflicted by a colonial power on its subject peoples.

In the Dutch East Indies, following a rebellion against Dutch rule, a military force was sent against the rebels, and nearly a thousand women and children were killed. In the Dutch Parliament a member of the government's own Party declared that the Dutch soldiers had behaved like 'Huns and Tatars', massacring the women and children for the commercial ends of mining and oil exploration.

The conflicts of imperialism and nationalism were everywhere intertwined. Within the Russian Empire, the Governor-General of Finland was shot dead in June by the son of a Finnish senator. The next month the Minister of the Interior, Vyacheslav Plehve, was killed by a bomb. In November, at a conference in St Petersburg, the usually docile presidents of the local provincial assemblies demanded the establishment of a constitution for Russia, and civil and religious liberties.

In Ireland, the desire for independence was inspired by other national struggles. In 1904 the Irish nationalist leader Arthur Griffith wrote of the achievement of the Hungarians in 1867 in obtaining their own parliament: 'Hungary won her independence by refusing to send members to the Imperial Parliament at Vienna or admit any right in that Parliament to legislate for her.' A year later Griffith founded Sinn Fein – Ourselves Alone – dedicated to an Ireland independent of the United Kingdom. Fourteen years later, as a Sinn Fein member of the British Parliament, he was to be one of the leaders of Sinn Fein's refusal to sit any longer in the Parliament in London, but to establish its own Irish Parliament in Dublin.

In India, where more than a million Indians died of plague in 1904, the Indian National Congress was searching for a means of challenging British rule. From South Africa, where his work on behalf of Indian rights had been tireless, Mahatma Gandhi advocated the method he was using there: non-co-operation. Peaceful but all-embracing protest was 'the only weapon', he wrote to a friend, 'that is suited to the genius of our people and our land, which is the nursery of the most ancient religions and has very little to learn from modern civilisation – a civilisation based on violence of the blackest type, largely a negation of the Divine in man, and which is rushing headlong to its own ruin.'

China was also on the verge of an internal transformation. A Chinese revolutionary, Sun Yat-sen, who had trained as a doctor in both Hawaii and Hong Kong, pressed for an end to the imperial dynasty and the 'regeneration' of China. In 1904 he and his followers published a document entitled 'Summary of the Revolution'. It was a far-ranging call, strongly influenced by Socialist doctrines: 'The Revolution having been inaugurated by the people, it shall be democratic, i.e., all citizens shall possess equal rights.' It was a revolutionary manifesto for a country where such ideals would have to be fought for in the streets and on the battlefields.

In 1904 the third modern Olympic Games was held in St Louis, Missouri. The United States won eighty gold medals – by far the largest number – with the next largest, five each, going to Germany and Cuba, and four to Canada. Several of the inventions of 1904 were to have a permanent place in the coming century. Among them were King C. Gillette's safety razor and Thomas Sullivan's tea bag.

At the World Fair held in St Louis at the same time as the Olympics, German immigrants produced two items of food that, as a result of the Games, were popularized throughout the world: the ice cream cone and the hamburger.

In St Petersburg, tension had been building up as a result of the dismissal of four workers from the Putilov factory, the largest factory in the Russian capital. When the Putilov workers went on strike they were widely supported: on 7 January 1905 more than 80,000 people from enterprises across the city were on strike, closing down the capital's electricity. A mass demonstration was planned to demand increased wages and liberal reforms. On January 8 the demonstration's leader, Father Gapon, informed the Tsar that it would be peaceful, and that a petition would be presented which it was hoped the Tsar would receive in person, as the demonstrators had no faith in his ministers. But in another petition that day, peasant and working-class demonstrators warned the Tsar they had reached 'that terrible moment when death is to be preferred to the continuance of intolerable suffering'.

On Sunday January 9 Father Gapon – whom the Tsar described in his diary as 'some kind of priest-socialist' – led thousands of unarmed men, women and children towards the centre of the city, singing hymns and carrying crosses and religious banners. As they approached the Winter Palace, Cossack troops tried to drive them away with whips, but the crowd was too large and too determined to be whipped back. The Cossacks then used their rifles and swords. When several thousand striking workers reached the centre of the city, determined to help the crowd reach the Winter Palace, fighting ensued. When it ended 200 demonstrators lay dead.

On the following day strikes took place all over Russia. During mass demonstrations in Riga, troops charged and seventy demonstrators were killed. In Warsaw, on January 14, strikers marched through the streets looting and burning shops as they went. Russian troops opened fire and ninety-three marchers were killed. In prolonged fighting in Odessa, 2,000 demonstrators were killed. On February 17 the Tsar's uncle, Grand Duke Serge, who until a few weeks earlier had been Governor of Moscow, noted for his harshness towards any form of dissent, was assassinated.

Despite the revolutionary turmoil at home, and the military setback of the surrender of Port Arthur to the Japanese on January 1, Russian troops in Manchuria continued to fight, but in each confrontation their casualties were much higher than those of their enemy, and on March 9 they were forced to abandon Mukden, the principal town in southern Manchuria. During three weeks of fighting, 27,700 Russian soldiers had been killed.

The Russian Baltic Fleet had continued its long, slow voyage towards the Far East. On May 27 it reached the Tsushima Strait, the open waterway between Korea and Japan. The Japanese fleet was waiting. Battle ensued and within three-quarters of an hour all eight Russian battleships were out of action, as were seven of the twelve Russian cruisers and six of the nine destroyers. The Battle of Tsushima sealed the fate of the Russian war effort. On land the Japanese continued to advance, Japanese troops landing on Russian soil for the first time in the war, occupying the island of Sakhalin.

As Russia's humiliation intensified, President Roosevelt invited both Russia and Japan to accept a cease-fire, and to open negotiations in the United States. After less than three weeks of negotiations a treaty was signed. A war in which 58,000 Japanese and 120,000 Russian soldiers had been killed was over. Korea was recognized as a Japanese dependency, the first successful assertion of Japanese control on the mainland of Asia. Port Arthur was ceded to Japan. The southern half of Sakhalin island was annexed by Japan. Both belligerents agreed to evacuate Manchuria, which was returned to Chinese sovereignty.

In the final months of the Russian war against Japan, strikes, riots and violence had spread throughout Russia. In many rural areas, peasants murdered landlords, and looted houses, factories and sugar refineries. During April, in St Petersburg, a meeting of lawyers and professors from all over Russia called for a democratic constitution, based on universal suffrage and secret ballot. Their call was supported by the many unions that had sprung up, including those of medical personnel, engineers and technicians, agronomists, journalists, writers and school teachers. But, asserting its autocratic powers, the government forbade all public discussion of the lawyers' and professors' call.

The ability of the autocracy to stifle debate was under daily challenge. On May 8 a congress of fourteen unions, meeting in Moscow, advocated a general strike throughout Russia to end tyranny. In the Polish provinces of Russia, unarmed processions, mostly of working men, were attacked by Russian troops, and many marchers were killed. In Finland resolutions were passed demanding the abolition of the dictatorship and censorship, the restoration of Press freedom, and the removal of all Russian police forces. Municipal buildings in the Baltic provinces were attacked and portraits of the Tsar destroyed.

On August 19, realizing he could no longer resist the pressures of more than seven months' agitation and near-anarchy, the Tsar announced that 'while preserving the fundamental law regarding the autocratic power' he had decided 'to summon elected representatives from the whole of Russia to take a constant and active part in the elaboration of laws'. The new body would be called the State Council, in Russian, Gosudarstvennaia Duma – known simply as the Duma. It would be responsible 'for the preliminary study and discussion of legislative proposals'. These proposals, when decided upon, would be 'submitted to the supreme autocratic authority'.

The promise of an elected assembly was a massive concession for the Tsar, but a grave disappointment for those who wanted a democratic assembly with legislative powers, independent of the Tsar's authority. Not only the Duma's authority, but the franchise of the voters, was limited: owners of property could vote, as could proprietors of industrial establishments and also peasants. But working men and the professional classes, whose part in the demands for reform had been so strong, were both excluded. In St Petersburg, with a population of 1,500,000, there would only be 9,500 voters. In addition, the Tsar could dissolve the Duma when he chose. Nor were the public to be admitted to its sessions.

Unrest continued. In October there were strikes in both Moscow and St Petersburg, when troops again clashed with the strikers. On October 16, in the Estonian capital, Tallinn, Russian troops opened fire on a mass meeting of Estonians, killing 150. On October 26 a railway strike was declared throughout the empire, paralysing the ability of Russia to maintain trade or order. The constitutional reform parties believed only drastic action could force the Tsar to transform the Duma into a truly democratic constituency assembly. Decrees forbidding open-air public meetings without permission were ignored. In November people speculated that if the Tsar refused to accede to the demands of the Liberals for constitutional reform, he might be forced aside altogether by revolution.

On November 9 the sailors and artillerymen at the Kronstadt naval base, guarding the sea route to St Petersburg, mutinied. Troops sent to suppress the mutiny were only able to do so after severe fighting. An appeal on November 16 for workers to end the general strike was ignored. In Vladivostok, soldiers in the reserve mutinied, rampaging through the town, looting, and setting ships on fire. On November 25 there was a revolt of soldiers, sailors and workmen in the Crimean port of Sebastopol. Twenty thousand loyal troops had to be sent to crush it. The battleship *Potemkin*, under the control of its crew, flew the red flag of revolution, and bombarded government buildings in Odessa and other Black Sea ports with its powerful naval guns.

The Tsar had decided on his course. Harsh restrictions on press freedom were re-imposed, and new Governor-Generals appointed for the Baltic provinces and the Caucasus with authority to repress all agitation. Still the unrest continued. In Warsaw a demonstration by more than 400 Roman Catholic clergymen demanded autonomy for Poland, a separate Polish Parliament and the restoration of the Polish language in all local government business. There was a strike of postmen and telegraphists throughout the empire. The Tsar issued a new scale of heavy penalties for those who incited strike action. In response, the revolutionaries urged the public not to pay taxes, and called on soldiers to mutiny.

On December 21 revolution broke out in Moscow. The revolutionaries seized several railway stations and set up barricades. Councils of Workers' Deputies, many under Bolshevik control, were established throughout the city to direct the revolutionary effort. But government troops, remaining loyal to the Tsar, retained control of one of the railway stations, and of several fortified positions within the areas held by the revolutionaries, and were able to advance, bombarding revolutionary-held positions with artillery. The fighting continued for ten days. On December 28, 300 armed revolutionaries forced their way into the house of the Chief of the Secret Police and killed him. But the authorities were gaining the upper hand, and on the same day Tsarist police arrested all the members of the Social Revolutionary Committee in the city. A Bolshevik attack on the main police barracks was driven off. When the fighting in Moscow ended more than a thousand revolutionaries had been killed.

On December 26, while fighting was still intense in Moscow, the Tsar had issued a decree considerably widening the numbers who could vote for the Duma. Among the new voters would be house owners, tradesmen paying taxes, civil servants and railway employees. This concession calmed a considerable amount of Liberal unease in St Petersburg and Moscow. Elsewhere in the Empire, however, men and women were inspired by the revolution in Moscow to believe that the whole edifice of autocracy could be overthrown. There was fighting in several cities in the Polish provinces. In the Baltic provinces the revolutionaries fought, although in vain, to seize power, and in the Caucasus there were revolutionary outbreaks in several towns. On the Black Sea attempts were made to take over the main ports. In Odessa, after the declaration of martial law, Cossack troops cleared the whole centre of the city of strikers. In Estonia workers roamed the countryside looting and burning Russian-owned mansions until Russian troops hunted them down. Several hundred Estonian workers were killed by the troops. Five hundred more, arrested and court-martialled, were executed. Hundreds more were exiled to Siberia.

Other Empires faced other problems: in the British Parliament there was a call on May 9 for the 'gross disabilities' under which the Aborigines of Australia suffered to be removed for all time. On the following day the Archbishop of Canterbury said that the conditions under which the Aborigines had been put to work 'had many of the characteristics of slavery'. A week later, the conditions under which Chinese labourers were toiling in the mines in South Africa was cause for British parliamentary concern. These labourers had been brought from China under contracts which made their conditions of work harsh in the extreme.

In German South-West Africa the rebellion of the Herero and

Witboi tribesmen continued. The German commander in the colony, General von Trotha, threatened the whole tribe with 'extermination' if it did not surrender. The Herero leader, Morenga, having offered in vain to open negotiations with the Germans, attacked one of the main German army camps and overran it. He then challenged the Germans to a full-scale battle. When this took place, forty German soldiers were killed. More German troops were sent from Germany. In the fighting that winter, the Witboi chiefs surrendered but the Hereros fought on. Against them the Germans instituted the policy the British had used against the Boers: concentration camps in which Herero women, children and old people were confined behind barbed wire, to try to force their menfolk to surrender. But the Hereros fought on, as the Boers had done.

In Austria-Hungary the Hungarian demand for universal suffrage culminated in a mass Socialist demonstration in Budapest. The Emperor was indignant, and prorogued parliament. Austrian Socialists then united with their brethren in Budapest, and on November 28 a demonstration of working men, marching with red banners, assembled in front of the parliament building in Vienna while parliament was in session. Inside, the Austrian Prime Minister agreed to introduce a franchise bill based on universal suffrage. The Hungarian Prime Minister did likewise in Budapest.

In British India, the plague that had taken so many lives each year since the beginning of the century took even more in 1905, when 1,125,652 plague deaths were reported. The death of more than a million people in one year was a terrifying testament to the power of disease, and the inability of even the most beneficent rulers to control it.

The growing prosperity of the industrial nations, and the desire of those who were making the wealth to live in greater comfort, was reflected in 1905 by the purchase, in the United States, south of Kansas City, of land on which to build an exclusive residential district. The era of the Country Club had begun. With the growth of wealth there came, for some, a sense of communal responsibility. The year 1905 saw the founding in the United States of the Rotary Club, whose members, businessmen and professionals, met regularly both for the pleasure of each other's company, and to do beneficial work in their local communities.

The instinct for the preservation of natural resources continued to be most noticeable in the United States, where in 1905 President Roosevelt established a Forest Service for the proper management and preservation of the country's vast woodland resources. The founding of the Audubon Society that year was an earnest of the recognition to protect birds in the wild. Parallel with this guarding of nature came the continued expansion of industry: that same year saw the creation in Pennsylvania of Bethlehem Steel, a giant of steel production. In Gary, Indiana, the rival steel company, the United States Steel Corporation, constructed a 'company town' which could house 200,000 workers in conditions of comparative comfort. In Britain, the continuing expansion of the motor car industry was seen in the founding of the Austin Motor Company, and of the Automobile Association. Cars were to be made accessible not only to the rich, but to the middle classes. And motor omnibuses – the 'bus' of today's cities worldwide – opened their first regular service in London in 1905. The internal combustion engine, which a decade earlier had been a curiosity, was becoming an integral part of the life, work and leisure of the twentieth century.

On 10 January 1906 one of Britain's most popular newspapers, the *Daily Mail*, coined a new word, 'suffragette'. It referred to those women who, in search of the vote for women in national elections – one such election had just taken place, with an entirely male electorate – were adopting increasingly outspoken, even violent, tactics. In New Zealand, women, including Maori women, had received the vote more than a decade earlier. In Australia women had been entitled to vote in Federal elections since 1902; but unlike in New Zealand the Aborigines of Australia were denied the vote until 1967. In the United States, where an all-male franchise was still in place, there had for many years been a strong tradition of campaigning for votes for women. In the state of Wyoming, women got the vote as early as 1889, in Colorado in 1893 and in Indiana and Utah in 1896.

The question of the electoral franchise was momentarily over-shadowed in the public mind on February 10, when King Edward

VII launched a new battleship, the *Dreadnought*, the most powerful and fastest warship then in existence. This new class of battleship constituted a revolution in naval armaments, starting a race between the Great Powers that was to divert considerable financial resources from social policies.

In Russia, the turmoil of 1905 continued into the new year, despite hopes that the Duma, which was to be elected according to the wider franchise extracted from the Tsar, would be able to institute substantial reforms. The first election was to be held on April 4. Before then, in an attempt to curb political dissent, the government closed down eighty-eight newspapers and arrested more than fifty editors. Thousands of political agitators were sentenced to exile in Siberia or imprisoned. Thousands more fled the country for exile.

The first session of the Duma opened in the Winter Palace in St Petersburg on May 10. The Tsar's speech of welcome left the delegates puzzled that no reference was made to constitutional reform, or to the opportunities opened up by the very existence of an elected assembly. Instead the Tsar stressed his hope to bequeath to his son 'as his inheritance, a firmly established, well-ordered and enlightened State'. The deputies then transferred, through cheering crowds, to the Tauride Palace, where they were to hold all future meetings. In their first session there, that same day, they called for an amnesty for political prisoners – 'those who have sacrificed their freedom for their country' – and the replacement of the autocracy by a constitutional monarchy. They then called for elections to be held by universal suffrage, free education, the distribution of some private land to the peasants and the abolition of privileges based on class, religion or race.

The Tsar took the view that an amnesty, the first of the Duma's requests, would encourage another revolution, and rejected it. When the Duma asked that the death penalty be not carried out on eight workmen who had been arrested during the riots in the Baltic provinces, its plea was ignored and the men were shot. When the Duma criticized the government for not having taken steps to prevent a massacre of Jews in the Russian-Polish town of Bialystok, the Tsar then announced that he was 'cruelly disappointed' that the representatives of the nation had 'strayed into spheres beyond their competence' and declared the session of the Duma closed.

A number of deputies, incensed at having been dissolved before they had been allowed to make any legislative progress, moved to the town of Vyborg, in Russian Finland. From there they issued a manifesto protesting against the dissolution and urging the population to give the government neither money nor soldiers. For its part the government sent a circular to all provincial governors, ordering that 'disturbances must be repressed, and revolutionary movements must be put down by all legal means'.

The provincial governors, the conduit throughout Russia for the Tsarist government's instructions, often lacked the authority to carry out those instructions. In Odessa, after a Jewish deputation told the city's governor that anti-Jewish riots were imminent, he replied that while he could certainly prevent government troops from joining in the attacks he would be unable to control either the Cossack troops, who had their own commanders, or armed gangs of anti-Semites – the 'Black Hundred' – or the public at large. Shortly afterwards, Cossacks and Black Hundreds joined a mob that rampaged through the Jewish districts, killing, maiming and plundering. The army stood aside.

That autumn many provincial governors and police chiefs were killed by revolutionaries. Field courts martial were established in many provinces at which the trial of someone accused of revolutionary activity was held in secret, and could take no longer than eighteen hours. The sentences had to be carried out within twenty-four hours. During September and October, 300 people were shot or hanged by order of these courts martial.

Japan, the victor of the Russo-Japanese War, was imposing its own imperial rule in Taiwan, a Japanese possession since 1895. Expeditions against the aboriginal population of the island had led by 1906 to the killing of tens of thousands. With the country apparently 'pacified' it was opened up to foreign investment. Gold production, the island's chief source of revenue for Japan, rose considerably. But 'pacified' proved to be a relative term for the Japanese in Taiwan, as it was for some of the European Powers in Africa. Within a year of the pacification having been declared complete, new outbreaks of revolt took place.

In South Africa the Zulu population in the British province of Natal rose in revolt in 1906. In an attempt to deter the rebels the Natal government sentenced to death twelve Zulus who had been convicted of murdering two police officers at the outbreak of the rebellion. The twelve men were executed, but the rebellion continued. Its suppression was conducted with severity, and more than 3,000 Zulus were killed. The Anglican Bishop of Zululand charged that the conduct of the troops was 'a deep disgrace to Englishmen'.

French efforts to assert authority over Morocco were challenged by Maclain, a Muslim leader described in the European press as 'a fanatical sorcerer from the Sahara', who incited the local population to attack Christians and Jews. At Marrakech he and his followers burst into the Jewish quarter, murdering and looting. At the port of Mogador only the arrival of a French gunboat protected the Jews of the town from another Berber chief.

A British expedition to find and punish rebels in Northern Nigeria was successful, British newspapers reporting that the rebel forces at one town had been 'almost exterminated'. In South-West Africa the German colonialists' war against the Herero, Hottentot and Witboi had continued with heavy casualties on both sides. The German public were shocked when they were told, in June 1906, that almost 2,000 German troops had been killed in the fighting. German military reinforcements were sent, and the last of the Witboi leaders surrendered. A month later the Hottentot chief gave himself up. A German military force then set out against the ever-defiant Hereros, but heavy casualties were inflicted on the Germans throughout the autumn.

In Berlin, a majority of the Reichstag deputies, including the Centre Party on which the government relied for support, demanded a reduction in the number of troops in German South-West Africa. The Chancellor was indignant at this attempt to curtail German imperial policy, and when a motion to increase the money allocated to South-West Africa was rejected by 178 votes to 168, he dissolved the Reichstag. Of the 80,000 Hereros in South-West Africa at the start of the century, only 15,000 were alive a decade later.

*   *   *

That year, in the United States, Upton Sinclair's novel *The Jungle* exposed the terrible conditions, moral as well as sanitary, in the meat stock yards and packing houses of Chicago. In a letter to President Roosevelt, Sinclair urged an investigation. At first Roosevelt was reluctant to instigate one, but public pressure mounted, and when two undercover agents confirmed what Sinclair had written – that grave breaches of public health were involved in the slaughter and packing of meat – action was taken, and two pieces of binding legislation, the Meat Inspections Act and the Pure Food and Drug Act, were passed through Congress. These acts imposed severe penalties on anyone whose canned meat was adulterated in any way, or did not clearly show the date of manufacture.

Natural disasters continued to take their toll. In Hong Kong, a typhoon killed 10,000 people. In Italy, 500 people were killed when Vesuvius erupted in the first week of April. On the morning of April 18 San Francisco was struck by an earthquake. There had been no warning, only an unexplained nervousness of dogs and horses on the previous evening. As fires spread, Federal troops were deployed throughout the burning city to stop looting. Four looters, caught in the act, were arrested and shot. When a large crowd of looters attacked the Mint, which was ablaze, fourteen of them were shot dead.

More than a thousand people were killed in the earthquake. The people of Japan subscribed $100,000 to earthquake relief. But President Roosevelt declined all foreign help, asserting that the United States was able to help its own homeless and destitute. The United States was not the only earthquake victim in 1906. On August 16 an earthquake struck Chile, killing 3,000 people.

President Roosevelt's determination to protect the natural and historic wealth of his country continued to lead to legislation. The Antiquities Act, 1906, gave the President authority to set aside Federal lands 'for the protection of objects of scientific, prehistoric, or historic interest', and the authority of the National Forests Commission, established a decade earlier, strengthened. In Britain the creation of rural suburbs as integral parts of a city was inaugurated in 1906 with the founding of Hampstead Garden Suburb, on the northern outskirts of London. That year, the Liberal government also instituted reforms in the conditions under which merchant seamen worked. Internationally, a convention was signed which forbade night-shift work for women.

In the realm of music 1906 saw the invention of the jukebox and the debut of the singer Maurice Chevalier. In the United States the W. K. Kellogg Toasted Corn Flake Company launched a new breakfast cereal, Kellogg's Corn Flakes. That same year the Coca-Cola Company replaced the cocaine in its popular drink with caffeine. Two technological advances, both of which were to have wide repercussions in the years ahead in the life of every nation, also took place in the United States in 1906: the opening in New York of a film studio, and the first radio broadcast, transmitted on December 24, when music, a poem and a short talk were heard not only in New York City but by ships' radio operators at sea.

In Russia, at the opening session of the second Duma in 1907, the Prime Minister, Peter Stolypin, created a sense of hope and expectation when he announced: 'Our country must be transformed into a constitutional State.' What constituted the essential parameters of a 'constitutional State' differed in the mind of the government and that of the members of the Duma. When the Duma voted to expropriate land from landowners for distribution to needy peasants, the government refused to agree. In June, Stolypin demanded the suspension of all the Social Democratic party members, sixteen of whom were at once arrested, and a further fifty-five of whom were charged with carrying on revolutionary propaganda in the army and navy, in the form of pamphlets, widely distributed, calling on all soldiers and sailors to disobey the orders of their officers. The Duma wanted a committee of deputies set up, before which the government could present its evidence against the Social Democratic deputies. But before the committee could meet, the Tsar dissolved the Duma, and fixed a date for new elections in three months' time.

Before the new elections could be held the Tsar changed the basis of voting. This was itself an unconstitutional act which violated a provision accepted when the Duma had been established in 1906, that the electoral law could not be changed without the Duma's consent. Under the new franchise more votes were to go to landlords and fewer to peasants, and two-thirds of the seats allocated to Poland and the Caucasus were taken away. Before the elections could take place, newspapers critical of the government were fined and confiscated, and more than a thousand people were exiled to Siberia. In Vilna, a Polish bishop who had been a member of the second Duma was removed from his bishopric for having supported the demands of the Poles in his diocese for equal treatment with the Russians.

Before the second Duma could assemble, there was a mutiny of the garrison at Vladivostok which took several days to suppress. In his opening address to the Duma, Stolypin stressed that revolutionary excesses could only be met by force. By the end of the year more than a hundred newspaper editors had been exiled to Siberia, and twenty-six left-wing members of the second Duma had been sentenced to imprisonment with hard labour. To avoid arrest, Lenin, leader of the Bolshevik faction of the Social Democratic Party, left Russia for exile in Europe: he was to remain in exile for ten years.

In France a 'crusade of beggars' served as a focal point for other discontents. During rioting in Narbonne, French troops were taunted by the crowd to use their bayonets, and did so; in Perpignan the town hall was burned down. In Italy, peasant farmers and unsuccessful immigrants returning from Central and South America demanded government help in regions where there was agrarian distress, disrupting railway services as part of their protest. At Bari an attempt to launch a general strike was crushed. Social unrest also flared in the rural areas of the Roumanian provinces of Moldavia and Wallachia in the spring of 1907, when thousands of peasants who had witnessed the growing prosperity of Roumania through its grain exports without being the beneficiaries of that prosperity, rose in revolt. On a fierce rampage against those whom they accused of exploiting their labour, the peasants destroyed crops and burnt homes. In savage reprisals, the Roumanian government forces, 140,000 strong, killed more than 11,000 of the peasant rebels.

At an International Socialist Congress held in Germany in August, attended by the Socialist and labour party leaders from all over the world, delegates listened as the German Social Democratic Party leader, August Bebel, spoke of his conviction that wars came, not from conflict between the working classes, but from the desire of capitalist interests to provoke international conflicts. Bebel was strongly critical, however, of a French Socialist motion that in the event of war soldiers in all armies should desert, and even revolt. Another German Socialist then declared that love of humanity would never prevent his party from being 'good Germans', and he dismissed as 'foolishness' the idea of those delegates who believed that a European war could be brought to a halt by a working-class general strike.

The delegates were agreed that colonialism inevitably led to 'slavery, forced labour, the extermination of the natives, and the exhaustion of the natural riches of the countries colonized'. The cost of the colonies, the congress declared, should be born entirely by those who profited from their spoliation. It also agreed that Socialist members of all parliaments should vote against 'war budgets', and that Socialist workers should demonstrate whenever there was the 'slightest danger' of war.

In Vienna, during the first European elections held under universal male suffrage, the largest number of votes cast went to the mayor, Karl Lueger, head of the Christian Socialist party, whose platform was a mixture of Roman Catholicism, anti-Semitism and Socialism.

Every nationality of the Austrian Empire was represented in the parliament in Vienna, but in his address to the newly elected members Franz-Josef spoke of his confidence that 'a comprehensive widening of the juridical foundations of political life may go hand in hand with a concentration and increase of the State's political power'. This did not bode well for the national aspirations of the minorities. The principal national unrest in Austria-Hungary that year came from the most easterly peoples of the Empire, the Ruthenians, who, never having been independent, but always under the rule of some distant capital, resented the growing German influence in their main city, Lemberg. In the parliament in Vienna two Ruthenian deputies disrupted the proceedings by singing Ruthenian songs at the top of their voices, while another, who tried to make his speech in Russian, was forced to fall silent when informed that only the eight official languages of Austria could be used in the debates, and that Russian was not one of them.

In Prussia, the German authorities continued to press forward with the Germanization of the Polish areas. Polish-language newspapers were confiscated and their editors arrested, and a law was passed forbidding Polish peasants to build houses on their own land. The culmination of the anti-Polish measures came on November 26, when a bill was introduced into the Prussian Parliament for the compulsory expropriation of land owned by Poles. Money would be raised through local taxation to give cash compensation to those whose land was to be taken; thus the Poles would have to pay for their own eviction.

Slav discontent in Germany was small compared with that in Austria-Hungary. In the province of Bosnia-Herzegovina, which since 1878 had been under Austrian military occupation, the Serbs, who formed nearly half the population – the other half being Muslims – demanded complete autonomy, the election of a popular assembly on the basis of universal suffrage, and government of the province, not by Austrian military rulers, but by parliamentary majority. Austria rejected all these demands.

In the Hungarian portion of Austria-Hungary, the Croat minority was demanding a greater voice. The issue around which the agitation centred was language. When Croat members of the Hungarian Parliament insisted on speaking in Croat, the Hungarian deputies refused to listen to them. In anger the Croats walked out of the chamber. When the Governor of Croatia, appointed by the government in Budapest, supported Croat language demands, he was replaced by a governor known to support Magyar predominance in Croatia. One of the first of the new governor's ordinances made Magyar the official language on all Croatian railways. Croat travellers would have to discuss any surcharge of their train ticket in Hungarian, study the luncheon menu in Hungarian, and listen to all station announcements in Hungarian.

Similar language unrest affected the Slovak-speaking regions of northern Hungary. In one Slovak village a parish priest was imprisoned for two years for having insisted that the Slovak language be used in the schools and law courts. While the priest was in prison the villagers built a new church for him at their own expense, but refused to consecrate it until he was set free. The bishop, a Magyar, sent another priest, escorted by Hungarian troops, to consecrate the church. The villagers resisted and the troops opened fire. Eleven villagers were killed, among them five women and two children. When the Slovak deputies in the Hungarian Parliament protested, the Minister for Home Affairs replied that the villagers had committed 'an act of rebellion against the State'.

In Portugal's western Africa colonies, Guinea and Angola, native uprisings led to the despatch of troops from Lisbon and short but intense punitive expeditions. In German South-West Africa, the last of the Herero rebels were being hunted down. Reports reaching Europe suggested that, in the systematic sweeps being made against Herero villages, the whole tribe was being 'annihilated'. In German West Africa, and in nearby French West Africa, Muslim rebellions were crushed.

In the Far East, Japan was learning the problems of imperial rule. In Korea, an uprising against the Japanese presence led to bloodshed. A Korean regiment, refusing Japanese orders to disband, opened fire on the Japanese forces that eventually overcame it. More than 200 Japanese police and postal officials were murdered in the course of the uprising. Reprisals were severe.

No year was free from disasters which made headlines throughout the world. Accidents on the railways of the world were taking a steady toll. In Britain more than a thousand people lost their lives in 1907, and had done every year for the past decade. In 1907 an earthquake struck the central Asian region of Bukhara, a predominantly Muslim region over which Tsarist Russia had been sovereign for the previous forty years. In one town, 15,000 people were killed.

In India, the death toll from plague for the twelve months ending in September 1907 was 1,206,055, bringing the death toll for the previous seven years to more than five million. Drastic measures were recommended by the Government of India's medical experts, including the evacuation of hundreds of thousands of rat-infested houses, and the mass destruction of rats, even the possible inoculation of rats. Famine also struck Russia in 1907, when the widespread failure of the harvest led to the deaths of several million people.

Disasters in some parts of the world were parallelled by advances in the quality of life elsewhere: 1907 saw the manufacture in the United States of the first electric washing machine, and in Germany the invention of Persil detergent. The first synthetic plastic, Bakelite, was also invented that year, and on July 8 in New York, *The Follies of 1907* music and dancing show had its opening night: the Ziegfeld Follies that were to entertain millions of people for another half century.

Within the Ottoman Empire there were those determined to turn their backs on sloth and corruption, and create a modern empire. In 1908 the Committee of Union and Progress, established in Salonika two years earlier by Turkish reformers, mostly young army officers, demanded the salvation of Turkey through constitutional reform. One catalyst for the Young Turk revolution was the growing anarchy in Macedonia, where the continuing fighting between Greeks, Bulgarians, Serbs and Roumanians, the burning of each other's villages and the murder of civilians, threatened to bring Austrian and Russian troops into Macedonia to restore order, at Turkey's expense.

On July 23 the Young Turks in Macedonia declared the Ottoman constitution restored. Turkish troops based in Salonika then threatened to march on Constantinople if the Sultan did not accept their demands. On learning of the force that was about to descend on the capital, the Sultan agreed to restore the constitution that he had granted his subjects in 1876, which briefly instituted a parliamentary system, but had been 'suspended' fourteen months later. He also agreed to abolish censorship and release political prisoners. A Frenchman was appointed financial adviser to the new government, and an Englishman adviser on irrigation. But a request by the Young Turks for an alliance with Britain was rejected in London. Despite its revolution, Turkey was not regarded as on a par with the European Powers.

The Russian revolution had been crushed at the end of 1905, but discontent, terror and repression had returned. In the two years 1908 and 1909 more than 3,000 Russians were sentenced to death for political crimes, and more than 4,000 to hard labour. In July 1908 Leo Tolstoy published an appeal in which he declared that government repression was 'a hundredfold worse' than the criminal and terrorist violence in Russia because it was carried out in cold blood. On Tolstoy's eightieth birthday that September, the Russian newspapers were forbidden to make any mention of the anniversary.

The European Powers were searching for agreements that would help avert European conflict. In April, France and Germany agreed a common frontier between the German Cameroons and the French Congo. The border was delineated along rivers and streams so that accidental clashes between troops could be minimized. But the German navy continued to grow, becoming the largest naval force in the Baltic, and alarming both Russia and Britain. In the autumn of 1908 a retired German civil servant, Rudolf Martin, caused uproar in Britain when he advocated building a fleet of Zeppelin airships to be used for invasion, 'each to carry twenty soldiers, which should land and capture the sleeping Britons before they could realize what was taking place'. One result of Martin's outburst was to create interest in British government circles in the aeroplane as a weapon of war.

The French Army had just ordered fifty Wright aeroplanes to be built in France, and was experimenting with bombs containing inflammable liquid that might be dropped from these planes. The British Government asked Sir Hiram Maxim, the inventor of the Maxim gun, for advice. Maxim, who believed the aeroplane would become an effective weapon of war, spoke bluntly: 'If you were going to bombard a town, you might have a thousand of these machines, each one carrying a large shell, because it is the large shell that does the business. If a thousand tons of pure nitroglycerine were dropped on to London in one night, it would make London look like a last year's buzzard's nest.'

In Austria-Hungary, racial and national animosities were in no way diminished in 1908. When the Bohemian Diet met in Prague, the Germans, who constituted a majority, obstructed all legislation proposed by the Czech members, or in any way advantageous to the Czechs. In the southern province of Slovenia, German and Slovene citizens of the empire clashed in the streets. In Vienna, German and Italian students fought, the Italians demanding an Italian university in the Austrian port of Trieste, the majority of whose inhabitants were Italian. In the parliament in Vienna, the Czech Radical deputies sought to prevent the passage of the annual budget measures by drowning the voices of the debaters with whistles and penny trumpets.

In retrospect, the national tensions within Austria-Hungary were the prelude to that empire's territorial disintegration, but at the time it seemed that Austria-Hungary could only grow in strength and cohesiveness, even expanding its influence southward into the Balkans. Following the decision of the Young Turks in Constantinople to call a parliament – something hitherto unknown in the Ottoman Empire – Austria-Hungary feared that the province of Bosnia-Herzegovina, under Austrian control since 1878 but still under nominal Turkish suzereinty, would seek representation in that parliament, and challenge the often harsh nature of Austrian rule. Austria-Hungary was determined to forestall this. Since 1878, Bulgaria, while autonomous, had been nominally a Turkish possession. It too feared that the Muslims in its midst would look to the new rulers in Constantinople for representation and redress.

Austria-Hungary and Bulgaria took co-ordinated action. On October 5 Bulgaria declared its independence from Turkey, and on the following day – a fateful day for European stability – Austria-Hungary announced the annexation of Bosnia-Herzegovina. The annexation alarmed Serbia, which found itself with the full panoply of Austrian sovereign power along its longest border, from the Danube to the Adriatic Sea. It also alarmed Russia, which feared that Austria-Hungary would move against Serbia, many of whose most vociferous nationalists lived within the annexed areas. When the Crown Prince of Serbia arrived in St Petersburg on October 28 he was met with enthusiastic Russian crowds denouncing Austria's acquisition of Bosnia-Herzegovina. But Germany, taking Austria-Hungary's side, was emphatic that no action should be taken against the annexation. Russia, following her defeat by Japan, was in no position to act as the protector of the South Slavs. Instead, she urged Serbia not to take any 'provocative steps' which might lead to hostilities with Austria and threaten a wider war.

The new Turkish Parliament was opened in Constantinople on 10 December 1908. In conformity with the mood of reform and toleration, a Greek was appointed Minister of Mines, Forests and Agriculture, and an Armenian became Minister of Commerce and Works. Of the 250 elected deputies, fifty were Arabs from Arabia; there were also eighteen Greeks, twelve Albanians, four Bulgarians, two Serbians and three Jews. These constitutional advances, which raised great hopes among the Turkish population, were parallelled by anger that the provinces of Bosnia-Herzegovina and Bulgaria had both been lost.

Far from Europe, the European Empires continued to face the anger of their subject peoples. In the Dutch East Indies, sporadic rebellions against Dutch rule on several islands were put down, the harshest measures being described as 'pacification'. British 'pacification' efforts were also in evidence in 1908. Along the north-west frontier of India, two Muslim tribes, the Mohmands and the Zakka Khels, whose rebellion more than a decade earlier had been crushed, rebelled again. A punitive expedition against the Zakka Khels was successful before the Mohmands could come to their assistance, despite the call by the Mohmand mullahs for their people to participate in *Jihad*, or Holy War. When 7,000 Mohmands crossed into British India they were driven back and a second punitive expedition sent against them. The Mohmands, their forts and watch towers having been destroyed, gave up the struggle.

Within India, the British rulers were confronted by increased nationalist agitation. In Bengal an attempt was made to blow up the train in which the Lieutenant-Governor was travelling. At Muzaffarpur two British women were killed when a bomb was thrown at their carriage by two Bengalis who mistook the carriage for that of a local magistrate. In a garden in Calcutta, police discovered a cache of arms, bombs and bomb-making instructions. In July the Bengali nationalist leader and newspaper editor, Bal Gangadhar Tilak, was convicted of sedition and sentenced to six years' transportation. In December the Indian Criminal Law was amended, denying the accused in any case of sedition, disturbance or murder, the right to be present at his own trial, or to be represented by his own defence lawyer, unless the magistrate specifically allowed it. If committed for trial, the accused would be sent before a panel of three judges. He would have no right to trial by jury.

In the German Empire, the question of the treatment of the Poles continued, year by year, to be the subject of harsh legislation and internal division. New measures were introduced in the Prussian Parliament on 26 February 1908 to expropriate land from the Poles and transfer it to Germans. A liberal German newspaper denounced the expropriations 'in the name of justice and humanity', but a majority of the members of the German Parliament supported their Prussian counterparts. The German Parliament also debated a Polish request to allow the use of the Polish language at public meetings. It was agreed that where more than sixty per cent of the local inhabitants spoke Polish, Polish could be the language of the meeting, provided three days' notice of the meeting was given to the police. So rigidly was the law upheld that where even as many as fifty-five per cent of the local population were Polish, they were not allowed to use their own language at public meetings. The Poles were tenacious in their national cause, holding 'mute' public meetings at which there were no speeches, but where the resolutions were written up in Polish on a large blackboard, and passed by a show of hands.

In South Africa, an attempt to expel Indians who were said to have entered the country without permission was met by widespread protest, and the organization of passive resistance to the government's registration laws. When Gandhi and several other leaders of the demonstrations were sentenced to two months' imprisonment with hard labour, Jan Christiaan Smuts, the South Africa Boer leader, denounced the sentences as too lenient. In answer to criticism from Britain of the severity of the punishments, Smuts replied that the Transvaal was 'a White man's country' and should be 'kept that way'.

Smuts agreed to open negotiations with Gandhi, but made it clear he hoped no more Indians would reach South Africa, and that in due course the Indian population would wither away. A new law sought to deprive the Indians already in the country of religious teachers, doctors and educationalists. When the act came into force Gandhi renewed his call for demonstrations, always stressing that no violence should be employed. He was convinced that morality would prevail over prejudice. It did not do so in South Africa.

In the United States, Theodore Roosevelt remained a firm believer in the importance of preserving his country's natural resources. Having set up the system of National Parks that would be protected from both urban and industrial exploitation, he called a conference of State Governors and prominent men which determined that the 'conservation of our natural resources is a subject of transcendent importance, which should engage unremittingly the attention of the nation'. The conference also called for laws to prevent waste in coal, oil and gas mining and extraction, 'with a view to their wise conservation for the use of the people'.

The ravages of nature continued to take human life. In June more than a thousand Chinese were killed when an earthquake created a fissure several miles long, swallowing up both homes and their occupants. The next month, in the Canadian province of British Columbia, fire destroyed the town of Fernie, killing a hundred people. In British India, plague deaths during the twelve months to September were calculated at 201,575. The worst natural disaster in Europe in 1908 came when an earthquake struck southern Italy. An estimated 200,000 Italians were killed.

The motor car made a significant advance in 1908, when Henry Ford announced that his Ford Motor Company would be making a Model T car, priced within the capacity of hundreds of thousands, even millions, of people. To the benefit of millions more, that year saw the introduction in the United States of the electric iron and the paper cup. The cinema was becoming a popular vehicle for the spread of culture to the masses: among the films of 1908 was *Tosca*, starring Sara Bernhardt. The location of the main film studios in the United States was about to change from the East Coast to the West. When filming of *The Count of Monte Cristo* was completed that year in an open air studio near Los Angeles, a new venue, and a new word, entered the vocabulary of entertainment: Hollywood.

A story that might have come from Hollywood had its origins in 1908. On August 4 that year the Waterman's Fountain Pen

Company of New York engraved the date of manufacture on one of its new gold-tipped fountain pens. The pen later became the property of Alexandre Villedieu, a Frenchman. He had it in his pocket in May 1915, while fighting on the Western Front. During the battle he was killed. His body, like that of tens of thousands of others, was never found, until, in the spring of 1996, a local farmer, ploughing the field, chanced upon it. Alongside Villedieu's body were his pipe, a pocket knife, his military belt – and the Waterman's fountain pen.

In 1909 a British writer, Norman Angell, argued in his book *The Great Illusion* that even a victorious warring Power would suffer economic and financial loss as a result of any future war. Angell stressed that the great industrial nations: Britain, the United States, Germany and France, were 'losing the psychological impulse to war' because of the interdependence and profits of trade and commerce. But the Chief of the German General Staff, General Schlieffen, had devised a plan for the rapid swing of German troops through neutral Belgium, in order to reach Paris and defeat France within six weeks – before the cumbersome Russian army could have time to make any significant advance against Germany in the east. With France having surrendered, Germany would then turn, under Schlieffen's plan, to attack Russia, and advance with superior forces. This was, of course, only a plan, not a policy. Indeed, the German policymakers made a major conciliatory gesture in 1909, when a Franco-German agreement was signed, whereby Germany agreed to pursue 'only economic interests' in Morocco, while recognizing the special interests of France in the 'consolidation of order and of internal peace'. Germany also agreed not to carry out, or encourage, any measure that might lead to the creation of German economic privilege in Morocco. Following this agreement the German Government prevented a German mining company from pursuing 600 mining claims which it had negotiated with the Sultan of Morocco, on the grounds that these claims, if upheld, would constitute a German monopoly, and thus a breach of the new agreement.

It was in the Balkans that the seeds of a European war were planted. Following the Serb protests against Austria-Hungary's annexation of Bosnia-Herzegovina, the Austrians warned Serbia against any provocative action. There were demonstrations inside Russia in favour of Serbia. In protest against these demonstrations the German Government warned Russia that if she intervened militarily on behalf of Serbia, and attacked Austria-Hungary, then Germany would be bound by treaty to take the side of her Austro-Hungarian ally.

Faced by German pressure, the Russian Government advised Serbia to halt all anti-Austrian demonstrations and accept the Austrian annexation of Bosnia-Herzegovina. Serbia, far too weak to act alone against Austria, deferred to Russia's advice. Many Russians, with their sense of solidarity with Slavs everywhere, felt humiliated that German pressure had forced them to 'abandon' Serbia.

Inside Russia, the Duma continued to debate, but the powers of the autocracy were undiminished. Official figures released in St Petersburg in 1909 revealed that 782 political offenders had been executed in the previous year, an increase of more than a hundred from the year before that. The number in exile for political offences, mostly in Siberia, was an astonishing 180,000.

There was a growing call for greater Russification in Russia's Polish provinces, which had been a hotbed of revolt in 1905. Even among the liberal groups in the Duma, the idea of increased Russification found favour, with the result that the Polish deputies in the Duma lost half their representation. At the same time, the Polish Educational Society in Kiev, which catered for the large Polish minority living throughout western Ukraine, was closed down.

In Turkey, an attempt was made by forces still loyal to the autocratic powers of the Sultan to overthrow the Young Turks. On April 13 they seized power in Constantinople, but the troops in Salonika, the original base of Young Turk activity, remained loyal to the constitution, and Constantinople was recaptured eleven days later. The Turkish National Assembly, in an emergency session, voted unanimously to depose the Sultan, and he was sent into exile. He was succeeded by his brother.

Among the minorities inside Turkey who hoped the Young Turk revolution would bring them the political equality they had long been denied were the Armenians. There were as many as two million Armenians in the Ottoman Empire, by far the largest Christian group, living mostly in eastern Anatolia. Their hopes of equality were dashed, however, when in 1909 several thousand Armenians were massacred in southern Turkey.

In British India – where plague was in its tenth year, the total number of victims for the year being officially noted, with the extraordinary precision of the clerks of empire, as 129,756 – the Liberal government initiated reforms that would bring Indians into many levels of government. The first Indian to be appointed a member of the Viceroy's Executive Council took his place on the council in March. The appointment of an Indian had been strongly opposed by one member of the Viceroy's Council, who warned: 'An Indian colleague would be the admission of the thin end of the wedge which is to bring about the downfall of British administration.'

The British Liberal Government was in the final stages of negotiating an Act of Union with the Boer rulers in South Africa. There was distress in London when the Boers revealed their determination not to allow any form of equality for black Africans, Indians or people of mixed race, but would enforce a colour-bar as part of the constitutional legislation. A delegation of black Africans and Indians, Gandhi among them, went to Britain to put their case, and to have race equality made a part of the Union legislation. Many British Members of Parliament felt that the exclusion of non-whites from the right to vote was not only wrong in itself, but an abdication of imperial responsibilities. The white population of South Africa was determined, however, that their new parliament would be a parliament of whites, elected by whites, and that there should be no prospect of this franchise being extended in the future.

The British Government sought reconciliation with the Boers, the former enemies, and an attempt to satisfy Boer needs and prejudices overrode considerations of morality. Two Liberal principles were in conflict: that of equality and that of non-interference in colonial legislatures. With the passage of the Act of Union, the principle of equality with regard to skin colour in South Africa was ignored, and was to remain so for more than eight decades.

The British Empire was still expanding. On the Malayan Peninsula the Siamese Government transferred four Malay States to Britain, and agreed that British subjects throughout Siam would enjoy 'the rights and privileges' of Siamese citizens, but would be exempt from military service and all forced loans and military contributions. In Egypt, the British rulers promulgated a law placing under police supervision and village confinement anyone who agitated against British rule. Two months after the law was passed, the Egyptian National Congress met in Geneva, the Egyptian speakers stressing that they were competent to govern themselves, and that conditions under British administration were 'intolerable'. The British had no intention of leaving Egypt: control of the Suez Canal seemed an imperial necessity, guarding the sea route to India and the Far East. The actual Egyptian administration, like that of the Anglo-Egyptian Sudan to the south, was considered a model of colonial rectitude and advanced thinking. There was also the moral imperative, as seen by the Liberal Government in London, of suppressing the slave trade and the arms trade still being carried on in the more remote regions. The British civil servants were convinced they were better suited than the local population to advance the causes of health and welfare. These officials were proud of the fact that, as a result of a persistent British campaign against mosquitoes, an increase in infant mortality had been halted at Port Said. The Egyptian call for an end to British rule seemed, in British eyes, retrogressive and subversive, harmful not only to the fabric of empire but to the well-being of its native populations.

Every imperial power faced conflicts within its Empire. In Spanish Morocco, 6,000 Rif tribesmen attacked the 2,000-strong Spanish garrison, killing eleven Spanish soldiers before being driven off by artillery fire. Reinforcements were sent from Spain, but the Moors attacked again. In the ensuing battle, 300 Spanish soldiers were killed and more than a thousand Moors. Inside Spain there were anti-war demonstrations in those towns from which reservists had been called to the colours. On July 18 the demonstrations spread to Barcelona. That same day, in Morocco, Rif tribesmen launched an attack on Spanish supply lines. The news that reached Spain was inflamed by rumours that exaggerated the scale of the losses. Anti-war demonstrations in Barcelona and Madrid spread to railway stations in other cities from which conscripts were leaving for North Africa.

In Barcelona, anarchists and socialists called a general strike for July 26. On the following day, in the Rif, more than 500 Spaniards were killed. Three days later troops were called out to put an end to the anti-war demonstrations in Barcelona. Artillery fire was effective in dispersing the demonstrators, almost 2,000 of whom were subsequently arrested, and five of whom were sentenced to death.

When the strength of Spain's military forces in Spanish Morocco reached 50,000, the Moors lost hope of driving the Spaniards out. Negotiations were opened on November 12, and three days later the tribesmen of the Rif surrendered. Militant Islam was once again suppressed.

The first decade of the twentieth century was coming to an end. Its achievements were considerable. In Germany in 1909, women were admitted to the universities for the first time. In Britain the first Town Planning Act was passed, regulating the unchecked spread of urban sprawl. The first department store also opened in Britain that year – the creation of an American, H. Gordon Selfridge. In Palestine, under Turkish rule, the first Jewish collective farm, or kibbutz, was founded on the shore of the Sea of Galilee. It was the brainchild of Arthur Ruppin, a German Jew. Most of the farmers who practised its collective ethos were Jewish immigrants from Russia.

The year 1909 also marked a milestone in the history of the cinema. A permanent location, the nickelodeon, which had been introduced in the United States four years earlier, raised cinema attendance to more than twenty million a week. One of the very first feature films was issued that year, Vitagraph's *The Life of Moses*. In Italy, Milano Films produced *Dante's Inferno*.

The science of flight made a great leap forward in 1909. On July 25 a Frenchman, Louis Blériot, flew across the English Channel. He flew twenty-three miles, from a field near Calais to a meadow behind Dover Castle. The flight took him just under an hour and twenty minutes. In New York, Orville Wright made two flights around the Statue of Liberty, then hastened by transatlantic liner to Berlin, where, in another remarkable flying display, he took the German Crown Prince up with him to a height of a thousand feet.

CHAPTER TWO

The Paths to War

1910—14

Tsarist power continued to be exercised throughout the vast territories of the Russian Empire in favour of Russification, sometimes dramatically so. During 1910 Finland was deprived of her autonomy, and that same year the Polish subjects of the empire were denied even the limited rights of local self-government that had been accorded to the Russians. Restrictions on Jewish residence and higher education were similarly maintained, as was the refusal to allow Jews to participate in local government.

The death of Leo Tolstoy in November was marked by a time of mourning throughout Russia. One of his last acts was to write an article opposing capital punishment. It stimulated a rally in St Petersburg by a thousand students demanding an end to the death penalty, and a student strike in protest against the ill-treatment of political prisoners.

The United States faced an upsurge of nationalist feeling in the Philippines. In July, the Secretary of the Interior was attacked on Palawan island. In August there was an uprising in the north of Luzon. In October, tribesmen on Mindanao rose in revolt. But the efforts of the United States to introduce a beneficial administration were continuous: road-making, water-supply and improved sanitation were much in evidence, trade in sugar and tobacco flourished, and there was pride in Washington at the end of the year when it was announced that bubonic plague had been eradicated on the islands and cholera greatly reduced.

In the Turkish province of Macedonia, almost the last possession of Turkey-in-Europe, the heavy hand of Turkish rule was much in evidence. The Young Turks were no less nationalist in their outlook than their predecessors. Bulgarian and Greek inhabitants of Macedonia who refused to give up their firearms were flogged and tortured; many fled across the borders into neighbouring Bulgaria and Greece. All Bulgarian political clubs in Macedonia were closed down, and efforts were made to interfere in the lessons taught in Bulgarian schools in the province.

Macedonian revolutionary activity, which had been suspended when the Young Turks came to power in Constantinople in the hope of a more tolerant future, was revived during 1910, mainly in reaction to the growing Muslim influence in the province. The reaction was intensified after the hanging, following secret trials by Turkish military tribunals, of Macedonians accused of anti-Turkish activities. The main thrust of the renewed agitation was among Bulgarians in the province, who found a ready source of money and bombs for their terrorist actions across the border in Bulgaria, where the government looked with favour on their activities.

The Greeks in Turkish Macedonia were likewise treated with harshness by the Turks, who insisted that disputes among Christians could only be adjudicated by Muslim officials. In Turkish Albania, the Albanians took up arms when the Turks insisted they use the Arabic script in all Albanian schools, rather than their own Latin script. As the Albanians fought on, 17,000 Turkish troops were sent against them. In a humiliating reverse for the Turks, 3,000 Albanians ambushed a Turkish military train, capturing a large quantity of supplies and disarming the soldiers. It was not until two weeks later that the Albanians were driven off, after a thirteen-hour battle with a substantially larger Turkish force. By the end of the year the Turks had 50,000 troops in their Albanian province, but it was estimated that a million Albanians were under arms, many of them in remote mountain areas almost inaccessible to military columns.

In Britain, the year 1910 witnessed considerable industrial unrest, with working men and women unconvinced that the Liberal government would reform their pay and conditions sufficiently to make life tolerable. New legislation was introduced, considerably improving working conditions. In France, a rail strike threatened to bring the

communications and commerce of the nation to a halt. It was brought
to an end when the government arrested the leaders of the strike and
ordered the mobilization into the army of all railwaymen and engine
drivers, thereby making them subject to military discipline should
they refuse to obey the order to start work. In parliament, deputies
who supported the strike prevented the Prime Minister, Aristide
Briand, from speaking by hissing, hooting and banging their desks.
At one point Briand declared that if the government had not found
a lawful means to stop the strike it would have resorted to illegal
means. There was such an outcry at this 'dictatorial' remark – an
outcry unprecedented in living Parisian memory – that the session
was suspended.

In parliament, deputies

There was also serious industrial unrest in Berlin in 1910, when
police protected non-union workers who were being employed by a
coal merchant whose own men were on strike. A demonstration of
workers in sympathy with the strikers, and denouncing the
strikebreaking support of the police, attacked the police with stones.
The police drew their swords and charged. The struggle continued
for two days, with many policemen and workers being injured. A
group of British and American journalists, who had police permission
to visit the scene of the confrontation, were attacked by the police
with their swords, and some were seriously injured. The German
Government, despite diplomatic pressure, refused to censure the
police.

In the United States there were strikes in New York and Chicago,
as men demanded higher wages, shorter hours of employment and
the right for an all-union work force. An explosion that destroyed
the *Los Angeles Times*, which had attacked the trade unions, was
attributed to the labour unrest.

In Budapest, in his annual speech from the throne, Franz-Josef
spoke of the need for a universal suffrage system that would maintain
'the unitary national character of the Hungarian State'. For the non-
Magyars in that State these fine words were of no help in furthering
their desire for much greater rights and autonomies. Croats in particular felt aggrieved at Magyar ascendancy.

Inside the Austrian half of Franz-Josef's domains, racial strife
was even more acute. In Lemberg, Ruthenian university students

who had already been denied a Ruthenian faculty attacked Polish students in the university building; a student was killed and a professor badly injured. In Bosnia-Herzegovina, during the first session of the local parliament, Serb, Muslim and Croat deputies made common cause in pointing out their political and economic subservience. The constitution, declared the Sarajevo deputies, 'does not correspond to the expectations of the country'.

In French Indo-China, forces hostile to France continued to attack French military columns. In a confrontation in April four hundred Vietnamese were killed. Many of those captured were deported to French Guiana, on the other side of the globe. In Egypt, British rule was under continual threat from nationalists who wanted an end to the imperial administration. Individual Egyptians who were part of the higher reaches of that administration were as much at risk as the British. In February the Prime Minister, Boutros Ghali Pasha, was assassinated by an Egyptian nationalist. He was the first native Prime Minister of Egypt and a Christian Copt – eighty-two years later his grandson was to become Secretary General of the United Nations.

Germany continued to have trouble in its colonial empire. In German South-West Africa there was a revolt of Kaffir labourers protesting at the low wages and meagre rations during railway building. The revolt was quickly put down, and several labourers were killed. In the German Cameroons, following the death of a German trader and his seventeen Cameroonian porters, murdered by a tribe that practised cannibalism, punitive measures were undertaken and several hundred tribesmen were killed in an attempt to strike at the perpetrators and their villages.

In India, plague, which had taken more than six million lives since the beginning of the century, but was believed to be on the wane, suddenly increased its depredations. In the year ending September 1910 almost half a million Indians died. Inoculation, the most valuable protection, could not be used because of popular prejudice against it, a British inquiry noting that the attitude of the population towards inoculation varied 'from apathy to active hostility'.

Manchuria was also affected by plague in 1910; nor was any way found to prevent it from spreading southward into China. That year there was also a famine in two Chinese provinces. Hundreds of thousands died. The first overseas military action in 1910 by a European Power was taken by France, when a Berber attempt to break into the Moroccan city of Fez was beaten off. A week after the French relief of Fez, Spanish troops occupied a town in Spanish Morocco that was under Berber attack. Spanish politics, already in turmoil as a result of the growing republican movement, were further convulsed by this forward move. An anti-war meeting in Barcelona was followed by mutiny on a Spanish warship anchored off Tangier. The leader of the mutiny was not so concerned by the military action in Africa as with the ending of the Spanish monarchy and establishing a Republic. He was arrested, condemned to death and executed. Strikes broke out all over Spain: in docks, mines and factories. Troops were called in to restore order; cavalry charges broke up demonstrations, and artillery was brought up as a final intimidation, but the strikes continued to spread. On September 19 the King signed a decree suspending the constitutional guarantees of personal liberty, and of freedom of the press. Within a few weeks the prisons were filled with republican agitators. When there was no room left in the prisons, army barracks were converted into places of incarceration. The unrest was quelled, partly because the financial resources of the strikers ran out; but the discontent did not diminish. One result was a dramatic increase in working-class emigration, mostly to the Argentine.

In Southern Nigeria, the murder of a British Assistant District Commissioner, two policemen and three boat boys was followed by a punitive expedition against the tribe responsible. In the Gold Coast, tribes in the northern territories who refused to submit to British rule were 'reduced to subjection' – in the words of the official British report – after one week's fighting by a native force led by a British army captain. In German South-West Africa, yet another Hottentot revolt broke out, and was suppressed.

The most distant European possessions were those in the Pacific. During 1911 there was a revolt on Espíritu Santo, one of the islands of the New Hebrides, an Anglo-French condominium. It was quickly suppressed. In the German Carolines a revolt of men who had been forced to work at road-making on the island was likewise suppressed: fifteen, who were found guilty of the murder of German traders, were executed; the rest of the population was deported to another island.

The coronation of King George V on June 22 was followed by a naval review at Spithead, when 167 British warships were assembled as a sign of the power of Britain. But it was a thousand miles to the south that a small naval episode threatened to escalate into a conflict between the Powers. For some time Germany had been hoping to develop a port on the Atlantic coast of Morocco, and at the beginning of July sent a gunboat to the tiny port of Agadir. The reason given by the German Government was that the gunboat was needed to protect German subjects in Agadir, whose personal safety and property were being threatened by Berber attacks. A few days later, the gunboat was replaced by a larger warship. No attempt was made to put German troops ashore, but the warship trained her guns on shore installations. She would leave Agadir, the Germans told the French, 'as soon as peace and order are restored to Morocco'.

The French insisted that the presence of a German warship, for whatever reason or pretext, was a breach of their rights in Morocco. There were rumours in Paris of impending war between France and Germany. When France asked Britain for support, the British Government entered the dispute, demanding that the Germans withdraw their warship. On July 26 the British Atlantic fleet, which was to have gone northward that week to Norwegian waters, was sent instead to the English Channel, within much shorter steaming distance of the Moroccan coast. The Germans backed down. For a short while the Agadir crisis had seemed a prelude to war, but within a month calm was restored, and at an international naval regatta in Britain, at Spithead, a yacht belonging to the Kaiser took part, and was among the victors.

Inside Britain, 1911 saw further industrial unrest. A strike of dock workers which began in May, spread during July and August until the docks at London, Liverpool and Manchester were at a halt. On August 1, more than twenty ocean liners in the London docks were unable to sail. Some workers, mostly coal porters and lightermen, agreed to accept arbitration, but the main body of the strikers would not settle. On August 11 the government made plans to send 20,000 troops into London. At a mass meeting of transport workers in Liverpool two days later, 200 people were injured in clashes with the police. Troops were sent to the city and, after stones were thrown at them, opened fire, killing two men. A warship was sent to the River Mersey and armed sailors landed to protect the docks. There was also rioting among the black dockworkers in Cardiff, who claimed that the rise in wages brought about by the strike caused shipowners to prefer white crews.

The dock strike was followed by a railway strike, reducing Britain's rail traffic by half and seriously affecting trade. Troops were sent to guard stations and signal boxes, and to protect workers who were still operating the trains. At Llanelli, in South Wales, troops fired on a crowd of rioters, killing two men. When the government finally promised that the strikers would not be penalized, and their grievances would be settled by arbitration, most railwaymen went back to work, but there was further rioting in South Wales, where the ugly spectre of anti-Semitism was raised in a series of attacks on Jewish shops and homes.

These British domestic upheavals had hardly abated when, on August 27, in a speech at Hamburg, the Kaiser spoke of the need for an increase in the size of the German navy. His speech rang alarm bells in Britain, where it seemed to herald a direct German challenge to British naval supremacy.

Inside Russia's universities, radical students were in the ascendancy. In February 1911 the Russian Government announced that much of the administration of the universities would be transferred to the police. Students who continued to agitate were expelled, and many were conscripted into the army. But the Russian Prime Minister, Stolypin, sought to initiate reforms. An act for medical care which he put on the statute book was in many respects more advanced than those in Britain or Germany. Land sales to peasants were such that within five years the peasants owned almost 90 per cent of all arable land and more than 94 per cent of all livestock: a true revolution in a countryside hitherto dominated by landowners with large estates.

But Stolypin's energies were soon to be cut short. At Kiev during a gala opera performance in the presence of the Tsar, he was shot by an anarchist while standing in the front row of the stalls. He died in hospital four days later.

In North Africa, only two regions were not yet under the control of a European Power: Tripolitania and Cyrenaica – today combined as Libya. Both had been under Turkish rule since the sixteenth century. The rest of the North African coastline was ruled by France, Spain and Britain. The Italian Government had long coveted a place on the southern shore of the Mediterranean. Italian national sentiment was roused by charges made against the Turks of unfairness towards Italian residents in Tripolitania, and of 'intriguing' by Germany, which was said to have its own territorial desires on Cyrenaica.

On 26 September 1911 a Turkish transport ship arrived in the Tripolitanian port of Tripoli with guns and ammunition. The following day the Italian Government gave the Turks forty-eight hours in which to accept the occupation of Tripolitania and Cyrenaica by Italian troops, and the establishment of an Italian administration. Before the ultimatum expired ten Italian battleships and cruisers took up war stations off Tripoli. On the following day Italy declared war on Turkey, and for two days Italian naval guns bombarded Turkish fortified positions. The Turks returned fire for as long as their ammunition held out, and then withdrew. Tripoli was occupied by the Italians on October 5, Benghazi on October 20.

In the interior, the local Arabs called on their fellow Muslims inside Tripoli to resist the Italian occupation. The call was answered by an uprising in which 374 Italian soldiers were killed, and terrible cruelties were perpetrated on those Italians who were captured. Italian reprisals were also cruel: hundreds of Arabs were killed by Italian soldiers in scenes of brutality which, being fully reported by the journalists and later supported by newspaper photographs, created indignation in the European capitals. 'Horrible atrocities,' a British commentator noted at the end of the year, were committed on both sides. That the 'half-savage Arab tribes' should have committed them, he added, 'was perhaps to be expected, but one would have thought that the civilised Italian soldiers would at least have abstained from such acts as the indiscriminate slaughter of unarmed men, women, and children for three days after the attack on the Italian rear by the Arabs had been repulsed.'

On November 1 an Italian airman, flying over a Turkish military encampment at an oasis in Tripolitania, leaned out of his aicraft and dropped a few small bombs by hand. No serious damage was done but a new, and in due course terrible, era had been inaugurated: that of aerial bombardment. On November 6 the Italian Government announced that Tripolitania and Cyrenaica were under the 'full and entire sovereignty' of Italy. The Turkish Empire in North Africa was at an end.

In British India, extremist nationalist agitators continued to use the bullet and the bomb, killing both British officials and Indians working for the British police. But the confidence of Empire could not easily be dented: at the end of 1911 the King-Emperor, George V, and his Queen-Empress, Mary, travelled throughout India as part of his coronation celebrations. At the Coronation Durbar in Delhi, 132 ruling chiefs paid homage. One concession announced that day was that in future Indian soldiers would be eligible for the highest British military award for bravery, the Victoria Cross, from which they had hitherto been excluded.

Hopes in India that the plague deaths would diminish and wither away were dashed when the number of deaths rose in 1911 to almost three quarters of a million. The total number of Indian plague deaths since the start of the century had risen to more than seven million.

In China the rule of the Manchu dynasty was ending, as revolutionaries established a republic. Any Manchu garrison which resisted was massacred. Among the students recruited to fight for the republican cause was eighteen-year-old Mao Tse-tung. One by one the provincial capitals fell to the revolutionary forces. In November, the Emperor, in an attempt to ward off disaster, agreed to accept a constitution, as demanded by the republican-dominated National Assembly, under which his imperial powers would be limited to the formal appointment of a Prime Minister who had already been elected by the parliament. Parliament would control all treaties and budgets.

The revolutionaries were determined that the Manchu dynasty

would disappear altogether and proclaimed a republican government at Canton. The organizer of the revolution was Dr Sun Yat-sen, a Christian, and a graduate of an American university. For the previous fourteen years he had been an exile from China, publishing a 'Summary of Revolution' in which he pledged 'equal rights' to all Chinese. He was also a supporter of a greater role for women in Chinese life.

In early December the Manchu troops were defeated in Nanking, and on December 31 the republicans elected Sun Yat-sen President of the Chinese Republic. He assumed office on the following day, abolishing the ancient Chinese calendar with its ten-day periods based on lunar calculations and replacing it by the Western solar calendar with its weeks of seven days. The final act of the establishment of the republic in China was the abdication of the Emperor on 12 February 1912.

Fire in cinemas and workplaces continued to take a heavy toll. In a Russian town halfway between Moscow and St Petersburg a wooden cinema building caught fire during the showing of a film to mark the jubilee of the emancipation of slaves in Russia; ninety people, including many children, were killed. During a cinema show in the United States, near Pittsburgh, panic arose after the cry of 'Fire!' was heard and although it was a false alarm twenty-five people, mostly children, died in the crush to leave the building. In New York, fire at a blouse workshop at the top of a ten-storey building killed 141 women working there. Most of the dead were Italian, Irish and Hungarian immigrants. Two issues long at the back of the public mind came to prominence as a result of the fire: inadequate safety standards in workplaces and the exploitation of immigrant labour. Other disasters in 1911 included the death in Alabama of more than a hundred convicts, killed when there was an explosion in the underground mine in which they were working as forced labourers.

A social disturbance rocked the United States that year – a lynching in Pennsylvania, when a black man who had tried to commit suicide to avoid arrest for theft was taken from hospital in his bed and burnt alive. Three times he tried to get out of the bed, and each time was forced back into the flames. The lynching was particularly shocking to enlightened Americans because those carrying it out were prominent citizens of the town, and because, when the lynch mob was brought to trial, the sympathy of the local whites was such that two successive juries refused to convict.

A new instrument of war was being developed, the submarine, designed to operate both on the surface, using automatic weapons against merchant ships, and beneath the sea, using torpedoes against warships. In January 1911 the German submarine *U-3* sank in Kiel harbour. When she was raised on the following morning her crew of twenty-six were dead. It was Germany's first U-boat fatality. Air accidents also continued to cast a pall. At the start of the Paris-Madrid aeroplane race in May, before a crowd of half a million people, a pilot who tried to avoid hitting a group of cavalrymen as he crash-landed, killed the French Minister of War and badly injured the Prime Minister. On a single day in September, three airmen were killed in crashes in France and one in the United States. The total number of fatalities in the air in the previous twelve months was seventy-six. The seventy-seventh aviator to die that year was killed in Spain two days later.

The need to regulate flight was becoming urgent. On November 26 the French Government announced that all aviators must obtain flying certificates; that their machines must be numbered and carry lights; and that they could land only when signalled to do so. Flights over towns and crowds were forbidden.

The first air mail experiment took place on 18 February 1911 in India, when, as part of an exhibition mounted by the local British administrators and traders, a French aviator, Henri Piquet, flew with a small bundle of letters from Allahabad to Naini, a distance of five miles. Beginning on September 9, the pioneer aviator Gustav Hamel made a series of flights between London and Windsor to deliver mail by air. In three weeks he carried 25,000 letters and 90,000 postcards. Even as Hamel's experiment was coming to an end in Britain, an American aviator, Earle Ovington, based on Long Island, likewise demonstrated, during nine days of flights, that mail could be delivered in bulk by air on a regular basis.

*　　*　　*

Film studios were being established in every European country. The films were silent, but in 1911 dialogue inter-titles first appeared on the screen. In San Francisco a local ordinance forbade 'all films where one person was seen to strike another'.

The boundaries of exploration were reaching the furthest extremities of the globe. On 14 December 1911 the Norwegian explorer Roald Amundsen reached the South Pole, the first person to do so. A British explorer, Robert Falcon Scott, with ten men, reached the Pole on 17 January 1912, too late to secure the triumph for Britain. He and all those with him died on the journey back to their base.

Aware of the pressure in Germany for an increase in naval expenditure, at the beginning of 1912 the British Government proposed a halt to the building of warships for a fixed period of time on both sides of the North Sea – a 'Naval Holiday'. The Kaiser replied he was not interested, and that a substantial increase in German naval construction was imminent. In a speech in Glasgow, the British First Lord of the Admiralty, Winston Churchill, stressed that Britain had the resources and ability to build faster and cheaper, and on a larger scale, than any other Power, but he was certain that if naval rivalry led to war it would benefit neither side. 'If two great and highly scientific nations go to war with one another,' he told a London audience later that year, 'they will become heartily sick of it before they come to the end of it.'

Germany faced internal strains in Alsace-Lorraine, where opposition in the former French province to Germanization led the Kaiser to declare that if the agitation continued he might incorporate the two provinces into Prussia. Germany's ally Austria-Hungary was in greater turmoil. In Budapest, Hungarian Socialists declared a four-day strike in support of universal male suffrage, smashed thousands of street lamps, and burned dozens of trams. In the Bohemian Parliament in Prague the German minority showed its powers of disruption on the day a Czech woman deputy was due to take her seat, by preventing the session being held. In the Galician Parliament in Lemberg, Ruthenian deputies continued to obstruct the proceedings by demanding their own university. In Croatia, the Hungarian-appointed ruler continued to seek to suppress Croat nationalism. His efforts led to street demonstrations in favour of greater Slav autonomy, not only in the Croat capital Zagreb, but also in Bosnia-Herzegovina.

In Libya, despite Italian success in driving the Turks from Tripoli and Benghazi, the tribes of the interior refused to accept Italian rule. As fighting continued the Italians machine-gunned the tribesmen from the air. They also attacked the Turks elsewhere. On July 19, Italian warships opened fire on the Turkish forts at the Dardanelles. All the Italian political Parties reacted with enthusiasm, except for the small Socialist Party, whose leader, Benito Mussolini, opposed the war on the grounds that 'We Socialists are not Italians but Europeans'.

For all their public bluster the Italians were wearying of the struggle with Turkey. Peace was signed on October 15. The Italians would administer Libya, but it would remain under Turkish sovereignty. In this way, the Koranic law which forbade the cession of the lands of Islam to the 'infidel' would not be broken.

In Albania, the insurrection against Turkish rule gained renewed momentum that summer, when 20,000 Albanian soldiers captured the garrison town of Pristina. In July the Turks tried to calm the Albanians by announcing that from then on the use of armed force against them was forbidden, and that the Albanian peasants would be indemnified for damage done to their farms and fields by Turkish soldiers. But the Albanians, determined to acquire full autonomy, if not to see an end to Turkish rule altogether, occupied the Macedonian town of Uskub (Skopje) and threatened to advance on Salonika. The Turkish Government sent some of its best troops to the region, and the Albanians were driven northward into the mountains.

The Serbs and Bulgarians under Turkish rule in Macedonia were both clamouring for the Governments of Bulgaria and Serbia to drive the Turks from the province. A Balkan League was established, in which – for the first time in 500 years of squabbling and fighting – Bulgaria, Serbia, Montenegro and Greece united against Turkey. On September 30 the Balkan League mobilized. The Turks mobilized a day later. On October 8 Russia and Austria-Hungary issued a joint declaration 'energetically condemning' any measures that might lead to war. They were ignored, and hostilities began on October 18.

For seven weeks the armies of the Balkan League advanced. Within a month much of Macedonia and large parts of Albania were under Serb control. The Greek army was also successful, driving the Turks from Thrace. Many Christian soldiers, whom the Turks had drafted into the army, deserted to the attackers. On November 8, Greek forces entered Salonika, the largest city in the Ottoman Empire after Constantinople. The Bulgarians also advanced, reaching Turkey's principal European defences, the Chatalja Lines. But the defence lines held firm.

On November 28 Albania proclaimed its independence. Serbia at once advanced into Albanian territory, determined to gain an Adriatic coastline. Serbia's action angered Austria-Hungary, which saw its own influence in the Balkans virtually disappear. The Serbian Government, unable to risk war with Austria-Hungary, withdrew its claims to Albania and accepted an arrangement with Austria that would establish a trading outlet on the Adriatic for Serbian goods, without the need for Serb sovereign territory. On 16 December 1912 a conference of delegates from the Balkan League met in London. Four days later agreement was reached on Albanian autonomy, and on Montenegrin, Bulgarian, Greek and Serbian territorial annexations at Turkey's expense.

Turkey remained in Europe but with her land area greatly reduced and her 400-year rule of Macedonia ended. Macedonia was divided between Serbia and Bulgaria. Thrace was divided between Bulgaria and Greece.

Accidents at sea remained a frequent occurrence, seizing both the newspaper headlines and the public imagination. When a German transatlantic liner struck a British submarine off Dover, slicing it in two, all but one of the fifteen submariners on board were drowned. When a British battleship engaged in trials in the English Channel ran into an Italian steamer, all thirty-six Italian seamen went down with their ship. But the disaster that most riveted attention that year was when the ocean liner *Titanic*, the largest vessel afloat, struck an iceberg on its maiden voyage from Southampton to New York, with the loss of 1,635 lives.

Among the industrial nations, social welfare programmes were increasingly bringing support to those who were out of work, often due to injuries sustained in the workplace, or who faced long periods of unemployment through illness. In Britain the Liberal government brought in a National Health Insurance Act whereby the workers' right to financial support in ill-health was underpinned both by the employer and the State. Another answer being advocated for the ills of capitalist society was Socialist revolution. In January 1912 a small gathering took place in Prague, organized by Lenin, a meeting of the Bolshevik section of the Russian Social Democratic Labour Party. At Lenin's urging a Bolshevik Central Committee was elected, with seven members and four 'candidate' members. This was the close-knit professional organization Lenin believed essential if revolution was to be brought to Russia. During the meeting in Prague he was given the power to co-opt others on to the Central Committee. He nominated two people, a metal worker, I. S. Belostotsky – of whom little more was heard – and a Georgian revolutionary then in exile in Siberia, Josef Stalin.

Excesses on the part of the Tsarist authorities continued. Three months after the Prague meeting of Bolshevik exiles, Tsarist troops killed 170 desperate, half-starved workers in the Siberian gold mines on the Lena River. The men had dared to ask for an improvement in their harsh and degrading conditions. The Russian Government, the master of repression, also tried social innovation: a national health insurance system, whereby hospital funds to which workers and employers contributed would provide for medical assistance in the case of illness; and accident insurance, where the whole financial responsibility of compensation fell on the shoulders of the employer. This compensation included pensions for the widows and orphans of those killed in accidents in the workplace.

Would these measures help lessen internal Russian discontent? Social Democrats of all factions – Menshevik, Bolshevik and Bundist – insisted that only revolution could end inequality, and that strikes and conflict, not legislation and amelioration, were the way forward. The right to strike remained persistently denied, giving the social conflict its sharpest weapon.

*   *   *

In the United States, 1 March 1912 saw the first use of a parachute for jumping from a moving aircraft, and reaching the ground safely. That year the first regular passenger Zeppelin air service was inaugurated between Berlin and Friedrichshaven. In the fifth Olympic Games, held in Stockholm, the races were timed electronically for the first time. On August 13, in the United States, the first regulation of broadcasting was brought in, the Radio Act, whereby radio operators had to obtain a licence. Films also continued to gain in popularity. In 1912 there were 400 cinemas in London; in the United States that year, an estimated five million people visited the cinema every day.

On 11 January 1913 the last horse-drawn omnibus carried its passengers through the streets of Paris. The internal combustion engine was master of the brightest capital in Europe. In London, some horse-drawn buses continued to ply their routes, but only for another three years. In every European capital, culture and commerce flourished side by side, as did the extremes of wealth and poverty. This was also true in the United States, which had emerged as the world's most prosperous nation. In 1913 its manufacturing output exceeded that of France, Britain and Germany combined. Also in the United States a new screen star, Charlie Chaplin, made thirty-five short films in 1913. Advertising, to encourage spending, made a leap forward that year with the launching of a campaign throughout the United States for the sale of Camel cigarettes.

While culture and commerce flourished, war and destruction also marked the new year. In February, when the Bulgarian army attacked the Turkish city of Adrianople (Edirne), the First Balkan War was renewed with even greater intensity than in the previous year. On March 28, Adrianople fell to a combined Bulgarian and Serbian assault, and 30,000 Turks were taken prisoner. An armistice was signed on April 20, under which Turkey gave up yet more territory in its Macedonian and Thracian provinces. Peace had been signed, but the Bulgarians were determined not to allow Greece or Serbia to have the main territorial advantage. The Bulgarian army had lost 30,000 dead in the war, but this did not deter its leaders from sending the Bulgarian army back into battle, not against Turkey, but against its recent allies Greece and Serbia. With that attack, on June 30, the Second Balkan War began. Roumania, which had stayed out of the First Balkan War, decided to enter the Second, and advanced towards the Bulgarian capital, Sofia. The Greeks, taking advantage of the Roumanian attack, seized the Thracian towns which Bulgaria had taken from the Turks during the First Balkan War. The Bulgarians retreated, committing atrocities against Greek civilians which shocked Europe. In the town of Demi Hissar a Bulgarian gendarmerie captain forced the bishop, two priests, and a hundred leading citizens into the courtyard of a school, and killed them.

Even as the Bulgarians, who had precipitated the Second Balkan War, fled back to their borders, the Turks decided to re-enter the conflict. On July 12 the Turkish army advanced towards Adrianople, then still under Bulgarian occupation, and recaptured it on July 20. As the Greek army advanced into the territory Bulgaria had conquered from the Turks a year earlier, further atrocities were reported, the Greeks taking revenge on the Bulgarians for what they had done a few weeks earlier. When, on August 10, the Treaty of Bucharest was signed, all five Balkan combatants – Bulgaria, Greece, Roumania, Montenegro and Serbia – agreed to new frontiers. The port city of Salonika, coveted by Bulgaria, was assigned to Greece.

The rest of Europe was shocked by the destruction of life in the Balkans and the fighting between nations so recently allies. Not only in Europe, but in the United States, there was a sense of bewilderment and helplessness that so much misery could be inflicted by neighbours upon each other. In the hope that the lessons of the two Balkan Wars might be of service to mankind, an international commission of enquiry was set up. In the words of Nicholas Murray Butler, the leading spirit behind it: 'If the minds of men can be turned even for a short time away from passion, from race antagonism and from national aggrandisement to a contemplation of the individual and national losses due to war and to the shocking horrors which modern warfare entails, a step and by no means a short one, will have been taken toward the substitution of justice for force in the settlement of international differences.' Within two years these hopes were to be cruelly dashed.

A second Treaty of Peace was signed on September 29 by Turkey, Greece and Bulgaria. Adrianople was returned to Turkey. Bulgaria ceded territory to Roumania. The Bulgarian-inhabited regions of

Macedonia, over which so much Bulgarian – as well as Serbian and Greek – blood had been shed, were allocated to Serbia. In the main, Serbia was the principal territorial beneficiary of the Balkan Wars, having occupied much of Albania, where fighting continued. The European Powers insisted that an independent Albania must be one of the main results of the defeat of Turkey. Serbia ignored them.

One aftermath of the Second Balkan War was that Crete was incorporated into Greece. The Greeks failed, however, to acquire the twelve Dodecanese islands, including Rhodes and Kos, which they had hoped to annex following Turkey's defeat. In a move almost unnoticed during the fighting, Italian forces had occupied the Dodecanese, and refused to be dislodged. Surreptitiously, the Italian empire had been extended.

The disputes in the Balkans had a disturbing impact on the relationship between the European Powers, even those who were allies. In February 1913, the German Chief of Staff, General von Moltke, told Conrad von Hötzendorf, the Austrian Chief of Staff, that he was convinced 'a European war is bound to come sooner or later, in which the issue will be one of a struggle between Germandom and Slavdom'. To prepare 'for that contingency', von Moltke believed, was 'the duty of all States which are the champions of Germanic ideas and culture'. Introducing a new Army Bill on April 7, the German Chancellor, Bethmann-Hollweg, pointed out the harmful effect on Germany of the Balkan wars: 'If it should ever come to a European conflagration in which the Slavs would be ranged on one side and the Germans on the other, this newly developed vitality of the Slavs in the Balkans would be a disadvantage to Germany, as they would hold the balance of forces in that quarter which had hitherto been occupied by Turkey.'

Slav and German were in opposite constellations. 'Nobody could conceive the dimensions of a world conflagration, and the misery and trouble it would bring upon the nations,' Bethmann-Hollweg warned. 'All previous wars would probably be as child's play, and no responsible statesman would be disposed lightly to set the match to the powder.' As to the new Army Bill, although Germany desired peace, he explained, 'if war came, she wanted to win'.

*   *   *

Serbia's occupation of Albania was a short-lived triumph. On 18 October 1913 the Austro-Hungarian Government, determined to show that Serbia could not extend its territory to the Adriatic, demanded the Serb evacuation of Albania within eight days. To the Austrian Chief of Staff, General Conrad von Hötzendorf, the Kaiser expressed support for any Austrian action to force Serbia out of Albania, telling von Hötzendorf: 'Within a few days you must be in Belgrade. I was always a partisan of peace; but this has its limits. I have read much more about war and know what it means. But finally a situation arises in which a great power can no longer just look on, but must draw the sword.'

The Serbs, fearing an attack from across the Danube on their capital, Belgrade, complied with the Austrian demand. Albania became an independent State, the European Powers deciding that she was best governed by the prince of a European dynasty. Their choice was a German officer in the Prussian army, Prince William of Wied. The Kaiser's encouragement for an Austrian invasion of Serbia was to prove an ominous precedent.

Within the German Empire the repression of minorities continued. In Alsace-Lorraine meetings called to celebrate events connected with French rule and the history of France were banned. German settlers whose ultra-German sentiments could be guaranteed were brought into the provinces. French was only allowed to be taught in government schools in Alsace-Lorraine for one hour a week, and could not be spoken at all in the debating chamber of the local parliament. The language question also erupted in Schleswig, which Germany had annexed from Denmark in 1864. The Norwegian explorer Captain Amundsen was refused permission to give a scientific lecture in Norwegian, a language near enough to Danish to be understood by those who did not speak German. The head of the Government of Schleswig, a German, warned those Danish-speakers who dared to hope Schleswig would be lost to Germany in war, that Germany's 'ready army and no less ready navy would afford the best answer'.

Finding himself at the centre of so much bellicose talk, Bethmann-Hollweg told a friend that April: 'I am fed up with war and the clamour for war and with the perennial armaments. It is high time that the great nations calmed down again and occupied themselves with peaceful pursuits, or there will be an explosion which no one desires and which will be to the detriment of all.'

In Spanish Morocco, several Spanish outposts in the mountainous regions were overrun by Muslim rebels. During the fighting, a Spanish lieutenant with a small force of local Moorish mercenaries won a victory over the tribesmen and was awarded the Military Merit Cross. His name was Francisco Franco – the future dictator of Spain. There was also fighting between French and Moroccans that September, when twenty French soldiers were killed. A punitive expedition received the submission of the local tribes. In Italy's newly conquered province of Libya, Arab resistance to Italian rule resulted in more than 200 Italian soldiers being killed. The Italian punitive expeditions that followed led to an even heavier loss of Arab lives.

Among the first overseas initiatives of President Woodrow Wilson in the United States was the completion of the disarmament of Muslim rebels in the Philippines.

South Africa saw an upsurge of white discontent in 1913, when, in Johannesburg, white mine workers rioted in protest at the harsh conditions of work underground. Cavalrymen drew their swords and charged into a crowd of demonstrators, whereupon the strikers rushed to the power station and cut off the electric current to the city. In three days of fighting, twenty strikers were killed. At their collective funeral, a wreath was placed on the grave with the words: 'In memory of our martyrs who were foully murdered in cold blood by the capitalist class.'

In the Transvaal legislation prevented Indians trading or farming, or owning houses. Offenders would be deported. The terms of the restrictions, explained the Transvaal Minister of the Interior, were 'a matter of self-preservation'. The Indian cause was championed, as earlier, by Gandhi, who led a non-violent protest march from the Natal coast towards the Transvaal. At the border of the province he was arrested, and sentenced to nine months in prison with hard labour.

Gandhi's sentence was reduced to two months, but the unrest

continued, and there were strikes by Indian miners and sugar workers throughout Natal. In a struggle on one sugar plantation, where police tried to arrest a number of Indian workers, six Indians were killed. Black South Africans found the restrictions enshrined in the constitution being rigidly upheld. No black African was allowed to acquire land in an area scheduled for whites. In a speech setting out his philosophy of apartheid, General Botha explained that he did not believe in ruling the blacks with a truncheon; rather, they should be regarded as minors, and the whites as their guardians. He wanted a policy which would lead to peace between whites and blacks, but he added, 'equality was not to be thought of'.

The European Powers were edging towards war. To Germany's alarm, British naval expenditure for 1914 was the highest on record. In Germany and Austria-Hungary, Russia's intentions were stimulating war talk. In May the German Chief of Staff, General von Moltke, confided to the German Secretary of State, Gottlieb von Jagow, that he was afraid that in two or three years Russia would have built up her maximum war armaments. Von Moltke believed Germany had no choice but 'to wage preventive war in order to beat the enemy while we still have some chance of winning'.

Colonel House, President Wilson's emissary, wrote to the President from Berlin in May: 'The situation is extraordinary. It is militarism run stark mad. Unless someone acting for you can bring about a different understanding there is some day to be an awful cataclysm.' Reaching London, Colonel House told the British Foreign Secretary, Sir Edward Grey, how in Berlin 'the air seemed full of the clash of arms, of readiness to strike'.

On June 12 the Kaiser went for the weekend to Konopischt, near Prague, to stay with the heir to the throne of Austria-Hungary, Archduke Franz Ferdinand. During their meeting Franz Ferdinand asked if Germany would still be willing, as the Kaiser had intimated during the Albanian crisis eight months earlier, to support Austria-Hungary in destroying the Serbian 'hornets' nest', the source of anti-Austrian feeling in Bosnia-Herzegovina. The Kaiser replied that Austria should 'do something' before the situation worsened. He doubted that Austria need fear Russian intervention on behalf of Serbia. The Russian army, he said, was not yet ready for war.

A week later, as Inspector-General of his nation's army, Franz Ferdinand was in Sarajevo, capital of the annexed province of Bosnia. The Serbian Foreign Ministry had warned him the visit was unwise, in view of pro-Serb agitation in Sarajevo, but he decided to go ahead, taking his wife with him. On June 28, as they were being driven through the city, a Serb student, Gavrilo Princip, shot and killed them both.

For the Austro-Hungarian Chief of Staff, Conrad von Hötzendorf, eager to find an excuse to attack Serbia, the assassination of Franz Ferdinand was 'a godsend, or rather, a gift from Mars'. When the Kaiser learned the news he noted in the margin of a telegram from his Ambassador in Vienna: 'The Serbs must be disposed of, *and* that right soon!' Against the Ambassador's remark that 'only a mild punishment' might be imposed on Serbia, the Kaiser wrote, 'I hope not.'

The German attitude towards Austria was crucial. On July 4 the German Ambassador in Vienna, Count Tschirschky, told a senior Austrian official that Germany would support Austria-Hungary 'through thick and thin'. Tschirschky advised the Austrian: 'The earlier Austria attacks the better. It would have been better to attack yesterday than today; and better to attack today than tomorrow.' The Kaiser took the same view, telling the Austrian Ambassador to Germany on July 5 that Austria would regret it if she did not 'make use of the present moment' which was 'all in our favour'. The Kaiser added: 'Should war between Austria-Hungary and Russia prove unavoidable' Germany would be at Austria's side; Russia was 'in no way prepared for war'. He then left in the imperial yacht for his annual three-week summer cruise in Norwegian waters.

Austria-Hungary's leaders were confident they could chastise Serbia without involving war with any other European power. On July 7 the Austrian Foreign Minister, Count Berchtold, proposed an immediate armed attack on Serbia. Its aim, he and his Cabinet colleagues agreed, would be to reduce Serbia territorially, and make her dependent upon Austria. A deciding factor in this decision was the Kaiser's assurance two days earlier that should war between Austria-Hungary and Russia prove unavoidable, 'Germany would be at Austria's side'. These six words signalled the death knoll of caution in Vienna, and the destruction within a month of peace in Europe.

A key figure in the events that followed was the German Ambassador in Vienna, Count Tschirschky. Asking to see Berchtold on July 7, he stressed Germany's desire for Austria-Hungary to take military action against Serbia. Tschirschky told Berchtold of a telegram he had just received from Berlin – the reason for his visit – in which the Kaiser instructed him 'to declare here, with all emphasis, that in Berlin an action against Serbia is expected, and that it would not be understood in Germany if we allowed the opportunity to pass without striking a blow'.

As Austria's leaders contemplated war with Serbia, and were responsive to German encouragement, a secret report from Sarajevo reached them, emphasizing that there was no evidence to implicate the Serbian Government in the Archduke's assassination. In calmer times this report might have decided the policy-makers against punitive action, but calm was not the dominant feature of the Austrian mood towards Serbia, and on July 14, a day after learning that Serbia was not the guilty party, the Austrian Council of Ministers decided to issue an ultimatum to Serbia.

In Berlin, the German Secretary of State, von Jagow, like the Kaiser, was convinced Russia would not intervene in the dispute between Austria-Hungary and Serbia, even if the Serbs rejected the ultimatum and Austria declared war. 'The more resolute Austria shows herself,' von Jagow informed the German Ambassador in London on July 18, 'and the more energetically we support her, the sooner will Russia stop her outcry. To be sure, they will make a great to-do in St Petersburg, but when all is said and done, Russia is at present not ready for war.'

The Austrian ultimatum was delivered in Belgrade on July 23. Linking the Belgrade Government with the assassination – something the secret Austrian report of ten days earlier had specifically denied – it insisted the Serbian Government condemn all anti-Austrian propaganda, and agree to a joint Austro-Serbian commission to investigate Franz Ferdinand's murder. There must be a Serbian army order condemning Serbian military involvement with the murders, and a Serbian promise of no further Serbian intrigue in Bosnia. Serbia must undertake to punish anyone who circulated anti-Austrian propaganda, in schools or in Serbian nationalist societies. Finally, Austrian officials would participate in the trial and punishment of those connected with the plot.

Whether one sovereign State could accept such demands from another was much debated. The British Foreign Secretary, Edward Grey, called it 'the most formidable document that was ever addressed from one State to another'. British diplomats doubted that Britain would be able to stay clear of war if it widened beyond the Balkans. 'We shall be lucky', one British diplomat wrote to his wife two hours before the Austrian ultimatum was due to expire, 'if we get out of this without the long-dreaded European war, a general bust-up in fact.'

The Serbian Government understood that even if Russia were eventually to enter the war against Austria-Hungary, Serbia's ability to resist an onslaught across her exposed frontiers was limited. She therefore sent a conciliatory reply to the Austrian ultimatum, agreeing to everything demanded of her. The only qualification regarded the demand that Austrian officials participate in the trial and punishment of those connected with the assassination. This demand, the Serbians asked, should be submitted to the International Tribunal at The Hague. If the tribunal accepted its legality, Serbia would agree to it.

Serbia had effectively capitulated. But in Berlin, the German Government pressed the Austrians to strike at Serbia before wider complications ensued. 'We are urgently advised to act at once and face the world with a *fait accompli*,' the Austrian Ambassador in Berlin informed Vienna by telegram on July 28. When the Austrians pointed out to the Germans that it would be another two weeks before Austrian mobilization was completed, the Germans pressed Austria not to wait so long. The mood in Berlin was bellicose, but it was not untinged with panic; Austria must crush Serbia before the Russians could respond, and Germany herself be drawn in as a result, not of her national interest, but of her alliance with Austria.

The Austrians recalled their Ambassador, Count Giesl, from Belgrade. But did Serbia's conciliatory reply to Austria's ultimatum really provide cause for war? Suddenly even the Kaiser had his doubts, which he expressed in private on the morning of July 28, when finally he read the full text of the Serbian reply – of three days earlier. Reading it side by side with the full text of the Austrian ultimatum, he could see no reason why Austria should embark on a full-scale war. 'A great moral victory for Vienna,' he wrote in the margin of his copy of the Serbian reply, 'but with it every reason for war is removed and Giesl ought to remain quietly in Belgrade. On the strength of this we should never have ordered mobilization.'

Having blown hot for so many days, the Kaiser suddenly blew cold. A full-scale Austrian invasion of Serbia was not needed, he felt. All that was required, he wrote, 'as a visible *satisfaction d'honneur*' for Austria, was that the Austrian Army 'should temporarily occupy Belgrade as a pledge'. Negotiations could then begin to end the brief military conflict. 'I am convinced', the Kaiser wrote to his Secretary of State, von Jagow, 'that on the whole the wishes of the Danube monarchy have been acceded to. The few reservations that Serbia makes in regard to individual points can in my opinion be well cleared up by negotiations. But it contains the announcement *orbi et urbi* of a capitulation of the most humiliating kind, and with it every reason for war is removed.'

An hour after the Kaiser penned these words – 'every reason for war is removed' – Austria declared war on Serbia, confident of German support if the war widened. During July 29 the Austrian naval flotilla on the Danube opened fire on Belgrade. The Tsar panicked. 'To try to avoid such a calamity as a European war,' he telegraphed, in English, to the Kaiser, 'I beg you in the name of our old friendship to do what you can to stop your allies from going too far.' But Austria-Hungary was not to be restrained. The Kaiser's reply – 'I am exerting my utmost influence to induce the Austrians to arrive at a satisfactory understanding with you' – showed how out of touch he was with the warlike mood in Austria to which, less than three weeks earlier, he had himself contributed so much.

The Tsar, desperate to keep Russia out of the war, cancelled Russia's order for general mobilization. The Kaiser wanted to do likewise, but the German General Staff refused. The Tsar, too, was soon prevailed upon by his generals to renew mobilization. The generals feared that unless Russia mobilized, the Polish provinces of the Russian Empire would be at risk of a German annexation. That day the American Ambassador in London, Walter Page, wrote to President Wilson: 'It's the Slav and the German. Each wants his day, and neither has got beyond the stage of tooth and claw.'

Confident of German military support, Austria continued with its mobilization. The German Government then sent an ultimatum to Russia to 'cease every war measure against us and Austria-Hungary' within twelve hours. Russia rejected this ultimatum, wherupon the Kaiser and his General Staff prepared to go to war against Russia. To avoid France coming to Russia's assistance on the battlefield, Germany asked France to state categorically that she would remain neutral in the event of a Russo-German war. France refused to make such a commitment. She would neither abandon her ten-year-old alliance with Russia, nor give Germany a free hand to march eastward. As proof of French determination to help Russia, orders went out from Paris to more than four million Frenchmen to make their way to their barracks.

'Three hundred million people today lie under the spell of fear and fate,' a London evening newspaper declared on August 1, and went on to ask, 'Is there no one to break the spell, no gleam of light on this cold, dark scene?' On the following day André Gide reached Paris from the countryside. 'Crowds on the platform, both serious and vibrant,' he wrote. 'A workman shouts as he goes by: "All aboard for Berlin! And what fun we'll have there!" People smiled but did not applaud.'

At five o'clock in the afternoon of August 2, Germany delivered an ultimatum to Belgium, demanding that German troops be allowed to pass through Belgium in their attack on France. In return, Germany promised to 'maintain the independence of Belgium and her possessions'. Should the passage of German troops be refused, Germany would 'treat Belgium as an enemy'. Belgium rejected the German demand, and awaited events.

On the morning of August 3, Germany declared war on France. The sweep towards Paris would start through Belgium. The violation of Belgium's neutrality would give Britain the right, by a treaty of 1830, to declare war on Germany. Britain informed Germany that if German troops crossed the Belgian border, Britain would declare war. That morning, August 3, the German army crossed the Belgian border at five separate points. On the following morning the British Government again warned Berlin to respect Belgian neutrality or face war. The German army continued to advance. At eleven o'clock on the evening of August 4 the British Government declared war on Germany.

CHAPTER THREE

First World War

1914—18

THE FIRST FIVE MONTHS OF WAR saw all the expectations of the warring powers disappointed. The German dash through Belgium and France, to Paris, successful for forty days, came to a halt on the forty-first day, when a combined British and French force halted the German armies less than thirty miles from the capital, driving them back across the River Marne. Russian hopes of a swift victory over Germany were also frustrated, as the rapid, deep thrust of the Russian forces into East Prussia was halted at Tannenberg. The Austro-Hungarian forces also hoped for the swift defeat of Serbia, but the Serbs, like the French and British on the Marne and the Germans at Tannenberg, reversed the fortunes of war, and Austria failed to secure a victory. Indeed, a rapid Russian advance threw the Austrians into consternation. News of the loss of Lemberg (Lvov), the main city of Eastern Galicia, on September 3 was kept secret from the Austro-Hungarian public for almost a week.

The end to the ambitious military plans of Germany, Russia and Austria-Hungary did not lead to an end to the war. Instead, each disappointed war machine tried to redress the unexpectedly unfavourable balance. In the west, the Germans established a line of trenches that ran through a corner of Belgium and across eastern France. In the east, the frustrated Russian armies prepared to defend the Polish provinces of the Russian Empire. The Austro-Hungarian army prepared to renew its assault on Serbia. 'No one can describe this vast wreck,' the American Ambassador in London wrote to President

Wilson on August 25. 'It will be ours to preserve civilization. All Europe is shooting it to pieces.'

The numbers of dead rose within the first five months of the war to the highest in modern warfare, creating an ever-widening circle of war widows and war orphans, of bereaved parents and grieving relatives and friends. The French alone were mourning 300,000 dead as the year 1914 came to an end. The Russian losses were as high. At sea, the loss of hundreds, even thousands, of men in a few minutes soon became commonplace.

On Christmas Day, along a twenty-seven mile sector of the Western Front, twenty-one incidents were recorded of British and German soldiers meeting in No-Man's Land, taking photographs of each other, and even playing football. 'Just think,' one British soldier wrote home to his family, 'that while you were eating your turkey, I was out talking and shaking hands with the very men I had been trying to kill a few hours before.'

On the Eastern Front, in the first months of 1915, the Germans steadily reversed their initial defeats and advanced into Russian Poland. In the southern sector it was the Russians who advanced, pushing back their Austrian adversary. In a secret message to the German Chancellor, during Easter, the Austrian Foreign Minister, Count Czernin, suggested that the time had come to make peace with Russia. Austria-Hungary, he argued, had regained almost all the territory which it had lost to Russia in the opening months of the war, while Germany had made massive strides into Russian territory. It ought therefore to be possible to bring the conflict to an end. Both sides had shown their strength and courage, both had lost heavily in men and weaponry. Russia had shown that she was prepared to risk all for Serbia; and Serbia was still independent, the Austrians having failed to enter Belgrade or make any serious inroads into her territory.

Czernin's logic held no appeal to the leaders in Berlin. For them, the victories over Russia were only just beginning.

On the Western Front, the first military initiative of 1915 was taken by the British. Their aim, which was not achieved, was to drive the Germans from the French village of Neuve Chapelle. On

March 10, in the opening British artillery barrage, intended to pulverize and demoralize the German defenders, more shells were fired than in the whole of the Boer War. But one sector of the German front line was not hit by the barrage, the guns allocated to it having fallen short of their target as the result of an aiming error. It was the Germans who attacked next, hoping to drive the British from the Belgian town of Ypres and reach the Channel ports. The German artillery bombardment was so heavy as to make Ypres virtually uninhabitable, but they were unable to breach its defences or push further west.

A German initiative in April, the use of chlorine gas, was intended to enable the trench lines to be pierced. The first Allied soldiers to face the gas were French Africans from Senegal, who immediately began pushing to the rear, through the British reserve lines. 'It was impossible to understand what the Africans said,' the official British historian wrote, 'but from the way they coughed and pointed to their throats, it was evident that, if not suffering from the effects of gas, they were thoroughly scared.' In a second German gas attack three days later, 2,000 Canadian troops were killed.

The British War Council decided that Britain should use gas against the Germans. But this new, harsh element failed to end the stalemate of trench warfare. Even before the failure of gas to secure a breakthrough, the British had begun to search for a new war zone which might offer a swifter victory than trench warfare. Strategic planners looked towards Turkey, the only non-Christian power among the belligerents, which had entered the war as Germany's ally in October 1914, as an area where victory might be secured, and the Central Powers seriously weakened.

The British leaders were spurred into action by an appeal from Russia for military action to take pressure off the Russian front in eastern Anatolia. On 5 January 1915, after receiving the Russian appeal, Lord Kitchener, the Secretary of State for War, suggested that Russia could be helped by an Anglo-French attack on the Dardanelles. If the Turks could be driven from the Dardanelles, he argued, and Constantinople itself threatened, then three neutral States, Greece, Bulgaria and Roumania, might enter the war on the side of the Allies. Each would be influenced by the possibility of acquiring Turkish territory. Italy too, having failed to persuade Austria-Hungary to give up territory in return for joining the Central Powers, might join the Allies in search of spoils.

The Secretary to the British Cabinet, Colonel Hankey, suggested that victory at the Dardanelles would give the Anglo-French forces access to the River Danube 'as a line of communication for an army penetrating into the heart of Austria', and bring British sea power to bear 'in the middle of Europe'. The first attack at the Dardanelles was to be made by ships alone, with the enthusiastic support of the First Lord of the Admiralty, Winston Churchill, who was convinced that Britain's warships would blast their way through the waterway known as The Narrows and penetrate the Sea of Marmara.

The attack on the Dardanelles took place on March 18. Within a few hours most of the Turkish mines which had been laid in the waterway were located and destroyed. But then the advancing fleet reached an unlocated line of twenty mines, and three of the ten Allied battleships were sunk. On one of them, the *Bouvet*, 620 French sailors were drowned. The British lost forty-seven men. Faced with the unexpected minefield, and the loss of ships and men, the British admiral called off the attack. He was willing, however, to try a second attack in a few days' time, convinced he could sweep the remaining minefields and push past the last Turkish defences. Churchill also wanted one more naval push. But the balance of opinion in London, especially at the War Office, was that the next stage of the attack ought to be by troops, not ships: troops who would land on the Gallipoli Peninsula and destroy the Turkish defences facing the waterway. Once that was done, but only then, would the warships push on into the Sea of Marmara, freed from the risk of unswept minefields and the harassment of Turkish artillery defences.

The military landings on the Gallipoli Peninsula took place on April 25. The troops succeeded in landing at Cape Helles, although losses on some of the beaches were heavy. The attackers were also able to scale the cliffs overlooking the beaches, and further north, at Anzac Cove, to secure a beachhead on the Aegean side of the peninsula. At Anzac Cove the objective of the first day's assault was the high ground along the central spine of the peninsula, dominated by the ridge of Chunuk Bair. Australian troops approached the ridge shortly after the Turks guarding it had run out of ammunition and withdrawn down the far slope, but a Turkish counter-attack drove them back. The second and third days' objectives, to push down the eastern slope to the shore of the Marmara, less than four miles away, was likewise not achieved, then or later.

Twenty-four hours after the Gallipoli landings, Britain and France accepted Italy's territorial demands on Austria-Hungary and Turkey, and welcomed Italy as an ally. As Italy prepared to do battle with the Austro-Hungarian army along their high mountain frontier, the British and French went on seeking the defeat of Turkey on the Gallipoli Peninsula, and on the Western Front.

In the eastern region of Turkey, the large Armenian Christian population, long denied its national rights by the Muslim Turks, hoped that a Russian victory over Turkey, which seemed possible that spring, would lead to the recognition of Armenian national aspirations. Great savagery marked the Turkish treatment of the Armenians under their rule. Starting on April 8, Turkish soldiers shot dead tens of thousands of Armenian men, and drove hundreds of thousands of Armenian women and children from their homes, forcing them across the mountains southward to the inhospitable deserts of Syria. The number of Armenians murdered was formidable: 600,000 during the massacres in Anatolia and a further 400,000 as a result of brutalities and privation during the deportations into the deserts of Syria and Mesopotamia. On May 24 the British, French and Russian Governments, each at war with Turkey, issued a joint public denunciation, describing the mass killings of Armenians as 'a crime against humanity and civilization'.

In May, the main New York newspapers published an advertisement, sent to them from the German Embassy in Washington, stating that travellers intending to embark on an Atlantic voyage 'are reminded that a state of war exists between Germany and Great Britain and her allies', that the zone of war included the waters adjacent to the British Isles, and that vessels flying the British flag or a flag of her allies 'are liable to destruction in those waters'. Travellers sailing in the war zones to Great Britain or her Allies 'do so at their own risk.' This warning was published next to a British Cunard Line advertisement for the sailing, at ten that very morning, and again a month later, of the *Lusitania*, which the advertisement described as 'Fastest and Largest Steamer now in Atlantic Service'. She sailed as planned. Six days later she was sunk by a German submarine off the coast of Ireland. Of the 2,000 passengers on board, 1,198 were drowned; 128 of them were United States citizens.

The United States was shocked by the sinking, and by the loss of so many American lives. Referring to the German newspaper notice, President Wilson said that 'no warning that an unlawful and inhumane act will be committed' could be accepted 'as a legitimate excuse for that act'. But Wilson had no intention of abandoning American neutrality, seeking only an apology, which in due course the German Government delivered. A month after the sinking of the *Lusitania*, the Kaiser issued a secret instruction to all German submarine commanders. They were henceforth to spare all large passenger ships.

On the Western Front, on May 6, the British army launched an attack against Aubers Ridge, the high ground which it had failed to capture during the battle of Neuve Chapelle two months earlier. It was a failure. A shortage of artillery shells limited the preliminary bombardment to forty minutes, and fewer than eight per cent of the shells fired were high explosive. As at Neuve Chapelle, the German barbed-wire defences were left virtually intact. In a single day of battle, with not one of the objectives reached, the British and Indian death toll was in excess of 11,000 men.

The failure at Aubers Ridge, attributed to the shell shortage, led to a demand in Britain for a change in the political direction of the war. Hitherto the Liberal government had excluded the Conservative opposition from all part in war direction. The Conservatives were now brought in to the highest places of war direction, with A. J. Balfour, a former Conservative Prime Minister, replacing Churchill as the Cabinet Minister in charge of the Royal Navy. But neither these political changes, nor the employment of women in growing number in the munitions factories in Britain, led to any rapid improvement in Britain's military situation on the Western Front or at sea. The Germans were likewise caught in the destructive stalemate, a renewed German gas offensive failing to secure a break-through. A British attempt to drive the Germans from the Ypres salient was likewise unsuccessful. At the end of July, the Germans used flame-throwers for the first time. The men caught in the direct blast of the fire, one British eyewitness wrote, 'were never seen again'. But still the trench lines held, the death toll mounting with every renewed attack.

At Gallipoli, one more attempt was made, on August 6, to take the heights of the peninsula. Landing at Suvla Bay, north of Anzac Cove, twenty-five British battalions were put ashore virtually unop-posed. Their attack was matched by the simultaneous advance of Australian and New Zealand troops from the Anzac area. 'Heavy fighting has been going on since yesterday at the Dardanelles,' the German Naval Chief of Staff, Admiral Tirpitz, wrote in his diary on the second day of the renewed assault, as British, Indian, Australian and New Zealand troops pushed inland and reached the lower slopes of the ridge. 'The situation is obviously critical,' he added. 'Should the Dardanelles fall, the World War has been decided against us.'

At first it seemed that Tirpitz's apocalyptic vision might be a true one. After three days of battle, New Zealand troops reached the summit of Chunuk Bair, the strategic height from which the Sea of Marmara was visible far below. One of Turkey's boldest soldiers, Mustafa Kemal, led the counter-attack on the following morning, as he had done in May, driving off the crest the Lancashire soldiers who had replaced the New Zealanders during the night. They had never been in battle before. The Turks on the ridge were experienced fighters. Further north, on the even higher ridge of Koja Chemen Tepe, a small British and Gurkha force which had also reached the crest on August 9 repelled a Turkish counter-attack with a bayonet charge, and was about to drive the Turks down the far slope when British naval gunners, not knowing the summit was secured, and too far off to make out the situation on the crest with binoculars, opened fire, blasting the attackers with the full force of naval high explosives. Those who survived the bombardment retreated down the slope whence they had come. Both crests remained in Turkish hands, and Kemal was promoted General. Three further attacks were beaten off in the foothills. When the peninsula was evacuated, nine months after the first landings, 48,000 British, French, Australian and New Zealand soldiers had been killed, and 66,000 Turks.

A spate of disasters suffered by the Russian armies on the Eastern Front led the Russians to appeal to Britain for a renewed offensive on the Western Front, hoping to take the pressure off Russia in the east. An attack was launched on September 25, at Loos, where the British used poison gas for the first time: 600 German soldiers were killed, but German superiority in machine-guns brought the attack to a halt a few hundred yards from its starting point. So shocked were the German machine-gunners at the sight of row after row of British troops walking towards them and being mown down, that when a fifth British advance failed, and the wounded men who could walk or crawl were working their way back to the British lines, no shot was fired at them. Among the British dead was Rudyard Kipling's only son, John. Among the wounded was a future British Prime Minister, Harold Macmillan, who was shot in the hand.

That September there was an anti-war riot in Odessa by 2,500 wounded Russian soldiers, due to be sent back to the front when their wounds were healed. The Bolsheviks encouraged soldiers every-where to demand an end to the war, and to refuse to be sent back to the front. In St Petersburg, 500 reservists attacked the police at the railway station where they were being embarked for the war zone. 'News from Russia testifies to the growing revolutionary mood,' Lenin wrote with some satisfaction in a private letter from his exile in Switzerland.

On the Eastern Front, German troops entered Vilna, the largest of the cities of Lithuania, taking 22,000 Russian soldiers captive.

A second war front had been opened against the Turks in the spring of 1915, in Mesopotamia, where the initial advance from Basra towards Baghdad augured well for the British and Indian troops. But the conditions were even harsher than on the Gallipoli Peninsula, with the temperature climbing by the end of June to 115 degrees

Fahrenheit (45 degrees Celsius), and fierce, biting mosquitoes attacking the advancing troops with unexpected ferocity. There was also a sinister aspect of the battle: those wounded British and Indian soldiers who had not been found by search parties were robbed by marauding Arabs, many of the injured men were mutilated, and some of them were murdered. Baghdad was unconquered.

In the Balkans, the Austro-Hungarian army, under a German commander, renewed the offensive against Serbia on 7 October 1915. Belgrade was captured, and seven days later Bulgaria, hitherto neutral, joined in the assault, overrunning the eastern half of Serbian Macedonia. Britain had warned Bulgaria that if she attacked Serbia, Britain would come to Serbia's assistance. To implement this pledge an Allied Expeditionary Force of 13,000 men landed at Salonika, followed nine days later by 18,000 French soldiers. The Anglo-French force failed, however, to break through the Bulgarian lines and push into central Serbia. By November 23 the Serbian army had been pushed back to a tiny corner of land in the mountains around Kosovo. To these sacred fields, the scene of Serbia's defeat at the hands of the Turks more than five centuries earlier, the Serbian army retreated. With it came thousands of civilian refugees.

From Kosovo, soldiers and refugees fled, through treacherous winter conditions, across precipitate mountain paths to the Adriatic Sea. Of the 300,000 who set off, 20,000 perished on the march. Austria-Hungary occupied Serbia. The Anglo-French force remained at Salonika, reinforced by Serbian soldiers who had managed to make their way southward, but despite two years of fighting, only a single border town was liberated from the Austrian and Bulgarian occupying forces. Following the Austrian conquest of Serbia, the Austrian Chief of Staff, General Conrad von Hötzendorf, advised his Emperor to seek a negotiated peace with Russia. The defeat of Serbia fulfilled Austria's war aims. But there was no way Austria could make peace without Germany's approval, and the Kaiser, confident of victory in both east and west, insisted that the war go on.

The first military initiatives of 1916 were taken by Austria-Hungary: the conquest of Montenegro, followed by the conquest of Albania. It was a time of triumph for the Central Powers. In the Aegean,

the Anglo-French army completed its evacuation of the Gallipoli
Peninsula, 35,268 troops being taken off Cape Helles in eleven days.
In Mesopotamia, where the town of Kut had been captured from the
Turks but was then beseiged, a British and Indian relief force, sent
from Basra to break the siege, was defeated only twenty miles from
Kut and forced to retreat. A second attempt to relieve the siege
reached within two miles of Kut but was also beaten back. The
besieged troops surrendered, more than 11,000 being led into captivity, brutally ill-treated by their guards as they were marched
northward. Of the 2,500 British soldiers on this march, 1,750 died.
Of the 9,300 Indian soldiers, 2,500 died.

On the Eastern Front, the German army had overrun the whole
of Russian Poland and the Lithuanian provinces of the Russian
Empire. Inside Russia, the anti-war movement in Russia grew with
every military setback. In January, 10,000 workers went on strike
in the Black Sea naval base of Nikolayev. Two weeks later, 45,000
dock workers in St Petersburg went on strike. Inside Austria-
Hungary, where war weariness was also strong and national aspirations growing, the Chief of Staff, General Conrad von Hötzendorf,
again pressed for peace before the whole fabric of the hitherto triumphant Habsburg domains was endangered. 'England cannot be
defeated,' he warned Count Tisza on 4 January 1916. 'Peace must
be made in not too short a space, or we shall be fatally weakened,
if not destroyed.' These fears were at odds with the confidence of
most of the Austro-Hungarian leaders, who had conquered Serbia,
Montenegro and Albania, and driven the Russian army away from
their soil. That month German was declared the sole official language
in Bohemia, and in the streets of Prague the police used truncheons
against people whom they overheard speaking Czech.

The German military planners, whose scheme for the rapid defeat
of France had been left in tatters in September 1914, devised a new
plan to bring the fighting on the Western Front to a victorious end,
an attack on the French fortress at Verdun. The French having made
clear they would hold Verdun to the last man, the German military
planners reasoned that if Verdun could be under continuous attack,
more and more French soldiers would be brought in to defend it,
and, as the Chief of the German General Staff, General Falkenhayn,

explained to the Kaiser, whether the Germans captured Verdun or not 'the forces of France will bleed to death'.

The German attack on Verdun began on 21 February 1916. The commander of the French forces, General Pétain, watching French troops returning from the battlefield, wrote: 'In their unsteady look one sensed visions of horror, while their step and bearing revealed utter despondency. They were crushed by horrifying memories.'

Determined to defeat Britain, on March 28 the Reichstag in Berlin voted for immediate, unrestricted submarine warfare. In a further effort to weaken Britain's war effort, the German Government encouraged an Irish nationalist, Sir Roger Casement – who a decade earlier, as a British diplomat, had exposed the cruelties perpetrated in the Belgian Congo – to recruit Irish soldiers in German prisoner-of-war camps to fight against the British. Casement was unsuccessful; of the several thousand men he hoped to recruit into an Irish Brigade, only fifty-two joined. While in Germany, he was urged by the Sinn Fein leaders in Ireland to obtain arms for an Irish uprising. He asked for 200,000 rifles. When the Germans, who did not regard the Irish revolution as a promising one, offered only 20,000, Casement was distraught. The revolution – the seizure of power in Dublin – was fixed for April 22, Easter Sunday. In order to warn Sinn Fein they could not count on German support, Casement returned to Ireland on board a German submarine, pretending to the Germans that he would help foment the uprising. He was put ashore on the Atlantic coast of Ireland. At the same time, a small German merchant ship brought the 20,000 rifles, and a million rounds of ammunition, to the Irish coast. But a British ship intercepted the merchantman, which scuttled itself, and the cargo was lost. Casement was arrested four days later, after he landed, and before he could get to Dublin. He was taken to London, brought to trial, found guilty of treason, and executed.

Despite the loss of the rifles and ammunition, the Irish national uprising went ahead. On April 24, in Dublin, a proclamation was read out from the steps of the main Post Office establishing 'the Provisional Government of the Irish Republic'. For a week the rebels held out against the troops sent against them, mostly men from Irish regiments who had been fighting on the Western Front for more than a year. By the end of a week of fighting the rebels were crushed. Sixty-four had been killed, as had more than 200 civilians caught in the crossfire and in British artillery attacks on rebel-held buildings. More than a hundred troops and police had also been killed. Fifteen of the rebel leaders were tried in secret and sentenced to be shot. A sixteenth, Eamon de Valera, a professor of mathematics, was saved from execution because he was an American citizen. He spent the rest of the war in various English prisons. Later he was to lead Southern Ireland in its first years of independence.

Emerging from their North Sea ports on the last day of May, a force of 103 German warships steamed northwards to attack Allied merchant shipping off the Norwegian coast. The expedition, the largest German naval initiative since the outbreak of war, was foiled when the attackers were themselves attacked by 51 British warships. The German naval commanders and the Kaiser had always hoped for a battle in which they might break the British naval blockade of the German North Sea ports. The British had always hoped to destroy the German High Seas Fleet, leaving only submarines as their German naval adversary. In addition to the ships sunk by both sides, more than 6,000 British and 2,551 German sailors were killed. After the Battle of Jutland, the German High Seas Fleet, unwilling to risk the losses of another major naval confrontation, never again challenged the British in the North Sea, and the British blockade of Germany remained in force.

On the Western Front, at Verdun, the Germans used a new phosgene gas, Green Cross, which wiped out a whole French division, 5,000 men in all. But the Germans did not have enough gas to renew the attack. In the hope of taking German pressure off Verdun, the British Commander-in-Chief, General Haig, brought forward by four days the artillery barrage of his imminent offensive on the Somme. The barrage was then continued an extra two days because heavy rain made an infantry attack impossible. The attack finally began on July 1. During the prolonged British artillery bombardment many of the German defenders were in deep, well-fortified shelters.

When the British soldiers moved forward, most of them weighed down by sixty-six pounds weight of equipment, they were confronted by a hundred German machine-gun positions, hidden in armoured emplacements. These too had survived the ferocious bombardment. In the first day's fighting more than a thousand British officers and 20,000 men were killed, the highest death toll for any single day of the First World War.

Among the troops in action on July 1 was a Newfoundland battalion. Typical of the fate of all the attacking forces that day, of the 810 men who advanced, 710 were either killed or wounded. 'It was a magnificent display of trained and disciplined valour,' one of Haig's staff informed the Newfoundland Prime Minister, 'and its assault only failed of success because dead men can advance no further.'

The main beneficiaries of the British attack were the French. The first day of the Battle of the Somme was the 132nd day of the German attack on Verdun; the relief provided for Verdun was immediate, with tens of thousands of German troops being transferred from Verdun to the Somme. Among those who fought on the Somme was Donald Hankey, the brother of the British Cabinet Secretary, who sent an account of what he had seen to the editor of the *Spectator* magazine. The editor, in what he regarded as the interest of patriotism, refused to publish it. Hankey had written: 'Day and night we have done nothing but bring in the wounded and the dead. When one sees the dead, their limbs crushed and mangled, one can only have revulsion for war. It was easy to talk of glory and heroism when one is away from it. But here, in the presence of the mutilated and tortured dead, one can only feel the horror and wickedness of war. Indeed it is an evil harvest, sown of pride and arrogance and lust of power.' Hankey was killed later in the battle, leading his men over the top. He was thirty-one.

After nine days of fighting on the Somme, the British to the north of the river and the French south of it had pushed the Germans back between one and two miles. There would be no breakthrough. At Verdun, a final German assault using gas and flame-throwers failed to capture the last fort between the German front line and the city: in the two and a half weeks since the new gas had first been used the French soldiers had been issued with effective gas masks. Science, which had been enlisted to shorten the war, served only to prolong it.

On the Eastern Front, by the end of July, the Russians had crossed back into Austria-Hungary and taken 40,000 Austrian prisoners. A further 7,000 Austrian and 3,500 German soldiers were captured on August 7. The German High Command began to despair of its Austrian ally. General Hoffman, appointed by Berlin to take command of the Austrian defences, noted bitterly in his diary that within the Austro-Hungarian army there were 'no less than twenty-three distinct languages. No one understands anyone else.'

For two years Roumania had remained neutral. Alerted, however, to the possibility of territorial gains for herself as a result of Russia's successes in Eastern Galicia, on August 27 she declared war on Austria-Hungary. Nine days earlier the Roumanian government had signed a secret treaty with the Allies, whereby Roumania would acquire three long sought-after regions of Austria-Hungary: Transylvania, the Bukovina and the Banat. As Roumanian troops pressed forward across the border into Austria-Hungary, the Kaiser, seeking stronger men and more ruthless military measures to counter the Roumanian threat, replaced his Chief of the General Staff, General Falkenhayn, by the legendary Field Marshal, Paul von Hindenburg, who was given, as his deputy, the hero of Tannenburg, General Ludendorff. The Hindenburg-Ludendorff combination produced an immediate upsurge of morale in the German army, and among German civilians, each searching for the hope that the war could be won, and, more importantly, ended.

Hindenburg-Ludendorff's first initiative was to double munitions production and treble the production of artillery and machine-guns. Their second initiative was to take effective command of all the armies of the Central Powers. Not only the Austrians, but the Turks and Bulgarians, agreed to this, recognizing the predominance of Germany's military skills. As the Roumanians advanced deep into Transylvania, the Central Powers played their trump card, a declaration of war against Roumania by Bulgaria, its southern neighbour, wherupon Bulgarian troops invaded Roumania in conjunction with German troops who had been sent to Bulgaria.

As the advance into Roumania began, and Bulgarian aircraft bombed Roumanian military depots and munitions factories in Bucharest, the Roumanian High Command appealed for a renewed British military offensive on the Somme, to force the Germans to take troops back from the Roumanian front. The renewed offensive took place, and succeeded in driving the Germans from two villages, but it was not enough to force the Germans to withdraw any of their troops from the Roumanian Front.

On September 10 a new weapon of war, the tank, was in action with the British forces on the Somme. An armoured, tracked vehicle, it could crush barbed wire and cross the lines of trenches, impervious to machine-gun bullets, while behind it infantrymen could move forward protected by the tank itself. But the military planners had not been prepared to wait until sufficient numbers of tanks were available to offer the chance of a breakthrough.

Among the infantrymen participating in the advance in which tanks were first used, and killed during the attack, was Raymond Asquith, son of the British Prime Minister. Badly wounded that day, for the second time, was a future British Prime Minister, Harold Macmillan. As a result of his wound, he had to remain on crutches until the end of the war.

On the Italian Front, in September, Italy launched its sixth military offensive along the Isonzo River: three to four miles of Austrian territory was gained along a fifteen-mile front, and 50,000 Austrian soldiers were captured. But the cost of this success was appallingly high: as many as 20,000 Italian soldiers were killed.

The Italian line had held, but the Roumanian army was in retreat. On December 6 German troops entered Bucharest, and the campaign was over. Germany, having defeated the largest of the Balkan States, then intensified the submarine offensive, confident of being able to force Britain to its knees. The Allied Powers were equally confident of victory. The setback on the Somme was interpreted as a victory, in view of the few miles gained and the 72,901 German soldiers taken prisoner. France, despite the heavy loss of life at Verdun, had held the town itself, making good the boast that 'Verdun will not fall'.

In Russia a storm was brewing that might bring the Eastern war to an end. In October and November there were almost 200 strikes, by an estimated 200,000 working men, demanding an end to the war. That winter the Tsar was warned by his Chief of Staff that there were sufficient reserve troops for only another five months' fighting. The offensive into Austria-Hungary was halted and pushed back. The Russian army was incapable of further offensive action. 'The plain truth,' wrote a British officer attached to Russian military headquarters, 'is that without aeroplanes, far more heavy guns and shell and some knowledge of their use, it is butchery, and useless butchery, to drive the Russian infantry against German lines.'

On December 20, Woodrow Wilson, having been re-elected President six weeks earlier, addressed a Peace Note to all the warring Powers, asking them to give him their views 'as to the terms upon which the war might be concluded, and the arrangements which would be deemed satisfactory as a guarantee against its renewal, or the kindling of any similar conflict in the future'. Small nations, Wilson added, had to be made secure from any future aggression. Rival leagues and alliances had to be avoided. But a 'league of all nations' might be formed 'to preserve peace throughout the world'. In the continuation of the war, Wilson warned, there was the risk that 'an injury be done to civilization itself which can never be atoned or repaired'.

Wilson's Peace Note was rejected by all the belligerents. The new British Prime Minister, David Lloyd George, who had come to power two weeks earlier, pledged to fight the war with increasing vigour, answering Wilson: 'We shall put our trust rather in an unbroken army than in broken faith.' In answering Wilson's insistence that there was no place for conquest and annexation, the Kaiser told his confidants that when the war was over 'the coast of Flanders must be ours'. In Austria-Hungary, the death on November 21 of the eighty-six-year-old Emperor Franz-Josef was followed by a patriotic statement by his successor, the twenty-nine-year-old Emperor Charles, that the war must be continued 'until the enemy powers realized that it was impossible to overthrow the monarchy'. In Russia, the Prime Minister, Boris Stürmer, an advocate of a negotiated peace, was replaced, the Tsar insisting that the war be fought 'to a finish'. The new Prime Minister, Alexander Trepoff, stressed in his first speech that when the war was over Russia must acquire Constantinople and the Dardanelles. Russia would continue the war until 'complete victory'.

Although none of the warring Powers was willing to make peace, each was busy positioning itself for influence in the post-war world. Following the defeat of Serbia, the heir to the Serbian throne travelled to London with the Serbian Prime Minister to obtain British support for the creation an independent South Slav State (Yugoslavia). In London and Paris, Czech national leaders sought assurances that after the war an independent Czechoslovak State would emerge. Zionist leaders in London were trying to persuade Britain to establish a Jewish National Home in Palestine after Turkey's defeat.

Russia and Germany were competing to assure the Poles of their support for an independent, or at least autonomous Poland once the war was won. In Belgium, the Germans tried to encourage Flemish support for the future incorporation of Belgium into Germany, or into the German sphere of influence. To counter this the Allies pledged they would not end hostilities with Germany 'until Belgium has been restored to her political and economic independence'.

Germany initiated unrestricted submarine warfare on 1 February 1917: the first United States ship to be sunk was a cargo ship, torpedoed off the south-west coast of Britain. Its crew was saved by a British ship, but its cargo of grain was lost. That same day, President Wilson told Congress he was breaking off diplomatic relations with Germany. Although not a declaration of war, it was an indication that such a declaration might not be far distant.

For the Allies, Russia was the weak link. A German intelligence assessment that the Russian army could not hold out 'longer than the autumn' was widely accepted. More than a million Russian soldiers had been killed in action. More than half a million more were in hospital, too badly injured to return to the front. A further million had deserted. The number of men in front-line and reserve units was insufficient to meet the demands of the battlefield in 1917. With the start of a strike in the Putilov munitions works in Petrograd on March 3 – February 18 in the Russian calendar – Russia's warmaking capacity was further eroded. By March 9 there were between 200,000 and 300,000 factory workers on strike. Marching crowds declared: 'Down with the autocracy!' and 'Down with the war!'

On March 10, from his military headquarters 450 miles south of Petrograd, the Tsar ordered the suppression of the Petrograd riots by force. When, on the following morning, Tsarist troops opened fire on a crowd that refused to disperse, forty civilians were killed. Leaving his headquarters by rail for Petrograd, the Tsar hoped to exert his authority there to end the strikes and demonstrations, but even as he was on his journey the soldiers of the Petrograd garrison – 171,000 men in all, plus 152,000 in nearby towns – the men on whom he was hoping to rely, joined the street demonstrations whose slogans included 'Down with the Tsar!'

On March 12, soldiers and police still loyal to the Tsar were unable to prevent the burning of the Law Courts, or attacks on police stations throughout the city. In many instances the strikers persuaded the troops who were sent against them not to open fire. In the clashes which did take place, 587 demonstrators were killed, as were 655 soldiers and 73 policemen. The Duma decided to act without Tsarist authority, forming a Provisional Committee for the Restoration of Order in the Capital – known as the Provisional Government.

On March 13 the captain of the Russian cruiser *Aurora*, which was undergoing repairs in Petrograd, was murdered by his own sailors. Forty more officers were murdered at the nearby island base of Kronstadt. On March 14, as the Tsar continued towards Petrograd, an officer went into his carriage to tell him the tracks ahead were in the hands of 'unfriendly troops'. The train made a detour westward to Pskov, where it was met by the commander of the Northern Front, General Ruzsky. He urged the Tsar to acknowledge the authority of the Provisional Government. The Tsar refused to do so. That day, the Petrograd Soviet, an assembly which had been elected by striking factory workers and disloyal soldiers, issued its Order No. 1: all saluting of officers by men who were not on duty was abolished, and all weapons would be controlled by elected committees loyal to the Soviet.

The Bolsheviks, a minority in the Soviet, and whose leaders, including Lenin, were still in exile, called for an immediate end to the war and the establishment of the 'dictatorship of the proletariat'. But power in the Soviet was in the hands of the Mensheviks, with Alexander Kerensky, a member of the Provisional Government, favouring the continuation of the war. On March 15, while still at Pskov, the Tsar received telegrams from each of his army commanders, urging him to abdicate. They doubted the Russian army could continue the war if he remained on the throne. Bowing to the unanimity of senior military opinion, the Tsar abdicated. To the relief of the Allies, the Provisional Government announced it would continue with the war, and do so 'to a victorious conclusion'. At the same time, the Menshevik majority in the Petrograd Soviet declared its support for a 'defensive' war against the Germans.

On March 21 a United States tanker was sunk by a German submarine in a specially declared 'safety zone' inside Dutch waters. Twenty American crewmen were killed. President Wilson called an emergency session of Congress for April 2. The day before it convened, an armed American steamer was torpedoed off the French coast and twenty-eight of her crewmen drowned. 'The world must be made safe for democracy,' Wilson told Congress on April 2. Four days later the United States declared war on Germany.

In Petrograd, the leaders of the Provisional Government made every effort to revive the warmaking spirit, pledging Russia's commitment to the defeat of Austria-Hungary, and to punitive reparations against Germany. But whole Russian divisions were throwing down their arms and crossing into the German trenches to fraternise and to surrender. On April 29, the Russian Commander in Chief, General Alexeyev, informed the Ministry of War in Petrograd: 'The army is systematically falling apart.' By the end of May, 30,000 deserters a day were reaching Kiev from the front, hurrying home.

On the Western Front, by the end of May more than 30,000 French soldiers had left the trenches and made their way to the rear. Courts martial were instituted and swift punishment imposed: fifty of the mutineers were shot. Later the mutiny spread to the French troops at Salonika.

During the week when the French mutinies were at their most intense, the first 1,000 American combat troops reached France. It was to be another twelve months, however, before the Americans had arrived in sufficient numbers to take part in the fighting, other than as small detachments amid British and French units. But Haig was determined to launch a new offensive in the Ypres salient before the Americans arrived, and even if the French would not be able to participate on the British flank. In preparation for the battle, the British exploded nineteen enormously powerful mines under the Messines-Wytschaete ridge. Ten thousand German soldiers were killed, most of them by the blast, or buried alive in the vast mounds of earth thrown up by each explosion. Thousands more were stunned, the German front-line trenches overrun, and more than 7,000 German soldiers taken prisoner. Among the British officers who took part in the battle for the ridge was Captain Anthony Eden, a future Prime Minister. The German pilots in action above the battlefield included Lieutenant Hermann Goering, who from 1935 to 1945 was to be in charge of the German air force. During the German retreat from the ridge Goering shot down his first British aircraft. Eden was twenty years old, Goering twenty-four.

As the German submarine attacks intensified, the Allies instituted the convoy system, armed warships protecting groups of merchant ships as they crossed the Atlantic together. The first west–east transatlantic convoy sailed from Hampton Roads, Virginia, on July 1. Only one merchant ship was lost: it had fallen behind the convoy. During the rest of July, sixty merchant ships crossed the Atlantic in convoy without loss. Most distressing to the German High Command, more than a million American troops were brought across the Atlantic in convoy with the loss of only 637 men.

On July 1, the day the first Allied convoy set sail across the Atlantic, General Brusilov launched the Russian summer offensive to which the Provisional Government was committed. It was initially successful. As the Russian armies moved forward through Eastern Galicia they captured 17,000 Austrian soldiers and approached their objective, the oilfields of Drohobycz. But even as Drohobycz fell, Brusilov's hopes were dashed as the Austrians halted the Russian advance and took thousands of Russians prisoner. On July 7, Alexander Kerensky, Minister of War and the Navy, became Prime Minister. Repeatedly visiting the front, he urged the soldiers to fight on. His efforts were in vain. Following a German-led counter-attack, tens of thousands of Russian soldiers threw down their rifles, fled the battlefield, and headed for home. Hundreds of their officers, trying to halt the flight, were shot by their own men. On the last day of of July, 40,000 Russian soldiers were in flight. That day, Austrian and German forces recovered the last Austrian territory which Brusilov had recaptured. In Petrograd, a Bolshevik attempt to seize power was crushed; Lenin fled from the city and went into hiding.

In Berlin, almost as war-weary as Petrograd, a majority of German Reichstag deputies signed a Peace Resolution urging the government to work for 'a peace by agreement and permanent conciliation'. To the relief of the German General Staff, a new German Chancellor, Dr Georg Michaelis, declared: 'I do not consider that a body like the German Reichstag is a fit one to decide about peace and war on its own initiative during the war.' When the leader of the British Labour Party, Ramsay MacDonald, tried to persuade the House of Commons to endorse the Reichstag Peace Resolution, his proposal was defeated by 148 votes to 19.

The third British offensive in the Ypres salient – Third Ypres – began on July 31 and continued for more than three months. Despite the fiercest fighting, it failed to take even its first day's objective, the village of Passchendaele, only four and a half miles from the starting point. Within a month, heavy rain had turned the battlefield to liquid mud, into which men and horses were sucked in and drowned. On October 30, Canadian troops entered Passchendaele, but their casualties were heavy and they were driven out. Two weeks later, after a renewed Canadian advance across five hundred yards of mud, and in the face of a German artillery bombardment by 500 guns assisted by German air attacks, the offensive was called off. The next day a senior British staff officer made his first-ever visit to the front line. As his car drew closer to the trenches he was appalled by the conditions around him. Reaching the furthest point the car could go he burst into tears and said: 'Good God, did we really send men to fight in that?' The man sitting beside him, who had earlier been in action, replied, expressionless: 'It's worse farther on up.'

The number of British and British Empire dead in the Third Battle of Ypres has been estimated at between 62,000 and 66,000, German deaths at 83,000. Commenting on the high but imprecise nature of the British figure, the official British history noted: 'The clerk-power to investigate the exact losses was not available.' On the Italian Front, German troops called in to help the Austrians advanced across the Isonzo river, entered the town of Caporetto, and took 10,000 Italian prisoners. Frightened that Italy might be driven to seek a separate peace, and as anti-war demonstrations broke out in Milan, Lloyd George sent two British divisions, both badly needed on the Western Front, to Italy.

At the end of October an estimated one million Russian railway and transport workers were on strike, and supplies were unable to reach the Eastern Fronts. From Petrograd, the Bolsheviks called daily on the soldiers and sailors not to fight. A new Russian Minister of War, General Verkhovski, assured the British Military Attaché that he would restore the Russian army and 'make it in a fit condition to fight by the spring'. The attaché was sceptical, writing in his diary that on the basis of what he knew and saw 'there is evidently not the slightest hope that the Russian Army will ever fight again'.

Efforts were being made to stimulate patriotism in Russia. In issuing a declaration to the Jews of the world on November 2, stating that the British Government 'view with favour' the establishment of a Jewish National Home in Palestine, the British Foreign Secretary, Arthur Balfour, hoped that this promise would encourage the millions of Jews in Russia to support the war effort, and exert every possible influence to secure an Allied victory over the Central Powers. On November 3 the British Foreign Office asked three leading Zionists then in London to go at once to Petrograd, to rally Russian Jewry to the Allied cause. 'With skilful management of the Jews of Russia,' Balfour was told by Lord Hardinge, Permanent Under-Secretary of State at the Foreign Office, 'the situation may still be restored by the spring.'

Neither General Verkhovski nor Lord Hardinge was right. It was not the spring that was the crucial time, but that very week, the first week of November. On November 3, the day of Hardinge's hopeful note, it was learned in Petrograd that Russian troops on the Baltic Front had thrown down their arms and were fraternizing with the German soldiers facing them. On the following day, when the Provisional Government ordered the 155,000-strong Petrograd garrison to go to the front, a Bolshevik 'Military Revolutionary Committee' persuaded them not to go. The Provisional Government decided to act against the Bolsheviks. On November 6 the Bolshevik printing presses were seized and closed down, and the telephone lines to Bolshevik headquarters at the Smolny Institute were cut. The bridges over the River Neva were raised, to prevent Bolshevik detachments crossing them.

For a moment it seemed that the Bolsheviks had been outwitted and outmanoeuvred. But that afternoon, armed Bolshevik units recaptured the printing works, lowered the bridges, and seized two crucial centres of communication in the city, the Central Telegraph Office and the Russian Telegraphic Agency. The telephone lines to the Smolny Institute were reconnected. Lenin, in hiding since the defeat of the attempted Bolshevik uprising in July, reached the Smolny that evening, his face bandaged as a disguise.

That night, without bloodshed, the Bolsheviks occupied the principal buildings in the capital, including the railway stations, post offices, telephone centres, State Bank and bridges. At nine o'clock in the morning Lenin drafted a proclamation declaring that the Provisional Government had been deposed, and that government authority was in the hands of the Bolshevik Military-Revolutionary Committee. Despite having been 'deposed' by the Bolsheviks, the Provisional Government met the next morning, November 7, in the Winter Palace, whereupon 18,000 Bolshevik supporters, protected by a thousand soldiers loyal to the revolution, surrounded the palace and demanded the surrender of the deputies. During the day 9,000 sailors from the Kronstadt naval base reached the capital and declared their support for the revolution, as did the crews of two Russian destroyers which arrived that day in the River Neva.

Throughout November 7 the members of the Provisional Government remained inside the Winter Palace, insisting on their sole right to govern Russia. That evening the sailors on board the cruiser *Aurora*, which had been anchored in the Neva for several weeks, announced they would open fire on the Winter Palace if the Bolsheviks were not admitted. A few blank shells, harmless but noisy, were fired by the *Aurora* as proof of its seriousness. The Bolsheviks, supported by 14,000 soldiers and sailors, stormed the Winter Palace. By one o'clock on the morning of November 8 its defenders had fled. That morning, Lenin was elected Chairman of the Council of People's Commissars. In Moscow, armed Bolsheviks occupied the Kremlin. Throughout Russia, hundreds of towns declared themselves for the revolution.

Lenin's first decree was the Decree of Peace, four million copies of which were sent to the soldiers at the front. The troops could come home. When, on November 11, forces loyal to the Provisional Government, led by Kerensky, marched to within shelling distance of the capital, they were met by a larger Bolshevik force and driven off. Leon Trotsky, Commissar for Foreign Affairs of the new Bolshevik government, informed the Germans that Russia wished to make peace, and two days later asked for an immediate armistice. In Paris, the new French war leader, Georges Clemenceau, exhorted the French Chamber of Deputies: 'War, nothing but war.'

On November 20, only ten days after the Passchendaele offensive had been finally halted by mud and carnage, another British offensive was launched on the Western Front, at Cambrai: 376 tanks took part in the opening attack. 'The triple belts of wire were crossed as if they had been belts of nettles,' one British officer recalled. The defenders were driven back five miles, and 7,000 German soldiers taken prisoner. But German reinforcements, rushed back to the Western Front from Russia, where the enemy had collapsed, prevented the long-anticipated British cavalry breakthrough. Cambrai, the objective of the new attack, remained in German hands. The British then withdrew in order to straighten their line.

On December 1, a formal cease-fire was declared throughout the Eastern Front. The Russian war was over, and the former Tsarist

Empire breaking up. Estonia was the first of the old imperial provinces to declare its independence, followed by Finland. They were
the first new countries to come into being as a result of the First
World War. Latvia was the next to declare its independence. Turkey
was also losing its empire. British forces had entered Baghdad on
March 11: the Arab revolt had driven the Turks out of Arabia. On
December 9, Jerusalem surrendered to a British army.

In the hope of detaching both Austria and Turkey from Germany,
Lloyd George authorized secret talks, with Austrian and Turkish
emissaries, in Switzerland. The talks broke down. With Russia out
of the war and Germany in the ascendant, both Turks and Austrians
saw the peace negotiations about to take place between the Bolsheviks
and Germans, and themselves, as a chance to acquire Russian territory. Greed overrode war-weariness.

On 8 January 1918, Woodrow Wilson issued a 'peace programme'
consisting of Fourteen Points, setting out a democratic, liberal ideology as the basis for the post-war world. At Brest-Litovsk, where
the Bolsheviks were negotiating peace, negotiations broke down on
February 17. The German terms, which included the separation of
Russia from Poland, and the German annexation of Lithuania and
southern Latvia, were too harsh for the Bolsheviks to accept.

The Germans re-opened hostilities and advanced. 'This beast
springs quickly,' Lenin commented to Trotsky. Acting equally
quickly, Lenin and Trotsky accepted the terms they had rejected two
days earlier, but the Germans were in no hurry to sign, and continued
to advance. Lenin appealed to the Germans to end the fighting. The
German terms had grown to include the annexation of Poland, the
Baltic States and parts of the Ukraine – territory already under
German occupation. At a meeting of his ruling council, Lenin was
bitterly attacked for urging acceptance, which he only secured after
threatening resignation. By the time the peace treaty was signed at
Brest-Litovsk on March 3 the Germans were in control of almost
half of Russia east of Moscow. Under the treaty, Russia gave up all
claims to seven of the provinces that had been an integral part of
Tsarist Russia: the Baltic provinces, Poland, Byelorussia, Finland,
Bessarabia, Ukraine and the Caucasus. These vast areas contained one

third of Russia's pre-war population, one third of her arable land and nine-tenths of her coalfields, as well as almost all her oil.

In the West, Ludendorff was convinced he could drive a wedge between the British and French armies, force the British back to the Channel Coast, and enter Paris. The offensive began on March 21. Within twenty-four hours, 21,000 British soldiers had been taken prisoner. On the following day German troops crossed the Somme, driving a wedge between the British and French and bringing to 45,000 the number of Allied soldiers captured in four days. To co-ordinate the Allied effort, on March 29 Marshal Foch was given charge of all the Allied forces. The Germans regained all the ground they had lost on the Somme two years earlier, but the Allied line held, and American troops were reaching the battlefield in large numbers. Ludendorff decided to switch the German attack further north, drive the British out of the Ypres salient and reach the North Sea coast between Calais and Dunkirk. The attack was launched on April 9, with 2,000 tons of gas shells fired against the British troops, incapacitating 8,000, many of whom were blinded.

The high ground around Passchendaele, reached at such heavy cost five months earlier, was evacuated on April 15. Five days later American troops were in action in the St Mihiel salient. At first they were driven back, outnumbered, and caught unawares by the German gas shells, but then they regrouped and held the line. At Ypres, French troops prevented the Germans taking the town. Ludendorff's hopes of a knock-out blow were ended. In three weeks more than 30,000 German and 20,000 Allied soldiers had been killed.

On May 12 the Kaiser and the Emperor Charles agreed to share the economic exploitation of the Ukraine. The 'bread basket' of Russia would be giving its 1918 harvest to the Austro-German war effort. But Charles's problems within his empire were intensifying. On the day of his meeting with the Kaiser, Slovene soldiers mutinied, demanding an indepent Slovakia and an end to the war. Within a week both a Ruthenian and a Serbian unit in the Austro-Hungarian army mutinied. They too demanded independence and an end to the war. Czech troops in barracks a hundred miles north of Prague mutinied on May 21. Setting off by train to Prague, they declared that when they arrived they would 'put an end' to the war. They were intercepted on the journey and disarmed. Ten were sentenced to death and 560 imprisoned. 'Had the rebels succeeded in advancing southward,' the local Governor told the authorities in Vienna, 'and had they found support – and this was by no means impossible – among the civilians in these regions, we might by now have faced a regular revolution in parts of Bohemia.'

On May 27, Ludendorff tried one more offensive on the Western Front. The initial attack was successful, but the Allies were able to counter-attack elsewhere. One German-held town, Cantigny, was attacked on May 28 by an American brigade, in the first sustained American offensive of the war. Nearly 4,000 American soldiers took part, Cantigny was overrun, and seven separate German counter-attacks driven off. The American troops who were in action gave courage to all those who saw them. 'We all had the impression that we were about to see a wonderful transfusion of blood,' a French Staff Officer commented. 'Life was coming in floods to re-animate the dying body of France.'

On June 7 a massive German assault was launched along the French sector of the line. Three quarters of a million German gas shells were fired: 15,000 tons of gas. The line broke and the Germans, advancing five miles before nightfall, took 8,000 prisoners. On June 10 the German army was within forty-five miles of Paris, but on the following day French and American troops launched a counter-attack, and the Germans were driven back. As Ludendorff called off the offensive, the Allies pressed home their advantage. On June 30 the French attacked with a new type of tank as their surprise weapon. It weighed more than five and a half tons. A thousand Germans were taken prisoner.

Ludendorff did not give up, and chose July 14 for the preliminary bombardment of one more offensive. As the bombardment began, there were those in Berlin who expected German troops to be on their way to Paris within a few days, and the Allies to sue for peace within two months. But at one of the main points of attack, opposite the American Rainbow Division, Pétain had created a complete line of bogus, virtually unmanned trenches, and it was against these that much of the gas attack was expended, leaving the fully-manned trenches further back almost untouched by the bombardment. When German troops reached the parapets of the real trenches, and the uncut wire and unimpeded machine-gun fire of the defenders, they were, one American officer recalled, 'exhausted, unco-ordinated, and shattered, incapable of going on without being reorganized and reinforced'. After the battle that officer was haunted by 'the vision of those writhing bodies hanging from the barbed wire'. He was Douglas MacArthur, who a quarter of a century later commanded the United States forces in the Pacific.

On July 18, Foch launched an Allied counter-attack. The German line was broken and by the end of the fourth day 30,000 Germans had been killed. 'Never have I seen so many dead men, never such frightful battle scenes,' a German officer later wrote. Among the German soldiers who fought throughout the retreat was Corporal Hitler. On August 4 he was awarded the Iron Cross, First Class, the citation speaking of his 'personal bravery and general merit'. On the day Hitler was awarded his Iron Cross, the American Assistant Secretary for the Navy, Franklin D. Roosevelt, made his only visit to the battle zone. During the day he saw 'two hundred limping, exhausted men come out of the line – the survivors of a regiment of a thousand that went forward forty-eight hours before'.

The Germans fell back, the German Chancellor, Georg von Hertling, noting in his diary: 'On the 18th even the most optimistic among us knew that all was lost. The history of the world was played out in three days.'

On August 8, British, French and Dominion troops began a new offensive, and by at the end of its third day, 24,000 German soldiers had been taken prisoner. On August 14 Ludendorff recommended immediate peace negotiations. He was supported by the Emperor Charles, who warned the Kaiser that Austria-Hungary 'could only continue the war until December'. On August 17 the French attacked again, as did the British four days later. On the Somme, so strongly contested in 1916, the Germans withdrew ten miles in a single day. In Vienna, on August 30, the Austrian Foreign Minister, Baron Burian, informed the German Government that Austria-Hungary intended to begin peace negotiations with the Allies whatever

Germany might say. An estimated 400,000 Austro-Hungarian soldiers had deserted from their units, he said, a situation not unlike that which had brought the Russian war effort to a halt a year earlier.

The Germans fought on, the Kaiser hoping that if a positive change occurred in German fortunes on the battlefield, even for a short time, Germany would be in a better position to make a negotiated peace. No such positive change seemed likely, however. On September 8, French and American troops drove the Germans out of the St Mihiel salient. Among the American soldiers in action were George S. Patton Jnr, who in 1944 commanded the United States Third Army, and George C. Marshall, the Chief of Staff of the United States Forces throughout the Second World War.

On the Salonika Front, Bulgarian troops had continued to hold the mountain ridges which they had manned for two years, but on September 15, having been ordered not to retreat in the face of a massive Allied onslaught, they mutinied, and the retreat began. Ten days later British troops entered Bulgaria, and the Bulgarians asked for an armistice. They were the first of the Central Powers to do so.

On the Western Front, September 26 was the first day of a new French and American offensive. Among the American artillerymen in action that day was Captain Harry S. Truman, a future President. 'I slept in the edge of a wood to the right of my battery position,' he later recalled. 'If I hadn't awakened and got up at 4 a.m. I would not be here, because the Germans fired a barrage on my sleeping place!' Within twenty-four hours, 23,000 German soldiers had been taken prisoner. Near Cambrai, British troops, supported by a thousand aircraft, attacked the Hindenburg Line, taking 10,000 prisoners. On September 28, Haig launched his fourth offensive against the Germans in the Ypres salient. Passchendaele was quickly taken, and in two days, along the whole Western Front, 37,000 German prisoners were in Allied hands. That evening, Ludendorff told Hindenburg that Germany must seek an armistice. On the following day, the Bulgarians were granted the armistice they had sought four days earlier and hostilities ceased on the Salonika Front.

*   *   *

On October 2, as a thirty-mile sector of the main German defences – the Hindenburg Line – was being overrun by the Allies, Germany acquired a new Chancellor, Prince Max of Baden. Hindenburg advised him to seek an immediate peace, but Prince Max was for the continuation of the war. 'I hoped I could fight down pessimism and revive confidence,' he later explained, 'for I myself was still firmly convinced that in spite of the diminution of our forces we could prevent our enemy from treading the soil of the fatherland for many months.'

Ludendorff pleaded with Prince Max for an immediate armistice. 'Every day lost,' he wrote, 'costs thousands of brave soldiers' lives.' But the Prince still hesitated, not wanting Germany to lose Alsace-Lorraine and the Polish districts of Prussia, an Allied condition for any armistice. On October 3, however, when Prince Max brought two Social Democrat deputies into his government, they immediately urged him to seek an armistice or risk revolution in Germany. Recognizing the truth of this, on the following day he told the Reichstag that peace was essential. Obtaining the agreement of the Austro-Hungarian Government to contact the Allies, he telegraphed Washington requesting an armistice. But he did so in terms not likely to be acceptable to Wilson, seeking to end the war without any pre-conditions harmful to the pre-war territorial integrity of either Germany or Austria-Hungary.

On October 8, having consulted Lloyd George and Clemenceau, Wilson rejected Prince Max's request. The first condition of any armistice, he replied, was the evacuation of all territory occupied by Germany. The war would not end until there were no German troops on French or Belgian soil, and no Austro-Hungarian troops in Serbia. The fighting on the Western Front continued. On October 9 a British cavalry unit made an unprecedented eight-mile advance, taking 500 German soldiers prisoner as it galloped forward. Five days later Adolf Hitler was among those temporarily blinded by a British gas shell and evacuated to hospital in Germany. On October 18 a senior German army commander, Prince Rupprecht of Bavaria, told Prince Max that his troops were short of ammunition, artillery support, horses and officers, and could not go on much longer. 'We must obtain peace,' he urged, 'before the enemy breaks into Germany.'

*   *   *

The Habsburg Empire was disintegrating even more rapidly than the German. On October 25 the Hungarian nationalist leader, Count Michael Karolyi, set up a Hungarian National Council in Budapest, the first stage of the complete separation of Austria and Hungary. On October 26 the Turks began armistice talks on board a British battleship which three and a half years earlier had bombarded the outer forts of the Dardanelles. From Vienna, the Emperor Charles telegraphed to the Kaiser on the following day: 'My people are neither capable nor willing to continue the war. I have made the unalterable decision to ask for a separate peace and an immediate armistice.'

On October 28, Austria-Hungary asked the Allies for an armistice. That day, in Prague, an independent Czech State was proclaimed. Two days later the Anglo-Turkish armistice agreement was signed, and the Allies took possession of the forts at the Dardanelles that had kept them out in 1915. All German and Austro-Hungarian troops in Turkey were given a month to return home.

On November 2 the Americans launched a new offensive on the Western Front, using mustard gas for the first time. An attempt by the German High Command to transfer troops from the Eastern to the Western Front to meet the new offensive was a failure. The troops mutinied rather than go to the war zone. On the following morning the Austro-Hungarian armistice was signed and all fighting on the Italian Front ended. Only Germany was at war with the Allies, but on November 3, German soldiers in reserve near Metz mutinied, refusing to go forward to the front. Germany's ability to continue the war was at an end. On November 7 a German armistice delegation crossed into France. In Munich the Social Democrat leader Kurt Eisner proclaimed the establishment of a Bavarian Socialist Republic.

On November 8, as the German armistice negotiators reached the Forest of Compiègne and their first meeting with Marshal Foch, Prince Max went to the Kaiser's headquarters at Spa, in Belgium, and told him he must abdicate, to avert further revolution. Eleven German cities were already flying the Red Flag. The Kaiser refused, telling his Chancellor he would return to Germany and lead his army against the forces of revolution. But with revolutionaries in control of all the main railway junctions, there was no way he could get

back to Germany. Aachen, only twenty miles from the his headquarters, was in the hands of anti-war and anti-monarchist forces.

Hoping to preserve the monarchy by establishing a regency for
the Kaiser's eldest son, Prince Max announced that the Kaiser had
abdicated and that a regency was in place. But the Kaiser had not
abdicated, and Prince Max resigned. He handed the Chancellorship
to Friedrich Ebert, the socialist leader. On November 9, as Ebert
took up his duties in the Chancellery, and announced his intention
of ruling according to parliamentary procedures, the Spartacists –
German Communist revolutionaries – seized the nearby Imperial
Palace, where Karl Liebknecht, speaking from the palace steps,
declared the establishment of a German Soviet Republic.

That afternoon the Kaiser decided to resign, and the following
morning, while the German delegates at Compiègne were still discussing the clauses of the armistice, he left his headquarters for
Holland, and exile.

At half past five on the morning of November 11 the Germans signed
the armistice. It was to come into effect at eleven o'clock that morning
– the eleventh hour of the eleventh day of the eleventh month.
Among the artillery batteries in action in the final six hours was that
of Harry Truman, who fired his last round at 10.45 a.m. At two
minutes to eleven, at a village on the French-Belgian border, a Canadian private, George Price, was killed by a German sniper bullet.
He was one of the very last casualties of the First World War.

The Allies had lost more than five million men killed in action;
the Central Powers three and a half million. At the very moment
when these war deaths were being calculated, an influenza epidemic
was wreaking havoc among civilians and soldiers alike. More American soldiers died of influenza than were killed in action. Worldwide,
the epidemic killed twelve million people, six million in India. One
other statistic may give cause for reflection: 48,909 American soldiers
had been killed in action in 1917 and 1918, but in those same two
years 55,985 Americans were killed in car accidents in the United
States. They have no memorial.

CHAPTER FOUR

Aftermath of Armageddon
1919—25

ON 6 JANUARY 1919 vast crowds gathered in Berlin called for revolution, but one of their most fiery leaders, Rosa Luxemburg, urged them not to seize power, warning that their Spartacist movement did not have enough popular support. Revolutionary ardour was not to be dampened, however, and the crowd seized a number of public buildings, raised the Red Flag and proclaimed a German Soviet Republic. The German army, loyal to the parliamentary regime under the Chancellor, Friedrich Ebert, attacked the revolutionaries with artillery and machine-gun fire. Those who tried to escape were hunted down, and 1,200 were executed. The two leaders, Karl Liebknecht and Rosa Luxemburg, were captured and shot.

Nine days after the crushing of the revolution in Berlin, the delegates of the victorious Allied powers arrived in Paris for the opening of the Peace Conference. To make sure the German delegates did not have second thoughts about signing the final document, the wartime Allied naval blockade of Germany remained in force, something on which France had insisted.

The German people had elected a National Assembly, which met on February 6 at Weimar. The constitution which it devised guaranteed 'basic personal liberties' and introduced universal suffrage for both men and women over the age of twenty. It confirmed the office of President of the Republic, elected directly by the people. The President would choose the Chancellor. The first President was Friedrich Ebert. Nine days after his election, 15,000 Spartacist-Communists in Munich marched under the slogans 'All Power to the Soviets', 'Remember Liebknecht and Luxemburg', 'Long Live Lenin and Trotsky', and 'No politician can forbid the sovereign people to make a revolution'. Power in Munich resided with Kurt Eisner, head of the Bavarian Social Democrats. But the Communists, forming a Bavarian Soviet, demanded power. On February 21 Eisner was shot dead, not by a Communist insurgent but by a right-wing aristocrat and army officer, Count Anton von Arco Valley. Shortly before the assassination, the Count had written in his diary, about Eisner: 'He is a Jew, he is not German. He betrays the fatherland, therefore . . .' The rest of the sentence was left blank. The Count had shot Eisner in the back.

Revolution broke out in Hungary on March 22. The dominant figure, Béla Kun, wanted to link forces with the Russian Bolsheviks and help bring revolution to both Munich and Vienna. As he consolidated power in Hungary, the Bavarian Communists made their bid for power in Munich, establishing the First (Anarchist) Bavarian Socialist Republic on April 6. Its head was Ernst Toller, a poet and playwright who had fought on the Western Front until invalided out in 1916. After street fighting in several towns, a rival government was established in northern Bavaria headed by Johannes Hoffman, a member of Kurt Eisner's former Socialist government. On April 13 troops loyal to Hoffman advanced on Munich and arrested most of the Communist leaders, but fighting continued until evening, when Eugen Leviné, who had been sent from Berlin by the German Communist Party to restore the Party's fortunes, declared the Second Bavarian Soviet Republic. In Moscow, Lenin told a vast crowd gathered for the May Day celebrations: 'Today the liberated working class is celebrating its anniversary freely and openly – not only in Soviet Russia but also in Soviet Hungary and Soviet Bavaria.'

In fact, there were no celebrations in Munich that day, but fierce street fighting as 35,000 soldiers converged on the city with orders from Berlin to crush the Communist regime altogether. Their weapons included flame-throwers and artillery. By nightfall only the railway station was in Communist hands; it was captured the following morning. Revenge was swift. Among the 142 Red Guard prisoners shot after being captured were fifty-five of the Russian prisoners-of-war who had joined the battle. Forty-four civilians were also shot. Eugen Leviné was captured, found guilty of treason and shot. Ernst Toller was sentenced to five years in prison.

In Paris, the victorious powers, pressed to do so by Woodrow Wilson, established a League of Nations, and with it 'mandated territories', nominally under the authority of the League, which were given to the victors. France acquired Syria and Lebanon, Britain acquired Mesopotamia (Iraq) and Palestine. In eastern Palestine, known as Transjordan, Britain set up an Arab ruler. Within western Palestine, between the Mediterranean and the River Jordan, Britain was pledged to establish a 'Jewish National Home'. The League of Nations confirmed that Jews could immigrate there 'as of right', leaving Britain to work out how to satisfy the conflicting aspirations of Arabs and Jews. Japan, New Zealand and Australia shared Germany's Pacific territories. Germany's African empire was also distributed among the victors. Japan was given all Germany's coal mining and railway concessions in China. France and Britain received most of Germany's pre-1914 treaty rights and commercial concessions in Morocco, Egypt, Siam and Liberia.

The Rhineland remained sovereign German territory, though many Frenchmen had hoped it would become a separate State controlled by France. The one restriction imposed on the Rhineland was that no German military forces could be stationed there and no military fortifications built. This 'demilitarization' was not a territorial loss to Germany, but served from the outset as a reminder of defeat. As part of the creation of Poland, Germany had to give up the city of Posen – which became Poznan – and the province around it. Danzig, an important pre-war German Baltic port, was made a Free City under League of Nations control. The loss to Germany in Europe amounted to 13 per cent of her pre-war territory and 12 per cent of her pre-war population. Most significant for Germany's economic future, the loss constituted 16 per cent of her pre-war coal production and 48 per cent of her steel production.

The exploitation of the coal mines of the Saar basin was transferred to France 'in full and absolute possession', as compensation for Germany's wartime destruction of coal mines in northern France. Germany could neither build nor buy submarines, nor have an air force. Her army was limited to 100,000 men. What Germans resented most, however, was Article 231 of the treaty, asserting 'the responsibility of Germany and her allies for causing all the loss and damage to which the Allied and Associated Governments and their nationals have been subjected as a consequence of the war imposed upon them by the aggression of Germany and her allies'.

This clause became known as the 'War Guilt' clause. It was followed by another, stating that Germany 'will make compensation for all the damage done to the civilian population of the Allied and Associated Powers and to their property'. The amount of reparations was to be settled by a commission on which Germany should not take 'any part whatever'. Germany also agreed 'to the direct application of her economic resources' to pay reparations. To ensure compliance, the Allies would occupy the Rhineland and the three bridgeheads to the east of it for fifteen years. Until the Germans signed the treaty, the Allied naval blockade of Germany, preventing the import of vital foodstuffs, would remain in force.

Under the treaty, all German warships would also have to be handed over to the Allies. Anticipating this, the German commander of the ships that had been interned for the previous six months at Scapa Flow, off the north coast of Scotland, gave orders on June 21 for them to be scuttled. Within a few hours, seventy-four German warships, including fifteen of the most powerful warships then in existence, were at the bottom of the sea. On the following day the German delegates in Paris were asked to sign the Versailles Treaty. They indicated they would not sign the war guilt clauses. As discussion continued, news reached the delegates of the scuttling of the German fleet. This hardened the Allied attitude. They would allow no alterations to the treaty, and would give the Germans only twenty-four hours to sign it. When the German delegates asked for forty-eight hours, this was refused, Lloyd George being the most emphatic of the Allied leaders that twenty-four hours was enough. The sinking of the ships was, he said, 'a breach of faith'.

On June 28, four hours before the Allied deadline was due to expire, the German delegates signed the treaty. They did so, they protested, 'yielding to overwhelming force, but without on that account abandoning its view in regard to the unheard of injustice of the conditions of peace'. Versailles was followed by three other treaties. Under the Treaty of Neuilly, Bulgaria had to transfer the province of Thrace, her only outlet on the Aegean Sea, to the Allies, who later gave it to Greece. Yugoslavia acquired land in Bulgarian Macedonia. Like Germany, Bulgaria was to have no air force, no submarines and a limited army. Like Germany she was to pay reparations. She had also to give Yugoslavia 50,000 tons of coal a year for five years.

Under the Treaty of St Germain, Italy acquired considerable territory from Austria, as did Roumania and Poland. Serbia gained the Slav regions of the defunct Hapsburg Empire: Slovenia, Croatia, much of Dalmatia and Bosnia-Herzegovina. Czechoslovakia was given the former Austrian provinces of Bohemia and Moravia, and the German-speaking Sudetenland region, formerly Austria-Hungary's main source of coal. Austria was to have no air force, and an army of no more than 30,000 men. She was also forbidden to unite with Germany, despite a unanimous vote by the Provincial Assembly in Vienna in January, declaring 'German-Austria' to be a part of the 'German realm'.

Under the Treaty of Trianon, which related to the Hungarian provinces of Austria-Hungary, Roumania acquired Transylvania. Czechoslovakia obtained Slovakia and Ruthenia. Yugoslavia acquired Croatia and the Banat, and Poland a small mountainous area in the north of Slovakia. Most of the province of Burgenland was transferred to Austria. Having lost more than two-thirds of her pre-war territory, Hungary was truncated and aggrieved. In June, Béla Kun's Communist forces won several victories against the Czechs and recovered some Magyar-speaking territory in Slovakia. In July they attacked Roumania, hoping to regain the even larger Magyar-speaking regions there. But the Roumanians quickly drove the invaders back, and on August 1, Kun resigned. The Roumanian army entered Budapest three days later, imposing a severe tribute, including half Hungary's railway engines and wagons, a third of her livestock and a third of her agricultural machinery. When the Paris Conference protested, the Roumanians replied that this was reparation for the damage done to Roumania during its occupation by the Central Powers during the war.

The Roumanians remained in Budapest until November. When

they left a new Hungarian Government was set up, dedicated to the elimination of what remained of Communist sympathies of the short-lived Béla Kun era. Action against the officials of the former regime was swift: thirty Hungarian Communists were executed officially, and a further 370 were sought out by the mob and killed.

In the former Tsarist empire, 300,000 Russian Bolsheviks – the 'Reds' – were being attacked by 300,000 Russian anti-Bolsheviks – the 'Whites' – the latter being led by several former Tsarist generals. Fighting alongside the Whites were 180,000 Allied troops: British, French, American, Serbian, Czech, Greek, Italian, Finnish, Polish, Korean and Japanese. For a whole year, the democratic, liberal, monarchical and reactionary hopes of millions of Russians struggled against the Communists, with their one-Party State and instruments of repression.

By mid-February there were more than half a million anti-Bolshevik Russians under arms. In South Russia, General Denikin advanced from the Caucasus and Ukraine, with Cossack support, hoping to reach Moscow. In the west General Yudenich was securing control of the Baltic region. In Siberia, Admiral Kolchak was pressing in on the Russian heartland from the east. At that very moment, Lloyd George, fearing a pro-Communist backlash in Britain, persuaded the British Cabinet to withdraw all British troops. On April 5 the last French troops sailed, taking with them 30,000 Russian civilians and 10,000 anti-Bolshevik Russian soldiers.

The anti-Bolshevik forces were not united, either in leadership or policy. Some wanted to set up a constituent assembly based on a democratic franchise. Others wanted to restore the monarchy. Some wanted to recognize the independence of Poland, the Baltic States, Finland and the newly declared independent Caucasian republics of Georgia, Armenia and Azerbaijan. Others wanted these regions to return to Russian rule. Denikin in particular was opposed to allowing the Caucasian nationalities to retain their independence, but Britain had made Georgian independence a British pledge at the Peace Conference. Yudenich liberated all Estonia and most of Latvia from Bolshevik control, yet it was by no means certain he would agree to their independence.

In July, the last 700 American troops left North Russia, and in August the last British troops began to leave. The anti-Bolshevik Russians fought on. By September 20 Denikin was only 300 miles south of Moscow. As he advanced, fifty British pilots and cavalrymen advanced with him, volunteers who had been allowed by the British Government, as a final gesture of support to the anti-Bolsheviks, to help organize his aircraft and troops. By October 13, Yudenich's troops were less than forty miles from Petrograd. British naval units supported him in the Gulf of Finland. On the Siberian Front, Admiral Kolchak, having been driven back several hundred miles, was again advancing to the Volga. But suddenly the advancing anti-Bolshevik Russians were plunged into disarray, as the Ukrainian anarchist leader, Nestor Makhno, turned his peasant army against Denikin, seeking to carve out a substantial southern Russian region for himself. A week later several Cossack units transferred their allegiance from Denikin to the Bolsheviks. Lenin granted them an amnesty and drafted them into the Red Army. On October 18 the tribesmen of Daghestan, on the Caspian Sea, turned against Denikin, forcing him to divert 15,000 troops to the south.

On October 19, when Yudenich was only twelve miles from Petrograd, a British general was selected in London to join 'the entry into Petrograd'. By the evening of October 21 the anti-Bolsheviks were holding the heights of Pulkovo, overlooking the city. The future of Bolshevism was in the balance. As Yudenich prepared to cut the Moscow–Petrograd railway line, Makhno seized two railway junctions in the south on which Denikin was dependent for all military supplies coming up from the Black Sea. At that moment the Red Army launched a counter-attack against Denikin, and his troops were driven back, all hopes of reaching Moscow ended. On Lenin's orders, Trotsky then drove Yudenich back from Petrograd. In Siberia, Kolchak was driven back 1,500 miles. In a final blow to Denikin, Lenin authorized secret talks with the Poles, who agreed to a military truce with the Bolsheviks, and then advanced rapidly against Denikin, acquiring substantial territory for Poland.

In India, where the Anarchical and Revolutionary Crimes Act effectively suspended all civil liberties in peacetime, Gandhi launched an

All-India Satyagraha – literally, 'truth-force' – a peaceful protest involving fasting, boycotting British manufactured goods, strikes, demonstrations and the deliberate courting of arrest. At its centre was the *hartal*, a day given up to closing all shops and stopping all work. It was non-violent. When one revolutionary group, the Ghadrites, resorted to terrorist actions, Gandhi denounced them, but his protests were ignored. Railways were attacked, telephone and telegraph wires cut, and Hindu and Muslim protesters joined forces. In one incident, police opened fire on protesters and twenty-eight were killed.

In the Punjab it looked for a while as if British control had been lost. At Amritsar, where a British missionary was attacked and injured, as a collective punishment the British officer commanding the troops in the city, General Dyer, ordered all Indians passing the spot on which she had been attacked to crawl on their hands and knees. Indians protested at what the British Government itself later called 'racial humiliation'. On April 13, shortly after issuing the 'crawling order', General Dyer was confronted by a large crowd of Indian demonstrators in the confined space of the Jallianwalla Bagh. The Indians facing him were virtually unarmed; a few had staves. Determined, in his own words, 'to teach a moral lesson to the Punjab', he ordered his Indian troops to open fire with machine-guns and rifles. In less than ten minutes, 379 Indians were killed and more than a thousand injured.

What became known as the Amritsar Massacre intensified the Indian desire to see an end to British rule. But Gandhi was so shocked at how his non-violent Satyagraha campaign had been perverted by those who had threatened British lives, that he described the campaign as a 'Himalayan blunder', called it off, and fasted for three days 'as a penance'.

In Ireland, nationalist gunmen attacked British policemen and official property every day. The British Government sent tanks, armoured cars and machine-guns to prevent further violence. Sinn Fein responded by appealing for volunteers to enlarge its own military force, the Irish Republican Army (IRA). It also established an alternative government to British rule. Eamon de Valera, the one leader of the Easter 1916 uprising who had not been executed – because he was an American citizen – was made President of the Republican government.

On September 7 a British soldier was shot dead in the predominantly Catholic town of Fermoy. On the following day a crowd of 200 soldiers, incensed by their colleague's death, rampaged through the streets of Fermoy, smashing windows and looting shops. On September 10, Sinn Fein was outlawed in several southern Irish counties. Two days later all newspapers favourable to Sinn Fein were suppressed. Britain was determined not to make any political concession to terror. The Republicans were equally determined to end British rule altogether.

On 10 January 1920, eight weeks after the United States Senate, in a fit of isolationist pique, had rejected the Treaty of Versailles, the treaty came into force. As part of the treaty, the League of Nations also came into existence, committed to preventing wars by bringing the conflicting powers to the negotiating table. The brain-child of Woodrow Wilson, the League had lost its American patron as a result of that Senate vote. But its hopes were still high, the twenty-six articles of its Covenant providing for collective consultation, arbitration and 'the acceptance of obligations not to resort to war', as well as agreements to curb the arms trade, to secure the 'just treatment' of native peoples, to combat the drug and white slave trade – the sale of women and children for prostitution overseas – and to provide for the international prevention and control of disease. Article sixteen provided for collective action in the event of unprovoked aggression by one State against another.

At the first session of the League Assembly in Geneva on 15 November 1920, it was agreed that all Powers should limit their arms expenditure; the search for arms reduction was to become a major element of the League's activities during the next decade. One of the first fruits of the new policy was the French decision to reduce the period of national military service from two years to eighteen months.

The former Allies had not disbanded their wartime alliance. In order to secure compliance with the treaties they set up a Supreme

Allied Council, with Britain and France as the leading members. The United States, the Supreme Council's natural leader, withdrew from its deliberations when it withdrew from the League of Nations. The Supreme Council possessed the military strength the League lacked: when Yugoslav troops entered the Carinthian region after a plebiscite had determined by a large majority the area should become part of Austria, the Supreme Council ordered Yugoslavia to withdraw its troops or face Allied troops. The Yugoslavs complied, and Carinthia remains part of Austria to this day.

In Germany, the Conservative Party, encouraged by its right-wing elements, contemplated the overthrow of the republican government. On March 13 Dr Wolfgang Kapp, a former President of East Prussia, supported by a regiment of German soldiers who had earlier volunteered to fight against the national independence movements in the Baltic, marched into Berlin and declared himself the acting Chancellor.

Having fled to Dresden, the President and the Chancellor, Friedrich Ebert and Gustav Bauer, supported by the Minister of War, Gustav Noske – who had helped crush the Bavarian Communist regime a year earlier – appealed to the German working class to launch a general strike. The strike brought the life of Berlin to a halt, making it impossible for Kapp to govern, and four days after seizing power he resigned. At that very moment the Spartacists sought to revive their revolutionary fortunes by using the strike to their advantage. In the predominantly working-class area of Berlin, local Soviets were established, a German Communist Republic declared, and Communist governments – Soviets – were set up in a dozen towns throughout Germany. One by one they were suppressed by the army, which had remained loyal to the government.

The sole area of Germany beyond the government's military power was the Ruhr, Germany's industrial heartland, which had been demilitarized by the Treaty of Versailles, and in which Germany was not allowed to have troops. To crush the revolutionary forces there, the German Government sought permission of the Allies to send in troops. Britain and Italy agreed, but France refused. The revolutionaries, having seized control of two towns in the Ruhr, proclaimed the 'union' of 'Red' Germany with Bolshevik Russia. In an attempt to discredit the revolutionaries in German eyes, the government in Berlin pointed out that several of the leaders of the new revolt were Jews just as Eisner, Toller and Leviné had been in the Bavarian revolution a year earlier.

Fearing a repetition of the Communist uprising of January 1919, and without waiting for Allied approval, the German Government, under a new Chancellor, Hermann Müller, sent German troops into the Ruhr. More than a hundred soldiers were killed, but the Spartacists were crushed. The French, incensed at this unilateral German action – which was technically a violation of the Treaty of Versailles – and without consulting Britain or Italy, ordered French troops to enter part of the demilitarized zone, and to occupy Frankfurt-on-Main and Darmstadt. There was anger in Germany because many of the French troops were African soldiers from Senegal: part of France's black colonial army that had fought on the Western Front throughout the war.

After a few days of tense negotiations between France and Britain, during which the French refused a British request to invite the German Government to the discussions, the French agreed to withdraw the Senegalese troops, and to act in future only with the agreement of their Allies.

Germany and the Supreme Allied Council entered negotiations to carry out the disarmament and reparations clauses of the Versailles Treaty. France was to receive 52 per cent of the total sum, the British Empire 22 per cent, Italy 10 per cent, Belgium 8 per cent and Serbia 2 per cent. Two million tons of coal a month were to be delivered from German coal mines to France. Vast quantities of livestock were to be handed over to France and Belgium, including 36,000 horses, 132,000 cattle and 135,000 sheep. These were part of the material price of defeat. The psychological price was to be much higher.

With the disarmament clauses of the Versailles Treaty enforced, Germany could no longer wage war, except within its own borders and in defence of the German republic. Poland and Russia were under no such restraints. With the collapse of the anti-Bolshevik forces, the Poles launched a great eastward offensive and on May 8 entered Kiev, the capital of the Ukraine. In June the Bolsheviks counter-attacked, driving the Poles out of Kiev and advancing rapidly westward, towards Warsaw. The Poles appealed for help from the Allies. France responded by sending General Weygand, one of Marshal Foch's best known staff officers, as a military adviser to the Polish army. The British also sent a general. Speaking in Moscow on July 24, Trotsky declared that Poland would soon become 'a bridge by means of which the social revolution could be spread from Russia to Western Europe'.

On August 3 the Red Army reached the River Bug at Brest-Litovsk, on the direct road and rail line to Warsaw. That day, the Russians set up a Soviet regime – the temporary Polish Revolutionary Committee – in the conquered areas of eastern Poland. On August 8 the Red Army cut the Warsaw–Danzig railway line, depriving Poland of her outlet to the sea and her main link with Allied supplies. On August 14 units of the Red Army reached a village only twelve miles from Warsaw. It seemed inevitable that the Polish capital would fall, and that Communism would reign supreme less than 200 miles from the German border.

On August 15 the Poles launched a counter-offensive, known in Poland as the Miracle of the Vistula. Within a week they had taken 35,000 prisoners. A week later the number had increased by a further 65,000. As the Russians retreated eastward, a peasant army of up to 20,000 men, known as the Green Army, rose deep inside Russia against the harsh decrees of Communism, including the requisition of that year's harvest. Lenin ordered the total suppression of the revolt, and the shooting, in batches, of peasants who were suspected of supporting the rebellion. Complete villages were also burnt down as the authority of Moscow was reasserted.

Another rebellion broke out that August in the North Caucasus, led by a Muslim cleric, Imam Najmuddin Gotsinskii. Seizing control of Daghestan and Chechenya, he led his soldiers to the Caspian Sea, where, after a nineteen-day street battle, they seized the town of Derbent, replacing the local Soviet. Troops loyal to Moscow attacked the rebels but were defeated, and their commander beheaded. In reprisal, Soviet forces, who had already lost more than 800 men in the fighting, burned down a mosque in which a hundred rebels were besieged, killing all of them. The fighting continued for several months. Even after Soviet rule was restored, Muslim insurgents set up guerrilla bases in the mountains and continued to harass their Communist masters.

Since driving the Red Army back from Warsaw, the Poles had advanced deep into Russia, almost as far as the Byelorussian capital, Minsk. On October 11 the Soviet Government accepted the Polish armistice terms, and a day later signed the Treaty of Riga. Poland acquired much of Byelorussia and the whole of Eastern Galicia, with a Byelorussian and Ukrainian minority of six million out of a total population of thirty million. She also had three million Jews.

In Paris, the Supreme Allied Council negotiated a peace treaty with the Turkish Government. The Dodecanese Islands, occupied by Italy since the Italo-Turkish war of 1912, were to become Italian sovereign territory. A large Anatolian region centred on Smyrna (Izmir) was to become an autonomous region under Greek administration, with the right to attach itself after five years, by plebiscite, to Greece.

The Dardanelles, the Sea of Marmara and the Bosphorus – the Zone of the Straits – were to be controlled by a commission nominated by Britain, France, Italy and Japan. Turkey was not to be represented on the commission, nor would any Turkish troops be allowed in the zone, in which Allied garrisons were to remain 'in permanent occupation'. The Turkish navy and air force were to be abolished, and the Turkish army limited to 50,000 men. Tax-gathering powers throughout Turkey were given to a Finance Committee made up of representatives of Britain, France and Italy.

The Turkish Government argued against many of the proposed terms, especially the removal of the Smyrna province from Turkish rule, but the only modification the Allies would allow was to permit a Turkish representative to join the Straits Commission. In answer to the other points of protest, the Allies declared that the time had come 'when it is necessary to put an end once and for all to the empire of the Turks over other nations'. Not only had the Turkish Government 'failed to protect its subjects of other races from pillage, outrage and murder, but there is abundant evidence that it has been responsible for directing and organizing savagery against people to whom it owed protection'. This was a reference, principally, to the massacres of the Armenians.

The Turkish Government in Constantinople knew it had no choice but to accept the terms of the treaty, punitive though they were. At the same time, a growing movement against the treaty was being led by Mustafa Kemal who, having gathered an army of several thousand men, set up his headquarters at Angora (Ankara), marched westward, occupying the former Ottoman capital of Bursa, and the southern shore of the Sea of Marmara. On June 17 a specially summoned meeting of British Cabinet Ministers denounced him as a 'bandit', but did not feel it had the ability to use the British troops already in Constantinople to drive him away. Authorized by Britain and France to take military action against him, Greek forces, which had occupied Smyrna a year earlier, moved rapidly northward, driving Kemal from Bursa.

The Turkish peace treaty was formally signed at Sèvres, outside Paris, on August 10. In protest against its terms, Mustafa Kemal established a Turkish Parliament in Angora, denounced the treaty and declared war on the Allies. The Angora government would, he said, when ready to do so, drive the Allies and the Greeks from Turkish soil. Then, after negotiating an agreement with the Bolsheviks, he sent his troops into the area designated by the Supreme Allied Council as the new State of Armenia. During the fighting between the Kemalists and the Armenians, the Armenians asked for admission to the League of Nations, but this was refused. By the end of the year, Kemal's forces had overrun what was to have been the independent State of Armenia in eastern Anatolia. It remained Turkish to the end of this century and beyond.

In return for Bolshevik acceptance of Turkish rule in what the Supreme Allied Council had designated western Armenia, Kemal agreed not to hamper the Bolshevik incorporation of eastern Armenia into the Soviet Union. At the new Turkish-Soviet border, Bolshevik and Turkish troops stood guard over the extinction of Armenian independence on both sides of the frontier. Bolshevik rule was also established in the briefly independent republics of Georgia and Azerbaijan. These two Caucasian nations, which had raised the flags of independence two years earlier, set up their own parliaments, spoken their own languages and printed their own stamps, and had been accepted by the rest of the world as independent States, fell once more under the rule of Moscow. The Bolsheviks also moved against Bukhara, in Central Asia, where, after the fall of the Tsarist regime, an independent Emirate had been set up by the local Muslim leader, Sayid-Mir-Alim-Khan. In August 1920, just as Lenin and Trotsky were expecting imminent victory over Poland, they sent a large Bolshevik army to conquer the Bukhara. The Muslim forces fought tenaciously, but were overrun.

The anti-British movement in Ireland gathered momentum throughout 1920. To combat the continuing attacks by the Irish Republican Army on British soldiers and police, 40,000 British troops were sent to Ireland. In search of a political solution, the British Government introduced a Home Rule Bill to Parliament on February 25, whereby there would be two parliaments, one, in Dublin, with 128 members, the other in Belfast, with 52 members. Britain would retain control of foreign policy and defence, customs and excise, land and agricultural policy, and the machinery for maintaining law and order. The Dublin parliament would enable Catholic Ireland to govern itself.

For Sinn Fein this was not enough. It wanted to govern the whole of Ireland, freed completely from British rule. Full independence, not limited autonomy, was the goal. The Home Rule Bill, Sinn Fein declared, was designed solely for the 'plunder and partition of Ireland'. The IRA continued to shoot at British troops, who continued to raid the homes of suspects. More than 500 such raids were reported every week. Often they were accompanied by considerable violence on the part of the troops. IRA violence was also shocking to the British public. In March, the Resident Magistrate in Dublin, sixty-year-old Alan Bell, who was investigating the attempted assassination of the Lord Lieutenant of Ireland, was dragged from a train and shot dead. 'De Valera has practically challenged the British Empire', Lloyd George complained in a private letter.

A secret report to the British Cabinet in May stated that the Dublin police could not be relied upon to combat the IRA, nor could the civil service. Nor would Catholic judges impose the death penalty on members of the IRA who had been convicted of murder, even though Lloyd George had approved hanging as the essential punishment and deterrent. The killings by the IRA continued. When a senior police officer, Colonel Smyth, who had lost an arm in the war and been twice decorated for bravery, was shot dead in Cork by thirteen or fourteen IRA men, his murder provoked riots in which thirteen people were killed. To increase pressure on the IRA, a new Irish police force was set up, consisting of 8,000 former soldiers. Known from its uniform as the Black and Tans, it served as an auxiliary arm to the existing police force, the Royal Irish Constabulary, and was feared for its often brutal tactics.

Catholics and Protestants were at war. In one month, forty people were killed in attacks and reprisal actions. When, in Dublin, the IRA pulled six British officers out of their beds and shot them in front of their wives, the reprisal took place later that same day, soldiers opening fire on a crowd, including several IRA men, which had gathered at a football ground. Nine people were killed. The six murdered officers were honoured by the British Government at a memorial service in Westminster Abbey.

In December, Lloyd George declared martial law in four southern Irish counties, and called for the surrender of all arms within seventeen days. Anyone found with arms after that would be tried by court martial. The penalty for carrying arms would be death. It was felt, Lloyd George told his Cabinet on December 13, that 'the decent public in Ireland' desired a truce and an end to violence. Churchill shared this view, suggesting that once a truce could be in force for a month, and the murders stop, it would 'give a chance for the murderers to go off to America'.

In Mesopotamia, where 14,000 British and Indian troops were stationed, more than 400 were killed during an Arab uprising in 1920. British retaliation took the form of machine-gunning the rebels from the air. In Somaliland a Muslim leader known as the 'Mad Mullah', despite five military campaigns against him over a decade, took the offensive. This time British aircraft dropped bombs on his encampments. It was not, however, to British bombs that the Mullah finally succumbed, in November 1920, but to influenza.

*   *   *

The armistices and peace treaties with which the First World War had ended were not followed automatically by the spirit of reconciliation. When, in August 1920, the VIth Olympiad was held, Antwerp was chosen for the Games as a gesture to 'brave little Belgium', Germany's victim of a previous decade. None of the ex-enemy countries were invited to attend the Games.

That year, by far the worst disaster took place in China, where drought destroyed the harvest over a vast area, and fifteen million Chinese died of starvation.

In 1921 the League of Nations set up a Permanent Court of International Justice, whose judges represented the different legal systems of the thirty participating States. States wishing to do so could submit to the Court all disputes capable of resolution by judicial process. Other League activities in 1921 included the administration of both the Free City of Danzig and the Saar Valley, and efforts to secure the financial rehabilitation of Austria, improve sanitary conditions in Mediterranean ports, and reduce the white slave traffic – especially between South America and Europe.

In British India, non-co-operation, as urged by Gandhi, was growing. His attempts to persuade people not to buy imported cloth, but to use materials homespun in India, gained momentum. Parallel to Gandhi's non-co-operation movement, which found its greatest, though not its exclusive support among Hindus, a more aggressive Muslim independence movement, the Khilafat movement, made inroads among the Muslim population. It gained its name, and some of its strength, from opposition to Britain's policy towards the Sultan of Turkey, the Caliph, who was effectively a prisoner of the British in Constantinople. At an All-India Khilafat Committee meeting in Karachi in July, two of the leaders of the movement, the brothers Mohammad and Shaukat Ali, advocated a Muslim religious ban on service in the army: Indian Muslims had distinguished themselves on all the war fronts during the First World War. Both men were arrested, as they had been in 1914 for denouncing Britain's war with Turkey, charged with incitement, convicted and imprisoned yet again.

That August a Muslim uprising took place in the Malabar district of India, where the million-strong Moplah people, who regarded all non-Muslims as infidels, and who had been influenced by the Khilafat movement, declared two independent Muslim kingdoms. They then attacked both Europeans and Hindus, burnt and looted government offices, sacked Hindu temples and forced many Hindus on pain of death to covert to Islam. Hindus who refused to convert were beheaded. Gandhi, in what many Hindus considered utterly mis-judged even-handedness, spoke of 'the brave, God-fearing Moplahs, fighting for what they consider as religion, and in a manner which they consider as religious'. The Government of India responded by putting Gandhi in prison.

British and Indian troops were rushed to the district and the Moplah insurgents attacked: 1,826 Moplahs were killed, 5,000 were captured and 14,000 surrendered. The remnant of the rebels, 700 in all, who took to the hills and continued fighting, were slowly hunted down. The government, which had gained considerable Indian sym-pathy in suppressing the rebellion, lost some of that sympathy when, in a much-publicized incident, seventy Moplah prisoners, locked in an airless railway carriage without water, suffocated to death.

The French and Spanish Governments were also embroiled in a col-onial struggle in Morocco during 1921. In the Rif district the Spani-ards were continually challenged by a Muslim leader, Abd el-Krim, who seized seventy Spanish fortified posts. More than 9,000 Spanish soldiers were killed during the fighting, many of them slaughtered as they sought safety inside their garrisons.

Spanish military reinforcements sent to Morocco included 75,000 front-line troops and 100,000 reservists. In a series of battles they uncovered evidence of Moorish mutilations on Spanish soldiers killed earlier. Major Francisco Franco – the future Spanish dictator – who took command of the Spanish Legion during the Moroccan campaign, later wrote of 'feeling in our hearts a desire for revenge, for the most exemplary punishment ever seen down the generations'. Revenge was taken. During one engagement, each of the twelve volunteers whom Franco asked to liberate a besieged blockhouse returned with a trophy – the severed head of a Moorish attacker.

In the Sudan, which was under joint British and Egyptian rule, there was a Muslim uprising in 1921 led by Abdul-laqhi-es-Soghayer. After two British officers and three civilians were killed, the British launched a punitive expedition. Soghayer was caught and hanged, and the uprising suppressed. The demonization of Islam was a feature of the European response to these essentially national uprisings.

It was not only in the colonial empires that violence marred the year 1921. In Italy, riots broke out in several cities between socialists and the increasingly active Fascisti, who denounced not only Socialism and Communism but also parliamentary institutions. In October the Fascisti held a congress in Rome, transforming their movement into a political Party: they already had 20 seats in the 535-seat parliament. Their programme was diffuse. Land would belong 'to him who works it', but large 'capitalist' farms would not be dismantled. The 'practical degeneration' of socialism would be opposed. An increase in armaments needed to sustain an aggressive foreign policy would give work to the unemployed in the armaments factories and war industries. Even after the Fascists had constituted themselves a political Party, violence underpinned reason and debate. Benito Mussolini, the leader of the movement, spoke publicly of using force to impose Fascist goals.

The year 1921 saw another Communist uprising in Germany, in the centre of the republic, when a thirty-year-old Communist, Max Hölz, who had served in the trenches in the First World War, put himself at the head of a military formation which, for several weeks, fought off numerous attacks by a much larger body of government troops. With the defeat of the uprising, Hölz escaped, but was betrayed to the police and captured. Two thousand of his fellow-insurgents were captured and imprisoned.

At his trial, Hölz defended the path of Communist revolution on the grounds that all other paths had failed to redress the inequalities of society. Sentenced to life imprisonment, he was amnestied seven years later. Among the Communists, he was a hero, and it was assumed in 1933 that he would take a prominent part in the Communist opposition to National Socialism. For internal Communist Party reasons, however, he was sent to the Soviet Union, where he was among the many foreign Communist victims of Stalin's purges.

It was the right, not the left, that was gaining the initiative in the streets of Germany. An estimated 40,000 former army officers were at the centre of frequent anti-government demonstrations, demanding a return of the monarchy. In Bavaria, Adolf Hitler was building up the National Socialist (Nazi) Workers' Party from a dozen members to several hundred, and hoping for many more. Denunciation of the Versailles Treaty was a main theme of his speeches. In Munich, in February, 6,500 people – 500 more than his Party membership at that time – gathered in a circus tent to hear him denounce the Allied demand for reparations. In every speech, Hitler denounced those whom he characterized the enemies of Germany, principally the signatories of the Versailles Treaty and 'the Jews'. In 1921 he created a paramilitary arm, the 'SA'. In order to get round the Versailles ban on paramilitary groups, the initials stood for Sports Division. Later the same initials were taken to stand for a more threatening title, *Sturmabteilung* – the Stormtroops. From the uniform that the Stormtroops wore, they were also known as the Brownshirts. They were, Hitler explained in the first issue of their own newspaper, the SA *Gazette*, not only an instrument for the protection of the Nazi movement, but were 'primarily the training school for the coming struggle for freedom on the domestic front'.

In Russia, the Bolsheviks were confronted in 1921 by an insurrection in Siberia by peasants who were refusing to hand over their grain and livestock. As many as 60,000 peasants took up arms, cutting several stretches of the Trans-Siberian railway and occupying two large towns. It took several months, and many executions, before the authority of the central government was restored.

Discontent with the autocratic nature of the Soviet regime also broke out in what had once been its citadel, the naval barracks at Kronstadt. Within a few days strikes also broke out in Petrograd and Moscow. The desire everywhere was for an end to the self-proclaimed 'dictatorship' of the Commissars through whom all authority passed. Trotsky, as Commissar for the Army, instructed a former Tsarist officer, General Tukhachevsky, Commander-in-Chief of the Red Forces, to destroy the Kronstadt rebellion. Tukhachevsky acted with great ruthlessness. In the North Caucasus, the Chechen and Dagestani

Muslim rebels led by Imam Gotsinskii continued to hold out in the mountains. The Red Army went after them, crushing the last resistance. Imam Gotsinskii escaped and went into hiding but when he was caught five years later he was shot.

By early spring, Lenin had to face the fact that, after more than three years, Communism had failed to feed the Russian people, and that the economic methods he and his Party imposed led to bankruptcy and widespread starvation. In March, in a dramatic abandonment of Communist dogma, he introduced the New Economic Policy (NEP), designed to restore elements of capitalist commerce and exchange, and to enable trade to begin with the outside world. Trade agreements were signed with Britain, Poland and Germany, and exports began, after a lapse of several years, to western Europe and the United States.

Inside Russia, as the last of the peasant revolts in Siberia was being crushed, the compulsory requisitioning of grain was abolished, and compulsory deliveries of agricultural produce was replaced by a tax in kind to the State amounting to just over half the produce that had earlier been requisitioned compulsorily. Peasants were also allowed to put any surplus grain, potatoes and hay on the market. By an Agrarian Law of March 21, small landowners were allowed to keep their land for at least nine years. Lenin recognized that he could not feed the workers in the factories if the small landowners were driven from their land, and the fields distributed in even smaller packets to peasants who could not manage them better, and produced less. 'We cannot prevent the progress of capitalism,' Lenin declared on May 6, 'but we can try to develop it into Russian State capitalism'. A further decree enabled nationalized factories to be transferred to co-operatives, and even to private individuals. Shops could be opened in the towns, and trade conducted in the markets, without being hampered by the authorities.

The New Economic Policy gave Russia, for the first time since the 1917 revolution, a modicum of prosperity for those who could embark on trade or manufacture. But it came too late to prevent a widespread famine that summer throughout most of the agricultural districts of Central Russia. Hopes that the newly conquered Caucasus would provide the much-needed supplies of grain and food were not realized. Through inefficiency and lack of economic incentives for producers, only half the quota reached the cities and towns where food was in desperately short supply.

As famine spread, appeals were made to the United States for immediate help, and an American Relief Administration was established, which appealed to the American public for help. This was forthcoming, and substantial supplies were despatched. An International Conference of all Red Cross societies agreed that two men – the League of Nations Commissioner for Refugees, Dr Fridtjof Nansen, the Norwegian scientist and explorer, and the former American President, Herbert Hoover – should exercise 'supreme control' of relief work in Russia. 'The conditions are even worse than I expected', Nansen – who was to be awarded the Nobel Peace Prize for his work in Russia – telegraphed to a British newspaper on December 19: 'Words cannot possibly describe the misery and horrors I have seen. People are dying in their houses and in the village streets in the pitiless cold of a Russian winter without food or fuel to feed them. Millions must unavoidably die.'

A thousand tons of grain were sent from the people of Spain. The German and Czech governments sent aid to regions where Germans and Czechs lived. From Jews in Britain and the United States came help for the Jews of the region. Lenin also made another compromise to prevent disaster, setting up an All-Russian Famine Relief Committee in which non-Communists, including former Constitutional Democrats and Socialist Revolutionaries, hitherto outlawed, could participate. Co-operatives were given the right to buy goods from abroad for the purpose of barter inside Russia. On November 23, hoping to attract foreign capital – five years after the revolution which was meant to destroy capitalism for all time – Lenin authorized foreign capitalists to acquire concessions inside Russia, and to invest in profit-making enterprises, including the leasing and renting of property. Under an Agrarian Law that December, peasants could retain whatever produce was needed to sustain themselves and their households.

Despite the famine and the New Economic Policy, Lenin had reason to be confident with the control exercised by his regime. A secret police system was in operation, and thousands of politicians and citizens who spoke openly against the regime were in prison. Even at the height of the New Economic Policy, sixty-one people were executed in Petrograd for 'conspiracy against the Soviet Government': one was the well-known poet Gumilev.

In Ireland, as the struggle by the IRA against British rule continued, and thirty to forty people were being killed every week, two parliaments were set up, one in Dublin and one in Belfast, and the political separation of Ulster from the rest of Ireland became a reality. The government in London, having no intention of relinquishing British sovereignty over any part of Ireland, invited the IRA to the negotiating table, and called for a truce. The IRA accepted: all killing would end on July 11. Three days later the hitherto hated enemy of Britain, Eamon De Valera, met Lloyd George in the Cabinet Room at 10 Downing Street. Six days later Lloyd George presented the British Government's proposals: Southern Ireland would be offered Dominion Home Rule, with complete control of her own taxation, finance, police and army. Britain would control imperial defence.

De Valera rejected the proposals and demanded complete independence. On October 11 the Southern Irish leaders, including the leaders of the IRA, went to Downing Street to renew negotiations. Only De Valera refused to attend, claiming that as he was the 'President' of his country and Lloyd George only the Prime Minister, he was too senior to attend. Michael Collins, Minister of Home Affairs and Finance in the Sinn Fein Government, offered Britain the permanent neutrality of Southern Ireland in the event of a conflict in which Britain became involved in Europe or elsewhere. After two months of negotiations, the Sinn Fein and British delegates reached agreement. 'We had become allies in a common cause', Churchill, one of the British negotiators, later wrote, 'the cause of the Irish Treaty and of peace between the two races and two islands.'

The Irish Treaty was signed on December 6. Northern Ireland would remain an integral part of the United Kingdom. Southern Ireland became to all intents and purposes independent, but Britain remained 'solely responsible' for the security of Britain and Ireland 'and the seas around them'. The southern Irish ports would be part of a British defence strategy in the event of war. Southern Ireland would remain under the British Crown, with the same degree of independence as Canada, Australia, New Zealand and South Africa, and with its own Parliament and Law Courts. All taxes raised by the British in Southern Ireland that year were transferred to the Dublin Government 'for Irish internal administration'.

De Valera, angered that the treaty did not secure full independence, resigned as President, and, seeking re-election, was defeated. Michael Collins became Prime Minister. British troops were withdrawn and the Black and Tans disbanded. The Southern Irish Government then granted an amnesty for all British forces, policemen and civil servants who had committed or assisted 'acts of hostility against the Irish people', and declared, in explanation: 'We must not suffer ourselves to be outdone by our late enemies in seeking that the wrongs of the past may be buried in oblivion.'

Northern Ireland remained a part of the United Kingdom. Southern Ireland, despite its relative poverty, embarked upon the challenges and achievements of statehood, evolving a year later into the Irish Free State, and in due course successfully negotiating her neutrality, the withdrawal of the British naval bases and transformation into a Republic.

Under Woodrow Wilson's successor, Warren G. Harding, the United States was confronted by agitation in the Philippines for an end to American rule, while in Santo Domingo there were protests against the continuing American occupation. In the American South there had been a revival of activity by the Ku Klux Klan, with fifty-nine black Americans being lynched, five of them burnt to death, and five of them burnt after they had been killed. There were also mutilations, branding with acid, floggings, tarring-and-feathering, and kidnappings. At Tulsa, Oklahoma, a violent racial attack took place on May 31 which resulted in the death of 200 blacks.

In reaction to these killings, a privately initiated Inter-Racial Committee Movement was established. It grew in strength, with all its members dedicated to the elimination of racial animosity. Its success by the end of the year in gaining considerable local support on both sides of the racial divide led the President to establish a Federal Inter-Racial Commission. But the evil of racism remained strong: in the following year there were fifty-one reported lynchings, thirteen of those lynched having been taken from jails, and seventeen from law officers outside jails.

For the first time in United States history, the size of the urban population overtook that of the rural population. That year, 1921, a stock market crash wiped out the savings of millions of people.

For more than a year the United States had sought to secure a comprehensive naval disarmament treaty for the Pacific and the Far East. This reached fruition in Washington on 6 February 1922. Not only was there agreement among the five signatories – Britain, France, Italy, Japan and the United States – for a reduction in naval armaments, but agreement was also reached denouncing the use of poison gas in warfare, and condemning as 'piratical' under international law all submarine attacks on merchant ships, whether these merchantmen were armed or not. With the stroke of a pen, two of the most hated weapons of the First World War, gas and the submarine sinkings of merchant ships, were abolished, at least on paper.

In Germany, discontent against reparations was widespread, but no reparations had yet been paid. Two dates were set by the Allies for the first two reparations payments, January 15 and February 15. The German Government asked for a postponement of both amounts, explaining it did not have the financial or material resources to pay. The Supreme Allied Council met in emergency session at Cannes – where Lloyd George was on holiday. German delegates had been asked to attend. When their leader, Walther Rathenau, set out Germany's financial problems, it made a strong and positive impression on the Council. As a result, Germany was granted a year's postponement on its first two monthly payments.

While the Cannes conference was in session, the French President, Raymond Poincaré, accused the German Government of 'maliciously avoiding' the fulfilment of her obligations. But after a month and a half of further negotiations, the Reparations Commission, set up under the Treaty of Versailles, recognized Germany's dire economic situation, and agreed to a series of lesser amounts as proposed by the German Government. When, however, it then urged the German Government to introduce stringent tax-gathering measures to ensure that the reparations obligations could be met, the German Government denounced this proposal as 'an intolerable infringement' of German sovereignty.

The German delegates, proceeding from Cannes to Paris, continued to negotiate the reparations payment schedule, reaching an agreement, much to Germany's satisfaction, that all the 1922 payments could be postponed. The German Government also gained agreement to its proposal that the new schedules of payment would only be met once an international loan to help Germany was raised. As discussions proceeded in Paris as to how to secure this loan, discussions in which the United States played its part, Rathenau was assassinated in Berlin. His assassins were three Nationalists who considered Rathenau, as a Jew, a traitor to Germany. In the Reichstag, the Chancellor, Dr Wirth, denounced the extremist organizations which touted anti-Semitism, extreme nationalism and monarchism. Pointing to the almost empty benches where the Nationalist deputies normally sat, he called out in angry tone: 'The real enemies of our country are those who instil this poison into our people. We know where we have to seek them. The Enemy stands on the Right!'

In Italy, as many as 200,000 men were in Fascist military formations, Blackshirts whose uniform struck terror into those whom they assaulted, or who saw them on the rampage. Speaking at a Fascist rally on September 20, Mussolini declared that violence could be a 'moral necessity' if it was used to resolve what he called a 'cancerous' political situation. The task of Fascism was to weld the nation into an organic whole that would work for the greatness of Italy. The Fascist aim was not to destroy the fabric of the State, but to demolish the 'social-democratic superstructure' which had served Italy so badly in the past.

On October 6 Mussolini discussed with his closest confidants the prospects of a march on Rome. Three Fascist armed columns were established within thirty miles of Rome. One had 4,000 men, one 2,000 and the third, at Civitavecchia, 8,000. There was also a reserve formation of 3,000 men. Speaking in Naples on October 24, Mussolini told 40,000 Fascists who had marched past him in review in military formation: 'I assure you in all solemnity that the hour has struck. Either they give us the government or we shall take it, by marching on Rome. Now it is a matter of days or hours.' The next day Mussolini left Naples by train for Milan.

In secret, October 28 was the day set for the seizure of Rome by the three military columns. As news reached Rome of the Fascist military preparations on October 27, the Prime Minister, Luigi Facta, went to the King and resigned, explaining he did not have the means to halt the Fascist preparations. He proposed that the King proclaim a state of siege in the capital, but the King preferred to postpone such a drastic measure. Facta remained in charge of the government until a successor could be found, as provided for by the constitution. During the night of October 27/28 reports reached his office of Fascist seizures of power in towns throughout Italy.

On the morning of October 28, Facta asked the King to proclaim a state of siege, but the King refused to do so. Instead, he invited Mussolini to Rome. The implication was that Mussolini would be asked to join the next government, with several other important portfolios given to other Fascists. But when the Fascist representatives in Rome urged Mussolini to accept this outcome, he replied tersely that it was 'not worthwhile mobilizing the Fascist army, causing a revolution, killing people' for the sake of joining a government headed by someone else. Mussolini told the king he would only leave Milan for Rome if it was he who was to be entrusted with forming a government. He would be Prime Minister or nothing.

During October 29 the only rival for the premiership, Antonio Salandra, under whom Mussolini had refused to serve, advised the King to ask Mussolini to form a Government. Mussolini insisted that any such request must be made in writing. He wanted a telegram sent to him in Milan, stating that the King intended to appoint him Prime Minister. The telegram arrived at noon. As there was no train to Rome that afternoon, Mussolini had to wait in Milan until evening. Then he took the night train, telling the stationmaster who saw him off: 'I want to leave exactly on time. From now on everything has got to function perfectly.'

At 10.30 on the following morning Mussolini's train reached Rome. He was then driven to see the King, who formally entrusted him with the task of forming a government. Mussolini became Prime

Minister and Minister of the Interior. His Fascist militia were still awaiting the call to march on Rome and seize power, but they were no longer needed for this task, as he was already in power. At the King's invitation, Mussolini then invited the militia to the capital, where they took part in a military review which the King attended, and were then sent away. On November 16, Mussolini laid his programme before both houses of the Italian Parliament. The new government, he told the legislators, was willing to assume full responsibility, and was therefore asking for full powers. If the deputies refused, the government would take the powers 'of its own accord'. The full powers were granted him nine days later, by 275 votes to 90. Italian Fascism, hitherto a movement of street violence and the seizure of municipal power, became, by vote of parliament, the governing Party, in the hands of a man who believed the State must rule with an iron fist.

In Turkey, Mustafa Kemal, proclaiming himself head of a provisional government, set up the banner of national regeneration at Angora. Reviling the efforts of the Sultan's government in Constantinople to work with the Allies, he built up an army and waited until he felt strong enough to drive out the foreign troops, mainly Greeks, who controlled enormous areas in the west of Anatolia. By August, his army was driving the Greeks further and further westward. The British, French and Italian occupation forces at Constantinople and the Zone of the Straits could only watch, and wait. Lloyd George, who had negotiated the Treaty of Sèvres which had set up the Zone of the Straits, told his Cabinet colleagues: 'In no circumstances could we allow the Gallipoli Peninsula to be held by the Turks. It was the most important strategic position in the world, and the closing of the Straits in the war had prolonged the war by two years. It was inconceivable that we would allow the Turks to gain possession of the Gallipoli Peninsula, and we should fight to prevent their doing so.'

In Chanak, opposite the Gallipoli Peninsula, a British force of a thousand men awaited the arrival of Kemal's army. In all, 7,600 British, French and Italian troops in the Zone of the Straits faced

11,000 Turkish troops already in the region, and a further 40,000 moving northward from Smyrna, soldiers who had just defeated the Greeks in a hard fought, even savage campaign. Many of the Greeks had been driven, literally, into the sea, and hundreds of Armenians had also been massacred.

On September 18 the British troops at Chanak were confronted by a considerably larger Turkish army advancing towards them. As if to underline that Britain would have to act against the Kemalists alone, both France and Italy withdrew their troops from the Asian to the European shore. At the same time the French Government instructed its High Commissioner in Constantinople to enter into direct negotiations with Kemal. The unity of the Allies had collapsed, even before it had been put to the test. As far as France was concerned, Poincaré remarked, the Turks could 'cross to Europe when they pleased'. Lloyd George resisted this, telling his Cabinet Secretary on September 22: 'No Kemalist forces must be allowed to cross the salt water. The moment a Kemalist gets afloat he must be dealt with.' But on September 23, without Lloyd George's knowledge, Poincaré, Count Sforza – the Italian Ambassador in Paris – and the British Foreign Secretary Lord Curzon, who were in Paris, issued a Joint Note stating that they 'viewed with favour' the Turkish claim to Eastern Thrace, including the city of Adrianople, which was then occupied by Greece. The three statesmen also favoured, once a new peace treaty was signed with Turkey, the withdrawal of all Allied troops, High Commissioners and administrators from Constantinople.

The Paris Note offered Kemal the prospect of making a satisfactory peace with the Allies. On September 27 the commander of the British forces at Constantinople and the Straits, General Harington, made contact with him and offered to talk. In London, Lloyd George was emphatic that if Chanak was attacked it must be defended. Its evacuation, he told his colleagues, 'would be the greatest loss of prestige which could possibly be inflicted on the British Empire'. On September 29 a British ultimatum was sent to Harington in Constantinople, for delivery to Kemal: unless the Turks withdrew their forces from around Chanak by an hour to be determined by Harington, 'all the forces at our disposal, naval, military and aerial, will open fire'.

Harington did not deliver the ultimatum. He had learned from Kemal on the morning of September 30 that the Turkish troops at Chanak would not 'provoke any incident', and that Kemal was eager to negotiate a truce. The British Cabinet was uneasy. In a telegram to Harington, drafted by Churchill, the general was told that while the British Government wanted peace, 'we do not however desire to purchase a few days of peace at the price of actively assisting a successful Turkish invasion of Europe. Such a course would deprive us of every vestige of sympathy and respect and particularly in the United States. Nor do we believe that repeated concessions and submissions to victorious orientals is the best way to avert war.'

Harington was confident he could convince Kemal, without delivering the ultimatum, to withdraw from the Straits and await the outcome of peace talks in which all his demands would be met. Negotiations began at Mudania on October 3, when the senior Turkish negotiator, Ismet Pasha, victor of the recent battle of Inönü against the Greeks – from which he later took the name Inönü – and a veteran of the Gallipoli campaign of 1915, agreed to halt all Turkish military movements in the region of the British forces, and withdraw a thousand yards from the British line.

Ismet also demanded the right to occupy Eastern Thrace immediately. The French and Italian delegates were willing to accept this, the British not, and on October 6 the conference broke down. The British Cabinet once more contemplated war, but on the following day a leading British Conservative, Andrew Bonar Law, published a letter in the newspapers stating that Britain could only keep the Turks from Constantinople and Thrace if the Allied Powers and the United States joined in such an action. Without at least French support, he argued, military action must be avoided. 'We cannot act alone as the policeman of the world.'

The negotiations at Mudania were resumed on October 8. After two days the Turks accepted the Paris Note, giving Allied recognition to the Turkish claim to Turkey-in-Europe, including Adrianople, and committing the Allies to the withdrawal of their troops and administration from Constantinople. The Mudania Convention was signed on October 11. The Greeks would leave Eastern Thrace at once, and a Franco-British-Italian administration would take over until Turkish rule was restored. Britain had avoided war with Turkey, but the spectre of more fighting had roused strong Conservative hostility against Lloyd George, and on October 19 the Conservative Party Members of Parliament, meeting in London, voted to leave the coalition that had ruled Britain since 1915, and stand for election as an independent Party. In the election which followed they were returned to power for the first time since 1905. Bonar Law, the man who had raised the standard of revolt against military action, became Prime Minister.

Kemal's authority was secured. On November 1 the National Assembly at Angora voted to abolish the Sultanate and made Turkey a republic. On November 17 the Sultan left the city where his family had ruled for more than 400 years; a British battleship took him to Malta. The Ottoman dynasty, like those of the Romanovs, Hohenzollerns and Habsburgs, was over, and a new treaty with Turkey was negotiated at Lausanne, whereby Kemal became ruler of a republic.

In Ireland, the establishment of the Irish Free State, giving Southern Ireland virtual independence from Britain, did not satisfy those who wanted complete severance from the British Crown and Empire, the establishment of a republic, and the extension of that republic to Northern Ireland. The most serious blow to the settlement, though it did not destroy it, was the assassination of Michael Collins, who, after signing the treaty, had become Commander-in-Chief of the Irish Army. Collins, an Irish patriot, was ambushed by Irish fanatics while driving through the remote countryside in County Cork.

Collins was never forgiven by some for his signature of the Irish Treaty, but a majority of citizens wanted peace to be preserved, and his funeral in Dublin was the scene of a demonstration in favour of an end to the killings. The forces of disruption continued however to pursue their destructive path. In December, after several officers of the new Irish army had been assassinated, the Free State Government executed seven IRA men found guilty of killing their fellow-Irishmen.

During 1922 the first Soviet show trial was held in Moscow. The chief accused, Abram Gots, had been a Siberian exile from 1906 to

1917 and subsequently a member of the Petrograd Soviet. At the end of the trial the death sentence was pronounced against all the accused, all former revolutionaries, deemed enemies of the regime. The French writer Anatole France, whose sympathy for the new Russia was well-known, declared: 'I will have nothing to do with these methods. By such acts as this, an irreparable, crushing blow is dealt to every liberating movement in the world. In the name of humanity, in the name of the highest interests of the world proletariat, I protest against such actions!'

That winter, Lenin suffered a second stroke. Shortly afterwards, on December 22, he dictated his testament, a series of notes which showed how aware he was of the struggle for power that would follow his death. Trotsky was his chosen successor. 'Stalin is too rude,' he wrote, 'and this defect, though quite tolerable in our midst and in dealings among us Communists, becomes intolerable in a General Secretary. This is why I suggest that the comrades think about a way to remove Stalin from that post and appoint another man who in all respects differs from Comrade Stalin in his superiority, that is, more loyal, more courteous, and more considerate of comrades, less capricious, etc.'

As General Secretary of the Communist Party since the beginning of 1922, Stalin was in a commanding position to outwit Trotsky. Lenin intended his testament to become widely known, but it was suppressed for thirty-three years, until after Stalin's death.

On November 14 the first radio news bulletin was transmitted in London, from the rooftop of the Marconi building in the Strand. At first, the daily broadcasts were limited to news bulletins and dance music in the evening. But a revolution had begun which was to bring the events of the century rapidly, with increasing frequency, and sometimes with great urgency, into an ever-growing number of homes throughout the world.

At the beginning of 1923 the German Government sought to postpone reparations payments for another year. The French Prime Minister, Raymond Poincaré, who had been angered by the previous year's postponement, announced that France would seize from Germany various productive enterprises, retain control of them and exploit them, until Germany fulfilled its reparations obligations. On January 10, French and Belgian troops entered the Ruhr. Britain, in its most open breach with France since the end of the First World War, declined to participate in the French move.

In the factories which they had occupied in the Ruhr, the French ordered German workers to continue production. But a passive resistance movement began, and spread rapidly. It was clear that France would not be able to extract reparations by actually working the German industrial system. Poincaré then announced that France would only withdraw from the Ruhr 'in proportion' as the German Government paid its reparations dues. It took almost twelve months before Britain, with the help of the United States, was able to persuade Poincaré at least to set up a committee to examine the question of Germany's capacity to pay. Meanwhile, the French occupation of the Ruhr led to the total cessation of all German reparations payments, and to considerable poverty among the striking workers. The occupation also deprived the French ironworks in Lorraine of the German coke on which they were dependent in order to maintain production. In an incident in Essen, on March 31, when French troops were trying to requisition lorries at the Krupp factory, the workers stopped work and gathered in protest outside the factory. For several hours troops and workers faced each other. Then a French soldier with a machine-gun opened fire and thirteen German workers were killed. The French Government blamed the factory's German managers for inciting their workers to passive resistance.

The economic distress caused by the French occupation of the Ruhr and the German passive resistance was enormous. The German Government began to print money to pay subsistence wages to the two million workers who had downed tools. By August the value of the mark fell to one-fortieth of its value at the beginning of April. In many of the Ruhr towns there were repeated and widespread acts of looting and plunder. Both left-wing and right-wing extremists sought to make capital from the distress. In Frankfurt, the Communists organized a demonstration of 'fighting unions' – the Proletarian Hundreds – which led to bloodshed. In Munich, where the Bavarian Government was less strong than its Prussian counterpart, a Fighting

League of right-wing extremist groups had been set up – a loose alliance of many discontented groups. Among the members of the Fighting League, Hitler's National Socialist Party was prominent, and in several Bavarian towns Hitler's Brownshirts fought street battles with the Proletarian Hundreds.

As Hitler's adherents gained in strength and vociferousness, dominating the Fighting League, the Bavarian Government suspended civil law and placed the executive power of the State of Bavaria in the hands of a former Bavarian Prime Minister, Dr von Kahr, a supporter of the monarchy. He at once forbade a number of Nazi meetings. He also suppressed the Socialist self-defence organization. Violent separatist activity spread throughout Germany. 'There are now only two alternatives before us,' Hitler told a mass audience on September 12, 'the swastika or the Soviet star, the world despotism of the communist international or the Holy Empire of the Germanic nation,' and he added: 'The first act of redress must be a march on Berlin and the installation of a national dictatorship.'

Bavaria was on the verge of separating from the rest of Germany. When the Bavarian troops were ordered to swear a special oath to the Bavarian Government, the government in Berlin accused Bavaria of violating the German constitution. Encouraged by the almost daily confrontations, Hitler made plans for a Nazi seizure of power, not just in Bavaria, but throughout Germany. He looked to the chaos in the Ruhr to help his cause. By November 1923, as a result of the continuing French occupation and the almost total collapse of German industry, terrible hardships affected the middle class as the value of their savings disappeared overnight. The cost of basic foodstuffs became prohibitive. Physical hardships touched every family in the country. That month it took a million million (1,000,000,000,000) paper Marks to equal the purchasing power of a single German Mark in 1914.

Hitler exploited the economic collapse by blaming it on all those whom he wished to portray as enemies. First and foremost this meant to him the government in Berlin and its alleged allies, Jewish financiers and Marxist subversives. These were the same enemies, he declared, as the 'November criminals' who had deliberately brought about Germany's defeat in 1918. Hitler had an important ally in his campaign in General Ludendorff, the second most senior figure, after Hindenburg, in the German First World War military pantheon. Ludendorff stood to become the chief beneficiary of the 'stab in the back' legend, for it was he who had been at the helm when defeat came. It suited him to put the blame on others. He was also the beneficiary of a gift of 100,000 gold Marks from the German industrialist Fritz Thyssen, who wanted to see greater action against the Socialists, both in and out of government. Ludendorff parcelled out his money to other activists, Hitler among them.

Hitler's plan was to seize power in Munich, and, with Bavaria as his base, to launch a march on Berlin, not unlike Mussolini's march on Rome of a year earlier, but without first being invited to take power, as Mussolini had been. Unlike Mussolini in 1922, Hitler in 1923 was unimportant in political terms, without a single deputy in the Reichstag, and with no accepted overall leadership of the forces of the right, such as Mussolini had commanded. Still, he was determined to act.

On November 8 a meeting of 2,000 Munich citizens was held in the Bürgerbräu beer cellar. The heads of most Bavarian Government departments were there, many industrial leaders, and the directors of various municipal and patriotic organizations. Before the political speeches had begun, Hitler, supported by his Brownshirts, burst in, fired a single shot into the ceiling to command attention, and told the startled gathering: 'The national revolution has begun. The hall is surrounded by 600 heavily armed men. No one may leave the premises. Unless quiet is restored immediately, I shall have a machine-gun placed in the gallery. The Bavarian government and the national government have been overthrown, and a provisional national government is being formed.'

Hitler then proclaimed a new German Government. He would be its leader. Ludendorff would be the Commander in Chief of the German army in its march 'on that sinful Babylon, Berlin – for the German people must be saved. Tomorrow morning will either find Germany with a German nationalist government – or us dead!'

At midday on November 9, Ludendorff took charge of the forces of the Fighting League and, marching with Hitler and the other Nazi leaders at the head of a column of several thousand Brownshirts and others, marched towards the Odeonsplatz, one of Munich's main squares. A line of policemen stood across the road leading to the square. As the marchers approached, the police opened fire. Fourteen of the marchers were killed. Ludendorff marched on, upright and determined, right through the police cordon. Hitler, who had been pulled to the ground when the police opened fire, and had dislocated his arm, got to his feet and fled the scene, finding refuge that night in a suburb of Munich. Two days later he was arrested by the police and taken to prison to await trial for treason.

Since April, incidents of Nazi hooliganism had spread across the Bavarian border into Austria. Wearing swastika armbands like their German counterparts, the Austrian Nazis attacked Social Democrat meetings. The Police President (and former Chancellor) Dr Johannes Schober advised the Social Democrats to ignore these Nazi elements. They were, he said, of 'no importance'.

In Spain, democracy was overthrown in September 1923, when Miguel Primo de Rivera, Marquis de Estella, who was both an army general and a senator, suspended the Spanish constitution and set up a Directorate of army and navy officers to take control of Spanish political life. King Alfonso XII, who had come to the throne in 1886 – he was born after the death of his father, so that he had become King at birth – remained on the throne, surrounded by the trappings of elegance, but stripped of all power.

The powers of the Spanish Parliament (the Cortes) were drastically curtailed. Political opponents of the new regime were banished to an island in the Canaries. When, on November 6, King Alfonso refused to receive a petition presented by several leading Spanish politicians in defence of the constitution, there was despair among the parliamentary forces. In the provinces, the civil governorships were abolished, and Military Regions established.

Primo de Rivera also acted swiftly and with harshness against the separatists in Catalonia, the region which for many years had sought some form of autonomy. Catalan extremists responded by a campaign of bomb-throwing against Spanish officials and government buildings in Barcelona. 'Determined to hispanicize Catalonia,' one British commentator noted at the end of the year, 'the Marquis de

Estella had by the end of the first quarter of 1924 all but succeeded in reviving the movement for Catalan separatism.' The Directorate rejected all Catalonian requests for autonomy. Extremist activities grew, culminating in a plan, which the police discovered before it could be put into operation, to blow up the train in which King Alfonso and Queen Ena would be travelling to Barcelona. The Queen – a granddaughter of Queen Victoria – commented bitterly that it looked as if she and the king 'might have to pay' for Primo de Rivera's policy towards Catalonia.

Primo de Rivera had also to deal with a worsening Spanish position in Morocco, where an uprising of several of the Muslim tribes of the Rif had broken out a month before his seizure of power in Madrid. During November and December more than 4,000 Spanish troops were killed. Strict press censorship was imposed throughout Spain to prevent the extent of the disaster from being known. 'The Moroccan question,' wrote Sir Horace Rumbold, the British Ambassador in Madrid, 'is like a cancer in the life of the country.' As the Moroccan uprising spread, Primo de Rivera was forced to withdraw Spanish troops from many of the forts and outposts which they had established in the interior.

Anarchy in China increased during 1923, following the deposition of the child-emperor the previous year. Violence was widespread, and a dozen independent armies rampaged for food and loot, and kidnapped prosperous citizens for ransom. In the south, Dr Sun Yat-sen, the founder and leader of the Nationalist Party, the Kuomintang, made a move to seize the Chinese Government customs revenues of Canton, the city in which his own power resided. British and French warships intervened to prevent the seizure.

China had still to pay a penalty which had been imposed after the Boxer rebellion at the turn of the century. During the First World War, France, Britain, Italy, Japan and Belgium had agreed – China then being an ally – to postpone their share of this Boxer Indemnity until December 1922. When that date passed, the Chinese Government in Peking, which was in permanent conflict with the Sun Yat-sen's Kuomintang Government in Canton, stalled over the renewal of the payments. It wanted to retain whatever financial independence it could, and the ability to purchase arms and munitions for its conflict with the Kuomintang.

With the wild inflation in Germany, and the uncertainty of many European currencies, the question of debt repayments had become a touchy one. France was reluctant to see any diminution of the value of the money owed to her by China, even with a debt that went back almost a quarter of a century. The main grievance of the United States with the outside world in 1923 also concerned war debts – the money owed to the United States by dozens of governments. Four of the debtors – France, Italy, Belgium and Estonia – each declined even to suggest a repayment plan. Czechoslovakia, having agreed the amount that she owed, had made no repayment. Several other countries were unwilling to embark on detailed negotiations, among them Greece, Liberia and Nicaragua. Armenia no longer existed as a country and could not pay any of the money which her leaders had been advanced at the time of the First World War, when an Armenian State seemed one of the certainties of an Allied victory. Payment by Austria of the substantial sum of $27 million had, by reason of Austria's desperate economic situation as a truncated and impoverished nation, been postponed by Act of Congress for twenty years. When that date, 6 April 1942, was reached, Austria had been annexed to Germany for four years, and the United States was at war with Germany.

Only Britain had negotiated a debt-repayment plan. So delighted was President Harding at Britain's willingness to work out a method of funding its debt – partly by borrowing more money from America to pay the interest on the debt – that he told Congress: 'This settlement means far more than the mere funding and ultimate discharge of the largest international loan ever contracted. It is the re-commitment of the English-speaking world to the validity of contract; it is, in effect, a pledge against war and war expenditure.' This enthusiasm was not fully reflected in Britain. The insistence by the United States on having its bond fulfilled, even under extremely favourable terms, was interpreted as mean and greedy.

One of the worst natural disasters of the twentieth century took place in 1923, when, on September 1, an earthquake struck Japan. In

Tokyo, more than 100,000 people were killed. In Yokohama, where a tidal wave added to the destruction, the death toll exceeded 25,000. Another 100,000 were killed elsewhere in Japan. More than a million people were made homeless. From all over the world, money poured in for earthquake relief. Britain and the United States were particularly forward in sending aid. A natural disaster, in which as many as a quarter of a million people were killed within a few hours, succeeded, for a short while at least, in uniting the goodwill of many nations.

On 21 January 1924 Lenin died in the Soviet Union. He had never fully recovered from an assassination attempt four years earlier, and for the last year of his life, after a series of strokes, had been an invalid, unable to govern. He was only fifty-three years old when he died. Under his leadership, Russia had been transformed from an authoritarian monarchy into a Communist dictatorship. Following the assassination attempt on his own life he had established terror as an instrument of State policy.

In the battle for Lenin's succession, Leon Trotsky, one of the main architects of the revolution in 1917 and the founder of the Red Army, was outmanoeuvred by Joseph Stalin, who, as General Secretary of the Communist Party, emerged as the strongest political figure in the State. Under Stalin, the steps which Lenin had taken towards capitalism in his New Economic Policy were halted, the harsh tenets of Communist economic policy were restored, and a campaign was launched to eliminate the once-flourishing, educated, politically active middle class. Children of the 'bourgeoisie' were denied the right of attending high school or university. Apartment owners deemed 'bourgeois' were denied the right of voting on the house committees that determined the fate of their own apartments, in which they were invariably reduced to living in one room, while their other three or four rooms were redistributed.

While extending Bolshevik control, Stalin sought to restore relations with the very nations which, five years earlier, had tried to destroy it. The first country to offer recognition was Britain, in February, followed by Italy. The French recognition in October gave particular pleasure in Moscow, as it included a mutual agreement of non-interference in each other's internal affairs.

Despite trade agreements and solemnly negotiated non-interference pacts, the Communist ideological imperative remained the spreading of revolution far beyond the Soviet borders. Based in Moscow, and controlled by it, the Third International sought to stimulate revolution wherever it could. With the intensification of its propaganda in the Balkans, Yugoslavia, Bulgaria and Roumania formed an Anti-Bolshevik League. Yugoslavia would neither recognize the Soviet Union nor trade with it. In Estonia, the Communist party was suppressed and local Communist groups arrested. On December 1 there was an attempted Bolshevik uprising in the Estonian port of Tallinn, in which emissaries from Moscow played a prominent part. The main railway station and several military buildings were seized, and the Minister of Transport, in trying to prevent a coup, was shot dead at the station. The uprising was suppressed and its leaders sentenced to penal servitude for life.

So incensed was the British Government by the revelation of secret Soviet financing of British Trade Union activity that year that it broke off diplomatic relations with the Soviets. Mustafa Kemal's Turkey also refused to recognize Russia while Constantinople was being used as a base, not only for Bolshevik propaganda in Turkey, but also throughout the Balkans. In Moscow, one of the most dynamic leaders of the Third International, Karl Radek, was removed from his post because he was considered too moderate with regard to revolutionary activity inside Germany.

Soviet control over regions far distant from Moscow was extended in 1924, when a Muslim revolt in Turkestan was crushed and an anti-Bolshevik uprising in Georgia suppressed. So fierce were the Russian reprisals in the Georgian capital, Tbilisi, that in September a resolution was brought forward by France to the League of Nations, calling on the League to mediate. Britain supported France in this proposal, but when it was put to the Soviet Union, whose assent was essential under the rules of the League for it to be implemented, it was ridiculed by Moscow and dismissed with contempt.

During 1924, the Fifth Assembly of the League, meeting in Geneva, completed what was known as the Geneva Protocol. This was based on the aspiration, expressed in Article 8 of the League Covenant, whereby all members of the League of Nations undertook to reduce their national armaments, as a first step to the total abolition of war. At the core of the Geneva Protocol lay the willingness of large and small nations to entrust their security to an international body rather than to their own military strength, and to have confidence in the ability of that international body to assert its collective power whenever aggression threatened. The arbitration envisioned by the protocol would be both compulsory and pacific; those who framed it were convinced that there was an almost 'universal desire' among nations and peoples to accept compulsory arbitration, and that arbitration awards made under the protocol would carry great weight both with the parties in dispute, and with international opinion.

The security provisions of the protocol were based on the abolition of the 'right' of nations to make war. All the States who were members of the League agreed that 'in no case' would they go to war unless called upon to do so by the Council of the League, in order to repress an act of aggression by a 'recalcitrant' State. War would be a collective enterprise against the aggression of a single, rogue power, not the result of conflicting alliances, pacts, ambitions and armaments. The nature of any war to be conducted by the League was spelt out clearly in the protocol. It would start, not with actual hostilities, but with economic and financial pressure. If military action was required, the League Council would call on all its members to co-ordinate their land, naval and aerial forces in physical combat. No State could take military action in pursuance of any alliance until the Council of the League had called on it to do so.

By the end of 1924, seventeen governments had signed the Protocol. Britain hesitated, fearing it would undermine its imperial, dominion and colonial responsibilities.

In Poland, the largest of the new European nations, strenuous efforts were made during 1924 to resolve the country's minority problem. One long-standing demand, which had plagued Austria-Hungary's relations with the Ukrainians of Eastern Galicia, was for a Ukrainian University in Lvov. This was granted by the Poles in 1924. At the same time, Poland's three million Jews were granted representation in the Warsaw parliament.

In Czechoslovakia, social reform was high on the political agenda. In 1924 a law provided for the insurance of all workers against sickness, disablement and old age, and by the end of the year this law was extended to include the self-employed. Czechoslovakia was fortunate economically, in that her ability to export raw materials, especially coal, enabled her to build up a favourable balance of foreign trade, and to compete with Germany. With regard to its minorities, however, Czechoslovakia had less success than Poland: both the Ruthenians in the east and the German and Hungarian minorities elsewhere were dissatisfied with their subordinate status, feeling excluded from the inner decisions of the Czech leaders and denied the full economic benefits of citizenship.

In Turkey, its territory reduced under the Treaty of Lausanne to Asia Minor and a small area of Thrace, Mustafa Kemal asserted dictatorial powers, abolishing the Caliphate, closing all religious schools in Istanbul – as Constantinople became known – removing the Minister of Religion from the Cabinet, and sending the Caliph into exile. Another religious leader in Istanbul, the Armenian Patriarch, whose jurisdiction had covered all Ottoman areas with Armenian inhabitants, was encouraged to transfer his patriarchate to Palestine. A republican constitution was promulgated, and Kemal strove to create a secular and literate society. The Muslim religion was separated from the State, and the State machinery was secularized. As part of the Westernizing of all dress, the fez was abolished. Women's rights were also asserted in a way hitherto unknown in a Muslim country, culminating, in 1934, with votes for women.

Most revolutionary of all, Kemal abolished the Ottoman form of Arabic writing, replacing it by an alphabet written in Latin characters. With four-fifths of the population illiterate, the new alphabet was to have both a unifying and educational influence, combined as it was with a massive campaign against illiteracy. Newspapers were ordered to publish several columns a day in the new script. Post offices and government offices were ordered to use it at once. Kemal engaged personally in propaganda for the new alphabet, visiting hundreds of villages and explaining the new script on the blackboard. All government and semi-official employees were ordered to learn and employ it. Several schoolmasters were arrested for 'carrying on propaganda' against it. Bank notes printed in Arabic characters continued to circulate; apart from that, Arabic characters disappeared from Turkey on 3 November 1928.

In Italy, Mussolini's dictatorship was consolidating its power. The elections that were held in April 1924 were characterized by Fascist violence against opposition parties. Politicians and intellectuals who criticized Mussolini and Fascism were denounced as traitors to Italy, much as, forty years earlier, in Germany, Bismarck had denounced his political opponents as 'enemies of the Reich'. After the election those districts where the Fascist majority had not been as high as Mussolini had hoped saw renewed Fascist violence against opponents of the regime. Parliamentary opposition continued, but suffered a severe blow when a Socialist deputy, Giacomo Matteotti, disappeared from his home. He had openly denounced the corruption and intimidation which had been practised by the Fascist Party during the elections. Forty-eight hours after Matteotti disappeared it became clear that he had been murdered: the car into which it seemed he had been bundled was found with bloodstains on it.

Among those implicated in Matteotti's murder was a member of the Fascist Party Directorate. Mussolini, whom many Italians assumed must have given the order, immediately denounced the murder, removed those implicated from office and promised stringent measures to restore constitutional law in Italy. For the time being these assurances were enough to allay foreign distress; but they did not weaken for a moment Mussolini's resolve to eliminate the influence of parliament on the conduct of national policy. One of the first measures that he imposed after the murder was a strict curtailment of freedom of the press. The opposition newspapers would no longer have recourse to the courts if they were censored or shut down.

The French were still determined to secure reparations payments from Germany, even if it meant, as it had done in 1923, physically operating the main German industrial plants, or extracting German raw materials, lorries and railway rolling stock by force. In a defiant statement, the commander of the French occupation forces in Germany, General Dugoute, announced that the French army would remain in the Ruhr, if necessary, for a thousand years. Was it this that later gave Hitler the idea of declaring a 'thousand-year Reich'?

On January 14 a special commission set up to resolve the Ruhr crisis met in Paris, under the auspices of the Reparations Commission. Two United States experts, General Charles G. Dawes and Owen D. Young, although acting as private citizens, lacking the authority they might have had if the United States had been a member of the League, impressed on the other participants – from England, France, Italy and Belgium – the need to give Germany even greater flexibility in the annual payment of the reparations than had been secured in earlier negotiations.

Under the Dawes Report, German repayments became conditional on a balanced German budget and stabilized currency. To secure these goals, the Allied nations established a Bank of Issue in Germany, which was to be the fiscal agent of the German Government. The bank was to be administered by a German president and management boards, but in all matters relating to creditor nations and reparations payments was to have a General Board of Control made up of seven Germans and seven foreigners. Thus France could feel that its demand for reparations would not be undermined. Reparations payments were to be made through the Agent-General for Reparation Payments. The first Agent-General was Owen Young; the second was also an American, Parker Gilbert. At a conference in London the German delegates accepted the Dawes Plan, and the French Government agreed to withdraw from the Ruhr.

Inside Bavaria, the separatist ambitions which had surfaced with such violence during 1923 were stilled. Hitler was awaiting trial for his part in the failed Munich putsch. The Nazi Party had been banned by the Bavarian Government. But the forces of racism and extremism found a focus in the establishment of an ultra-nationalist alliance made up of Nazis and like-minded extremists and anti-Semites throughout Bavaria. One of the alliance's leaders, Dr Rudolph Buttman, who was to devote his political life to Hitler, declared: 'We will carry the nationalist idea into the last mountain village.' The Jews, he warned, and the other 'mortal enemies', would no longer rejoice as they had done when the putsch was crushed the previous November.

Throughout Bavaria, small groups of Nazis continued to gather, illegally, brandishing the swastika flag as a symbol of German regeneration, and demanding war against the 'international powers' who, they insisted, were bent on destroying Germany: the Allies, Marxism, the Jews, the Catholic church, capitalism, and parliamentary democracy.

Hitler was sentenced in April 1924 to five years in detention, on a charge of high treason. In the German general election held in May, not a single Nazi Party member was elected. That December, Hitler, who had repeatedly petitioned the Bavarian authorities, was released from prison. 'What will you do now?' asked a friend who met him at the prison gate. 'I shall start again, from the beginning,' he replied.

The first woman Cabinet Minister was appointed in 1924, Nina Bang, Denmark's Minister for Education. In the United States, American Indians were allowed full citizenship for the first time. Also in the United States, an unspoilt area of natural countryside, the Gila Wilderness in New Mexico, was the first to be given protected status. In the cinema, the first talking film system was being developed, and Walt Disney produced his first film cartoon, *Alice's Wonderland*.

In March 1925, negotiations opened in Paris between Britain and France, in which Germany was included, and also Italy and Belgium. The culmination of the negotiations was the signature, on October 16, of the Locarno Treaties. The frontiers of Western Europe across which the armies had marched in 1914 were all accepted as permanent by the former adversaries, and protected against aggression by mutual agreement. Not Germany, but Morocco, became the bane of French political life that year. The leader of the Muslim rebels, Abd el-Krim, who took up arms against the French in May, indicated he was prepared to negotiate some form of autonomy for his people. The French Prime Minister, Paul Painlevé, who was also Minister of War, decided instead to crush the rebellion. The Spaniards, who had withdrawn from much of the interior of their zone in Morocco the previous year, were encouraged by the strong line taken by France, and embarked on new initiative of their own, the dictator, Primo de Rivera, taking personal command of the Spanish troops in Morocco. A line of fortified blockhouses was established, known as the Primo de Rivera Line, which repeated attacks by the Moors failed to breach.

In French Morocco, Abd el-Krim persuaded the tribes of the Rif to declare a Holy War against both the French and Spanish. He had attacked and destroyed the villages of tribes still friendly to France, but by the end of July the French were pushing his warriors back into the interior. A turning point came when General Pétain, the 'victor' of Verdun, was appointed to plan a major French attack.

A joint French and Spanish offensive was opened on September 2, when 12,000 troops landed at a bay which was under Abd el-Krim's control. The first Spanish troops to go ashore were commanded by Colonel Franco. Those defenders who are too tenacious', he wrote in his diary, 'are put to the knife.' Within a month, recognizing that he did not have the manpower or artillery force to maintain his position, Abd el-Krim offered to negotiate. The French, supported by Spain, demanded unconditional surrender. The war continued. In Britain the harsh Spanish methods of warfare led to widespread sympathy for what was seen as Abd el-Krim's struggle for independence.

The failure of the harvest, and a typhus epidemic, provided a bitter background to Abd el-Krim's struggle, with continuing French and Spanish military successes. A year after raising the standard of revolt, he surrendered. Some of his followers continued to resist, but when, six months after his surrender, his former lieutenant was killed in battle, the resistance of the tribes was virtually at an end. An agreement was reached in Paris (on 13 July 1926) between Spain and France, delineating their Moroccan frontier, and giving each the right to pursue rebels across it. Abd el-Krim, who was not even mentioned in the agreement, was sent into exile on the French island of Réunion, in the Indian Ocean. Franco was promoted general; aged thirty-three, he was said to be the youngest general in Europe.

In Germany, on 26 February 1925, two months after his release from prison, Hitler held a public meeting to refound his Nazi Party. Three thousand people attended. What the party needed, he explained, was 'fighters, not parliamentarians'.

On the day after Hitler's refounding of the Nazi Party, the first President of the German Republic, Friedrich Ebert, died. On becoming Chancellor in 1918, he had helped to ensure the triumph of the forces of moderate socialism against those of Marxist and Bolshevik extremism. In the election for his successor, the candidates included Ludendorff, the candidate of the extreme nationalists and 'racialists', who had been at the forefront of Hitler's putsch two years earlier; and Ernst Thaelmann, the German Communist leader. The main parties of the Weimar coalition chose the Prime Minister of Prussia, Wilhelm Marx, as their candidate. The Nationalists chose the seventy-seven-year-old war hero, Marshal Hindenburg, hoping he would support an end to the republic and a return to the monarchy.

In the election, Hindenburg's stature as a venerable warrior was decisive, and he was elected President by 48.3 per cent of the voters; Marx received 45.4 per cent and Thaelmann only 6.3 per cent. Ludendorff polled less than 5 per cent. On May 12 Hindenburg took office, swearing on oath to support the constitution. The Republic was in safe, if elderly hands. If, in hindsight, there was any dark cloud on the horizon, it was the publication on July 18 of the first volume of a two-volume work, hardly noticed at the time by reviewers or readers. It had been written in prison during the previous year and a half by Adolf Hitler. Entitled *Mein Kampf* (My Struggle), it made clear that Hitler had strong pretensions to ruling Germany, which he considered to be in danger. There were, he argued, two perils threatening 'the existence of the German people': one was Marxism and the other was Judaism. While he was living in Vienna before the First World War he had discovered what he called 'the truth' about the Jewish conspiracy to destroy the world of the 'Aryan' by means of political infiltration and corruption.

The word 'Aryan', hitherto a linguistic term referring to the Indo-European group of languages, took on, in Hitler's book, a new meaning, that within a decade was to capture the minds of millions of Germans. It was a British-born racist, Houston Stewart Chamberlain, whose work Hitler admired, who at the turn of the century had given the concept of Aryan its racial connotations, using it to denote superiority over the 'Semitic' races. Yet the term 'Semitic' itself was originally not a racial but a linguistic term, and related, not to Jews and non-Jews, but to a language group which includes Hebrew and Arabic. These realities did not trouble Hitler. For him 'Aryan' was synonymous with 'pure'. By contrast 'Semitic' was synonymous with 'Jew', hence 'impure'.

Hitler presented himself in *Mein Kampf* as a man who had seen, and who would prevent, not only the destruction of German life, but the destruction of life on earth, by 'the Jew'. The dangers, as he presented them, concerned the racial integrity of the German people, and a deliberate assault on that integrity. Hitler told his readers that 'the Jew systematically endeavours to lower the racial quality of a people by permanently adulterating the blood of the individuals who make up that people'.

In *Mein Kampf*, Hitler outlined his mission: he would expose and then destroy the threat posed by a worldwide Jewish effort against the foundations of 'Aryan' life. Germany could only become a great nation again if it first recognized, and then repelled, the Jewish danger. Germany's defeat in 1918 could have been prevented, but for 'the will of a few Jews', traitors inside the German Reich. 'There is no such thing', Hitler concluded, 'as coming to an understanding with the Jews. It must be the hard-and-fast "Either-Or".'

Hitler also explained his own part in combating those dangers: 'Should the Jew, with the aid of his Marxist creed, triumph over the people of this world, his Crown will be the funeral wreath of mankind, and this planet will once again follow its orbit through ether, without any human life on its surface, as it did millions of years ago. And so I believe today that my conduct is in accordance with the will of the Almighty creator. In standing guard against the Jew I am defending the handiwork of the Lord.'

Few heeded such hate-mongering in the summer of 1925. The Weimar Republic had established a democratic, parliamentary and republican regime in Germany. Marshal Hindenburg, a venerable old soldier, with no political ambitions or disruptive ideology, had been elected President. Hans Luther, a moderate middle-of-the road politician of no political party, was Chancellor. Gustav Stresemann, a master of conciliation and moderation abroad, was Foreign Minister.

The reparations demands of the Allies were being lessened year by year. The crisis of whirlwind inflation had passed. Employment was slowly rising. International conferences offered Germany, for the first time since her defeat, equal participation in European diplomacy. On 16 October 1925, three months after the publication of Hitler's first, bitter volume, Germany signed the Locarno Treaties, in which Germany and France, and Germany and Belgium, mutually undertook 'that they will in no case attack or invade each other or resort to war against each other'. In seven years, Germany had emerged from the beaten enemy to the equal partner.

Also signed at Locarno were Arbitration Treaties between Germany and Poland, and Germany and Czechoslovakia. These protected the eastern borders of Germany against German eastward expansion.

Women's participation in national life continued to find new expression in 1925. In Belgium the first woman Mayor was appointed, in the United States, the first woman State Governor. Also in the United States, an Institute for the Coordination of Women's Interests was founded.

In the world of art, the first Surrealist exhibition was held that year, in Paris. Also in Paris, the term 'Art Deco' was formulated. In Soviet Russia, Dmitri Shostakovich published his first symphony and Serge Prokofiev his Symphony No. 2, but Russia's artistic life was deeply troubled. The poet Akhmatova, who refused to leave Russia for exile – 'I am not with those who abandoned their land' – found her poems banned. The poet Yesenin, of peasant origin, a Social Revolutionary seven years earlier, dreaming of agricultural communes of the most egalitarian sort, committed suicide in Leningrad, aged thirty, disillusioned with what the revolution had brought.

Art in the United States suffered from no such traumas. Aaron Copland published his first symphony in 1925, the year in which the first regular broadcasting of country music began – from Nashville, Tennessee – and Paul Robeson gave his first recital of Negro spirituals. In an attempt to combat what he saw as the evil influence of jazz, the American industrialist Henry Ford organized a series of nationwide folk dances, but the dance that took America by storm that year was the Charleston.

Inventions continued to benefit those in more affluent lands. An American, Clarence Birdseye, made use of the existing deep-freezing process to deep-freeze food that had already been cooked. A Hungarian designer, Charles Breuer, designed the tubular steel chair. And the first 'motel' opened that year, in California, the year in which 17,671 Americans were killed on the roads. Slowly but surely the motor car was imposing itself on the lives of the nations, as motor-car deaths became commonplace in all prosperous societies.

CHAPTER FIVE

Between Two Storms
1926—32

A NEW DICTATOR entered the European scene in 1926 – Marshal Jozef Pilsudski – who in 1892 had founded the Polish Socialist Party. Contemptuous of post-war Polish parliamentary democracy, he put himself at the head of a number of army regiments, surrounded Warsaw, and marched into the city. Elected President by a large popular majority, he refused to take office, saying that under Poland's constitution the President did not have enough powers. Five months later he made himself Prime Minister, and for the next nine years, until his death in 1935, he ruled Poland as autocrat.

In neighbouring Lithuania a Liberal-Socialist government which had been in power for most of the year was overthrown during a night attack on government buildings in the capital, Kovno. About 250 leading Communists were arrested, and four were executed. A new government was then formed, in which the right-wing Clerical Party held power. In Latvia, a Socialist government was warned by the newspapers that what had happened to the left-wing government in Kovno was the fate of all those who 'betrayed the national interest'. But the Latvian Government survived, carrying out a moderate social policy, and proving tenacious of Latvia's seven-year-old independence.

In the Soviet Union, Stalin, the General Secretary of the Communist Party, was placing his nominees in charge of the highest offices. As his control spread, he faced concerted opposition within the Communist Party. On October 1 a meeting was held in a small factory in Moscow, at which Trotsky was the main speaker. Zinoviev, another of the Bolshevik leaders of 1917, accused Stalin of betraying the revolution. Stalin took rapid action. On October 23 the leaders of the opposition were warned to abstain from any further 'insubordination to the rules of the Party'. Trotsky was expelled from the Politburo – the controlling body of the Communist Party – and Lev Kamenev was struck off the list of candidate members. Three days later Stalin summoned the Fifteenth Congress of the Communist party of the USSR. Trotsky, Kamenev and Zinoviev were each allowed to speak, but the overwhelming majority of the delegates were vociferous in their support for Stalin, several of whose close colleagues were given new posts and new authority. Nikolai Bukharin was appointed editor of the Party newspaper, *Pravda*, and also replaced Zinoviev at the head of the Moscow-based Communist International organization, the Comintern. Control of the secret police was given to another close colleague of Stalin, Vyacheslav Menzhinski, who used his powers to supervise the draconian collectivization of agriculture and to extend the slave labour camp system.

Stalin wasted no time in depriving his enemies of all influence. Zinoviev had to stand down as President of the Leningrad Soviet, and from the Politburo. Kamenev lost his post as President of the Moscow Soviet.

In Italy, Mussolini supervised the establishment of the Corporate State. Service to the nation and its Fascist ideology was to be the overriding duty. Representation in parliament would be by trades and professions, not by wealth or position in society. Strikes were made illegal, and all workers' and employers' associations placed under the control of the State. All labour disputes would be resolved by compulsory arbitration. The 'education and thrift' of workers and employers alike were put under a Ministry of Corporations, headed by Mussolini himself. To stifle criticism, all opposition newspapers were censored, and more than 500 opponents of the regime were put under preventative detention. Democratic elections, which Mussolini derided as 'paper chases', were abolished, as was the Italian system of elective mayors. Henceforth a list of mayoral candidates would be submitted by the inhabitants to the government, which would then make the choice.

With an adverse trade balance, Mussolini looked to austerity to enhance both the economic and moral development of the nation. Spending on luxuries was discouraged. No further licences were to be issued for cafés, dance halls and restaurants. Expensive private housing was to be replaced by mass construction for the lower and middle classes. Italian products were to be purchased in preference to foreign imports. In foreign policy Mussolini sought to enhance Italy's prestige and position in the world. The German and Austrian Governments complained that a policy of 'ruthless Italianization' was being carried out in the South Tyrol, the area – reaching as far north as the Brenner Pass – which Italy had acquired from Austria after the war. Mussolini replied that he had no intention of 'knuckling down' to Germany or any other power. If necessary Fascist Italy would 'carry the Italian flag beyond the Brenner'.

On August 7, Italy signed a treaty of friendship with Spain, in which 'mutual defence in Africa' was a feature. A treaty with the Yemen was signed on September 2, consolidating Italy's position as a maritime power in the Red Sea, giving her the right of economic penetration into the Yemeni hinterland, and challenging Britain's position at Aden. Two weeks later a treaty was signed with Roumania, aimed at moving Roumania away from its alignment with France – its friend and patron since 1918 – and towards Italy, and giving Italy an economic interest on the lower Danube and on the Black Sea. Three more Italian treaties followed: with Greece on November 24, with Albania five days later – creating an Italian counterweight to Yugoslav influence in the Balkans – and with Germany on December 29.

In Germany, a high point in 1926 was the country's admission to the League of Nations. The parliamentary system established after the war was in its ninth year. But with the rise in unemployment to more than a million, support for the Communists was growing. As the economic crisis worsened, unemployment reached two million and continued to rise. The Nazi Party gained a mass of recruits from among the unemployed. At the beginning of 1926 its membership stood at 17,000, but within two years it had more than doubled, to 40,000. Among the most active, and most feared members of the Party were the black-uniformed Protection Squad (*Schutzstaffeln*, or

SS), set up to provide Hitler and the Nazi leadership with personal protection. On July 6 the Hitler Youth movement was inaugurated, under Hitler's personal patronage. It provided what quickly proved to be an attractive array of sporting activities, camping, rousing songs and a fiercely defended national ideology. The youngsters wore brown shorts and marched behind swastika-waving leaders.

On December 10, Hitler published the second volume of *Mein Kampf*. Once again anti-Jewish venom permeated its pages. 'At the beginning of the war,' Hitler wrote 'or even during the war, if twelve or fifteen thousand of these Jews who were corrupting the nation had been forced to submit to poison gas, just as hundreds of thousands of our best German workers from every social stratum and from every trade and calling had to face it in the field, then the millions of sacrifices made at the front would not have been in vain.' On the contrary, Hitler continued, 'if twelve thousand of these malefactors had been eliminated in proper time, probably the lives of a million decent men, who would be of value to Germany in the future, would have been saved'.

Hitler's readership was still small. Every effort was being made by the German Government to normalize life, attract tourists to the many beautiful regions with which the country was endowed, and to enhance trade. At the beginning of the year British troops evacuated Cologne, after seven years of occupation, ending a visual daily reminder of the defeat of 1918. Germany also negotiated a treaty with Russia in 1926, each country agreeing that it would remain neutral if the other was attacked, and would not join in with the attacker. Each country also pledged not to join any financial or economic boycott that might be imposed on the other.

That there might be some secret clauses in the treaty was strenuously denied by both sides. In fact, a series of secret arrangements was already enabling Germany to breach the disarmament clauses of the Treaty of Versailles. Starting in 1922, and reaching a high point in 1926, nine separate facilities were set up inside the Soviet Union, at secret locations, to enable German military training and research to go ahead. At four locations, Russian armaments factories produced weapons and munitions under German supervision. At another, German engineers manufactured tanks. At two others, the Germans established a poison gas plant and a chemical warfare research centre. At yet another there was a flying school for German pilots, and nearly every German air force officer who was to hold a high position during the Second World War attended a flying course there between 1926 and 1931.

Aircraft production, forbidden to Germany by the Treaty of Versailles, was being undertaken in strictest secrecy both inside and outside the German borders. By 1926, with the encouragement of the German Government, Hugo Junkers was operating an aircraft factory in Germany which, while ostensibly manufacturing civilian aircraft, was making their conversion to war purposes an integral part of their design and construction. Also with government support, Ernst Heinkel set up an aircraft factory in Sweden, and Claude Dornier set up factories in Italy and Switzerland.

In Britain, 1926 was marked by a prolonged coal strike that divided the nation. The miners were being told by the mine owners that they must accept a reduction in their already low wages, or face dismissal. With unemployment high, many miners accepted the reduced wages for fear of being unable to get other work. On May 1, when the miners' leaders insisted on no further reduction of wages anywhere in the industry, the whole work force was locked out by the owners. In sympathy with the miners, the Trades Union Council – the TUC – called a general strike, which began on May 3. Commerce and industry were brought to a standstill throughout Britain. But a massive volunteer effort was made to keep essential services running. Buses were driven by volunteers, many of them students who disapproved of the strike. At many ports, fish was unloaded by volunteers.

The government refused to force the mine owners to make concessions. After a week, the TUC, representing the mass of British workers, recognized the urgency of a return to work, and felt it could no longer support the miners in their determination to continue on strike. On May 12 the general strike was called off. The coal strike went on throughout the summer.

The United States was drawn into a conflict in Nicaragua in 1926, when the Socialist leader Emiliano Chamorro seized power, but immediately faced a counter-revolution headed by a more left-wing group. In order to 'protect American property', which was under attack by counter-revolutionary troops, President Coolidge authorized the landing of American Marines. The counter-revolutionaries were driven out, and a government acceptable to the United States was formed. Within a year, the Marines withdrew. American interests, which included lumber, sugar, rice and banana plantations, had been secured. An American collector of customs was appointed to collect the interest on the Nicaraguan debt to the United States.

To secure control over the Panama Canal, the United States signed a treaty with Panama whereby, in the event of the United States being at war, Panama would 'turn over to the United States' the control of its radio communications, aircraft and aviation centres. Also under the treaty, Panama ceded to the United States 'in perpetuity' part of a small but strategically placed island off the Atlantic terminus of the canal.

In 1926 the profits and productivity of every branch of the American economy reached record levels. In automobile production, steel, copper, oil and cement, building construction and the manufacture of newsprint, all previous records were broken. But for Europeans, this success contrasted with the insistence of the United States that war debts must be paid. Despite European attempts to gain further reductions, the Italian debt of $2,000 million, although spread over sixty-two years, was confirmed by Congress. Also confirmed were debt agreements with Belgium, Czechoslovakia, Roumania, Estonia and Latvia. The French debt, of more than $4,000 million, had to be paid off, like the Italian, in sixty-two annual instalments. Each debtor country negotiated its own terms, often to the anger of the others. Under the agreements reached, Britain was repaying between 70 and 80 per cent of her debt, France only 50 per cent and Italy a much-envied 26 per cent.

Inside the United States, organized crime continued to disturb the daily life of the major cities, as the maintenance of Prohibition since 1919 enabled considerable fortunes to be made by the illegal manufacture and distribution of alcohol. In Chicago, Chief Detective William O'Connor asked for 500 volunteers among policemen who had served in the American army in France in 1917 and 1918.

Forming them into a special armed detachment, he explained why they were to use the same weapons as the gangsters. 'Men, the war is on,' he said. 'We have got to show society that the Police Department, and not a bunch of dirty rats, are running this town. It is the wish of the people of Chicago that you hunt these criminals down and kill them without mercy. Your cars are equipped with machine-guns and you will meet the enemies of society on equal terms. See to it that they do not have you pushing up daisies. Shoot first and shoot to kill . . . If you meet a car containing bandits pursue them and fire. When I arrive on the scene my hopes will be fulfilled if you have shot off the top of the car and killed every criminal inside it.'

Gangsters also fought gangsters. Three years later, on 14 February 1929, St Valentine's Day, seven members of one Chicago gang, headed by George 'Bugsy' Moran, were shot dead by members of another gang – headed by Al 'Scarface' Capone – in a hail of machine-gun fire. The dominant weapon of the First World War had become an instrument of gangland power.

In China, the struggle between north and south intensified during 1926, with different warlords in command of the various provinces, and with the Nationalist Party, the Kuomintang, with its head-quarters in Canton, gaining considerable ground. Working closely with the Kuomintang was the Chinese Communist Party. In 1924 the Soviet Union had signed a treaty with the Kuomintang leader, Sun Yat-sen, whereby the Kuomintang army was to be trained by Soviet instructors. The senior Soviet general whom Stalin sent to Canton, Mikhail Borodin – under his original name, Mikhail Grusenberg, he had been active in the Jewish Socialist Workers Movement at the turn of the century – became personal adviser to the Kuomintang generals. A Chinese Communist, Chou En-lai, was made the head of the political department of the army.

Stalin was sceptical of the ability of the Chinese peasants to make any practical contribution to the advancement of the Communist cause. But the leading ideologist of the Chinese Communist Party, Mao Tse-tung, stimulated by the enthusiasm shown by peasants in Hunan province for political activity, consulted Borodin as to the best way of organizing a rural Communist movement. The Kuomintang-

Communist alliance was effective. In Canton, Mao Tse-tung ran the Propaganda Department for the Kuomintang Central Executive Committee, and edited the Kuomintang political weekly newspaper. At the same time he took charge of a specially created Peasant Department under the direct auspices of the Communist Party Central Committee, and began training peasant agitators at the Kuomintang's Peasant Movement Training Institute.

'If we want our revolution to succeed,' the Kuomintang leader, Chiang Kai-shek, declared in August, 'we must unite with Russia to overthrow imperialism.' The Chinese Communists, he explained, did not want 'to apply Communism, but want rather to carry out the national revolution'. But having used the Communists as allies and co-fighters, Chiang Kai-shek broke with them after power in Shanghai was seized by the city's workers. Although they then handed the city over to him, he turned savagely against them. This ended the Chinese Communists' hopes of co-operation with the Kuomintang as the road to early revolution. At the same time, Stalin also turned against them, denouncing the Chinese Communist Party's alliance with the peasants, and pouring scorn on those like Mao Tse-tung who believed that it was through the peasants that Chinese Communism would triumph.

Perhaps the event of 1926 with the most long-term impact on the twentieth century, certainly upon the daily lives of thousands of millions of people, took place on January 26, when, from a room in London, John Logie Baird carried out the first transmission of a new invention, television.

At the beginning of 1927, anti-foreigner riots flared up in China. Many British and other foreign traders were attacked, and the British Concession at Hankow was overrun. A division of British troops left Liverpool on an ocean liner *Megantic* on January 25. Among their weaponry were gas shells. On March 24 six British traders were murdered at Nanking. Foreign warships on the river opened fire and six Chinese were killed. The American, French, Italian and Japanese Governments sent naval reinforcements to Chinese waters. But the Chinese nationalists under Chiang Kai-shek were determined to avoid foreign intervention – 20,000 British troops were then gathered at Shanghai – and apologized for the Nanking incident.

Entering Nanking himself, Chiang Kai-shek established a government of his own and opened negotiations with the foreign powers for economic assistance. He also clamped down on the Communists in the city, striking at his former allies with considerable ferocity. Flushed with a sense of victory, he then advanced as far north as Hsuchow, where he was besieged by the Northern Army commanded by Marshal Sun Chuan-fang. In the battle that followed, which ended with Sun Chuan-fang recapturing the town, 50,000 men were killed. Chiang Kai-shek retreated.

In Peking, an independent warlord, Marshal Chang Tso-lin declared himself Dictator, or Generalissimo. The Governor of Shansi province, General Yen Hsi-san, at once declared himself an adherent of the Kuomintang and marched towards Peking. Tens of thousands of soldiers were killed in the battles which followed, but the capture of Peking was beyond the Nationalist capacity. As the rival armies continued to battle, China remained without a central government. When Chiang Kai-shek appealed for negotiations to revise the 'unequal' treaties that had been signed by China before the war with the foreign Powers, the American Secretary of State, Frank B. Kellogg, insisted that only when there was a government that could speak for the whole of China could negotiations start.

Inside the continental United States, the Ku Klux Klan sought to revive its fortunes by staging a parade in New York. On May 30, Memorial Day, a thousand 'knights' of the Klan, in robes and white caps, together with 400 members of their women's organization, the Klavana, walked four miles through the streets to their reviewing stand. Throughout the march they were jeered and attacked by hostile crowds.

There was other violence in the streets of New York that day. Two Italians who were on their way to join a detachment of 400 black-shirted Fascists in the Memorial Day parade, were attacked by an anti-Fascist group and killed. The murdered men were both war veterans, one having served with the American and the other with the Italian army. Meanwhile, police clashes with the Klan continued throughout the day. No deaths took place in New York, but in the American South, following the pattern of previous years, there were sixteen recorded lynchings of black Americans. There were also forty-two incidents where police prevented lynchings.

On 7 January 1927 a telephone conversation between the President of the American Telephone and Telegraph Company, and the Secretary of the British Post Office, inaugurated the first commercial transatlantic telephone link. Not only was it possible to talk across the airwaves, but also to hold two-way conversations with sufficient clarity to make possible both personal contact and commercial discussions. The only drawback was that wireless amateurs were able to 'listen in'. On that first day, thirty-one telephone calls were made. (On the day that I wrote this sentence – 15 August 1996 – more than 1,800,000 transatlantic telephone calls were made within twenty-four hours.) Within two months, improvements on the land-line connection between New York and San Francisco made it possible to conduct a telephone conversation between San Francisco and London, eight time zones away.

On May 20, Captain Charles Lindbergh, a twenty-four-year-old United States air mail pilot, made a record transcontinental flight across the United States on May 10–12. Eight days later he flew non-stop from New York to Paris, the first ever solo flight across the Atlantic. His plane, the *Spirit of St Louis*, covered the 3,610 miles in thirty-three and a half hours. Eight years had passed since the first transatlantic flight, by two English aviators, Alcock and Brown, who flew from Newfoundland to Ireland in sixteen hours, but the impact of Lindbergh's solo flight was considerable. When it became known in France that his plane would be landing at Le Bourget airport after dark, the Paris police appealed for owners of cars to drive out to Le Bourget and use their headlamps to light a landing path for him. When he returned to the United States – by sea – vast crowds, many cities and innumerable institutions, headed by Congress, honoured him. Flying to every State in the United States, he visited seventy-eight cities by air, after which he made a non-stop flight from Washington to Mexico City, followed by flying to sixteen countries in Latin America.

As a result of Lindbergh's achievements, writes the air historian R.E.G. Davies, 'the American people were suddenly seized with the idea that the aeroplane was a safe, speedy, and useful vehicle. This realization awoke the interest of ordinary folk who just wanted to experience the thrill of flying, and more important, perhaps, the awareness of businessmen that aircraft building and operating could be a profitable investment. There had been nothing like it since the railway boom of the previous century.' Within three years, three commercial air lines were operating routes from coast to coast.

On May 12 the British police raided the London premises of the Soviet Trade Delegation, and of Arcos Ltd, a trading company with close links to Russia. The police had been made aware of efforts by members of the delegation to obtain military information. Two days later the Soviet Chargé d'Affaires was asked to leave Britain, and the Foreign Office announced that 'the existing relations between the two governments are suspended'. They were not to be renewed for two and a half years, until after the advent of a Labour government.

In British India, the year 1927 was marked, as its predecessors for the past five years had been, by continual strife between Hindus and Muslims. Within the wide spectrum of Indian classes, castes, languages and ethnic groups, and political aspirations, it was this religious conflict that created the greatest tensions. The Indian National Congress, the main body of Indian national activities and agitation, was made up of Hindus and Muslims working together, in harmony, but since 1906 an All-India Moslem League had made itself the instrument of specific Muslim hopes and the protector of Muslim interests.

During a seventeen-month period between 250 and 300 people were killed in Hindu-Muslim clashes and more than 2,500 injured. There were riots in the predominantly Muslim city of Lahore after a newspaper article denigrated the founder of Islam, the Prophet Mohammed. In an attempt to lessen the immediate tension, and to find a long-term solution to Hindu-Muslim violence, the head of the All-India Moslem League, Muhammad Ali Jinnah, convened a Hindu-Muslim Conference, known as the Unity Conference, at Simla.

But it was unable to find a way to halt the communal riots, which continued to take their toll in human lives.

An attempt was made by the Government of India to introduce a new section in the Indian penal code, to make it a criminal offence to insult the religion, or intentionally to outrage, or attempt to outrage, the religious feelings 'of any class of His Majesty's subjects'. This proposed new section of the law was submitted by the government to the Simla session of the Indian Legislative Assembly – the highest level of Indian participation in the government of India. During the ensuing debate it became clear that nothing could be done: the Muslim members of the assembly supported the new section, the Hindu members opposed it.

The British Government in London was committed, under the Government of India Act of 1919, to set up a Statutory Commission on Indian Reforms, to review the whole future nature of British rule. The commission was announced in November 1927, headed by a distinguished Liberal parliamentarian and jurist, Sir John Simon. Many Indian nationalists objected to the lack of any Indians on the commission, but the British Prime Minister, Stanley Baldwin, explained that the British Parliament could not escape from its 'ultimate responsibility' for any legislation that might follow. Protest meetings were held throughout India. The Indian National Congress decided to boycott the Simon Commission altogether. One large group in India did welcome the commission, however, and offered to co-operate fully with it. This was the Untouchables, those millions of Indians who were outside the rigid Hindu caste system – men, women and children who were obliged to undertake the most menial and degrading tasks. At their own Conference of the Depressed Classes, held at the end of the year, the Untouchables expressed their hope that the Simon Commission would give them a better place and a better life in any future Indian constitutional arrangement.

Even as the Simon Commissioners were on their way to India, the Government of India altered its policy with regard to Indian participation in the army, opening the gates to the substantial employment of Indians in the higher ranks. A massive irrigation project was also inaugurated, which was to irrigate almost twelve million acres of arid land. Another leap forward was the appointment of an Indian member of the Legislative Assembly, Srinavasa Sastri, as the first Agent of the Government of India in South Africa, responsible for ensuring that the treatment of Indians in South Africa was conducted fairly.

In Austria, the acquittal of two Fascists on charges of murdering two Socialists led to a workers' strike and clashes with the police. On July 15 there were riots in Vienna, and eighty-five people were killed.

The spread of dictatorial regimes in Europe continued. In Portugal, the right-wing government of General Carmona systematically reversed the social legislation of the Democrat Party, and the efforts of the deposed Prime Minister, Antonia Maria da Silva, to introduce a liberal regime. All town and district councils were dissolved, and replaced by Administrative Councils nominated by the dictatorship.

Anti-government demonstrators in Oporto were dispersed by artillery fire. This did not end the protests. In the capital, Lisbon, anti-government demonstrators, including sailors and policemen, tried to sieze control of the main government buildings. Troops loyal to the government barred their way and opened fire. Barricades were set up and for three days the centre of Lisbon was the scene of severe fighting. The army drove the rebels out of their positions in the streets, then the Portuguese air force bombed them in their stronghold, and they were forced to surrender.

In Spain, the anti-dictatorial forces sought some means of removing Primo de Rivera, but the plotters were exposed before they could go into action, and their leaders arrested. Eight days later King Alfonso opened the National Assembly; it was entirely consultative, the deputies having no power to make laws.

In the Soviet Union, Stalin hesitated to expel his critics, including Trotsky, whose support was widely based. However, when fourteen members of the Left Opposition, as they were called, set up their own printing press – an illegal act under the existing law – they were summoned to a special Party Tribunal and expelled from the Party. Trotsky was among those who tried to defend them, but after he used the occasion to attack the Party bureaucracy, he was expelled from the Executive Committee of the Comintern – the Communist

International – and then from the Party itself. When the Fifteenth Party Congress opened in December, the merits of Stalin were proclaimed by every speaker. He himself demanded of the delegates 'complete acceptance' of the Party's policies and tactics. Trotskyism was declared an 'anti-Soviet force' and Trotsky's followers were denounced. When a specially established Commission of Enquiry recommended to the Congress that ninety-eight leaders of the opposition should be expelled from the Party ranks, the Congress unanimously agreed. Those expelled included Karl Radek, one of those who had travelled to Russia with Lenin in 1917.

Stalin's secret police were vigilant in seeking out any remaining dissenting voices. A manifesto issued under the one-word signature 'Kremlin' threatened severe punishment for anyone committing offences against Soviet rule. That winter, twenty people, most of them former Tsarist officers, and including the leader of the former Constitutional Democrat Party, Prince Dolgoruki, were shot without trial.

Inside Germany, the Governments of both Bavaria and Saxony agreed early in 1927 to end their ban on Hitler's public speaking, imposed after the failed putsch. He gave both governments an assurance that he would not pursue any 'unlawful' aims or use any 'unlawful' means in his renewed political activity. That year Hitler spoke in public fifty-six times. How the Party proposed to come to power was unclear. That year one of Hitler's staunchest followers, Dr Josef Goebbels, published a pamphlet about what the Nazi Party should do if it could not win power through the ballot box. 'What then?' asked Goebbels, and went on to answer his own question: 'Then we'll clench our teeth and get ready. Then we'll march against this government; then we'll dare the last great coup for Germany; then revolutionaries of the word will become revolutionaries of the deed. Then we'll make a revolution!'

One of the fathers of modern racial theory, Houston Stewart Chamberlain, an Englishman who had made his home in Germany, was dying. His life's work had been to show that the Anglo-Saxon race was the superior one, and that although up till then the cross-breeding of races had not damaged the German race, the German race was in danger. The threat, he asserted, came from the Jews.

As Houston Stewart Chamberlain was on his deathbed, Hitler called on him. He had derived the core of his Nazi racial theories from him, and, in Chamberlain's dying moments, showed his homage by kissing his mentor's hand.

Having eliminated the Left Opposition as a political force in the Soviet Union, Stalin set about the destruction of the Right Opposition, those leading Communists who had supported him a year earlier against Trotsky, Kamenev and Zinoviev. When the Central Committee met in April 1928, Stalin accused Bukharin, Rykov and Tomsky, his three main allies of the previous year's struggle, of 'dangerous deviations' and lack of Party discipline. Bukharin, he said, had been guilty of 'treacherous behaviour'.

Action was swift; Bukharin was removed from the editorship of *Pravda* and chairmanship of the Comintern, and Tomsky from the leadership of the Trade Unions. Rykov was allowed to remain as head of government, but under notice. Then, in a display of the political cunning for which he was quickly to become notorious, Stalin turned to the Left Opposition and invited them to return to the Party. Radek, Zinoviev and Kamenev did so. Having been humiliated, they accepted the pardon and hastened to play a part once more in Party life. But their influence was small, their tasks minor, and their prospects of authority nil.

The pattern of Communist totalitarianism did not change. On December 17 it was decreed that all rural land belonged to the community and that the 'socialization' of agriculture was essential. The more prosperous peasants, the Kulaks – whose success as farmers was the result of reforms two decades earlier, in Tsarist times – were deprived of the right to be elected to the local Soviets, and declared the enemies of socialist agriculture. The campaign against the Kulaks, thus begun, became one of the cruellest persecutions of the twentieth century.

Public show trials were also instigated as a regular feature of Communist control. After a secret police chief in a coal mining town had reported direct to Stalin on co-ordinated sabotage by fifty Russian

1. British troops in action in South Africa, 1900.

2. Orville Wright and his aeroplane, 1903.

3. Sarajevo: the Archduke's car, 28 June 1914.

4. Turkish troops at Gallipoli, 1915.

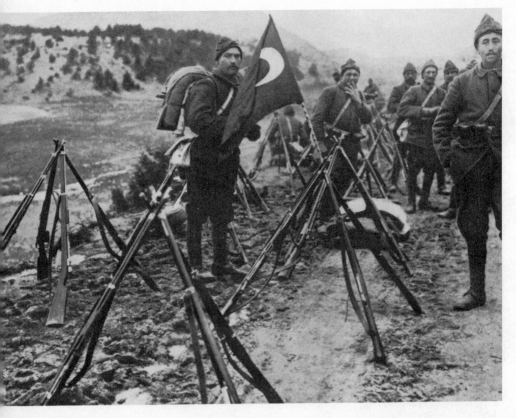

5. Serbian troops in retreat, winter 1915–16.

6. Roumanian troops on their way to war, 1916.

7. Lenin, disguised.

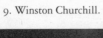

8. Stalin, 1917.

9. Winston Churchill.

10. Wilhelm II.

11. Revolution in Petrograd, November 1917.

12. American tanks on their way into action, 1918.

13. American wounded, 1918.

14. German prisoners of war.

15. Berlin, 1918: revolution crushed.

16. Hunger in Russia, 1920.

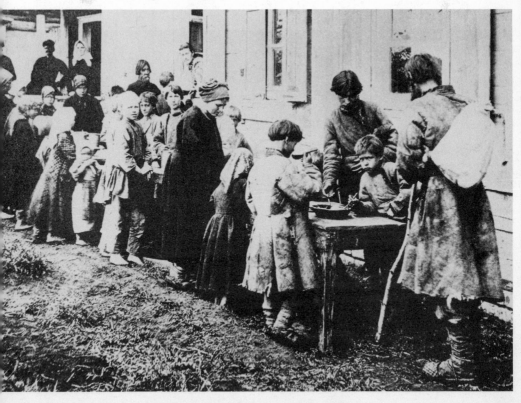

17. *Above* Franklin D. Roosevelt.

18. *Right* Jawaharlal Nehru.

19. *Below* Hindenburg and Hitler in Berlin, 1933.

and three German engineers in the local coal mines, Stalin ordered the case to be brought to trial. The charges were a deliberate fabrication. The presiding judge, Andrei Vishinsky, who was to preside over most subsequent show trials, had been in prison with Stalin in Baku before the revolution.

Everything about the show trial was stage-managed. The slogan 'Death to the Wreckers!' was hung in large banners on public buildings. The twelve-year-old son of one of the accused demanded the death penalty for his father. Confessions were read out that had been extracted by force and fraud. Two of the accused, who had first been tortured, then promised their freedom if they signed confessions implicating not only themselves but others, tried to say this in court, but were howled down.

Five of the Russian engineers were executed. The aim of the trial was to encourage the denuniciation of the 'class enemy' and make any charge plausible. From that moment 'bourgeois specialists', experts of pre-revolutionary upbringing who were loyally serving the new regime, could be rooted out and executed, or sentenced to long terms of imprisonment and forced labour. Although, in the coal mine case, the charges against the three German engineers were withdrawn, it too set a pattern for linking the 'class enemy' with outside forces allegedly intent on undermining the Soviet Union. At later show trials, spying for a foreign power became a standard charge.

In Europe, where every year war memorials were being unveiled to the dead of the First World War, the desire to avoid a renewal of conflict was strong. In 1928 the American Secretary of State, Frank B. Kellogg, promoted a Peace Pact which he invited all members of the League of Nations to sign. Its aim was to outlaw war altogether: 'The unqualified renunciation of all war as an instrument of national policy'.

The Peace Pact was supported by the French Foreign Minister, Aristide Briand. But the three States of central Europe – Czechoslovakia, Yugoslavia and Roumania – fearful that Hungary would seek to regain some of the territory she had lost in 1918, united to denounce all attempts to change their borders. Inside Hungary, resentment at the existence of large Hungarian minorities across its borders was acute. In December a secret shipment of arms bound for Budapest was discovered in Vienna. It was labelled 'oil engines', but when one of the crates accidentally broke open it was found to contain machine-gun belts. On January 19, Hungary's Prime Minister, Count Bethlen, condemned both liberalism and democracy as 'antiquated political forms'.

In securing support for his policies, Bethlen formed a political alliance with the Hungarian Fascist leader, Gyorgy Gömbös, who brought fifty more members of parliament to the government side. Gömbös was rewarded by being made Minister of Defence, and drew Hungary closer to Mussolini's Italy. His influence also led to a rise in anti-Jewish activities throughout Hungary. After the admission to Budapest University of seventeen Jewish students above the derisory quota established for the admission of Hungarian Jews, there were violent attacks on Jewish students in the capital.

In Vienna, the Austrian Fascist *Heimwehr* organization had formed its own armed force, with which it attacked its opponents, principally the Social Democrats. One of the demands of the Austrian Fascists was *Anschluss*, union with Germany. Even moderate opinion in Austria favoured such a union. When the Tenth German Song Festival was held in Vienna, hundreds of thousands of 'Anschluss Day' programmes were printed, and the festival became a call to the world to accept the 'racial unity' of Germans living in the two countries, with a common language, common culture and common border. Shortly after the song festival, the Austrian Fascists announced that 40,000 of their number would assemble in the largely Socialist industrial town of Wiener Neustadt as a gesture of defiance to the Social Democrats. A Socialist counter-march was organized. Only the intervention of 12,000 Austrian troops – one third of the total strength of the Austrian army as laid down by the Peace Treaties – armed with machine-guns and a plentiful supply of ammunition, prevented direct confrontation.

Another country plagued by internal dissent was Yugoslavia, where the Croats resented their position of inferiority in the administration and in the Belgrade parliament. The Yugoslav Communist Party was also flexing its muscles. On May 1 it organized demonstrations in the Croat capital, Zagreb, and there were many arrests, among them that of the city's Communist Party Secretary, Josip Broz, who was imprisoned for two weeks. The Communist Party, he declared, 'is now fighting unreservedly for the independence of Croatia'. Twenty years later, Broz, then Tito, was to lead a Communist Yugoslav State, where Croat independence and breakaway minorities were absolutely forbidden.

Frustrated by Serb dominance of the legislature, Croat deputies in the Belgrade parliament disrupted the proceedings for four consecutive days, after which four of their number were dragged out of the chamber by the police. On June 20 a Serb deputy opened fire and killed a Croat deputy. Anti-Serb riots broke out in Belgrade, the police opened fire, and five rioters were killed. Many Croats felt that without autonomy for Croatia the wider concept of Yugoslav unity was dead, but on July 4 the Serbs rejected a Croat demand for new, 'honest' elections.

Power in Belgrade passed to a coalition, in which Serbs and Slovenes came together under a Slovene Prime Minister, Father Korosec. The Croats were excluded. There was rioting in Zagreb, in which the Communist Party took a leading part, even distributing arms. Josip Broz had to go into hiding, but was caught and brought to trial. Asked by the prosecutor, 'Are you in communication with Moscow?' he answered at once: 'Certainly we are in communication with Moscow. We are Moscow's organization.' He was sentenced to five years in prison.

A new Croat leader, Dr Macek, in search of a compromise that would preserve the unity of the Yugoslav State, argued for a much looser union between Croatia and Serbia, with separate parliaments, separate legislatures and separate Prime Ministers. The Crown would provide a purely personal union between the two countries. In Zagreb, in support of this plan, Croat university students went on strike. In street riots, one person was killed and many injured. On December 5, when the Belgrade government appointed a Military Governor for Zagreb, the Croats feared the imposition of a Serb dictatorship. On December 26 a Serbian secret police agent was murdered in a Zagreb café. In Belgrade there were calls for the trial of the Croat leaders for high treason. It was a conflict that could not be resolved.

*   *   *

In Italy, in a measure designed to strengthen the hold of the Fascist Party, Mussolini incorporated the Fascist Grand Council, which had been in active existence since 1923, into the Italian constitution. The Grand Council would advise on any political, social or economic question 'submitted to it by the government', and would have to approve all constitutional changes brought before parliament. Members of the Grand Council would 'enjoy freedom from arrest'. Mussolini alone would summon it, and he alone would set the agenda for its meetings, which would be held in secret.

Mussolini had already boasted that under Fascism the trains 'ran on time'. In 1928 he announced schemes to drain the malarial areas of Italy and put them under cultivation, providing impoverished villages with irrigation, drainage, roads, water and electric power. Summoning 80,000 farmers to Rome, he told them that agriculture had a 'foremost place' in the government's policies. Their loyalty had been assured beforehand by a rise in the tariff on wheat, giving them a guaranteed minimum price when the cost of wheat fell as a result of deliberate overproduction.

In Germany, a proliferation of political Parties prevented any one Party securing an absolute majority in the Reichstag. Elections were called in May 1928. Thirty-one Parties put forward candidates, including the Nazi Party, which was disappointed in securing only twelve seats. It had gained 810,000 votes out of more than thirty million cast.

The largest Party in the new parliament was the Social Democrats, with just under thirty per cent of the poll. They formed the government, and faced an acute economic crisis. As foreign loans increasingly became a feature of industrial production, many factories were unable to continue. Employers were unable to maintain the existing rates of wages, and men were laid off. For several months a strike of 50,000 dockworkers demanding no more redundancies brought the shipping industry to a virtual stop. In the Ruhr almost a quarter of a million iron workers were locked out by their employers for a month, after a government arbitrator accepted the workers' demands for higher wages, but at the same time shortened the working week, thereby effectively reducing their wages.

Hitler, despite securing only twelve seats in the Reichstag, was certain that what he called the 'fighting spirit' of Nazism would gain him more and more adherents. He took comfort that so many votes had been won by the German National People's Party and the Communists, both of them his rivals, but both, like him, opponents of the democratic system. It was his belief that if they could succeed, so could he. Until the spring of 1928, Nazi Party meetings in Berlin had been banned, but on November 16, six months after the election, Hitler spoke in the Sportpalast in Berlin, asserting the need for racial and national 'regeneration'. 'The bastardization of great States has begun,' he declared. 'The negroization of culture, of customs – not only of blood – strides forward. The world becomes democratized. The value of the individual declines. The masses are apparently gaining the victory over the idea of the great leader.' Hitler was convinced that he could become the 'great leader' in Germany, just as Stalin had become in Russia and Mussolini in Italy.

Unknown to Hitler, or to the other critics of the alleged pusillanimity of the German Government with regard to German rearmament, considerable strides were made secretly in 1928 to rebuild the German army. The Minister of Defence, General Groener, was assiduous in preparing core cadres for a future substantial army. Inside the Soviet Union, the training facilities set up six years earlier for German aviators, chemical warfare specialists and other branches of army ordnance, continued to operate, despite Stalin's show of anti-foreigner feeling. His army, too, was the beneficiary of the work being done.

At German army manoeuvres, the British Military Attaché, James Marshall-Cornwall, had seen a motor truck with canvas screens around it, designed to simulate a tank, and carrying out 'tank' practice and 'tank' operations, both forbidden under the Versailles Treaty. While visiting Stockholm, for he was also Military Attaché to Sweden, he found German engineers working at the leading Swedish munitions factory.

In China, fighting between the Nationalists and their opponents was overshadowed in 1928 when, in the northern province of Kansu, a revolt of the predominantly Muslim population threatened Chinese control. By the time it was suppressed, 200,000 Muslims had been killed. A rebellion by Barga Mongols early in August, while the suppression of the Muslim revolt was still taking place, led to further slaughter.

Slowly, the Kuomintang was asserting its authority over a wider and wider area. On October 3 a new constitution was promulgated in Nanking, with Chiang Kai-shek appointed President. By the end of the year, even Manchuria was under Nanking's control. China was effectively one country again, after more than a decade of fierce division. As a first measure of national unity, the Nanking Government announced that all 'unequal treaties' with foreign governments were abrogated. The Danes were told that the Danish-Chinese Treaty of 1863 had expired, the Italians that the Italian-Chinese Treaty of 1866 was valid no more. France and Japan received similar communications. At the same time, the United States announced its recognition of the Nanking Government and concluded a treaty with it, granting China complete tariff autonomy. The German Government hastened to follow suit, signing a similar agreement a few weeks later. By the end of 1928, ten other nations, including Britain, had signed individual treaties with China, accepting that their former special status, a relic of the era of Great Power imperialism, could no longer be maintained. Only Japan still fumed at having lost its special status in China and refused to sign a new treaty. The assertion of Chinese sovereignty over Manchuria was a blow to Japanese ambitions there.

Having turned against the Chinese Communists a year earlier, the Kuomintang faced fierce Communist hostility. From a rural hiding place, Mao Tse-tung directed a number of uprisings, calling on the peasants of the region 'to massacre the landlords'. Local Soviets were established in rural areas. In a move which paralleled the persecution of the Kulaks in Russia, Mao ordered the execution, not only of the more prosperous peasants, but of peasant landowners. It was the landless peasants, the poorest of the peasant class, who were to be the chosen ones of the new dispensation. Ironically, Mao's efforts were regarded as too moderate by the Communist Party authorities in Hunan. Ordered by his superiors to undertake a large-scale military expedition, Mao and his forces did so, and were defeated. He was able, however, to recruit 8,000 peasants into his militia, and to defeat a Kuomintang force which, in his absence, had overrun his base.

The Chinese Communist Party's Central Committee, located in Shanghai, had an exaggerated view of the strength and potential of the men under arms. Instructions sent to Mao at the end of June made it clear that the Party leaders believed the time had come to destroy forever the political and military power of the landlords, and to make plans for a Communist uprising throughout China. As a first step, Mao's forces were ordered to make another military sortie. Mao rejected this order and was removed as Secretary of the local Special Committee. Rather than believing in a seizure of power by force of arms, on the Russian model of 1917, he considered revolutionary activity to be a long-term aspect of the Chinese Communist struggle, that must be conducted more on the lines of guerrilla warfare than through direct confrontations with the far superior military forces of the Kuomintang.

Mao pursued the policy he believed would alone lead to revolution: the slow education of the peasants, and the maintenance of a guerrilla movement that could neither be pinned down nor brought to battle by superior forces. 'The vast forces of the oppressed classes have not yet been set in motion,' he wrote. 'So we are reduced to contending for the country in this cold atmosphere.' An unusually severe winter added to the hardships facing the small and isolated army, against which the Kuomintang, buoyed up by its victories elsewhere in China, launched yet another offensive. Mao had to abandon his base, but hardly had he done so than his force was attacked and lost half its fighting men. He was then forced to retreat. With the remnants of other Communist forces joining him over the next few months, he could muster less than 3,000 men. A rebuke from the Central Committee in Shanghai expressed its 'complete lack of confidence' in what he had done. He was ordered to resign from the army. He declined to do so. 'The more adverse the circumstances,' he replied to his distant, city-bound critics, 'the greater the need for concentrating our forces and for the leaders to be resolute in the struggle.'

In this firm, disobedient response lay the seed of the steady build-up of peasant power, the subsequent Long March, and the Chinese Communist revolution two decades later.

1929 marked the tenth year of the existence of the League of Nations. It was also the year the Kellogg-Briand Pact, outlawing war, came into force. As if to underscore the importance of the pact, a new American President, Herbert Hoover, made it clear that he would look with favour on a return of the United States to the European, and indeed global responsibilities, which it had set aside a decade earlier. The United States also joined the Permanent Court that year, becoming an equal party to the settlement of all disputes between States that were capable of judicial resolution. That summer a comprehensive treaty, known as the General Act, came into force, for the peaceful settlement of all disputes between nations by conciliation. Under its terms the League States accepted the compulsory arbitration of the Permanent Court for all disputes where conciliation failed.

In seeking to secure the prevention of future war, it was disarmament that proved the hardest objective. When negotiations began in 1929 it became clear that the more heavily armed States were reluctant to reduce their arms, while those which had been compulsorily disarmed were eager, in the first instance, to rearm, before contemplating disarmament. A series of formulae were proposed, whereby the strong would disarm in the same proportion as the weak would rearm. But the more disarmament was discussed, the clearer it became that agreement lay a long way off. How large, for example, should reserve military forces be? How much training could they undergo, once the regular armies were reduced? What form of international supervision would be adequate? How could the budgets and financial arrangements of member States be controlled to prevent clandestine expenditure on arms, through apparently innocuous government departments which did not have the word 'war' or 'defence' in their title? Trust was essential, but in the matter of national armaments, basic concepts of national self-preservation were also involved. The German army was being secretly built up by army officers confident that one day the Versailles restrictions would be thrown off.

*   *   *

For more than a year the British Mandate authorities in Palestine had been involved in a Jewish-Muslim dispute in Jerusalem, centring around the Western, or Wailing Wall. On August 15 a group of young Jews marched to the Wall to reiterate Jewish demands for its ownership, and swore an oath to defend it at all costs. On the following day an Arab crowd reached the Wall, where by chance there were no Jewish worshippers at that time. The Arabs overturned a table and burned the Jewish religious books there. Elsewhere in Jerusalem a Jewish schoolboy was stabbed to death when he wandered by accident into a Muslim quarter.

On the following Friday, August 23, Arabs worshipping at the al-Aksa mosque were incited to violence by a sermon warning of Jewish plots. After prayers they attacked, with knives and sticks, any Jews they could find. In the vicinity of Jerusalem, Arab villagers, many of whom had returned home after praying at the al-Aksa mosque, attacked the Jewish villages nearest to them. The attacks quickly spread to the southern city of Hebron, the site of the tombs of the Patriarchs – holy to both Jews and Muslims – and fifty-nine Jews were murdered. In the holy city of Safed, in the north, twenty Jews, mostly children and old people, were killed.

In all, 133 Jewish civilians were murdered in Arab attacks. The British Mandate authorities intervened to prevent further attacks, and in the process of defending Jewish homes and driving off Arab attackers, the Mandate police killed 113 Arabs. Two British officials were also killed while trying to restrain the Arab attackers. As a result of the 1929 riots, the cause of Jewish-Arab reconciliation, which had hitherto been the hope of moderates on both sides, was dealt a severe blow.

In Germany, the Nazi Party gained ground throughout 1929. A Party Congress at Nuremberg, staged with spectacular use of swastika flags and banners, was an emotional demonstration of loyalty for Hitler. As unemployment rose in Germany, reaching three million, affecting the middle as well as the working class, Nazism gained a wider appeal. Hitler's repeated denunciation of Jewish 'big business' and Jewish 'wealth' appealed to those eager to find a scapegoat for their misfortunes. At the same time Hitler made contact with wealthy

German businessmen, presenting himself as a man who would bring order and discipline to Germany and protect their investments.

In an attempt to win over the millions of army veterans, Hitler joined forces in 1929 with the nationalist veterans' association, the *Stahlhelm*. With his twelve Reichstag seats, he also combined with the German National Party, under Alfred Hugenberg, which had seventy-eight seats. Initially they came together to oppose a formula put forward by the United States for a much less rigid scale of reparations. Their call was: 'No payments at all.' The 'shame' of Versailles had to be eliminated, not appeased. Hitler also added another enemy in his speeches, 'American Jewish bankers', who alone would profit from Germany's sweat and toil.

Hugenberg and Hitler had, between them, ninety seats in the 491-member Reichstag, and were the masters and manipulators of a large segment of public opinion. Both realized the appetite of many millions of people for a scapegoat. 'War Guilt' was still a potent factor in rousing an audience to anger, and they called for a referendum to renounce the War Guilt clause. Enough public signatures were secured, one tenth of those entitled to vote, to hold one. The total number of those voting was 21,000,000. Those who voted in favour of renouncing the War Guilt clause totalled 5,800,000. While this was a long way from the 50 per cent needed to turn the referen dum into law, it was an indication of growing hostility to the settled order, a hostility exploited by the Nazis for their political purposes.

In February 1929, Trotsky, having refused Stalin's demand to give up all political activity, was expelled from the Soviet Union. He went first to Turkey and then to Mexico. The instruments of Soviet terror continued to be wielded to great effect. In May, amid officially orchestrated public denunciations, three railway officials were shot. The charge against them was sabotage. In October several Red Army generals were executed, accused of having discussed a 'counter-revolutionary' plot. In the Caucasus, forty people, including several army officers, and several Kulaks – well off and less well off peasants who owned land, sometimes only small plots – were executed for allegedly wanting to bring back the Tsar. Bukharin was expelled from the Politburo for having 'slandered the Party with demagogic accusations'. Stalin, the real demagogue, found that accusations of demagogery levelled against others were a plausible stick with which to beat those who dared suggest he was the one who had exceeded his powers.

Meanwhile, the mass executions of Kulaks continued, most widely in the Ukraine. On November 25 Stalin announced that the 'socialization of agriculture' would be continued 'at all costs'. A new Commissariat of Agriculture was appointed, Yakov Yakovlev, who endorsed with enthusiasm Stalin's statement that the object of collectivization was 'the liquidation of the Kulaks as a class'. Yakovlev set a one-year target for the collectivization of those peasants who remained. More than fifteen million peasants were taken from their individual farms and smallholdings and forced into State farms. Rather than let their cattle fall into the hands of the State, many of these peasants, before being deported, slaughtered their cattle. As much as half the country's herd was destroyed. The so-called rich peasants, the hated and denounced Kulaks, were deported, not to State farms but to vast labour camp zones above the Arctic Circle, in North Russia and in Siberia. An estimated fifteen to twenty per cent of the deportees – mostly the women, children and old people – died in the cattle trucks and on the forced marches to their new 'homes'. The survivors were told that they must build their own huts and grow their own food. An official Soviet estimate – published in Moscow in 1990, just before the disintegration of the Soviet Union – puts the number of peasant deaths in the Ukraine alone at about four million. The American historian Robert Conquest, who spent a lifetime studying Soviet tyranny, puts the number at about five million.

Religion was also under attack in Stalin's Russia. On May 22 the Soviet constitution was amended to make 'religious' propaganda illegal, while stressing the legality of 'anti-religious' propaganda. Churches, mosques and synagogues were closed down, many being turned into youth clubs, cinemas, or government and Party offices. Thousands of priests, imams and rabbis were imprisoned. Hundreds of monasteries and cathedrals, many of them the priceless architectural and historical treasures of medieval Russia, were pulled down.

*   *   *

In the Kingdom of the Serbs, Croats and Slovenes, as Yugoslavia was then officially known, the struggle between Serbs and Croats intensified. On the night of 5–6 January 1929 a proclamation was posted on the walls of Belgrade, signed by King Alexander, suspending the constitution, appointing the commander of the royal bodyguard as Prime Minister, and approving a Cabinet made up mostly of Serbs. The few Croats who were invited to join were not politicians but specialists in the field of the ministry concerned, without political experience.

The King had become dictator. The very name of the State – the Kingdom of Serbs, Croats and Slovenes – was abolished. In its place came the name by which the country would be known until its disintegration in the 1990s: 'Yugoslavia'. The long-recognized borders of Serbia, Croatia and Slovenia were declared irrelevant, and new borders were established for nine specially designated regions through which the country would be governed on non-racial, non-national, grounds. Local patriotism was to be replaced, if possible, by Yugoslav national sentiment. The individual Croat, Slovene and Serb youth associations, which in Croatia had been a focal point of Croat national identity, were dissolved, and a single Yugoslav youth association was established. The Croat association, angered at losing its base of influence and authority, where the Croat spirit was nurtured among the young, dissolved itself but refused to join the Yugoslav association.

Arrests of Croat dissidents were frequent; but newspapers were forbidden to refer to the arrests. Several leading Croats fled abroad, joining a growing Croat national exile movement.

In India, the work of the commission headed by Sir John Simon on the country's constitutional future was coming to an end. But before Simon could issue his report, the Labour Prime Minister, Ramsay MacDonald, anxious to mollify Indian nationalist opinion, announced that Britain would grant India eventual self-government. Under the title Dominion Status, the inhabitants of the subcontinent would be elevated to the same status as the inhabitants of Canada, Australia and New Zealand. They would govern their own internal lives, with only the very broadest defence and foreign affairs considerations to be retained by British officials.

On October 31 the Viceroy, Lord Irwin, a leading figure in the Conservative Party, announced that the 'natural issue' of India's constitutional progress was 'the attainment of Dominion Status'. It was 'important to make clear to India', he wrote to a friend a week later, 'that the ultimate purpose for her is not one of perpetual subordination in a white Empire'. Less than two months after Irwin's public declaration in favour of Dominion Status for India, an attempt was made by Indian nationalist extremists to kill him. As his train was entering Delhi, a bomb placed on the tracks exploded a few seconds after the Viceregal carriage had passed over the spot. That afternoon, shaken but unharmed, he received a delegation of leading members of the Indian National Congress, led by Gandhi. After expressing the delegation's concern at the assassination attempt, Gandhi told Irwin that the British promise of eventual Dominion Status was not enough; it must be immediate Dominion Status. As to the retention of defence policy in the hands of a British Viceroy, this too, the Congress leaders insisted, must not be allowed to stand. It was the Indians of India, not the British Parliament or its representatives, who must decide the country's defence policy. Indians were as capable of defending India from outside attack as was Britain.

Before the delegation withdrew, Gandhi told Irwin that he and his colleagues were doubtful that even the Labour government, let alone the Conservative opposition, was sincere when it said that it would agree to eventual Dominion Status. Six days later, on December 29, at a session of the All-India Congress in Lahore, anger was expressed at the idea of any delay in implementing the British Government's pledge. 'Eventual' Dominion Status was seen – wrongly – as having been offered by the British Government as a temporary sop to nationalist sentiment, and was denounced as a promise that would not be fulfilled.

Congress then elected as its President forty-year-old Jawaharlal Nehru who, in his first speech as leader, pledged to work for an end to every facet of British rule. This was not mere oratorical bravado. At midnight on December 31, on the banks of the Ravi River, watched by a gathering of more than 1,700 members of Congress, Nehru hoisted the banner of independence atop a tall flagpole. Dominion Status had been rejected. Indian nationalism had moved from accommodation with British rule to total rejection of British India.

In the United States, an unprecedented boom had raised stock prices to their highest point ever, reducing memories of the stock market crash of 1921–2 to a bad episode well and truly in the past. But ominous signs were increasing during the autumn, as the prices of basic commodities began to fall, including those of timber, caused largely through the reappearance on the world market of Russia as a serious competitor able to undercut prices. Excessive sheep farming in Australia was leading to a collapse in the price of wool. Over-production, as well as a fall in individual purchasing power, was threatening a worldwide economic crisis. At the beginning of October there was a sudden fall in the price of wheat. This affected not only American farmers, but farmers in Canada and Australia.

Despite these signs, the United States, with its vast resources of raw materials, did not seem vulnerable to economic disaster, but on October 23, large-scale selling of shares took place on the New York stock market, and shares fell back to their 1927 level. President Hoover immediately took the unusual step of issuing a reassuring statement, pointing out that the 'fundamentals' of American prosperity were sound, and that the United States was 'more prosperous and more industrious than ever before'. This was fundamentally true, but the reassurance came too late. On the day that it was issued, Thursday 24 October 1929 – 'Black Thursday' – the New York stock market collapsed. Even those who had bought shares not as a speculation, but as part of savings portfolios, found that the value of their funds had dropped to a third, and even to a quarter, of their value on the previous day. On September 3 the average price of the thirty leading American industrial shares had stood at $380. By the close of trading on October 24 it stood at $230, a loss of $150. That night, a leading American financier, dining with some of his close associates, addressed them laconically as 'Friends and *former* millionaires.'

At first, it seemed that only the rich owners of stocks would suffer: wealthy men who been made even more wealthy by stock market trading and speculation. But when the scale of private investment became known it was clear, from one New York brokerage house alone, that three million families were involved in its market operations, and in the resultant loss.

A second downward lurch of the stock market on November 19, when the price of the thirty leading industrial shares fell further, to $198, accelerated the distress of millions of Americans across the country. Everyone who had set aside some savings, including the most prudent, suffered. The national income fell, to be halved within three years. Foreign trade could not be sustained. Shopkeepers who feared that Christmas trade would be adversely affected, cancelled their orders, further weakening the manufacturing and trading base. The motor-car manufacturing centres of Michigan were badly hit.

President Hoover made every effort to calm the public and to restore some kind of confidence. At a series of conferences in the White House at the end of October, with leading bankers and industrialists, he discussed how to cushion the fall in manufacturing and halt the slide towards widespread unemployment. The railway companies promised him that they would not reduce wages, and would continue and even increase their equipment and renewal plans. The leaders of the electricity and power industries promised to increase their construction budgets for the following year by eight per cent. In a meeting with State Governors, Hoover secured a promise that the State expenditure on highways would be raised 'to the utmost'. Congress agreed to almost double the amount of Federal aid for the road construction programme. Public projects, Hoover argued, should be 'pushed their hardest' during a time of threatened depression. But as the year drew to a close, the prognosis was not good. As many as three million of the work force – some eight per cent – were out of work.

In British India, at the beginning of 1930, the Bengali nationalist leader, Subash Chandra Bose, was sentenced to a year in prison for leading a demonstration in Calcutta under the banners 'Long Live Revolution' and 'Up with the Republic'. Three days later, the day which the Indian National Congress had declared Independence Day, a bomb placed in a school that had been intended to kill a British official wounded four Indian children.

Gandhi offered to call off civil disobedience in return for concessions by the Government of India, including a general amnesty for political prisoners, a free licence for firearms, and an end to the government salt monopoly. When his demands were rejected he embarked, on March 12, on a protest march to the Indian Ocean. Reaching the ocean on April 6, after a short swim in the sea he scooped up a handful of sand and salt water: a deliberately illegal act. That day he declared the start of a week of civil disobedience.

On April 23, supporters of the Indian National Congress clashed with British and Indian troops in the city of Peshawar. A British soldier who was riding a motor cycle in front of an armoured car was seized by the mob and hacked to death with a hatchet. Two other soldiers were burnt to death when petrol was poured over their armoured car and ignited. The loyalty of the Indian troops was uncertain, and during the attempt to suppress the riots, one battalion of Indian troops was withdrawn after two of its platoons refused to return to the scene of the confrontation when ordered to do so.

On May 5, Gandhi was arrested and, wearing only a loin cloth, his usual garb, was taken to prison in Poona. Riots spread rapidly throughout India. On May 8, at Sholapur, in the Bombay presidency in which Gandhi had been arrested, a large crowd attacked the police station and several policemen were killed. Within three days a police force reduced to eighty men was trying, in vain, to restrain a mob of 10,000. On May 13 martial law was proclaimed and troops sent to the city. That month the President of the Legislative Assembly, V.P. Patel, resigned. The British had placed high hopes on his presidency, and on the assembly, where Indians were serving at the centre of the legislative process, their highest position within the governing hierarchy. In resigning, Patel stated unequivocally that, even while occupying the chair of the assembly, he was in complete sympathy with 'every movement designed to create a condition which might make it difficult, if not impossible, for the British rulers to carry on in the country'.

V.P. Patel's resignation, and his words of defiance, encouraged the nationalists, just as Gandhi's defiance had done. Patel was later sentenced to six months in prison for 'breaches of the law'. When new elections were called for the Legislative Assembly, they were

boycotted by the Congress Party. On election day, Congress volunteers, including many educated women, picketed the polling booths
to prevent people from voting. In November, Britain accepted that
Indians would be responsible for their own government both at the
legislative and provincial level. Britain would retain control of foreign
affairs and defence. On condition that Gandhi, Nehru, Patel, and
other leaders were released from jail, Congress agreed to discuss these
proposals.

In Germany, the fourth decade of the twentieth century opened with
an attack by Hitler's stormtroops on Jewish civilians in Berlin. Eight
Jews were killed. Throughout the year Jews were attacked with fists
and truncheons as they sat in cafés and theatres, and synagogue
services were interrupted with sudden incursions, beatings and
derision.

The number of unemployed in Germany had reached 2,500,000.
In the Reichstag, Hugenberg's German National Party was
demanding a revision of the Polish frontier in Germany's favour. Nor
was this an extremist position. 'I have not met a single German of any
authority', the British Ambassador, Sir Horace Rumbold, reported to
London that February, 'who is content to accept Germany's eastern
frontier as definitive.' Equally ominous, the British Air Attaché in
Berlin discovered that the Junkers aircraft factory, which was strictly
forbidden to manufacture war planes, was offering aircraft to foreign
governments 'which are readily convertible into military machines'.

On March 12 the Reichstag ratified the Hague Agreements,
whereby the 'Occupying Powers' – Britain, France and Belgium –
agreed to withdraw their troops from German soil, in return for
Germany's acceptance of a final reparations figure. This new figure
had been substantially scaled down from the original demands of a
decade earlier. This was a considerable achievement for the predominantly Social Democrat government. Hugenberg's Nationalists and
Hitler's National Socialists were vehement, however, in denouncing
the fact that any reparations were still to be paid at all.

On March 27, as Nazi-led anti-Versailles protests intensified, the
Social Democrat Chancellor, Hermann Müller, one of the German
signatories of the treaty, resigned. Three days later Dr Brüning,

leader of the Centre Party, formed a government. Although he governed without the help of the nationalist parties, their activities, particularly those of the Nazi Party, were gaining in strength and disruptiveness. Hitler still had only twelve seats in the Reichstag, a fact which lulled his parliamentary opponents. That summer, as the number of unemployed in Germany rose to 3,000,000, Nazi Party membership also rose, and dramatically so, from half a million at the beginning of the year to almost two million in the summer.

In order to secure the budgetary measures he believed essential, Brüning resorted to a measure never before used by the republic: emergency legislation that suspended the powers of parliament. The means whereby he did this were embedded in the Weimar Constitution of 1920, paragraph forty-eight of which stated, without equivocation: 'In cases where public security and order are seriously disturbed or threatened in the German Reich, the President of the Reich is empowered to take the measures necessary for restoring public security and order.'

This Enabling Act, as it was known, was promulgated by Brüning on July 17. It was the first suspension of the rule of parliament since the creation of the German Republic more than a decade earlier. When the Reichstag met the following day and passed a resolution calling for the cancellation of the Enabling Act, Brüning dissolved the Reichstag. Then, for three months, he ruled by emergency decree, until, hoping for a new Reichstag that he could control more effectively, he called a general election.

Elections were set for September 14. During the election campaign the efforts of the Nazi Party made a strong impression on foreign observers. 'The movement', wrote the British Ambassador, 'is a new and vigorous one and obviously appeals to youth; and now, during the electoral campaign, its youthfulness and vigour are obviously appealing to all those in Germany who are feeling dissatisfied.'

Nazi Brownshirts were active throughout the campaign, terrorizing Communists and Jews. Hitler's adviser on propaganda, Dr Josef Goebbels, organized 6,000 local Nazi Party meetings. Innumerable torchlight parades were held. Among those who rallied to the Nazi Party was Prince August Wilhelm, one of the Kaiser's sons. Like many others, he feared the spread of Communism in Germany, and saw the Nazi party as the best weapon against it. When the election results were announced the Nazi Party had increased its seats in the Reichstag from 12 to 107. Its voters, 810,000 hitherto, numbered more than 6,000,000: just over 18 per cent of the electorate. With five per cent more votes than the Communist Party, Hitler's was the second largest Party in the Republic. On the day the Reichstag opened to its new political composition, Brownshirts attacked Jews in the streets of Berlin, and the windows of Jewish-owned department stores were broken. As the 107 Nazi deputies walked in a triumphant phalanx to the Reichstag building, supporters lining the streets cheered them on with one of the Party's popular cries: '*Deutschland erwache, Juda verrecke!*', 'Germany awake, death to Judah!'

Brüning had no intention of letting the Hitler-Hugenberg bloc, which commanded 148 seats in all, five more than the Social Democrats, form a government. Instead he continued as Chancellor, using as the basis for his authority the Enabling Act he had introduced before the election. The Social Democrats, alarmed at the strength of the forces of the Right, no longer sought to have the Enabling Act reversed.

By the end of the year the number of those without work in Germany had risen to almost 5,000,000. The Nazi Party continued to offer them a direction both for their emotional bitterness, and for their physical energies, that the government could not provide.

In Austria, the emergence of a right-wing militia, the Heimwehr, and the question of reparations, was a double burden for the government. In January 1930 Dr Johann Schober, the Austrian Chancellor, travelled to The Hague, where he secured a complete liberation for Austria from the sums claimed by the succession States of the Habsburg Empire, principally Czechoslovakia and Yugoslavia, calculated on money owed at the time of the break-up of the Empire eleven years earlier. Schober astonished Allied circles, however, when three months later, after seven weeks of negotiations in Berlin and Vienna, he announced the signature of an Austro-German treaty. This was not the political union forbidden by the post-war treaties, but a bilateral commercial treaty. Given the rise of nationalism in both Germany and Austria, however, it alarmed foreign observers.

On September 30, sixteen days after Hitler's electoral success in Germany, Karl Vaugoin, head of the Austrian Clerical Party, formed a government of Clericals and Heimwehr, an essentially Fascist coalition. Prince Starhemberg, the Commander-in-Chief of the Heimwehr, was appointed Minister of the Interior, and the leader of the Salzburg Heimwehr became Minister of Justice. Within a few days, the railways were put under Heimwehr control.

Elections were fixed for November 9. During the campaign there were repeated confiscations of any newspaper that criticized Heimwehr plans. In the four days before the election, the army and the local police, who were sympathetic to the Heimwehr, raided factories, working-men's clubs and local Socialist Party headquarters. But at the polls, Clericalism and Fascism were rejected by a majority of the voters, and the Socialists emerged as the largest single Party, with seventy-two seats. Vaugoin's Clericals won sixty-six seats, a loss of seven. The Heimwehr and its allies, standing as the Homeland Block, won only eight seats. Democracy, despite the challenge against it, had been preserved.

In the Soviet Union, democracy was a term of contempt. On January 30 the Commissariat of Agriculture proudly announced that four million farms were already under State control; ten days later, ten million; ten days after that, more than thirteen and a half million; and by March 1, more than fourteen million. For two and a half years there had been no Communist Party Congress. Stalin had not felt the need to have his draconian measures scrutinized, even by a carefully selected band of the Party faithful. That summer he was confident enough to summon the Sixteenth Congress. Two thousand delegates attended the opening ceremony in Moscow, and listened to a speech by Stalin which lasted an incredible ten hours. The collectivization of agriculture must continue, he insisted; so also must the industrialization of the Soviet Union. He made no reference to the work of the secret police, who were imposing a reign of terror that made even the mildest opposition to the leader a dangerous risk. That September the secret police announced that it had uncovered a plot of 'counter-revolutionaries' who had wanted to cut the food supplies from the working people. Three days after the announcement, forty-eight people were shot, half of them officers and industrialists of the Tsarist time.

Slowly, Stalin replaced the senior and middle leadership of every branch of Soviet life, including the Party centre. On December 19, A.I. Rykov, one of the most senior members of the Party, who had earlier sided with Stalin against Trotsky, was removed from his post as President of the Council of People's Commissars and replaced by Vyacheslav Molotov, a devoted Stalinist. Within three months the trial of three officials accused of conspiring to overthrow the Soviet Government and put the 'Mensheviks' in power opened in Moscow. The 'machinations of the accused', declared the Attorney-General, N.B. Krylenko, had caused 'great damage to the Soviet economic system, but they had no support among the masses of the people'. The evidence was non-existent, but the ten-year prison sentences were real, and the deterrent effect considerable.

In the United States, following the stock market crash of October 1929, there had been 22,109 business failures. President Hoover was hopeful, however, that the economy would recover, and had brought together business and industrial leaders to inject confidence, and also Federal money, into their endeavours. For the first four months of 1930 the economy seemed to steady, and there was even some recovery; by April 1930 the steel mills that had been so hard hit six months before had risen from 40 to 80 per cent of their capacity.

In June, however, when it became clear that the number of those out of work was still rising, and that more and more small businesses were unable to find markets for their products in the general depression, there was another crash. By the end of the year the number of businesses that had failed – 26,355 – exceeded that of the previous year. The number of bank failures was multiplied threefold: in 1930 it was 1,326. It was also estimated that the number of people without paid work was between two to three million (the Department of Labour's estimate) and 5,300,000 (the American Federation of Labour's estimate). The population of the United States was 122 million.

A fall in the price of grain made it impossible for farmers to make profits. Nature also played its part in the downward spiral of confidence and the spread of distress, with severe flooding on the lower Mississippi and a severe drought spreading westward from the Pacific Coast, destroying crops and driving many small farmers to bankruptcy and penury. In cities, 'bread lines' became a familiar and distressing sight. In rural areas, food riots took place as farmers and their families looted village food shops and demonstrated against the local authorities.

Congress passed emergency measures of food relief, and the American Red Cross, which a few years earlier had been at the forefront of sending help to the famine areas in Russia, undertook to feed three quarters of a million people. But the economic decline was not evenly distributed or universal. Although wages fell steadily throughout the year, savings increased, reaching a record level in October. Two products reported a considerable increase in sales in 1930: soap and chewing gum. Manufacturers of refrigerators sold 25 per cent more than in their 'boom year' of 1929.

Economists and statisticians took heart at these two facts, believing that the American people had the numbers and the resources to pull out of the depression by strength of character and national pride. The award of the Nobel Peace Prize to Frank B. Kellogg – who had become a justice at the World Court at The Hague – for his success in having negotiated the Paris Treaty for the 'outlawry of war' was a reminder, too, of the place the United States had in the world, despite the continuing official policy of isolation. Only the vehemently isolationist Chicago *Tribune* pointed out the irony that the prize for the outlawing of war was given in a year in which 'Belgium was increasing its fortifications against Germany, France is fortifying every inch of its frontier towards Italy, and Mussolini is feeding tonic to the eagles of war'.

In Florence, on May 18, after praising the 'stern and warlike face of Fascist Italy', Mussolini told his audience that although 'words are beautiful things, rifles, machine-guns, ships, aeroplanes and cannon are still more beautiful'. Mussolini was also enhancing his dictatorship. That year many Italian Communists were arrested, tried and imprisoned. Two Italians who distributed a clandestine newspaper calling for a coalition of all the non-Communist parties to oppose Fascism were sentenced to fifteen years' imprisonment – two years longer than Mussolini's regime was to last.

In Italy in 1930, an earthquake killed 2,000 people. In the United States that year, 29,080 people were killed on the roads. In France, the death toll on the roads was 2,042. To protect itself against a more traditional enemy, France began the construction of the Maginot Line, a string of fortifications from the Belgian border to the Swiss Alps, hoping to keep out any future German invader. More prosaically, it was in 1930 that ready-sliced bread was first marketed, under the brand name 'Wonder Bread' – yet another advance in ease of life for millions of people.

In Germany, throughout 1931, the Nazi Party, while holding the second largest number of seats in the Reichstag, refused in the most vulgar language to take any part in any coalition government. The only terms on which the Party would agree to enter government was if Hitler were appointed Chancellor.

In February German unemployment approached five million. How could the Nazi Party be kept from power? On March 4 the British Ambassador, Sir Horace Rumbold, argued in a secret despatch to London that Britain's only chance of averting a Nazi triumph was to support Dr Brüning and to enable him to remain Chancellor. The only way of supporting Brüning, he wrote, was to give Germany economic help, to come to an arrangement, possibly a moratorium, on reparations, or to organize some international credit operation on Germany's behalf.

Under Brüning's government, clandestine rearmament and military training continued without pause. Work by German engineers on the manufacture of tanks, specifically forbidden by the Versailles Treaty, was carried out secretly, not only in the Soviet Union, under Stalin's benign eye, but in Sweden, whose arms manufacturers were glad to turn any amount of profit, large or small. Over several months, the British Military Attaché, Colonel James Marshall-Cornwall, had collected evidence of a number of infringements of the military restrictions. He estimated that there were about 7,000 soldiers in excess of those allowed by treaty undergoing training in military depots. He had been shown photographs of an armoured motor-cycle combination, fitted with a machine-gun, which had already been constructed in Germany.

Hitler pursued his own agenda for creating the unity of hatred. That year, the SS – Hitler's personal bodyguard – which had already been enlarged by Heinrich Himmler as a 'protection squad' that could initiate violence in the streets, set up its own Intelligence Service, the Sicherheitsdienst, or SD, headed by Reinhard Heydrich, to keep a close watch on dissenters inside the Nazi Party.

In March 1931 Brüning took a sudden initiative in foreign policy which aroused immediate antagonism in France and deep suspicion in England. On March 19 it was announced that Germany and Austria intended to form a Customs Union. On the following day the French, Czechoslovak and British Governments protested, the British Government warning Austria that such a union might be a direct breach of Article 88 of the Treaty of Saint-Germain, whereby Austria agreed not to commit any act 'which might directly or indirectly or by any means whatsoever compromise her independence'. The German Government insisted that the agreement had no political significance; it was no more than the first step in the creation of a free trade area, which other nations were welcome to join. The British Government was not impressed by this line of argument. If the German aim was a wider economic plan, it asked, why had this not been mentioned to some of the other nations who might be asked to participate?

Winston Churchill, then in opposition to the Labour government of Ramsay MacDonald, was not averse to the proposed Customs Union. If it were to be a strictly economic union, he wrote in an American newspaper article, it might help to control the new extremism in Germany. If it were to be seen, by the mass of ordinary Germans, as a success for Brüning's foreign policy, it would have an important sequel by robbing 'the much more dangerous Hitler movement of its mainspring'. Churchill went on to ask his readers: 'Will not the mastery of Hitlerism by the constitutional forces in Germany be a real factor in the immediate peace of Europe?'

Churchill's reasoning did not prevail. In protest against the Customs Union, the French Government withdrew its considerable financial deposits from the Austrian Creditanstalt bank. This bank was already, at the request of the Austrian Government, trying to bolster up another of Austria's banking institutions. With the sudden withdrawal of French funds, it was on the verge of collapse, and on May 11 it notified the Austrian Government that it could no longer meet its obligations. The effect in Vienna was as devastating as Black Thursday had been in New York two years earlier. First Austria, then in rapid succession Germany and Hungary, were plunged into a banking crisis which left millions of small investors penniless.

Britain also suffered from the collapse of the central European banking system, so much so that the Labour government was forced to impose drastic measures, including cuts in unemployment benefits, that were unacceptable to the Socialist idealists. The result was a political crisis, and the formation, on August 24, of a National Government, still led by Ramsay MacDonald, but with the Conservatives forming the largest grouping in his Cabinet. When a General Election was held the Conservatives were returned as by far the largest Party. For the sake of national economic stability they agreed that the National Government should remain in place, with MacDonald as Prime Minister, but it was a Conservative victory.

The reduction of unemployment benefit, a sign that the new National Government was prepared to be ruthless in putting its finances in order, led to the United States advancing financial credit to the Bank of England. This staved off the possibility of national bankruptcy. Similar American economic help in 1941 was to carry Britain over a grave war emergency. Fifteen years later, during the Suez crisis of 1956, when American economic aid was deliberately withdrawn in protest against Britain's action, a major British military initiative collapsed overnight.

In Germany, Brüning had continued to rule by emergency decree since the elections the previous September. The greatest fear of a majority of the deputies, that the Nazis would come to power, gave him considerable strength. The Social Democrats, despite their deep disagreement on social policy with Brüning's Centre Party, supported him in order to keep the government in office and exclude the Nazis. But whereas, in the previous year's general election, the Nazi Party

had secured 18 per cent of the total vote, in the local elections held
in 1931 it secured a substantially higher share of the poll: 37.4 per
cent at Oldenburg in May, and 37.1 per cent in Hesse six months
later. The total suspension of reparations for a year, and a suspension
of all Germany's foreign debts for six months, was ignored by Nazi
propagandists. Racism was their main card. That September, on the
eve of the Jewish New Year, squads of young Brownshirts attacked
Jews as they were returning from synagogue. One eyewitness recorded
how, in one incident, 'while three youths beat an elderly gentleman
with their fists and rubber truncheons, five other young men stood
round to protect them'. This scene, the strong helping the strong to
attack the weak, had become a Nazi trademark. So too was the
deliberate choice of a holy day in the Jewish calendar, or a place of
worship, for anti-Jewish violence. Fifty synagogues were desecrated
in 1931 throughout Germany, and several thousand tombstones
broken or scrawled with anti-Semitic graffiti in cemeteries all over
the German Republic.

By the end of the year, the number of unemployed in Germany
had risen to five and a half million, and unemployment relief was
falling to below subsistence level. But Hitler reiterated on every
public platform that he had no intention of coming to power by
force. He would, he said, reach his goal through the democratic
system he so despised. He would, he insisted, wait – as indeed he
did wait – until summoned by the President to take on the duties
of Chancellor.

Mussolini had turned to overseas adventure to unite a nation in
patriotic zeal. At the beginning of 1931, Italian troops captured the
Kufra Oasis in Libya, driving the Senussi Muslim tribesmen into the
desert. The hoisting of the Italian flag over the Senussi stronghold
caused enthusiasm throughout Italy. In September, Italy captured
the Senussi leader who had been their most feared opponent, and
hanged him publicly.

While Mussolini was consolidating his imperial control in North
Africa, the British Empire was facing a crisis in India. Gandhi had
been allowed out of prison by the Viceroy, Lord Irwin, in return for
calling a halt to civil disobedience by his followers. On February 17,

the two men held the first of eight meetings, and on the morning of March 5 they announced the conclusion of the Delhi Pact – also known as the Gandhi-Irwin Pact. Gandhi agreed that the boycott of British goods 'as a political weapon' would end, as would civil disobedience in all its forms. Congress would send representatives to London to a Round Table Conference to discuss the future of India. Britain would retain 'safeguards' in the areas of defence, foreign affairs, India's overseas debts and the interest of the minorities, including the Depressed Classes – the Untouchables. But throughout his discussions with the Viceroy, Gandhi was adamant that India must have the right to ultimate withdrawal from the British Empire.

Under the Gandhi-Irwin pact the Government of India agreed to release all Indians arrested as a result of previous non-co-operation and disobedience, to remit all fines, and to return all confiscated property. One phrase in the agreement – 'it has been agreed that' – gave Gandhi the status, not of a supplicant but of an equal negotiator. But the expectations raised that the pact would somehow prove a panacea to all ills were dissipated somewhat when Irwin rejected pleas for the commutation of the death sentence passed on three men for the murder of a police officer in Lahore three years earlier. When Hindus in Cawnpore called a strike in sympathy for the condemned men, Muslims refused to join the strike. Riots broke out on March 24, with murder, arson and looting rampant. By the time the riots had been put down by the police, 300 Hindus and Muslims were dead. Four months later further Hindu-Muslim riots broke out in Kashmir. In Bengal, terrorist actions against the British grew in intensity. Three British officials were shot dead on April 7, and the District Magistrate of Midnapore on the following day. A judge was murdered, as he sat in court, on July 27. Later in the year a District Magistrate was killed by two Indian girl students as he sat in his bungalow. Two other civilians and two Indian police inspectors, were also killed. In August, the standard of revolt was raised in the North-West Frontier Province by Abdul Ghaffar Khan, leader of the Muslim 'Red Shirt' Army. Abdul Ghaffar Khan was one of the political prisoners who had been released from prison under the Gandhi-Irwin Pact. He at once demanded full independence for the province. Lord Irwin's successor as Viceroy, Lord Willingdon, declared the Red Shirts an illegal organization, and Abdul Ghaffar and 200 of his followers were arrested.

The Round Table Conference in London, which Gandhi attended, opened on September 8. When it ended on December 1, he intimated that the Indian national movement and the British Government had come to a parting of the ways, and that non-violent civil disobedience might soon be revived. Returning by sea to India, he was met at Bombay on December 28 by an enormous demonstration of welcome. In a speech in Calcutta two days later, the new Viceroy warned both Congress and the Bengali terrorists that the government would meet their challenge to its authority 'by resolute determination'. The 150,000 British officials in India were confident that they could rule, and rule with justice, their 353 million Indian subjects.

The United States was not in a strong position to give a lead in world affairs in 1931. For three years her economy had been in disarray. Bank failures were still frequent, millions of people had their savings wiped out, and the number of unemployed reached seven million. Destitution was widespread. Throughout the country the drill halls used by the National Guard for territorial training were turned into dormitories for homeless men and women, even for whole families. At baseball games, appeals were made and collections taken up for the unemployed. Above the skyscrapers of New York a loudspeaker system fitted to an airship called upon the citizens below to remember that they had jobs, and urged them to remember those less fortunate, asking them: 'Give until it hurts.'

The spread of crime led to lists being published of the most violent cities: Memphis, Tennessee, came first with nearly sixty murders for every 100,000 citizens. In Chicago the equivalent figure was fourteen, in New York only seven. When Chicago launched a city-wide campaign against crime, Al 'Scarface' Capone was sent to prison for eleven years for 'evading his income tax payments'. His real crime was to have been chief of the 'racketeers' who exploited Prohibition to make – or extort – a fortune in the illicit alcohol trade. That year, seventy 'gangsters' were killed in Chicago: twenty-nine by police, twenty-six by citizens, five by watchmen and ten in gang warfare.

But by far the highest loss of life in the United States in 1931 came from road accidents, when 34,000 Americans were killed, only slightly fewer than the number of American soldiers killed on the Western Front in two years of fighting.

The economic distress led the Democrats to look for someone who could challenge the Republicans in the presidential election of the following year. They chose Franklin D. Roosevelt, the Governor of New York State, who had expressed his view that it was 'time for the country to become fairly radical for at least one generation', because, he added: 'History shows that where this occurs occasionally, nations are saved from revolutions.' In New York, where economic distress was such that revolution, or at least serious social unrest, might seem a possibility, Roosevelt created a Temporary Emergency Relief Administration to give local authorities the funds to find work and relief for the unemployed. Almost one in ten families in New York State were on relief. Roosevelt also encouraged a 'back-to-the-land' movement, whereby families could avert starvation, and even earn a small livelihood, as farmers and cultivators.

In China, where Cantonese separatists had challenged Chiang Kai-shek's authority within the Kuomintang, he was both defending himself against them and pursuing his former allies, the Communists. For ten days, Communist forces managed to hold the city of Changsha, establishing a Communist government. When the Kuomintang re-entered Changsha, Mao Tse-tung's wife and younger sister were among those executed. Within a period of twelve months, Chiang Kai-shek launched three 'Encirclement Campaigns' against the Communists, but largely as a result of the guerrilla tactics devised by Mao Tse-tung – and criticized by the Communist Party's Central Executive Committee, which wanted its troops to fight in pitched battles in direct confrontation with the enemy – Chiang Kai-shek's forces were unable to break the pattern of revolt. The guerrilla principles Mao adopted enabled small Communist armies to survive against the far larger armies sent to destroy them. One principle was concealment, another was striking at the enemy at its weakest point, a third was the strategy of 'luring the enemy' deep into the base area. Even so, the Kuomintang were preparing for an advance into the heartland of Mao Tse-tung's self-declared Chinese Soviet Republic when news came to Kuomintang and Communist alike, on September 18, that Japan had invaded Manchuria.

A quarter of a century earlier the Japanese had battled with Russia for this same region. In the face of the Japanese action, the rival Chinese nationalist factions recognized that they must give up their quarrel, and unite to defend the soil of China. Within the Kuomintang, supreme power was restored to Chiang Kai-shek, but the Cantonese rebels were given a predominant part in his administration.

On September 18 Japanese forces attacked Mukden, overrunning the Chinese army barrack, the arsenal and the aerodrome. A Japanese-controlled administration was then set up; Japan had effectively annexed a Manchurian city. Demands by the Nanking Government that Japan evacuate Mukden were ignored. The Japanese insisted that they had no territorial designs on China, but stressed that the rights of the Japanese civilians in Manchuria had to be protected. Those rights had not in fact been violated, but Japanese troops remained in Mukden, while the Japanese worked to encourage a separatist movement among the local Chinese. When the League of Nations, asked to do so by China, offered to mediate, Japan rejected mediation, and soon renewed its advance deeper into Manchuria, an area one fourth the size of China.

The fighting between China and Japan in Manchuria had taken the pressure off the Chinese Communists. On November 7, at the opening of the First All-China Soviet Congress, the delegates proclaimed the Chinese Soviet Republic. A Council of People's Commissars was also established, of which Mao Tse-tung was chairman, but with circumscribed powers. Control over the Red Army passed to Chou En-lai, who more cautiously rejected Mao's plans to link up the various forces fighting the Kuomintang in different areas into a solid geographic whole.

A natural disaster overshadowed these political manoeuvres. No one knew how many tens of thousands of Chinese – perhaps hundreds of thousands, possibly a million – were drowned that year during floods which turned the province of Hupeh into a lake the size of Scotland. They were the worst floods in China in living memory.

Tens of millions of people lost their homes, and were destitute and without food. Large quantities of wheat were sent from Canada and the United States, but these were not a gift: the Chinese Government had to agree to pay the market price for them, payment to be spread over five years.

In British India, on 4 January 1932, the Indian National Congress voted to revive civil disobedience, calling on the Indian people to refuse to obey British laws, and to resist, without violence, all British orders. Gandhi was arrested. Boycotts and picketing spread. The trade of Bombay was brought to a virtual halt by the declaration of *hartals* – days of strike and mourning. By the end of the year, 66,000 Indians had been imprisoned, including 610 women. From prison, Gandhi spoke of the inevitable end of British rule as a result of the will of the Indian people.

Presidential elections were held in Germany on March 31. There were three candidates, eighty-five-year-old Field Marshal Hindenburg – the incumbent President – Ernst Thaelmann the Communist candidate, and Hitler. In the final ballot, held on April 10, the Marshal won 19,000,000 votes and the former corporal more than 13,000,000. Thaelmann secured less than 4,000,000. Hitler's share of the poll was 37 per cent. Following the election of President, Dr Brüning was replaced as Chancellor by Count Franz von Papen. Although the Nazi leaders were not invited to join the new government, von Papen hoped that he could remain in power for several years with Hitler's tacit support. In local elections the Nazi Party continued to do well, often winning up to 40 per cent of the vote.

Von Papen was an aristocrat and an extreme right-wing member of the Centre Party. He had never been a member of the Reichstag or held elected office. On becoming Chancellor he resigned from the Centre Party. He would rule as an individual, he said, not as a Party adherent; his aim was a 'combination of all national forces'. He then dissolved the Reichstag, knowing he would be unable to command a majority, and so dispensed with parliamentary rule altogether. He then reversed Brüning's edict dissolving the Nazi Brownshirts, who were once more free to terrorize the streets. Bavaria and Baden both insisted on maintaining the ban, but von Papen, using the Emergency

Decree system introduced by Brüning, forced them to allow Nazi militias to operate legally within their jurisdictions.

That summer, in Prussia alone, seventy-two people were killed in street violence within two months. On June 19, in the provincial elections at Hesse, the Nazi Party vote increased from 37 to 44 per cent, making it the largest Party in the province. Street violence continued. Von Papen, alarmed at the prospect of civil war, issued a Terror Emergency Decree which authorized special courts to be set up to try political offences. In Silesia, five Nazis were condemned to death for killing a Communist workman.

An international conference on reparations opened at Lausanne on June 16. The anarchic situation inside Germany was in the minds of all the participants. The aim of the conference was to bring back stability in Germany by reducing Germany's remaining reparations liability to an absolute minimum. On July 9 the conference accepted everything Germans had asked for. The only reparations that were retained were a final and nominal demand for a mere 3,000 Marks. Commenting on Germany's rising inflation, Hitler mocked that those 3,000 Marks would be worth only 3 Marks — a few pennies — in a few months' time. It was too late for the ending of reparations to help the moderate elements in Germany. In the streets, Nazi Brownshirts continued to demand Germany's release from the 'shackles' of Versailles. When a General Election was set for the end of July, Hitler flew by aeroplane to up to ten different cities in a day, speaking at each and then flying to the next.

The election was held on July 31. The Nazi Party won 230 seats, an increase of sixty-three. The Social Democrats secured 133, a decrease of ten. The Communists raised their number of seats, but only to eighty-nine. While still not able to form an absolute majority in the Reichstag, the Nazi Party was by far the largest, with 37.1 per cent of the total poll. Von Papen remained Chancellor and declined to invite Hitler to join his government. Hitler's reaction to his exclusion from power was to intensify the terror in the streets. Writing to London on August 4, the British Ambassador to Germany, Sir Horace Rumbold, described how in the East Prussian capital Königsberg 'prominent Socialists and Communists were surprised at night and murdered in their beds or shot down at the doors of their houses.

The windows of shops owned by Jews were smashed and their contents looted.'

On August 13, bowing to the force of terror, von Papen received Hitler in the Chancellery and offered him the post of Vice-Chancellor. Hitler refused. His aim, he said, was the Chancellorship, nothing less. As the 'idol' of thirteen million voters he must, he insisted, have 'the same degree of power' as had been granted Mussolini after – in fact, before – the march on Rome. Hitler added: 'I consider it my duty to mow down the Marxists.' He then returned to his hotel. Later that afternoon he was invited by Hindenburg to the Presidential Palace. The interview lasted only fifteen minutes, during which time Hindenburg rebuked Hitler for not keeping the promises of 'toleration and co-operation' he had earlier made to the government. After Hitler left the room, Hindenburg told his State Secretary: 'That man for a Chancellor? I'll make him a postmaster, and he can lick the stamps with my head on them.'

The Nazi Brownshirts continued unhindered in their work of violence and terror. On September 29, at the start of the Jewish New Year, several thousand Nazis converged on the Kurfürstendamm, the main street of Berlin's West End, attacking any Jews they saw and knocking them to the ground. As they did so, they cried out with glee the Nazi slogan 'Perish Judah!' In an attempt to show how patriotic the Jews of Germany had been, the Reich Association of Jewish Front-Line Soldiers published a memorial volume giving the names of more than 12,000 Jewish soldiers who had been killed in action in the First World War. To stress the significance of this Jewish contribution to the German war effort, the first copy was presented to Hindenburg on October 2, the President's eighty-fifth birthday.

Germany had become a focal point of world attention, but what had seemed the inevitable advance of the Nazi Party to power was challenged in new elections in November 1932, when the Nazi share of the vote fell from 37.1 per cent to 33.1 per cent, and its seats in the Reichstag from 230 to 197. They were still a formidable popular and parliamentary force, but it seemed their influence was on the wane. The Communists increased their seats from 89 to 100. The Social Democrat representation fell from 133 to 121. Despite relief in liberal and democratic circles that the Nazi Party had fallen back, it remained the largest Party in the Reichstag.

Von Papen offered to bring Hitler into his new government with several Ministries for Nazi Party members, and – as he had been offered three months earlier – the Vice-Chancellorship for himself. Hitler reiterated that he wanted the Chancellorship or nothing. When Von Papen put this to Hindenburg, and offered to make way for Hitler as Chancellor, Hindenburg refused. Von Papen, unable to command a majority in the Reichstag, resigned.

Hindenburg had no choice but to ask the leader of the largest Party in the Reichstag to try to form a government. This was Hitler's chance. He could take the post of Chancellor and form a power-sharing coalition with the other right-wing and centre parties. But his aim was complete power, not sharing power with others, even under his Chancellorship. He would only form a government, he told Hindenburg, if he was authorized to form a 'presidential Cabinet', whose powers would derive not from the will or votes of parliament but from the Presidency. He would agree to rule Germany, he said, only if he could rule without the Reichstag.

Hindenburg ended his negotiations with Hitler and turned to a political outsider, General von Schleicher, who had been Minister of Defence under Brüning, and asked him to take over the Chancellorship, ruling as best he could with a divided and hostile Reichstag. Von Schleicher accepted, and tried to win the confidence of the political Parties. 'I am a heretic enough', he said in a radio broadcast on December 15, 'to confess I am an adherent neither of capitalism nor of Socialism. My programme consists of a single point – to create employment.'

By the end of 1932 there were 6,000,000 unemployed in Germany. Von Schleicher hoped to create work for them by means of a massive State building programme of roads, canals and railways. He also wanted to encourage the return of industrial workers to the land. Both of these were relatively long-term projects, especially land resettlement and the creation of a rural labour market to absorb the urban unemployed.

In Austria, 'Hitlerites', as they were called, made their first appearance that year, demanding union with Germany and embarking on violent street demonstrations. On April 24, in the elections for the provincial Diets, they made large gains, and in the Vienna Diet obtained fifteen seats where previously they had none. Their first appearance in the Diet was marked by a violent pro-Nazi demonstration in the streets. But the balance of power in the Diets, as in the national parliament, lay firmly with the nationalist Heimwehr, and the Clerical and Social-ist deputies, and on May 20, after a two-week government crisis, an administration was formed by Dr Engelbert Dollfuss, a leading member of the Clerical Party, who brought two strong Heimwehr supporters into his Cabinet. The Hitlerites, without any place in the national parliament or the government, continued their activities in the streets. An anti-Semitic protest march at Vienna University on May 30 forced the university to close for a week. In search of 'wealthy Jews', a Hitlerite gang entered the International Country Club in Vienna, injuring not only Jews and other Austrians, but also the diplomats of four nations. International protests followed but the Hitlerites were not deterred. On October 16 they marched through one of the Socialist quarters of Vienna, attacking the Socialist sec-retariat. When the Socialists unexpectedly defended the building by force, two Hitlerites were killed.

In the United States, the Depression continued, and unemployment reached its highest level, as many as 11,000,000 out of work, out of a total work force of 58,000,000. As work could not be found, 'Barter Exchanges' were organized, where, in more than 500 communities, members who enrolled would offer to work in exchange for food, clothing or shelter. Even the professional classes were drawn in. Doctors accepted chickens or eggs for their services. Some Barter Exchanges issued their own banknote-style 'scrip' to facilitate the work-for-goods exchange system.

As the distress continued, First World War veterans, forming themselves into an America Legion, demanded an immediate cash bonus. President Hoover resisted what he feared would be a dangerous inflationary move, the equivalent to printing a vast amount of money without security. The veterans converged on Washington, 20,000 ex-soldiers in all, many of them with their wives and children. They called themselves the Bonus Expeditionary Force. Living in tents and shacks, they announced they would not move from Washington until their demand was met. On June 14 they crowded into the Capitol building and persuaded Congress, amid rousing cheers, to vote in favour of the bonus. When the Senate rejected this three days later, there was disorder in the streets which continued for several days. On July 28, Hoover called out the troops. The tent camps were broken up and burned, and the marchers expelled by force from the Capitol.

The Democrats were working with great energy to produce a programme of their own. On July 1, Franklin Roosevelt was nominated as the Democratic presidential candidate. The Democrats, he said, would champion the 'forgotten man at the bottom of the economic pyramid'. He would replace the high protective tariff, which made it difficult for America to sell its goods overseas, with commercial treaties to create a reciprocal reduction in trade barriers, and lead to the freer and faster flow of goods in both directions. He would reduce the money owed by farmers in mortgages and loans. He would decentralize industry, bringing industrial production, and with it greater employment and prosperity, to towns and areas outside the industrial belts. He wanted the Federal Government to enter the electric power industry, and to undertake four major Federal projects to bring prosperity and employment to remote and neglected areas. 'Each one of these,' he said, 'in each of the four quarters of the United States, will be for ever a national yardstick to prevent extortion against the public, and to encourage the wider use of that servant of the people – electric power.'

Roosevelt also pointed the way forward to a fairer society. In San Francisco he declared: 'Every man has a right to life, and this means that he also has a right to make a comfortable living. He may by sloth or crime decline to exercise that right; but it may not be denied him. Every man has a right to his own property; which means a right to be assured, to the fullest extent attainable, in the safety of his savings.'

The election, held on November 8, produced a Democratic landslide, with Roosevelt carrying forty-two States as against six for Hoover. Twenty-two million votes were cast for Roosevelt, fifteen million for Hoover. The nation and the world had then to wait until 4 March 1933 before Roosevelt's inauguration, and for his presentation of a programme to revive America's fortunes.

In the Far East, the Japanese began a systematic advance through Manchuria, despite a strong protest by the United States. Elections in Japan had given the war party a clear victory – 303 seats against 146 – and on February 18 the Japanese Government established a Manchurian Republic. Entirely independent of China, it was to be known as Manchukuo. To rule it, the former Chinese boy emperor Pu Yi, who had been deposed in 1922, was made Chief Executive. He was twenty-six years old. Later the Japanese declared him 'Hereditary Emperor of Manchukuo'.

Anti-Japanese demonstrations broke out in Shanghai. Japanese warships were despatched to protect the 30,000 Japanese living there, and a Japanese expeditionary force of 12,000 men landed and advanced towards the area where the Japanese were living. When the Japanese military commander, General Ueda, issued an ultimatum to the Chinese to let his troops enter Shanghai, it was rejected. He then ordered his troops forward, helped by the Japanese air force, which bombed the Chinese quarter of the city. Hundreds of Chinese were killed before a cease-fire was declared, as a result of British and other European pressure. A truce was signed on March 3, and fighting ceased. Two months later the Japanese troops withdrew from Shanghai. But when Japan transferred the customs receipts of the Manchurian ports to the Government of Manchukuo, it deprived China of an important annual source of revenue.

Inside the Soviet Union, the continuing forcible collectivization of agriculture had led to acute peasant hardship, mass deportations, and a collapse of rural productivity. At the meeting of the Communist Party Central Committee in October, sharp criticisms of the collective farm system were put forward, and an agitation to give up collectivization began. Not only did collectivization continue, however, but those who fell below the targets set by Moscow were put on trial, accused of sabotage and shot. Yet the peasants could not produce the amounts demanded of them, however hard they tried: the total amount of grain deliveries demanded from them in 1932 exceeded the total crop. The delivery of whatever grain had been harvested was so ruthlessly enforced that starvation became widespread. That winter several millions of Russians died of starvation.

In the previous famine after the Bolsheviks came to power, appeals had been launched by the Soviet regime for help from the capitalist world, which had responded with massive aid, supervised by the League of Nations and the Red Cross. For this second famine, which was on a much larger scale, no such appeal was made. Rumours of hunger were denied. When, at a closed and secret meeting in Moscow, the Secretary of the Kharkov Provincial Committee spoke of the scale and horror of the famine, Stalin intervened personally to belittle him. 'We have been told that you, Comrade Terekhov, are a good speaker,' Stalin said. 'It seems that you are a good storyteller, you've made up such a fable about famine, thinking to frighten us, but it won't work. Wouldn't it be better for you to leave your post of provincial committee secretary and the Ukraine Central Committee, and join the Writers' Union? Then you can write your fables and fools will read them.'

'You live in interesting times,' Paul Valéry told a graduating class in Paris on 13 July 1932. 'Interesting times are always enigmatic times that promise no rest, no prosperity or continuity or security,' and he added: 'Never has humanity joined so much power and so much disarray, so much anxiety and so many playthings, so much knowledge and so much uncertainty.'

CHAPTER SIX

Towards the Abyss
1933—39

ON 30 JANUARY 1933 Hitler became Chancellor of Germany, invited to do so by the President, Marshal Hindenburg, according to constitutional procedures. The Nazi Brownshirts, for so many months the terror of the streets, marched everywhere in triumph with their cries of 'Germany awake', 'Down with the Jews' and 'Heil Hitler!'

Hitler acted quickly to extinguish democracy in Germany, and to promote racism. An Emergency Decree, passed by the Reichstag on February 5, expropriated all Communist Party buildings and printing presses, and closed down all pacifist organizations. Brownshirts attacked trade union buildings, and beat up political opponents in the streets.

On February 27, fire broke out inside the Reichstag building. Even before the blaze had been extinguished, and before any guilt could be established — the culprit was a deranged Dutchman with no political leanings — Hitler demanded new rules legalizing arbitrary imprisonment without warrant or trial. Elections were held on March 5. Although the Nazi vote increased to more than seventeen million, it was still not a majority of the forty million electors. In a move only possible because of the strength of Brownshirt terror in the streets, the eighty-one newly elected Communist deputies were told they would not be invited to the opening of the Reichstag.

Beginning on March 9, terror found a hidden base behind barbed wire. Starting on that day the SS sent thousands of critics of the regime, including Communists, Social Democrats, Trade Unionists and Jews of all backgrounds, to a so-called 'concentration camp' set up in Dachau, near Munich, run by the one of the most brutal SS platoons in Bavaria.

On March 23, at the opening of the Reichstag in its new Berlin quarters, the Kroll Opera House, Hitler, wearing a Brownshirt uniform, promised to end unemployment and pursue peace with France and Britain – even with the Soviet Union. To do this, he said, he needed a special law to be enacted as soon as possible. It was an Enabling Law far more drastic than the one through which Brüning had ruled. Hitler's law would enable the government to pass any legislation it chose, without the need for a parliamentary majority.

When Hitler submitted his Bill, the Social Democrats opposed it. The Centre Party, with its seventy-three seats, supported it. As a result the Bill passed. Those seventy-three votes gave Hitler the power he wanted. An era of German elections and parliamentary life was over. An era of dictatorship and terror had begun.

The first change Hitler instituted after passing the Enabling Bill was to remove all Jews from their positions in the civil service and in the teaching professions. Then, in the last week of March the Nazi Party announced an imminent and open-ended Nazi boycott of Jewish shops. The proposed boycott was given considerable publicity outside Germany. In protest, on March 27 a mass rally in New York threatened a counter-boycott of all German-made goods unless the anti-Jewish boycott was called off. The Nazi leaders bowed to the threat of economic reprisals and limited themselves to a single, one-day, boycott of all Jewish-owned shops, cafés and businesses.

The boycott began at ten in the morning on Saturday, April 1. Brownshirts, standing outside Jewish-owned shops, carried placards urging 'Germans' not to enter. A week later the German Government ordered the immediate dismissal of all civil servants 'not of Aryan descent'. Jewish schoolteachers, university lecturers and professors, being civil servants, were all dismissed. By giving German non-Jews the status of 'Aryan' – an imaginary ethnic concept based upon spurious scientific theories of racial purity – Hitler formally divided German citizens into two groups.

To terrorize all political opponents, concentration camps were set up at Esterwegen and Sachsenhausen, in addition to Dachau.

Daily beatings and harsh treatment were the rule. By the beginning of April 1933, there were a thousand Germans, of whom a hundred were Jews, being held at Dachau without warrant or trial. On April 26 one of the main instruments of State control in the German Republic, the Geheime Staatspolizei, or Secret State Police, was taken over by the Nazi Party. Known as the Gestapo, it was given the power to shadow, arrest, interrogate and intern, without reference to any other State authority. The apparatus of dictatorship was complete.

On March 3, thirty-three days after Hitler came to power in Germany, Franklin Roosevelt was inaugurated as President of the United States. In his inaugural address he spoke with ringing words of hope that were to mark out the mood and philosophy of his Presidency, telling the nation: 'So, first of all, let me assert my firm belief that the only thing we have to fear is fear itself – nameless, unreasoning, unjustified terror which paralyses needed efforts to convert retreat into advance.'

On March 9, Congress passed an Emergency Banking Act, giving Roosevelt the power to reopen banks on the condition that they proved sound. Three days later he broadcast to the American people his first 'fireside chat'. The restoration of confidence was his goal, and it succeeded. The special session of Congress that followed Roosevelt's inaugural produced more legislation than any other comparative period in American history. This was the beginning of the New Deal, whereby the United States would recover not only its economic power, its industrial productivity and its agricultural strength, but its confidence, energy and creativity.

In the Soviet Union, Stalin had ordered the construction of a canal linking the Baltic Sea and the White Sea. The project was placed under the authority of the secret police – the OGPU, later the KGB – who provided the labour needed from hundreds of prisons and labour camps under its jurisdiction. Among the prisoners were Communists who had never knowingly acted against the Soviet State. They had been selected for imprisonment solely to deter any form of dissent among those left behind. As many as 300,000 slave labourers worked on the construction of the White Sea–Baltic Canal at any one time. An estimated 200,000 died before the canal was completed.

That April a public manifestation of Soviet power took place, for the world to witness. Starting on April 12, an eight-day trial was staged in Moscow, accusing British and Russian engineers of sabotage. Their task had been to maintain various power stations in the Soviet Union. Stalin used the trial, and the guilty verdicts, to assert the need to combat 'wrecking and espionage' by the tightening of State control over every aspect of national life.

The tyranny within Germany grew with every day. On May 2 the buildings of the Socialist Trade Unions were occupied by the Nazis, and all German trade union leaders arrested. Eight days later, all Socialist newspapers were confiscated and the assets of all Socialist organizations seized. That midnight, in the square facing the Berlin Opera House, a bonfire of books was lit, photographs of which would appear within twenty-four hours on the front pages of hundreds of newspapers around the world. They included books on philosophy and psychology, books of Communist, Socialist, democratic or humanistic outlook, books by Jews and books which failed to glorify war.

On May 16 President Roosevelt appealed to all governments to work towards a successful conclusion of the World Disarmament Conference at Geneva. On the day after this appeal, Hitler insisted that the sole purpose of the Brownshirts and the SS was 'to protect Germany against Communism'. He was supported in his disingenuous assertion by the Governments of Italy, Austria and Hungary.

The United States continued to take a lead in trying to maintain a momentum of negotiations, and to work out an acceptable formula for disarmament. Britain proposed a 'probationary period' during which a method of arms supervision would be tested, before actual disarmament began. Hitler rejected any such supervision outright. Disturbed by the implications of Hitler's reiterated call for the revision of the Treaty of Versailles, three nations of central Europe – Czechoslovakia, Yugoslavia and Roumania – under the leadership of the Czech Foreign Minister, Edouard Beneš, strengthened their existing Little Entente, creating a Permanent Council, a Secretariat and a Permanent Council: a virtual diplomatic federation.

Hitler's appeal, and that of the Nazi Party, grew: it was not restricted to Germany. On October 1, Konrad Henlein, a former German subject of the Austro-Hungarian Empire, founded a pro-Nazi movement inside Czechoslovakia. The German-speaking group he led were the Germans of the Sudetenland, who had never been part of Germany, but of Austria-Hungary. To help start Henlein's Sudeten German Party, the German Foreign Office financed his newspaper and paid his Party debts. Within a year he called his first mass meeting, to which 20,000 Sudeten Germans came.

On October 14 Hitler announced that, as Germany had been denied 'equality of rights' with regard to armaments, she was withdrawing from both the World Disarmament Conference and the League of Nations.

Inside Germany, the coalition that Hitler had formed at the beginning of the year was at an end. On July 14 a German Government decree made illegal the existence of any political party other than the Nazi Party. At the General Election held on November 12, only the Nazi Party was allowed to campaign, and the only candidates allowed were Nazi Party members. Hitler obtained 95 per cent of the votes cast. His power was absolute. There were still four million unemployed, but in the three months since he had come to power, 1,300,000 former unemployed had been given work on public work projects.

By the end of 1933 at least 100,000 Germans were being held in brutal concentration camps. It was widely known throughout Germany, and far beyond its borders, that several hundred Germans had been murdered that year. The ability of German Catholics to act as a force for moderation was undermined when Hitler negotiated a Concordat with the Pope. Under its terms the Catholic Church agreed not to carry out any political activities. In return, Hitler's Government promised not to interfere with Catholic life inside Germany.

On July 25 the German Government published a decree under which compulsory sterilization was ordered for all who were blind, deaf, deformed or suffering from mental disorders. Hitler was confident that the racism he wished to promulgate would win wide acceptance. 'Only in our own day does the significance of the laws of race and racial heredity dawn upon mankind,' he declared at Nuremberg on September 2. In a series of sermons, the Catholic Archbishop of Munich, Cardinal Michael von Faulhaber, spoke courageously against the racial policies. 'The individual must not be deprived of his own dignity,' he said, 'or be treated as a slave without rights of his own.' The Protestant Evangelical clergy publicly opposed the introduction of Nazi ideology into its ranks. The man who inspired this act of defiance was Pastor Martin Niemöller, who, as a U-boat commander during the First World War had been awarded Germany's highest decoration for bravery. But at Hitler's urging, and to Niemöller's disgust, the Protestant Church agreed to pass an ordinance whereby only those of 'Aryan descent' could be ordained priests, and under which all clergy who were married to 'non-Aryans' were dismissed.

The consolidation of Nazi power during 1933 was matched by an upsurge in emigration. By the end of 1933 more than 60,000 Germans had left Germany. At least half of these were Jews. Forty-five Jews were killed that year in Germany. Everywhere towns and villages had put up placards: 'Jews not wanted'. In some villages the names of Jewish war dead had been erased from the war memorials. By the end of the year 30,000 German Jews had left Germany and been admitted into Britain, the United States and the countries of Western Europe. A further 5,000 gained entry into Palestine. Among the first Jews to establish himself in exile was Albert Einstein. Not only was he a Jew, but in 1914 he had emerged in Berlin as one of the leading opponents of the war, an unforgivable sin in the new climate of national regeneration.

Beyond the immediate borders of Germany, Hitler's propaganda machine, directed by Dr Joseph Goebbels, stimulated pan-German feeling. Following elections in the Free City of Danzig, the Nazi Party gained control of the city's administration, its first success beyond the Versailles Treaty borders of Germany.

On July 1 the German Government carried out the first of a series of propaganda flights over Austria, to drop leaflets denouncing the Austrian Chancellor, Dr Dollfuss. In September, to prevent the Austrian Nazis trying to overthrow the government, Dollfuss assumed dictatorial powers. The activities of Austria's Nazis were centred on their call for union with Germany. To further this aim, they organized anti-Dollfuss riots in the universities. On the evening of November 5, when Dollfuss was about to speak in Klagenfurt, the Nazis cut off the electricity and plunged the city into darkness.

Hitherto the United States had refused to enter into diplomatic relations with a country which showed 'an active spirit of enmity to our institutions', but on November 17 the United States officially recognized the existence and legitimacy of the Soviet Union.

Inside the Soviet Union, the process of eliminating all opposition to Stalin's rule continued. As 1933 came to an end, more than a thousand Red Army officers and soldiers were arrested. Within a few months almost a million Communist Party members were deprived of their membership, and of the power and privilege that went with it.

In Hungary, anti-Semitic acts became a feature of 1933, with anti-Jewish demonstrations on the university campuses, where Hungarian students infected by Nazi propaganda demanded that their Jewish co-students be restricted to the benches at the back of the lecture hall. Jewish students who defended themselves against physical attack were given the same punishments by the university authorities as their attackers. In Roumania, the ultra-nationalist Iron Guard served as a focus for violent and fascist activities and anti-Semitic outrages.

In Switzerland, its long border with southern Germany offering tempting access to Nazi propaganda, all Party uniforms had been forbidden by a parliamentary vote on May 12. Among the groups to which this ban applied was the Swiss National Socialist Front, which was hostile to Jews. By the end of 1933, several thousand German Jews and other opponents of Nazism had been admitted to Switzerland as refugees.

In Iraq, several thousand Assyrian Christians were shot down in cold blood by Muslim troops. In Palestine, Arab demonstrations against Jewish land purchase were broken up by the British in several towns, but not until twenty-four Arabs and one British policeman had been killed. In the Far East, Japanese troops were driving the Chinese out of Manchuria and back to the Great Wall. In British India, the home of 255 million Hindus and 94 million Muslims, the Indian National Congress continued to demand 'home rule' as a prelude to full independence. Under Gandhi's leadership, innumerable acts of peaceful but effective civil disobedience caused havoc. The British had brought in Indians to the Viceroy's Legislative Council, but the Indian National Congress demanded an Indian presence on the Executive Council as well, where power resided. When this was refused they declared a boycott of the central legislature and took no further part in its work.

In the Dutch East Indies, thirty-four Indonesian naval mutineers were killed when the training ship they had commandeered was bombed from the air. In Morocco, sixty French troops were killed during the final phase of the 'pacification' of the tribes of the Atlas district. The tribes to the south remained uncurbed.

In the United States, President Roosevelt persevered with his New Deal designed to ensure the recovery of the American economy. In June, Roosevelt submitted to Congress the National Industrial Recovery Bill, a milestone in his measures to increase employment. The use of child labour was to be abolished. Adult hours of work were to be reduced without a reduction in wages. Minimum rates of pay were to be maintained and exceeded. The act was passed on June 16. It was, Roosevelt said, 'the most important legislation ever enacted by the American Congress', and he immediately set its provisions in train. One of his devices to increase employment was the growth of expenditure on defence, including thirty-two new warships. Money was also put up for 'public works' to be carried out in States with the highest unemployment, and for road-building and road improvement. Most ambitious of all, a new government authority was set up, the Tennessee Valley Authority (TVA) to build dams and hydro-electric plants across a region hard hit by the Depression.

The science of flight continued to make rapid strides in 1933. On July 15 an American aviator, Wiley Post, flew direct from New York to Berlin, the first aviator to do so. This was but a prelude to his complete aerial circumnavigation of the globe in just over seven days.

In France the maintenance of democracy had been a matter of continual struggle. On 6 February 1934 there was a demonstration in Paris by the right-wing Union Nationale des Combattants (the UNC), denouncing the failures of democracy. There were violent clashes with police and sixteen demonstrators were killed. On February 12 there was a general strike throughout France in protest against the killings. That same day, in Vienna, there was far greater violence when the Chancellor, Engelbert Dollfuss, leader of the Christian Socialist Party, tried to crush his principal rivals for power, the Social Democrats. Artillery and tanks were turned on the Socialist strongholds in the city. When the fighting ended, eleven of the workers' leaders were seized and hanged.

Beyond Germany's borders a debate was raging about how best to deal with the reawakened German nationalism. The French Government sought safety in armaments, and in drawing closer to the Soviet Union. The Polish Government felt that it could come to some satisfactory agreement directly with Germany, and negotiated a non-aggression treaty. The British Government wanted to secure peace by a universal reduction of arms. Inside Germany, anti-Jewish excesses continued. In his book *These Times*, the British journalist J.A. Spender wrote of 'something nasty and brutish in the German Revolution, which was worse than primitive savagery'. On May 1 the anti-Semitic magazine *Der Stürmer* produced a special fourteen-page issue in which the Jews were accused, as they had often been during the Middle Ages, of murdering Christian children in order to use their blood in making Passover bread and other 'Judaic rituals'. This was a libel on a whole people: no such rituals had ever existed. As in every province, the villages of Franconia competed during the summer of 1934 to be 'free of Jews'. On May 26 the *Frankische Tageszeitung* described the moment a few days earlier when 'the swastika flag was hoisted on the property of the last Jew to leave Hersbruck'. The newspaper was certain that other districts would soon follow this lead, 'and that the day is not now far off when the whole of Franconia will be rid of Jews, just as one day that day must dawn when throughout the whole of Germany there will no longer be one single Jew'.

Since the beginning of 1931, Hitler's private army, the SA Bownshirts, had been commanded by Captain Ernst Roehm. By the start of 1934 the SA numbered more than two million. Roehm wanted them to become the sole military arm of the regime, absorbing the regular armed forces within their structure, but for Hitler this was unacceptable. On June 30 he confronted Roehm directly, accusing him of plotting rebellion, and placed him under arrest. He was then shot.

With full control of the SA, Hitler arranged the arrest of more than a hundred and fifty SA leaders in Berlin, where they were killed by an SS firing squad. The assassinations of other suspected potential opponents began in the early hours of June 30 – the Night of the Long Knives. Among those killed was a former Chancellor, General von Schleicher, who had been in retirement since Hitler came to power a year and a half earlier: six assassins shot him down. Hitler defended the killings in a speech to the Reichstag two weeks later, warning that 'Everyone must know that in all future time, if he raises his hand to strike at the State, then certain death will be his lot.'

On August 1 a law was passed combining the offices of 'Führer and Reich Chancellor' with that of President. On the following morning, President Hindenburg died. Hitler became President and remained Chancellor. Before the day was over all German soldiers had to swear an oath of personal loyalty to 'the Führer of the German Reich and People, Adolf Hitler'.

Within a month of the Night of the Long Knives, Austrian Nazis, with the full support and encouragement of Berlin, began a campaign of terror throughout Austria. Anti-Dollfuss and pro-Nazi propaganda was broadcast daily into Austria, calling for the absorption of Austria into Germany. On July 25, in connivance with the German Government, Dollfuss was assassinated. The murder of Dollfuss was intended as the prelude to the seizure of power by the Nazis in Vienna, and the annexation of Austria by Germany. But Austrian Government forces, led by the Minister of Justice, Dr Kurt von Schuschnigg, won control of the Chancellery.

*   *   *

In the Soviet Union, a thirteen-year-old schoolboy received a cash prize for reporting that his mother was stealing grain. Theft of grain was a crime punishable by death. His mother was arrested and shot.

In China, following a short lull, the battles between the Kuomintang and the Communists resumed. After a series of defeats, Mao Tse-tung ordered a withdrawal, and on October 16 began a journey of almost 6,000 miles from their bases in the south to a safer, distant haven, somewhere beyond the reach of the Kuomintang. As they prepared to leave, the Nationalists attacked them and after five days' continuous fighting 4,000 Communist soldiers had been killed. The 'Long March' went ahead, a twelve-month ordeal that established Mao Tse-tung's leadership. When the march ended, he became Party Chairman, committed to extending to the maximum the area of China under direct Communist control.

Another remote Chinese-controlled region of Asia, Inner Mongolia, came under Japanese rule that year. At the same time, Japanese control of Korea was consolidated by the widespread arrest of Communists throughout the province. By the end of the year, twenty-two Korean Communist leaders had been brought to trial and sentenced to death. During negotiations in London at the end of 1934, Japan formally abrogated the Washington Naval Treaty. Henceforth, she would build her navy to whatever strength and scale she wished.

In London, the British Parliament legislated for Indian constitutional reform, bringing Indian politicians and civil servants into even higher positions of authority than hitherto. In response, Gandhi called off civil disobedience.

The main short-term challenge to the British and Indians alike was the challenge of nature. On the afternoon of January 15 an earthquake had struck northern India with hitherto unrecorded ferocity. In Bihar and Nepal, 10,000 people were killed. The first photographs of the disaster were flown to Britain by air for distribution to the newspapers. In August there was severe flooding in the Ganges Valley, where many villages were totally submerged. But the general economy of India was improving, and, convinced that the progress of constitutional reform would continue, Gandhi retired from the leadership of Congress. His intention was to devote himself to the improvement of the lot of the Untouchables, the poorest of Indians, despised by most Hindus, whom Gandhi called Harijans – the Children of God.

In 1914, the assassination of the Archduke Franz Ferdinand of Austria-Hungary by a Serb nationalist had precipitated the First World War. Twenty years later, on 9 October 1934, another assassination, that of King Alexander of Yugoslavia, caused a tremor of fear. The king was killed, together with the French Foreign Minister, Louis Barthou, at Marseille. His assassin was a Macedonian who had been trained by Croat extremists in Hungary. Immediately following the assassination, the Yugoslav Government ordered, as an act of retaliation, the mass expulsion of its Hungarian minority. Alexander's cousin, Prince Paul, was appointed Regent, and appealed for justice to the League of Nations. Fearing that Hungary and Yugoslavia would find themselves at war, Britain and France prevailed upon Hungary to take a conciliatory tone. Yugoslavia accepted this, and stopped the mass expulsions of Hungarians.

Hopes that the Regent might offer some long-term gesture of conciliation to the Croats were not fulfilled.

In Turkey, the process of modernization undertaken by Mustafa Kemal continued, with Kemal taking the surname Atatürk – father of the Turks. In education, not the imam and the mosque, but the schoolteacher and the schoolroom, were held up as the way forward. Higher education became a status symbol of the new Turkey: German Jewish refugees from Hitler were welcomed in, to teach in the professions.

As republican Turkey moved towards Western modernity, republican Spain moved towards civil war. Throughout 1934 the forces of Socialism and separatism sought to test their respective strengths against the centrist, Catholic-dominated government. In February common cause was made in Madrid among Socialists, Syndicalists and Communists, who co-ordinated a series of strikes. In both Catalonia and the Basque country, separatist movements demanded greater political authority. With the support of the Socialists, both Basque and Catalan separatists held mass demonstrations, which the

Prime Minister, Ricardo Samper, ordered to be broken up. In retaliation, Catalan separatists set fire to the law courts in Barcelona.

Samper's government fell, and he was succeeded by Alejandro Lerroux. The Socialists declared a general strike. There were armed attacks on police stations and army barracks. In Barcelona, Catalan independence was proclaimed. Lerroux declared martial law and in Madrid the army broke up the Socialist forces. In Barcelona the Catalan separatists surrendered or fled. But in the Asturias the miners fought on. In the first week of October the revolutionaries gained two major successes, seizing Oviedo, the capital of the region, and Gijón, its principal port.

On October 6 a Communist government was proclaimed throughout the Asturias. The Madrid government took immediate military action, much of it directed from Madrid by General Franco, a strong anti-Communist who was convinced that the workers' uprising in the Asturias had been 'deliberately prepared by agents from Moscow'. Gijón was retaken, with Franco directing operations from Madrid over the telephone. Troops of the Spanish Legion and Moorish Regulars were rushed at Franco's orders from Morocco, and entered Oviedo a week after the Communist regime had been established there. Vengeance was swift. Workers believed to have been leaders of the insurrection were arrested and shot. All local trade unions were dissolved, and Catalan autonomy suspended.

On December 1 one of Stalin's closest colleagues, Sergei Kirov, was assassinated in Leningrad. The Soviet authorities announced that the murder was the work of the disgraced former revolutionary leaders, Trotsky, Kamenev and Zinoviev. The assassin, Leonid Nikolaev, was said to have been part of a secret 'Trotskyite-Zinovievite terrorist organization'. No such organization existed. Nikolaev was shot. Those closest to Kirov were also killed, on Stalin's orders.

On the day of Kirov's murder a draconian decree amended the Soviet Criminal Code. It was done on Stalin's own initiative, without any discussion at the Politburo. The decree read: 'The investigating authorities are instructed to expedite cases of those accused of planning or carrying out terrorist acts. Judicial bodies are instructed not to delay carrying out death sentences involved in crimes of this category on the assumption of possible clemency, as the Presidium of the Central Executive Committee considers clemency in such cases to be unacceptable. Agencies of the Commissariat of Internal Affairs are instructed to carry out the death sentence on criminals in the above category as soon as possible after sentence has been pronounced.'

Within hours Kamenev and Zinoviev were among those arrested. At public meetings held across the Soviet Union demands were made for action against 'terrorists'. The personnel of the secret police was substantially increased. The public were warned that enemies of the people were lurking in every factory and collective farm, in every educational and technical institute. The preparation of public show trials intensified. From every region came accounts of enemies unmasked, continual interrogations and sentences of death.

Of the 1,225 Communist delegates at the Party Congress that February, 1,108 were arrested within a year. Most died under interrogation in prisons or slave labour camps. Of the 139 members and candidate members of the Central Committee elected at the congress, 98 were arrested and shot. Meanwhile, the murdered Kirov was elevated into a hero, his name being attached to myriad institutions and towns, including the Leningrad ballet, and main roads everywhere.

The democratic nations might not have had the means or will to oppose tyranny, but did have faith in their own way of life. On June 19 the National Archives were opened in Washington. Above its portals were inscribed in stone the proud assertion: 'This building holds in trust the records of our national life and symbolizes our faith in the performance of our national institutions.'

On 13 January 1935 the League of Nations supervised the plebiscite in the Saar, under which the inhabitants were to decide whether to be part of France or of Germany. They voted by an overwhelming majority for union with Germany. Within six weeks Nazi rule and ideology were imposed, and many liberal and left-wing Saarlanders fled to France.

In the Soviet Union, following the murder of Kirov, the year 1935 was dominated by Stalin's secret police drive to eliminate every trace of opposition, or potential opposition. Zinoviev and Kamenev, both of whom had stood at the centre of the revolutionary effort in 1917, were sentenced to death. Only a direct appeal to Stalin from Lenin's widow led to the death sentences being commuted to imprisonment. This proved a short-term respite, however, as both were shot within a few years.

The Russian Orthodox Church was another target of Stalin's hostility. In every city, ancient churches were demolished to make way for roads and parks. At the same time, Soviet Communism set itself up as the model of modernity and efficiency. Individual industrial output was increased by groups of workers providing back-up to a colleague who, as if working on his own, would then break all individual work norms. Goals were set to encourage spectacular achievements: statistics of such achievements became the focal point of daily newspaper and radio coverage and exhortation.

On 5 December 1934, Abyssinian troops on the border of Italian Somaliland had attacked an Italian frontier garrison. On the following day Italian military reinforcements drove the Abyssinians back and inflicted heavy casualties. In mid-January negotiations began at the League headquarters in Geneva. On January 29, while these talks were still in progress, another border clash took place and five Italian soldiers were killed. Within a month, Italian troops embarked for Africa. In the second week of March, all Italian men born in 1911, 1912 and 1913 were mobilized. On March 17, Abyssinia complained about this to the League, but nothing was done.

As the military build-up continued, it took considerable efforts by the League to persuade the Italians to accept League-appointed arbitrators. Italy agreed to this on May 25. But on July 7 Mussolini announced: 'There can be no turning back. Government and nation are now engaged in a conflict which we have decided to carry on to the bitter end.' On August 1 a British Member of Parliament, Colonel Josiah Wedgwood, warned: 'If one dictator cannot be stopped from attacking Abyssinia, nothing can stop another dictator from attacking Lithuania, and Memel, and Austria.' If the League of Nations failed to prevent war, Wedgwood added, 'security will leave, not only the small nations, but France, and Czechoslovakia, and Italy as well'.

The Sixteenth Assembly of the League of Nations opened in

Geneva on September 11. The British Foreign Minister, Sir Samuel Hoare, spoke forcefully of the need 'for the collective maintenance of the Covenant in its entirety, and particularly for steady and collective resistance to all acts of unprovoked aggression'. France and the Soviet Union joined in the call for decisive action in defence of Abyssinia. On September 12 the American Secretary of State, Cordell Hull, intimated that even for his country there might be a limit: 'Armed conflict in any part of the world cannot but have undesirable and adverse effects in every part of the world.'

The League Council set up a Committee of Five to prepare a report. The report, submitted on September 26, made every possible concession to Italy. Mussolini rejected these concessions. In response the League Council ordered a report to be drawn up, as a matter of urgency, about the future of Abyssinian sovereignty. On October 3, before the report could be completed, Italian troops advanced into Abyssinia on three separate fronts. The League Council, meeting in emergency session four days later, declared Italy to be the aggressor. The League Council then activated Article 16 of the League Covenant, under which sanctions could be imposed. On November 18 four sets of sanctions were put into force: an arms embargo, financial measures including an end to loans and credits, the refusal to take imports from Italy, and an embargo on the export to Italy of materials needed to make war, including oil.

For the French Prime Minister, Pierre Laval, good Franco-Italian relations were the cornerstone of his foreign policy, as a counterweight to Germany. In secret conversations in Paris, Laval persuaded his British opposite number, Sir Samuel Hoare, to support a 'peace plan' very much in Italy's interest. Abyssinia was to be partitioned and part of her territory transferred to Italy. The Hoare-Laval Pact was meant to be an entirely secret basis for a joint Franco-British approach to Italy. But it was leaked to the newspapers, and then, as it could no longer be denied, published officially in Paris. Those who supported the League's strong stand against Italian aggression were shocked by the cynicism of the pact. Mussolini, having rejected with contempt the plan which was meant to help him, warned that any embargo on oil for Italy would be regarded as an 'act of hostility', and that he would reply to it with 'acts of war'.

With the opening of hostilities in October, the Italian troops faced fierce opposition, and many units were forced back. In the air, however, the Italians held virtual mastery.

In France the year 1935 witnessed an intensification of the political and social divisions. Municipal elections in May showed a marked swing to the left. In the suburbs of Paris the Communist Party made impressive gains, and joined the Popular Front, led by Léon Blum, which demanded a forty-hour working week, large-scale public works to be financed by a tax on the wealthy and the nationalization of heavy industry. On December 6, a member of the right-wing Croix de Feu proposed the disarmament of all rival groups. The Popular Front acceped this. The danger of escalating street violence was averted.

On August 2, British Royal Assent was finally given by George V – the King-Emperor – for the Government of India Act. The central feature of the Act was the establishment of provincial autonomy. Gandhi could focus his efforts on an all-India campaign for the improvement of the conditions of village life, as well as the abolition of 'untouchability'. On June 25 a Hindu who opposed equality for the Untouchables had thrown a bomb into a car, mistakenly believing that Gandhi was in it.

In the Punjab there were violent clashes between Hindus and Muslims, and between Sikhs and Muslims. During riots in Karachi and Lahore forty people were killed. To reduce the possibility of further killings the government forbade the carrying by Sikhs of the dagger that is one of the five symbols of their faith. Insulted by this, many Sikhs embarked upon a campaign of civil disobedience. In northern India, a local Muslim leader, the Haji of Turangzai, raised the Islamic banner of revolt. A substantial force of Indian troops was sent against him, and the rebellion was crushed.

It was the ravages of nature that led to by far the greatest loss of life in India in 1935. On May 31, a second earthquake within a year killed more than 30,000 people, 20,000 of them in the city of Quetta.

*   *   *

Germany continued its rearmament. In the secrecy of his entourage Hitler spoke openly of what he intended to do. On March 22, from what he described as a 'reliable source', the British Ambassador noted that Hitler 'talks not only about Russia but also about Czechoslovakia whose existence he considers a regrettable smudge on the map of Europe. The German minorities numbering 3,000,000 must be restored to the Reich when Austria joins Germany.'

Hitler continued in public to express peace-loving sentiments. On May 3 he sent an open letter to the owner of the *Daily Mail*, Lord Rothermere, whose newspapers in Britain were advocating good relations with Germany. Hitler wrote: 'I am no new advocate of an Anglo-German understanding. In Germany I have made between four and five thousand speeches to small, large, and mammoth audiences, yet there is no single speech of mine, nor any line that I have written, in which I have expressed anything contrary to this conception, or against an Anglo-German understanding.' An agreement between England and Germany, Hitler added, 'would represent the weighty influence for peace and common sense of 120,000,000 of the most valuable people in the world.'

What did Nazi 'common sense' involve? By September 1935 at least a quarter of all German Jews – 100,000 in all – had already been deprived of their livelihood. Then, on September 15, Hitler personally signed two decrees, known as the Nuremberg Laws, which redefined German citizenship. Under the first of the two laws, German citizenship could only belong to 'a national of Germany or kindred blood'. Under the second law all Jews were defined as being 'not of German blood'. Marriages between Jews and German 'nationals' were forbidden. All marriages conducted 'in defiance of this law' were invalid. Sexual relations outside marriage were forbidden between Jews and Germans. Jews were forbidden to fly the German flag.

Under the headline 'The Shame of Nuremberg', the *New York Herald Tribune* described the two laws as the realization 'of nearly the whole anti-Semitic portion of the Nazi programme'. That year tens of thousands more German Jews emigrated, many of them to Palestine. To facilitate their emigration had been the task of the League of Nations High Commissioner for Refugees, James G.

McDonald. But on December 27 McDonald resigned, having come
to the conclusion that the cause of Jewish emigration – Nazi racial
policy – ought to be challenged directly by the League.

It was not only through the racist laws promulgated at Nuremberg that Nazism defined its purpose and its plan. At the Nuremberg
rally that September, 54,000 members of the Hitler Youth marched
past Hitler in the stadium. Afterwards he told them that what was
required of them was unlike anything required of previous generations. The 'dull, philistine youth of yesterday' had been replaced by
the upright athlete, 'swift as a greyhound, tough as leather, hard as
Krupp steel'.

On March 16 Hitler struck a body blow to the League of Nations
by introducing compulsory military service. Henceforth, German
rearmament, hitherto often disguised as civilian sports activities such
as amateur flying clubs, would be in the open. On November 1 all
physically fit German males aged twenty-one were called up for
twelve months' military service. At the same time the four main
classes of weapons forbidden by the Treaty of Versailles were to
be reintroduced: tanks, heavy artillery, aeroplanes and submarines.
Within a year, aircraft production reached a scale that outstripped
Britain and France. That November the Swastika flag was recognized
as Germany's only official flag.

Persecution of the German Catholic Church intensified. There
were mass arrests of monks and nuns accused of conspiring to smuggle
money out of the country and sentenced to long terms of hard labour.
Heavy fines effectively secured the confiscation of a large part of the
church's property. A Minister for Church Affairs was appointed, who
was given supreme authority over the Evangelical Church. Church
Committees were established under the Ministry's auspices, which
sought to impose the Nazi doctrines in churches and church schools.
The leading opposition pastors were sent to concentration camps.

In China, the Communists' Long March moved steadily further away
from the areas Mao Tse-tung had earlier controlled. Eighty thousand
marchers had to cross terrain at 16,000 feet, and the Nationalists
bombed them from the air. After eight months half had died or been
killed. Finally, in October, they reached Yenan, where Mao Tse-tung

established a new headquarters. That December he declared that, despite its heavy losses, the Long March 'has proclaimed to the world that the Red Army is an army of heroes, while the imperialists and their running dogs, Chiang Kai-shek and his like, are impotent'. It was to be another fourteen years before the impotent ones could be driven out of China.

Once again, the ravages of nature brought the most death and destruction to China. During heavy rains in May, the Yellow River burst its banks and more than 50,000 peasants were drowned. In July the Yangtse overflowed, with an equally high death toll.

In the United States, President Roosevelt pursued his New Deal despite Republican opposition to Federal 'interference'. There were still at least ten million unemployed. More than sixteen million people were receiving Federal, State or Municipal relief. But there were setbacks to the New Deal when some of Roosevelt's programmes were rejected by the Federal Courts. The most serious of these setbacks concerned the enforcement of codes of fair competitive practices on industry, and the enforcement of agreements with regard to hours and wages. On May 27 the Supreme Court held that these aspects of New Deal legislation – specifically as enshrined in the National Industrial Recovery Act – were unconstitutional.

Roosevelt persevered. In June, by Executive Order – whereby the President had the power to execute a law passed by Congress under his constitutional rights as Chief Executive – he created the National Youth Administration (NYA), which provided jobs for hundreds of thousands of youngsters. The man chosen to be the director of the NYA in Texas was a future President, Lyndon Baines Johnson, at twenty-seven the youngest director in the United States.

In August, Roosevelt obtained the passage of a Social Security Bill which established, for the first time in United States history, unemployment insurance, health insurance, non-contributory old age pensions, maternal and child welfare, vocational rehabilitation and pensions for the blind. The Act provided that the Federal government would match, more or less equally, local State funds. Signing on August 14 in the full glare of the newsreel cameras, Roosevelt used twenty pens in signing his name: a means of providing souvenirs for the faithful which has persisted to this day. 'This social security system,' he said, 'will give at least some measure of protection to 30 million of our citizens who will reap direct benefits.'

Other citizens – citizens by conquest – were beneficiaries of Roosevelt's legislation that year. It was almost forty years since the United States had acquired the Philippines from Spain. On November 14 the New Commonwealth of the Philippines was inaugurated. For ten years the Philippines would have a large measure of self-government, after which they would become 'automatically free'. The first act of the new President of the Philippines, Manuel Quezon, was to ask Roosevelt to lend the Chief of Staff of the United States Army, General Douglas McArthur, to reorganize the Philippine defence forces. Roosevelt agreed. Six years later, McArthur was to defend the Philippines against Japanese attack, to capitulate, and in due course to return as victor.

In Canada, as the Prime Minister Richard Bennett announced his own 'New Deal', Roosevelt proceeded with yet further stages of his own New Deal. A Resettlement Administration was set up to help farm owners and tenants move to better land. One of its decisions was to hire a film maker, Pare Lorentz, to make films showing what the New Deal was achieving. The first film, *The Plough that Broke the Plains*, did well in independent cinemas – its final dust storm sequence was a cinematographic masterpiece. Roosevelt then set up the United States Film Service to portray the efforts of government departments, as well as the problems confronting those who were struggling to overcome economic hardship.

Also set up were Federal public work programmes, loans to companies to construct electricity supply networks in rural areas, pensions for those over sixty-five, financial help for the blind and the disabled, and unemployment assistance to be paid from individual contributions rather than from taxation.

The life of millions of individuals continued to be centred on everyday pleasurable pursuits. A new game was launched, 'Monopoly', invented by Charles B. Darrow of Philadelphia. George Gershwin's opera *Porgy and Bess* was given its first performance. Among films launched in

1935 were *Anna Karenina*, starring Greta Garbo, *The Bride of Franken-stein* with Boris Karloff, and *A Night at the Opera* with the Marx Brothers. In Britain, the first streamlined steam locomotive was introduced on the main railway line from London to Newcastle, and broke the world speed record. At the League of Nations, Australia stressed the importance of 'nutrition', urging the need to increase world consumption of fresh food products, in order to improve global health. But the shadow of an impeding clash of nations and armies was everywhere in evidence. In Britain, 1935 saw the construction of the first practical radio equipment for detecting aircraft in flight: radar. Ten years later radar was to provide vital warning of incoming enemy aircraft intent on mass destruction.

In Spain, in elections on 16 February 1936, victory went to the Popular Front coalition of the Parties of the Left. Four days later the new Prime Minister, Manuel Azana, announced his commitment to wide social changes to favour smallholders, peasants and the working class. Regional autonomy would be restored to Catalonia. He then appealed to the working class for unity in the work of reform and reconstruction, but rioters attacked those they blamed for their distress during the previous three years, looted right-wing political clubs, and occupied land on large estates, unwilling to wait for the legislation to transfer the land, eager for possession in time to plant their grain.

Churches were burnt, and property belonging to the rich was destroyed. A Fascist vigilante group, the Falange Espagnola, denouncing these activities as a Red Terror, went on a rampage of its own. Azana appealed for an end to all extra-parliamentary activity by all groups. This, he said, was the last chance for democratic Spain. The right called for the army to take power. Parliament was suspended for a week to prevent violence in the chamber. The army decided the time had come to act, and on July 18, in Spanish North Africa, General Franco seized the city of Melilla and took control of Spanish Morocco. That day, army officers seized control of four Spanish cities. Franco, still in North Africa, placed himself at the head of the insurgent government. With the authority of President Azana, trade unions throughout Spain were authorized to call general strikes wherever the army tried to impose martial law. In Madrid and Barcelona there was severe fighting between the army and forces loyal to the government, which gained the upper hand. But the army was confident of victory: on July 27 Franco told an American journalist, Jay Allen: 'I shall continue to advance. Shortly, very shortly, my troops will have pacified the country, and all of this will soon seem like a nightmare.' When Allen commented, 'That means you will have to shoot half Spain,' Franco replied: 'I repeat, at whatever cost.'

The government in Madrid, headed from September 4 by Francisco Largo Caballero, ruled through a Cabinet that included Socialists, Communists, Republicans, and Catalan and Basque Nationalists. The Anarcho-Syndicalists were also represented. The insurgent government under Franco – known as the Junta – functioned from Burgos. Its armed forces reached the outskirts of Madrid on November 6. But Madrid held out, its defences augmented by volunteers of the International Brigade, who came from many lands: French, Germans, Austrians – many of them refugees from Nazism, Poles, and even Italians, opponents of Mussolini. Russians came from the Soviet Union to fight for the Republic, as did volunteers from the United States and Britain. Other volunteers included Yugoslavs, Czechs and Hungarians, Scandinavians, Swiss, Canadians, Mexicans, Albanians, Irish, Chinese, Korean, Japanese, Peruvians and Jews from Palestine. The British writer Stephen Spender, who was living in Vienna when the Spanish Civil War began, found that the Austrian Socialists living there in fear of arrest and persecution no longer felt alone and abandoned. For them, as for anti-Fascists throughout Europe, the cause of republican Spain became a rallying point of activity and hope.

On October 24 the Portuguese Government, the first foreign government to turn its back on the elected rulers of Spain, broke diplomatic relations with Madrid.

In Germany, the modernization Hitler had promised continued. Fast motor roads were built, without traffic lights to impede vehicles' progress. On February 26, Hitler opened the first factory to make the affordable 'People's Car' – the Volkswagen. He also, more sinisterly, ordered his General Staff to prepare to send German troops into the Rhineland.

On March 6 German troops entered the Rhineland, a sovereign and integral part of Weimar Germany which had been demilitarized after the First World War as part of the Versailles Treaty. That same day, Hitler offered Non-aggression Pacts to France, Belgium and Britain. Having unilaterally abolished one demilitarized zone, he then proposed the establishment of another, on both sides of the Franco-German and Belgian-German frontiers. He also sought an alliance with Italy. This German-Italian 'Axis' had its price: Hitler had to give up Austrian claims for the South Tyrol. But he soon found another territorial cause, demanding greater rights, powers and even autonomy for the German-speaking peoples of the Sudetenland, then an integral part of Czechoslovakia.

Nazi Party activity inside the Sudetenland increased. Many Sudeten Germans, among them Socialists and trade unionists, regarded every aspect of Nazism as vile. But the Sudeten German Party, led by Konrad Henlein, began to demand autonomy for the Sudetenland. The Czech President, Eduard Beneš, rejected this call, fearing that it was a prelude to annexation. Henlein's Party, which continued to call for Sudeten autonomy, could not be discounted. In the Czech Parliament his forty-five deputies, elected in 1935, represented 60 per cent of Czechoslovakia's German-speaking citizens. He was also well-funded, receiving a monthly subsidy from the German Foreign Office, and denouncing the Czech Government for inequalities which did not exist. At the same time Czechoslovakia, which had signed its own pact with the Soviet Union, was denounced from Berlin as an 'outpost of Bolshevism'.

In the Free City of Danzig, the League of Nations High Commissioner complained about the 'unconstitutional activities' of the local Nazi Party. The League took no action, and in October, using terror tactics learned in Germany, the Danzig Nazis forced their two main German rivals, the Socialists and the German Nationalists, to dissolve.

In Roumania there was also sympathy with the general aims of German Nazis. Early in 1936 a new political Party had been formed, made up of several well-established existing Parties, whose aim was the elimination of both Jews and Hungarians from Roumanian public life. Roumanian Communist leaders were imprisoned. The Communist Party was also at the centre of political conflict in Poland. On March 26 it organized the occupation of the coal mines at Chropaczowa, and a hunger strike. The police moved in and broke up the strike. They also arrested the Communist leaders, among them Wladyslaw Gomulka, who was sentenced to eight years in prison. He would emerge as the leader of Communist Poland in 1956 – twenty years after his first imprisonment.

In France, the General Elections that ended on May 3 brought to power a coalition of Parties of the left – the Popular Front. This was the first time in French history that the Socialists were the largest single parliamentary Party. Léon Blum, the Socialist leader, became Prime Minister. But the Communist Party, even before Blum took up office, called for a strike of workers in the capital. Within a week, 300,000 workers were out on strike. Arbitration took place at Blum's official residence, the Matignon Palace, and ended with the Matignon Agreement. Employers recognized collective labour contracts negotiated by the unions, and granted wage increases. At the same time, Blum introduced wide-ranging measures of social reform, including a forty-hour week, collective labour agreements, levies on the salaries of civil servants and paid holidays.

Inside Germany, membership of the Hitler Youth Movement was made compulsory. As a result, the Church Youth Movement was outflanked. On June 17, Hitler placed all German police forces under the direct control of the SS.

Hitler was ready to show German Nazi achievements to the world. In August, Berlin was host to the Olympic Games. Never before had the Games been staged with such elaborate ceremonial. In September, at the annual Nazi Party Congress at Nuremberg, the theme was the launching of a crusade against the 'world danger of Bolshevism'. The first practical manifestation of this crusade was the help sent to Franco in Spain. This included aircraft and munitions, pilots, engineers and technical advisers. By the end of the year at least 10,000 German infantrymen had arrived in Spain to fight for Franco.

*   *   *

In April, in Abyssinia, the Emperor Haile Selassie's forces, rather than fall back towards the capital, Addis Ababa, decided to risk everything in a direct military confrontation with the advancing Italians. Within four days he and his troops were forced to retreat, in large measure due to the use of poison gas by the Italians. Making his way to Palestine and exile, Haile Selassie appealed in vain for the restoration of his kingdom. Italian troops entered Addis Ababa, and in a mass rally in Rome, Mussolini announced the annexation of Abyssinia to Italy. With this new conquest, Italy controlled a large swathe of East Africa: Abyssinia, Eritrea and Somaliland. 'Pacification' was undertaken in Abyssinia throughout the summer and autumn. At the same time Mussolini wanted to be seen by his people and by the world as an enlightened ruler. Italian factory corporations, ironworks, brickworks and cement works among them, were encouraged to transfer their factories to the new territory. Italian farmers were encouraged to emigrate, and promised that at a later stage the land they cultivated there would become their own property. At the same time, echoing Hitler's Nuremberg Laws of the previous year, strict racial rules were introduced – in this case to prevent a mingling of Italian and Ethiopian blood.

German preparations to wage war were becoming more evident. On October 3 the German Government launched a battle-cruiser, the *Scharnhorst*. At 35,000 tons, it was 10,000 tons above the Versailles Treaty limit. In November, Germany unilaterally denounced the section of the Versailles Treaty which established international control over five waterways that flowed through Germany: the Rhine, the Danube, the Elbe, the Oder and the Niemen. In response, France strengthened its defensive Maginot Line. In September, Germany held army manoeuvres: their secret objective was to test France's defensive abilities against a German invasion.

On November 24 there was a sign of the contempt with which the Western democracies held Nazism when the Nobel Peace Prize was awarded to one of Hitler's most outspoken opponents, the leading German pacifist Carl von Ossietzky, who had been held in the concentration camp at Esterwegen since 1933. The award was described in the German newspapers as 'an insult to the new Germany'. In the sphere of propaganda, Dr Goebbels justified food shortages with the slogan: 'The German people must temporarily do without butter in order to produce the guns necessary for their defence!' On December 8 a second battle-cruiser, the *Gneisenau*, was launched.

Inside the Soviet Union, forced labour was in operation throughout the country in an unprecedented road-building campaign, and on two ambitious canal systems, the White Sea–Baltic Canal in the north, and the Caspian–Black Sea Canal in the south, which employed tens of thousands of slave labourers from the prison camps. Thousands died working on these canals, in conditions of extreme hardship.

Trials and purges turned into a tidal wave of destruction. Those associated with Trotsky in the past at the highest level of government, men who had devoted their lives to the establishment and maintenance of Soviet Communism in its early years, were arrested and accused of treason. On August 22, the last day of the purge trial of 1936, the prosecutor Andrei Vyshinsky demanded that all sixteen of the accused should be shot. His final demand, 'Shoot all the sixteen mad dogs', was greeted by what *Pravda* described as 'stormy applause'. They were all executed, or died soon afterwards in prison and labour camps.

Amid great secrecy Germany had been putting pressure on Austria for closer links with Germany. On July 11 an agreement was signed, whereby Austria promised that her policy would always be based on the recognition that she was 'a German State'. An amnesty was granted to Austrian Nazis then in prison, and the Chancellor, von Schuschnigg, agreed to take two pro-Nazi Austrians into his Cabinet.

Democrats everywhere looked with alarm as the Swastika emblem was flown in Austria and banned Nazi newspapers made their reappearance, and as the Nazi anthem, the Horst Wessel Song, was again heard in the streets.

In Britain, the Fascist movement under Sir Oswald Mosley took to the streets wearing black shirts in imitation of Mussolini, and promoting anti-Jewish sentiment in imitation of Hitler. Provocative marches were organized through the predominantly Jewish areas of London's East End. The Jews defended themselves, and on October

11, a week after a Fascist march through the East End, they took part in what they described as a 'victory march' of their own. During it, groups of Fascist youths raised their arms in the Fascist salute. The marchers responded by the clenched fist salute and chants of 'Ban the Blackshirt Army.' Finally the marchers drew near to their destination, led by ex-service men, many wearing medals and carrying banners inscribed: 'National Ex-Service Men's League Against Fascism'. Others in the procession carried Communist red flags. When fifty young Fascists advanced towards the platform, the police charged them and they were dispersed.

Within three months the British Government passed a Public Order Act, banning uniforms in street processions and giving the police the power to forbid such processions altogether. The Fascist movement failed to win a single seat in parliament.

Violence broke out in British Mandate Palestine in 1936, when Arab attacks on Jews and Jewish property were followed by bloody clashes between the Arabs and the British. In some instances Arabs killed Arabs: the Mayor of Hebron was shot dead outside his house because he had opposed the acts of violence by his fellow-Arabs. The death toll when the disturbances ended in 1936 was 187 Arabs, 80 Jews and 28 British soldiers and police. A Royal Commission put forward the radical proposal of partition: the creation in Palestine of two separate States, one Jewish and one Arab, with Britain retaining control of Jerusalem. The Jews were tempted by Statehood, even if it excluded the city they regarded as holy. The Arabs rejected partition altogether, demanding sovereignty throughout Palestine. All that emerged was a British curb on Jewish immigration, which Britain hoped would mollify Arab hostility.

In Egypt, as negotiations for independence began in the early months of 1936, anti-British rioting provided a violent background to the talks. On August 26 a treaty was signed, granting Egypt's sovereignty and independence. Britain's one strategic demand, to retain control of the Suez Canal, was accepted.

In the United States, the Works Progress Administration, which gave out an average of two million jobs a year during its seven-year history, was in its second year. But Roosevelt continued to find his New Deal legislation being undermined by the Supreme Court. The intensity with which his policy of Federal intervention was resented by those who believed in the powers and legitimacy of laissez faire was enormous. In June the Supreme Court struck down a central plank of Roosevelt's legislation, the New York State Minimum Wage Law for women and children. As a result of the imposition of a minimum wage, the Supreme Court ruled, the property rights of employers were being violated. Following this ruling, minimum wage laws in seventeen States had to be revoked.

Roosevelt, however, continued on his course, inaugurating the Hoover Dam on the Colorado River to provide hydro-electricity, and telling the Democratic Convention on June 27: 'We have taken the businessman out of the red. We have saved his bank, and given it a sounder foundation; we have extended credit; we have lowered interest rates; we have undertaken to free him from the ravages of cutthroat competition. We will keep him on the road to freedom and prosperity.' When the nation went to the polls on November 3, Roosevelt carried every State but two.

As European tensions rose, German verbal attacks on Czechoslovakia created sympathy for the Czechs. But neutrality legislation proposed by Congress to keep the United States clear of European entanglements would prevent American help being sent to Czechoslovakia if she were to be attacked by Germany. Czechoslovakia was allowed, however, to buy supplies, but not munitions, in the United States, and to pay for and transport them to Europe at its own risk. This was known as the 'cash and carry' policy. The Neutrality Law, strengthened by Congress on the last day of 1936, already prevented the shipment of war material to either side in the Spanish Civil War.

The First World War was remembered that summer when the German and French Governments agreed to establish a preserved area around Vimy Ridge, on French soil, as a permanent war memorial to the war dead of all the combatants. Four thousand Canadian veterans gathered at the ceremony of dedication. Three days later they were addressed in Westminster Hall, London, by the British Prime Minister, Stanley Baldwin. 'I am confident of this,' he told them. 'If the dead could come back today there would be no war. They would never let the younger generation taste what they did. You all tasted that bitter cup of war. They drank it to the dregs.' Baldwin added: 'If Europe and the world can find no other way of settling disputes than the way of war, even now when we are still finding and burying the bodies of those who fell twenty years ago – if they can find no other way, the world deserves to perish.'

Roosevelt's efforts to introduce New Deal legislation were meeting with increasing opposition from the Supreme Court. American conservatism had always rejected the Federal interventionist approach. On 6 February 1937 Roosevelt decided to strike at the root of the problem, calling for a reorganization of the whole Federal judiciary. 'The judiciary, by postponing the effective dates of Acts of Congress,' he said, 'is assuming an additional function and is coming more and more to constitute a scattered, loosely organized and slowly operating Third House of the National legislature.'

Roosevelt proposed that he be given power to appoint extra judges whenever a Federal judge – each of whom had life tenure – who had reached seventy and had served for ten years failed to resign or retire. Under his plan, the nine judges of the Supreme Court could be expanded to fifteen. The Republicans claimed that Roosevelt was aiming to 'pack' the Supreme Court with his nominees, but he stood his ground.

Under the threat of Roosevelt's changes, the Supreme Court declared that Roosevelt's Moratorium Act for keeping down farm mortgages was in keeping with the constitution. On May 24 the Supreme Court approved the Social Security Act. Although his proposal to change the basis of the senior judiciary was then defeated in Congress, the aim of its passage had been achieved. The Supreme Court was no longer a political opponent.

In Europe, on February 27 the French Government took measures designed to protect France against a German attack: the creation of a Ministry of Defence and the extension of the Maginot Line of forts. The leading arms factory was also nationalized.

*   *   *

The only fighting in Europe during 1937 was in Spain, but no one side could gain the ascendancy. Hitler and Mussolini sent soldiers and armaments to help the Nationalists. The Republican capital, Madrid, suffered repeated Nationalist bombing and artillery attack, and in February there was a fierce battle south-east of Madrid, when members of the International Brigade faced Moorish soldiers from Spanish North Africa. A British Communist member of the Inter-national Brigade, Jimmy Younger, wrote to a friend: 'It was slaughter. At the end of the first day my Battalion . . . 400 strong to start with, was reduced to less than one hundred. I could hear the wounded moaning and calling to us as they lay between the lines. At the end of a week I knew the meaning of war.'

Supported by a naval bombardment, and with the participation of Italian and Moroccan troops, the Nationalists captured Malaga. An Italian military column took part in the triumphal entry into the city, and throughout Italy the 'Italian victory' was proclaimed. The loss of Malaga caused the Madrid government to reconsider the organizational structure of national defence. Conscription was introduced, and a single military command established.

Soviet war material continued to reach the Republican forces, but the number of Soviet citizens who were allowed to participate in the fighting was never more than 2,000. Italy sent 70,000 soldiers, including complete military formations. The number of German participants on the side of the Nationalists was at least 10,000. By the end of February, the Nationalists were in control of thirty-three out of Spain's fifty provincial capitals, but the three main capital cities, Madrid, Barcelona and Bilbao, as well as the most heavily populated and prosperous areas, remained loyal to the Republicans.

Franco focused his main efforts on the conquest of the Basque provinces. As his forces advanced slowly and with mounting difficulty through Basque country, German pilots bombed the towns through which they believed the Basque troops were passing. On April 26 the German target was the historic Basque capital of Guernica. The first attack was made by German Heinkels dropping bombs near the station and machine-gunning the area around it. The next wave of bombers were the heavier Junkers 52s. The bombing lasted for three hours, leaving 1,645 people dead, many of them shot down as they fled by the machine-guns of the Heinkels. The Nationalists entered Guernica three days later.

Outside Spain the impact of the bombing of Guernica was immediate. In Paris, Picasso painted his large black and white mural *Guernica*, which helped fix the bombing of the town in the public mind worldwide as one of the worst evils of the century.

Behind the front lines, the Spanish Republic was faced with deep dissent between its active political groupings. In the first week of May, fighting broke out: the Communists seized the Barcelona telephone exchange, and in four days of fighting, 1,000 were killed. The Republican Prime Minister, Largo Caballero, who refused to allow the suppression of the Catalan Marxists, was replaced by Dr Juan Negrin. As soon as Negrin became Prime Minister, orders went out for the arrest of the Catalan Marxist leaders. The Nationalists took full advantage of this internecine struggle among the Republicans. Within three months, Franco's forces had eliminated almost all Basque resistance. In the centre of Spain, however, Republican forces made considerable gains. There was to be no swift victory for either side.

In the Soviet Union, the purges of 'enemies of the State' intensified during 1937. Among the institutions from which an increasing number of members were taken away to execution, prison or labour camp were the main sources of Communist activity and zeal: the Young Communist Movement, the trade unions, the Academy of Sciences, and the Union of Soviet Writers. A military court also sentenced to death one of Stalin's leading military commanders, Marshal Tukhachevsky, and seven other generals, all of whom had been charged with treason and spying 'on behalf of an unfriendly State'. The accused were denied defence counsel or the right of appeal. After a summary trial lasting for only three hours, all were found guilty and shot. Even close friends of Stalin could not count on his goodwill. One such was his fellow-Georgian, Avel Yenukidze, for fifteen years Secretary of the Central Executive Committee of the Soviets. He was shot for 'high treason'.

On July 31 a Soviet Politburo directive instructed the commandants of all labour camps to submit 'arrest quotas' of their prisoners. The directive laid down that twenty-eight per cent of those whose names were put forward should be shot, and the rest given eight to ten years additional labour camp sentences. The number to be shot was listed precisely: 72,950.

Of the eleven non-Russian Republics of the Soviet Union, ten had their heads of government removed from office during 1937. In August, the Chairman of the Council of People's Commissars in the Ukraine, Lyubchenko, killed himself so as to avoid arrest as an 'enemy of the USSR and a betrayer of Ukrainian interests'. His successor Bondarenko – appointed by Stalin – was arrested three months later, and charged with maintaining treasonable contact with Ukrainian separatists in an 'anti-Soviet' centre in Berlin. In November, the acting President of Byelorussia – another Stalin appointment – and the Vice-President, were both removed from office. Similar purges of the leaders of the peripheral republics took place in the Caucasus, the most dramatic being the trial of thirteen senior members of the Abkhazian Government on a charge of 'counter-revolutionary conspiracy'. In the autumn of 1937 all Soviet diplomatic representatives to the border States were summoned back to Moscow, never to reappear again in any diplomatic list.

Since the failure of Communist revolutions outside Russia after 1918, several hundred European Communists had found refuge in Moscow, where they had been given a place of honour in a hotel facing the Kremlin, and from where they spoke lyrically of the achievements of their Soviet hosts, and of Stalin. In 1937 they too became the victims of the purges. Among them was Béla Kun, who had led the Hungarian Communist government in 1919.

In Germany, in the early months of the year, Catholic priests, monks and nuns were brought to trial. The favourite charges, being the most salacious, were of sexual depravity. Others were of 'complicity with Communism'. Catholic parents whose children went to religious schools were encouraged to remove them. Special 'plebiscites' were held among parents to hasten this decision. On May 27, Pope Pius XI issued an encyclical on the condition of the Catholic Church in Germany. It was entitled *Mit brennender Sorge*: 'With Deep Anxiety'.

In it he deplored the persecution of Catholics in Germany as 'illegal and inhuman'.

Undeterred by Papal protest, on June 25 Hitler issued a special decree depriving the Protestant Church of control of its finances. That summer more than a hundred Protestant clergymen were arrested and imprisoned, among them Pastor Niemöller, the former U-boat commander.

On September 7 a German decree imposed a 25 per cent tax on all Jewish wealth. On November 8 an exhibition opened at Nuremberg entitled *Der ewige Jude* – 'The Eternal Jew', which portrayed Jews as the 'taskmasters for international Bolshevism'. With a bravery born of desperation, a group of Austrian anti-Nazis, led by a devout Christian, Irene Harand, entered the exhibition hall and stuck labels showing Jewish 'benefactors of humanity' on the walls and display cases.

Anti-Jewish measures were not confined to Germany. In the Free City of Danzig, and in Poland, there was a spate of anti-Jewish actions. The Polish Government began talks that December with the French Government, hoping to facilitate Jewish emigration to the French colonial territory of Madagascar, in the Indian Ocean.

In the summer of 1937 the Japanese army began full-scale war in northern China. As the Japanese pressed relentlessly forward, the Chinese forces withdrew, evacuating Peking and withdrawing south-ward. On September 15 the Chinese Ambassador to the League, Dr Wellington Koo, was applauded by the representatives of fifty nations, an unprecedented gesture of support. When it came to action, however, the only decisions reached were to reduce China's financial contribution to the League, and to pay £30,000 towards fighting epidemic diseases inside China. On October 10 the Chinese forces, having fallen back from Peking, were defeated in a battle during which 30,000 Chinese soldiers were killed. Those who survived, 200,000 in all, fled southward.

Shanghai was the next target for the Japanese, which they bombed incessantly and eventually overran. The United States Ambassador to Japan, Joseph Grew, described the bombing of Shanghai in his diary as 'one of the most horrible episodes in modern times'. When the battle was over, and Shanghai under Japanese rule, a European eyewitness, the Swedish mining engineer, Gunnar Anderson, asked: 'What is it really worth, this wonderful machine civilization, if it has no inherent force to prevent a destruction like this?'

In Britain, on May 26, Neville Chamberlain became Prime Minister, at the head of a predominantly Conservative administration. Winston Churchill, to whom he offered no place, continued to advocate increased rearmament and support for collective security within the Covenant of the League of Nations. Speaking to the Anti-Nazi Council on June 14, in London, he told those who shared his concerns: 'I feel our country's safety is fatally imperilled both by its lack of arms and by the Government's attitude towards the Nazi gangsters.'

In parliament, Churchill focused on the persecution of the Jews in Germany. 'It is a horrible thing', he said, 'that a race of people should be attempted to be blotted out of the society in which they have been born.'

On November 19, Japanese troops, advancing in their war of conquest, reached Souchow. For four days the city was looted and burned. Thousands of Chinese women were raped, or taken away by force to Japanese army brothels. Thousands more were murdered. Three weeks later, on December 13, the advancing Japanese entered the Nationalist capital, Nanking, attacking the Chinese civilian population in an orgy of destruction.

Japanese officers used their swords to chop off the heads of their prisoners. Soldiers bayoneted prisoners to death, often tying them up in batches first. Old people, women, children, and wounded soldiers were shot down in the streets. Shopkeepers, having been ordered to open their shops, were then killed, and the shops looted. In the weeks that followed at least 20,000 rapes were committed by the Japanese soldiers in Nanking – one Chinese estimate puts the figure at 80,000. A Japanese soldier, Takokoro Kozo, later recalled: 'Women suffered most. No matter how young or old, they all could not escape the fate of being trapped.'

As news of the mass raping in Nanking reached the outside world there was an outcry. In response the Japanese army instituted a system of official military brothels into which women from the nationalities and races under Japanese rule were forced.

The atrocities committed by the Japanese in Nanking were witnessed by the twenty-two foreigners – mostly Europeans and Americans – who were members of the small foreign community there. A Presbyterian Minister from the United States, W. Plumer Mills, who wanted to set up a protected zone in Nanking, was supported by the Americans, English, Danes and Russians in the city, as well as by several German residents, who were members of the Nazi Party. One of these Nazi Party members, John Rabe, was made head of the Nanking Safety Zone, which took in a quarter of a million Chinese. But not everyone who entered it could be saved. Several thousand Chinese soldiers, having laid down their arms and been given sanctuary in the zone, were found when Japanese troops entered the zone: in the first search 1,300 were taken away and executed. The Japanese also took thousands more men from the zone and killed them: men who had not been soldiers, but rickshaw pullers and manual labourers. The Japanese soldiers who searched the zone said that the calluses on these men's hands were proof that they were soldiers.

John Rabe protested to the Japanese about the raping of women inside the zone. He also intervened to stop individual rapes. A European eyewitness noted in his diary that when Rabe confronted Japanese soldiers he 'thrusts his Nazi armband in their face and points to his Nazi decoration, the highest in the country, and asks them if they know what it means. It always works!' Another Nazi in Nanking, Eduard Sperling, used his Swastika armband to order Japanese soldiers to desist from raping and looting. More than 200,000 civilians, a third of the population, and 90,000 soldiers were killed in Nanking, after the city's surrender.

'How our modern civilization drifts back towards medievalism,' William Dodd wrote in his diary on December 14, shortly before returning to the United States after four years in Berlin as ambassador.

On 4 February 1938 Hitler declared himself Commander in Chief of the German Army. Eight days later he invited the Austrian Chancellor, Kurt von Schuschnigg, to his mountain retreat at Berchtesgaden, overlooking Austria. Hitler told Schuschnigg that he must grant an amnesty to all Nazis serving sentences in Austrian prisons, and allow full freedom of movement for the Nazi party inside Austria, as well as transfer the Ministry of the Interior to a leading Austrian Nazi, Artur Seyss-Inquart. Addressing Schuschnigg as if he were a despised adversary rather than a Head of State, Hitler screamed: 'I demand obedience, and I shall enforce it, if necessary with my armies.' Having been shown Germany's strategic plan for the occupation of Austria, Schuschnigg agreed to Hitler's demands.

Desperate to save the independence of Austria, Schuschnigg took a dramatic initiative, announcing a nationwide plebiscite to decide whether or not the people wanted an independent Austria. Hitler decided he could not risk such a vote. On the morning of Friday March 11, two days before the plebiscite was due, he sent an ulti- matum to Schuschnigg demanding its cancellation. Schuschnigg refused. That afternoon a second ultimatum demanded not only that the plebiscite be cancelled, but that Schuschnigg resign.

Schuschnigg accepted defeat, telling the Austrian people: 'So I take leave of the Austrian people, with the German word of farewell, uttered from the depth of my heart – "God protect Austria".' That night Hitler's forces crossed into Austria. There was no resistance and no fighting. In many places the Germans were welcomed with Swastika flags and flowers. On March 12 Austria was decreed part of the German Reich. Two-thirds of the officers in the Austrian army were at once interned, and thousands of Austrian patriots, democrats, Catholics, Socialists and Communists were sent to concentration camps in Germany. Within a few days every aspect of German Nazism was introduced into Austria. Anti-Jewish laws were imposed overnight. Jewish shops and homes were looted. Of Austria's 200,000 Jews, 30,000 were arrested and sent to German concentration camps. Ten thousand committed suicide. Tens of thousands more made their way as refugees to whatever countries would receive them.

As a result of the German annexation of Austria, Czechoslovakia was surrounded on three sides by Germany. The Sudeten German leader, Konrad Henlein, was confident that, as a result of Hitler's pressure, the Sudeten Germans would soon gain autonomy, telling them on March 13: 'Victory is certain.' The French Government offered to go to Czechoslovakia's aid if she were attacked, but Britain rejected this dramatic course. Instead, Chamberlain and his Cabinet agreed on March 22 that pressure be put on Czechoslovakia to make concessions to its Sudeten minority.

On April 16, in a gesture of conciliation, the Czech Prime Minister, Edouard Beneš, declared an amnesty for all Sudeten Germans who had been imprisoned, many of them for high treason. The German-language newspapers controlled by Henlein denounced the gesture as 'quite worthless', and on April 24 Henlein announced the Karlsbad Programme, which included complete autonomy for the Sudetenland. The Czech Government rejected this, while at the same time pledging to continue with plans to satisfy all minority claims. But when municipal elections were held throughout Czechoslovakia on June 12, the Henleinists won 90.9 per cent of the votes cast in the Sudetenland.

Hitler contemplated war, telling the head of the German Armed Forces on June 18: 'I will decide to take action against Czechoslovakia only if I am firmly convinced, as in the case of the demilitarized zone and the entry into Austria, that France will not march, and that therefore England will not intervene.' On August 7 the British Military Attaché in Berlin reported secretly to the Foreign Office that Hitler had already decided to attack Czechoslovakia in September, whatever agreement Beneš might reach with the Sudeten Germans.

Desperate to avoid war with Germany, Beneš made a further offer to the Henleinists, on September 8, of a massive loan to benefit local Sudeten industry, local police autonomy and absolute language equality, as well as the full cantonal self-government. The offer was rejected, and throughout the Sudetenland there were demonstrations in favour of annexation by Germany. The war crisis intensified. On September 10, in a speech at Nuremberg, Hermann Goering, who had brought the German Air Force to a high point of combat readiness, fulminated against the Czech people, telling an ecstatic German audience: 'This miserable pygmy race without culture – no one knows where it came from – is oppressing a cultured people, and behind it is Moscow and the eternal mask of the Jew devil.'

Czechoslovakia looked to Britain and France to warn Hitler not to invade, but Britain had no intention of going to war in order to prevent Hitler acquiring the Sudetenland. Speaking at Nuremberg on September 12, Hitler declared that the 'oppression' of the Sudeten Germans by the Czechs must end. The Henleinists took his speech as a call for revolt. The Czechs declared martial law, and Hitler called for a plebiscite. On September 15, Neville Chamberlain flew from London – his first ever flight by air – to see Hitler at Berchtesgaden. Hitler assured him that, while he would accept the results of a plebiscite in the Sudetenland that called for annexation with Germany, he 'did not wish to include Czechs in the Reich'. For his part, Chamberlain told Hitler that he was not opposed to the separation of the Sudetenland from Czechoslovakia, if that were the result of a plebiscite.

On September 20 Britain and France prepared a plan which they believed would satisfy Hitler: a plebiscite, followed by the cession to Germany of those German-speaking areas of Czechoslovakia that voted for it. Two days later, Chamberlain flew for a second time to see Hitler, who was then at Bad Godesberg, on the Rhine, and sought Hitler's approval for the Anglo-French plan. While accepting it in principle – for the plan was essentially his own – Hitler then insisted that German troops must be allowed to occupy the German-speaking area at once. Only after that could the plebiscite take place. He further insisted that all fortifications and war materials in the Sudeten areas should be handed over to Germany intact.

On September 27 the British Government took a further initiative, aimed at accelerating the timetable of the transfer of Czech territory to Germany. The British plan was that the Czechs should withdraw from the frontier towns of Eger and Asch in four days' time, and from all the other areas with more than 50 per cent German speakers by October 10. Any further withdrawals, as determined by plebiscite, must be completed by October 31.

On the afternoon of September 28 Hitler invited Chamberlain to fly to Munich, with the French Prime Minister Edouard Daladier and Mussolini, to settle the Sudeten question. As Chamberlain prepared to make his third flight to Germany in fourteen days, Lord Halifax telegraphed to the senior British diplomat in Prague: 'It is essential that Czechoslovak government should at once indicate their acceptance in principle of our plan and timetable. Please endeavour to obtain this without delay.' This telegram was sent from London to Prague at 8 p.m. At 10.40 p.m. Beneš accepted in principle what had become the combined Anglo-French and German plan.

On the morning of September 29, Chamberlain flew to Munich where, during twelve hours of talks, he, Daladier, Mussolini and Hitler worked out the details of the transfer of the Sudetenland from Czechoslovakia to Germany. Chamberlain asked that the Czech representatives participate in the discussion, but Hitler refused, and they were kept in a room near the conference hall. When the decision was finalized after midnight, the Czechs were asked to accept it. When they asked if they could make some comments on the agreement, they were told that everything had been settled. Beneš, who had remained in Prague, was given no opportunity to make any changes.

Returning to London, Chamberlain was met by large and enthusiastic crowds, first in Downing Street and then outside Buckingham Palace. He was confident that as a result of the Munich agreement, the danger of an Anglo-German war had receded, telling his Cabinet on October 3 that Britain was 'now in a more hopeful position, and that the contacts which had been established with the Dictator Powers opened up the possibility that we might be able to reach some agreement with them which would stop the armaments race'.

In the House of Commons, the Leader of the Labour Party, Clement Attlee, warned: 'This has not been a victory for reason and humanity. It has been a victory for brute force.' The Leader of the Liberal Party, Sir Archibald Sinclair, told the House: 'A policy which imposes injustice on a small and weak nation, and tyranny on free men and women, can never be the foundation of lasting peace.' Churchill stressed the moral aspect, insisting that there never could be friendship between Britain and 'that Power which spurns Christian ethics, which cheers its onward course by a barbarous paganism, which vaunts the spirit of aggression and conquest, which derives strength and perverted pleasure from persecution, and uses, as we have seen, with pitiless brutality the threat of murderous force. That Power cannot ever be the trusted friend of the British democracy.'

German troops began their occupation of the Sudetenland on October 1 and completed it ten days later. As with the annexation of Austria, no shot was fired, no armies fought, and there was no resistance. To escape the imposition of Nazi rule, many Sudeten Social Democrats – German speakers who were as German as the Henleinists and pro-Nazis – fled across the Sudetenland border into the truncated Czechoslovakia. At Hitler's insistence they were sent back to Germany, where many were immediately arrested and sent to concentration camps. The agreement that sealed their fate in this way was signed two weeks after Munich. The British and French Governments acceded to it.

Hitler's next decision was to expel all 12,000 Polish-born Jews who lived in Germany. Many of them were immigrants from the 1920s. Beginning on October 28, they were taken by train and truck to the German border with Poland, and forced across it. One of those expelled, Sendel Grynszpan, wrote to his seventeen-year-old son, Herschel Grynszpan, who was in Paris, describing the suddenness and humiliations of the expulsion. The son went to the German Embassy in Paris and shot a young diplomat there. 'My dear parents,' he wrote to them on a postcard, 'I could not do otherwise. May God forgive me. My heart bleeds at the news of 12,000 Jews' suffering. I must protest in such a way that the world will hear me. I must do it. Forgive me. Herschel.'

Using his diplomat's assassination as an excuse, Hitler launched a massive attack on Jewish homes and synagogues throughout Germany, Austria and the newly annexed Sudetenland. Starting in the early hours of November 10, Jewish shops and synagogues were set on fire. This orgy of destruction was known as Kristallnacht, 'the Night of the Broken Glass'. It marked a turning point in how the Nazi Party was perceived abroad. A leading article in *The Times* on the following day declared: 'No foreign propagandist bent upon blackening Germany before the world could outdo the tale of burning and beatings, of blackguardly assaults upon defenceless and innocent people, which disgraced that country yesterday.'

In the Soviet Union, the purges and show trials continued, culminating in 1938 in the 'Trial of the Twenty-One'. Among the accused were two founding members of Soviet Communism, Aleksei Rykov and Nikolai Bukharin, both of whom had been expelled from the

Communist Party in 1937. Also brought to trial were the former head of the secret police, G.G. Yagoda, and Christian Rakovsky, who had established Soviet rule in the Ukraine after the revolution. Unlike the hundreds of trials which lasted a few hours and were held in secret, the Trial of the Twenty-One lasted ten days, in the presence of invited journalists from all over the world. All the accused were sentenced to death, with the exception of Rakovksy, on behalf of whom the British Labour Party leadership, headed by Clement Attlee, appealed direct to Stalin, recalling Rakovsky's days as Soviet Ambassador to Britain. Much was made in Britain of Stalin's generosity when Rakovsky, aged seventy, was not sentenced to death, but to twenty years penal servitude. He was shot a few years later.

In the course of two years, according to the precise records of the Soviet secret police, 33,514 'enemies of the people' had been shot and 5,643 imprisoned.

In Spain, the Madrid Government continued to defend the capital, and the considerable regions under its control, despite the constant acquisition by Franco and the Nationalists of war supplies from Germany and Italy. The Germans and Italians urged Franco to exploit air power to the full, despite the international outrage at the bombing of Guernica the previous year. On January 28, nine Italian bombers struck at Barcelona, killing 150 of its citizens during a single swoop on the city which lasted only a minute and a half. Further bombing raids on Barcelona killed 815 people. Leaflets dropped over the city stated: 'We shall bomb you every three hours unless you surrender.'

Barcelona refused to surrender. Then, in a renewed military offensive towards the Mediterranean, on April 15 – Good Friday – the Nationalist forces reached the sea, driving a wedge between the Barcelona province and the rest of Republican-controlled Spain.

In July the Republicans counter-attacked, crossing the River Ebro. In October, after Franco ordered the heaviest artillery and aerial bombardment of the two-year struggle, the Republicans were driven back across the river. Franco's field orders were severe. A British Field Marshal, Sir Philip Chetwode, was unable to mitigate the plight of the Republican prisoners-of-war. 'I could not stop him executing his unfortunate prisoners,' Chetwode wrote.

On December 23 the Nationalists launched a massive offensive against Catalonia and the defenders were overwhelmed. Slowly the Republic was being crushed.

At a conference in London, held at St James's Palace, the British government found itself under heavy pressure from the Governments of Egypt, Iraq and Saudi Arabia to curtail Jewish immigration into Palestine. Deferring to this pressure, Britain imposed an upper limit of 75,000 more Jews to be allowed to enter, with a further 25,000 in emergency cases. When this total of 100,000 Jews had entered, majority rule would be established: that is, power would be transferred to the Arab majority. This would prevent the emergence of a Jewish State in Palestine.

In the United States, Roosevelt's measures to create employment were slowly having an effect. By the end of 1938 more than a million of the unemployed had found work. But 23,000,000 people were receiving some form of public relief. To stimulate the economy Roosevelt announced a massive Federal programme of 'spending and lending' for public works and industrial expansion. Two industries, textiles and steel, took immediate advantage of this 'pump-priming', as Roosevelt called it, and saw a rise in production. The boot and shoe industry followed, as did the building industry. Minimum wages and maximum hours of work were introduced for all industries whose products were sold across State borders. By the end of the year the construction of residential homes was breaking all recent records.

It was in foreign policy that the greatest changes took place in the United States in 1938. In May, after Hitler had annexed Austria, Secretary of State Cordell Hull warned that isolation during a period of totalitarian advance was a 'bitter illusion'. He ended his speech with a bold assertion. 'There was never a time in our national history when the influence of the United States in support of international law was more urgently needed than at present – to serve both our own best interests and those of the entire human race.' In September, during the Munich crisis, Roosevelt had appealed directly to Hitler not to break off negotiations with the Czechs.

With a growing number of European refugees seeking entry to

the United States, Roosevelt ruled that the 12,000 to 15,000 German refugees already in the country under temporary permits could stay. After Kristallnacht, Britain agreed to take in 10,000 German children. The United States would allow its existing quota of 27,370 German refugees a year to be maintained, but would make no extra entry permits available. Only three countries, Holland, Denmark and the Dominican Republic, and one city, Shanghai, agreed to allow refugees in without restrictions.

The first days of 1938 had seen the Japanese forces in China continue their advance, capturing a number of coastal towns. Their superiority in aircraft and tanks was decisive. Canton was entered on October 21 and Hankow, the seat of the Chinese Government, five days later, giving Japan control of the whole length of the Canton–Hankow railway, the route along which the Chinese forces had received most of their arms and ammunition from overseas. The only route open to the Chinese after October was the mountainous and winding 'Burma Road', which linked India to Chungking, Chiang Kai-shek's third capital in less than a year. It was travelled by up to 5,000 trucks and 8,000 pack mules at any one time, maintained by a quarter of a million Chinese labourers.

On 30 January 1939 – the sixth anniversary of his coming to power – Hitler told the Reichstag that in order to to feed its population Germany would need Lebensraum – living space. He then called on Czechoslovakia to reduce the size of its army, give him overall control of its foreign policy, and provide Germany with whatever raw materials it required. He also pressed the Prague government to introduce Germany's Nuremberg Laws of 1935, to turn the Jews of Czechoslovakia into second-class citizens. Beneš rejected these demands, but on March 13 Hitler summoned the President of Czechoslovakia, Dr Hacha, to Berlin. It was an ominous summons, reminiscent of that of Schuschnigg before the destruction of Austrian independence.

On the morning of March 14, while Hacha was preparing for his journey, the Slovak Diet, meeting in Bratislava, called for the separation of Slovakia from Czechoslovakia. The Diet then adopted a Declaration of Independence. That same day the Slovak leader,

Father Tiso, who had just returned to Bratislava from Berlin, tele-graphed Hitler asking him to act as the 'protector' of the new Slovak State. Dr Hacha was on his way to Berlin, together with the Czech Foreign Minster, Dr Chvalkovsky. They were received with full mili-tary and diplomatic honours: national flags, national anthems and all the impressive protocol of a State visit. Then, in an interview with Hitler that lasted until four in the morning, they were presented with Germany's demands. The Czech heartland of Bohemia and Moravia would become a 'Reich Protectorate'. Slovakia, and the most easterly province, Ruthenia, would become independent States. If these changes were not accepted, Hitler said, he would reduce Prague to 'a heap of ruins' by aerial bombardment.

Dr Hacha knew the fate of Guernica, primarily the work of German pilots. On March 15 his government capitulated. That day German troops marched into Bohemia and Moravia. The Czech armed forces laid down their arms. Germany had aquired enough military supplies to equip a million and a half soldiers. The gold reserves in the Czechoslovak National Bank were taken over by Reichsbank officials from Berlin. Hundreds of Czechs were imprisoned, and thou-sands taken to Germany as forced labourers. The universities were closed. Jews felt the full severity of the Nuremberg Laws. All manifes-tations of Czech culture were suppressed.

With Germany's agreement, Slovakia retained the independence it had declared during the immediate run up to the break-up of Czecho-slovakia. She also provided military bases for tens of thousands of German troops who, as the summer months proceeded, began to mass along the southern Polish border.

Ruthenia also took the opportunity of the disintegration of Czechoslovakia to declare its independence. The Prime Minister of the new State was a Ruthene, Father Volosin. But he did not have time even to form a government before Hungarian troops marched in. The Ruthenes had no army of their own with which to offer resistance. Father Volosin fled across the border into Roumania, and Hungary annexed Ruthenia. Fear stalked central Europe: on March 20, five days after the German Protectorate was proclaimed over Bohemia and Moravia, Roumania agreed to set aside for Germany one half of its considerable petrol production. On March 21, the Lithuanian Foreign Minister was invited to Berlin as a matter of urgency, and in the course of a few hours signed an agreement ceding the territory of Memel to the German Reich.

Hardly had Hitler acquired Memel than Mussolini invaded Albania. For the loss of only twelve Italian soldiers in action, Albania was conquered.

The Spanish Civil War entered its final phase. On January 26, Franco's forces entered Barcelona. In the bloodletting that followed 3,000 Republicans were killed. On February 6 the President of the Republic, Don Manuel Azana, fled to France and exile, urging the Republicans to surrender. The Prime Minister, Dr Negrin, followed into exile three days later. In and around Madrid the Communist forces within the government ranks wanted to fight on. Thirty per cent of the land area of Spain was still under government control. But the departure of the President and Prime Minister was a serious blow. When a successor to the President, Diego Martinez Barrio, who was himself in exile, was appointed at the end of February, he refused to return to Spain.

Those on whom the defence of the Republic depended were at each other's throats. On March 7 one pro-Communist commander ordered his troops to surround Madrid. On March 10, after four days intense fighting, another commander, an Anarchist, won the military initiative. Several senior Communist officers were arrested and shot. On March 27, Franco's forces entered Madrid. The remaining Republican-held cities fell in rapid succession. By March 31 the whole of Spain was under Nationalist control. Thirty-two months of civil war was over. In Catalonia and the Basque country, regional liberties were suppressed with rigour. The restoration of the land to its 'rightful owners', one of the main pieces of legislation of the Negrin government, was halted and then reversed.

Returning to the Soviet Union, those who had led the Russian effort in Spain were almost all arrested, imprisoned and shot. Stalin wanted no one to live who had participated in the Spanish struggle. Among those who vanished without trace after returning to Russia was the Soviet Consul in Barcelona, fifty-five-year-old Vladimir

Antonov-Ovseenko, who had been at the centre of the destruction of the Catalonian Marxists in 1937. Antonov-Ovseenko had been active in the 1905 Revolution, was one of the organizers of the seizure of the Winter Palace in 1917, and Lenin's first Commissar for Military Affairs.

Brigade Commander Skoblevsky had taken a leading part in winning the Battle of Madrid for the Republic. On his return to the Soviet Union he was hailed as the 'Hero of Madrid'. This did not save him. Denounced as a traitor, a wrecker and a spy, he was shot. His arrest took place only two days after he had received the prestigious Order of Lenin for his services in Spain.

The Japanese were bombing Chiang Kai-shek's capital, Chungking. On May 4 more than 1,500 Chinese were killed, and on May 23 at least 5,000. On the coast, the Japanese continued to capture port after port, depriving the Nationalists of the possibility of sea-borne supplies. One barrier to the consolidation of the Japanese military conquests was the growth of Chinese guerrilla activity. More than a million Chinese were participating in guerrilla activity, some Kuomintang led, others Communist led. There were also repeated clashes between the Kuomintang and Communists: it was an ongoing civil war. Although, according to chillingly precise Japanese figures, 1,218,462 Chinese had been killed in the fighting since 1937, the Japanese aim, to destroy the Chinese armies in the field, had been denied them. American aeroplanes, pilots and machine-guns were beginning to reach the Chinese forces.

In January, Roosevelt gave permission for the French Government to purchase United States warplanes. On March 20, five days after Hitler's forces entered Prague, he issued a direct challenge to Hitler, listing thirty-one countries whose independence the United States wished to protect, and asking if Hitler was 'willing to give assurance' that his armed forces would not invade them. The countries included Britain, France, Poland, Yugoslavia and Greece. This was not the sort of question usually put by any Head of State to another, certainly not to Hitler. Yet Hitler answered it in a speech during which he offered to make a non-aggression pact with any of the countries mentioned in Roosevelt's list.

Any attempt by Germany 'to dominate Europe', Neville Chamberlain warned, 'would rouse the successful resistance of this and other countries who prize their freedom'. Within a few weeks Britain signed agreements with Poland and Turkey. In a speech on April 28, Hitler accused Poland of seeking to join Britain in the encirclement of Germany, telling the Poles that all Germany wanted was the return of Danzig and the Polish Corridor, with their predominantly German populations. He could tolerate no longer, he said, as leader of the German people, that East Prussia should be cut off territorially from Germany.

Hitler insisted that he had no desire to rule over a single Pole. His sole aim, he said, was the restoration of German sovereignty over German people. If Poland continued to resist these just demands, the German newspapers warned, she would be 'wiped off the map with a mailed fist'.

In the second week of August, Hitler ordered German troops to concentrate along the Polish border. On August 11 he summoned Professor Carl Burkhart, the League of Nations High Commissioner in Danzig, to Berlin, and told him: 'If the slightest incident happens I shall crush the Poles without warning in such a way that no trace of Poland can be found afterwards.' Britain, hoping to protect Poland's eastern frontier, began negotiations with the Soviet Union. But Stalin had no particular desire to fight for Polish independence. The eastern third of Poland had been conquered from Russia in 1921. It contained, outside the cities, a majority of Byelorussians and Ukrainians.

In total secrecy Stalin began negotiation with Hitler. Even while British negotiators were in Moscow, Soviet negotiators were in Berlin. In return for Stalin leaving the fate of Poland to him, Hitler would allow the Soviet Union to annex its eastern provinces. The two dictators would partition the country between them. For Stalin, an attractive feature of the German offer was that it gave him control of the three Baltic States of Estonia, Latvia and Lithuania. The Nazi-Soviet pact was signed on August 23. Poland was to be partitioned between Germany and the Soviet Union.

On August 25 the British Government signed a formal treaty of alliance with Poland. France had a similar alliance already. Suddenly

Hitler was confronted by the very real possibility of a two-front war, against Poland in the east and Britain and France in the west. He hesitated, but then convinced himself that Britain and France would not honour their treaties by embarking on a full-scale war against Germany.

On August 29, in the style of the previous Sudeten, Austrian and Czech crises, Hitler demanded that a Polish negotiator, equipped with full powers to come to a final agreement about the transfer of Danzig and the Polish Corridor to Germany, arrive in Berlin 'by midnight' of August 30. The Polish Government refused to be pushed into negotiations without having seen the German terms in advance. Late on the night of 31 August 1939 the German Government informed the world that Polish troops had broken into a German radio station in Upper Silesia, and, after killing a number of Germans working there, had broadcast an appeal to the Polish people calling the population to war.

No such Polish provocation had taken place. The Polish troops were Germans dressed up as Poles. The dead German – for there was indeed one – was a common criminal taken from a concentration camp and killed by his fellow Germans to give credence to the tale of a Polish attack. The incident was a crude fabrication, but in the early hours of September 1, citing this bogus incident as the reason, Hitler ordered German troops to cross into Poland.

CHAPTER SEVEN

Second World War
1939—45

IN THE VERY FIRST HOURS of the German attack on Poland, on 1 September 1939, German planes destroyed many Polish aircraft while they were still on the ground. That afternoon forty-one German bombers took part in the first German bombing raid on Warsaw. A hundred civilians were killed. On the following day, more than a hundred Polish refugees were killed when their train, which was evacuating them from the border area, was bombed while standing at a railway station. German tanks and armoured vehicles – the Panzers of Hitler's modern army – advanced against battered and often bewildered defenders. In every Polish city, town and village occupied by the Germans, prominent local Poles – priests, teachers, municipal officials – were executed in order to deprive the citizens of those who would be their natural leaders in adversity. Random arrests were made of Polish civilians to be shot as a reprisal for an attack – often not a fatal attack – on a German soldier. For the death of a single German soldier, ten, twenty, thirty, even more people could be taken out of their homes and killed. Polish Jews were also killed at random from the first days of the war. Hundreds were murdered each day.

On September 3 Britain and France declared war on Germany. The rest of the world was neutral. That evening in the Atlantic the passenger liner *Athenia*, on its way from Liverpool to Montreal, was torpedoed without warning by a German U-boat. Of the 1,418 passengers and crew on board, 112 were killed, most of them American students returning home, and refugees from Europe seeking a new life in Canada and the United States. That night ten British bombers flew from their bases in southern England across the North Sea to Hamburg, Bremen and nine other cities in the Ruhr, and dropped more than five million leaflets denouncing Germany's action in invading Poland. Britain and France saw no scope for any meaningful military initiative that might help the Poles. French troops did cross the German frontier at three points in the Saar on September 7 but there was little fighting and the Germans were content to let France hold a few square miles of German territory.

On September 17, as the German army drove the Polish forces further and further eastward, Soviet troops began to occupy Eastern Poland in accordance with the Nazi-Soviet pact. The German and Soviet armies linked up east of Warsaw. The Polish capital was completely isolated. On September 26 Warsaw surrendered. Poland's twenty-year-old independence was over: 60,000 Polish soldiers had been killed on the battlefield, and 25,000 Polish civilians had been killed in the bombing and artillery bombardment of Warsaw. On October 5 Hitler took the salute at a march past of German troops in Warsaw, and told the foreign journalists who had been invited to witness his triumph: 'Take a good look round Warsaw. This is how I can deal with any European city.'

The German death toll was 14,000. On October 9 Hitler set out for his commanders his plans for a new German offensive, through Holland, Belgium, Luxembourg and Northern France. It was, he wrote, 'to serve as the base for the successful prosecution of the air and sea war against England'. The war at sea took a turn for the worse for Britain four days later, when the battleship *Royal Oak* was torpedoed and 833 sailors drowned while the warship was at anchor in Scapa Flow. On November 24 the German battle cruiser *Scharnhorst*, the first warship to be built after Hitler broke the Versailles Treaty prohibition on German warship construction, sank the armed British merchant cruiser *Rawalpindi* after a fourteen-minute bombardment, and 270 British sailors were drowned. In early December, in the South Atlantic, the German pocket battleship *Graf Spee* sank three British merchant ships in five days. Tracked down by two British and a New Zealand cruiser, she sought safety in Uruguayan territorial waters. Four days later her captain ordered her to be scuttled. He then shot himself in a hotel bedroom in Montevideo. The sinking of British merchant ships continued.

In German-occupied Poland, Poles and Jews were being murdered every day, shot at random. That November, a German army staff officer, appalled by what he saw, wrote to his wife: 'The wildest fantasy of horror propaganda is as nothing to the reality, the organized gangs who murder, rob and plunder with what is said to be the tolerance of the highest authorities.' He added: 'It shames me to be a German!' By the end of the year more than 10,000 Poles and Polish Jews had been murdered.

On 30 November 1939, as Hitler imposed his cruel regime in Poland, the Soviet Union launched an air, land and sea attack on Finland. On December 14, after a four-day emergency debate at Geneva, the Soviet Union was expelled from the League of Nations. The main Finnish line of defence, the Mannerheim Line, resisted all Soviet efforts to break through it. In one battle, two Soviet divisions were driven back to the Soviet frontier, and then across it. After four days of fighting, more than 25,000 Soviet troops lay dead in the snow, killed in action or frozen to death.

The German conquest of Poland provided the German war effort with a mass of forced labourers. Under an order of 25 January 1940 a million Polish workers were to be deported to Germany to work in factories and fields. Czech civilians were already being taken to Germany as forced labourers. Thousands died in harsh conditions.

In mid-January, Stalin ordered a new offensive against the Mannerheim Line, but the line held. Two days later, at the Anglo-French Supreme War Council, the British and French Prime Ministers, Chamberlain and Daladier, agreed to send an expeditionary force to Finland, to join the line against the Soviet force. Chamberlain told his colleagues: 'Finland must not be allowed to disappear off the map.' The Supreme War Council agreed that in order to deprive Germany of Swedish iron ore, crucial for its war effort, an Anglo-French force should land at the northern Norwegian port of Narvik, cross into Sweden, and take control of the Swedish iron-ore fields. This same force could then continue eastwards to Finland, to assist the Finns, thus, in Chamberlain's words, 'killing two birds with one stone'.

On February 10 the Soviet forces broke through the Mannerheim Line. The Finns retreated to a second defence line. On March 8 that line was also broken. Five days later Finland acceded to the Soviet demands, retaining its independence and most of its territory, but granting the Soviet Union fifty miles of Baltic coastline, a swathe of Finnish territory in the north, and a thirty-year lease on the Finnish naval base at the entrance to the Gulf of Finland. The 'Winter War' had lasted for three and a half months: 58,000 Russian and 27,000 Finnish soldiers had been killed.

Germany had a signals intelligence success early in 1940; one of its very few. By decoding British naval signals, Hitler learned of the Anglo-French plan to land troops in Norway. A counter-move was organized, involving the landing, in advance of the British, of far larger numbers of German troops. The plan was then widened to include the invasion of Denmark, to secure the lines of communication between Germany and Norway.

At Narvik, a million and a half tons of iron ore was in warehouses and at the quayside, awaiting shipment to Germany. The British and French set April 5 for the laying of mines in Norwegian territorial waters, hoping to force the ore-bearing ships out to sea. As British ships set off across the North Sea to begin the minelaying operations, Chamberlain declared publicly: 'Hitler has missed the bus.' On April 7, as the British minelaying armada was still on its way to the Norwegian coast, ten German destroyers destined for Narvik steamed northward. As dawn broke on April 9, German warships were in position off the Norwegian coast. Other German warships were entering Oslo Fjord. At each port, superior German fire power, artillery and air support enabled them to land and advance. The minelaying armada, so suddenly and unexpectedly forestalled, was ordered back to Britain. That morning German forces also landed in the Danish capital, Copenhagen. The King of Denmark knew his army could not resist and ordered a cease-fire. Denmark was Hitler's second military conquest, six months after Poland.

The Norwegian capital, Oslo, fell to the Germans on April 9.

At Narvik, five British destroyers managed to penetrate the port's defences in the early hours of April 10, sinking six German invasion transports and two of the ten German destroyers. On April 13 the remaining eight German destroyers were sunk. That day, British troops landed at two ports in central Norway, supported by French troops, French Foreign Legionnaires and Polish naval units which had escaped capture by the Germans six months earlier. But the Germans had air superiority and mounted repeated dive bombing attacks on the Allied forces and shipping. The German ability, secured by skilful cryptography, to read more than 30 per cent of the British naval signals in the North Sea and Norwegian area, enabled them to attack ships carrying troops and munitions that might otherwise have evaded them.

On April 30, as Hitler confidently awaited a victory in Norway, he gave instructions for the final preparations to attack Belgium, Luxembourg, Holland and France. British troops, despatched to France six months earlier, awaited the German onslaught. The German attack began on May 10. In Britain, Winston Churchill replaced Chamberlain as Prime Minister. On May 13, as the Germans drove forward, Queen Wilhelmina of Holland sought refuge in Britain. That afternoon Churchill told his new government: 'I have nothing to offer but blood, toil, tears and sweat.' He repeated those words a few hours later in the House of Commons, telling Members of Parliament 'You ask, what is our policy? I will say. It is to wage war, by sea, land and air, with all our might and with all the strength that God can give us; to wage war against a monstrous tyranny, never surpassed in the dark lamentable catalogue of human crime. That is our policy.' As to Britain's aim: 'It is victory, victory at all costs, victory in spite of all terror, victory however long and hard the road may be; for without victory there is no survival.'

On May 14, German bombers struck at the bridges over the river at Rotterdam. Many bombs missed their target and fell on the city centre, killing almost a thousand Dutch civilians. In Norway the sustained German air bombardment made it impossible for Britain to hold any coastal points, and a general evacuation began. 'The small countries are simply smashed up one by one, like matchwood,' Churchill telegraphed to Roosevelt. On May 17 the Germans

entered Brussels, their fifth conquered capital in nine months. On
May 18 Belgium's principal port, Antwerp, fell to the Germans.
Three days later German troops reached the Channel Coast, cutting
off the British Expeditionary Force. 'My estimate is that the war will
be won in a fortnight,' one German general, Erwin Rommel, wrote
to his wife on May 24.

The evacuation of British troops began on the following day,
first from Boulogne and Calais, which were quickly occupied by the
Germans, and then from Dunkirk. On May 27, Belgium surrendered
unconditionally. French troops fought on, demoralized by intense
German air attacks, which were also aimed at French civilians fleeing
the battle zone. On the roads, chaos ensued, as refugees fled southwards, and soldiers tried in vain to stop the militarily overwhelming
German onslaught.

By midnight on 2 June 1940 the Dunkirk evacuation was completed: 338,226 soldiers, French as well as British, had been evacuated
in seven days. More than 34,000 British soldiers had been captured
in the Dunkirk perimeter, many while fighting rearguard actions to
keep the perimeter open. Large quantities of arms and ammunition,
heavy guns and armoured vehicles had to be left behind.

On June 6 the King of Norway broadcast to his people to say
that all military operations in Norway were at an end. He then
embarked in a British warship for England and exile.

On June 10, realizing France's days of fighting were nearly over,
Mussolini moved his troops forward into the French provinces along
the Italian border. Four days later German troops entered Paris. They
were unopposed. On June 16 Marshal Pétain, the heroic defender of
Verdun in the First World War, became Prime Minister of France
and immediately asked for an armistice. Hitler allowed Pétain to
remain at the head of a government based in the remote spa town
of Vichy. Churchill broadcast to the British people. 'Whatever has
happened in France makes no difference to our actions and purpose.
We shall defend our Island home, and with the British Empire we
shall fight on until the curse of Hitler is lifted from the brows of
mankind. We are sure that in the end all will come right.' That day,
June 18, the French Under-Secretary of War, General de Gaulle,
reached Britain, where he called on all Frenchmen who wanted to

continue to fight to join him. 'Today we are crushed by the mechanized forces hurled against us,' he said, 'but we can still look to a future in which even greater mechanized forces will bring us victory.'

On June 18 France signed the armistice. More than 92,000 Frenchmen, 7,500 Belgians and 2,900 Dutchmen had been killed in the fighting. The British had lost 3,500 soldiers, the Germans 5,000. Hitler was master of Poland, Denmark, Norway, Belgium, Luxembourg, Holland and France.

On July 3 a British plan was put into operation to seize or neutralize all French ships wherever they might be, to prevent them being used by Germany. The largest number were at Oran. When the French admiral refused to hand them over, British warships opened fire. Most of the French ships were still at anchor. Three were destroyed. Seven managed to sail across the Mediterranean to Toulon, and German protection. More than 1,250 French sailors were killed. If the Royal Navy had not acted, Churchill told the House of Commons, 'mortal injury' might have been done to Britain. The French ships could have become part of a German invasion fleet.

Inside the Soviet Union, 15,000 Polish soldiers who had surrendered to the Russians in October 1939 were taken to three execution sites, one in the forest of Katyn, and shot. Stalin did not want an independent Polish leadership to emerge after the war. A month later he annexed the three Baltic States. On the following day, July 21, Hitler ordered his staff to prepare a plan of attack on the Soviet Union. The date 'May 1941' soon appeared in the inner circles of Hitler's advisers as the one most favoured for the attack.

In Britain, preparations against a German invasion were continuous. On August 3 a contingent of Canadian troops arrived in Britain. On the following day several thousand Australian troops arrived, followed two days later by pilots and airmen from Southern Rhodesia. The German air offensive against British air targets was launched on August 9. That day – the first day of the Battle of Britain – 300 German aircraft flew over south-east England and the Channel coast. Their targets were the radar stations which enabled the British to identify the raiders in time to intercept them. Eighteen German aircraft were shot down. On August 13, with Britain's radar defences still essentially intact, the German Air Force attacked airfields and aircraft factories. Of the 1,485 German aircraft which crossed the English Channel that day, forty-five were shot down, for the loss of only thirteen British fighters.

On August 14 poor weather limited the number of the attacking aircraft to five hundred. Even so, seventy of them, an even larger number than on the previous day, were brought down, for the loss of twenty-seven British fighters. That day the German army began looking for a site in East Prussia which could serve as Hitler's head-quarters during the invasion of the Soviet Union.

The Battle of Britain continued, a daily and ferocious challenge in the skies. On August 20, speaking of the airmen who were in action every day, Churchill told the House of Commons: 'Never in the field of human conflict was so much owed by so many to so few.' Churchill then warned that British bombers would continue to strike at German military industries and communications, air bases and storage depots 'upon an ever-increasing scale until the end of the year, and may in another year attain dimensions hitherto undreamed of'.

On the night of August 30, German bombers dropped incendiary bombs on London. A new phase of the air battle had begun: the Blitz. The main targets were no longer airfields and aircraft factories, but docks, railway yards, railway stations and factories. On September 7, 300 German bombers, escorted by 600 fighters, flew over the London docks. Many bombs fell on nearby residential areas, and 448 civilians were killed. On September 15, eight British ports were attacked.

In German-occupied lands, tyranny and terror went hand in hand. In Belgium a punishment camp was opened by the SS on the outskirts of Antwerp. The number of Germans and Poles in concentration camps that autumn exceeded 100,000. In October, a special task force was set up to seize and transport valuable cultural objects to Germany. More than 5,000 paintings were removed from museums and private homes. On October 3 the Jews of Warsaw, some of whom lived in every district of the city, were ordered to move to the predominantly Jewish district, which was to be walled in, forcing more than 400,000 Jews to live in an already crowded space where 250,000 had lived before. Those Jews who had to move to this specially created 'ghetto' could take with them only what they could carry, or load on handcarts. The rest of their possessions, including stoves, ovens, wardrobes, books, tables and chairs, carpets and beds, had to be abandoned.

'The war is won!' Hitler told Mussolini when they met at the Brenner Pass on October 4. 'The rest is only a question of time.' Ten days later Hitler told another Italian visitor, 'Let's wait and see what London looks like two or three months from now. If I cannot invade them, at least I can destroy the whole of their industry.' On the following night, October 15, German bombers caused 900 fires in London, and the death of 400 Londoners. During the month of October, 6,334 British civilians were killed, of whom 643 were children under sixteen.

Britain had one ally Hitler could not touch. On October 24 an Anglo-American Agreement was signed 'to equip fully and maintain' ten additional British Divisions, their weapons to be manufactured in the United States, and everything to be ready to send them into combat in time for 'the campaign of 1942'. The agreement also contained a pledge by the United States to 'ensure priority' for the material needed to maintain these divisions in the field. Half of all munitions produced in the United States would go to Britain, irrespective of America's own defence needs. At Roosevelt's suggestion Britain was also provided with seventy American destroyers which had been kept in store since the end of the First World War, and would build 300 new merchant ships for British use. The United States would pay for these vessels, which she would then 'rent' to Britain. A similar system, later known as Lend-Lease, would be applied for all arms purchases.

A British bombing raid on Munich on the night of Hitler's anniversary celebration of the beer hall putsch so angered Hitler that he ordered a series of counter-raids. On November 14, 500 German bombers struck at the factory zone around Coventry. In the course of the raid, during which seven munitions factories were hit and production stopped for many months, the city centre was also bombed, and 568 men, women and children killed. Of the 75,000 buildings in the city centre, 60,000 were destroyed or badly damaged. That November the month's civilian death toll from German bombing of Britain was 4,588.

On October 28 Mussolini had invaded Greece, using his troops in Albania. Within a week the Greeks halted the Italian advance. They then launched a counter-offensive that within five months drove the Italians back across the border deep into Albania. Hitler feared that Britain would be able to use air bases in Greece to bomb the Roumanian oilfields. Hitler, who needed this oil for his invasion of Russia, decided to postpone the attack on Russia in order to defeat Greece first.

Just as Hitler had known of Britain's Norwegian intentions, so Britain knew of Hitler's Greek, Balkan and Russian moves. Since the fall of France, British cryptographers had been reading, on a daily basis, the top secret messages sent from German headquarters to the German commanders-in-chief in the field by the most secret system of German communication, the Enigma machine. At times these top secret German military, naval and airforce orders were read in Britain simultaneously with the despatch of the orders from Berlin to the field commanders.

Another potentially serious threat for Hitler came on December 29, when Roosevelt told the American people that the United States 'must be the great arsenal of democracy'. These words gave courage in Britain to those who wondered how they could survive the continuing aerial bombardment. That night an air raid over London destroyed or severely damaged many famous buildings and churches, and engulfed St Paul's Cathedral in flames. It also brought the British civilian death toll for December to 3,793.

Far from the European war, on August 21, on Stalin's orders, Leon Trotsky was murdered in Mexico, stabbed with an ice-pick. His assassination showed how long the arm of vengeance could be. Nor did vengeance stop there. As soon as news of Trotsky's death reached Moscow, Stalin's secret police chief issued an order for the 'liquidation of active Trotskyites in the camps'. Once again the labour camp regions were combed, and hundreds, perhaps thousands of victims executed.

Another camp had been set up in the autumn of 1940, not in Russia but in German-occupied Poland, a German 'quarantine' camp where Poles were punished for 'acts of rebellion or disobedience'. The camp was Auschwitz. Hundreds of Poles were put to death there in its first few months, many executed in front of the other prisoners. That autumn, in preparation for what the SS called the 'final solution' of the Jewish question, tests were carried out at Auschwitz using a commercial pesticide, Zyklon-B. Those experimented on were Soviet soldiers being held as prisoners-of-war. The test was hailed as a success by those who devised it.

Hitler prepared to invade Greece in 1941. His generals warned him of the difficulties if the invasion of Russia had to be delayed, but Hitler brushed their fears aside, and continued to plan for the invasion of Russia after the defeat of Greece. British troops, alerted to Hitler's plans through Enigma, began to arrive in Greece from March 5.

In Yugoslavia, the Regent, Prince Paul, bowed to German pressure to allow German troops through Yugoslavia on their way to attack Greece. In protest against the alignment with Germany, on March 27 the Belgrade government was overthrown and a new Prime Minister pledged to oppose the passage of German troops. Summoning his military commanders, Hitler postponed the invasion of the Soviet Union from May 1 until June 22 and instructed them to plan for the conquest of Yugoslavia 'with merciless harshness'.

On the morning of 6 April 1941 German bombers attacked Belgrade. In a single day 17,000 Yugoslav civilians were killed. In response, eighty British aircraft bombed Berlin on the night of April 8–9, when Hitler was forced to spend part of the night in his air raid shelter. No Berliners were killed. In a German counter-retaliation on London on April 16, more than 2,300 Londoners were killed, as well as forty Canadian soldiers who were on leave in the capital.

On April 10 the German army entered Zagreb, and then handed the city to the Croat nationalists, who declared a separate Croat State.

Three days later German forces occupied Belgrade. In northern Greece
a stand was made by Greek and Allied forces, among them many
New Zealanders, and for a few days the Germans were checked, but
by April 16 the line was breached. On April 23 the Greek army
surrendered. The Allied troops – British, Australians, New Zealanders and Poles – began their evacuation on the following day, 50,000
being taken off, mostly to Crete. On April 25 Hitler ordered preparations to be made for an airborne invasion of Crete.

On April 27 the Germans entered Athens. A month later, on May
20, German airborne forces landed on Crete, the largest parachute and
glider landing ever undertaken. At first it seemed the Germans might
be defeated by the land forces arrayed against them, but German air
power proved decisive and German dive bombing deadly. On May
27 the Allied forces began yet another evacuation: 17,000 men were
taken off in five nights.

On May 24, while the battle for Crete was at its height, the
German battleship *Bismarck* opened fire in the distant North Atlantic
against the British battlecruiser *Hood*. After eight minutes, shells
from the *Bismarck* pierced the deck of the *Hood*, blowing up her
munitions magazine. The warship sank immediately. All but three
of her 1,418 officers and men were killed. Three days later the
Bismarck was herself tracked down by British warships and attacked.
As she burned her captain gave orders to scuttle the ship: 2,107 of
her crew of 2,222 were drowned. The pride of Hitler's navy was at
the bottom of the sea.

The long-awaited German invasion of the Soviet Union began on 22
June 1941. During the first day, in an indication of what was to
come, dozens of Russian villages were burned down after the German
army had passed through them. Many of their inhabitants – Russian
peasants and Russian Jews – were murdered on the spot. 'We have
only to kick in the door and the whole rotten structure will come
crashing down,' Hitler told General Jodl at his new headquarters at
Rastenburg, in East Prussia.

On the fourth day of the German invasion, the commander of
the 47th Panzer Corps, General Lemelsen, protested to his subordi-
nates about the 'senseless shootings of both prisoners-of-war and

civilians'. The shootings went on. The hundreds of thousands of Russian soldiers who were taken prisoner were denied the most elementary rights accorded to prisoners-of-war. Many were put into the fields without any form of cover, surrounded by barbed wire and guards, refused medical attention, food and even water, and in the course of a few weeks were deliberately starved to death. Others, who were being marched to the rear, were beaten and shot down as they marched. Yet others, when winter came, were allowed no shelter, and froze to death in their hundreds of thousands.

From the first days of the German invasion of the Soviet Union the SS Special Task Forces took Jews out of their homes to the nearest wood or ravine, and shot them down. Tens of thousands of Jews were murdered in the first few weeks; hundreds of thousands in the months ahead; as many as a million by the end of the year. As the executions spread from town to town and village to village, babies and small children were thrown into the deep pits in which their parents had been shot.

On June 29 Stalin ordered the destruction of everything that could be destroyed, to deny it to the Germans. This 'scorched earth' policy was to be carried out in every locality that was about to be abandoned. What could not be evacuated must be destroyed, 'leaving the enemy with not a single locomotive, not a truck, not a loaf of bread, not a litre of fuel'. At the same time, newly formed partisan groups were instructed to blow up bridges, railway tracks, telephone and telegraph wires and installations behind the lines.

On July 2 a decision was made in Moscow to evacuate all factories on the line of the German advance throughout the industrial regions of Southern Russia. In one day, twenty-six armaments factories were given the order to move. On July 16 the last Soviet defence line protecting Moscow was broken. Hitler was jubilant. 'We must now face the task of cutting up our cake according to our needs in order to be able, first to dominate it, second to administer it, third to exploit it.' He even welcomed the Russian partisan activity behind the lines, telling the senior officers at Rastenburg: 'It enables us to exterminate everyone who opposes us'.

The British Government realized that if the Soviet Union were defeated, as she might well be, by late autumn, Hitler would turn against Britain. At Churchill's urging, Stalin was sent military equipment of the highest quality, much of which had just arrived from the United States, intended for Britain's war arsenal. At their first ever meeting, held on board ship off Newfoundland, Churchill and Roosevelt agreed to give immediate aid to the Soviet Union 'on a gigantic scale'. Each shipment, whether of planes or war material, ran enormous risks. The British merchant seamen who maintained the lifeline to northern Russia were among the unsung heroes of the Second World War.

On September 1 the German forces attacking Leningrad cut the city off from all rail connection with Moscow. With its million civilian inhabitants, including tens of thousands of refugees, Leningrad was being bombed every day from the air, and pounded by artillery fire. In Moscow, as the German army drew closer, Stalin found time to settle old scores. On September 5 he signed a list on which were the names of 170 people, most of them already prisoners, who were to be shot. One of them was Christian Rakovsky, the former Soviet Ambassador to Britain who had been spared the death sentence three years earlier by the intervention of the British Labour Party leadership. At the time of his execution he was seventy-three.

In the third week of September it was announced from Berlin that 86,000 German soldiers had been killed since the invasion of the Soviet Union almost three months earlier, an average of more than 1,000 a day. But on September 19, when German troops entered Kiev, the capital of the Ukraine, half a million Soviet soldiers were taken prisoner. Almost all of them were to die in the months ahead as a result of deliberate starvation and brutality. Cruelty was a daily occurrence. When three SS sentries were killed in a Russian village in mid-September all the villagers, several hundred old men, women and children, were machine-gunned. In Yugoslavia, a hundred Serb hostages were being shot for every German killed. In Greece, villages which gave support to Greek partisans were burned down, and hundreds of their inhabitants shot. In France, fifty hostages were shot at Nantes in reprisal for the assassination of the local German military commander. In Kiev, only ten days after the German occupation, 33,000 Jews were taken to a ravine at nearby Babi Yar and killed during three days of savagery.

Allied aid to the Soviet Union was intensified. In the last week of September the whole of that week's British tank production was sent to Russia, and all the fighter planes (1,800), tanks (2,250), anti-tank guns (500) and Tommy guns (23,000) sent from the United States to Britain were diverted to Russia. But Allied aid might prove in vain if Hitler could achieve his goal of victory before the winter. On October 2 he launched the campaign for the capture of Moscow. 'Today begins the last, great, decisive battle of the war,' he announced in a radio communiqué.

On October 15 Stalin ordered the evacuation of all government offices from Moscow to the Volga. In front of Moscow, anti-tank ditches, one of them four miles long, were being dug by women labour detachments brought from the capital. On October 19, German troops were only sixty-five miles away. Six days later, the first deep snow fell on the Moscow Front. It offered the prospect of growing difficulties for the attackers, and a protective shield for the defenders.

On November 12 the temperature on the Moscow Front fell to -12°C, bringing frostbite, a nightmare, to the German soldiers. No provision had been made to enable them to fight at such low temperatures. It had been assumed in Berlin that the war would be won well before winter. By contrast, the Russian army, whose training had always included winter fighting, possessed specially trained ski troops, who first went into action on November 16.

On November 25 Hitler confided to his adjutant: 'We started one month too late.' The adjutant added: 'Time is his greatest nightmare now.' On December 1 a German attempt to break through the snow-covered defences of Moscow was unsuccessful. When ordered to renew their efforts, many of the German soldiers screamed out in agony that they could not go on. German sentries who fell asleep at their post were found in the morning frozen to death. Despite a ferocious blizzard on December 2, some German troops managed to reach a village twelve miles from the centre of Moscow, but they were pushed back.

Not only the freezing weather but the high scale of casualties was breaking the German morale. In the last two weeks of November and the first four days of December, 85,000 German troops were killed in action on the Moscow Front, the same number as had been killed throughout the whole Eastern Front between mid-June and mid-November. The rate of deaths in action had risen from an average of just over 400 day to almost 5,000.

Hitler knew he must capture Moscow or face a prolonged and possibly interminable war. A further German attack was ordered on December 4. The temperature had fallen to almost the coldest ever recorded in the Moscow area: 35°C below zero. In that temperature the German tanks could not be started. Even after lighting a fire underneath a tank it took four hours before the engine could be made to start. Thousands of men froze to death in their trenches. On December 5 the Russians began a counter-attack. Hitler ordered his troops to hold on 'at all costs', but by nightfall the German front line had been driven back. Hitler would not enter Moscow that year in triumph. Nor, as he had often told his listeners at Rastenburg, would he be able to burn it to the ground.

On Sunday December 7, as the Germans were being pushed back from Moscow, a combined force of 366 Japanese bombers and fighters attacked the United States warships at anchor at Pearl Harbor. This was the climax of Japan's ambition to establish its control throughout the Far East and the Western Pacific. Four American battleships were blown up, or sank where they lay at anchor. Four more were damaged. Eleven other warships were sunk or disabled, and 2,403 Americans were killed, 1,777 of them on the battleship *Arizona*.

Japan had also bombed American airfields in the Philippines and the British airfield in Hong Kong, where all but one of the aircraft on the tarmac were destroyed. In a simultaneous Japanese bombing raid on Singapore, sixty-one civilians were killed. At the same time the northernmost island in the Philippines was occupied by Japanese soldiers, and a Japanese fleet carrying 24,000 combat troops reached Malaya. Elated at what he thought would be a rapid Japanese victory over the United States, on December 11 Hitler declared war, by this act bringing the United States in as a belligerent in the struggle for Europe. Within two and a half years a vast American army was to land in Northern Europe and penetrate into the heart of Germany.

Off the coast of Malaya, two days after the Japanese troop landings, Japanese torpedo-carrying aircraft sank the British battleship the *Prince of Wales* and her sister ship the *Repulse*: 840 officers and men were killed. Japan overran the American island of Guam, Hong Kong, the Dutch East Indies, Malaya and the Philippines. The Japanese are occupying all the islands, one after another,' Hitler told Himmler on December 18. They will get hold of Australia too. The White race will disappear from those regions.' In Europe the systematic deportation had begun of Jews from ghettos throughout Poland, and in due course from towns throughout Western Europe, to remote camps where they were murdered by gas. The first such death camp was established in a forest near the village of Chelmno, in German-occupied western Poland, where as many as 300,000 Jews were murdered within a year. Several other camps – among them Auschwitz – were to exceed even Chelmno's destructive power.

In the Far East the prisoners of war of the Japanese quickly learned that their captors did not consider them worthy of decent treatment. The first Western soldiers to experience Japanese methods were British and Canadians captured in Hong Kong. In batches of fifty and more, they were routinely roped together and bayoneted to death.

At a prisoner-of-war camp in German-occupied Poland, 100,000 Soviet soldiers died during the winter after being herded together in vast open fields, surrounded by barbed wire and guards, and given no food. They dug holes in which to try to get shelter from the wind and snow, and ate grass and roots to try to keep alive. But it was not long before all the grass and roots were used up. Any Polish villagers caught trying to throw them food were shot.

The battle front also had its horrors other than war itself. In a single day in December on the Eastern Front 14,000 German soldiers submitted to the amputation of their frozen, gangrenous limbs. Few of them survived more than a few hours. In Leningrad, more than 3,000 people were dying every day of starvation, 3,700 on Christmas Day alone.

On 1 January 1942, from London, Washington and Moscow, the Allies declared their war aims: 'to ensure life, liberty, independence and religious freedom, and to preserve the rights of man and justice'. Twelve days later, in London, the representatives of nine occupied countries signed a declaration that all those guilty of 'war crimes' would be punished after the war. The bluntness of the declaration did not, however, stop those crimes. At a meeting a week later, at Wannsee outside Berlin, German officials, with SS guidance, discussed the planned deportation and destruction of more than six million European Jews. The destruction was carefully recorded. In sending his summary of the mass murder of Jews in Lithuania over the previous seven months, the SS Colonel in charge itemized the shootings day by day and village by village. He then added them up for his superiors to see at a glance: in all 138,272 Jews had been murdered, of whom 34,464 were children. On January 30, while Hitler celebrated the ninth anniversary of his coming to power, he told a vast crowd in Berlin: 'The war will not end as the Jews imagine it will, namely with the uprooting of the Aryans, but the result of this war will be the complete annihilation of the Jews.'

In the Far East, Singapore surrendered to the Japanese on February 15 after incessant Japanese shelling and bombing. The British Empire's largest city east of India had fallen. The soldiers who surrendered included 32,000 Indians, 16,000 British and 14,000 Australians. In the years ahead more than half of them were to die as prisoners-of-war in circumstances of the harshest deprivation and cruel treatment. On February 16 twenty-five British soldiers who had surrendered in Malaya were taken to the shore, bayoneted and shot. Sixty-five Australian nurses who were with them were then ordered to march into the sea. As they did so, Japanese machine-gunners opened fire. Only one nurse survived. Two days later, on Singapore Island, 5,000 Chinese civilians, most of them prominent members of the island's thriving Chinese community, were rounded up and taken into captivity. After two weeks all of them had been killed.

In a Japanese air raid on the Australian city of Darwin, on February 19, all seventeen ships in the harbour, including an American destroyer, were sunk. In the air battle twenty-two Australian and American planes were shot down, for the loss of only five Japanese planes. The death toll on the ground was 240.

On the Eastern Front, Russian partisans, often hundreds of miles behind the front line, had begun to control large areas of forest and swamp, destroying German army stores and disrupting rail and road communications. Armaments and even soldiers were parachuted to them by the Soviet army. At the beginning of March Hitler was told that more than 200,000 German soldiers had been killed in Russia since June 1941.

For almost two years Auschwitz had been the place of the execution of hundreds of Poles, and of terrible tortures. In the early months of 1942 a new camp was being built there, in the nearby hamlet of Birkenau. More than a million Jews were to be brought to Birkenau by train from all over Europe, mostly in sealed railway trucks in conditions of the utmost squalor, during which many died. Most trains brought a thousand deportees to Birkenau. Of those thousand, half were usually murdered by gas within a few hours of their arrival. Heinrich Grüber, a German Protestant pastor who had been imprisoned in Dachau for having denounced the murder of Jews, later recalled the arrival in Dachau of railway wagons from Auschwitz filled with clothes: 'We were shaken to the depths of our soul when the first transports of children's shoes arrived – we men who were inured to suffering and to shock had to fight back tears.' Later thousands more children's shoes arrived. 'This was the most terrible thing for us, the most bitter thing, perhaps the worst thing that befell us.'

Japanese troops crossed the border of Thailand into British Burma. During an air attack on Mandalay, 2,000 Burmese were killed and much of the city set on fire. Rangoon was evacuated on March 7. That day the Dutch on Java surrendered, and 100,000 Dutch, British, Australian and American troops were taken prisoner. More than 80,000 Dutch civilians were also interned: 10,000 of them died in captivity. In a prisoner-of-war camp on Java, an Australian medical officer recorded in his clandestine diary how three Dutch prisoners-of-war, who had been caught while trying to escape, were 'tied to poles and bayoneted to death like pigs before their comrades'.

*　　*　　*

On the Eastern Front, a sustained German attack on Soviet partisan units was launched on March 19. Dozens of Russian villages were set on fire and their inhabitants killed. But these murders – in one area at least 3,500 villagers were killed in a few days – only served to strengthen partisan determination. In Yugoslavia a German army directive ordered the destruction of whole villages wherever partisan activity had taken place. 'Removal of the population to concentration camps can also be useful,' the directive noted. In Poland, after a German patrol was attacked in a small town on March 20, a hundred Poles working in a nearby labour camp were taken to the town and hanged in the square, the inhabitants being forced to watch.

As part of Britain's scheme to help the Soviet Union before the German 1942 offensive, Lübeck on the Baltic was bombed on the night of March 28–29. Eighty per cent of the medieval city was destroyed, including the Marienkirche, known as the 'mother church of Northern Germany'. A factory making U-boat components was also destroyed. That night 312 citizens were killed in Lübeck, the highest German civilian death toll thus far in a British bombing raid.

Hitler retaliated by bombing British cities with medieval town centres. In the raids on Bath, Norwich and York, starting on April 23, many ancient buildings were destroyed and 938 civilians killed. In the raid on York the medieval Guildhall was destroyed.

At the beginning of April the Japanese completed the conquest of the Philippine island of Luzon, where American and Filipino troops had fought tenaciously on the Bataan peninsula. The Japanese took 76,000 prisoners, of whom 12,000 were American. They were marched northward for sixty-five miles, and treated so brutally that 5,000 Filipinos and 600 Americans died. Those who fell while marching were clubbed or bayoneted to death as they lay on the ground. In their first few weeks behind barbed wire, a further 16,000 Filipinos and 1,000 Americans died of starvation, disease and the brutality of their Japanese guards.

On April 29, Japanese troops in Burma seized the terminus of the Burma Road, ending the possibility of further Allied overland supplies to Nationalist China. It did not seem the tide of war could turn in the Far East or the Pacific, but on May 2, in the Coral Sea, American warships intercepted a Japanese invasion fleet on its way to New Guinea, and in the ensuing battle, seventy Japanese and sixty-six American planes were shot down. The Japanese losses made it impossible for the invasion fleet to continue.

The heaviest British bombing raid yet carried out over Germany was launched on the night of May 30–31 against Cologne. More than a thousand bombers took part. Within ninety minutes 1,455 tons of bombs were dropped and enormous damage done. Thirty-six factories were unable to continue production. This was almost the equivalent of the total of all the destruction caused in all previous British bombing raids over Germany.

As many as 2,500 separate fires were started in Cologne that night, and 3,330 buildings destroyed, among them nine hospitals, seventeen churches, sixteen schools, six department stores and two cinemas. The number of dead was between 469 and 486, the highest yet caused by a British bombing raid. British civilian deaths in the Blitz had been more than ten times as high.

As the German army launched its new onslaught against Russia, it also secured a dramatic victory in North Africa. There, British and Commonwealth troops based in Egypt had earlier pushed their Italian and German adversaries back across the deserts of Libya, but then General Rommel overran Tobruk, taking 30,000 British, Australian and other Allied prisoners. The fall of Tobruk was followed ten days later, on the Eastern Front, by the German capture of the Crimean city of Sebastopol. The German army was moving forward both to the Suez Canal and the Caucasian oil fields. It would reach neither, but in the fighting for both, the Allies were to come to the brink of disaster.

In the summer of 1942 Germany and Japan were both confident of a continuing series of victories. But neither was able to achieve its aims without high losses. In the first week of June, alerted by the daily reading of Japan's top secret radio signals, American warships intercepted a Japanese invasion fleet on its way to Midway Island, the two-square-mile indispensable stepping stone for the planned

Japanese invasion of the Hawaiian Islands, and the last outpost between Japan and Hawaii still under American control. An American aircraft attack on June 5 sank all four Japanese aircraft carriers, three of which had been among the five that had taken part in the attack on Pearl Harbor six months earlier. The Japanese lost 332 aircraft and 3,500 men in the battle. American losses were 150 aircraft and 307 men. Like the Battle of the Coral Sea a month earlier, the Battle of Midway was a defeat in the arm of warfare which Japan had chosen for conquest: air power.

On June 23 the Japanese sent 300 British prisoners of war to a base in Thailand. Three months later 3,000 Australian prisoners of war were sent to a camp in Burma. Between the two camps lay hundreds of miles of jungle and ravines. The Japanese wanted to have a railway between the two, along which they could move troops and military supplies from Thailand to Burma. Prisoners of war of all nationalities were the builders: 15,000 perished.

The German drive towards the Caucasus opened on June 26. That week the German advance into Egypt was halted by a combined force of British, Indian, South African and New Zealand troops. Rommel would never reach the Suez Canal.

Sensing victory against Russia, on July 16 Hitler left his East Prussian headquarters and moved to the Russian town of Vinnitsa, closer to the front. Behind the lines mass murder continued daily. On July 22 the German SS in Warsaw, helped by Ukrainian and Latvian SS men, rounded up 6,250 Warsaw Jews and deported them to the death camp at Treblinka and their deaths. Deportations then continued every day. After seven weeks more than 250,000 of Warsaw's Jews had been deported and killed.

On August 7 the Americans launched their first land-based offensive in the Pacific, landing 16,000 troops on Guadalcanal in the Solomon Islands. In a month of fighting, much of it hand-to-hand, 1,600 Americans and 9,000 Japanese were killed. Most Japanese soldiers, when capture was imminent, committed suicide rather than face what for them was the personal humiliation of captivity.

Two days after the American landing on Guadalcanal the German army reached Maikop in the Caucasus, the first oilfield on their line of advance. The oil wells had been blown up by the Soviet defenders as they withdrew. The German advance to the much larger oil wells of Grozny and Baku continued. On August 19, partly to take some pressure off the Eastern Front, an Allied landing on the French channel port of Dieppe, in which almost 5,000 Canadians and just over a thousand British troops took part, was driven off: 907 Canadians and more than a hundred British soldiers were killed, and 2,000 of the attackers taken prisoner. Dieppe was a costly but important prelude to the Anglo-American cross-Channel landings. It would be almost two years before a permanent Allied foothold could be secured in northern Europe.

On August 21 the Swastika flag was raised by German soldiers on the highest mountain in the Caucasus. Two days later German soldiers reached the outskirts of Stalingrad. Russian troops resisted them in every street, building and cellar. On September 27 the Swastika flag was raised over the headquarters of the Stalingrad Communist Party. Hitler, elated, flew back from his Russian headquarters to Berlin to await the moment, which he expected within twenty-four hours, when he could announce the fall of Stalingrad.

Another three weeks of stubborn Russian house-to-house resistance followed. When, on October 20, German soldiers finally reached the Volga river bank near the centre of the city, Soviet soldiers were in possession only of a thousand yards of shoreline. 'The Führer is convinced the Russians are collapsing,' one of his Field Marshals reported on October 21. 'He says that twenty million will have to starve.' Three days later, however, with Stalingrad still resisting, Rommel's forces in Egypt were defeated at El Alamein. It was a blow to Hitler's plan to take over the Middle East, where, as in the Caucasus, oil was to be found in abundance. But on November 6 Hitler learned that the German advance in the Caucasus had been driven back from the outskirts of Grozny. The main Caucasian oilfields were never to fall into German hands. More bad news for Hitler came a day later, on November 7, when American troops landed in French North Africa. Within three days the Allies were in control of 1,300 miles of Atlantic and Mediterranean coastline. The Vichy regime in North Africa collapsed.

By November 9 Rommel had been driven back 200 miles. To try to prevent Germany's ejection from North Africa altogether, Hitler ordered several hundred German transport aircraft to fly there at once with military reinforcements. To do this the planes taking troops to Stalingrad and the Caucasus had to be brought back from the Eastern Front. In addition, of 500 fighter aircraft moved to Tunisia, 400 had to be brought from Russia. But despite Hitler's denuding the Russian front of crucial aircraft, on November 13 Rommel was driven out of Tobruk, his capture of which that summer had been such a blow to Britain. Realizing that sooner or later the American troops pushing in from the east and the British from the west must crush him, Rommel asked Hitler for permission to withdraw from North Africa altogether. Hitler refused. It was a 'political' necessity, he said, for Germany to have a bridgehead in North Africa.

On November 19 the Red Army began the encirclement of all the German forces inside Stalingrad. But when the German commander, General von Paulus, asked permission to withdraw before the trap was closed around him, Hitler insisted he remain in the city.

On December 2, in an atomic pile located at the University of Chicago's disused football stadium, an Italian émigré scientist, Enrico Fermi, who had fled from Italy because his wife was Jewish, was conducting an experiment. By mid-afternoon he produced what he was looking for: the first self-sustaining nuclear chain reaction. The next step was to find and process the uranium needed to manufacture an atomic bomb.

In the Pacific, on the fringes of their newly won conquests, the Japanese had begun to retreat. Under fierce American pressure, the Japanese forces on Guadalcanal, to which repeated Japanese reinforcements had been beaten off, were abandoned, although some troops, refusing to surrender, fought on until they were all killed. In New Guinea, when the last Japanese stronghold surrendered, many of the garrison swam out to sea to drown rather than be taken prisoner.

The Germans, like the Japanese, were facing a gradual but definite retreat at every extremity of their conquests. On 14 January 1943, Roosevelt and Churchill, meeting at Casablanca, in recently liberated

French North Africa, agreed that the bombing of Germany both by day and by night should be intensified. Thirteen days later, the United States bombers, based in Britain, carried out their first bombing raid over Germany.

Trapped inside Stalingrad, von Paulus asked Hitler permission to surrender. Hitler replied: 'The Sixth Army will hold its positions to the last man and the last round.' To encourage von Paulus to continue fighting he then appointed him Field Marshal. That same day, January 31, von Paulus surrendered. During the siege of Stalingrad 160,000 German soldiers had been killed; 90,000 were taken into captivity, marched eastward to Siberia. Tens of thousands died on the march, and tens of thousands more in captivity.

On the night of March 5–6 British bombers struck at Essen: 160 acres of factories, railways and stores were hit, fifty-three factory buildings destroyed or damaged, 3,000 homes destroyed and 457 people killed. Goebbels wrote in his diary: 'If the English continue their raids on this scale, they will make things exceedingly difficult for us.' Three nights later, British bombers struck at Nuremberg. Six hundred buildings were destroyed, several factories damaged and 284 citizens killed. On the following night, Munich was bombed. As a result of a strong wind the main weight of bombs missed their targets, hitting instead the cathedral, four churches and eleven hospitals. More than 200 people were killed. It was not only over Germany that the Allied bombers sought their targets. On April 5, when American bombers attacked the Renault assembly lines near Paris, 228 French civilians were killed. That same day an American daylight raid on Antwerp, the aim of which was to destroy an aircraft factory, failed because of a navigational error to find the factory. Most of the bombs fell on a built-up area of the city, killing 936 civilians. Among the dead were 209 schoolchildren who were at school.

At the beginning of March the Japanese tried to send reinforcements to New Guinea. The movement of their ships was betrayed by the interception of their own top secret signals, which they could not conceive were being read by the Americans, any more than the Germans could conceive the British were reading their most secret operational orders and tactical secrets. As a result of this knowledge,

American bombers intercepted the invasion fleet, sinking all eight of the Japanese troop transports: 3,500 Japanese soldiers were drowned. Of the 150 Japanese warplanes that took part in the battle, 102 were shot down.

Japanese cruelty against captured Allied servicemen knew no bounds. On March 29 an American flight-lieutenant was shot down over New Guinea. He was sentenced to be decapitated. A Japanese officer described the sequel: 'The unit commander has drawn his favourite sword. He taps the prisoner's neck lightly with the back of the blade, then raises it above his head with both arms, and brings it down with a sweep. All is over. The head is dead white like a doll's.'

On the last day of April, as part of the daily deportation of Jews to their deaths from all over German-dominated Europe, 2,000 Polish Jews were taken by rail from the town of Wlodawa to the nearby death camp at Sobibor. On reaching the camp the Jews, sensing something terrible was in store for them, attacked the SS guards with pieces of wood torn from the carriages. The Jews were killed by machine-gun fire or grenades. It was a courageous, hopeless act of resistance.

There was profit in the mass destruction of human life. In the three months up to the end of April the personal belongings of murdered Jews, delivered to Germany, included 94,000 men's watches, 33,000 women's watches and 25,000 fountain pens. The men's watches were distributed to combat troops, to men of the submarine service and to guards in concentration camps. The 5,000 most expensive watches went to the Reichsbank in Berlin for their gold to be melted down. Others were retained by the SS for their personal use.

On May 8 the German Air Force abandoned its remaining North African airfields and withdrew to Sicily. A day later, German forces in Tunisia surrendered unconditionally to the Allies. The pace of Allied warmaking intensified. On May 14 the British and American Chiefs of Staff agreed to a combined Anglo-American bomber offensive, from bases in Britain, under which the Americans would bomb

German industrial targets by day and the British by night. On the night of May 16–17 a spectacular raid on the Möhne and Eder dams, making use of a new invention, the 'bouncing bomb', led to severe damage to the dams and massive loss of water needed for the industries of the Ruhr. Widespread flooding disrupted road, rail and canal communications. The cost of the raid in human terms was high, on both sides. The attack was made by nineteen planes. Eight failed to return. Of the total aircrew of fifty-six of the eight planes, fifty-three were killed. The Germans who died that night were mostly civilians, drowned when the dams broke. Among the dead were several hundred Russian women who had been brought from the Ukraine to work on farms in Germany, and were in a camp five miles downstream from the Möhne Dam. The total death toll of 1,260 was the highest thus far in any air raid on Germany.

On April 18 the Jews in the Warsaw ghetto rose up in revolt. The Germans used machine-guns, artillery and flame-throwers against men and women with pistols and hand-made Molotov Cocktails. In the course of the fighting 14,000 Jews were killed. Almost all those still alive – 42,000 in all – when the revolt was finally crushed on May 16 were sent to labour camps where, before the end of the year, they were murdered. How could the evils of Nazism be ended? At a meeting in the White House on May 19, three days after the crushing of the Warsaw ghetto revolt, Churchill and Roosevelt agreed that the cross-Channel landing should take place as soon as possible in 1944. Meanwhile, Allied bombers continued their almost nightly raids. A British air raid on the night of May 29–30 on Wuppertal, in the Ruhr, created an intense firestorm in the narrow streets of the old town. A thousand acres of buildings were destroyed, including five of the six largest factories, and 3,400 people were killed, by far the highest death toll yet in a single bombing raid against Germany. Watching a Royal Air Force film of the raid, taken from one of the bombers, Churchill asked: 'Are we beasts? Are we taking this too far?'

The bombing went on. On the night of June 11–12, a raid on Düsseldorf destroyed 130 acres of factories, industrial buildings and homes, started more than 8,000 fires, and killed 1,292 people.

*   *   *

Undeterred by the disaster at Stalingrad, Hitler planned a third German offensive against the Soviet Union. In a message to his troops in the Kursk salient on July 4, he told them: 'More than anything else, your victory will show the whole world that resistance to the power of the German Army is hopeless.' But two and a half hours before the offensive began the next morning, alerted by British Intelligence's reading of the German generals' instructions, the Russians opened a massive artillery bombardment on the German troops forming up to attack, and on their artillery positions. The German element of surprise was lost, and much damage inflicted on the German forces before they could advance.

The largest tank battle in history then began, with 6,000 tanks on the battlefield. In the skies 4,000 aircraft were in combat. On July 10, the fifth day of the battle, as the Russians held back the German assault, the Allies invaded Sicily. Hitler was suddenly fighting a war on two fronts simultaneously. Neither went his way. Sicily, the stepping stone to Italy, was captured by the Western Allies, and Kursk, the way back to the Volga, was held by the Russians. On July 22 the Americans entered Palermo, on the northern coast of Sicily. Two days later the Fascist Grand Council, meeting in Rome, voted for Mussolini's dismissal. One Fascist dictatorship was ended.

On the night of July 28–29 the British bombed Hamburg. The raid lasted forty-three minutes. A firestorm was created in the city centre as hundreds of fires merged into one and 42,000 people were killed: more civilians in this one raid than in all the German raids on London together. Albert Speer, who was about to be put in control of all German raw material and industrial production, warned Hitler that if three or four other cities were bombed as Hamburg it could lead to 'an end of the war'. But no city was to be bombed in this way, with a firestorm leading to tens of thousands of deaths, until the bombing of Dresden a year and a half later.

The German army was in retreat on two fronts. The evacuation of Sicily began on August 11 and continued for six days. On August 22 the Germans withdrew from Kharkov, the main city of the eastern Ukraine. Half a million German soldiers had been killed in Russia since June 1941. 'It is a curious thing,' Goebbels wrote in his diary, 'that although every individual soldier returning from the Eastern Front considers himself personally superior to the Bolshevik soldier, we are still retreating and retreating.'

In Greece, partisans attacked German patrols, storehouses and communications, derailed trains and seized stocks of raw materials needed for the German war effort. In reprisals, in the course of a year, 10,000 civilians were killed. The Greek guerrillas fought on, often engaging the Germans in armed combat. Resistance activities were also growing in Denmark, Holland, France, Belgium, Poland, Yugoslavia and Norway.

On September 3, after Allied troops landed on mainland Italy, the Italian Government agreed to an armistice. German troops, hurrying southward to forestall the Allies, entered Rome five days later. Mussolini was being held by anti-Fascist Italians in a ski resort hotel 9,000 feet up in the Abruzzi mountains. On September 12 ninety German soldiers using gliders and a small plane, led by the German commando leader, SS Colonel Otto Skorzeny, landed on the mountain, outwitted the 250-strong Italian garrison, and flew off with Mussolini to a small airstrip near Rome. He was then flown to Hitler's headquarters in East Prussia. Hitler then established him as ruler of a small puppet administration in northern Italy: the Italian Social Republic, known as the Republic of Salo.

The German occupation of northern Italy put all the Jews there at risk. When the SS tried to seize all 5,000 of Rome's Jews for deportation to Auschwitz, 4,000 were given shelter in private homes, monasteries and convents, 477 of them in the Vatican. In Milan, where 600 Jews were seized and deported to Auschwitz, a further 6,000 were sheltered in Christian homes and survived the war.

Behind the German lines in Russia, anti-partisan sweeps that autumn led to the deaths of thousands of Russian villagers. Polish acts of resistance, which Goebbels noted in his diary on September 17 had 'increased enormously', were likewise met by executions and reprisals. In Paris, after French resistance fighters assassinated the German official responsible for rounding up Frenchmen for forced labour, fifty

Parisians were seized at random and shot. In Italy, as a reprisal for the capture of two German soldiers by Italian partisans, thirty Italian civilians were executed. On the other side of the globe ninety-six Allied prisoners of war being held by the Japanese on Wake Island were made to sit down on the beach in one long line with their backs to the sea. They were then blindfolded and, with their hands tied behind their backs, shot dead.

In North Borneo, local Chinese and the native Suluk people rose in revolt against Japanese rule and tyranny. Forty Japanese were killed. In reprisal, 189 suspects were rounded up and executed. But resistance never died. In the Philippines an American mining engineer, Wendell Fertig, led a force of several thousand Filipinos. In Burma an Englishman, Hugh Seagrim, organized a guerrilla force of 2,000 Karens. So savage were the Japanese reprisals on Karen villagers that Seagrim gave himself up to spare them further executions. He was shot. The Karen revolt continued. On 4 January 1944 a sustained Anglo-American air drop of munitions and supplies was inaugurated to help resistance groups in France, Belgium, Holland and Italy. In Denmark, executions were carried out by a special German squad whose task was to create docility through terror. Among the first people to be executed, on January 4, was a clergyman and poet, Kaj Munk. His funeral procession became a demonstration of Danish defiance. Five days after Munk's execution in Denmark, twenty-two Frenchmen held as hostages in prison in Lyon were shot dead as a reprisal for the death of two German soldiers in the city.

The Red Army crossed into Poland on January 6. Stalin, while celebrating the military achievement, sought political advantage from it. Five days earlier he had established a Communist-controlled Polish National Council, which was to be the 'supreme organ of democratic elements' in Poland, bypassing the Polish government in exile in London, which contained many members of the pre-war Polish Government. Communism would come to Poland with the Red Army. The London Poles continued to encourage resistance inside Poland with their Armia Krajowa, the National Army. The Polish National Council promoted a rival anti-German movement, the Armia Ludowa, the People's Army. Both were supplied with arms by their respective patrons in London and Moscow. Both fought tenaciously against the Germans and suffered massively in German reprisals. Both, conscious of the struggle ahead for the mastery of post-war Poland, fought each other.

A similar struggle between the forces of Communism and anti-Communism was taking place inside Yugoslavia, where two resistance groups, one headed by Drazha Mikhailovic and the other by Tito, competed for support from the Allies and struggled to drive the Germans out of areas in which they then established their respective political control. On January 15 the Germans launched their sixth military offensive against Tito's partisans in just over three years, driving them from their headquarters, but Tito, to whom Britain, the United States and the Soviet Union were each sending weapons, ammunition and advisers, moved the centre of his operations and continued to fight.

In Greece, partisan activity had also increased considerably. On January 18 Kurt Waldheim, an Austrian-born German intelligence officer – later Secretary General of the United Nations and President of Austria – estimated the number of Greek partisans active in northern Greece at 25,000. The Germans carried out repeated anti-partisan sweeps and executed villagers suspected of supporting the partisans. On May 1, two hundred Greek hostages were shot in Athens. Hitler urged his generals to combat resistance with severity, telling them on January 27: 'You can't smash terror by philosophizing, you have to smash it by even greater terror.' In five months, in Warsaw, 4,300 Poles were executed. When the head of the SS in Warsaw, General Kutschera, was killed by Polish partisans, 1,600 Poles were executed as a reprisal.

On 22 January 1944 an Allied army was put ashore at Anzio, half way between the Allied front line in Italy and German-held Rome. Within twenty-four hours more than 36,000 troops were ashore, for the loss of only thirteen of the attacking force, but then the Germans besieged the men who were meant to be linking up with the Allied line further south and pushing on to Rome.

On that Southern Front, despite repeated attacks by British, American, Polish and other Allied troops, the fortified hill and monastery of Monte Cassino, which blocked the route north, continued to be held by the Germans. In the monastery more than 500 civilian refugees were sheltering, together with the bishop. On February 14 the Allies dropped more than 400 tons of bombs – a fifth of the tonnage usually dropped during a night raid on the city of Berlin – reducing the monastery to ruins, and killing the bishop and 250 of the Italian civilians. But an Allied infantry attack later that day, in which Maori troops from New Zealand as well as Gurkhas from Nepal and Indian soldiers took part, fighting bayonet to bayonet, failed to drive out the German defenders.

At the end of February the Allies launched another Anglo-American air offensive against German aircraft factories, airfields, air storage parks and ball-bearing factories. These raids were seen as an essential preliminary to the cross-Channel landings, planned for the summer. German air power had first to be significantly reduced. In the British air raid on aircraft factories at Augsburg on the night of February 25–26, in which 700 citizens were killed, almost the whole of the medieval centre of the city was destroyed. The Germans made extraordinary efforts to restore production, and to move factories away from cities. In the last half of 1943 the average German monthly production of single-engine fighters was 851. By the summer of 1944, despite the bombing, it had almost doubled, to 1,581.

As part of the preparations for the cross-Channel landing, on the night of March 6–7, bombing raids began on railway marshalling yards, bridges and communications centres in northern France. During one raid in April, 640 Parisians were killed. Three days later, during an American daylight raid on the railway yards at Rouen, many bombs fell in error on the medieval centre of the town, and 400 citizens were killed.

Soviet forces were within a hundred miles of the border of Hungary. There was fear in Berlin that the Hungarian Regent, Admiral Horthy, might seek an agreement with Stalin rather than risk the destruction of his country and his regime. On March 19, German troops entered Hungary. Within two months more than 400,000 Jews, who hitherto had been protected by Horthy from deportation, were being deported to Auschwitz and killed.

In Italy, the Germans holding Monte Cassino continued to

frustrate the Allied hope of reaching Rome. In a massive bombing raid on the monastery on March 15 almost a thousand tons of bombs were dropped. Some bombs fell several miles from the target, killing 96 Allied soldiers and 140 Italian civilians. An infantry assault by British, Maori, Indian and Gurkha troops failed to drive the Germans out.

The German move against partisans was relentless. On March 23, after an Italian partisan threw a bomb at an SS unit in Rome, killing thirty-three SS men, the Germans rounded up 335 Italian men and boys and took them to the Ardeatine Caves, where all of them were shot. Of those executed in the caves, 253 were Catholics and 70 were Jews. Twelve were never identified. In the French Alps 8,000 German soldiers, with air support, tracked down a French resistance unit of 450 men and women. More than 400 of the French fighters were killed. In the second week of April, during an anti-partisan sweep in the rapidly dwindling areas of German-occupied Russia, 7,000 Russians were killed. Most of them were villagers who had taken no part in partisan activity.

A renewed Allied military offensive in Italy began on May 11. British, American, Indian, French, Polish and Moroccan troops were among those taking part, as was a force of Palestinian Jews, fighting under the symbol of the Star of David. In seven days Monte Cassino was overrun. The flag raised on the ruins was that of the Polish troops who had been prominent throughout the battle. More than 8,000 Allied troops had been killed in the last phase of the six-month struggle to break the German line at Cassino.

In the Pacific, American troops advanced from island to island. Each Japanese garrison, loyal to the emperor and the Japanese military code of honour, refused to surrender, even when confronted by over-whelmingly larger forces. On the northern coast of New Guinea the 15,000 Japanese defenders fought for more than six months, refusing to surrender. When the struggle was over 12,811 Japanese lay dead. The Americans lost just over 500 men. When the Admiralty Islands were overrun – at the height of the Cassino battle in Italy – 3,820 Japanese soldiers were killed and only seventy-five surrendered. Most of those who surrendered had been too badly injured to be able to kill themselves. The American death toll was 326. In the fighting for Saipan Island, 20,000 Japanese were killed in battle and a further 7,000 committed suicide, many of them in deliberately suicidal rifle and bayonet charges against the American troops facing them. In the battle for Guam 18,500 Japanese defenders were killed or committed suicide rather than surrender. More than 2,000 Americans also fell in the twenty-day battle. On Tinian, more than 6,000 Japanese soldiers were killed, and 290 Americans. Slowly, inexorably, massively, the Japanese forces were bleeding to death.

As the Allied army in Italy advanced northward from Cassino, the troops who had been trapped in the Anzio bridgehead for four months broke out. On May 25 the two forces linked up. The Normandy landings were only two weeks away. Allied air raids on railway lines and marshalling yards in France intensified. One raid against Lyon, intended to impede the movement of German reinforcements from southern France to the Normandy area, destroyed many of the designated targets but also killed 717 French civilians. By the last week of May, 3,000 French civilians had died as a result of Allied bombing judged essential if the Normandy landings were to succeed.

On the evening of June 4, American troops reached the centre of Rome. In the English Channel, during the night of June 5–6, a vast naval armada was on the move: 2,727 merchant ships, 2,500 landing craft in tow and 700 warships. At five minutes to midnight, as June 5 came to an end, several hundred British infantrymen went in by glider and captured two bridges on the eastern flank of the landing grounds. By dawn on the morning of June 6, more than 18,000 British and American parachutists were on the ground. At 6.30 that morning the first troops landed. They were Americans, with amphibious tanks, landing under fire. Within the hour, British and Canadian troops were ashore. Hitler instructed Rommel to drive the invaders back 'into the sea' by midnight, but when midnight came 155,000 Allied troops were ashore.

Behind the lines in Normandy members of the French Resistance were sabotaging bridges and railway lines. One resistance unit was operating near the town of Tulle. On June 9, as a reprisal for its activities, a German SS division seized 200 men at random in Tulle and, forcing wives and children to watch, hanged them on lamp posts and balconies outside their homes. In another reprisal, for an attack on a German military formation on its way to Normandy, a small village, Oradour-sur-Glane, which had no connection with the attack, was surrounded by SS troops who then murdered 642 of the villagers, of whom 190 were schoolchildren. Only two villagers managed to escape.

On the Normandy battlefield, Rommel struggled to prevent the Allies breaking out of the bridgehead, holding the city of Caen, a crucial German communications centre, and the chief Allied objective for the fourth day of the landings, for two months. As the battle for Caen began Hitler launched his much-vaunted 'secret weapon', a small pilotless, jet-propelled plane which carried a ton of explosives that detonated on impact. It was known as the V1 – the 'V' standing for Vergeltungswaffe (Reprisal Weapon). On mainland Britain, against which it was first launched on June 14, it was known as the flying bomb, Doodlebug, and Buzz Bomb. The only flying bomb to explode that day, in London, killed six people, the youngest an eight-month-old baby killed with his mother. Three days later two flying bombs which fell on London killed thirty-seven people, including thirteen patients, most of them children, and five nurses, in a hospital. On the following day, a Sunday, a flying bomb hit the Guards Chapel during a church service. Fifty-eight civilians and sixty-three service personnel were killed, including many American soldiers.

On June 22, three years to the day since the German invasion of the Soviet Union, Stalin launched his 1944 offensive. Hitler faced half a million advancing troops in the west – their numbers to be doubled within three weeks – and 1,700,000 in the east. Both armies had superior fuel resources and superior air power. Both had as their objective the conquest of Germany itself. The battle in the east proceeded with a swiftness that left Germany no time to establish meaningful defence lines. By the end of the first week 38,000 German troops had been killed and 116,000 taken prisoner.

German army officers, some fearful of defeat, others hating the Nazi and Gestapo system, were plotting to kill Hitler. When the conspirators approached Rommel for support, he passed back the message: 'Tell the people in Berlin they can count on me.' But on July 17, while in his car, he was severely wounded by machine-gun fire from an Allied fighter bomber. Taken to hospital, he was no longer able to serve either as a commander or a conspirator. The assassination plans continued. One of the plotters, Count Claus von Stauffenberg, who was often present at Hitler's military briefings, was given a bomb small enough to hide inside a briefcase, with a silent fuse.

On July 20 the German ring around the Allied forces in Normandy was broken. Hitler, at Rastenburg, held his briefing in a wooden hut near his bunker. He was studying a map on a large table when Stauffenberg activated the fuse of the bomb in his briefcase, then pushed the briefcase under the table with his foot and hurried out of the room. When he was 200 yards away the bomb went off. Watching the hut exploding, he assumed Hitler was dead and drove rapidly to the airfield at Rastenburg, then flew to Berlin. What he did not know was that one of the generals around the table, in trying to get a better look at the map, had inadvertently pushed the briefcase with his foot to the far side of the wooden frame holding up the table.

The wooden frame saved Hitler from being killed outright. He was injured, but was well enough to greet, a few hours later, a long-awaited visitor – Mussolini – and show him the ruins of the hut and how narrowly he had escaped assassination. That evening Goebbels broadcast over German radio to tell the German people that their leader was alive and in full possession of his faculties. A terrible vengeance was taken on the conspirators. Stauffenberg was arrested that same evening and put in front of a firing squad. In the months ahead more than 5,000 Germans were executed for their part in the conspiracy, or for their alleged sympathy with the conspirators. Rommel was given the choice of suicide, and a military hero's funeral, or a public trial and execution as a traitor. He chose suicide.

On July 22, as soon as Russian troops crossed the River Bug, the limit of the territory of Poland he wished to annex, Stalin set up a Polish Committee of National Liberation. Almost all its members were Polish Communists. In Warsaw, with the Soviet army only a few hundred miles away, there was concern that the Soviet Union would impose a Communist government as soon as its troops reached the capital, and on July 25 a Polish national uprising began. Members of the Home Army loyal to London joined forces with the Communist People's Army and seized two thirds of the city. But an attempt by the insurgents to capture the airport, as a base into which the British and Americans could fly supplies, was defeated.

On the night of August 4, flying from their base in southern Italy, thirteen British bombers, mostly manned by volunteer crews, reached central Poland, a distance of more than 750 miles, and the extreme limit of their range. Only two were able to get as far as Warsaw, where they dropped twenty-four containers of arms and ammunition. Twelve of the containers fell into the hands of the insurgents. The other twelve fell into German-controlled parts of the city. Five out of the thirteen bombers failed to return. Neither then nor later would Stalin let them make the forty- or fifty-mile flight beyond Warsaw to a Russian air base, where they could refuel. Stalin's aim was to see his own Communist Polish nominees installed in power. When the Soviet Army entered Lublin, at the height of the Warsaw battle, Stalin established the Polish Committee of National Liberation there as the interim Polish government, and declared Lublin to be the temporary capital of Poland.

On August 4, as the agony of Warsaw was in its early yet already terrifying stages, an episode took place 700 miles to the west, in Amsterdam. Eight Jews who had been hiding in an attic for almost two years were betrayed to the Gestapo and deported to Auschwitz. One was Anne Frank, a German-Jewish girl who had escaped to Holland before the war with her family. Only one of the eight, Anne Frank's father, survived the war. Anne and her sister Margot died in Belsen.

In Warsaw, the Polish insurgents fought on. By August 5 more than 15,000 Poles had been killed, many of them women and children. Within three days a further 30,000 civilians had been killed, including hundreds of patients in the hospitals and casualty stations. Stalin having refused a direct appeal from Churchill to help the Warsaw insurgents from the nearby airfields under his control, on August 12 Churchill authorized the despatch of twenty British bombers from their base in southern Italy. Each bomber carried twelve large containers of arms and ammunition to be dropped by parachute. Twenty-eight bombers set out. Among those who volunteered were Polish, British and South African crews. Fourteen of the bombers reached Warsaw, where three were shot down by German anti-aircraft fire. The rest dropped their containers. Of the thirty-five tons of supplies loaded on the bombers, less than five tons reached the insurgents. But even five tons was welcome assistance.

On the night of August 15 a further ten British bombers set off from southern Italy. Six failed to return. Among the aircrew killed that night were twenty South Africans. In all, of the 306 aircraft which set off for Warsaw from southern Italy, and also from Britain, forty-one were shot down, and 200 airmen killed. One American airman, captured by the Germans near a village outside Warsaw, was beaten to death by his captors.

On August 16 the Canadians fighting in Normandy entered Falaise. For twenty-four hours they were forced to fight inside the town, street by street and house by house, but finally, on August 17, Falaise was in Allied hands. During the final resistance in the Falaise pocket 10,000 German soldiers had been killed and 50,000 taken prisoner.

The Allies were poised to liberate Paris where, on August 19, there was an uprising by Resistance fighters. In Lyon, one of the last acts of the Gestapo before the Allies arrived was to take a hundred French hostages from prison, where they were being held on suspicion of being connected to the Resistance, drive them to a disused fort outside the city, and kill them.

On August 23 Roumania signed an armistice with the Russians. This defection cut Germany off from the oil of Ploesti. The Allies intensified their bombing of synthetic oil plants in Germany. In a daylight raid on an armaments factory, bombs falling wide of their target hit the nearby Buchenwald concentration camp. Four hundred prisoners, mostly Jews, and also eighty SS men, were killed. Also killed were several privileged prisoners being held as possible hostages, among them the tyre manufacturer Marcel Michelin – a French citizen – and Princess Mafalda, daughter of the King of Italy.

In an act of retaliation for the death of the SS men, the camp commandant ordered sixteen British and French parachutists who had been captured while on clandestine missions inside France to be hanged. Another of those killed that day as a reprisal was Ernst Thaelmann, the German Communist leader who had challenged Hitler for the Presidency in 1932. Sent to a concentration camp on 28 February 1933, by the time of his execution he had been a camp prisoner for more than eleven years. On August 24 a Free French armoured force entered Paris. In the days that followed, several thousand French men and women who had collaborated with the Germans during the occupation were killed in acts of vengeance. The elation of victory could not spare those who had served the conqueror.

On September 7 Hitler ordered the firing of a second 'secret weapon', the V2: Revenge Weapon-2. This was not a pilotless plane like its predecessor, but a rocket that carried an explosive charge. Missile warfare had begun. When a V2 hit a Woolworth department store in South London, 160 lunchtime shoppers were killed.

The Japanese were evacuating the Philippine Islands. Thousands of Allied prisoners of war, being taken to camps in Japan, were put in the holds of ships, allowed almost no food or water, and reduced to near starvation and madness. On September 7 an American submarine sank a large Japanese freighter. The submarine commander did not know there were 675 American prisoners of war on board. Only eighty-five survived the sinking. They were fortunate to be able to swim ashore, where they were sheltered by Filipino guerrillas.

Dozens of Japanese transport ships were sunk by the Americans during September. Many had prisoners of war in their holds, battened down, starving, tormented by thirst and fear. On September 18, in one of the worst maritime disasters of the Second World War, a British submarine sank a Japanese freighter off Sumatra, and 5,620 of those on board were drowned: they included 1,377 Dutch civilian internees being taken to Japan, sixty-four British and Australian internees, captured American merchant seamen, and Asian slave labourers. Of 50,000 Allied prisoners of war whom the Japanese transported on board ship, locked in the cargo holds and bilges, more than 10,000 died at sea.

*   *   *

On September 10 the first Allied soldier in Western Europe crossed into Germany. A week later British and American parachute troops, together with Polish troops, and British and American infantrymen and tanks, took part in an attempt to outflank the German defensive lines and establish a bridgehead across the lower Rhine at the Dutch town of Arnhem. The operation failed. More than 1,400 of the 35,000 airborne force were killed, and 6,000 taken prisoner.

In October there was an uprising by the Jewish slave labourers inside Auschwitz who were being forced to take out the corpses from the gas chambers to the crematoria. They succeeded in blowing up three of the gas chambers. The explosives which they used had been smuggled into the camp by five Jewish women slave labourers working in an ammunition factory just beyond the camp perimeter.

The revolt inside Auschwitz was crushed and all those who had taken part in it were killed. The five women who had made it possible were also executed: hanged in front of the whole camp. Despite severe torture they refused to betray their accomplices.

Hitler was almost at the end of his ability to conduct the war. A senior German army officer who visited him at Rastenburg on September 26 noted in his diary: 'It was a tired, broken man who greeted me, then shuffled over to a chair, his shoulders drooping, and asked me to sit down. He spoke so softly and hesitantly, it was hard to understand him. His hands trembled so much he had to grip them between his knees.'

That day, Hitler signed a decree for the setting up of a People's Army for the defence of German soil. Every able-bodied man between the ages of sixteen and sixty was to be called up. Efforts intensified to punish those regarded as enemies of the regime. In October, seventeen Post Office employees in Vienna were caught taking chocolate and soap from badly wrapped army parcels being sent through their sorting office. All seventeen were marched to a central square and executed in public.

On October 6 the first German jet aircraft entered combat. It was spotted by a Canadian air force squadron and shot down. Although more jets later took to the air, they did not do so in sufficient numbers to halt the Allied advance into Germany. The warmaking powers of Japan were about to take a new turn, as Japanese pilots volunteered to crash their planes on the decks of American warships. These suicide pilots were known as *kami-kaze* – from the Japanese characters for 'God-wind' or divine wind. The first kamikaze attacks took place on October 24, on the start of the three-day Battle of Leyte Gulf, off the Philippines. The first suicide pilot hit an aircraft carrier, killing sixteen men, but the carrier was not disabled and remained in formation. Several kamikaze planes were shot down before they reached their targets. The new 'weapon' created considerable damage. On one American cruiser 131 men were killed. But the tide of war could not be turned by suicide pilots.

During the Battle of Leyte Gulf twenty-six Japanese warships were sunk, including a 'super-battleship' with hitherto unprecedented eighteen-inch naval guns. During a sustained American assault she was hit by twenty torpedoes and seventeen bombs, and blown to pieces.

President Roosevelt was elected to an unprecedented fourth term as President of the United States on November 7. Five days later British bombers sank the *Tirpitz* in its Norwegian fiord. At least a thousand German sailors were drowned. The sinking of Germany's last warship in Western waters released several powerful British warships for service against the Japanese in the Pacific.

In East Prussia the Russians were advancing deep into historic German lands. On November 20 Hitler left Rastenburg and returned to Berlin. He was never to see Rastenburg or East Prussia again. Three days later, American and French troops entered Strasbourg, and the capital of Alsace returned to France. Hitler had one last strategic plan, a German offensive, starting in the Ardennes Forest and driving to the port of Antwerp, through which was passing the bulk of the supplies needed by the Allied armies already on German soil. German troops did break through the American lines – a quarter of a million German troops against 80,000 unsuspecting Americans – but never reached Antwerp. An essential part of the plan, a parachute drop behind the American lines to disrupt American communications, was a failure. Within twenty-four hours most of the parachutists had been captured.

In co-ordination with the Ardennes offensive against Antwerp, the Germans launched a series of V2 rocket attacks on the city, hoping to create panic. When a V2 hit a crowded cinema, 567 people were killed, almost 300 of them Allied servicemen. In all 3,752 Belgian civilians and more than 700 Allied servicemen were killed by the rockets sent against Antwerp. But they served no military purpose. Realizing the sweep to Antwerp was beyond his powers, Field Marshal von Rundstedt asked Hitler if he could withdraw his troops into Germany. Hitler refused. The appearance over the battlefield on December 24 of sixteen German jet aircraft was ineffectual. Their numbers were too few.

At the end of December the Russian army reached Budapest and prepared to besiege it. Realizing the Germans would fight to the last around the city and inside it, as Hitler had ordered them to do, the Hungarian Government broke away from the Axis and declared war on Germany.

Throughout the Far East the Japanese occupation had stimulated national forces determined not to allow the colonial powers to return. In Vietnam, the Communist leader Ho Chi Minh set up small, highly trained political-military units to spread Communist influence. The first of these units went into action on December 24, attacking two French military outposts. In future years that day was celebrated in North Vietnam as the 'birthday' of the Vietnamese armed forces.

Also on Christmas Eve 1944, Winston Churchill flew to Athens to secure an all-Party government and prevent a Greek Communist seizure of power. During two days of talks he persuaded the Greek Communist leaders to call a halt to their battle against their fellow-Greeks, and join an all-Party government.

On the Eastern Front, where just over three million German soldiers faced six million Russians, the Soviet forces launched their winter offensive on 12 January 1945. Three days later Hitler left his headquarters near the Ardennes for Berlin. During the journey one of his staff, an SS colonel, commented wryly: 'Berlin will be most practical as our headquarters: we'll soon be able to take the tram from the Eastern to the Western Front!' Hitler laughed at the colonel's sense of humour. Henceforth the Chancellery, and in due course the bunker under it, was to be his command post.

On January 17, Soviet forces entered Warsaw. The following day they took the surrender of the 62,000 German troops trapped inside Budapest. After five days and nights of continuous street fighting, more than 35,000 German soldiers lay dead. On January 23 the Russians entered Hitler's former headquarters at Rastenburg, where three and a half years earlier he had celebrated his early triumphs against them. Four days later they reached Auschwitz, where, amid the charred ruins of twenty-nine storehouses the SS had not had time to burn, they found some of the clothes of the victims: 836,255 women's dresses, 348,000 sets of men's suits and 38,000 pairs of men's shoes.

On January 30, the twelfth anniversary of Hitler coming to power, 8,000 German soldiers and refugees from East Prussia reached Kiel harbour on board the transport ship *Wilhelm Gustloff*, named after a Nazi who had been assassinated by a Jew before the war. As the ship entered harbour it was torpedoed by a Soviet submarine. More than 6,000 of those on board were drowned, the highest maritime loss on a single ship of the Second World War.

On January 31 the Soviet High Command asked for British and American air support to prevent the Germans transferring as many as twenty-nine divisions to the Silesian Front. To meet the Russian request, Allied bombers planned an attack on Dresden, through which the German troops had to pass. The British would bomb by night and the Americans by day. Up till then Dresden, a city of Baroque palaces, art galleries and opera houses, had not been a British or American target. The first part of the raid took place on the night of February 13–14, when British bombers attacked the city. Their target was the city's railway marshalling yards. During the raid a fire storm was started as ferocious as that in Hamburg two years earlier. Eleven square miles of the city were burned out. On the following morning American bombers struck the marshalling yards. Some of the fires were still burning seven days later. The number of bodies officially identified and registered by the city officials was 39,773. At least 20,000 more bodies were buried under the ruins or incinerated beyond recognition, even as bodies. The inscription on the mass grave in Dresden's main cemetery addresses the question of how many died with two short sentences: 'How many died? Who knows the number?'

American carrier-based aircraft attacked the Japanese home islands for the first time on February 11. To bomb the Japanese mainland most effectively the Americans needed the airfield on the eight-mile wide island of Iwo Jima. An amphibious landing took place on February 19, but although the American flag was raised on the island's highest point, Mount Suribachi, on the third day – resulting in one of the most famous photographs of the war – it took fifty more days of fighting for them to conquer the island. The death toll was high: 6,821 American marines and 20,000 Japanese soldiers. Nine hundred American sailors were also killed in the battle for Iwo Jima. Of the six flag raisers in the photograph, three were to be among the American dead.

On the night of February 23–24 there was a massive Anglo-American bombing raid over railway yards, canals, bridges and vehicles throughout Germany. Nine thousand bombers took part, attacking without pause for twenty-four hours. At Pforzheim, where 1,825 tons of bombs were dropped in twenty-two minutes, a firestorm was caused which killed 17,600 people. This was the third highest death toll during the bombing of a German city after Dresden and Hamburg. When Cologne was bombed by a force of 834 British bombers on March 2, the death toll could not be ascertained: the city was almost in the front line and no official register of the dead could be compiled. American troops, entering the city four days later, cleared 400 bodies from the streets. On March 3, in an attempt to forestall further rocket bomb attacks, the British sent a bomber force to destroy the launch sites near The Hague. Many bombs fell wide of the target, hitting a residential area and killing 520 Dutch civilians.

The last rocket bombs were fired on March 27. One fell on Antwerp, killing twenty-seven people. During its six months' existence the V2 'reprisal' weapon had killed 2,855 people in Britain and 4,483 in Belgium, and had destroyed several thousand homes. But it failed to affect the course of the war, serving only to intensify anti-German feeling and strengthen the belief that it was a 'just war'.

On March 9 more than 300 American bombers dropped 2,000 incendiary bombs on Tokyo. The raid lasted for less than three hours. When it was over a firestorm greater than that in Dresden was raging, and sixteen square miles of Tokyo were burned out. The first official death toll was put at 83,793. Later, when the ruins had been searched and many more charred remains discovered, the total was put at 130,000. In the following three months five more Japanese cities were to face the terrifying rigours of firestorm and mass destruction. The Japanese civilians did not even have the benefit of a competent anti-aircraft defence, as the bombers flew too high for the guns of the defenders. In the whole campaign, 243 American airmen were killed, the same number as in a single night during a British air raid over Berlin a year and a half earlier. Japanese deaths, when the carpet bombing raids came to an end, were more than a quarter of a million.

On the morning of March 7, American troops reached the Rhine, at the small town of Remagen. Its citizens put out white flags, and there was no fighting. To the surprise of the American soldiers the bridge over the river was intact. By nightfall a hundred American soldiers had crossed the Rhine. British and Canadian forces reached the Rhine two days later. Germany's western maritime highway was under Allied control. In the struggle for it, 10,333 British, 7,300 American and 5,655 Canadian soldiers had been killed. The German losses were much higher: 45,000 in the area facing the Americans and 22,000 among those facing the British and Canadians.

The Germans were still putting jet aircraft into action. During a counter-attack on the Remagen bridgehead, sixteen of the twenty-one attacking German aircraft were shot down. At least half of them were jets. But on March 21, in a co-ordinated attack, British and American aircraft made almost all the remaining German jet airfields unusable, and on March 25 American forces overran the two last working jet airfields near Darmstadt and Frankfurt-on-Main.

In the Far East, on April 1 – Easter Sunday – 50,000 American troops landed on Okinawa, the final stepping stone for the invasion of Japan. They were opposed by twice the number of Japanese defenders. In the battle for air supremacy above the island, 5,900 Japanese combat planes were shot down for the loss of less than 800 American planes. On one occasion, instead of sending a group of ten or twelve kamikaze pilots into action against the American warships off Okinawa in a single attack, the Japanese High Command ordered 355 into the air at the same time. The tactic was successful, with two American ammunition ships, two destroyers and a tank landing ship being sunk, but the vast armada was effectively intact. All 355 kamikaze pilots were killed.

On April 1, Hitler moved from his offices to the underground bunker deep below the Chancellery. On the following day, Soviet and Bulgarian forces captured the Hungarian oil fields at Nagykanizsa, cutting off the Third Reich from its last supply of fuel oil. When Hitler ordered General Kurt Student, the victor of the Crete campaign in 1941, to retake the oil fields, the general replied that his tanks did not have enough fuel to do so. Hitler's order and the general's reply were both read by British Intelligence, confirming the desperate state of Germany's combat abilities.

On April 3 the Ruhr was encircled. That same day, an American armoured division deep inside Germany noticed a number of emaciated figures walking along the road. 'Cadaverous refugees' was how an American war correspondent described them. 'They were like none we have ever seen. Skeletal with feverish sunken eyes, shaven skulls.' The refugees spoke almost incoherently of 'people buried in a big hole' and 'death commando', and urged the soldiers to come to the camp where they had been held prisoner. On the following morning American troops entered the camp. Its name was Ohrdruf. Hundreds of corpses were piled up at the entrance. Each one wore a striped uniform and had a bullet hole at the back of the skull. It emerged that more than 4,000 prisoners had died at Ohrdruf in the previous three months. Hundreds had been shot as the Allied armies drew near. Some were Jews, others were Poles and Russian prisoners of war. They had been employed building a vast underground telephone exchange intended for use by the German army.

Ohrdruf was the first of more than fifty concentration camps and mass murder sites inside Germany that were uncovered by the Allied forces in the weeks ahead. Their names were to become synonymous with Nazi terror: Buchenwald, Dachau, Belsen, Flossenbürg, Mauthausen. The nature of the evil perpetrated in Germany under Nazi rule could no longer be hidden behind the secrecy of war.

In East Prussia, on the evening of April 9, Königsberg surrendered to the Russians after a prolonged siege in which 42,000 German soldiers and 25,000 civilians had been killed. On the following day, Soviet troops reached the centre of Vienna.

In the Far East on April 12, a new Japanese suicide weapon was used for the first time: a flying bomb – like Hitler's V1 but larger and with a pilot on board. He directed the bomb to its target and was blown up with it. The suicide bomb could be launched from a bomber twenty miles away from its intended target. The first target to be hit and sunk was a United States destroyer off Okinawa. Eighty-one officers and men were killed.

As American sailors in the Pacific faced a new and terrible weapon, and in Europe advanced to the very centre of Germany, their Commander-in-Chief, President Roosevelt, died. He was sixty-three years old. His death brought tears to the eyes of many battle-hardened American soldiers. Goebbels hoped Roosevelt's successor would agree to join Germany and fight against the Soviet Union, but the new President, Harry Truman, was determined to see Germany totally defeated. The daily revelation of Nazi atrocities only served to strengthen that conviction among the Allies, as two more concentration camps were reached: Buchenwald by the Americans and Belsen by the British.

On the morning of April 16 the Soviet forces opened their offensive against Berlin. American troops entered Leipzig on April 19. Germany was in imminent danger of being cut in two. On the following day Hitler celebrated his fifty-sixth birthday. The Americans were bombing Berlin that day, but during a lull between attacks he came up from his bunker to inspect the teenage soldiers of the Hitler Youth, as well as some much older men who had been conscripted into a newly formed SS division. Returning to his bunker, he spoke to his guests of his determination not to allow Bohemia and Moravia, Norway or Denmark to be overrun, and on the following day forecast that 'the Russians will suffer the greatest defeat of their history before the gates of Berlin'.

In the Ruhr pocket, 325,000 German soldiers, among them thirty generals, surrendered on April 21. Soviet troops, advancing that day south of Berlin, overran the headquarters of the German High Command. On April 22 Hitler learned that an SS general whom he had sent to the Elbe the previous day with orders to halt the Russian advance had failed to persuade a single unit to take the offensive. That day, three of Hitler's most senior generals urged him to leave Berlin for a secure mountain hideaway in Bavaria. Shouting at them that he was 'deserted', Hitler insisted on remaining in his capital, and in his bunker, to 'meet the end when it came'. On the following day he took personal command of the defence of Berlin, but never emerged above ground. On April 25, on the western bank of the Elbe, an American army officer chanced upon a Soviet soldier. Both men were foraging for food. Two attacking armies had linked up. Germany was cut in two. In Moscow a 324-gun salute was fired to celebrate, while in New York crowds in Times Square sang and danced through the night. On April 26 Soviet troops completed the encirclement of Berlin.

On April 28, at a lakeside village in northern Italy, Mussolini was seized by Italian partisans. He had sought to disguise himself in a German Air Force greatcoat and helmet, but was recognized and then shot. Executed with him were the Secretary of the Fascist Party and four Cabinet Ministers. Mussolini's mistress, Clara Petacci, was also shot. She had insisted on being with him to the last. Her body and Mussolini's were then taken by truck to Milan and hung up by the heels.

On the morning of April 29 the German armies in Italy – more than a million men – surrendered to the Allies. In his bunker in Berlin, Hitler, having married his mistress Eva Braun, was writing his political testament. The Jews, he wrote, were 'the real guilty party in this murderous struggle' and would be 'saddled' with the responsibility for it. Hitler added, with reference to his many pre-war and wartime public warnings: 'I left no one in doubt that this time not only would millions of children of European Aryan races starve, not only would millions of grown men meet their death, and not only would hundreds and thousands of women and children be burned and bombed to death in cities, but this time the real culprits would have to pay for their guilt even though by more humane means than war.' The 'more humane means' had been the gas chambers.

On April 30, American troops entered Munich. That afternoon, in Berlin, a Soviet soldier waved the Red Banner from a second floor window of the Reichstag, less than a mile from Hitler's bunker. An hour later, having finished lunch and said goodbye to those in the bunker, Hitler retired to his room with Eva Braun. Those waiting outside heard a single shot. Hitler had killed himself. Eva Braun had swallowed poison. A radio signal was sent from the bunker to Admiral Doenitz at Flensburg, to tell him he was Chancellor. In the bunker, Goebbels arranged for his six children to be given a lethal injection by an SS doctor. He then had himself and his wife shot by an SS orderly.

On the morning of May 2 the German forces in Berlin surrendered to the Russians. In southern Russia, the two most senior members of the German rocket bomb research team surrendered that day to the Americans. One of them, Wernher von Braun, later commented: 'We were interested in continuing our work, not just being squeezed like a lemon and then discarded.'

On May 4 the German armies in north-western Germany surrendered. In Austria the Americans entered Berchtesgaden, Hitler's mountain retreat, and also Flossenbürg concentration camp, yet another camp where battle-hardened soldiers were horrified by what they encountered: the sights and smells of death and starvation. Among the 'privileged' prisoners liberated at Flossenbürg were Pastor Martin Niemöller, the former leader of the German Confessional Church who had spoken out courageously against Nazi persecution, Kurt von Schuschnigg, the Austrian Chancellor who had challenged Hitler in 1938 by calling a plebiscite, and Léon Blum who, when Prime Minister of France before the war, had formed a government which favoured a common European front against aggression.

On May 5 the German forces in southern Germany surrendered, as did the German army in Holland. A few moments after midnight, the citizens of Prague rose up against their German occupiers. The Germans fought back, and more than 3,000 Czechs were killed.

On May 7, at Reims, General Alfred Jodl, since 1939 the Chief of the Operations Command of the German Armed Forces, signed the unconditional surrender of all German forces on all fronts. The Second World War in Europe was over. On May 8 – VE 'Victory in Europe' Day – a Soviet general took the surrender of the German troops who had continued to fight in and around Prague. In the United States, at Fort Oglethorpe, Georgia, a few minutes after Colonel Howard Clark, the commanding officer, had addressed his men to announce the end of the European war, he was handed a telegram announcing that his youngest son, First Lieutenant William A. Clark, had been killed in action in the Philippines three weeks earlier.

Heinrich Himmler, who had wandered about northern Germany for several days after the final surrender, went into a British army camp and gave himself up. He was identified, then kept under guard until he could be taken away for interrogation. On reaching the interrogation centre he bit on a cyanide capsule he had concealed in his teeth. He died a few moments later. Joachim von Ribbentrop, Hitler's Foreign Minister, was arrested in a Hamburg boarding house. He was taken under guard to the Palace Hotel at Mondorf, in Luxembourg, where those former German leaders who were to be charged with war crimes were being assembled.

In the Far East, the war continued. Despite the massive bombing of Tokyo, which showed the Emperor and his government the possibility of the eventual total destruction of every Japanese city, the Japanese Cabinet decided on June 8 'to prosecute the war to the bitter end'. Two weeks later American forces reached the Japanese command cave on Okinawa. During the night the two Japanese generals in the cave, dressed in full ceremonial uniform with medals and ceremonial swords, had been served a special feast, and then, kneeling on a clean sheet with their faces towards Hirohito's palace in Tokyo, using a specially sharpened sabre, killed themselves.

On the battlefield of Okinawa 107,500 Japanese soldiers had been killed in just under four weeks' fighting, their bodies counted on the battlefield. A further 20,000 were believed to have died in the caves into which they fled, against which the Americans used flame-throwers and explosives. Many local Okinawans were also killed in the fighting, at least 80,000. The American losses were lower, but formidable: 7,613 on land and 4,907 at sea, many as a result of kamikaze attacks. A small island had changed hands in battle, and more than 200,000 human beings were dead.

On American Independence Day, July 4, General MacArthur announced the liberation of the Philippines. There were still isolated pockets of Japanese resistance, but starting on July 11 these were attacked from the air using a new weapon, the napalm bomb, the petroleum component of which burned with a tenacious and terrifying fierceness on both buildings and human beings.

In preparing to repel the American amphibious landings on Japan – planned for November 1, though the Japanese did not know the exact date – two new suicide weapons were designed. One was a torpedo on which a man would be strapped and which he would guide onto its target. The other was a mine on which a Japanese soldier would likewise be strapped, and which he would then fix to the hull of a troop transport and detonate. Experiments were also being made with a third suicide device: sunken concrete shelters in which six-man squads would be waiting offshore, just beneath the water, to detonate themselves as the invasion barges filled with troops passed over them, a few minutes before they would have waded ashore.

These devices were about to be made otiose. On July 16 the first atomic bomb test was carried out near Alamogordo, in the desert of New Mexico. Within a mile radius of the explosion, all plant and animal life was killed.

At the Potsdam Conference, Churchill, Truman and Stalin were determining the future of post-war Germany. In the middle of the conference Churchill returned to Britain to learn the results of the general election. The Conservative Party had been defeated and he, its leader, was no longer Prime Minister. The leader of the Labour Party, Clement Attlee, Churchill's wartime Deputy Prime Minister, was the new Prime Minister. It was he who returned to Potsdam.

Under the Potsdam Agreement, Germany and Austria were both divided into Soviet, American, British and French zones of occupation. Berlin and Vienna were placed under joint Four-Power control. Poland lost the eastern third of its pre-war territory, including the predominantly Polish cities of Vilna and Lvov, to the Soviet Union. In return, Poland gained a substantial swathe of territory taken from the eastern areas of Germany: the industrial region of Silesia, the coastal region of Pomerania and the southern half of East Prussia. The Soviet Union acquired the northern part of East Prussia, including its main city, Königsberg – which was renamed Kaliningrad, after the Soviet President.

The Potsdam conference specifically agreed to 'the removal of Germans from Poland, Czechoslovakia and Hungary'. These Germans were already on the move, a vast array of refugees. As a result of the Soviet annexation of eastern Poland, millions of Poles were also on the move, into those parts of Germany which had been transferred to Poland. Millions of Germans and German-speaking peoples were expelled by the Soviets, Poles and Czechs from areas in which they had lived for many generations. East Prussia was being cleared of its German inhabitants in preparation for Russian and Polish partition and settlement. The Sudetenland was being emptied of its Sudeten Germans so that Czechs could live there.

Preparations were being made to drop the atomic bomb on Japan. On July 24 Truman noted that he had given instructions 'to use it so that military objectives and soldiers and sailors are the target and not women and children'. As he went on to explain: 'Even if the Japs are savages, ruthless, merciless and fanatic, we as the leader of the world for the common welfare cannot drop this terrible bomb on the old capital or the new.' The target would be 'a purely military one'. Truman added: 'we will issue a warning statement asking the Japs to surrender and save lives'.

The first target chosen was Hiroshima, which contained in fact many more women and children than soldiers and sailors. Nor was any warning issued. In the early hours of August 6 a specially adapted B-29 bomber, *Enola Gay*, dropped a single atomic bomb. It was detonated 1,885 feet above the ground. No single blast had ever killed so many people. Within two weeks the death toll reached 92,233. Many more died in the years that followed from the effects of radiation; by 1986 the cenotaph in Hiroshima listed 138,890 victims.

Two days after Hiroshima, the Soviet Union declared war on Japan, as Stalin had promised to do at Potsdam, and two million Soviet soldiers crossed into Manchuria. They were faced by 700,000 Japanese troops, and drove them southward in a series of ferocious encounters.

President Truman had agreed that if the Japanese did not accept unconditional surrender by August 11, a second atomic bomb would be dropped that day. But the weather forecast for August 11 was bad, and the date for the second bomb was brought forward two days, to August 9. This gave the Japanese three days rather than five in which to surrender. But they were not told either about the second bomb, or the change of date.

In the early hours of August 9 a second specially adapted B-29 bomber, *Bock's Car*, flew with the second atomic bomb to its objective, the city of Kokura. But when the pilot reached his target it was covered in industrial haze. His orders were to bomb only a visual target. He therefore flew on to the city of Nagasaki, ninety miles to the south-west, and dropped the bomb there. Forty thousand people were killed within a few minutes. Five thousand more were to die in the next three months. Thirty years later the final death toll was calculated at 48,857.

At the very moment of the second atomic bomb explosion, before news of it reached Tokyo, the Japanese Supreme War Direction Council, meeting in Tokyo, were discussing the Allied call, made at Potsdam, for unconditional surrender, and reflecting on the implications of the first atomic bomb. The Minister of War told the Council: 'It is far too early to say that the war is lost. That we will inflict severe losses on the enemy when he invades Japan is certain, and it is by no means impossible that we may be able to reverse the situation in our favour, pulling victory out of defeat.'

The Council was divided, three for surrender and three for fighting on. That evening, as news of the catastrophic destruction of the second atomic bomb reached Tokyo, Hirohito called a further meeting. It was held shortly after midnight in his bomb shelter. Hirohito said he was doubtful Japan could continue to wage effective war, or even defend its own shores, in the event of invasion. He then authorized the Prime Minister to accept unconditional surrender, but with one condition, that he, the Emperor, would remain on the throne.

As diplomatic exchanges began, through intermediaries in Switzerland, between Japan and the United States about whether the Emperor could keep his sovereign prerogatives, American bombers were still in action. On the morning of August 14, eight hundred bombers attacked Japanese military installations. The United States, meanwhile, agreed that the Emperor could continue to rule Japan, but under a Supreme Commander appointed by the Allied powers. At midnight on August 14 a Japanese radio announcer asked all listeners to stand respectfully in front of their radio sets. They then heard, for the first time in Japanese history, the broadcast voice of their Emperor. The enemy, he said, 'has begun to employ a new and most cruel bomb'. Its power to do damage was 'indeed incalculable, taking the toll of many innocent lives'. That was why he had agreed to the surrender of Japan.

Fighting continued in Manchuria. The Soviet Union, having entered the war against Japan only seven days earlier, was not going to be cheated of its prize. When the war in Manchuria ended on August 20, more than 40,000 Japanese and 8,219 Soviet soldiers had been killed. On August 23 the Russians occupied Port Arthur, which they had lost to the Japanese in the last Russo-Japanese war in 1905.

The ending of the war in Manchuria did not end the conflict in China. On the day after Japan's surrender, from his base in Yenan, Mao Tse-tung had ordered his troops to advance 'on all fronts' and disarm all Japanese troops they encountered. He was determined to extend Communist control as widely as possible. At the end of August he went to Chungking to negotiate with the Nationalists, but it soon became clear that there would be no solution but civil war.

At a ceremony held on board the American battleship *Missouri* in Tokyo Bay on September 2, General MacArthur supervised the formal signing of the Japanese surrender. Standing behind him as he put his own name to the instrument of surrender were two Allied generals captured early in the war: the British General Arthur Percival, who had been held captive since the fall of Singapore in February 1942 and the American General Jonathan M. Wainwright, who had been a prisoner of the Japanese since the fall of Bataan three months later.

New conflicts were emerging in the Far East, into which American troops were eventually to be drawn. On August 16, the day after the Japanese surrender, the Vietnamese Communist leader Ho Chi Minh ordered a 'general insurrection' throughout Vietnam, and Vietnamese Communist troops entered Hanoi. The Japanese had gone but the French had not yet returned. On September 2 Ho Chi Minh issued the Declaration of Independence of the Democratic Republic of Vietnam, and set up an interim Vietnamese government in Saigon. Six days later – scarcely three weeks after the ending of the war with Japan – French, British and Indian troops were landed in Indochina to reinstall the French colonial administration which the Japanese had ousted four years earlier, and to forestall the Communists. Because the number of Allied forces was limited, the French and British commanders enlisted the help of 2,000 Japanese troops who had surrendered to them, and who had so recently been the hated occupying power.

Before the end of the month the French had driven the Communist government from Saigon. The Communists took swift revenge, killing more than a hundred Westerners, including the commander of the American forces who a few months earlier had been helping them in their fight against the Japanese occupation.

The death tolls of the Second World War were still being calculated as 1945 came to an end, and were never finally ascertained. As many as fifteen million soldiers, sailors and airmen had been killed in action. At least ten million civilians had been murdered in deliberate killings – six million of them Jews. Between four and five million civilians had been killed in air raids. Four million prisoners of war had been killed or allowed to die in situations of the utmost cruelty after capture – three and a half million of them Soviet soldiers in

German captivity. Was the total death toll thirty-three million, or even more? As the Dresden war memorial expressed it: 'How many died? Who knows the number?'

CHAPTER EIGHT

Recovery and Relapse
1946—56

At THE FIRST MEETING of the General Assembly of the United Nations Organization, held in London on 10 January 1946, fifty-one nations were represented. Neither Germany nor Japan was as yet included. Under the Security Council of the League, a Military Staff Committee was set up to co-ordinate international military action in the event of aggression taking place anywhere in the world. Among elements of the pre-war League of Nations retained by the United Nations was the International Court of Justice at The Hague.

Speaking in New York on February 28, the United States Secretary of State, James Byrnes, former Director of War Mobilization, described his country's emerging international doctrine. 'If we are to be a Great Power,' he said, 'we must act as a Great Power, not only to ensure our own safety but to preserve the peace of the world.' The method which Byrnes and President Truman favoured was the maintenance of military strength, combined with clear warnings that force would be used against aggression. For Truman, America's ability to deter Soviet ambitions centred on the atomic bomb. On July 1, within a year of Hiroshima and Nagasaki, the first American post-war atomic bomb test took place on Bikini Atoll, in the Pacific. A fleet of several dozen Second World War vessels was deliberately destroyed in the explosion, which created an astonishing cloud 2,000 feet across at base, rising 5,000 feet into the sky.

Another reversal of American inter-war isolation was a sense of responsibility towards those who had suffered. This had been stimulated by the personal experiences of several million American soldiers, who had seen poverty and desperation in countries that had been under German occupation. Under the vision of Senator Fulbright, Congress agreed to sell American wartime surplus and put the proceeds towards the education in the United States of students from all over the world. The first of more than sixty States to sign into the Fulbright scholarship programme were China, Greece and the Philippines. The Philippines had been granted full independence from the United States on American Independence Day, 4 July 1946. It was the first of the countries that had been occupied by Japan to achieve statehood.

During the Fulbright scholarship debate, Congressman Lyndon Baines Johnson – a future President – declared: 'We in America are the fortunate children of fate. From almost any viewpoint ours is the greatest nation; the greatest in material wealth, in goods and produce, in abundance of things that make life easier and more pleasant.' Nearly every other people in the world, he added, 'are prostrate and helpless. They look to us for help – for that inherent courageous leadership'. By reason of its national wealth, the United States was the largest single financial contributor to the United Nations International Children's Emergency Fund (UNICEF), established on December 11 to give aid to mothers and children in Europe and Asia who were in need as a result of the war.

On October 1 the International Military Tribunal at Nuremberg, which had been in session for fourteen months, sentenced twelve German wartime leaders to death. One of them, Field Marshal Goering, cheated the hangman by swallowing poison in his cell. On October 16, the day after Goering's suicide, the other eleven were hanged. Among them was General Jodl, who had advocated 'terror attacks' on the British population in 1940 to 'paralyse the will of her people to resist and finally force the government to capitulate'.

Survivors of the Holocaust were not always safe in post-war Europe. On July 4, forty-two Jews were murdered in the Polish town of Kielce. These killings intensified the determination of the survivors to leave Europe, mostly for Palestine. But on July 30 the British Cabinet, fearful of antagonizing the Arabs of Palestine and beyond, began to deport all 'illegal' Jewish refugees it could catch to detention camps on the island of Cyprus. In fifteen months 50,000 Jews were intercepted. In Poland, meanwhile, more than a thousand Jews had been murdered by the end of 1946, stimulating a continuous exodus. Starting on August 14, 732 child and teenage concentration camp survivors, most of them Polish-born, were flown from Prague in British bombers to the north of England, where they were nursed back to physical health and mental vigour.

In Paris, Ho Chi Minh was negotiating with France for an armistice between his Vietminh soldiers and the French colonial forces. On November 20, while negotiations were still taking place, the French attacked a small ship in Haiphong harbour which they believed was carrying arms and munitions to the Vietminh. In retaliation, Vietminh soldiers seized the port. When the Vietminh refused to leave, the French opened fire with artillery, tanks and naval guns, and several thousand Vietminh soldiers were killed.

As fighting spread throughout Vietnam, the French gained control of the main cities and highways. But the Vietminh, moving their forces and administrative structure – the Communist government – to an area near the Chinese border, could not be dislodged.

In India, rebellion broke out in the Royal Indian Navy. In Bombay, during two days of rioting in support of the mutineers, sixty rioters and four policemen were killed. Recognizing that the naval mutiny was only a small indication of Indian nationalist discontent, the British Prime Minister, Clement Attlee, announced on March 14 that if India wanted full independence, Britain would agree. In talks which followed, Gandhi and Nehru sought to retain a united India with Hindus and Muslims working together in a single governing instrument. The Muslim League, led by Mohammed Ali Jinnah, demanded complete sovereign authority for the predominantly Muslim areas of India. As the debate intensified, there were violent clashes between Muslims and Hindus. In Calcutta 4,000 people were killed in four days. In eastern Bengal, a largely Muslim area, tens of thousands of Hindus were driven from their villages. Many were killed as they fled. As a reprisal, Hindus in the largely Hindu province of Bihar turned upon the Muslim minority in their midst, killing more than 7,000.

Despite this communal violence, independence could not be long delayed. In November the British Government announced that no more Britons would be recruited, even temporarily, into the higher echelons of the Indian Civil Service, and no more British officers into the Indian army, navy or air force.

In France, under a predominately Socialist government, coal, gas, electricity and the nine main insurance groups were nationalized. At the general election held on November 10 the Communists emerged as the largest single political Party, but without an overall majority. A fifteen-day political deadlock was only resolved when the elder statesman of the left, Léon Blum, agreed to form a government. Although it lasted less than five weeks, it did adopt measures to lower the cost of living.

The Italians, like the French, were struggling to find a form of government that would enable the damage and deprivation of war to be repaired. King Victor Emmanuel, whom the Allies had allowed to remain on the throne after Mussolini's fall, abdicated on May 9. His son proclaimed himself King, as Umberto II, but elections within a month showed a massive majority in favour of a republic. Umberto refused to abdicate. There were pro- and anti-monarchist riots in several cities, and some bloodshed. When the Cabinet authorized the Prime Minister, Alcide de Gasperi, to assume the powers of Head of State, Umberto left Rome for exile in Portugal. In the ensuing referendum the Italians voted, though by the narrowest of margins, for a republic.

In Germany, the Western Allies and the Soviet Union had each established the right to reparation. In Hamburg several war factories and shipyards were dismantled and sent to Britain. Others were blown up so that the Germans could not use them. The German merchant marine fleet was divided among fifteen Allied nations, with the Soviet Union receiving a third — which it promised to share with Poland — and Britain a half. There was a similar distribution of German machine tools. German trade secrets and patents were likewise distributed. But within a year this policy was reversed, as the existence of the three Western zones was regarded increasingly in London and Washington as a bulwark against Soviet attempts to expand westward. As the need to put the western German economy on its feet then became a priority for the former Western Allies, Britain, France and the United States each embarked on policies designed to encourage western Germany to remain a capitalist and democratic society. It was the Americans who first declared they were stopping reparations deliveries in order to safeguard the German economy. The British and French followed. The Russians had no such inhibitions, and continued to remove complete industries, including the Zeiss optical works in Jena, which was transferred to Russia together with almost the entire German personnel.

On 7 January 1946, diplomatic relations were restored between Austria and the rest of the world, and an Austrian Government given sovereign authority. Six months later the Soviet authorities, without consulting the three other occupying Powers, confiscated £5 million worth of industrial property in their zone, as reparations. As a gesture of support for Austria, six days later the United States handed 280 former German factories to the Austrian Government. The Austrian Parliament then passed a Bill nationalizing many of the industries the Soviets had seized. The Russians eventually agreed that the confiscated factories could remain in Austria and supply the Austrian market.

Behind the Iron Curtain, Communist regimes asserted their authority under the watchful eye of the Soviet Union. In Czechoslovakia, following elections in which the Communists received the largest single vote, though not an absolute majority, as soon as the Czech Communist leader, Klement Gottwald, became Prime Minister he broke off negotiations with Washington for a $50 million loan on the grounds that the United States was using credits and loans 'to further a policy of economic imperialism'. A $19 million loan from Canada was accepted, however, as was a smaller loan from Britain. Later the Foreign Minister, Jan Masaryk, son of a former president, fell to his death in Prague: almost certainly murdered.

In Hungary a political clash between the Communist and opposition deputies in the parliament was resolved by the expulsion of the opposition as 'reactionaries'. In Roumania, the opposition Parties agreed to join a Communist-led coalition. When elections were

called, the British and American Governments protested at widespread Communist intimidation and violence during the campaign,
in which several local opposition leaders were killed. When the
election results were announced the Communist Party had obtained
an overwhelming majority of the parliamentary seats. In Bulgaria,
where many voters were prevented from reaching the polling booths,
the Communist Party likewise secured a majority. Control of Albania
went to the wartime Communist partisan leader, Enver Hoxha. Five
weeks after he came to power he ordered the execution of two former
Regents and a former Prime Minister.

In Poland, under close Soviet scrutiny, the Communists dominated the political coalition. Polish opponents of Communism carried
out violent attacks on government installations and military barracks.
Using this unrest as a pretext, on the eve of the election the government arrested 10,000 politically active Poles, including many election
candidates.

The Soviet Union extracted substantial reparations from the countries
which had invaded her in 1941. Enormous quantities of raw materials,
industrial installations, railway rolling stock, trucks and cars were
taken from East Germany, Austria, Hungary and Roumania.
Although the Soviet Union refused any outside inspection, it was
clear that far more was taken than had been envisaged at the wartime
conferences. Goods in considerable quantities were also taken from
Poland, which had been Hitler's first conquest.

Inside the Soviet Union it was to need many years to repair the
ravages of the war. Of seventy-five coal mines in the Donbass only
four had managed to restart production fourteen months after the
end of the war. At the same time, hopes throughout the Soviet Union
that the rigours of Stalinist control might be relaxed were soon
dashed. Breaches of collective farm practice were severely punished.
A campaign was begun to eliminate from school text books all favourable references to agricultural improvements and industrial growth
at the time of the Tsars. Aspects of the Tsarist years which had been
stressed during the war to stimulate patriotism, such as the military
achievements of Peter the Great, were removed from the curriculum.
The cult of Stalin was intensified: songs, poems, doggerel, wall

posters, street slogans, radio programmes, films, plays – all had to
sing his praises.

In the Baltic States, which had been annexed to the Soviet Union
in 1944, Soviet soldiers were in armed conflict throughout 1946
with local nationalist forces. In Lithuania several hundred nationalists
were killed in clashes with Soviet forces. In western Ukraine more
than 8,000 anti-Communist partisans were killed or captured, and
large quantities of arms and ammunition seized. In combating the
nationalist forces, Soviet troops had also been killed. Stalin's order
was clear: 'Finish off the outlaws in the shortest possible time.'

Following the defeat of Japan, the Chinese Government and the
Chinese Communists each sought supremacy. In June, Chiang Kai-
shek ordered the arrest of Mao Tse-tung on charges of instigating
rebellion. Hundreds of Communist activists were arrested but Mao
Tse-tung evaded capture. In November, Chiang Kai-shek held elections throughout China, the first in its history. The Communist Party
was excluded from them. In Poland, it was the Communists who
did the excluding, when on election day, 16 January 1947, the
American Ambassador in Warsaw reported 'large-scale arrests,
intimidation of opposition voters, invalidation of registers, and forced
voting of Government and factory employees'. More than 2,000 opposition Party activists were taken to prison that day. The Communists
won the majority.

In March the United States took an important initiative in the
East-West divide. When Britain announced it could no longer be
responsible for the physical security or economic viability of Greece,
Truman announced that the United States would do all it could to
sustain Greek independence and solvency. Similar support, he said,
would be available to Turkey. American civilian and military personnel would train the Greeks and Turks to defend themselves. This
pledge, made on March 12, launched the 'Truman Doctrine'. A week
later a coup in Budapest brought the Hungarian Communist Party
into full power. The Hungarian Prime Minister, who was in Switzerland at the time of the coup, resigned by telephone. Truman called
the Communist seizure of power in Budapest an 'outrage' and protested against the Soviet involvement.

Even as Communists took power in Budapest, a new United States Secretary of State, George Marshall, the former Chief of Staff of the American armed forces and one of the architects of the Allied victory two years earlier, presented the 'Marshall Plan', a massive packet of aid and assistance to any nation in need as a result of the devastations of war. Marshall wanted Eastern Europe to benefit, and spent forty-six days in Moscow negotiating and explaining, but the Russians refused to allow the countries of Eastern Europe under their sway to be beneficiaries. Under strong Soviet pressure, the French Communist Party, a powerful participant in France's governing coalition, left the government in protest at its country's acceptance of the Marshall Plan.

Not one country in the Soviet bloc accepted Marshall's offer. The Foreign Minister of Czechoslovakia, Dr Vladimir Clementis, wanted to participate: this was later made into one of the charges against him when he was tried and shot. Stalin also forbade Finland to participate. In place of the Marshall Plan the Soviet Union created a Council for Mutual Economic Understanding (COMECON), which quickly became an instrument for systematically bleeding the economies of the satellite States, and a strong factor in the growth of anti-Moscow feeling throughout the Soviet bloc.

The first meeting of the fourteen countries who agreed to participate in the Marshall Plan was held in Paris on July 12. Over the coming four years the needy countries of Europe would receive from the United States both the essential supplies to restore their economic life, and the essential dollars with which to buy those supplies.

Communist control in Eastern Europe tightened throughout the year. When the United States and Britain protested to the Soviets at the dissolution of the Agrarian Party in Bulgaria and the execution of its leader, Nikola Petkov, their protests were rejected. In Roumania the veteran anti-Fascist politician and former Prime Minister, Julius Maniu, was brought to trial on October 29, accused by the Communist government of having put himself at the disposal of the 'imperialist camp' to transform Roumania into a base for launching an armed attack on the Soviet Union, and sentenced to hard labour for life. At the end of the year it was announced from Bucharest that King Michael – who had just represented Roumania at the wedding in

London of Princess Elizabeth – had abdicated, and that Roumania had become a People's Republic.

The British Empire was on the wane. On January 28 Britain and Burma reached an 'agreement to part'. Three weeks later Britain announced that British rule in India would end within a year and a half, on the basis of partition between the predominantly Hindu and predominantly Muslim regions. Gandhi opposed partition, calling it 'vivisection'. In order to avoid bloodshed, he said, the Muslims must be given 'all they asked' within a united India. The Muslims feared that under Gandhi's scheme they would be put under Hindu rule. As riots and killing spread, Gandhi's call for a united India was set aside. On April 18 Nehru stated that both the Punjab and Bengal would be divided. A Partition Council was established to work out the borders, and on August 15 India and Pakistan became two nations – independent, sovereign States. Two days later a Partition Council, which had devised a geographic line hopefully acceptable to both Hindus and Muslims, announced its award. The Government of Pakistan protested that too large an area had been handed to India.

Violence escalated. When Calcutta descended into bloodshed, Gandhi, who held no official position in the new Government of India, announced he would fast 'to the death' unless the killings ceased. Driving through Calcutta, he wrote of how he was overcome by 'a sinking feeling at the mass madness that can turn man into less than a brute'. After three days the violence in Calcutta subsided. In the Punjab, which was to be partitioned between the two countries, violence not only spread but created a massive exodus of seven million people: Hindus moving westward and Muslims moving eastward. Repeated butchery took place as they fled. At least a quarter of a million people were killed, many as they crowded trucks and trains, seeking desperately to reach the newly declared national territory of their co-religionists.

The arrival of the survivors, many of them seriously wounded, bringing stories of slaughter, inflamed the passions of those to whom they came. This was particularly true when a mass of Hindu refugees reached Delhi. Local Hindus and Sikhs attacked Muslims throughout the city. After several days of street violence almost all Delhi's

Muslims fled. Despite the Hindu-Muslim violence, the governments of India and Pakistan were desperate to avoid war. On September 21 they issued a joint statement that 'any conception of a conflict' between them was 'repugnant'. A major issue confronting them was that of Kashmir, where a Hindu ruler, whose family had been placed on the throne by the British a century earlier, governed a large Muslim majority. As Muslim tribesmen from outside his borders attacked Kashmir in force, the Maharaja asked to join India. On October 26 India accepted. The Muslim attackers redoubled their efforts, reaching the outskirts of the capital, Srinagar. The capital remained under Indian control, but large sections of Kashmir were occupied by Muslim troops.

On November 2 Nehru proposed a referendum in Kashmir under United Nations auspices. Meanwhile, he said, 'we have given our word to the people of Kashmir to protect them against the invader, and we will keep our pledge'. A year later the United Nations organized a cease-fire. In subsequent decades, war was to flicker again and again along the cease-fire line, and Kashmir remained partitioned, the largest section being part of India.

Britain was still the ruling power in Palestine, but the British will to rule had gone. An economic crisis in Britain added to the determination of the government in London not to take on the growing burden of extra troops and mounting expenditure needed to curb Jewish and Arab violence. Attlee and his Cabinet decided to hand the problem to the United Nations. As killings and chaos continued, a United Nations committee advocated two independent States, one Jewish, one Arab, in a partitioned Palestine, with Jerusalem to be put under direct United Nations control. The Jews in Palestine accepted this, but the Palestinian Arabs rejected any division of the land, or the creation of a Jewish State in any part of it. When the United Nations voted on November 29, thirty-three nations favoured a Jewish and an Arab State in a partitioned Palestine. Thirteen nations voted against, including all the Arab nations. Two of the States voting against partition were India and Pakistan, whose own independence and statehood had emerged only three months earlier as a result of partition.

As soon as news of the partition resolution reached Palestine, the Jews there rejoiced at the imminent coming of statehood. The Palestinian Arabs took up arms against them. Although British rule still had six months to run, the British authorities were powerless to restore law and order, and in a spiral of escalating destruction that could not be halted, Arabs and Jews fought and died. That winter, an Arab Liberation Army was formed inside Syria to resist the creation of a Jewish State by armed intervention. The Jews armed themselves, and awaited the day that the British would leave, and their independence, even their survival, would have to be fought for.

In Vietnam, more than 115,000 French troops, with armoured vehicles, artillery and air support, confronted a combined military and guerrilla Vietminh Communist force of about 100,000, ill-armed and with no air power.

The French general in Vietnam, Jean Etienne Valluy, told his superiors he was confident he 'could eliminate all organized resistance in three months'. On October 7 he launched a parachute landing to seize the Communist governmental and military headquarters, but Ho Chi Minh and General Giap, the Vietminh commander, escaped. The French parachutists were themselves then surrounded; it took nine days of intense fighting before they were rescued. The Vietminh disappeared northward to their bases near the Chinese border. Two further French offensives before the end of the year failed to capture the leaders or to destroy the Vietminh.

In his address to Congress on 7 January 1948, Truman stressed his desire to admit into the United States more than 200,000 Displaced Persons then in Europe, half of them Jews, and to give priority to the Marshall Plan. 'Twice within our generation,' he said, 'world wars have taught us that we cannot isolate ourselves from the rest of the world.' A day later Marshall urged the Senate to bring his plan in quickly. 'If we decide that the United States is unable or unwilling effectively to assist in the reconstruction of western Europe,' he said, 'we must accept the consequences of its collapse into the dictatorship of police States.'

Truman also told Congress on January 7: 'Our first goal is to secure fully the human rights of our citizens.' Three weeks later he

sent a civil rights message to Congress, the first American President
to send a special message on this divisive domestic theme. 'Not all
groups are free to live and work where they please, or to improve
their conditions of life by their own efforts,' he said. 'Not all groups
enjoy the full privileges of citizenship. The Federal Government has
a clear duty to see that the Constitutional guarantees of individual
liberties and of equal protection under the laws are not denied or
abridged anywhere in the Union.' It was necessary for Congress to
enact 'modern, comprehensive civil rights laws, adequate to the needs
of the day, and demonstrating our continuing faith in the free way
of life'.

Discrimination in interstate travel by rail, bus and aeroplane
should be ended. The right to vote should be protected. Black soldiers
serving in the army should not be subjected to racial abuse. Although
his own ancestors were Confederates, Truman said, 'my very stomach
turned over when I learned that Negro soldiers, just back from
overseas, were being dumped out of army trucks in Mississippi and
beaten. Whatever my inclinations as a native of Missouri might have
been, as President I know this is bad. I shall fight to end evils like
this.'

The demands and aspirations of the post-war world were beginning to be widely heard. At the centre of the Labour Party's election
victory in Britain in 1945 had been its promise to extend social
justice. This promise encompassed greater economic security for the
working class, wider opportunities in education, fuller employment,
and the application of national resources to rebuild the shattered
homes and cities on the basis of social equality. A National Health
Service, introduced in 1948, provided for free medical attention
and treatment. Other legislation brought in cheap and subsidized
housing.

The violence which had accompanied the independence of India and
Pakistan continued into 1948. On January 12, Gandhi announced
he was starting another fast until the killing stopped. As he became
weaker, leaders of all communities promised to try to restore communal harmony, and begged him to end his strike. He agreed to do so
on January 28. Two days later, on his way to hold his regular daily

prayer meeting, he was greeted by a young man who then fired three shots. Within a few minutes, Gandhi was dead.

Gandhi's assassin was a Hindu extremist fiercely opposed to Gandhi's message of reconciliation with Muslims and co-operation with Hindu Untouchables. But the assassination did not impede the progress of statehood. On June 21 an Indian politician, Chakravarti Rajagopalachari, took the oath of office as Governor General wearing the simple, homespun clothing Gandhi had advocated for all Indians.

In Hyderabad, the Nizam, a Muslim prince, refused to accede to the Indian Union. His country would, he said, remain independent. Nehru insisted that Hyderabad, situated in the centre of India, 'cannot conceivably be independent, and India can never agree to it'. The State was 86 per cent Hindu. On the morning of September 13, Indian troops crossed into Hyderabad. After five and a half days' fighting the Nizam accepted India's demands and ordered a cease-fire: 286 Muslim Hyderabadi soldiers and just over a hundred Indians had been killed. An Indian military governor was appointed, and Muslim insurgents who continued to fight were hunted down.

On March 14 the United States Senate passed the Marshall Plan. 'In all the history of the world we are the first great nation to feed and support the conquered,' Truman wrote privately after the Bill became law.

A sense of imminent conflict with the Soviet Union led Truman to bring back compulsory military training. Since the end of the war, he told Congress, 'the Soviet Union and its agents have destroyed independence and democratic character of a whole series of nations in Eastern and Central Europe. It is this ruthless course of action, and the clear design to extend it to the remaining free nations in Europe, that have brought about the critical situation in Europe today.' In response to this, on May 9 the Soviet Union accused the United States of seeking its 'encirclement'. The Soviet accusation included the American military occupation in South Korea – which had been part of the immediate post-war arrangement between the Soviet Union and the United States. This occupation ended on July 24, when Syngman Rhee was inaugurated as President, but American troops remained in South Korea as a protective force. In North Korea, on September 9, the Communist-led Democratic People's Republic of Korea was established, under the leadership of Kim Il Sung. The two Koreas faced each other across a fortified line. In South Korea, Syngman Rhee's government was not only anti-Communist, but rigorously suppressed dissent.

On May 14 the British Mandate in Palestine came to an end. Eleven minutes later the United States recognized the new State of Israel. The Soviet Union did likewise. By contrast, the Arab States bordering on the new country launched an immediate attack. Egyptian aeroplanes bombed Tel Aviv. Both the Transjordanian Arab Legion and the Syrian-based Arab Liberation Army advanced into the area allocated to the Jews by the United Nations. Arab Legion artillery bombarded the Jewish Quarter of the Old City of Jerusalem. In the centre of the country, troops from Iraq attacked Israeli positions.

The war lasted nine months, its temporary cease-fire lines serving as the borders of Israel for almost twenty years. The Palestinian Arab towns on the West Bank of the Jordan were occupied and annexed by Transjordan, which also occupied and demolished the Jewish Quarter of the Old City. Egypt occupied the Gaza Strip. During Israel's War of Independence, 6,000 Jews were killed, one per cent of the Jewish population of the new State. In the aftermath of the war more than a million Jews arrived from Europe and from Muslim lands, especially from North Africa and Iraq. Survivors of the Holocaust whom the British had interned on Cyprus made the short journey across the eastern Mediterranean to a new home.

Three quarters of a million Arab refugees had fled the fighting or been encouraged by Israel to leave. Some were forcibly ejected from their villages, which were then demolished. More than half a million were placed in refugee camps inside Lebanon, Syria, Egypt and Jordan – as Transjordan became known. Several thousand Arab homes in Jerusalem were taken over by the Jewish newcomers, many of whom had themselves been driven out of their homes in Arab lands.

Inside Israel 160,000 Arabs remained, or returned within a few months of the war. They became Israeli citizens, living for the first decade of statehood under Israeli military administration, but in due course voting in elections and represented in the parliament. Fifty years after Israeli statehood was declared, these Israeli Arabs, their numbers grown to more than half a million, constituted more than twenty per cent of the Israeli population. They were never to lose their sense of being second-class citizens.

Berlin, which lay within the Soviet zone of Germany, and which was itself divided among the Four Powers, became a flashpoint of Cold War confrontation in 1948. On April 1 the Russians announced far stricter controls than hitherto on all traffic going by road or rail to the city. Foodstuffs, freight and Allied military cargoes were allowed to proceed only after specific Soviet authorization. Soviet air vigilance was imposed on all Allied air traffic. On April 5 there was a mid-air collision between a Soviet fighter plane and a British airliner on the outskirts of Berlin. The fourteen people on the British plane, and the Soviet pilot of the fighter, were killed.

In May the Soviet Union denounced all Allied economic improvements in western Berlin, insisting the whole city was economically part of the Soviet Zone. The Western Powers disputed this. The divergence of views between West and East reached its climax on June 7 when, in London, a Six-Power pact was signed, under which a constituent assembly and a federal government would be established in western Germany, based on democratic institutions. As well as Britain, France and the United States, three other Western victims of Nazi aggression, Holland, Belgium and Luxembourg, signed the pact. On June 23 the Soviet Union countered this Western initiative at a conference in Warsaw attended by all Communist-bloc States, where the London Pact was condemned, and delegates demanded the complete demilitarization of Germany, as well as Four-Power control of the Ruhr – from which Russia was excluded under the Potsdam agreement – and the setting up of an all-German provisional government.

On June 24, Britain, France and the United States found their road and rail access to Berlin blocked by Soviet troops and tanks. Their only remaining access to Berlin was by air. To supply their own forces, and feed the German population in the Western sectors of the city, a massive air lift was begun. It quickly became a symbol

of Western resistance to Communist threats. The two million inhabitants of Western Berlin were fed, and the Soviet blockade, kept in
place for fifteen months, served as a stark symbol of the East-West
divide.

In December, as a culmination of three years' work in which the
United States had taken a major part, the United Nations approved
a Universal Declaration of Human Rights, which upheld the right
of every individual to leave any country, and to go to any country.
But its broad sweep and ambitious intentions were quickly challenged
by actual violations. The first of these took place within three weeks,
when, on December 27, after the Hungarian Catholic leadership
refused to make concessions to the Communist regime, the government arrested Cardinal Mindszenty. His right to leave Hungary was
immediately curtailed.

In China the Nationalists were being pushed back by the Communists
at every point of conflict. In October they lost their remaining strongholds in Manchuria. When Chiang Kai-shek's wife reached Washington on December 1, to appeal for American intervention on behalf
of the Nationalists, she found words of sympathy but no promises
and no action. On December 16 the State Department announced
that American 'hands off' policy towards China would not change.

The Soviet Union continued to absorb its territorial gains of
1945. On March 24 a decree was issued in Lithuania imposing the
collectivization of all farms there. Similar decrees were issued in Latvia
and Estonia where, at harvest time, many farmers were sentenced to
a year or two 'deprivation of liberty' for having refused to deliver
their quotas to the State. Lithuanian Catholic priests were denounced
for 'educating the youth in a spirit of opposition to the State'.

In Byelorussia and the three Baltic Republics, the Roman Catholic Church was singled out for denunciation. In the Central Asian
Republics, Islam and the Mullahs were accused of encouraging polyg-
amy, bride-barter and the wearing of veils. Another accusation against
the predominantly Islamic republics was that religious festivals were
reducing the productivity of collective farms. Soviet Jews were
denounced for continuing to hold religious services in private homes.
The leading Jewish actor and theatre director, Solomon Mikhoels,

was murdered on Stalin's orders, then given a public funeral. He had just helped compile a volume of documents about the Nazi Holocaust on Soviet soil. Stalin refused to allow the book to be published.

The wife of Stalin's foreign minister Vyacheslav Molotov, Polina Molotov, was a Jewish woman, and a member of the Soviet Anti-Fascist Committee set up during the war to make the Soviet suffering better known abroad. On November 8 she officially welcomed Golda Meir, the Israeli Ambassador to Moscow, to a diplomatic reception. Twelve days later the Anti-Fascist Committee was dissolved and almost all its members arrested. In due course most of them were shot. Polina Molotov was imprisoned. Jews were condemned as 'rootless cosmopolitans', alien to the Russian way of life and hostile to Russian needs. Jewish theatre critics were denounced as an 'anti-Party group'.

In Yugoslavia, the Soviet Union's wartime ally and associate, the Communist leadership had begun to resist the pressures from Moscow. In a brave act of defiance, President Tito broke with Stalin and declared his own form of Communism. On March 27 Stalin and Molotov sent him a letter warning of the dangers of the breach. But Tito would not allow himself or his country to be browbeaten, and Yugoslavia embarked on an independent Communist course. Within Western Europe, the strength of Soviet domination elsewhere behind the Iron Curtain led to calls for European unity. On March 17 a treaty was signed in Brussels by five Powers — Britain, France, Belgium, Holland and Luxembourg — establishing a Consultative Council which would meet whenever peace seemed to be threatened. The Council's Military Committee, later renamed the Defence Committee, held its first meeting in London on April 30.

In May, in parallel with the governmental work of the five Brussels Treaty Powers, an International Committee of the Movements for European Unity met in The Hague. Its object was to 'affirm the urgent need for close and effective unity among the peoples of Europe'. It was also determined to see Western Germany take its place around the European discussion tables.

In South Africa the segregation of white South Africans from the majority black and mixed-race — known as coloured — population was vigorously maintained. At the General Election on May 26 the

Nationalist Party won seventy-nine seats as against seventy-four for the opposition Parties. The new government had as its priority turning the system of apartheid from one of social to legal separation. Legislative acts defined three categories of citizen: white, coloured and African. Marriages were prohibited between whites and black South Africans. Under the Immorality Act, sexual intercourse between whites and 'coloureds' was also forbidden. Once legalized, the separation of people by colour was sustained by police coercion, and a secret police and informant system which, in maintaining unjust laws, undermined the rule of law.

That rule of law was exercised in Tokyo on November 12, in the former War Ministry building, when the International Military Tribunal, Far East, found seven Japanese wartime leaders guilty of war crimes. They were sentenced to death, and hanged on December 23.

Television was beginning to take its place worldwide as a purveyor of news and entertainment. The leisure of hundreds of millions of people was also enhanced in 1948 by the first long-playing gramophone record. That year the word game Scrabble was launched in the United States, as was the drive-in hamburger café, by Richard and Maurice McDonald, whose surname and distinctive red-and-yellow logo were, within five decades, to adorn shopping malls throughout the world, including Moscow and Jerusalem.

On the morning of 21 June 1948 six young scientists at Manchester University were carrying out an experiment. Nine times that morning they put a series of programmes through a computer – named Baby – without success. On the tenth try the experiment worked. The computer could 'remember' and calibrate any number of digits that were fed into it. Mathematical problems could be solved 10,000 times faster than hitherto. The team that carried out the successful experiment was led by Freddie Williams and Tom Kilburn, both of whom had worked on radar during the war. They had ushered in the computer age.

The rule of Stalin was in its third decade – tyrannical and malign. In the four-day period between 25 and 28 March 1949 thirty-three trains left Latvia for 'special settlement areas' in Siberia. On board were 43,000 Latvian civilians, of whom more than 10,000 were children, part of an operation under which 100,000 people were deported from the Soviet Baltic Republics. Among more than five million Soviet citizens imprisoned in labour camps, or in enforced exile, in 1949 were 503,375 women: this precise figure was given to Stalin by his Minister of the Interior. One of them – her case was typical – was a woman who, while queuing for milk in Moscow, had told those around her that she understood from her son in the Red Army in Vienna that people were no longer queuing for milk in the West. She was at once denounced by the whole queue, and sentenced to ten years in labour camp.

When Stalin was told that the cost of maintaining children in the camps was considerable, he agreed that women with children under the age of eleven should be released. Such mothers, he decreed, must continue to do forced labour, but they could do it in their home towns. Women who had been sentenced for 'counter-revolutionary activity', however, must remain in the camps with their children. President Truman's decisions were of a different order. On January 20 he presented his 'Fair Deal' policy, extending social security, raising the minimum wage and greatly increasing federal house-building. He had already provided federal funds for both slum clear-ance and low-cost housing for the poor.

Elected President for another four years, Truman's inauguration ceremony on January 20 was the first to be broadcast live on tele-vision, watched by an estimated ten million Americans: the largest number of people until then to watch a single event. Another hundred million listened on the radio. Truman told his listeners in unambigu-ous words: 'The actions resulting from the Communist philosophy are a threat to the efforts of free nations to bring about world recovery and lasting peace.' Within three months, the North Atlantic Treaty was signed in Washington, establishing the North Atlantic Treaty Organization (NATO). Twelve nations subscribed to the treaty: the United States, Canada, Britain, France, Luxembourg, Belgium, Hol-land, Italy, Portugal, Denmark, Iceland and Norway. Their aim was mutual military assistance in the event of aggression. The potential aggressor was no longer Germany but the Soviet Union.

Western Germany was not a party to the North Atlantic Treaty, but her post-war regeneration was in accordance with the Western democratic ideals which underpinned the NATO concept. On May 23 the Federal Republic of Germany – also known as West Germany – came into existence, with its capital in Bonn, on the Rhine. On September 12, following openly contested elections, Theodor Heuss was elected President and Konrad Adenauer Chancellor. Neither had been members of the Nazi Party. Both had opposed the excesses of the Hitler regime. Adenauer had been dismissed as Chairman of the Prussian State Council because of his opposition to Nazism, and was twice imprisoned – in 1934 and 1944.

The Soviet Union could do nothing to impede the emergence of democracy in West Germany. Within three weeks of the elections Stalin called off the Berlin blockade. East Germany and the Soviet sector of Berlin remained under tight Communist control.

After two decades of violent turmoil the political future of China was about to be resolved. The Communist forces were everywhere in the ascendant. Hoping to gain time, on January 8 Chiang Kai-shek asked the United States, Britain, France and the Soviet Union to 'mediate' between the two warring sides, but the Four Powers rejected his appeal. Two days later Mao Tse-tung announced that as a condition of joining a coalition government the Nationalists would have to purge all 'war criminals'. Heading the list of those criminals was Chiang Kai-shek.

On January 22, Communist forces entered Peking. Peace talks began, but to no avail, as the Communists, confident of further military successes in the south, continued to advance. One by one the Nationalist-controlled cities in the south were overrun. On September 21, in Peking, Mao Tse-tung proclaimed the establishment of the People's Republic of China. The new government set as its main aim 'opposing imperialism, feudalism, and bureaucratic forces', while at the same time 'eliminating counter-revolutionary forces'.

Mao Tse-tung became Chairman, and Chou En-lai both Prime Minister and Foreign Minister. On December 7 the Nationalist government left mainland China for the island of Taiwan, never to return to the mainland. On December 16 Mao Tse-tung travelled to Moscow for talks with Stalin. He had never been outside China before. Stalin's biographer Dmitri Volkogonov commented wryly:

'Even their Marxism gave them little in common, since Mao was
fond of mixing his with Confucianism, while Stalin generally confined
himself to quoting his own works.' As Stalin and his visitor talked
and ate, their officials drafted a thirty-year Sino-Soviet Treaty of
Friendship, Alliance and Mutual Assistance. As Chinese Communist
forces, in their accelerating advance against the Nationalists,
approached the northern border of French Indo-China, it seemed to
France that Ho Chi Minh and his Communist Vietminh insurgents
might be considerably strengthened by their proximity to China. To
counteract this, France made concessions to the former Emperor, Bao
Dai, to attract the Vietnamese people to a non-Communist regime.
Bao Dai visited Paris in March and reached a series of agreements
with France, whereby Vietnam would be autonomous, with its own
army, full internal sovereignty, and full civil, commercial and penal
jurisdiction. French military, naval and air bases would remain, and
French culture would be encouraged. In return, France would propose
Vietnam for membership of the United Nations. Vietnam would
remain within the French Union, as would the other two former
protectorates of French Indochina – integral parts of the Indo-Chinese
Union of 1886 – Laos and Cambodia.

Bao Dai was confident that as a result of the agreement with
France he could offer the Vietnamese people an attractive alternative
to Communism. He arrived in Saigon on June 13 and on the following
day was proclaimed Chief of State of the new State of Vietnam. The
reaction of the Vietminh was immediate. The Supreme Commander
of the Communist Armed Forces, General Vo Nguyen Giap, called
for a vigorous military offensive against the Vietnamese forces loyal
to Bao Dai and against the French lines of communication. The
Vietminh had 82,000 men under arms. The French and Bao Dai
forces numbered 110,000. Within a few months extra French troops
raised this figure to more than 130,000, but many of them were
sent to the north as a barrier against possible Chinese Communist
incursion.

The onward march of Communism in Asia was much feared by
those who might be in its path. During 1949, North Korean Communist forces began to mount armed attacks across the 18th parallel
into South Korea. This geographic line had been decided upon as

the North-South divide by the Soviet Union and the United States
in 1945. In the course of the year more than 2,000 armed Communist
infiltrators were killed by the South Korean army. The North Korean
leader, Kim Il Sung, was supported in the maintenance of Communism by the Soviet Union. The government in the south was sustained
by American aid. But unlike the Soviet Union, which sent tanks,
artillery and a hundred modern military aircraft to North Korea, the
United States limited the nature of the arms it was prepared to
provide and refused to give South Korea the means of making effective
war on the North. Efforts by the United Nations to open trade
between North and South were a failure. South Korean politicians
who favoured closer trade and contacts with North Korea were
imprisoned for 'unpatriotic activity'.

The Soviet Union and the Soviet bloc, although signatories to the
Universal Declaration of Human Rights – to which all the governments behind the Iron Curtain had appended their signature in 1948
– continued to disregard those rights, as Communist control was
strengthened beyond the Soviet borders. A Soviet soldier, Marshal
Konstantin Rokossovski, a veteran of the Spanish Civil War – who
had been born in Warsaw and was of Polish origin – arrived in the
Polish capital in February, with three Soviet generals. Their visit
followed the arrest of hundreds of former Polish officers of the wartime
underground army, the Armia Krajowa, which had been loyal to the
London government in exile – at that time the only legitimate Polish
Government. The independent-minded Polish Communist Party
leader, Wladyslaw Gomulka, was cut off from political influence and
expelled from the Party's governing body. At the end of March
measures were introduced which effectively abolished trial by jury.
They were justified on the grounds that they were for 'improving
and simplifying court procedure'. In a series of political trials the
accused were denounced as agents of Western imperialism.

On November 7, Marshal Rokossovski was created a Marshal of
Poland and made Minister of Defence in the Polish Government. On
the following day he accepted Polish citizenship. In an Order of the
Day on the anniversary of the Bolshevik revolution he called on
the Polish armed forces 'to tighten the ties of brotherhood with the

powerful Soviet Army and the armies of the People's Democracies'. He also ensured that the army's tasks included Communist political work.

In Czechoslovakia the Communist system was imposed at every level of society. Men were taken for forced labour and for ideological re-education. Children had to join Party organizations. Newspapers were strictly controlled and several foreign correspondents were expelled. As in Poland, citizens innocent of wrong-doing were brought to trial and accused of spying for the Western Powers. The Soviet Union also insisted on the export to Russia of large quantities of Czech railway rolling stock, armaments, machine tools, industrial instruments and uranium. In return the Soviet Union provided some food and raw materials which the Czechs had to transform into manufactured goods to be re-exported to Russia.

The Catholic Church in Czechoslovakia was under mounting pressure. After Archbishop Josef Beran denounced the government's attempt to set up an independent, pro-Communist Catholic hierarchy – having earlier issued a pastoral letter with an injunction addressed to himself: 'Don't remain silent, archbishop! You can't remain silent!' – he was confined to his palace and forbidden access to his followers. In retaliation, a Papal decree issued from the Vatican excommunicated all church members who were supporters of the Communist Party. In November a law was passed giving the Czech State control over the appointment of clergy and payment of their salaries.

The most publicized Communist political trial of 1949 was in Hungary. It opened in Budapest on February 3, when Cardinal Jozsef Mindszenty, the Prince-Primate of Hungary, was accused of spying on behalf of the United States and seeking the restoration of the Habsburgs: he had met the heir to the Habsburgs in Chicago in 1948. Throughout the trial Mindszenty was outspoken in his criticism of Communism. Found guilty of 'organizing conspiracy against the Republic', he was sentenced to penal servitude for life.

A second trial in Hungary that year struck at the inner circle of the Communist regime. One of the accused was the former Minister of the Interior and Foreign Minister, Lazlo Rajk. Another was the Chief of the General Staff. They were accused of preparing a military coup, the assassination of the other leaders, an alliance with Tito's

Yugoslavia in a war against the Soviet Union and the establishment of Hungary as a 'colony of American imperialist interests'. As in the Soviet purge trials in the 1930s, the charges were absurd and the rule of law absent in the way the cases were conducted. All the defendants were found guilty and executed. On December 28 the Hungarian Government nationalized all foreign-financed trading and industrial enterprises, and all privately owned shops and factories employing more than ten people.

The Roumanian Government was equally thorough in its imposition of Communist rule. On January 14 a law was promulgated whereby those found guilty of minor economic offences against the State were liable to the death penalty. In March, a Land Act enforced the collectivization of farms without compensation to landowners or farmers. Peasants were warned that failure to co-operate in the collective farm programme would debar them from receiving tractors and other agricultural equipment from the government stores which alone could provide them. The two remaining non-Communist Cabinet Ministers in positions of authority in Roumania were removed in April. Organized religion was also under pressure, with both the Roumanian Orthodox Church and the Greek Catholic Church being made subservient to the State system. The Roman Catholic Church fought a tenacious rearguard action, with the result that the Roman Catholic bishops of Alba Julia and Jassy were arrested, and a month later all Roman Catholic congregations were dissolved.

Joint Soviet-Roumanian companies were set up to control Roumania's natural gas, metal, coal and shipbuilding industries, giving the Soviet Union a voice in the daily running of the Roumanian economy. Roumania had also to give the Soviet Union priority over the exports of Roumanian oil and timber. Only in Yugoslavia did the Communist leaders strike a line independent of Moscow. In a twenty-five page letter to Tito, Stalin denounced Yugoslavia's continuing independent stance as 'deviation' and 'treachery'. When he summoned the Yugoslavs to a Cominform meeting in Bucharest they refused to go. Like the Comintern between the wars, the Cominform was the Soviet Union's attempt, after 1945, to maintain its control over the ideological conformity of other Communist Parties.

In Bulgaria, treason trials were held against non-Communist

politicians and Church leaders. In April, after all religious schools were abolished, the British Government raised at the United Nations the suppression of religious freedom in Bulgaria. The treason trials continued. The Soviet Minister of Defence, Marshal Nikolai Bulganin, visiting Sofia in September, explained publicly that 'treason' meant any act that weakened the ties of friendship between the Soviet Union and Bulgaria. During the intensification of Party discipline and control, the Chief of the General Staff, General Kinov, was arrested, then put on trial with a leading Central Committee member, Traicho Kostov, and ten other senior Communist figures. They were accused of plotting to allow Yugoslavia to annex Bulgaria, and of attempting to sabotage trade agreements with the Soviet Union. All the defendants except Kostov confessed to these imaginary crimes and were sentenced to long terms of imprisonment. Kostov protested his innocence and his impeccable Communist credentials, was found guilty, and executed.

On December 21 Stalin celebrated his seventieth birthday. In Moscow a gala performance was given in his honour by the Bolshoi Ballet. Among those present were the Chinese Communist leader Mao Tse-tung, the Spanish civil war veteran Dolores Ibarruri, and the ruler of Communist East Germany, Walter Ulbricht. Two months had passed since the successful Soviet testing of an atomic bomb. News of this test was made public, not by the Soviets, but by the American, British and Canadian Governments. Andrei Vyshinsky, who had become Soviet Foreign Minister earlier that year, explained to the United Nations in New York that atomic energy was being used in the Soviet Union, not as part of any military arsenal, but 'for razing mountains, irrigating deserts, cutting through jungles, and spreading life, prosperity and happiness in places where human footsteps had not been in a thousand years'.

Unknown at that time, outside a tiny circle, was the fact that Britain was also in the process of manufacturing its own atomic bomb.

In South Africa, riots against apartheid broke out in Johannesburg. But speaking in New York, one of the most vocal white South African opponents of apartheid, Alan Paton, was hopeful. 'I look for the day,' he said, 'when in South Africa we shall realize that the only lasting and worth-while solution of our grave and profound problems lies not in the use of power, but in that understanding and compassion without which human life is an intolerable bondage, condemning us all to an existence of violence and misery and fear.'

'Understanding and compassion' did not yet seem the predominant mood of the mass of mankind. A grave warning of the way the world might go was published that year by George Orwell. His novel *Nineteen Eighty-Four* was set in an imaginary totalitarian world where total control over the mass of the people was exercised with vigilance and psychological cunning by 'Big Brother'. When Winston Smith, the hero of the novel, dares to exclaim, 'Down with Big Brother!' his interrogator smiles at him and says: 'You are a flaw in the pattern, Winston. You are a stain that must be wiped out.'

The triumph of the Communists in China, and the knowledge that the Soviet Union not only possessed the atom bomb but was manufacturing it, led on 27 January 1950 to each NATO country signing a defence agreement with the United States. Four days later, in strictest secrecy, President Truman gave orders for work to begin on a bomb that could cause far more devastation than the atom bomb – the Hydrogen bomb. On February 14 the thirty-year Treaty of Friendship, Alliance and Mutual Assistance negotiated by Mao Tse-tung and Stalin was signed in Moscow. The Cold War had acquired a new axis.

On March 1 the atomic scientist Klaus Fuchs, a pre-war German refugee who had been living and working in England and the United States, was sentenced by a British court to fourteen years in prison for betraying atomic secrets to the Soviet Union. Fear of Communist subversion led to a witchhunt in the United States against alleged Communists in the administration. On January 9 Senator Joseph McCarthy declared that 205 Communists were working in the State Department. As the anti-Communist crusade gained in momentum, the Republican-dominated Congress voted in favour of a bill requiring all Communist organizations to register, and forbidding the employment of Communists in companies doing defence work. Truman vetoed the bill, but it was passed into law over his veto. The

McCarthyites suffered a setback, however, when the Senate accepted a Foreign Relations Committee report that the State Department had not been subjected to 'Communist infiltration'. But when the conviction of eleven American Communists on charges of 'conspiracy to teach and advocate the overthrow of the government' was sent for appeal, it was sustained by one of America's leading jurists, Judge Learned Hand.

In defence of freedom of expression, and of sane rather than hysterical inquiry, Arthur Miller's play *The Crucible* drew on the destructive interrogations and burning of alleged witches in Salem, Massachusetts, in the seventeenth century. Miller gave courage not only to Americans who were under attack, but, in the years to come, to people under tyranny everywhere, including Poland and China. Inside the Communist world, repressions and trials continued. Jan Masaryk's successor as Czechoslovak Foreign Minister, Dr Valdimir Clementis, was forced to resign because, although a Communist, he had opposed the Nazi-Soviet Pact in 1939 and the Soviet invasion of Finland later that same year. According to the public denunciation against Clementis, 'there must have existed germs of distrust towards the USSR and comrade Stalin before 1939 if that failure could happen'.

In Hungary, a government decree on September 7 led to the closing down of most religious orders. In Roumania, eight death sentences were announced on Roumanian citizens allegedly working for foreign powers. The aim of the sentences was intimidation, not justice. In the Soviet Union, yet another search was on for 'spies' and 'enemies of the people'. Those arrested had never been spies or enemies, but members of the Communist Party at its highest echelons.

Stimulated by the East-West divide, the cause of European unity gained momentum. On May 9 the French and German coal industries, and all French and German iron and steel production, were placed under a single authority. In September, a European Payments Union was established, linking fifteen European countries to Britain and the sterling area, in a settlement of trade deficits and surpluses. On June 15 West Germany was admitted to the Council of Europe. Increasingly, the economic recovery of western Europe separated it economically as well as ideologically from its eastern neighbours.

In Japan, still under American military occupation, the suppression of Communism intensified, with the Communist Party's Central Committee members forbidden to take any further part in public life. This ban was later extended to thirteen of the Party's thirty-six elected Members of Parliament. Communist Party newspapers were suppressed, Communist civil servants dismissed and the Communist-dominated Federation of Trade Unions dissolved. On the Asian mainland, Ho Chi Minh asked the world on January 14 to recognize his Vietminh regime as the legitimate and sole rulers of Vietnam. Four days later Communist China gave its recognition, followed by the Soviet Union. France was contemptuous of Ho Chi Minh's pretensions, however, and confident that despite the setbacks of previous years it could defeat him on the battlefield. For his part, Truman accelerated American military aid to French Indochina, and the despatch of a military mission.

A new war was about to break out in the Far East, not in Vietnam but in Korea. At four in the morning of June 25, North Korean forces invaded South Korea and pushed quickly southward. Truman, who was then in his home State of Missouri, flew back to Washington. He later wrote of how during the journey the pre-war fate of Manchuria and Abyssinia was on his mind. 'I remembered how each time that the democracies failed to act it encouraged the aggressors to keep going ahead. If the Communists were permitted to force their way into the Republic of Korea without opposition from the free world, no small nation would have the courage to resist threats and aggression by stronger Communist neighbours.' If the North Korean attack was allowed to go unchallenged 'it would mean a Third World War, just as similar incidents had brought on the Second World War'.

The United Nations Security Council passed a resolution by nine votes to nil demanding the withdrawal of North Korean forces. There was no Soviet veto, as the Soviet delegate had walked out of the Security Council five months earlier in protest at its refusal to give Communist China a place. The North Korean Government ignored the Security Council resolution and continued its southward advance. As it did so, Truman ordered all American forces in Japan, Okinawa and the Philippines to be made ready for action. When the United

Nations Security Council called on all member States of the United
Nations to 'render such assistance to the Republic of Korea as may
be necessary to repel the armed attack and to restore international
peace and security to the area', the United States was among sixteen
nations that responded to the call for troops.

At a meeting of his senior advisers on June 26, Truman authorized
American air and naval support to the South Korean forces, telling
his advisers: 'Everything I have done in the past five years has been
to try to avoid making a decision such as I had to make tonight.'
On the following day, when North Korean troops and tanks entered
the South Korean capital, Seoul, Truman declared: 'The attack upon
Korea makes it plain beyond all doubt that Communism has passed
beyond the use of subversion to conquer independent nations and
will now use armed invasion and war.' By the following day most
of the South Korean army had been destroyed.

On his first inspection in South Korea, General MacArthur saw
a demoralized and ill-led South Korean army. He at once asked
Truman for two divisions of American ground troops to be sent to
Korea and enter combat. Truman agreed, noting in his diary: 'Must
be careful not to cause a general Asiatic war.' The first United States
troops, flying the flag of the United Nations as well as their own,
landed at the port of Pusan, on the south-eastern corner of the Korean
peninsula on July 1. MacArthur, the victor over Japan, was appointed
Supreme Commander of all the United Nations forces in South Korea.

The American troops who were rushed to the front line had
neither the training, combat experience nor equipment to stand up
to the North Korean forces. Within hours they were outgunned,
outnumbered and outflanked, and forced to retreat. A larger American
force pushed the Korean line back, but this advance was short-lived.
On July 11 the North Koreans renewed their offensive and drove
the Americans back. A 'line of no retreat' was set up, but after a
thirty-six-hour tank battle, in which the North Koreans had numerical superiority, the Americans were forced to pull back yet again.

At his first press conference since the outbreak of war, Truman
declared: 'We have never had the tar licked out of us – and it won't
happen this time.' In a television broadcast, he explained that the
United States forces were fighting under the United Nations flag to

resist an act of 'raw aggression'. It was this that made the war a 'landmark in mankind's long search for a rule of law among nations', and he went on to ask: 'Surely, with the history of the last twenty years fresh in our minds, no one can doubt that it is vitally important that aggression should be halted at the outset.'

As North Korean troops swept southwards, there were fears that the port of Pusan, the main landing place for United Nations troops and supplies, would fall. By July 25, only a quarter of South Korea remained under the control of the United Nations forces. A 'last ditch' defence triangle was established, where American cooks, clerks and drivers fought alongside the regular infantrymen. As American troops pulled back towards the 'last ditch' perimeter, the North Korean artillery barrages were both intense and accurate, causing one American officer to describe them as 'sheer butchery'.

On July 29 the United States Eighth Army commander, General Walton H. Walker, issued an order that Pusan must not fall. 'There are no lines behind which we can retreat,' he said. 'This is not going to be a Dunkirk or Bataan. A retreat to Pusan would result in one of the greatest butcheries in history. We must fight to the end. We must fight as a team. If some of us die, we will die fighting together.' Pusan did not fall. The establishment of a 130-mile defensive perimeter around the port enabled the North Korean forces to be held off, albeit with heavy casualties. United Nations air forces were able to strike with effect at the much-stretched North Korean supply lines, and Pusan became the port of disembarkation of an influx of American arms and armour.

On September 12 the first British troops took up their position in the line. But even as the battle for the perimeter continued, MacArthur was deciding on a surprise amphibious landing far behind North Korean lines, at Inchon, a city only twenty-five miles from Seoul, and 200 miles from the men trapped at Pusan. The landing involved 262 ships and 70,000 American troops – half as many as were fighting in the Pusan Perimeter. To his critics in the American High Command, MacArthur said: 'I can almost hear the ticking of the second hand of destiny. We must act now or we will die ... We shall land at Inchon, and I shall crush them.'

MacArthur was concerned, as the final stages of preparation went ahead, that a landing at Inchon might bring in Chinese and even Soviet troops, in order to prevent the North Koreans being pushed back across the 38th parallel. He believed, however, that he could secure the city and make rapid progress before the Soviet or Chinese leaders realized what had happened. He was right. When the landings took place on September 15 the North Koreans were unprepared for an attack so far behind the front line. Advancing from Inchon, American troops entered Seoul within eleven days of the landing. This success was followed by the breakout from the Pusan perimeter.

On September 27, Truman authorized MacArthur to advance beyond the 38th Parallel, provided the general could assure himself there was no sign of Chinese or Soviet military intervention. Truman added that MacArthur must not carry the war northward into China or the Soviet Union. On October 1 the Americans reached the 38th parallel. South Korea was again under its own sovereignty. That day, impatient to exploit his success, MacArthur ordered South Korean and American troops to prepare to cross the 38th parallel and move into North Korea. His instructions from Washington were: 'The destruction of the North Korean armed forces'.

The North Koreans were moving hundreds of Americans – prisoners of war and civilian internees – northwards, away from the battle zone and towards the Chinese border. On one of these marches, a hundred American prisoners of war and civilian captives were killed because they were too weak to continue, or as a punishment for some alleged infringement.

On October 9, Americans and South Korean troops crossed the 38th parallel into North Korea. Ten days later they captured Pyongyang, the capital of North Korea. MacArthur then gave orders for the 'maximum effort' to advance to the border of North Korea, the Yalu River. The British Government, uneasy that a military advance up to the Chinese border might provoke Chinese intervention, proposed instead the creation of a buffer zone south of the Yalu. MacArthur rejected this with contempt.

*　　*　　*

It was not Chinese intervention to help the North Koreans that followed the American advance towards the Yalu, but Chinese military action elsewhere. On October 22, Chinese forces entered Tibet. Confident of its sovereign rights, Tibet appealed to the United Nations for help against China's aggression, but the United Nations was too deeply involved in Korea to embark on a new area of conflict, despite anguish among many member States that Tibet would fall under Chinese and Communist control. The Tibetan army, no match for its adversary, accepted defeat. It could not expect succour from the outside world.

On November 5, MacArthur reported to Washington that 30,000 Chinese troops were already inside North Korea and 'massing' in substantial numbers. In Washington the Joint Chiefs, echoing the British, suggested to MacArthur that he might halt his troops somewhere short of the border to avoid the risk of clashes with the Chinese. He replied that if peace and unity were to be restored in Korea, it would be necessary to destroy all 'enemy forces' within the borders.

On November 24, under MacArthur's confident command, the United Nations forces launched an offensive into north-east Korea. Two days later Chinese troops reached the fighting line. They had entered the combat to secure victory, and fought accordingly. Supporting them were Soviet-built MiG-15 jet fighters, flown by both Chinese and Soviet pilots from bases on Chinese soil north of the Yalu that were immune from United Nations attack. Within twenty-four hours the United Nations forces – which included American, British, Turkish and South Korean units – were in retreat. By the last week of November more than 200,000 Chinese soldiers had crossed the Yalu River. MacArthur pressed Washington to authorize further withdrawals. The United Nations Command, he warned, was 'facing the entire Chinese nation in an undeclared war'. His own troops were 'mentally fatigued and physically battered'.

On December 5 the North Korean capital, Pyongyang, was abandoned by those who had entered it in triumph only forty-seven days earlier. Two days later the United Nations condemned the Chinese action in crossing into North Korea. The numbers of Chinese troops inside North Korea by the second week of December was estimated at between 400,000 and 450,000. MacArthur ordered further withdrawals. On December 15 the American forces crossed back over the 38th parallel. On December 27 the Chinese Government refused a United Nations offer of a cease-fire, and Chinese troops, advancing southward in force, crossed into South Korea.

The American and South Korean forces had retreated 300 miles in thirty days, fighting every mile of the way in temperatures far below zero. Frustrated at this continual withdrawal, MacArthur pressed his superiors in Washington for direct action against China itself. On December 30 he proposed that the United Nations should recognize a state of war with China, and then authorize the United Nations Command – of which he was the head – to blockade the Chinese coast, and through air attack destroy China's industrial capacity to wage war. MacArthur also argued that if between thirty and fifty atom bombs were dropped on Manchuria and the cities of mainland China, the war would be over.

The American Joint Chiefs agreed that the atom bomb was the only weapon that could effectively defeat the Chinese, but Truman rejected such a course. The man who had authorized the dropping of two atom bombs on inhabited cities in Japan five years earlier was not going to authorize the dropping of a third.

As fighting between the French and the Vietminh intensified in Vietnam the French pulled back from the northern frontier areas, and took up defensive positions in the Red River Delta. During the course of the retreat, Moroccan troops, attacked by wave after wave of Vietminh soldiers, broke in panic and fled. In their terror many of them went berserk. It was the worst disaster in eighty years of French colonial history. In Paris the Socialist leader Pierre Mendès-France argued that the only way to secure Vietnam was by a greatly increased military effort which would harm the French economy at home. He therefore suggested opening negotiations with Ho Chi Minh. The government rejected this.

Arms, equipment and medical supplies began to reach the French in Vietnam from the United States, but there was no chance of reversing the humiliation of the withdrawal from the border areas. On November 22, in the Chamber of Deputies in Paris, the French

Government secured a majority of 337 to 187 'to reinforce the army as required', and to seek even more American military aid. As one war was being fought in Korea, another had intensified in Vietnam.

On 1 January 1951 a United Nations High Commissioner for Refugees was made responsible for almost two million refugees worldwide. That same day, on the Korean battlefield, which was itself generating hundreds of thousands more refugees, North Korean and Chinese troops who had crossed the 38th parallel renewed their push southward. As British troops went forwards to the front line on New Year's Day, American soldiers going back into reserve called out to them: 'You're going the wrong way, buddy!' That day, Chinese troops in Korea were ordered to collect the largest number of prisoners possible as a New Year gift for Mao Tse-tung.

On January 4 the South Koreans and Americans were driven out of Seoul, as they had been six months earlier in the first days of the war. Once more the Americans were retreating towards Pusan. But a new state of mind was about to dominate the American troops in Korea. In late December their Commander in Chief, General Walker, had been killed when his jeep collided with a South Korean army truck. His replacement was General Matthew B. Ridgway, a veteran of the fighting in the Ardennes in the Second World War, where a severe reversal had been met and countered. Within weeks, Ridgway's fighting qualities and professionalism affected all his troops, including those in retreat. Under Ridgway's influence a United Nations counter-offensive was planned, making use of the overwhelming American air superiority and the American ability to obliterate the Chinese supply routes.

On January 13 Truman sent MacArthur a telegram reiterating the American position that the war in Korea was meant to demonstrate 'that aggression will not be accepted by us or by the United Nations'. He went on, however, to impress upon MacArthur that 'great prudence' was needed in the future conduct of the war. 'In the worst case,' Truman explained, 'it would be important that, if we must withdraw from Korea, it be clear to the world that that course is forced upon us by military necessity and that we shall not accept the result politically or militarily until the aggression is rectified.'

'. . . if we must withdraw from Korea . . .' These six words were the harbingers of a change in United States policy. On January 13, the day of Truman's telegram to MacArthur, a United Nations committee, consisting of an Iranian, a Canadian and an Indian, put forward a plan for an immediate cease-fire and the withdrawal of all foreign forces from Korea 'by appropriate stages'. The Americans expressed willingness to consider these proposals. The Chinese rejected them, proposing instead a Seven-Power conference, to be held on Chinese soil, to consider a 'limited' cease-fire. This was strongly supported by twelve Arab and Asian States headed by India, as well as by Canada and Britain.

In Britain, it was the Soviet Union that seemed the greatest long-term danger. On January 26, Attlee warned that to protect against Russian intentions it was necessary to ensure a substantial British rearmament, requiring of the British people 'great exertions and serious sacrifices'. He added: 'Our way of life is in danger, our happiness and the happiness and future of our children are in danger; and it is both our privilege and our duty to be ready to defend them if they are attacked.' Attlee went on to say that the 'arid and unattractive doctrines' of Marxism-Leninism were as distant as they could be from 'true' Socialism, but were held by men who controlled 'great armies' and who 'rejected the moral values on which civilization is based'.

In August, *Pravda* expressed indignation at a statement in which the British Foreign Secretary, Herbert Morrison, deplored the fact that Soviet citizens were restricted in their access to information about foreign countries, in their contacts with foreign citizens, and in their right to travel abroad. If he were a Russian, Morrison declared: 'I would find no rule of law, no political and religious freedom and equality, no sort of constitutional safeguards, no right to turn the Government out of office, or even to vote for any candidate not hand-picked by the Kremlin. I would find a Parliament which is very rarely allowed to meet, and is then the tool of the government.'

Communist repression faced citizens of a dozen countries. In Poland, a number of Roman Catholic priests were brought to trial and there were further attempts to secularize education. In Hungary, Archbishop Grösz, the acting head of the Roman Catholic Church

– Cardinal Mindszenty being under house arrest – was arrested and brought to trial with eight other religious leaders. He was found guilty of a number of specious charges and sentenced to fifteen years in prison. In the Roumanian campaign against Roman Catholicism, the eighty-one-year-old Bishop of Timisoara was tried by a military court on charges of spying 'in the service of the Vatican'. He was sentenced to eighteen years solitary confinement. There was also a sustained campaign of Russification in Roumania, with as many as 10,000 workers being made to learn Russian, and to use textbooks that would serve as 'a day-to-day guide and material factor in the formation of the workers' Socialist conscience'. In Czechoslovakia, Communist Party rule was tightened by a series of purges. The culmination came when the Party's Secretary General, Rudolf Slansky, was dismissed from his post and charged with being an enemy of the people, an imperialist spy, and the agent of 'Jewish capitalism', which, it was alleged, he intended to restore.

In Korea, American troops began advancing northwards again on January 25, as General Ridgway inspired his men to reverse the tide of withdrawal and demoralization. Improved use of air power and artillery in striking at the Chinese and North Korean positions, and improved communications, were among Ridgway's changes. He also ensured better quality food, warmer clothing for the fierce Korean winter, and improved Mobile Army Surgical Hospitals (MASH) for the sick and wounded.

In Vietnam, only twenty-five miles north-west of Hanoi, 20,000 Vietminh troops attacked the 6,000 French defenders of Vinh Yen, who included many Senegalese and Algerian troops. French air power was decisive. The most effective weapon was the napalm bomb – a development of Second World War flame-throwing devices – which ignited fields, trees and attackers in one indiscriminate blaze. The Vietminh retreated, leaving 6,000 dead on the battlefield. The French losses were 700. In a second Vietminh attack, this time on the village of Mao Khe, three French destroyers pounded the attackers from their anchorage in the nearby river. Heavy naval gunfire and further use of napalm by the French air force saved the French defenders. In the final battle inside the village, 3,000 Vietminh were killed. A third and final Vietminh offensive was against the French fortified positions south-east of Hanoi. As many as 15,000 Vietminh troops were involved in the attack, assisted by 40,000 porters carrying ammunition and food. The Vietminh succeeded in advancing, but once more French naval and air counter-attacks, this time helped by the local Vietnamese Catholic militia, broke their lines of supply and forced them back. As they retreated, the French attacked with heavy air bombardment and napalm bombs, and 9,000 Vietminh troops were killed.

On February 21, the Canadian forces in Korea were in action for the first time. Together with British and Australian troops, and supported by New Zealand artillery, they took part in an advance that drove the Chinese back fifteen miles. Three weeks later United Nations forces retook the South Korean capital, Seoul, and within another two weeks again reached the 38th parallel, and crossed it and pushed northwards. But Ridgway had no plans to retake Pyongyang or press as far as the Yalu River. Instead, he formed a 115-mile-long defensive line from coast to coast, and made preparations to hold it against an imminent Chinese offensive.

From his headquarters in Tokyo, MacArthur continued to advocate air strikes against targets in China. But Washington no longer took his advocacy seriously. To prevent the arrival of any further Chinese reinforcements, MacArthur wanted to 'sever' Korea from China by laying down a zone of radioactive waste – what he called 'the by-products of atomic manufacture' – along the Yalu River. His request was rejected out of hand.

In the third week of March, Truman began to work out proposals for a cease-fire agreement which he hoped to put to his United Nations allies. He first approached MacArthur for his comments, but MacArthur refused to enter into the discussion, other than to oppose what he called 'further military restrictions' on his command. On March 21 Truman sent his cease-fire proposal to the other United Nations participants in the war. On the previous day the Chiefs of Staff in Washington had informed MacArthur that there must be no 'all-out war' with China. Angered, MacArthur decided to take his own initiative, and on March 24, at the very moment America's

United Nations allies were studying Truman's cease-fire proposals, he issued a proclamation stating that an American decision 'to depart from its tolerant effort to contain the war to the areas of Korea, through an expansion of our military operations to his coastal areas and interior bases, would doom Red China to the risk of imminent military collapse'. To avoid this, MacArthur said, he offered the Chinese truce negotiations.

On March 29 the Chinese rejected MacArthur's offer. Three days later the Indian Government made a public appeal for a truce. Britain, a participant in the United Nations war effort, did likewise on April 2. The momentum for compromise was in stark contrast to Mac-Arthur's threat of a wider, potentially nuclear, war. On April 10, Truman acted. He did something that had not been done since Abraham Lincoln almost a century earlier: he sacked his Supreme Commander. Lincoln had sacked General George B. McClellan, whose fault had been his refusal to attack. MacArthur's fault was his desire to attack above and beyond the limits assigned him.

There was indignation among the Republicans in Washington when MacArthur's sacking was announced. Senator Richard Nixon, charging that Truman had both heartened and 'appeased' the Communist world, urged the Senate to censure Truman, and to call on him to restore MacArthur to command. Truman ignored the outcry, explaining in a short broadcast on the night of MacArthur's removal: 'We do not want to widen the conflict.'

Truman appointed Ridgway as MacArthur's successor. On the battlefield the struggle continued without pause or amelioration. Many acts of extreme bravery were reported in all the United Nations armies. On the night of April 24–25 a Japanese-American soldier, Corporal Hiroshi H. Miyamura, from Gallup, New Mexico, protected his squad from an attack by vastly superior numbers, killing more than sixty attackers with his machine-gun. When his ammunition ran out, and he was severely wounded, he fought on with his bayonet, thereby enabling his fellow-Americans to withdraw. His citation for the Medal of Honour described how 'when last seen he was fighting ferociously against an overwhelming number of enemy soldiers'.

The need to increase defence spending in order to continue at war in Korea led the British Labour Government to impose charges on people using the National Health Service. The government insisted the charges were essential if Britain was to fulfil its defence commitments in Korea, and also in Western Europe. In protest, two members of the government resigned. One of them, Aneurin Bevan, was the founder of the Health Service. The other, one of the youngest members of the administration, was Harold Wilson, a future Prime Minister.

On April 22, after darkness fell, the Chinese launched a new offensive in Korea, driving back the United Nations line in many places. New Zealand, Australian, Canadian and British troops were among those who took the brunt of the attack and stemmed the tide. On the Imjin River, British troops, together with a Belgian unit, were in hand-to-hand combat with the Chinese during a four-day battle. The Chinese numbers were overwhelming. Three Filipino light tanks that tried to reach the surrounded British infantry positions and give them cover were forced back. Orders to withdraw came on the night of April 24–25, but by then the troops were surrounded. Those units that could break out did so, losing heavily on the way, more than sixty men being killed. A British regiment, the Glosters, was trapped. Some of the British soldiers had not eaten for forty-eight hours. The riflemen were left with just three bullets each. The battalion adjutant, Captain Anthony Farrar-Hockley, who had fought bravely in Europe in the Second World War, was forced to accept that the situation was hopeless: 'Feeling as if I was betraying everything that I loved and believed in, I raised my voice and called "Stop!"'

The Glosters were led into captivity. Farrar-Hockley was to make three attempts to escape in the days ahead, but was recaptured each time. One of his officers, Major Guy Ward, had been a prisoner of war of the Germans from 1941 to 1945. His first thought when he saw the Glosters surrounded by Chinese was 'Oh my God, here we go again.'

Captivity in North Korea, and also on Chinese soil, was a cruel experience. Of the 7,140 Americans who fell into Chinese hands, 2,701 died in captivity. Of the 1,188 British and Commonwealth prisoners, fifty died. In the camps there were savage interrogations, especially of air crew. Solitary confinement was a much-dreaded pun-

ishment. Hunger and starvation were daily enemies. Another implacable enemy was dysentery. Some men drowned when they fell into
the open latrines.

A renewed Chinese offensive launched on May 15 drove back the
South Korean troops facing it for as much as thirty miles. But
American troops who were also in the line did not pull back, despite
heavy casualties, and the Chinese failed in their objective, the recap-
ture of Seoul. Eleven days after the Chinese offensive had begun, the
United Nations forces once again crossed the 38th parallel and were
on North Korean soil.

On June 25, the first anniversary of the start of the Korean War,
Truman said he was willing to negotiate a settlement on the basis
of a Korea divided as hitherto along the 38th parallel. In response
to a Soviet request for an armistice, General Ridgway offered to meet
his Communist opposite number to discuss an end to hostilities.
Armistice negotiations opened on July 10, in the only area south of
the 38th parallel controlled by the North Koreans.

As the talks continued so did the fighting. By mid-August the
American death toll had reached 13,822. This was already a quarter
of the United States dead in the First World War. The American
bombing missions over North Korean and Chinese-held positions
also continued. On August 22 the Communists broke off the cease-fire
talks, claiming a United Nations aircraft had attacked the conference
area. To avoid a similar incident, Ridgway asked for the talks to be
moved to a place that was not wholly under Communist control.
The Communists agreed and on October 25 the talks were started
again at the village of Panmunjom, in No-Man's Land. After a month
of talks, it was agreed that the approximate future border between
North and South Korea should be the existing cease-fire line.

In Britain, the national indebtedness created by five and a half years
of war, and the continuing cost of the reconstruction of battered
cities, was damaging the economy. Socialism, despite its strong ideological and practical appeal for half the nation, had not proved the
panacea many had hoped. When a General Election was held in
October, the Labour government, which had only a narrow majority,
was defeated, and the Conservatives returned to power.

Churchill was again Prime Minister. As a former negotiator with the Soviet Union at the highest level, he brought with him the hope that it might be possible to build bridges with Stalin's Russia. 'Even if the difference between West and East are, for the time being, intractable,' he said on November 6, in his first speech to parliament after returning to office, 'the creation of a new atmosphere and climate of thought; and of a revived relationship and sense of human comradeship, would, I believe, be an enormous gain to all the nations.'

On November 7 the United States, Britain and France produced a disarmament plan covering the regulation, limitation and balanced reduction of all armed forces and all armaments. The atom bomb was included in the scheme. The three governments made clear that 'a first and indispensable step is disclosure and verification': international inspection of all armed forces, paramilitary forces, security forces and police forces. This was rejected by the Soviet Union. Two months later, on December 30, France, Italy, Luxembourg, Belgium, Holland and West Germany announced the formation of a European Defence Community (EDC). On the following day, the Economic Co-operation Administration of the Marshall Plan was replaced by a Mutual Security Agency.

Following a typhus epidemic in Manchuria and North Korea at the beginning of the previous year, which decimated many Chinese military units, both China and North Korea accused the United States of deliberately and systematically deluging the Communist forces with germ-laden insects – flies, fleas, mosquitoes. The Americans were even said to have dropped clams, having bred cholera organisms in them. On 22 February 1952 a formal charge of carrying out germ warfare was laid against the Americans by the North Koreans. On March 7 the United States informed the International Committee of the Red Cross: 'The United States has not engaged in any form of bacteriological warfare.' The Chinese then published the 'confessions' of American prisoners of war in Chinese hands, stating they had participated in germ warfare activities by dropping 'infected insects' on North Korea.

Seventy-eight American airmen had been interrogated. After as long as five months' solitary confinement and torture – both physical and mental – thirty-eight had 'confessed'. Dr Charles Mayo, the United States delegate at the United Nations, explained the cruel techniques that had been used to secure the confessions: 'human beings reduced to a status lower than that of animals, filthy, full of lice, festered wounds full of maggots, their sickness regulated to a point just short of death, unshaven, without haircuts or baths for as much as a year, men in rags, exposed to the elements, fed with carefully measured minimum quantities and the lowest quality of food and unsanitary water served often in rusty cans, isolated, faced with squads of trained interrogators, bulldozed, deprived of sleep and browbeaten with mental anguish'.

On February 26 Britain announced that it possessed its own atom bomb. It was tested in October. A month later the United States exploded the first-ever Hydrogen bomb, at Eniwetok island in the Pacific. In order to carry out the test, the H-bomb – as it became known – was suspended from a tower. The explosion blew the tower, and the island on which it was built, out of existence, leaving a 'hole' in the ocean several hundred feet deep. The atom bombs dropped on Hiroshima and Nagasaki had each generated the equivalent explosive power of 120,000 tons – as compared to the largest wartime bombs of 20,000 tons. The new H-bomb had an explosive power greater than five million tons.

On April 28, with the coming into force of the Japanese Peace Treaty, Japan became once more a sovereign and independent State. Hirohito remained Emperor, but with parliament and not the imperial palace as the centre of legislative power. Japan would pursue an anti-Communist policy and would align itself with the United States and the 'free nations'. One of the first measures of the new government was to pass a law that facilitated the release of convicted Japanese war criminals.

The Soviet Union refused to admit the validity of the peace treaty, and vetoed Japan's request to join the United Nations, but, accepting the reality of the situation, agreed to reduce substantially the size of the Soviet military mission in Japan. Also on April 28, the Japanese Government, in a further intimation of where its international alignment lay, signed a treaty of friendship with the Nationalist Chinese Government on Taiwan.

One of the first measures of the new Japanese Government was to pass a law that facilitated the release of Japanese war criminals imprisoned by the International Military Tribunal. One of those released from prison – he had never been formally convicted – entered national politics and within five years was Prime Minister.

Between May and July 1952 a series of trials was held in secrecy in Moscow. Those accused were Jews: writers, actors, poets, translators, physicians and noted theatrical figures. One who could not be brought to trial was the comic actor and producer, Solomon Mikhoels, who had been murdered on Stalin's orders four years earlier. All those brought to trial had served, at the request of the Soviet Government, on the wartime Jewish Anti-Fascist Committee, and had been sent to Britain and the United States to explain the Soviet war effort and the suffering of the Soviet people. Fourteen of the arrested Jews were brought to trial. All but one were sentenced to death and shot.

In Czechoslovakia, the former Secretary of the Czech Communist Party, Rudolf Slansky, who had been arrested the previous year, together with eleven other former senior Communist Party officials – all of them, including Slansky, were Jews – were accused of a range of espionage and treason charges. The accused were also charged with wanting to separate Czechoslovakia from the Communist bloc and restoring capitalism. The trial took place in the court room of a prison. Nine of the twelve, including Slansky, were hanged.

On June 23 the United Nations forces in Korea, which had watched with alarm the build-up of Chinese forces during the cease-fire negotiations, carried out a bombing attack on power plants in North Korea. One of these plants was near the Yalu River, the border between North Korea and Chinese Manchuria. In Britain there was unease that the United States had not consulted its British ally before ordering the air strikes so close to the border.

The fighting in Korea was no longer taking place up and down the peninsula, but in a narrow front across it, about fifty miles north of Seoul. Both sides were agreed that in any truce there should be a demilitarized zone (the DMZ) across the peninsula, along the line of the facing armies. But negotiations stuck on the issue of prisoners of war. The North Koreans wanted all 140,000 of their captured soldiers sent back. The United Nations insisted that half of them wanted to stay in the South, and that they should be allowed to do so. The conditions in the prisoner of war camps were bad. In one riot on Koje Island – the second – five prisoners and one American soldier were killed. In a second riot on Koje the American commander of the island was held hostage until better conditions were promised. At two other camps, at Cheju and on Pongam Island, riots, in part instigated by Communist prisoners demanding their return to the North, were suppressed by armed troops, and 138 prisoners were killed.

On July 23 a coup d'état in Egypt brought to an end the sixteen-year rule of King Farouk – who had come to the throne at the age of sixteen. He was overthrown, without bloodshed, by a group of army officers, led by General Mohammed Neguib, who resented Egypt's lack of assertiveness in the Arab and Muslim world. Farouk went as an exile, first to Italy and then to Monaco. Neguib took dictatorial powers for himself, and within a year proclaimed Egypt a republic. Such influence as Britain had been able to retain through the King was ended.

In Persia, a government headed by Dr Muhammad Musaddiq was also challenging both British and United States interests in his country, and doing so successfully. Supported by popular acclaim in the streets, and by-passing the moderate stance of the Shah, Musaddiq nationalized all foreign oil interests in his country. Since 1914 the British Government had been a majority shareholder in the Anglo-Iranian Oil Company.

The cruellest of the British overseas conflicts was in the Kenya Colony, where the Mau Mau secret society declared that its aim was to drive all Europeans from Kenya – rulers, farmers and tradesmen. One section of the Mau Mau oath read: 'When the reed buck horn is blown, if I leave a European farm before killing the European owner, may this oath kill me.' There was indignation in the House of Commons when the Mau Mau oath was read out. Those Kikuyu who were Christian rejected the barbarous pagan practices of Mau

Mau, including forceful mutilation. Between June and September more than sixty Kikuyu were murdered by the Mau Mau for refusing to join them. The killing by Mau Mau of Europeans began in the first week of October. Farmers and coffee planters were the principal victims. Thirty European civilians were murdered between October 1952 and the end of 1954, but, as law and order were enforced, only two in the five following years. During that same period more than 1,800 African civilians were murdered.

On October 7 Chief Waruhiu, who had ruled the Kikuyu for thirty years, and who wanted to work with the British, was forced out of his car on the road near Nairobi and killed. On October 20 a State of Emergency was declared. Two months later the Mau Mau leader Jomo Kenyatta – who had been educated at a Scottish missionary school and spent many years in England – was arrested and brought to trial, charged with administering unlawful oaths. He was sentenced to life imprisonment.

As well as in Kenya, British colonial rule was being challenged in Nigeria, the Central African Federation and Uganda. There were also uprisings in the Malayan Federation and British Guiana. In Malaya, a British-officered police force of 60,000 men had to maintain order among five million people. Tens of thousands of Malays were in detention. At any given time more than 5,000 were being held in prison without trial. Those found guilty of murdering British soldiers were executed. Chinese Communists – who predominated in the Malay insurgency – were deported to China. In the conflict between the police and the insurgents, 2,578 insurgents were killed, of whom more than 2,000 were Chinese.

The British Government was committed to maintaining the colonial administration until such time as it could win the war against the insurgents. Armoured vehicles, arms and equipment were obtained from the United States, as were chemical defoliants to clear the jungle on either side of the main roads. Within five years law and order were restored, and power was transferred to the Malays.

In South Africa, over which Britain had no control, the African National Congress warned the government in January, by letter, that unless the 'unjust laws' of apartheid were repealed by the last day of

February, there would be protest meetings held throughout the country. In reply, the Prime Minister, Dr D.F. Malan, warned that if a campaign of civil disobedience began the government 'will make full use of the machinery at its disposal to quell any disturbances and, thereafter, deal adequately with those responsible for initiating subversive activities of any nature whatever'. Malan added, in justification of the separations imposed by apartheid, that the differences between the black Africans and the whites were 'permanent and not man-made'.

On March 20 there was a triumph for the African National Congress when the country's Supreme Court ruled that the apartheid legislation of Malan's government was unconstitutional. A month later, on April 22, Malan introduced legislation to parliament – where he had a clear majority – making parliament itself a High Court, so that the Supreme Court ruling would be of no consequence, and the apartheid legislation would remain on the statute book unchallenged. One piece of legislation that was thereby 'legalized' was an amendment to the Native Laws Amendment Act, whereby no African was allowed to stay in an urban area for more than seventy-two hours unless he or she had lived there for fifteen years or worked for the same employer for ten years. Under another piece of legislation, entitled the Natives (Abolition of Passes and Coordination of Documents) Act, all black South African male adults had to carry at all times a so-called 'reference book' containing details of birth, taxation, movement and employment. This was the first of the 'pass laws' that were to be at the centre of liberal protest in South Africa for many years to come.

As apartheid was reaffirmed and intensified, the African National Congress embarked, on June 26, on a campaign of civil disobedience against 'unjust laws'. One form that the defiance took was to enter a railway station through the 'Europeans only' entrance. Those violating the law would be taken to court. Crowds of supporters would gather outside the court. The police would order them to disperse and they would refuse. The police would then use force. Several Europeans joined the protest movement, among them Patrick Duncan, the son of a former Governor-General of South Africa. By the end of the year, more than 6,000 Africans were in prison.

There were also deaths. After two Africans had been arrested at a railway station in Port Elizabeth, riots followed and seven Africans and four Europeans were killed. During a riot in Kimberley thirteen Africans were shot dead. It was forbidden for more than ten Africans to meet without government permission. The Minister of Justice, C.R. Swart, told his Nationalist Party followers: 'You cannot fight the law of the jungle with the rule of law. We are faced with a situation which we, as bearers of White civilization, can no longer tolerate.'

The Suppression of Communism Act gave the government sweeping powers of arrest and detention. As a result of the act, Sam Kahn, a South African Jew and one of the three members of parliament who represented African interests in the Assembly, was removed from parliament altogether.

In the United States the activities of Senator McCarthy in seeking to find and imprison Communists were unceasing. Under the Port Security Programme, which was given a spurious legitimacy by the alleged demands of the Korean War, employment tests were authorized for all maritime and dock workers in American ports. Many dockers lost their jobs, principally union leaders and those who were active in the unions. Even after a court decision declared the programme unlawful, and the firings had to cease, blacklisting continued.

A Grand Jury investigation reported a month later that 'an overwhelmingly large' group of Americans employed at the United Nations were 'disloyal' to their country. Within the State Department, diplomats had to appear before a Loyalty Board. The British-born actor and film-maker Charlie Chaplin was accused of having connections with 'subversive causes'. Leaving the Unites States, he vowed never to return. It was to be twenty-one years before he did so, at the age of eighty-four, to receive his second Academy Award (he had won his first in 1928).

That year the film *High Noon* was nominated for an Oscar. The screenplay had been written by Carl Foreman, who was among those being investigated by McCarthy. After Foreman refused to testify before a Committee set up by McCarthy – which had the finger-pointing name of the 'Un-American Activities Committee' – the Oscar went elsewhere, and was granted to Foreman only post-humously, thirty-two years later. Foreman, placed on a blacklist that prevented him from working in Hollywood, or in any American film studio, went to live in Britain. While in Britain he wrote the screenplay for *The Bridge on the River Kwai*, which won four Oscars.

Throughout the autumn the talks on a Korean cease-fire had continued at Panmunjom. The North Koreans continued to insist that all prisoners of war should be repatriated, not merely those who wanted to return. On October 5, while this proposal was still under consideration, the Chinese forces in North Korea launched their heaviest offensive of the year. Attacking with artillery and tank support along two-thirds of the front line, they engaged the United Nations forces in fierce fighting. Several hill positions held by United Nations forces were overrun. But there was no breakthrough, the attacking force being halted and eventually repulsed, as 23,000 Chinese troops were killed in two weeks.

In the United States, the issue of the Korean war held centre stage in the presidential election campaign throughout the autumn. The Republican candidate was General Eisenhower, who, calling upon all his authority as a soldier – and until April as the Supreme Commander, NATO – made use of the widespread weariness with the war to denounce Truman's handling of it, and to brand it as 'Truman's war'. In a national television broadcast on October 24, Eisenhower described Korea as 'the burial ground for twenty-thousand American dead' and promised that if he were elected President he would end the war. 'I shall go to Korea,' he said.

If Eisenhower had a way of ending the war, an angry Truman told an audience in Winona, Minnesota, he should tell him at once, and thus 'save a lot of lives'. What was the point of waiting until after the election. 'If he can do it after he is elected, we can do it now.'

The American presidential election took place on November 4. Eisenhower was elected by an overwhelming majority, winning all but nine of the forty-eight States, including Truman's Missouri. He then flew to Korea, spent three days touring the front lines, and returned to the United States. The way in which the war was being handled from Washington, he said, was 'intolerable'. When Truman was shown a poll in which 43 per cent of those questioned thought it had been a mistake for the United States to have gone to war in Korea, he wrote in a private note for himself: 'I wonder how far Moses would have gone if he'd taken a poll in Egypt? What would Jesus Christ have preached if he'd taken a poll in Israel?' It was not polls or public opinion which counted. 'It's right and wrong.'

Tyranny and dictatorship continued to flourish in many different forms and guises. Taking a leaf from Stalin's book, the Czech President, Klement Gottwald, turned against those Czechoslovak farmers who were resisting collectivization, denouncing them as 'kulaks' and 'village rich' who were acting as 'leeches' on the co-operative farming body. A tax based on the expected agricultural income of all farms was imposed on the independent farmers, who were regularly denounced as 'kulaks and speculators'. In a further punitive measure, all 'kulaks' were denied food rations and clothing coupons, even if their agricultural delivery quotas had been fulfilled.

In Poland, a Polish Government decree on 9 February 1953 gave the State the right to make and end all appointments within the Catholic Church, and to obtain an oath of loyalty to the Communist system from individual churchmen.

In Egypt, on February 10, General Neguib, who less than a month earlier had dissolved all political parties, was voted dictatorial powers by an emasculated parliament. Six days later, on February 16, at the other extremity of Africa, the passing by another emasculated parliament of the Public Safety Act gave the Governor-General of South Africa, and in some cases the Minister of Justice, power to declare a state of emergency and issue regulations that would override existing acts of parliament.

In South Africa, strikes by Africans were made illegal, and recognition refused to black African trade unions. Many urban facilities – including beaches and swimming pools – were restricted according to racial considerations. The African National Congress spoke out against these measures, but its members faced the prospect of arrest if they fell foul of the laws designed to inhibit black South African political activity. They were unable to preach the weapon of strike

20. Addis Ababa, October 1935: Abyssinian cavalrymen on their way to the front after the Italian invasion.

21. Mao Tse-tung talking to peasants in the early months of the Sino-Japanese War in 1937.

22. Japanese troops entering a Chinese village south of Hsuchow in June 1938.

23. Madrid: Republican militiamen in a trench dug round the Model Prison, which was cleared of prisoners and transformed into a fortress to keep out the Falangists.

24. London, September 1938: Communists call on the British Government to 'Stand by the Czechs'.

26. A German fighter plane shot down over Britain.

25. Esbjerg, Denmark, September 1939: the aftermath of a British bomb dropped in error. One Danish woman was killed.

27. Norwegian sharpshooters in the snow, April 1940.

28. Dunkirk, May–June 1940: British soldiers awaiting evacuation defend themselves against German planes.

29. Coventry, November 1940: a firestorm caused by a German air raid the night before is still blazing.

30. Japanese kamikaze pilots ready for action.

31. A kamikaze pilot tries to manoeuvre his plane onto the deck of an American warship.

32. *Above* Central Tokyo after an Allied saturation raid in September 1945.

33. *Left* Emperor Hirohito surveys the damage to his capital, October 1945.

34. Nehru and Gandhi at the All-India Congress meeting in Bombay at which Nehru took office as President of the Congress, July 1946.

35. *Left* On his retirement as Chief of Staff, General George S. Marshall receives a medal from President Truman, November 1945.

36. *Above* Ho Chi Minh in 1945, preparing for a mission against the French in Vietnam.

without immediate arrest and imprisonment. Some ANC members advocated violence, others called for restraint.

Among those who were caught up in this debate was a thirty-five-year-old lawyer, Nelson Mandela, who in 1952 had given up his law practice in order to travel the country advocating the need for a democratic and multi-racial society. During 1953 he took up the cause of the 60,000 and more Africans who were being forced, under the guise of 'slum clearance', to leave their Johannesburg suburbs and move to a tract of land bought by the government thirteen miles away.

On 5 March 1953, Josef Stalin died. He was seventy-four years old. The crowds that mourned in Moscow were so thick that several people were crushed to death. Yet even amid the outpouring of grief there were those who dared hope that change would come, that fear and tyranny would disappear. In the first days and weeks after Stalin's death, however, such hopes were seldom spoken.

Within a few months of Stalin's death the first cracks began to appear in the Soviet Union's control of its satellite countries. Food and housing shortages in Czechoslovakia were widespread, and there were protest demonstrations in many of the cities. In the industrial centres, factory workers went on strike. In Prague and Bratislava there were protest marches, in which many students took part. During rioting at Plzen the Red Flag was torn down and the busts of Lenin and Stalin were thrown into the streets. Portraits of Masaryk and Beneš – who had become 'non-persons' in the Communist pantheon – were hoisted aloft.

The riots and demonstrations were stopped by force. When tanks arrived the rioters in Plzen dispersed. Many of them were arrested and imprisoned. East Germany saw a similar turmoil, born of hope that with Stalin's death the Communist regime could be challenged with relative impunity. Tens of thousands of East Germans crossed into West Germany and sought refuge there. There was no wall at that time dividing East and West Berlin, and in a single day in March, 6,000 East Germans crossed the divide between the two sectors and obtained asylum in West Berlin. Within three months the number of asylum seekers had reached 184,793.

On May 28, in a further much-resented government order, it was announced that workers must significantly increase their productivity but would receive the same wages as before. Resentment grew, and on June 17 the workers in East Berlin went on strike and organized street demonstrations. Members of the People's Police (the much-feared *Vopos*) threw away their weapons and joined the demonstrators. To put down the uprising, Soviet troops and tanks were ordered from their barracks and deployed in the streets. Many East Berliners, not having weapons, beat on the sides of the tanks with their fists, or threw bricks and stones at them. Several Communist Party buildings were set on fire. The Red Flag, flying on the Brandenberg Gate as it had done on the day of the Soviet conquest of Berlin in 1945, was torn down.

On the afternoon of June 17 the Soviet commandant of Berlin proclaimed a state of emergency. Summary courts were set up where accusation, trial and execution could take place within an hour. Several hundred demonstrators were hanged or shot.

In Latin America, the image of rotating dictatorships, each one little different to its predecessor, was a strong one. But in the half century following the final end to Spanish rule, the aspirations of millions of Latin Americans continued to centre around the search for a less harsh, less corrupt government. On July 26 an attempt was made in Cuba by a group of revolutionaries to overthrow the newly installed regime of Fulgencio Batista – a former army sergeant who had earlier ruled Cuba from 1935 until the end of the Second World War, and had recently returned to power.

The rebels began their struggle with an attack on an army barracks in the town of Santiago de Cuba, the capital of Oriente Province, as far away from the capital, Havana, as any town in Cuba. They were outnumbered by ten to one, but hoped to capture the barracks by surprise and superior zeal. They failed to do so, six of the 134 attackers being killed. As the rebellion collapsed many of those who were captured were tortured and killed. The rebel leader, Fidel Castro, was fortunate: he was captured while sleeping by a humane army officer, brought to trial and imprisoned. 'With what joy I would bring revolution to this country from top to bottom,' he wrote from prison.

Castro had been sentenced to fifteen years in prison, but within two years he was released under amnesty and allowed to go to Mexico. There, he and his followers planned their return. Inside Cuba, Batista imposed harsh prison sentences on political opponents, and dictatorial control over the press, the universities and the national congress. After student riots, many students were arrested and tortured.

On the day after the attempted coup in Cuba, the long-drawn-out negotiations for a truce in the Korean War came to an end. That day, July 27, an armistice agreement was signed at Panmunjom. Within two weeks of the signing, the United States had signed a mutual defence treaty with South Korea. As had been the case before the start of the war two years earlier, North and South Korea became a symbol of the East-West divide.

In the aftermath of Stalin's death, Nikita Khrushchev's appointment as First Secretary raised hopes that he would lead his people towards a less monolithic regime. But reading the omens was always a speculative venture. On September 26, exactly two weeks after Khrushchev's elevation in the Soviet Union, the primate of Poland, Cardinal Stefan Wyszynski, was arrested in Warsaw. Throughout the year Wyszynski had defended the Roman Catholic Church against a series of attacks, including a death sentence and long prison sentences on priests accused of espionage, and a decree of February 9 under which the State arrogated to itself the right to make or terminate all ecclesiastical appointments.

When the Bishop of Kielce was sent to prison in September, Wyszynski protested. Two days later he was arrested. As part of Poland's commitment to the Communist bloc, a two-year agreement was signed with North Korea at the end of the year for 'Polish aid' in the form of steel, and industrial equipment.

In October a leading Polish delegate to the United Nations in New York, Professor Marek Korowicz, sought asylum. He was in a position to give many details about the nature of the Polish regime, and did so at a press conference in New York on November 24. There were at least seventy-three forced labour camps in Poland, he said, with about 300,000 people confined in them. 'Many a time on my bus trips from Katowice to Cracow,' he said, 'I passed the labour camp at Jaworzno, where there were approximately 20,000 forced labourers.' Thirty per cent of all prisoners were women.

Forced labour was also a feature of life in Communist Czechoslovakia. Short-term conscription of labour had been introduced by law on May 28. Twelve days labour service a year was the required period. People could be taken to their labour tasks at the weekends or while on holiday. In factories, extra 'peace shifts' took place on Sundays. Soldiers and civilians were also employed in work brigades to build houses. Much of this work was voluntary, but when three volunteers absented themselves they were sent to prison: a warning that absenteeism would be punished.

The checking of Communist ambitions in Korea was felt by the West to be a victory, even if North Korea remained under the most rigid type of Communist control. But there was a sense throughout the West of the need for vigilance in face of the apparent continual efforts of Communists worldwide to take advantage of national discontent. When it seemed that Communism might be successful in British Guiana, borne to victory on the votes won by the People's Progressive Party (the PPP), Britain sent troops to take over the colony. The troops landed on October 6. Three days later the British governor suspended the constitution and ruled under a state of emergency. The leaders of the PPP were arrested.

Not only Communism, but Islam, was offering an alternative political system to parliamentary democracy. On November 2 the Constituent Assembly in Pakistan declared the country a republic and designated it the 'Islamic Republic of Pakistan'. Henceforth laws based upon Muslim religious principles were to have an important place in national legislation. In Iran, Islamic clerics, among them the fifty-year-old Ayatollah Khomeini, were building up opposition to the secular aspects of the rule of the Shah and waiting for the day when they could denounce it publicly. The Shah, although autocratic, was trying to modernize his country and – much as Atatürk had done in Turkey two decades earlier – to set it upon a predominantly secular path, open to Western social and cultural influences. Two years earlier he had offered all his crown land, including 800 villages, for sale to the tenant farmers. The Islamic clerics saw no virtue in this: they wanted Iran ruled according to the tenets and ethics of Islam.

In the world of science and medicine, the discovery by Francis Crick and James Watson of the double helix structure of DNA, the basic material of heredity, opened up areas of understanding of human life hitherto unimagined – they called it the 'code of life'. In due course it was to provide a method of identification which could eliminate uncertainty over a wide range of otherwise unsolvable mysteries, including the identity of murderers, and the victims of murderers. In 1998 it confirmed the identity of Tsar Nicholas II, murdered with his family by the Bolsheviks eighty years earlier.

Figures made public in 1953 showed that life expectancy in the industrialized Western nations had risen dramatically since the start of the century. In the United States it was 68.4 years, having been 47 years in 1900, an increase of twenty-one years. In Britain there had been an increase of eighteen years. But in the two largest nations, India and China, the growth in population had hardly kept pace with the availability of food and medicine to sustain a life expectancy that never reached fifty years. The population of China had risen in the previous fifteen years from 475 million to 500 million, that of India from 310 million to 357 million. Each was to more than double its population in the half century ahead. The effect of the Second World War had been devastating with regard to food production. The year 1953 marked the first year that per capita food production worldwide had reached its 1939 level.

The cure and pattern of diseases was also changing. In the United States a vaccine designed by an American physician Jonas E. Salk, which promised to eliminate infantile paralysis (polio), was being used for the first time, and plans were being made to vaccinate half a million children. It was exactly a hundred years since the first British Act of Parliament made smallpox vaccination compulsory. In Britain, it was announced that deaths from lung cancer had overtaken those from tuberculosis, with 9,000 people having died of tuberculosis in the previous year and 14,000 from lung cancer.

Scientific investigations carried out in Britain and the United States in 1951 and 1952, and fully analysed in 1953, gave details of the relationship between smoking and cancer, and suggested that the risk of cancer was proportionate to the amount of tobacco smoked. Other research, in which a British professor, George Clemo, was prominent, showed another link with cancer, that of atmospheric pollution in large cities.

In the Soviet Union the resources of science were being used intensively by the defence establishment to seek Cold War advantages. To counter this, the United States continued to test its own atomic bombs. On March 17, at Yucca Flats, Nevada, more than 2,000 marines were given the order, seconds after a massive explosion, to charge across the desert to their 'objective' – the destroyed fortifications, trenches and arsenals of an imaginary enemy.

The 'real' enemy was the Soviet Union. At Bermuda in December, Churchill pressed Eisenhower to begin talk at the 'summit' with Stalin's successor, Malenkov. Eisenhower was not in a receptive mood, telling Churchill – in the words of the top secret minutes of the meeting – that if there were a 'deliberate breach' by the Communists of the Korean armistice the United States 'would expect to strike back with atomic weapons at military targets'. Speaking about future relations with the Soviet Union, Churchill told Eisenhower he would 'not be in too much of a hurry to believe that nothing but evil emanates from this mighty branch of the human family, or that nothing but danger and peril could come out of this vast ocean of land in a single circle so little known and understood'.

Eisenhower disagreed. The new Soviet Union, he said, like the Soviet Union under Stalin, was 'a woman of the streets', and he added: 'Despite bath, perfume or lace, it was still the same old girl.' There had been no change, Eisenhower argued, in the Soviet policy 'of destroying the Capitalist free world by all means, by force, by deceit or by lies'. This 'was their long-term purpose'. There had been 'no change since Lenin'.

Churchill continued to press Eisenhower to contemplate a meeting with Stalin's successors. 'Now, I believe, is the moment for parley at the summit,' Churchill wrote to the President in August 1954. 'All the world desires it. In two or three years a different mood may rule either with those who have their hands upon the levers, or upon the multitude whose votes they require.' Churchill was amazed that the United States did not grasp the opportunity of at least exploring a summit meeting. 'Fancy that you and Malenkov should never have met,' he told Eisenhower, 'or that he should never have been outside Russia, when all the time, in both countries, appalling preparations are being made for measureless mutual destruction.' Churchill added, in a final argument in favour of East-West discussions at the highest level: 'After all, the interests of both sides is survival and, as an additional attraction, measureless material prosperity of the masses.'

In his State of the Union Message on 7 January 1954 President Eisenhower stated that his aim during his second year of office would be 'to reduce the Communist menace without war', and went on to declare: 'We shall not be the aggressor, but we and our Allies have and will maintain a massive capacity to strike back.' To do this, the United States would 'take into full account our great and growing number of nuclear weapons and the most effective means of using them against an aggressor if they are needed to preserve our freedom'. Five days after Eisenhower's speech, his Secretary of State, John Foster Dulles, explained that the defence capacity of the United States would henceforth be based upon 'a great capacity to retaliate, instantly, by means and at places of our own choosing'.

On January 25 the Soviet, American, French and British Foreign Ministers met in Berlin, in an attempt to resolve the issue of the still-divided Germany and Austria. The Russians insisted that Russia retain control over East Germany and remain in occupation of Austria 'indefinitely'. Dulles told the conference that the fundamental difference between the Western participants and the Soviet Union 'revolved around the question of whether it was right, or indeed safe, to give men and nations a genuine freedom of choice'.

On October 3 a Nine-Power conference in London agreed that West Germany should become a member of NATO. On October 23, Britain, France and the Soviet Union agreed to end the occupation of Germany. That same day the Western European Union was established, to which both Italy and Germany were invited. Three days later, France and Germany signed an economic and cultural agreement.

*   *   *

On the morning of 1 March 1954 a Japanese fishing vessel, the *Fukuryu Maru* (*Lucky Dragon*), after a disappointing search for tuna off Midway Island, reached the Marshall Islands, hoping for a better catch. That morning her twenty-three-man crew were fishing east of Bikini Atoll, twenty miles outside the area that had been declared a 'danger zone' by the United States. As they were fishing, a vast explosion occurred, and they and their ship were covered with ash. The explosion was an American Hydrogen bomb. The ash was radioactive.

The Hydrogen bomb tested at Bikini was more than 500 times more powerful than that dropped on Hiroshima nine years earlier. On their return to their home port, the fishermen were found to be suffering from the effects of atomic radiation. At the end of September the wireless operator died of radiation sickness. The United States offered $1 million in compensation. The Japanese Government asked for seven times as much. But even as the debate over the American liability gained momentum, a new scourge was revealed. Japanese meteorologists reported that radioactive rain had fallen on Japan. Its source was not the Hydrogen bomb exploded by the United States, but a series of Hydrogen bomb tests by the Soviet Union.

Within the United States, liberal opinion was attempting to move away from racial segregation. On May 17 the Supreme Court ruled, in the case of *Brown versus Board of Education* (of Topeka, Kansas), that segregation in schools was unconstitutional, stating in its judgment: 'Separate educational facilities are inherently unequal.' This case was one of thirty-two that the black American lawyer Thurgood Marshall took to the Supreme Court, on which he himself eventually served. He won twenty-nine of those cases, including those which eliminated all-white primary elections and all-white juries.

The *Brown versus Board of Education* judgment was based on the assertion by the court, overruling current prejudice, that it was their environment, not their genes, that made black Americans 'inferior', and that no physiological or mental inferiority existed. While the court was limited by its legal brief to segregation in schools, by natural extension its ruling clearly applied to segregation in all public facilities. It was to take a decade, however, before a President –

Lyndon Johnson – felt strong enough and motivated enough to put civil rights at the top of his agenda.

In the sphere of national defence, on April 7 the United States announced, in conjunction with Canada, that a chain of radar defence stations was being set up to warn of any hostile aircraft approaching from the north: a Soviet surprise air attack across the Arctic Circle would thereby be noticed in time for counter-measures to be taken. This was the 3,000-mile Mid-Canada Line, which followed the 55th parallel and consisted of almost a hundred radar warning stations. On September 27 a second chain of radar stations, located above the Arctic Circle, and stretching from Alaska to Greenland, was begun. This was the Distant Early Warning Line (DEW Line). Three days after it was announced, the first atomic-powered submarine, the *Nautilus*, was commissioned by the United States Navy. Within two months, on December 11, the world's largest aircraft carrier, the 59,650-ton *Forrestal*, was launched in an American naval yard.

Televised hearings of Senator McCarthy's committee had begun on April 22. McCarthy's frequent interruption of the proceedings with the words 'point of order' became a national and much-mocked catch phrase. In the course of an argument over his right to quote a secret Federal Bureau of Investigation memorandum, McCarthy invited all Federal employees who had information about corruption or treason to give it to him, whatever directives to the contrary they might have received from their superiors. This incitement to disregard the law was repudiated by the Attorney-General.

While a hard core of McCarthy's followers continued to support him, large sections of the public on whose tacit support he was dependent had begun to turn away from him. On July 30 the Senate began a debate on whether McCarthy should be censured for 'conduct unbecoming to a Senator', and a committee of Senators was appointed to examine his conduct. Two months later, on September 27, he was found to have acted 'improperly' in urging Federal employees to hand over documents to him. McCarthy did his own cause no good by denouncing the Senate committee as a 'lynch party' and as the 'unwitting handmaidens of the Communist Party'. On December 2 his witchhunt was finally ended, when a Senate vote of 67 to 22 passed censure upon him. The Republican Senators had been evenly divided (22 to 22) for and against him.

Inside the Soviet Union, in the first decree signed solely by Nikita Khrushchev, Communist Party organizations were ordered to take a less harsh attitude towards the Russian Orthodox Church, and not to permit 'methods likely to hurt the feelings of believers'. The extent to which such an attitude would prevail, or be allowed to spread to other spheres, was uncertain. The publication of an article in the journal *Novy Mir* (*New World*) in which the author suggested with considerable deference that writers should 'obey the dictates of their own consciences' led to the dismissal of the journal's editor.

The future of Germany remained unresolved, highlighting the confrontations of the Cold War in Europe. That October the German Federal Republic entered NATO. As part of the NATO arsenal, the United States provided pilotless bombers capable of delivering an atom bomb.

While the military defence of Western Europe was predominantly the concern of NATO, the economic well-being of the non-Communist countries of the continent was being given a new impetus by the five-year-old Organization for European Economic Co-operation (OEEC). One initiative taken in 1954 was to reduce the indebtedness of the debtor countries by the creation of an instalment system, not unlike that which had been put in place after the First World War. Another initiative was a drive to reduce import restrictions on goods crossing from one member country to another. Britain took a lead in this, reducing the restricted goods by 80 per cent. The French followed swiftly along the same track, removing restrictions on 75 per cent of their commercial imports within a period of ten months. In a parallel measure of economic easement, the six members of the European Coal and Steel Community – France, West Germany, Italy, Holland, Belgium and Luxembourg – had established a single market for coal, coke, iron ore, steel and iron.

Western Europe was fortunate that its disputes and development centred upon the gradual coming together of nations in search of greater economic harmony. In eastern Europe and the Balkans the stresses and strains of Communism overshadowed the development of nations that were still struggling to overcome the long-term effects of the Second World War. In January the Yugoslav Communist Party expelled its Chairman, Milovan Djilas, who had argued strenuously in favour of greater freedom of expression. Djilas, who had had several talks with Stalin in Moscow a few years earlier, had a profound contempt for the Communist system as it had developed in the Soviet Union. With his authority as a Vice-President of Yugoslavia – and as a wartime partisan leader in Bosnia and his native Montenegro – Djilas had written a series of articles in the official Communist Party journal *Borba* (*Struggle*) and in his own magazine *Nova Misao* (*New Thought*) calling for greater liberalization, and warning that it was in the nature of oligarchies throughout the Communist world to usurp and preserve the class distinctions they had been expected to abolish.

In Vietnam, the position of the Vietminh had been much enhanced during the previous twelve months. It had been provided by China with the latest American military equipment, captured by the Chinese from the Americans in Korea, and was in many respects superior to the American equipment being sent direct to the French forces from the United States.

A new French Commander in Chief, General Henri Navarre, recognizing the impossibility of maintaining French control in northern Vietnam, proposed dividing Indochina into a northern and a southern military area, along the 18th parallel. North of the parallel the French forces would take up defensive positions and avoid a major battle with the more numerous Vietminh. South of the parallel France would launch a substantial 'pacification programme'.

A major achievement by General Navarre was to persuade an American military mission, sent to Vietnam by Eisenhower, to endorse the French plan of campaign and to agree to supply a massive amount of military aid – at least $400 million. It was General Navarre who also decided that the fortress of Dien Bien Phu, a strategic focal point in the north, 'must be held at all costs'. In November 1953 his troops had seized Dien Bien Phu from the Vietminh, in the hope of disrupting the Vietminh supply lines into northern Laos. In Navarre's mind Dien Bien Phu formed an essential barrier to the Vietminh penetration of northern Laos. He also envisaged it being used as a base for attacking the Vietminh in the surrounding region. What Navarre had not anticipated was that the Vietminh would themselves besiege Dien Bien Phu, making it not a launching pad for future French initiatives, but a trap for all those inside it.

By mid-March 1954 the Vietminh had encircled Dien Bien Phu and the French troops there were besieged. In April the United States Air Force provided transport aircraft to fly a French battalion to northern Vietnam to participate in the defence of Dien Bien Phu. They also provided United States Air Force mechanics to help with the repair of French aircraft. But all these efforts were to no avail. The 49,000 Vietminh combat soldiers were surrounding 7,000 French and Vietnamese fighting men, and overlooked them from the high ground less than two and a half miles away. Colonel de Castries, the besieged French commander, sent a message from his command post on April 3: 'I expect every man to die at the position assigned to him rather than retreat an inch.' He then ordered his staff officers, the headquarters clerks and cooks, and the crews of grounded aircraft, to man the trenches around the fort.

A meeting was held in the White House in Washington on April 3 at which President Eisenhower, several senior Senators, and the President's military advisers, considered a plan to send an American bombing force to destroy the Vietminh attackers around Dien Bien Phu. The bombing plan was put forward by the chairman of the United States Joint Chiefs of Staff, Admiral Arthur Radford. He proposed a raid by seventy-five to a hundred American bombers, based in the Philippines, taking place over three consecutive nights. There was even some talk about dropping three atomic bombs on the Vietminh positions. The Vice-President, Richard Nixon, was willing to see American ground forces sent to Vietnam if the bombing offensive failed.

Then, on April 6, the French Government informed the United States that French 'public opinion' would no longer support the war in Indochina, and that henceforth a negotiated settlement was the prime French aim. On May 7 the garrison at Dien Bien Phu was overrun. The French will to hold on to northern Vietnam was broken. The talks that took place in Geneva on May 8 centred on an attempt to provide a unified government for the country. It was agreed that elections would be held under joint French and Vietminh auspices, but the structure of the international control commission that would supervise them was in dispute. The Soviet Union, supported by China, wanted Poland and Czechoslovakia to be among the 'neutral States'. The French replied that this was 'totally unacceptable'. Speaking for China, Chou En-lai said that not only must the Communist States not be 'arbitrarily' excluded from the international commission, but that they must have the right of veto on anything that was being decided.

Partition of Vietnam was inevitable. The Vietnamese Communists agreed to evacuate South Vietnam and take their troops out of neighbouring Laos and Cambodia. On October 8, Ho Chi Minh's forces entered Hanoi, which was proclaimed the Vietminh capital. The United States felt strongly that the cause of a unified Vietnam should not be abandoned. 'In the case of nations now divided against their will,' the State Department announced, 'we shall continue to seek to achieve unity through free elections, supervised by the United Nations to ensure that they are conducted fairly.'

Within China, in a draconian – and unsuccessful – attempt to redress the balance of rural poverty, the Soviet system of forced collectivization was introduced. Mao Tse-tung in 1954, like Stalin fifteen years earlier, tackled the scale of the problem with drastic measures. Chou En-lai explained: 'The people have to bear some hardships for the time being . . . in order that in the long run we shall live in prosperity and happiness.'

During the first eight months of the year 100,000 collective farms had been established. At Mao Tse-tung's insistence, and amid great hardship, during the following six months the number rose to more than half a million. What was becoming known as the Bamboo Curtain denied experts, critics and well-wishers alike, any clear scrutiny of these events inside China. The American historian Kenneth Scott Latourette, Professor Emeritus of Missions and Oriental History at Yale University, after praising the reconstruction, railway rebuilding, land reclamation, irrigation and flood prevention projects being undertaken by the Communist regime, as well as the improvement of urban utilities, the control of 'gangsterism' and the elimination of prostitution, commented: 'Yet this record had been made possible at a terrific cost in lives, liberty, moral integrity, and China's inherited traditions. At a conservative estimate from 3,000,000 to 5,000,000 had been executed in the first two years of Communist mastery.' Scott Latourette added: 'Most of this was by shootings in large groups which the public were encouraged or required to attend. In despair untold thousands had committed suicide. Many suffered from mental breakdowns. Class consciousness was created and nurtured and with it class hatred. Mass hysteria was fomented. A strict censorship of the printed page and the radio was enforced.'

It was not only in Vietnam that a new conflict had emerged in the wake of French imperial ambitions. In Algeria, France's refusal to give up sovereignty led to armed and violent conflict. At the end of October, Algerian Muslim nationalists attacked French soldiers and police throughout Algeria. This co-ordinated assault marked the beginning of a sustained attempt by the Front pour la Libération Nationale (FLN) to establish an independent Algeria, free from French control. The struggle was momentarily set aside in September, when more than a thousand Algerians were killed during an earthquake at Orleansville. But it was a pause of only a few days. During December 1954 the French reinforced their garrisons in Algeria with 20,000 men. The new arrivals were plunged at once into the daily fears, hatreds and killings of a colonial war.

On 17 January 1955 the Chinese Communists began a heavy aerial bombardment of Chinese Nationalist positions on the Pescadores islands, just west of Taiwan. The security and survival of the Chinese regime on Taiwan was the declared policy of the United States. There was, however, a limit to what America was prepared to risk, and Eisenhower quickly put pressure on Chiang Kai-shek not to use the threat to the Pescadores to draw in the United States as a belligerent.

On February 7, United States warships began the evacuation of 14,000 Chinese Nationalist troops and 18,000 Chinese civilian refugees from the islands. Six days later, when the evacuation was completed, the Chinese Communist forces took over the islands. The crisis was not yet over. The issue moved to the two small islands of Quemoy and Matsu, north of Taiwan, which lay close to the Chinese mainland, and which were also under Nationalist control. Britain urged the United States not to go to war for these two islands, as did Canada. It was rumoured in Washington that Eisenhower's advisers wanted him to respond to any attack on Quemoy and Matsu by an atom bomb attack on cities on the Chinese mainland. Eisenhower at once denied the rumour, and in a gesture of conciliation towards China the State Department allowed seventy-six Chinese Communist students, who had been detained in the United States, to return home. Among those allowed to leave was the rocketry expert, H. S. Tsien, who had been held in the United States for five years. On his return to China he began work on creating China's own rocket and ballistic missile programme.

In the East-West alignment, the Western defences were shored up on February 24, when Turkey and Iraq signed a treaty of alliance, the Baghdad Pact. The basis of the new agreement was mutual support against Communist activity within their respective borders, and any Communist threat from beyond them. Both Britain and Iran joined the pact.

There was indignation among many of the countries set up only after the Second World War that they might have to take a stance in a quarrel that they did not see as their own. On April 18 the heads of twenty-nine 'non-aligned' nations, among which Communist China was included, gathered at Bandung, Indonesia. They came at the invitation of the Indonesian President, Achmed Sukarno, a Muslim who had collaborated with the Japanese occupation forces during the war in the hope of gaining independence after the defeat of the Dutch. Sukarno had then fought the Dutch (who before the war had imprisoned him for eleven years). Among those whose anti-imperial credentials were as good as his was Archbishop Makarios, who made a strong plea to the delegates to support the Cypriot islanders' struggle against Britain and in favour of union with Greece. The main thrust of the Bandung conference was hostility to the United States. Considerable excitement was caused when Chou En-lai told the other delegates that 'the population of Asia will never forget that the first atom bomb exploded on Asian soil'.

The United States did not intend to leave the non-aligned States unwooed. On April 20, two days after the opening of the Bandung conference, Eisenhower asked Congress for $3,530 million in foreign aid appropriations. The Soviet Union also offered aid, and, as the United States had done, arms. On May 14, three weeks after the Bandung conference ended, eight Communist countries, meeting in Warsaw at the initiative of the Soviet Union, signed the Warsaw Pact, a unified military command for all its members – the Soviet Union, Albania, Bulgaria, Czechoslovakia, East Germany, Hungary, Poland and Roumania. The command was put under a Soviet Marshal.

Austria was allowed to remain outside these alignments. On April 15, in an agreement with the Soviet Union, she had promised to remain 'permanently neutral' on what was called the 'Swiss model', in return for which Soviet troops would withdraw before the end of the year. A month later, on May 15 – the day after the creation of the Warsaw Pact – the Soviet Union, Britain, France and the United States signed a treaty in Vienna restoring Austrian independence. The conditions for independence included one that in 1919 had been an integral part of the Versailles Treaty: that Austria should not join Germany. The other main condition was that Austria should join neither of the Cold War alignments. The Allied zones of occupation disappeared, and the occupation forces withdrew.

On June 30, as Austria began its first steps as a neutral country, the West German Government signed a military aid agreement with the United States.

In Cyprus, the movement for union with Greece, on behalf of which Archbishop Makarios had spoken at Bandung, gained a new impetus that year with the launch of a military campaign against British rule by the National Organization of Cypriot Fighters (EOKA), a guerrilla organization which targeted British military personnel and their families. All the apparatus of British colonial resistance to challenge was asserted with vigour. Severe penalties were enacted for terrorist activity, and public meetings other than church services were banned.

In Malaysia, both Malaya and Singapore were given new constitutions, with elected assemblies and a ministerial system of government. The Chief Ministers of the two self-governing administrations made it clear to the local Chinese leader, Chin Peng, that they would never recognize the Communist party in their respective territories, or agree to any terms for a settlement that did not start with a military surrender. Chin Peng withdrew into the jungle, declaring that he and his followers would fight on 'to the last man'. Among the troops that entered the jungle to seek him out was a contingent from Australia.

The French Government, led since June 1954 by Pierre Mendès-France, hoped to find a compromise for Algeria acceptable to the Muslims who made up the majority of the country's inhabitants. This included the teaching of Arabic in schools, the admission of more Muslims to government employment, local self-governing Muslim institutions, and an end to French control over the Muslim religion. The plan was rejected by the Muslims as not offering enough – and was denounced by the French settlers as offering far too much. In February the left-wing Parties in his coalition denounced Mendès-France's failure to offer more, and he was forced out of office.

In Morocco, Moroccan nationalists led by the *Front de la Libération Nationale* (the FLN) attacked French soldiers and police throughout Algeria. Near Philippeville, seventy-one Europeans and fifty-two Muslims were massacred. In an army reprisal, 1,273 'rebels' were killed. The new French Prime Minister, Edgar Faure, spoke out on the radio: 'All of France's honour and its humane mission obliges us absolutely, unequivocally, and outspokenly to keep Algeria for France, and in France.' As the violence spread, the French Government had to withdraw military units from the NATO command in Europe to reinforce its garrisons. When the year began there were 76,000 French troops in Algeria. When it ended the number had reached 170,000, and was still rising.

In Tunisia the process of the transfer from French rule to independence involved long and complex negotiations. The Tunisian national leader, Habib ibn Ali Bourguiba – who had spent two years in prison for his call for full independence – participated in the final talks in Paris. On June 3 agreement was reached. Tunisia would obtain full internal self-government, to be followed a year later by full independence. Bourguiba returned to Tunis a hero, and as Prime Minister – and President – in waiting. A resolution also emerged by the end of the year as a result of which Morocco achieved self-government, followed by complete independence. The first entirely Moroccan Government was formed on December 7.

Inside the United States, all manifestations of white supremacy in the South were being challenged by law. In the late autumn the Interstate Commerce Commission, a Federal body, ordered an end to segregation in public transport. On November 25 Rosa Parks, a black woman, was arrested in Montgomery, Alabama, for sitting in the front of a bus, in the section reserved for whites. Following her arrest Dr Martin Luther King, who had just arrived in Montgomery as Baptist pastor, led 50,000 black protesters in a boycott of local buses, demanding an end to segregation. The bus boycott lasted thirteen months.

Following the Senate vote against Senator McCarthy in 1954, the Federal Court of Appeals overturned one of the most vexatious aspects of the McCarthyite period – the withdrawal of the right to travel abroad to those accused of Communist sympathies. Travel to other countries was a 'natural right', the court ruled. In another landmark judgment reversing the developments of previous years, the New York Court of Appeals declared that loyalty oaths – such as the one required by the New York Housing Association for all its tenants – must no longer be required.

The testing of nuclear weapons in the atmosphere continued, with the Soviet Union and the United States each seeking the most effective weapon. The ability to destroy a city, or 500 cities, became a focal point of scientific experimentation. It also became a focal point of scientific unease. In March the Federation of American Scientists appealed directly to the United Nations 'with some sense of desperation' to collect the evidence of the effect of these explosions and take action accordingly.

A British nuclear scientist, Sir James Chadwick, who had been involved in the development of the original atom bomb, stressed privately the moral aspect of the new weaponry. 'The original atom bomb is a weapon not very different from other bombs – of the same kind but more powerful,' he wrote. 'The H-Bomb can hardly be classified as a weapon at all. Its effect in causing suffering is out of all proportion to its military effect. The H-bomb does not offer any improvement in the waging of war, and it brings with it a risk of making the world uninhabitable.'

In April, Albert Einstein was one of seven Nobel Prize winners who signed a statement that 'a war with H-bombs might quite possibly put an end to the human race'. His signature was received by the organizers on the day of his death. A month later, on May 15, the fourteenth and last United States nuclear explosion of the 1955 atomic test series took place in Nevada, at Yucca Flats. One test involved an atomic detonation at a height of six miles. A leading German nuclear scientist, Professor Otto Hahn, warned publicly of 'a danger to humanity' in the genetic effects of radioactivity, against which there was 'no permanent protection'. Hahn, who had carried out nuclear research inside Germany during the war, had been awarded the Nobel Prize for his pioneering work in the discovery of nuclear fission.

On July 18 a group of Nobel Prize winners issued a stark warning. They 'saw with horror', they wrote, 'that science was giving mankind the means with which to destroy itself'. They went on to state, with all the authority of their scientific expertise, that modern weapons of war 'may contaminate the world with radio-activity to such an extent that entire nations may be wiped out'.

Nuclear weapons and nuclear power were very different sides of the same scientific coin. The first atomically generated power station began operation in the United States on the evening of July 17 – the day before the Nobel Prize winners warning about nuclear weapons. It took place in the small town of Arco, Idaho, where nuclear power was used that night to light some 550 buildings for about a thousand residents of the town. For two hours, between eight and ten o'clock that evening, Arco was taken off the national electricity grid and plugged into the new source of electric power.

Henceforth, the development of nuclear power was rapid, first in the United States and then in both Britain and Canada. Before the end of the year the United States produced a catalogue of atomic materials for the production of domestic use and industrial energy, together with a price list. Nuclear power for domestic energy production was to become a central feature of modern industrialized life.

The testing of nuclear weapons in the atmosphere continued. On November 27 the Soviet Government announced that it had successfully carried out a series of atom and Hydrogen bomb tests. This was indeed known outside the Russian land mass, as radioactive dust from the explosions had already been detected by scientists in Japan and in Western Europe, and Siberia pinpointed as the place of origin. Britain also announced plans to carry out more nuclear tests in the atmosphere in the following year at Monte Bello Island, off the west coast of Australia, and thereafter at Maralinga, in the desert in central Australia.

In China, the Bamboo Curtain, as impenetrable as the Iron Curtain, cut off the country from outside curiosity and inquiry. Mao Tse-tung's imposition of Chinese Communist rule took place amid secrecy and severity. Special committees were formed throughout the organizational structure of the Communist Party with the authority to enforce Party discipline and to denounce anyone suspected of seeking 'personal dictatorship'.

Intellectual control was imposed with the same severity as political control. On July 17 it was announced that the author and writer Hu Feng had been arrested. He had earlier made public a criticism of Communism as exerting a 'blighting influence' on literature. The control which the Party exercised over culture, he wrote – he was himself a Party member – 'exhausted' people so that they could no longer think straight. With one brief respite, he remained in prison for twenty-four years. Throughout China, meetings were held denouncing 'Hu Feng-ism', and asserting the Party's correctness in accelerating the pace of land reform as opposed to private initiative. Other dissidents accused of counter-revolutionary activity were executed or sentenced to long periods in prison.

Inside the Soviet Union, widespread public discontent – expressed far more openly than was possible in Stalin's time – at the shortages of foodstuffs, forced the government to make intensive efforts to improve the food situation. Under the leadership of Khrushchev, whose colourful, at times almost eccentric personality was beginning to impress itself on his own people and abroad, a 'Virgin Lands' scheme was devised whereby volunteers would go to the empty, barren wastes of Kazakhstan and begin to cultivate the wilderness. In all, more than seventy million acres of virgin and barren soil were ploughed, and fifty million acres were then planted. This involved the establishment within a few months of more than 400 collective farms, and the despatch to the region of half a million 'volunteers'.

The scheme did not go well. By the time the planting ought to have been begun, only ten per cent of the planned accommodation had been erected, and only five per cent of the granaries needed to store the grain had been built. In addition, severe drought – endemic to the region – meant that much of the area that was planted produced a poor crop, or no crop at all.

In Latin America, widespread poverty was in stark contrast with the evolving prosperity and consumer society further north, in the United States and Canada. Dictatorship, often brought to power by promises of social reform, invariably turned to tyranny and corruption, leaving most dissatisfied those for whom it had seemed to offer the most. In Argentina the initially populist regime of President Peron was under sharp attack by those whom he had alienated by his dictatorial rule. The Radical Party insisted on the complete restoration of individual freedom.

Peron's supporters were issued with arms. On September 1 a state of siege was declared in Buenos Aires. On September 16 the garrison of the city of Cordoba – a Catholic stronghold – rose in revolt, its anti-government forces led by General Eduardo Lonardi, a devout Catholic who declared that his insurrection was 'in defence of Catholic Christianity'. Other garrison towns joined in, demanding Peron's resignation. A senior naval officer, Admiral Isaac Rojas, threatened a naval bombardment of Buenos Aires unless Peron resigned. In face of such a challenge, the dictator had no forces on which he could fall back. On September 19 Peron resigned. Four days later, General Lonardi entered the capital and was proclaimed President. The Peronistas were removed from their positions of authority in government, the universities, the law courts, and in Argentine embassies abroad. Peron fled to Spain, where Franco granted him asylum.

The realities of tyranny, revolution, imprisonment, exile, revenge were in contrast to the pleasurable enjoyments of life that so many people craved. On 18 July 1955, there was a landmark in such pursuits of harmless fantasy when the Disneyland theme park opened at Anaheim, in California. 'For some brief periods,' commented the *New York Times*, 'the ceremonies took on the aspect of the dedication of a national shrine.' Disneyland offered a world of light-hearted entertainment to children and adults alike, and a magical environment that was both clean and without violence – an environment at variance with many of the urban centres in the United States, including some within only a few minutes' drive of Disneyland itself.

In a speech on 25 February 1956, entitled 'On the Personality Cult and its Consequences', Khrushchev astounded his Communist Party listeners by giving details of how, under Stalin, innocent people had been accused, confessions extracted and cases fabricated against 'enemies of the people' who had done no wrong. Thousands of Stalin's political prisoners were released from prison and labour camp. But many of those released were made to remain in the region of their labour camps as 'semi-free labourers'. After Khrushchev's speech the Soviet forced labour system remained in operation. By keeping released prisoners at work in the neighbourhood of the camps, the system was even made more efficient as far as the Soviet economy was concerned.

In Prague and Bratislava there were demonstrations in May demanding a free Press and Parliament, freedom to travel abroad, an end to the jamming of foreign radio broadcasts, and a reduction in Marxist-Leninist teaching. On June 28, in the Polish city of Poznan, as workers' strikes and riots broke out, demonstrators called out to many of the foreign visitors who were in the town for the annual international industrial fair: 'This is our revolution. Tell the world what we are doing. We want the Russians to get out and we want better conditions after eleven years. We want bread.' To suppress the uprising, Polish tanks and troops were sent into the centre of the city and opened fire. Thirty-eight people were killed, most of them protesters, but also some Communist officials whom the demonstrators had caught.

In Hungary, a group of writers and intellectuals held a public meeting and demanded an end to Communist repression.

The last British troops left Egypt on June 13, in accordance with a British-Egyptian Treaty of October 1954. Eleven days later Colonel Nasser was elected President of Egypt, and on July 26 announced that he was nationalizing the Suez Canal. In future Egypt alone would be the financial beneficiary of the fees and dues of ships in transit.

The Suez Canal Company was owned partly by Britain and partly by France. On September 30, at a secret meeting between France and Israel in Paris, the two delegations agreed to co-ordinate military action against Egypt, and Anthony Eden, the new British Prime Minister, and his Foreign Secretary, Selwyn Lloyd, travelled to Paris to participate in the plan.

Nasser had ordered military reinforcements into the Gaza Strip, posing a direct threat to Israel. On October 21 and 22 the Israelis, French and British met in Paris for the second time in three weeks, to co-ordinate their action. The Israelis would cross into the Egyptian Sinai and advance towards the Suez Canal. This would give Britain and France the excuse to intervene militarily, in order to 'protect' the canal.

In the second week of September the Hungarian Trades Union Congress demanded Workers' Councils to represent the needs of the workers in disputes with the Communist Party. On October 15 there was a mass student demonstration in Budapest. The demands of the students went far beyond anything a Communist government – let alone Moscow – could accept: a government based on free elections, Hungary's withdrawal from the Warsaw Pact, freedom of the Press and educational instruction, independent courts of justice, free religious instruction if wanted, the end of forced collectivization and forced delivery of agricultural produce, the right to strike for workers, free communication with the West, the removal of Soviet emblems, an end to uranium deliveries to the Soviet Union and support for the Polish national movement.

On October 19, amid persistent Polish criticism of the harshness of the Communist regime, Khrushchev flew to Warsaw and warned that such criticism must stop. Soviet troops based in Poland moved to the outskirts of Warsaw. But then Wladyslaw Gomulka – who had been imprisoned by his fellow Polish Communist leaders less than two years earlier for his 'nationalistic' views – was made First Secretary of the Party and persuaded Khrushchev to accept a non-confrontational path. On October 21 it was announced in Warsaw that Poland would go its 'own way' to Socialism. Collectivization was halted and a small measure of freedom of speech allowed. The 'Polish October' was judged in the West to be a setback for the Soviet Union, but Gomulka was careful to stress the binding defence links between Poland and the Soviet Union, insisting his was a variety of Communism, not a breach with it. In an editorial reflecting at least the temporary acquiescence of the Soviet leadership, *Pravda* gave cautious approval to the 'Gomulka variant'.

During demonstrations in Budapest on October 23, demonstrators demanded an end to Communist rule, the establishment of a democratic regime, the withdrawal of all Soviet troops from Hungary – where they had been stationed for more than a decade – and the release of Cardinal Mindszenty, who had been held under house arrest since 1948. They also demanded the return to power of a former Prime Minister, Imre Nagy, who had pursued a liberal Communist policy after coming to power in July 1953, been forced by Soviet pressure to resign in February 1955 and expelled from the Communist Party.

On October 24, Nagy was appointed Prime Minister. He promised immediate reforms, the 'democratization' of Hungary and the withdrawal of Soviet troops from the capital. These troop withdrawals were completed within a week. At the same time, troop reinforcements from inside the Soviet Union were brought up to the Soviet-Hungarian border. The Hungarian Minister of Defence, loyal to the old regime and to the Russians, ordered the Hungarian armed forces to crush the protesters. One of those to whom his instructions were sent was Colonel Pal Maleter, who was ordered to lead five tanks against the insurgents. 'Once I arrived there,' he explained two weeks later, 'it quickly became clear to me that those who were fighting for their freedom were not bandits, but loyal sons of Hungary. As a result I informed the Minister of Defence that I was going over to the insurgents.' That day Soviet tanks formed a ring around Budapest along a twenty-five-mile perimeter, and prepared to enter the capital.

In Poland, on the night of October 24, demonstrators in the industrial own of Lignica attacked the headquarters of the Soviet military command in charge of all satellite troops. They were dispersed by Polish militia using tear gas. There were also anti-Soviet demonstrations that day in the Polish port of Gdansk, and in Bialystok, only a few miles from the Soviet-Polish border.

Determined that Poland avoid the fate of Hungary, Gomulka appealed to the Poles not to call for the withdrawal of Soviet troops. A statement from the Central Committee effectively removed Poland from the conflict. In view of the 'perilous situation' in Hungary, the Central Committee declared, 'today, there is no time for demonstrations and public meetings. Calm, discipline, sense of responsibility, rallying around the Party and the people's authority for the realization of our just policy in this difficult and critical time – these are the most important requirements of the moment.'

Poland had become a spectator of the anti-Communist drama. On October 25, in Budapest, there was a mass demonstration in front of the parliament building. The Hungarian security forces opened fire and 600 demonstrators were killed. During October 26, groups of 'freedom fighters' attacked individual Soviet tanks with Molotov cocktails. Some brave individuals climbed on tanks to drop a grenade through the hatch.

On October 27 Imre Nagy released 5,000 political prisoners. Two days later, Soviet tanks and troops left Budapest.

On October 29 Israel invaded the Sinai peninsula. This was part of the plan that had been devised in Paris. Israel would advance westward across Sinai and, as it drew near to the Suez Canal, Britain and France would call for it to halt and pull back from the canal, call on the Egyptians likewise to pull back from the Canal Zone, and then land troops along the canal in order to protect it from attack and ensure the free passage of ships.

On October 30 Britain and France issued their ultimatum. It was addressed both to Israel – which was expecting it and had agreed in advance to comply with it – and to Egypt, which was required under the ultimatum to remove its troops from areas that were sovereign Egyptian territory. Both sides were told that their troops must be pulled back ten miles from the banks of the Canal. Israel accepted. Egypt refused. At the Security Council the United States put forward a resolution calling on Israel to halt her advance through Sinai and withdraw behind her frontiers. This resolution was vetoed by France and Britain.

During October 30, Cardinal Mindszenty was released. Dozens of members of the Hungarian security forces who were caught were beaten to death, or hanged upside down from lamp posts and then killed. Nagy's government announced that free elections would be held. Colonel Maleter placed his troops at the government's disposal.

Two struggles were being fought simultaneously. The Hungarian revolution and the Soviet attempt to crush it; and the Suez War. On October 31, British and French warplanes bombed the Egyptian airfields. By the morning of November 1 more than 75,000 Soviet troops and 2,500 tanks had crossed the Hungarian frontier and were moving rapidly towards Budapest. That afternoon Nagy withdrew Hungary from the Warsaw Pact, and on November 3 formed a new government. Colonel Maleter, promoted to general, was appointed Minister of Defence. Throughout the day the Soviet military advances towards Budapest continued. That evening Cardinal Mindszenty broadcast from Budapest. 'Our entire situation', he said, 'depends on what the Soviet Empire, the vast empire of 200 million inhabitants, will do with its troops within our borders. The radio has announced that the number of Soviet troops in Hungary has increased. We are neutral. We give the Russian Empire no cause for bloodshed. Do not the leaders of the Russian Empire realize that we will respect the Russian people even more if they do not oppress us?'

At eight o'clock in the evening of November 3 General Maleter drove to Soviet army headquarters to negotiate a halt to the Soviet military advance and the withdrawal of Soviet troops within a fixed period. The Russians had intimated that they would be willing to withdraw early in the new year. The talks began at ten o'clock. Two hours later the general and his delegation were arrested. By midnight almost all Hungarian industrial centres and military bases were surrounded by Soviet tanks. At four o'clock on the morning of November 4 the Soviet army entered Budapest.

Hundreds, even thousands of acts of personal defiance and heroism took place. Many insurgents acquired arms and took up positions on barricades. More than a thousand Soviet troops were killed in the fighting. Some deserted to the Hungarian patriots. Others proved so unreliable that they were withdrawn. But by eight o'clock on the morning of November 4, Soviet tanks had reached the parliament building on the bank of the Danube. The Hungarian Government was in session inside. To avoid capture, Imre Nagy took refuge in the Yugoslav Embassy. Cardinal Mindszenty found sanctuary in the United States Legation, where he remained for fifteen years.

Soviet tanks and troops battled throughout that afternoon and evening for control of the centre of Budapest, overrunning barricade after barricade. The United Nations General Assembly met in New York that evening – after midnight Hungarian time – and called on the Soviet Union to withdraw all its forces from Hungary 'immediately'. The Soviet Union took no notice. By mid-morning on Monday November 5, Soviet troops were in control of most of Budapest. Forty surviving soldiers in the Kilian barracks agreed to surrender under amnesty, and left the building. They were shot down.

In the early hours of Monday November 5, British paratroops landed at Port Said, at the northern entrance to the Suez Canal. At the same time, French troops landed at Port Fuad, on the opposite side of the canal. On the following day, in the United States, Eisenhower was re-elected President. He was determined to halt what he saw as the Anglo-French aggression against Egypt, and threatened immediate financial retaliation if the fighting did not stop.

Eisenhower feared that, as a result of the turmoil created by the Anglo-French and Israeli military actions, the Soviet Union would take advantage of the situation, and offer itself as Egypt's protector, bringing Soviet influence to the shores of the Red Sea. On November 6, Britain, France and Israel agreed a cease-fire, to come into effect that midnight, to be followed by their complete withdrawal from Egypt. As many as 500 soldiers had been killed in action.

In Hungary, 25,000 Hungarians and 7,000 Russians had been killed. Most of the Hungarians were civilians, and most of the Russians were soldiers. As many as 200,000 Hungarians fled their country, almost two per cent of the total population. Twenty-nine governments made offers of asylum. Each country that opened its doors was to find many facets of its national life greatly enriched by the newcomers. Inside Hungary, thousands were arrested and deported to camps in the Soviet Union. As many as 2,000 were executed. More than 20,000 were imprisoned. The border with Austria was sealed and mined.

The Soviet authorities had offered Imre Nagy a safe conduct out of Hungary. He accepted, and was deported to Roumania, where he was held in prison. Eighteen months later, having been brought back in secret to Hungary, he had been sentenced to death and shot. General Pal Maleter was also shot.

On December 5 the South African police, in a nationwide swoop, arrested 156 members of the African National Congress, the Indian Congress and the Congress of Democrats, three groups implacably opposed to apartheid. Among those arrested was the leading black lawyer, Nelson Mandela. All were accused of treason. 'It is not pleasant to be arrested in front of one's children,' Mandela later wrote, 'even though one knows that what one is doing is right. But children do not comprehend the complexity of the situation; they simply see their father being taken away by the white authorities without an explanation.'

In the United States, the struggle for civil rights reached a very different landmark on November 13, when the Supreme Court in Washington ruled that the segregation of bus passengers was unconstitutional. This enabled the boycott, begun the previous year in Montgomery, Alabama, to be called off, and pointed the way forward to further challenges to existing inequalities.

*   *   *

Another attempt at revolution was under way in the Caribbean. On the night of November 24–25 the ship *Granma* – a fifty-eight-foot yacht – left Mexico and sailed to Cuba. On board were Fidel Castro and eighty-one followers, including an Argentinian revolutionary, Ernesto (Che) Guevara. They landed secretly in eastern Cuba. It was the start of a sustained guerrilla war against the dictatorial regime of Fulgencio Batista.

A second landing of men and arms from the *Granma* took place on December 2. Three days later the main group of rebels was ambushed and twenty-four were killed. The rest were the object of repeated military searches, even of the use of napalm from the air. In the Sierra Maestra, Castro led a much-reduced group of twenty men, with scarcely more than twenty weapons. But they acquired arms and fought on. Steadily Castro augmented his numbers and, with growing peasant support, prepared the path to power.

The North Vietnamese Government of Ho Chi Minh had embarked on a Land Reform Programme. Its aim was both to give land to the peasants, and to establish full Communist control over the countryside. Those who opposed the programme were ruthlessly treated. In all, 100,000 peasants were executed. Agricultural output fell precipitately.

That October and November saw the triumphal appearance of the Bolshoi Ballet in London. It was the first visit of any Soviet ballet company to the West, and the first visit abroad of the Bolshoi in its two centuries of existence. People waited all night in the street at Covent Garden for the chance of a seat to see Galina Ulanova dance. 'You have given a most beautiful performance I shall always remember,' the Queen told Ulanova after watching her in *Giselle* on October 12. But as a result of the crushing of the Hungarian revolution the return visit of the Sadlers Wells Ballet to Moscow was cancelled. Nor did any official British representative go to the reception at the Soviet Embassy to celebrate the thirty-ninth anniversary of the Bolshevik revolution. In Moscow, during the celebration of that anniversary, Moscow Radio declared: 'The Soviet people rejoice from the bottom of their hearts at the victory scored by the Hungarian workers over the forces of reaction. We are firmly convinced that Hungary was, is and will remain a Socialist country.'

Another element in the intensification of the Cold War that year was the passing by the United States Congress of the Federal Aid Highway Act, which established a national road network, known as the National System of Interstate and Defence Highways. 'Our roads ought to be avenues of escape for persons living in big cities threatened by aerial attack or natural disaster,' Eisenhower explained. 'If such a crisis ever occurred, our obsolescent highways would turn into traps of death and destruction.'

CHAPTER NINE

Hopes Raised, Hopes Dashed

1957—67

ON 5 JANUARY 1957 President Eisenhower asked Congress to authorize him to employ the armed forces of the United States 'to secure and protect the territorial integrity and political independence of any nation or group of nations requesting such aid against overt armed aggression from any nation controlled by international Communism'. The phrase to 'employ the armed forces of the United States' went far beyond the use of American forces within a United Nations authorized conflict, as in Korea seven years earlier. Eisenhower's Secretary of State, John Foster Dulles, gave secret testimony that if any Communist 'volunteers' were sent to fight in the Middle East the United States would regard that as 'overt aggression'.

On January 10 the United Nations General Assembly established a special committee to inquire into the crushing of the Hungarian revolution. The committee, having been denied entry into Hungary by the re-established Communist government, took evidence from among the tens of thousands of Hungarian refugees in the West. Its conclusion was that the Hungarian revolt had been 'spontaneous', arising from grievances against the Soviet Union and conditions inside Hungary, and that the government which had succeeded that of Imre Nagy at the height of the struggle had been 'imposed' on Hungary by the Soviet Union. A special session of the General Assembly passed a resolution condemning the Soviet Union for depriving the Hungarian people of their liberty.

The General Assembly also appealed to the South African Government to reconsider apartheid. The appeal was ignored, and legislation continued to strengthen the racial divide. Separate university education was introduced, as well as racial segregation in the nursing profession. Other legislation allowed the government to enforce racial segregation in all places under local and public authority control, including libraries, concert halls and sports fields; and to evict black Africans from towns, and ban their entry into schools, hospitals, clubs, and even churches, in areas designated 'for whites only'.

Elsewhere in Africa the colonial structure was withering away. On March 6 the Gold Coast, renamed Ghana, became the first of Britain's African dominions to gain independence.

East and West Germany were drawing further and further apart. On January 7 a Soviet-German agreement was signed, giving the Soviet Union the right to intervene militarily in East Germany 'in the interests of security'. East Germany's economy was much less buoyant than West Germany's. Rationing remained in place. Raw materials continued to be sent to the Soviet Union under agreements that were little less than theft. Since 1953 more than 20,000 East Germans had fled to West Germany, and during 1957 that westward flow reached 5,000 a week. There was still no 'Berlin Wall' to stop East Berliners leaving. Any East German who came to East Berlin could make the westward journey.

West Germany moved forward economically with American loans and free enterprise. It also embarked within NATO on a self-defence policy that was denounced by East Germany as militarist, but offered protection for the economic and political achievements of the previous twelve years. During January registration for military service began in West Germany. Of 100,000 men called up only a hundred registered as conscientious objectors. On January 24 a West German officer was appointed Commander in Chief of the central sector of NATO in Europe.

On March 9 John Foster Dulles flew 9,000 miles from Washington to Canberra to appeal for a common defence policy throughout South-East Asia against Communist encroachment and subversion. Two days later he spoke at the opening session of the third annual meeting of the Council of Ministers of the South-East Asia Treaty Organization (SEATO). Speaking of North Korea and North Vietnam he criticized 'the open support given by Communist China to Soviet colonialism and imperialism'. This had 'ominous implications for all free Asian nations,' he said. Communist tyranny 'went about disguised in the pilfered clothes of liberty'.

During his speech Dulles alarmed the non-aligned nations, and the public of many of America's allies, when he remarked that the forces of the United States 'almost everywhere are equipped with atomic weapons . . . It is almost a normal part of their equipment.'

In China the Communist Party had struggled to improve rural productivity, and to create among the peasants of China – seventy per cent of the Party membership – a sense of national effort. Figures for grain production revealed however that the system was failing. During 1957 grain production rose by one per cent but the population by two per cent. Shortages of cotton led to a cut in the cloth ration. Three leaders of students who rioted and attacked Communist Party officials were executed.

Mao Tse-tung began an experiment – the Great Leap Forward – conscripting peasants for massive irrigation and water control projects. Within three months, 100 million peasants had been set to these tasks. Their wives, left at home, had to do the agricultural work of their absent husbands, mostly as agricultural labourers. Centralized schemes were devised for child care, and for feeding the wives whose work made it impossible for them to cook at home. To increase industrial production, some industries were moved from the cities to the countryside. The slogan for the Great Leap Forward was: 'More, faster, better, cheaper.'

The cause of European unity advanced without British participation. On March 25 six European nations signed the Treaty of Rome. 'The Six', as they became known, were Belgium, France, West Germany, Italy, Luxembourg and Holland, nations which since the end of the Second World War had been at the forefront of the push for a united Europe. The Treaty of Rome established a European Economic Community (EEC), known as the 'Common Market'. It was followed by a further agreement by the Six, also signed in Rome, for a European Atomic Energy Authority (Euratom) to enable the signatories to

share the development of atomic energy for fuel. In a third development towards greater unity among the Six, a European Court of
Justice was set up.

In the United States, as the legal reversal of many of the
McCarthyite judgments continued, McCarthy died. He was only
forty-seven years old. By his denunciations of Communist conspiracies
he had caused deep divisions in American society. A month after his
death, the Supreme Court ruled that FBI reports used in criminal
files, many of which had helped secure convictions in the McCarthy
era, had in future to be made available to the defendant, something
McCarthy had refused to allow. In a further ruling two weeks later
the Supreme Court laid down that membership of the Communist
Party was not sufficient ground for conviction.

On August 30 the Senate passed the Civil Rights Bill by sixty
votes to fifteen. The new Act, the first civil rights legislation in the
United States in the twentieth century, made the right to vote absolute, irrespective of colour, and gave power to federal prosecutors to
obtain court injunctions against any actual or threatened interference
with the right to vote. Anyone refusing to obey such an injunction
could be imprisoned by a judge, sitting without a jury.

Following the 1956 Supreme Court ruling for integration in
schools with 'all deliberate speed', American children had to be
admitted to senior high schools without discrimination based on
colour. On 4 September 1957, fearing mob violence from whites
who opposed the Supreme Court ruling, the Governor of Arkansas,
Orval Faubus, tried to prevent the admission of black children to a
school in Little Rock. Local National Guardsmen were used to turn
the children away. From Washington, Eisenhower took immediate
action, ordering a thousand Federal troops – paratroopers from an
airborne division – to escort the nine children to school. They did
so, and the children took their place in the classroom.

In 1957 an Asian influenza pandemic, known as 'Asian 'flu', constituted the worst global epidemic since the end of the First World
War, killing more than a million people in two years, including
16,000 in Britain and 70,000 in the United States.

*   *   *

Of great impact in 1957 was the first publication in the West, in Italian translation, of Boris Pasternak's novel *Dr Zhivago*. Attempts by the Soviet authorities to persuade Pasternak to produce a 'corrected' text were in vain. The book, with its realistic portrayal of the Bolshevik revolution, and of the revolution betrayed, was banned inside the Soviet Union. Copies that did circulate, in mimeographed versions, passed surreptitiously from hand to hand.

The atom and Hydrogen bomb tests in the atmosphere, carried out by the United States, the Soviet Union and Britain, were causing growing alarm. Unlike the American and British nuclear tests, the Soviet tests were not made public, but reports from scientists in Japan, Britain and the United States made clear that seven Soviet nuclear tests had taken place in the atmosphere in January, March and April. On April 23 the philosopher and philanthropist Albert Schweitzer sent a letter to the Norwegian Nobel Committee – the awarders of the Nobel Prizes – pressing them to 'mobilize' world opinion against the tests. Schweitzer, whose appeal was broadcast by the Nobel Committee in Norwegian, French, German, English and Russian, warned of the 'great and terrible danger to our descendants from radio-activity'.

On May 10 the Soviet Union appealed to Britain to stop all nuclear tests. Five days later Britain exploded its first Hydrogen bomb, and two further British tests followed on May 31 and June 19. Although on June 25 Eisenhower was given a report, quickly made public, that the American nuclear devices exploded in the Nevada desert were 'about 95 per cent free' of radioactive fall-out, within a month the United States Atomic Energy Commission stated that a 'clean' bomb was an impossibility. This report also made clear that a new type of conflict, 'radiological warfare', could be carried out using low altitude nuclear explosions which could contaminate large areas beyond the range of the physical damage.

Both the Soviet Union and the United States were developing an intercontinental ballistic missile (ICBM) that could carry a nuclear warhead, with a range of up to 5,000 miles. Britain was developing an intermediate range ballistic missile (IRBM) with a range of 2,000 miles. The United States and the Soviet Union were also developing this intermediate missile. To counter the threat of a Soviet air or missile attack across the Polar regions a joint American and Canadian radar defence line was completed in 1957, the Distant Early Warning (DEW) Line, its transmitter and receiver stations stretching from the far eastern tip of Alaska to eastern Canada. American and Canadian interceptor bomber squadrons were in the air at all times to respond to a warning of attack. But to obtain adequate warning of ballistic missiles flying at 24,000 miles an hour and descending on their targets at an angle of twenty-three degrees – a warning the DEW Line could not give – the United States embarked on a Ballistic Missile Early Warning System (BMEWS), also based on radar. The Soviet Union was building its own defensive line.

On October 4 the Soviet Union launched the first artificial earth satellite into space. The satellite, called *Sputnik*, circled the earth in a mere ninety-five minutes. A month later the Soviets launched *Sputnik II*, which was placed into orbit with a dog – named Laika – on board. The dog's presence enabled Soviet scientists to study living conditions in space. The 'space race' accelerated. On December 17 an American attempt to launch an intercontinental ballistic missile was finally successful, while at a rocket range in Australia, Britain tested a long-range missile capable of carrying nuclear warheads for 2,000 miles, travelling towards its target at 2,500 miles an hour.

The United States had no intention of allowing the Soviet Union to be the only Power in space. On the morning of 31 January 1958, the first United States satellite was sent into orbit, programmed to study cosmic rays. With its launch, wrote the *New York Herald Tribune*, 'the United States of America regained its national pride'. Meanwhile, as nuclear testing in the atmosphere continued, protests grew. On February 17 the British Campaign for Nuclear Disarmament (CND) held its first public meeting, in Trafalgar Square, London. On March 31 the Soviet Union announced it was suspending the testing of nuclear weapons for six months. One week later members of CND marched from the British nuclear research centre at Aldermaston to London. A day later, while the marchers were still on their way towards the capital, Eisenhower proposed the establishment of mutually agreed testing as a means of enforcing a total test ban.

On May 9 the Soviet Union accepted a Western proposal, first

put forward a year earlier, for technical talks to see if it was possible
to establish a system for controlling and monitoring the suspension
of nuclear testing. These talks began at Geneva on July 1 and made
some progress. As they continued, on July 23 a nuclear-powered
American submarine, the *Nautilus*, left Pearl Harbor and, passing
through the Bering Straits, which separate the United States from
the Soviet Union between Alaska and Siberia, made its way under
the pack ice and beneath the North Pole, emerging from the pack
ice east of Greenland on August 5. In its ninety-six-hour journey
under the ice it had covered 1,830 miles. Even in the Arctic pack
ice it found areas of open water and thin ice through which it could
have fired its missiles. At one point under the ice the submarine was
only 1,180 miles from Leningrad and 1,420 miles from Moscow,
well within missile range. In Geneva, the talks were set back on
September 18 when the Soviet Union announced it was about to
resume nuclear tests in order to catch up with the West – which
had continued its own test programmes during the summer.

In Algeria, the French settlers realized that the government in Paris
was willing to negotiate with the Muslim nationalist leaders. In a
gesture of defiance, on May 24 the settlers ordered French parachute
units based in Algeria to land on the French island of Corsica, and
set up Committees of Public Safety in Algeria, calling for General
de Gaulle to come to power in France and maintain French rule in
Algeria. Senior French army officers stationed in Algeria supported
this call. On May 29 de Gaulle agreed to the request of the French
President, Pierre Coty, to form a government, and on June 1 he
secured a parliamentary majority. On June 2 parliament granted him
emergency powers for three months. He at once curbed the powers
of the Committees of Public Safety in Algeria which had been among
the strongest advocates of his coming to power.

To the distress of those who wanted the Algerian nationalists
crushed, on June 4 de Gaulle offered to 'open the door to reconciliation'. Algeria's political future, he pledged on June 27, would be
settled by her elected representatives, Europeans and Muslims alike.
As Prime Minister, de Gaulle had been granted the power to draw
up a new constitution for France, establishing a Fifth Republic. It

was approved on September 23, and included recognition by France of the right of her overseas territories to independence.

In China, the Great Leap Forward was entering its second year. In April, twenty-seven co-operative farms in the Province of Honan were turned into a single commune of almost 10,000 households – 43,000 people in all. By the end of the year 740,000 co-operative farms had been merged into 26,000 communes. These encompassed 120 million rural households, virtually the whole Chinese peasantry. Hardship, starvation and economic disruption were widespread. Labour battalions received less than six hours rest each twenty-four hours. After working with almost no breaks from 5 a.m. to 6 p.m., commune workers had then to do compulsory small-arms drill.

The reality of the Great Leap Forward included the arrest of tens of thousands of 'rightists' and 'counter-revolutionaries', among them 3,000 members of the Communist Youth League. There were also charges that 'dangerous separatist activities' had emerged among China's Mongol, Turkic and Korean minorities, and 'rectification' campaigns were carried out to ensure loyalty and unanimity. So severe was the Tibetan resistance – described officially as 'subversive plots and splitting activities' – that all commercial traffic on the Lhasa–India highway was suspended.

Internal chaos, maladministration and the cruel rigidity of the Great Leap Forward led to famine. In the worst affected areas the monthly food ration for each adult was reduced to nineteen pounds of rice, three and a half ounces of cooking oil and three and a half ounces of meat – when there was meat. The death toll in the four years 1958 to 1961 has been estimated as thirty million.

In the Soviet Union under Khrushchev, the compulsory delivery of farm produce to the State remained, but was made more flexible. Emphasis was put on farms growing the crops most suitable for local conditions, rather than those which Moscow-based planners and controllers felt were most needed for the centrally managed economy. On August 10 Khrushchev opened the largest hydro-electric project in the world, on the Volga. Electricity flowed in abundance, but

ecologically the dams proved a disaster, leading to the steady evapor-
ation of the Caspian Sea.

On October 23 the Nobel Prize for Literature was awarded to
Boris Pasternak, whose novel *Doctor Zhivago* was still not allowed to
be published inside the Soviet Union. Pasternak, who was living in
Moscow, accepted the prize. The Soviet newspapers denounced him
as 'an enemy of Socialism' and denounced the award of the prize as
a 'Cold War manoeuvre'. Four days after Pasternak accepted the
award he was expelled from the Soviet Writers' Union, and the State
Publishing House was forbidden to reissue any of his earlier books
or sign any contracts with him for new books. There were public
calls, orchestrated by the authorities, for his expulsion from the Soviet
Union. Pasternak withdrew his acceptance of the award, and then
wrote to Khrushchev asking to be allowed to stay in his homeland.
His request was granted.

On December 21 de Gaulle was elected President of France, receiving
78.5 per cent of the vote. The Communist candidate received 13.1
per cent. Under the new constitution of the Fifth Republic, which
de Gaulle had promoted while Prime Minister, the powers of the
President were enhanced.

On December 30 all six States of French West Africa – Chad,
Congo, Gabon, Mali, Mauritania and Senegal – formed a federation
that would remain within the French Community. Elsewhere in
Africa the demands of national movements were more vociferous,
with 'self-determination' being the call that went out from the All
African Peoples' Conference which met in Ghana. Among the resolutions passed by the conference were the call for an end to 'racialism
and discriminatory laws' and condemnation of 'frontiers, boundaries
and federations'.

By the late 1950s motor-car accidents had created a serious depletion
of human life and individual productivity. It is impossible to calculate
how much the industrialized nations lost in terms of the value of
the manpower and productive lives, and future productive enterprise,
as, in the United States, 35,331 citizens were killed on the roads
in 1958, and in Britain 5,970. Efforts to reduce road deaths were

continuous. In Britain, radar was first used on 20 January 1958 to check car drivers for speeding.

The cause of faster air travel was advanced by the introduction of the first scheduled transatlantic jet services. On October 4 a British Overseas Airways Corporation (BOAC) Comet jet made a non-stop crossing of the Atlantic from London to New York. Twenty-two days later a Pan-American (Pan-Am) Airways Boeing 707 jet flew non-stop from Paris to New York.

Commerce also took a leap forward when the Bank of America in California launched the first multi-purpose credit card, and the first American Express credit card was also launched.

As many as 4,000 young people, many under twenty-five, including many professionals, were fleeing each week from East Germany to West Germany, across the open border between East and West Berlin. The refugees from East Germany were absorbed in West Germany, bringing with them their energy and talents, and further accentuating the political, economic and cultural divide between East and West.

In Poland, with all its borders touching other Communist States, the way out through emigration was effectively closed, and there was no 'West Poland' to which to go. Internally, a close watch was kept on all dissent – and incipient hostility to the Soviet Union – in the inner corridors of power, and those dubbed 'revisionists' were expelled from the Party. One of those denounced by the authorities was the writer Antoni Slonimski, who at a meeting of the Polish Writers' Union called for a minute's silence in memory of the murdered Hungarian leader, Imre Nagy.

The same strictness prevailed in Czechoslovakia, where the border with neutral Austria was strictly fortified and patrolled. In March several Czechs were sentenced to hard labour for 'listening to hostile radio stations and passing on the news to their friends in cafés'. In June a man was sent to prison for four months for 'anti-Communist chatter' in a tram.

'I still believe that kinder times will come,' Boris Pasternak had written in 1958. Those 'kinder times' were to elude much of mankind in the ensuing forty years. But the instinct for improvement was strong, seen forcefully in the United States in the work of a nationwide charity, the March of Dimes. Set up by President Franklin Roosevelt in 1933 to combat polio, in 1955 the March of Dimes saw its anti-polio work effectively concluded with the declaration that the Salk vaccine was 'safe, effective and potent'; in the United States alone, an estimated 135 million babies were saved by the vaccine in the ensuing four decades. This success led the March of Dimes to turn to a new challenge, saving babies from birth defects and related infant health problems, including mental retardation. By the end of the century the number of infant deaths from respiratory distress syndrome had been halved. Anna Eleanor Roosevelt, a granddaughter of the President, and a national trustee of the March of Dimes, commented forty years after the new orientation: 'Today, we are saving babies.'

The work of charitable organizations devoted to health and welfare is usually unsung. Yet it constituted a significant feature of national and international efforts for human well-being during the second half of the twentieth century.

On 1 January 1959 President Batista of Cuba and those most closely associated with his regime flew into exile. On January 8 Fidel Castro arrived in Havana, following which swift action was taken against perpetrators of excesses during the latter years of Batista's rule. More than 200 people were convicted of crimes against the Cuban people and shot. At the same time, land was transferred from large-scale landowners to those who would till the soil and grow their own food, including 700,000 unemployed. On January 27 Castro's lieutenant, Argentinian-born Che Guevara, expressed his wider regional aspirations: 'The example of our revolution for Latin America and the lessons it implies have destroyed all the café theories: we have shown that a small group of resolute men supported by the people and not afraid to die if necessary can take on a disciplined regular army and completely defeat it.'

On May 1 a hundred Panamanian rebels landed on the Caribbean shore of Panama. They were immediately trapped by the authorities. A month later, on June 1, two planes with rebels on board flew into Nicaragua from Costa Rica. They were quickly overcome. Later that month a rebel attack was launched on the Trujillo regime in the

Dominican Republic. The rebels had been trained in Cuba. They too were soon defeated. On August 13 there was an 'invasion' of Haiti by thirty Cubans. Three months later, eighty guerrillas crossed from Brazil into northern Paraguay. On November 13 there was a revolt in Guatemala against the presence of an American training base for anti-Castro Cubans. All these attempts at fomenting revolution were suppressed.

The Western defence system was strengthened on May 22, when Canada and the United States agreed to work together to develop the use of atomic energy for 'mutual defence'. The United States also agreed to sell Canada the nuclear warheads needed for her intercontinental ballistic missile programme. On June 14 the United States agreed to give Greece information about nuclear weapons and provide her with ballistic rockets. Eleven days later the Soviet Union proposed a nuclear-free zone in the Balkans and the Adriatic. This was rejected by the United States and Britain.

On July 22 the American Vice-President, Richard Nixon, reached Moscow. On the following day Khrushchev protested to him about the annual Captive Nations resolution, which had just been passed through Congress, as it had done each year since 1950. The resolution urged Americans to 'study the plight of the Soviet-dominated nations and to recommit themselves to the support of the just aspirations of those captive nations'. Khrushchev told Nixon: 'Hitherto, the Soviet Government thought Congress could never adopt a decision to start a war. But now it appears that, although Senator McCarthy is dead, his spirit still lives. For this reason the Soviet Union has kept its powder dry.'

Inside the United States the determination of the Governor of Arkansas, Orval Faubus, not to allow integration despite the rulings of Federal courts, was finally frustrated on January 10 when a District Judge ordered the School Board of Little Rock to integrate the town's schools. Forty-four teachers who had been dismissed because they were suspected of supporting integration were reinstated. Where Arkansas reluctantly led, other southern States followed, pushed into integration by their respective State Supreme Courts. On February 2 in Virginia twenty-one local schoolchildren were admitted as a result of the court ruling to a previously all-white school. On June 5, Georgia issued an order forbidding racial segregation in the schools in Atlanta. That October, however, Martin Luther King warned against the limitations of the current Supreme Court judgments: 'Full integration can easily become a distant or mythical goal – major integration may be long postponed, and in the quest for social calm a compromise firmly implanted in which the real goals are merely token integration for a long period to come.' King added: 'The Negro was the tragic victim of another compromise in 1877, when his full equality was bargained away by the Federal Government and a condition somewhat above slave status but short of genuine citizenship became his social and political existence for nearly a century. There is reason to believe that the Negro of 1959 will not accept supinely any such compromises in the contemporary struggle for integration. His struggle will continue.'

King rejected calls to violence. His answer lay, he explained, in 'the mass boycott, sitdown protests and strikes, sit-ins – refusal to pay fines and bail for unjust arrest – mass meetings – prayer pilgrimages etc.' Citing Gandhi as his inspiration, King urged his followers to use 'every form of mass action yet known – create new forms – and resolve never to let them rest. This is the social lever which will force open the door to freedom.'

The ending of empire, colonialism, racial discrimination, colour prejudice and foreign control was everywhere accelerating, but not everywhere uniformly resolved. On January 4 there were violent disturbances in the Belgian Congo, and five Belgian policemen were injured. The Belgian Government responded by sending in parachute troops. On the following day those troops clashed with Africans in the city, when thirty-five African protesters were killed. The Belgian Government announced four days later that it would grant substantial and meaningful reforms to the Congolese.

In London, on February 19, agreement was reached by the Prime Ministers of Britain, Turkey and Greece for the independence of Cyprus. It would not be given to Greece or divided between Greece and Turkey, or between Greek Cypriots and Turkish Cypriots. Instead, it would remain a single entity with full independence, as a republic with a president, and with the Greek and Turkish Cypriot communities each obtaining a wide measure of autonomy. Britain would retain two sovereign military bases. The desire of EOKA for union with Greece, a desire that had been backed up by force and terrorism, would have to be abandoned.

On February 22 the British Governor released all Cypriot prisoners held in detention. Five days later an amnesty for EOKA terrorists was declared. On March 1 Archbishop Makarios returned to Cyprus from exile. At the end of the year he become the independent republic's first President. EOKA was disbanded and Makarios – once the outspoken advocate of union with Greece – worked to reconcile the Greek and Turkish communities. One result of his ameliorating efforts was that former EOKA activists launched several assassination attempts against him. None succeeded.

In Nyasaland, the British colonial authorities, unwilling to bow to the threat of force, sought to control the nationalist movement and to curb its activities. Their determination was strengthened after the return to Nyasaland of the African National Congress leader, Dr Hastings Banda, from a prolonged exile, when airfield buildings and installations were attacked by stone-throwing crowds in several towns, and at mass protest meetings speakers demanded 'immediate control' of Nyasaland for its African inhabitants. After ten days of protests, a state of emergency was declared, the African National Congress was outlawed, and 166 of its members were arrested, including Dr Banda. When African protesters tried to release a group of prisoners held on board ship at Nkata Bay, troops opened fire and twenty protesters were killed. This brought the number of African dead in the disturbances to fifty-two. No European or African members of the security forces were killed.

A British Government inquiry concluded later in the year that the national aspirations of the Africans in Nyasaland were not limited to a small minority of political activists, but were shared by the 'great majority' of the people.

In Southern Rhodesia the Prime Minister, Sir Edgar Whitehead, seeking to avoid an African national challenge to white authority in his country, declared a state of emergency and banned four African National Congress Parties. In neighbouring Northern Rhodesia the

Zambia African National Congress was banned by the British authorities on March 12. The Congress had called for an African boycott of the elections eight days later. Many Africans did vote, but the system of representation was such, and the mix of official and elected members so contrived, that of the ten members of the executive council only two were Africans.

In Kenya, eleven Mau Mau prisoners who were being held by the British at Hola Camp were severely beaten on March 3, and died. The killings accelerated the pressure both in the colony and in Britain for Kenyan independence. In December the British Government agreed that in Tanganyika elected African members could form a majority in the legislative council. Singapore, founded by the British in 1819, became self-governing on June 3. A month later Jamaica was granted internal self-government within the West Indies Federation which had been established two years earlier.

On September 16 De Gaulle offered all the inhabitants of Algeria – French and Muslim – a referendum, in which they could either choose continued association with France, or independence. The referendum would be held, he said, within four years of an 'effective' end to the Algerian national rebellion. France's United Nations Trustee territories were also on the verge of independence. On December 6 the General Assembly voted to give the three million people of France's Togoland Trusteeship independence in four months' time.

In South Africa, the imposition of apartheid was taking harsher and more draconian forms with every piece of legislation. The Promotion of Bantu Self-Government Bill provided for the establishment of eight 'homelands' – known as Bantustans – for Africans, in which they would become citizens of their Bantustan, but would lose their already circumscribed right of representation in the Pretoria parliament. For Africans whose relegation into homelands was being arranged without their participation in the debate, or even in any discussion of the geographic areas involved, this was a policy of separation and exclusion. Despite the Bantustans, six million Africans would still be living in the 'white-designated' areas, and subjected to all the rigours of apartheid.

Legislation passed in Pretoria also brought to an end the existing racially integrated education at both Cape Town and Witwatersrand Universities, and set up separate institutions of higher learning for the three officially designated 'non-white' categories: Coloureds, Indians and Africans. Earlier legislation which forbade sexual intercourse between 'whites' and 'non-whites', and made even an 'invitation' to commit such an act illegal, was being rigorously enforced.

In February there was a national uprising against Chinese rule in Tibet. The Chinese took immediate military action. On March 17 Tibetans in Lhasa, the capital, attacked the Chinese garrison there. It was a bold but futile gesture of defiance. To escape capture by the Chinese, the Tibetan spiritual and temporal leader, the Dalai Lama, was smuggled out of Tibet, making his way 300 miles on horseback to the Indian border, where he was given asylum. The Chinese presented their own spiritual ruler to the Tibetans: the Panchen Lama. On April 10 he was proclaimed Lama at a short ceremony in Lhasa, in front of the palace of the man he was usurping. Three months later the Chinese began to expropriate monastic land in Tibet and to redistribute it. The power of the Tibetan leadership, and such wealth as it possessed, was systematically destroyed.

The Dalai Lama appealed on September 9 to the United Nations for international intervention to restore Tibetan independence. On September 22, before his appeal was heard, China was admitted to the United Nations. The General Assembly responded to the Tibetan appeal a month later, with a resolution calling for the restoration of civil and religious liberties in Tibet. The Chinese, from their seat in the Assembly, denounced the resolution and refused to implement it. When the century ended, China was still master of Tibet.

Inside China the persecution of Christians intensified. On October 18 the superior of the Maryknoll Mission in China, sixty-eight-year-old Bishop James E. Walsh, was arrested. He had been in China since 1918. Long service to Roman Catholicism in China was his sole 'crime': he was to spend twelve years in prison. Throughout that time he was allowed no news reports, and only one visitor, his brother, for a single visit in 1960. Among Chinese Christians arrested that year was Allen Yuan, an evangelical pastor. Charged with propagating falsehood, he was sentenced to the first of a series of incarcerations in labour camps that were to add up to a total of twenty-two years. Forty years later, aged eighty-three, and a free man at last, he was still preaching in China.

In Poland, Wladislaw Gomulka continued to pursue the specifically Polish 'road to socialism'. He also improved Poland's links with Tito's Yugoslavia, which had broken away from Soviet dominance a decade earlier. At the Party Congress in Warsaw in March, when new conditions for Party membership were laid down, insistence on 'ideological conformity' was abandoned. Party members were told that a special 'revising' commission had decided that neither a competence in Marxism-Leninism, nor a public repudiation of religious belief, should any longer be among the qualifications for Party membership. During a visit to Warsaw in July, Khrushchev himself gave specific support to a pledge by Gomulka that the Polish peasant farmers need have 'no fear' of collectivization.

The situation in Czechoslovakia was far more Stalinist than in Poland. Agricultural co-operatives were being extended, with 156,000 private farms absorbed into them. The President, Antonin Novotny, commented ominously that summer: 'Land is being wasted in the form of gardens attached to private houses.' To combat growing absenteeism at work the Communist Party warned: 'We shall have to return to a system of visits by comrades.' A cultural conference at the beginning of the year insisted that the work of writers and artists should have 'as its main concept the struggle against bourgeois survivals and ideas hostile to our system'. After a number of literary magazines were closed down, writers, artists and musicians were warned by the Party leadership: 'Pay heed that your art fully assists the Communist moral and aesthetic education of the working people.'

At the beginning of the year, three theological students were imprisoned for stating publicly that 'there is no religious freedom in Czechoslovakia'. An actor was sent to prison for three years for 'making rude remarks' about the Czech Communist leaders and for 'admiring everything Western'. Following the abolition of private medical practice several doctors were sent to prison – one for eighteen years – for helping what were described in court as the 'remnants of the bourgeoisie' to obtain private medical attention.

In Hungary, Communist rule was also harsh, with thousands of schoolteachers being 're-educated'. In Roumania, it was made illegal to hire agricultural labour or rent land. There was also an increase in the State expropriation of the small agricultural surpluses Roumanian peasant farmers were allowed to keep.

Not the East-West conflict, nor colonial conflict, but the motor car, remained by far the largest mass killer year by year. During 1959 a total of 6,520 people were killed on Britain's roads, 36,223 on the roads of the United States. Among the visitors to the United States in 1959 was Nikita Khrushchev, the first Soviet ruler to do so. To remind his hosts of Soviet prowess, at the airport on arrival he presented Eisenhower with a model of the Soviet rocket *Lunik 2* which had landed on the surface of the moon two days earlier.

On September 27 a joint declaration issued by Eisenhower and Khrushchev marked a turning point in the Cold War. The two men agreed that international disputes should be settled 'not by the application of force but by peaceful means through negotiation'. With regard to Berlin it was agreed to open talks 'with a view to achieving a solution that would be in accordance with the interests of all concerned'.

On 3 February 1960 the British Prime Minister Harold Macmillan told the South African Parliament in Cape Town: 'The wind of change is blowing through this continent and our national policies must take account of it.' On February 21 a constitutional conference in London reached agreement on a parliamentary system that would ensure the emergence of black majority rule in Kenya. On April 1 Dr Hastings Banda was released from prison after twelve months as a 'dangerous agitator' and invited to London to discuss an end to racially discriminatory legislation in Rhodesia and Nyasaland. A constitutional conference on the future of Sierra Leone – where the first British settlement dated back to 1790 – agreed to independence for the colony within the year. On June 26 British Somaliland became independent, followed five days later by agreement on the terms of the independence of Cyprus, where the transfer of power took place on August 16. On October 1 the Nigerian Federation became independent. The 'wind of change' was not felt everywhere in the British

Empire, however. In Southern Rhodesia, a Law and Order Maintenance Act, passed on November 25, gave the police extra powers
against black nationalist agitation.

On January 20 a month-long conference began in Brussels to
move the Congo towards independence from Belgium. The senior
Congolese negotiator was Patrice Lumumba, who had been serving
a six-month sentence for inciting riots the previous October. According to the timetable agreed in Brussels, elections were held in the
Congo on May 11. Although Lumumba's Party did not achieve
anything approaching overall majority – it won 41 of the 137 seats
– his was the largest single bloc, and he became Prime Minister.
The transfer of power was accompanied by violent attacks by units
of the Congolese army on Europeans, including rape, and looting
was also commonplace. Lumumba managed to restore order by dismissing all remaining Belgian officers and declaring that every soldier
in the army would be promoted one rank, with the attendant increase
in pay.

On July 14 a secessionist movement in Katanga province, led
by Moise Tshombe, declared independence. Lumumba, desperate to
maintain the territorial unity of the Congo, appealed for help to the
United Nations. On July 15 the first United Nations troops – Ghanaian and Tunisian soldiers – arrived in Léopoldville and took control
of the radio station in the capital. But Lumumba was deposed on
September 14, after only eleven weeks as Prime Minister, and
imprisoned. The troops who seized power were led by Colonel Joseph
Mobutu, a former sergeant in the Belgian colonial regiment who
had risen to prominence since independence four months earlier by
suppressing mutinies with severity.

Escaping from prison, Lumumba called on the United Nations
troops in Léopoldville both to protect him, and help him regain
power. They declined to do so, and on November 28 he fled. He
was captured three days later by forces loyal to Mobutu, tortured,
and executed.

Elsewhere in Africa, the moves to full independence had proceeded
without violence. On June 26 Madagascar became independent from
France and was admitted to the United Nations. On July 11 the

French Government granted immediate independence to seven of its dependencies: the Republics of Dahomey, Niger, Upper Volta, Ivory Coast, Chad, Central Africa and Congo Brazzaville. On November 28 Mauritania declared its independence from France and became an Islamic Republic. Only in Algeria had the Muslim national movement been frustrated. The offer made by de Gaulle of self-determination for Algeria led to riots by the French settlers, and fourteen policemen were killed. De Gaulle appealed on television to the rioters to lay down their arms. They refused to do so. The centre of Algiers was surrounded by troops loyal to the government in Paris.

Algerian Muslim nationalists were also active. After terrorists on a beach west of Algiers killed twelve people, including several holidaymakers, the French army attacked and thirty Algerians were killed. De Gaulle continued to try to advance the process of Algerian self-government. The settlers were furious; when he visited Algeria on December 9 there were four attempts to assassinate him, as European and Muslim demonstrators clashed in the streets. The police opened fire, killing 123 people, most of them Muslims.

Returning to France, de Gaulle announced a national referendum: and within three weeks, on 8 January 1961, the people of France voted in favour of independence for Algeria.

On 21 March 1960 there was a demonstration in the South African township of Sharpeville against the pass laws which forced all non-whites to carry identity cards, and which made it virtually impossible for them to spend the night in a designated 'white' area, even if it was their place of work. At the height of the protest a crowd of several thousand surrounded the local police station. The crowd was unarmed, the seventy-five policemen inside the station were armed. The police ordered the crowd to disperse, but they would not do so. The police then formed a single line and opened fire. Fifty-six Africans were killed, most of them shot in the back as they tried to flee from the shooting.

There was worldwide indignation at the Sharpeville shootings. The South African Government ignored all pleas and censure. After eleven days of protest by Africans throughout South Africa, demonstrations such as that at Sharpeville were made illegal. Both the

African National Congress and the Pan-African Congress were banned; their leaders went into hiding.

The defence preparations of the United States were at the forefront of experimentation. On May 24 the *Midas II* satellite was launched. Known as the 'Spy in the Sky', its aim was to test the feasibility of setting up orbiting satellites able to send back to earth almost instantaneous warning of the launching of a ballistic missile attack. On July 20 the second American nuclear-powered submarine, *George Washington*, test fired a Polaris missile from under water. The missile, which could be armed with a nuclear warhead, travelled 1,100 miles. Soviet defence experts noted that the distance from the Baltic Sea to Moscow was less than 500 miles, as was the distance from the Aegean Sea to Soviet naval bases at Odessa and Sevastopol.

A Ten-Power disarmament committee was in session at Geneva under the auspices of the United Nations, hoping to reconcile Soviet-American differences. Such hopes were dashed when Khrushchev announced that the Soviet Union had shot down an American high-altitude spy aircraft – the *U-2* – above the Ural mountains, and that the pilot had been captured. Two weeks later a summit meeting was to have begun in Paris. Khrushchev insisted he would only take part if the United States announced it would not in future 'violate the State borders of the USSR with its aircraft, that it deplores the provocative actions taken in the past, and will punish those directly responsible for such actions'. The most Eisenhower was prepared to do was to say that all overflights had been suspended 'since the recent incident'. There would be no apology and no punishment. The summit was abandoned.

In Eastern Europe, Communism was under intense strain. In Poland there were riots at the industrial town of Nowa Huta, just outside Cracow, when a plot of land set aside for a church was confiscated by the authorities. In Czechoslovakia a Communist Party newspaper attacked what it called a 'considerable part' of the Czech university student body for being 'still under religious influence'. Another news-paper criticized school teachers, telling its readers on March 22: 'Some teachers may keep to the principles of scientific materialism laid down in the syllabus, but when school is over we find them in church.'

Inside China, a sustained onslaught took place on the religious worship of the many millions of Chinese Christians. On March 17 the Roman Catholic Bishop of Shanghai, Monsignor Ignatius Kung Ping-mei, who had been held in prison for the previous five years, was given a life sentence. Twelve other Chinese Catholics were sent to prison for between five and twenty years.

In the United States, the struggle for racial equality continued. In Georgia, Martin Luther King was arrested for organizing sit-ins at 'whites only' restaurants. He had also organized 'freedom rides' in those towns and rural districts where segregation on buses was maintained. In the ten Southern States, while 62 per cent of all whites were registered to vote, only 25 per cent of blacks were registered. A new Civil Rights Bill was introduced, intended to end all obstacles being placed in the way of black voter registration. It found a determined supporter in the Senate, Lyndon Johnson of Texas, who used his southern credentials and deep knowledge of the political system to out-manoeuvre the manoeuvrers. As passed into law the Act gave authority to the courts to appoint federal 'referees' to safeguard what were then called 'Negro voting rights'. Any attempt to obstruct the exercise of those rights by force or threats of violence was made a Federal offence.

On September 23, at the United Nations General Assembly in New York, Khrushchev made a strong attack on the Western World. There was a moment of humour, caught by the television cameras, when Khrushchev took off one of his shoes and began banging it on the desk in front of him. Macmillan intervened to ask the President of the Assembly: 'Mr President, perhaps we could have a translation, I could not quite follow.'

The confrontation was based on more than public posturing. Five days later NATO announced a unified system of air defence command. On November 1, Britain agreed to provide the United States with a base and facilities for American submarines armed with Polaris nuclear missiles. An atomic-powered aircraft carrier, *USS Enterprise*, had been launched five weeks earlier at Newport News, Virginia, with the capacity to sail for several years without refuelling. The focus of interest in the United States had turned, however, to the forthcoming presidential election. The Republican candidate was the forty-seven-year-old Vice-President, Richard Nixon. His Democratic challenger was even younger, forty-three-year-old Senator John F. Kennedy. During his six years as a Congressman – he was first elected in 1946 after naval service in the Pacific war – and his subsequent eight years as a Senator, Kennedy had been an advocate of civil rights legislation and increased United States financial aid for underdeveloped countries.

In a speech on July 15, in accepting the Democratic Party nomination for President, Kennedy called for a 'peaceful revolution for human rights' and 'an end to racial discrimination in all parts of our community life'. On October 19, when Kennedy and Nixon were campaigning in Florida, Martin Luther King was arrested in a restaurant in Georgia for refusing to leave a 'Whites Only' table. He was sentenced to four months' hard labour. His wife was then six months pregnant.

Kennedy had already expressed his distaste for Southern segregationist policies. Following King's arrest, three Southern State governors warned Kennedy not to intervene on his behalf. On October 25, from Chicago airport, he placed a long distance call to King's wife, assuring her of his concern and offering to intervene. On the following day Kennedy's brother Robert telephoned the Georgia judge who had imposed the sentence and made a plea for King's release. King was released on October 27.

King's father, a Baptist minister like his son, who a few weeks earlier had endorsed Nixon's candidature on religious grounds, announced he had changed his mind. 'Because this man was willing to wipe the tears from my daughter's eyes,' he said, 'I've got a suitcase of votes and I'm going to take them to Mr Kennedy and dump them in his lap.' For Kennedy, who aspired to be the first Roman Catholic President, the endorsement of a prominent Baptist was a turning point. His campaign managers distributed to black churches throughout the country a million pamphlets describing what had happened.

The presidential election was held on November 8. In terms of the numbers of votes cast, the real result was incredibly close, with

34,221,531 votes being cast for Kennedy and 34,108,474 for Nixon. The black vote went substantially for Kennedy, who was the youngest President, and the first Roman Catholic, to take office.

The natural disasters of 1960 were dominated by an earthquake at Agadir, in Morocco, which killed 12,000 people. American servicemen stationed in Morocco were among those who participated in rescue activities. Another earthquake, less widely reported, created equal devastation. In took place in Chile, where 10,000 people were killed. In the United States, 36,399 citizens were killed in motor-car accidents in 1960, bringing the total number of motor-car deaths spanning the Presidencies of Franklin Roosevelt, Truman and Eisenhower to 923,432. This was a terrifyingly high death toll in a country that had avoided war on its soil, and had made continual progress against death from disease. The British road deaths in that same twenty-seven-year period totalled 171,533.

On 20 January 1961 John F. Kennedy was inaugurated President of the United States. Aged forty-three he was the youngest President in American history. In his State of the Union message he declared: 'Let the word go forth from this time and place, to friend and foe alike, that the torch has been passed to a new generation of Americans – born in this century, tempered by war, disciplined by a hard and bitter peace, proud of our ancient heritage – and unwilling to witness or permit the slow undoing of those human rights to which this nation has always been committed, and to which we are committed today at home and around the world . . . Let every nation know, whether it wishes us well or ill, that we shall pay any price, bear any burden, meet any hardship, support any friend, oppose any foe, to ensure the survival and the success of liberty.'

Within three months of Kennedy's inauguration, however, there was a miscalculation which enabled American isolationists and liberals alike, as well as America's foes, to mock his efforts. On April 17 a group of 1,400 Cuban exiles invaded Cuba. They had been armed and trained by agencies of the United States Government. Their point of disembarkation was the Bay of Pigs. After three days on the beachhead almost all of them had been killed or taken prisoner.

After initial American denials of any official involvement, Kennedy accepted full responsibility for the government's part in the attack. He had, however, ruled out direct American military participation, although urged to order this.

With regard to social reform, Kennedy found a Congress that did not want to move as fast as he did. Of the first 335 measures which he proposed, only 172 were approved. One of those which was passed was a $435-million retraining scheme for the unemployed. But among the proposals against which Kennedy faced fierce opposition was medical care for the aged. Twenty-one Democratic Senators joined with thirty-one Republicans to create an unbreachable wall of opposition.

One element of the idealism with which Kennedy sought to inspire the American people, especially the youth, was the Peace Corps. Its mission was to help poorer countries meet their need for trained personnel, to encourage non-Americans to understand Americans better, and to foster greater American understanding of foreign countries. Volunteers worked as teachers, health assistants, small business advisers and agricultural specialists. The first group left the United States that September: twenty-eight surveyors, geologists and civil engineers who went to Tanganyika. By the end of the year more than 500 volunteers were at work. No part of the world was excluded. Only the Communist countries, who a decade and a half earlier had rejected the Marshall Plan with all its economic benefits and opportunities, declined to participate, their refusal orchestrated by the Soviet Union.

Inside the Soviet Union a decree of July 1 instituted the death penalty for 'professional speculators'. Many of those who were executed were Jewish: identified in the Soviet newspapers by their Jewish-sounding names. All but one of the synagogues in Moscow was closed down. In December all manifestations of 'bourgeois psychology and private-property tendencies' became a crime.

The struggle for power in the Congo intensified following the murder of Patrice Lumumba. In Katanga forces loyal to Lumumba took control of Bakuvu and most of the northern province. In Stanleyville, capital of the Oriental province, Antoine Gizenga, who had been trained in Prague, proclaimed a separate regime and prepared to defend it with 7,000 armed men. In one of his first foreign policy initiatives as President, Kennedy warned the Soviet Union that the United States would defend the charter of the United Nations 'by opposing any attempt by any government to intervene unilaterally in the Congo'. His warning was heeded.

A resolution adopted by the Security Council on February 21 began a concerted effort by the United Nations to avert civil war and restore parliamentary institutions to the Congo. The Soviet Union refrained from casting its veto. Following the resolution, the Congolese head of State, President Kasavubu, allowed the Congolese National Army to be reorganized with United Nations' help. For its part the United Nations agreed to supervise the withdrawal of all Belgian military personnel, and all foreign mercenaries serving with the army of the breakaway Katanga province.

After a mob loyal to Moise Tshombe, the former Congolese Prime Minister attacked United Nations personnel at Elisabethville airport, United Nations troops moved against the foreign mercenaries who were a significant part of the effective forces of the Katangese army. During fighting that began on September 13 the United Nations forces were attacked by jet aircraft flown by mercenaries. On the ground an Irish company of the United Nations force was captured. The United States under Kennedy announced its support for forceful United Nations military action. In an attempt to avert greater bloodshed, the Secretary-General of the United Nations, Dag Hammarskjöld, flew from Léopoldville for talks with the Katangese. His plane disappeared. The next day its wreckage was found eight miles from its destination. Hammarskjöld was dead. He was posthumously awarded the Nobel Peace Prize.

Violence spread throughout the Congo. On November 11, troops of the regular Congolese Army, nominally under United Nations supervision, looted a United Nations base and murdered thirteen Italian aircrew members. Another Security Council resolution authorized the United Nations' new Burmese Secretary-General, U Thant, to take 'vigorous action, including the use of the requisite measure of force' to restore the rule of law and the non-violent ascendancy of the Congolese authorities. Tshombe agreed to begin talks with the central government on December 20, and accepted Katanga's subordinate status within the Congo.

By the end of the year more than a thousand Congolese were being trained under United Nations supervision in public health and medicine. Under United Nations' auspices schools were reopened, teaching materials brought in, and teachers trained. Public works programmes were set up with United Nations guidance to relieve unemployment. There was also severe hunger to be tackled in areas where the fighting had been fiercest. At the beginning of the year 200 people were dying each day of starvation. Within three months United Nations relief efforts reduced this to fewer than twenty a week.

On April 12 a Soviet air force pilot, Major Yuri Gagarin, orbited the Earth in an artificial satellite. His single orbit was a triumph for Soviet rocketry and a blow to the morale of the United States, which saw it as evidence of Soviet superiority. Frantic efforts began in the United States to emulate Gagarin's exploit. This came three weeks later when, on May 5, a United States navy pilot, Commander Alan B. Shepard, was catapulted into space in a *Mercury* space capsule on top of a rocket. Unlike Gagarin's flight, Shepard's was sub-orbital and short: fifteen minutes in time and 115 miles in distance. By contrast, Gagarin had orbited the Earth. But Shepard's achievement, which on Kennedy's instructions had been broadcast live on radio and television, provided a boost in national morale. On May 25 Kennedy announced that the United States must take 'a clearly leading role in space achievements, which in many ways may hold the key to our future on Earth', so much so that it would become 'a major national commitment' to put a man on the Moon, and to bring him safely back to Earth – and to do so before the end of the decade.

On June 5, immediately following talks between Kennedy and Khrushchev in Vienna, it was announced on the President's authority that 'if NATO forces are about to be overwhelmed by non-nuclear attack from Communist bloc countries, NATO would respond with nuclear weapons'. In recognition of the emergence of West Germany as an integral part of the Western defence system, the United States agreed to supply the West German army with short-range missiles

– the nuclear warhead of which could hit a target seventy miles away – as well as 400-mile and 700-mile range missiles. The nuclear warheads of all these missiles would remain, however, under American control. In November, a German Admiral was given command of all NATO forces in the Baltic.

The contrast between the Western and Communist ideologies was highlighted on June 16, when Rudolf Nureyev, a twenty-three-year-old Soviet ballet dancer touring with the Kirov Ballet in Paris, sought asylum in France. Two weeks earlier, during his meeting with Kennedy in Vienna, Khrushchev had produced a memorandum insisting that the German question must be 'settled' that year and a peace treaty signed. If this were not done, control of access to West Berlin would be handed over by the Soviets to the East German authorities. The East German leader, Walter Ulbricht, added a few days later that after any German peace treaty, all air and military traffic to West Berlin would also come under East German control.

On July 25 Kennedy spoke on American television about the Berlin crisis. 'We cannot and will not permit the Communists to drive us out of Berlin, either gradually or by force,' he said. 'We do not want to fight, but we have fought before. And others in earlier times have made the same dangerous mistake that the West was too selfish and too soft and too divided to resist invasions of freedom in other lands.'

Within East Germany, the hardships and tyranny of Communist rule were taking their toll on morale. By the end of July the influx of East Germans through Berlin to the West had reached 4,000 a week. Many were skilled workers, and most of them were young. On August 12 more than 2,400 crossed into West Berlin, the largest number so far. It was clear that, with the Berlin zonal borders having no effective physical barriers – only check points – the number of those leaving would continue to grow.

On August 13, East German troops and police took up positions along the whole length of the Soviet Zone border inside the city. That same night the East German authorities began building a brick and concrete wall between East and West Berlin. The Western governments responsible for the British, French and American sectors of the city protested to Moscow in a joint note four days later. The

Soviet government rejected the protest within twenty-four hours, as the American Vice-President, Lyndon Johnson, flew to Berlin to deliver a message from Kennedy that the United States 'guaranteed' the continual freedom of the people of West Berlin. In order to test Communist intentions Kennedy ordered a convoy of armed troops to be sent from western Germany along one of the access roads to West Berlin that traversed East Germany. It was not molested.

On September 1 the Soviet Union exploded a Hydrogen bomb. A truce in place for more than a year was unilaterally broken. On the following day, at a meeting of the Non-Aligned nations in Belgrade, Jawaharlal Nehru warned of 'a danger of war coming nearer by the Soviet Government's decision to resume nuclear tests'. The testing of several more Soviet H-bombs followed. The United States responded by announcing on September 5 that it would also resume testing its H-bombs, though it would do so, it said, underground, where the bombs and their aftermath would be rendered 'innocuous'. It was to take more than forty years before the harmful radiation impact of underground testing became public knowledge.

On September 25, at the General Assembly of the United Nations, Kennedy called for the abolition of nuclear weapons 'before they abolish us'. Disarmament was no longer a dream, he said, but 'a practical matter of life and death'. He wished to challenge the Soviet Union 'not to an arms race but to a peace race', and not only in the sphere of nuclear weapons but 'step by step, stage by stage, until general and complete disarmament has actually been achieved'. The United States was willing to accept 'effective international control'. The first step should be to end all nuclear tests.

The Soviet Union baulked at the idea of international control. On October 1 it began a series of tests in the Arctic. The H-bomb which was exploded in the atmosphere on October 9 was estimated to be almost as powerful as the most powerful United States bomb of 1 March 1954: fifteen megatons. On October 23 there was a further explosion, so strong that ground and air shock waves were felt in Sweden, Denmark, Norway, France and West Germany. British atomic research experts described it as 'significantly larger than any previously recorded'. It was a fifty-megaton bomb. 'The device today,' wrote *The Times*, 'generated the greatest explosive force ever produced by man.'

On October 27, as Radio Peking broadcast a fall-out warning to all major cities in China, the United Nations General Assembly appealed to the Soviet Union not to carry out its publicized intention to explode another Hydrogen bomb in the atmosphere before the end of the month. Three days later the bomb was exploded. On November 24 the General Assembly declared that the use of thermo-nuclear weapons was 'contrary to the spirit, letter, and aims of the United Nations, and as such, a direct violation of the Charter'.

Endangering life and saving life went side by side. On December 15 it was announced by the United Nations that of the 1,336 million people who two decades earlier had been at risk from malaria, 298 million were 'free from the scourge' and a further 612 million protected by the eradication programmes. As for plague, which at the start of the century had killed millions of people, particularly in India, the recorded death toll worldwide was a mere 360. Smallpox too was on the wane, with the 498,000 cases recorded a decade earlier having fallen to 60,000 in 1961.

The United States was steadily improving its military power. In February 1962 Robert McNamara, Secretary of Defence, told a news conference that the United States had a 'second strike' nuclear retaliatory capacity greater than the 'first strike' of any other country. This meant that however severe the first nuclear attack might be, the United States would be the victor in the second stage.

In South Vietnam, America's economic and military presence was growing. By the end of the year there were 10,000 United States servicemen there, training local troops in their struggle against the Vietminh, and providing logistic support for military action against the Vietminh. American soldiers were also in combat. In October it was announced in Washington that forty-six Americans had been killed in the previous nine months while serving in South Vietnam.

After the Soviet Union had exploded more than fifty nuclear devices in the atmosphere during a period of nine months – an average of one every five days – Kennedy authorized the resumption of American tests. The first one took place on April 25, in the Pacific

Ocean, near two American possessions, Johnston Island and Christmas Island. On July 9 an H-bomb was detonated 200 miles above Johnston Island. It was the equivalent of two million tons of TNT. The flash of the explosion was so intense that it was seen in New Zealand, 4,000 miles away.

On October 16 Kennedy was brought an astonishing intelligence report. On September 10 an American reconnaissance aircraft had photographed building activity in a remote part of Cuba. Further photographs taken on October 14 showed medium-range missiles already in position. These had a capacity to carry nuclear warheads, and a range of more than a thousand miles. This would put Texas, Oklahoma and Arkansas within range. Washington – Kennedy's White House – was only 1,100 miles from the Cuban capital. At several Cuban airfields, Soviet bombers were identified, of a type that was capable of carrying nuclear bombs. In the photographs these bombers could be seen being uncrated. They had arrived by sea. Other photographs showed sites being prepared to receive even longer-range missiles.

For the six days after Kennedy was shown these photographs, a remarkable exercise in secret diplomacy took place. To prevent anything approaching Soviet missile readiness, he wanted the total elimination of the Cuban missile sites before they could be made operational. His military advisers – trained in the art of possible scenarios – warned him that to attack the sites could precipitate a nuclear war. This could develop, they said, if either of the effective methods of attacking the sites were carried out: an American invasion of Cuba, or the bombing of the missile sites.

Kennedy chose a third course, a naval blockade of Cuba. If this blockade did not force the Soviets to remove the missiles, he was prepared to contemplate direct military action. American intelligence showed more than twenty-five Soviet, or Soviet-chartered ships on their way to Cuba, many of them inevitably bringing equipment to make the missile bases operational. On October 22 Kennedy spoke on television to the American people, reporting for the first time on the presence of the missile sites and the imminent imposition of the blockade – the word 'quarantine' was used instead of blockade, to avoid repercussion in international law, where the legality of blockading a sovereign State could be challenged. The American aim, Kennedy said, was 'to prevent the use of these missiles against this or any other country, and to secure their withdrawal or elimination from the Western hemisphere'.

All ships on their way to Cuba would be stopped and searched. Only those not carrying offensive weaponry would be allowed to proceed. From Moscow came a warning that 'no State which values its independence' could accept the blockade. In secret, Kennedy gave orders that any Russian ship seeking to break the blockade should be sunk.

The United States blockade went into effect on October 24, when several Soviet ships known to be carrying jet warplanes and other weapons altered course to avoid the American naval patrols and abandoned their Cuban destinations. On October 25 the first Soviet ship to reach the American patrols was stopped. It was an oil tanker, and, as it was carrying only oil, was allowed to proceed to Cuba. A day later Kennedy was shown further American air reconnaissance photographs showing work on the missile sites continuing. Talks in Washington that day focused on the possibility of direct attacks on the missile sites. As the tension rose an American reconnaissance plane was shot down over Cuba and its pilot killed.

How far the Soviet Union was prepared to risk a direct American attack on the missile sites without retaliation was not known. But on October 27, in what appeared to be a face-saving suggestion, Khrushchev proposed that in exchange for the withdrawal of Soviet air bases in Cuba, the United States would remove its air bases in Turkey. Kennedy rejected this, but wrote a moderately worded letter to Khrushchev, in which he described as 'generally acceptable' the Cuban side of the Soviet proposal: that the United States would end its quarantine and guarantee the 'territorial integrity' of Communist Cuba, in return for the removal of the Soviet bases in Cuba. These would have to be removed, Kennedy wrote, under United Nations supervision, and work on the missile sites would have to stop 'immediately'. If Khrushchev were to give instructions along these lines 'there is no reason why we should not be able to complete these arrangements and announce them to the world within a couple of days'. Were the crisis not to be resolved on these lines, however, it 'would surely lead', Kennedy warned, 'to an intensification of the Cuban crisis and a grave risk to the peace of the world'.

On October 28 Khrushchev backed down. He would, he said, remove all Russian missiles, bombers and troops from Cuba. The United States could inspect all departing Soviet ships to ensure that the missiles were being removed. Within a few days forty-two missiles passed through the American quarantine and back to Russia. On November 21 the Soviet Union agreed to remove from Cuba all its bombers capable of carrying nuclear warheads. On the following day Kennedy announced the end of the naval blockade. He had confronted the Soviet Union, and forced it to back down.

Negotiations between France and Algeria had opened at Evian on 7 March 1962 between Mohammed Ahmed Ben Bella, the founder of the Algerian National Liberation Front (FLN) and de Gaulle's confidant, Georges Pompidou – who would soon become French Prime Minister. Agreement was reached eleven days later. A cease-fire would come into effect the following day at midday. French troops would withdraw, and there would be a referendum on self-determination. The European Algerians would be able to 'keep their French nationality and return to France whenever they liked'. If they decided to stay in Algeria they would have to choose 'at the end of three years, either to remain French, in which case their linguistic, cultural and religious rights as a foreign minority in Algeria would be respected, or else to become Algerian citizens, in which case they would have minority representation at both local and national levels, in proportion to their numbers'.

Opposition to Algerian independence from the *Organization de l'Armée Secrète* (the OAS) was immediate and violent. There were terrorist bomb attacks not only in Algeria but in metropolitan France. A car bomb in Paris killed two policemen. In response, there were large anti-OAS demonstrations, in which university students took a leading part. As many as 1,200 OAS members were arrested and held in prison. Two attempts to murder de Gaulle were foiled. During one of them, on a road three miles outside Paris, shots were fired.

The Algerian referendum was held on July 1. The result was

decisive: 5,993,754 voters opted for independence and only 16,478 opposed it. Hardly any Europeans opposed to independence cast their vote. The new government entered Algiers on July 3. But the resentment by extremist Europeans, and the excess of zeal of extremist Muslims, led two days later to a day of violence in Oran during which more than a hundred Europeans were killed. This was followed by the kidnapping of more than 500 Europeans suspected of sympathy with the OAS. Some were tortured and then released; others were never seen again. European homes were looted and cars destroyed. By the end of the year 800,000 Europeans – 80 per cent of the total – had left. Within a year of independence, all French-owned estates in Algeria were nationalized. Travelling to New York, Ben Bella was present at the United Nations when Algeria was admitted as the 109th member.

In South Africa, after the government had withdrawn a year earlier from the Commonwealth and established South Africa as an independent Republic, a law was passed on May 12 imposing the death penalty for all acts of sabotage. A few months later it became a criminal offence to publish anything said or written by white or black journalists whose works had been banned. Regulations were also put in force under which those banned from speaking or writing could be held under house arrest for five years, could not use the telephone, could not receive visitors and could not communicate with any other banned person. By the end of the year, eighteen such orders had been issued.

Among the leaders of the black South Africans who were arrested was Nelson Mandela. He was sentenced to five years in prison on conviction for having incited workers to strike, and leaving the country 'without valid documents'.

In south-east Europe, NATO had begun to give economic aid to both Greece and Turkey. NATO's opposite number, the Warsaw Treaty Organization, held its spring manoeuvres in Hungary, when Soviet, Roumanian and Hungarian forces, under the watchful eye of the Soviet Defence Minister, participated in 'a simulated attack with tactical atomic weapons'. Autumn manoeuvres were held in East Germany, with Soviet, East German and Czechoslovak forces taking part. In October there were yet more manoeuvres along the border between Poland and East Germany, in which East German, Polish and again Soviet forces participated. During these manoeuvres it was made clear to the West that the armed forces of East Germany were as much an integral part of the Warsaw Pact's military preparations as West Germany's forces were within NATO. The military forces of each multi-Power grouping were commanded by a Soviet and an American general respectively.

Tension did not have to escalate without some counter-measure. On 5 April 1963 the Soviet Union agreed to set up a telephonic 'hot line' whereby Kennedy and Khrushchev could talk directly in the event of a renewed crisis. The search for an agreement to ban nuclear testing continued. Hitherto agreement had proved impossible because of the Soviet refusal to allow on-site inspection. This refusal was circumvented by excluding underground tests from the ban. All tests above ground, which experts on both sides of the divide recognized as extremely contaminating, were to be banned: they could be monitored from afar. The agreement was signed on June 20. It constituted a breakthrough which created a sense of relief among those millions who feared both the possibility of a nuclear war and the poisoning of the atmosphere through nuclear testing. With it went an agreement that more than any other pulled the divided world back from the brink: to prevent a surprise attack from space, both sides agreed not to fire nuclear weapons into orbit around the earth.

Inside the Soviet Union, Khrushchev continued to assert the primacy of the Communist Party and its methods. On March 8 he told a conference of Party officials that the era of the purges had been 'creative', and urged writers to treat controversial areas of Soviet history 'with restraint'. The poet Yevgeny Yevtushenko was made to apologize for his 'immodesty' in writing about the suffering exacted by the Bolshevik Revolution in 1917: his account had been published in the French weekly newspaper *L'Exprèss*. The death penalty for 'economic crimes', which Khrushchev had instituted a year earlier, continued to be imposed amid considerable internal publicity intended to act as a deterrent. Most of the hundred people executed were officials and 'speculators' from the non-Russian Republics, and

Russian Jews. Only when Bertrand Russell protested directly to Khrushchev were the death penalties abandoned. But the party continued to point the finger at Jews as an 'unreliable' element in society.

In Poland, large numbers of students in religious academies were called up for military service – from which they had hitherto been exempted – and many convent schools were closed down. For three days there were riots in the south-eastern town of Przemysl when the authorities took over a convent school being used to train church organists. But the anti-clerical measures continued, as the Party sought to assert its ascendancy. Bishops wishing to attend the Ecumenical Council in Rome were refused permission to leave Poland.

In Czechoslovakia, on May Day, a group of youngsters were arrested in Prague for chanting anti-government slogans. Denounced by the authorities as 'hooligans', the demonstrators were sentenced to up to three years in prison. A teenage girl who was refused the right to study textile designing was told that it was because her parents had escaped abroad when she was three months old, leaving her with her grandparents. University graduates were told that they had to spend a minimum of three years after graduation at a 'basic place of work' – a factory or building site, collective farm or agricultural co-operative. Archbishop Beran, and four other Catholic bishops, released from prison after twelve years incarceration, were forbidden to resume their ecclesiastical or pastoral work.

On June 4 the Ayatollah ('sign of God') Khomeini was arrested for preaching against the rule of the Shah. Part of the Ayatollah's anger was directed against plans proposed by the Shah for the social and political emancipation of women. The Ayatollah's arrest led to protest demonstrations in the capital, Teheran, and other Iranian cities. The Shah sent him into exile: he went first to Turkey, then to Iraq and finally to Paris, where he formed a focal point for Iranian religious conservatism.

For the rulers and military commanders of South Vietnam, United States financial aid and military advisers played an essential part in enabling the confrontation between North and South to continue without the North winning repeated advantage. But on January

25, *Life* magazine carried its first major Vietnam war coverage, a fourteen-page spread critical of American involvement. The article was headed: 'We Wade Deeper into Jungle War'. The photographs made no attempt to glamorize the war: they focused on dirt and grime, suffering and pain.

On September 2 Kennedy made a strong attack on the Saigon government's repressive anti-Buddhist measures. Only 'with changes in policy and perhaps of personnel' could confidence in South Vietnam be restored, he said. When General de Gaulle proposed turning Vietnam into a 'unified, neutral State', however, Kennedy replied that he would not support any call for the withdrawal of American troops from Vietnam until the Communist guerrilla movement there had been 'crushed'. That year more than eighty American soldiers were killed, mostly while helping to drive the Vietcong out of what were designated 'strategic hamlets' in the south.

The independence of West Germany, and of West Berlin, had become an integral part of United States policy. The line of the Iron Curtain as it ran though Germany constituted the most westerly advance of Soviet power. The United States, as a former occupying power, embraced West Germany as a frontline ally in the confrontation with Communism. On June 23 Kennedy began a five-day journey through West Germany which included a visit to Berlin. Everywhere he went he repeated the assurance: 'We shall risk our cities to defend yours.' American troops would remain in Europe for 'as long' as they were needed for its defence. In West Berlin he visited the Berlin Wall, and then told 150,000 ecstatic onlookers: 'All free men . . . are citizens of Berlin. And therefore, as a free man, I take pride in the words, '*Ich bin ein Berliner.*' Four months later, the American Secretary of State Dean Rusk told an audience in Frankfurt that six American divisions would be kept in West Germany for as long as they were needed there.

In South Africa, a climax to the government's measures to curb protest and dissent came on July 12, when security police surrounded a house in Rivonia, a Johannesburg suburb. Six whites and twelve non-whites were seized, among them Walter Sisulu, former head of the banned African National Congress. Also brought to trial that year was Nelson Mandela, who had already been arrested the previous year and sentenced to five years in prison. At his new trial he was sentenced to life imprisonment. His place of incarceration was Robben Island, a maximum security prison from which there was no escape. Mandela was the 466th prisoner to be admitted to Robben Island that year. He was forty-six years old, and was not to be released for twenty-six years.

Within the United States the pace of civil rights activities accelerated, as blacks found a powerful voice in Martin Luther King, and a receptive ear in President Kennedy. The year 1963 marked the hundredth anniversary of Lincoln's Emancipation Proclamation, offering an end to slavery. On February 28, when Kennedy asked Congress to grant him wide-ranging powers to introduce civil rights legislation in voting, education and employment, he pointed out that a black person in the United States had about half as much chance as a white person to become a professional; that he had the prospect of earning only half as much as his white counterpart; and that his life expectancy was seven years less. Racial bias, Kennedy warned, marred 'the atmosphere of a united and classless society in which this nation rose to greatness'.

Training programmes were set up, and employers and schools were urged to accept the new equality. But there was much resistance, even in cities outside the South which had large black populations, among them New York, Chicago and Los Angeles, where the demand for school integration and equality of employment was as strong as in the South. In the summer several hundred blacks were arrested in New York when they tried to prevent people entering or leaving a medical centre building site, hoping to call attention to the need for more black workers in the construction industry.

In the South, Martin Luther King led a campaign against segregation, choosing Birmingham, Alabama, for the focus of his protest. It was, he said, the 'most thoroughly segregated big city in the United States'. Starting in April there were daily protest marches through the city, and each day the city authorities arrested some of the marchers.

When two black students tried to enrol at the University of

Alabama at Tuscaloosa, the Governor of Alabama, George Wallace, himself barred their way at the entrance. But on June 11, as Kennedy insisted that Federal laws be obeyed, the commander of the Federalized National Guard ordered Wallace to stand aside, and the two students were enrolled. The troops of the National Guard had been used, Kennedy explained, to enforce a Federal court order to ensure the admission to university of 'two clearly qualified young Alabama residents who happened to be born Negro'. Every American, Kennedy declared, should 'stop and examine his conscience about this and other related incidents'.

In presenting his Civil Rights Bill to Congress on June 19, Kennedy urged that policies based on race and on racial discrimination had no place in American life. On August 28, as the Bill was being debated, black leaders organized a march on Washington. More than 200,000 people took part. From the steps of the Lincoln Memorial, Martin Luther King spoke of his dream that the inequalities would pass away: 'I have a dream that one day this nation will rise up and live out the true meaning of its creed: "We hold these truths to be self-evident, that all men are created equal".'

To Kennedy's intense disappointment the Republican-dominated House of Representatives Rules Committee prevented any progress on the Civil Rights Bill for the rest of that year. He did succeed in pushing through social measures to help college building, medical schools and vocational training, but two other Bills on which he had set his sights, the reduction of taxation and the provision of medical care for the elderly, continued to be blocked by the Republicans.

With elections less than a year ahead, on November 17 Kennedy went to Florida, where he was much encouraged by the enthusiastic crowds that greeted him wherever he went. From Florida he flew to Texas, a State which he had won in 1960 by only a small margin of votes, and where his presence would clearly help the next year's Democratic campaign. With him was his wife Jacqueline: it was her first public appearance since the death of their prematurely born son Patrick three months earlier. On November 21 they were in San Antonio and in Houston, where enthusiastic crowds cheered their motorcade. That evening they flew to Fort Worth, where they spent the night. So large was the crowd outside their hotel the next morning

– an estimated 10,000 people – that before breakfast Kennedy wandered through it, and then made an impromptu speech from an improvised platform. Pondering the East-West divide and the problems of seeking détente with deterrence, he told the crowd: 'No one expects our life to be easy, in this very dangerous and uncertain world . . . I don't think we are fatigued or tired. The balance of power is still on the side of the free.'

From Fort Worth the Kennedys flew to Dallas, where they had originally intended to drive directly from the airport to the Trade Mart, where Kennedy was to make a speech to a luncheon meeting. But because of the gathering, as in Fort Worth, of large and enthusiastic crowds, he agreed to a change of plan, and to drive through the centre of the city. During the drive he was shot by a lone and deranged assassin. He died in hospital half an hour later. The announcement of his death sent shock waves throughout the United States and the free world.

Kennedy's body was flown back to Washington. With it on the plane was his wife Jacqueline and the Vice-Present, Lyndon Johnson. On board the aircraft Johnson was sworn in as President of the United States, the oath of office being administered by a Federal Judge, Sarah Hughes, who was in tears throughout the brief ceremony. As the shock waves of Kennedy's assassination reverberated, Johnson had to grapple with many unfinished items of Congressional and national business. In pushing ahead with Kennedy's Civil Rights Bill, he told the Senate – in which the Republicans continued their stiff opposition – that no memorial or eulogy could 'more eloquently honour President Kennedy's memory' than the swift passage of the Bill.

Johnson set his heart on social reform. On his first night as President, unable to sleep, he outlined to his assistants how he would 'revolutionize' America with Federal aid to education on an even greater scale than Kennedy had secured. He would bring in tax cuts to help business, cuts of the sort that Kennedy had failed to secure. He would push the Civil Rights Bill into law and secure important conservation programmes. Yet Vietnam could not be put aside. On November 24, the day before Kennedy's funeral, Johnson told a group of advisers he was determined not to 'lose Vietnam'. In a memorandum for the National Security Council he stated that the

United States' aim, as under Kennedy, was to help the South Vietnamese to 'win their contest against externally directed and supported
Communist conspiracy'.

The American Joint Chiefs of Staff were confident they could
bring about South Vietnamese successes by 'more forceful moves'.
The air force commander, General Curtis LeMay, wanted American
bombing of North Vietnam. As he expressed it: 'We are swatting
flies when we should be going after the manure pile.'

Johnson had to stand for election at the end of 1964. At a
reception in the White House on Christmas Eve, 1963, he told the
Joint Chiefs: 'Just you get me elected, and then you can have your
war.'

The Berlin Wall, which had been under construction for more than
a year, was finally completed on 5 January 1964, and East Berlin
was sealed off from the West of the city. Until that date, more than
a million East Berliners and East Germans had crossed to the West.
With the wall in place, the East German police showed no compunction in shooting dead anyone who attempted to scale it.

The confrontation between East and West which the Berlin Wall
represented did not prevent President Johnson from proposing a
decrease in defence spending. His aim, he explained on January 8,
was to 'liberate the energies of the nation' for domestic reforms, of
which Civil Rights was central, and the elimination of poverty the
most urgent. There must, he said, be an 'unconditional war on poverty', and to launch it he called for a budget of little under $1,000
million. As the war on poverty received Congressional endorsement,
it was revealed that three days before he was assassinated, Kennedy
had asked his advisers to draft for him a programme against poverty.

The Civil Rights Bill passed the final stage on June 19, a year
to the day since Kennedy had sent it to Congress. The new bill
was a revolutionary document, recognizing without prevarication the
rights of black Americans to equality, and to protection of their
rights as citizens. 'Refusal of service' on racial grounds was made
illegal in all hotels, motels, restaurants, petrol stations, libraries,
parks, swimming pools, golf courses and stadiums. Discrimination
was also forbidden in any programme that was in receipt of Federal

assistance, or by any employer or union with a hundred or more employees.

Johnson achieved other wide-ranging social reforms. A Food Stamp Act substantially widened the provision of food to the poor and destitute. An Economic Opportunity Act increased educational opportunities for poor children and he established a domestic peace corps, Volunteers in Service to America (VISTA).

In Vietnam the military government in Saigon remained committed to destroying the political influence and military prowess of the Vietcong. On February 2 Johnson renewed the pledge he had given earlier, and Kennedy before him, that the United States would continue to give military aid against the Communist insurgency. But he hesitated to become more deeply involved in Vietnam, and through a Canadian citizen, J. Blair Seaborn, the chief Canadian delegate to the International Control Commission in Vietnam, proposed a deescalation of the conflict to Ho Chi Minh. If the North Vietnamese agreed to end their support for the Vietnamese Communists in the South, the United States would provide North Vietnam with economic aid, and even with diplomatic recognition. If such a deescalation was not acceptable, Johnson warned, the United States would be prepared to contemplate naval and air attacks on North Vietnam.

The negotiations failed. During the spring Johnson announced that the number of American advisers in South Vietnam, many of whom were taking part in the actual combat, would be increased from 15,000 to 20,000. The new men arrived just as the Vietcong embarked on their most effective long-term strategy, the creation of a supply line from north to south, the Ho Chi Minh Trail, which would avoid the Demilitarized Zone (the DMZ) by running through neighbouring Laos, and cutting back across the Laotian border into South Vietnam. The trail was built by engineers using modern Chinese and Soviet equipment. Its roads and bridges could carry trucks laden with supplies. Along its 500-mile length, underground barracks, workshops, hospitals, fuel depots and storage were built, essentially safe from aerial bombardment. By the end of 1964 as many as 10,000 North Vietnamese troops had used the trail to penetrate the south, and take up positions around most southern towns.

As the Vietcong infiltrated more and more effectively into the south, Johnson contemplated bombing their supply lines. This was a relatively easy task on paper. A glance at the map showed where the supply lines ran. But in many areas they were hidden under a canopy of dense foliage, and constructed so that the depots, staging posts and even troop concentrations would not be visible from the air, or indeed from a few hundred yards away on the ground.

A draft resolution was ready in June, giving Johnson authority to commit United States forces to the defence of any nation in South-East Asia threatened by Communist 'aggression or subversion'. An opportunity came on August 2, after a secret South Vietnamese raid against North Vietnam in which a United States destroyer, the *Maddox*, took part. Three Vietcong torpedo boats attacked the *Maddox* while it was in international waters off the coast of North Vietnam. The attack on the *Maddox* provided Johnson with his opportunity. His resolution – known as the Gulf of Tonkin resolution – was debated by Congress on August 6 and 7. A Democratic Senator, Ernest Gruening of Alaska, warned that 'all Vietnam is not worth the life of a single American boy'. Wayne Morse of Oregon declared that 'the place to settle the controversy is not on the battlefield but around the conference table'. When the vote was taken, only Morse and Gruening opposed the resolution. In the House of Representatives the vote in favour was unanimous.

Immediately following the passage of the resolution, American bombers attacked five North Vietnamese coastal installations. Four patrol boats and an oil installation were hit. In an address to the American people Johnson made it clear that the United States, while prepared to limit its retaliatory actions, would not allow itself to be attacked without effective military reaction. At the same time, in secret, he continued his attempt to persuade the North Vietnamese to pull back from war on the basis of the proposals already submitted through the Canadian mediator, J. Blair Seaborn, under which North Vietnam would receive 'economic and other benefits' in return for giving up its support for the Communist insurgency in the south. But if they continued to support the southern insurgents they would 'suffer the consequences'. The North Vietnamese rejected what they saw as a solution dominated by a threat. They also felt that victory was within their grasp.

On November 3, Johnson was returned in triumph to the White House which he had entered – unelected – after Kennedy's assassination a year earlier. He had defeated his Republican challenger, Senator Goldwater, with the highest proportion of votes – sixteen million – ever secured by a Presidential candidate. The Democrat majority in both Houses gave Johnson a power for legislative action that was virtually unchallengeable. With regard to Vietnam, however, he hesitated to take the action many of his advisers were advocating – to land American combat troops, as opposed to advisers, in the South, and to send American bombers against the North.

In Britain, a new Labour government, headed by Harold Wilson, came into office on October 16, pledged to move Britain forward into the age of modern science and technology. The government also reflected similar social reform concerns to those of Johnson in the United States. Among one of Wilson's first measures was the provision of free medical prescriptions.

While the United States found itself more and more deeply drawn into the Vietnamese quagmire, the Soviet Union struggled to balance its enormous spending on defence with the economic needs of its often deprived citizens. Chaos seemed to loom when, with unexpected swiftness, opposition to Khrushchev crystalized at the highest level of the Communist Party hierarchy. Khrushchev's overbearing manner, his crude authoritarianism, and above all the failure of the Virgin Lands project, in which he had invested so much energy with so little return, were crucial factors. One catalyst was his indication to his closest and most senior colleagues that he was about to put forward another plan to reorganize agriculture. They did not want more upheaval, or more failure. While Khrushchev was on holiday on the Black Sea coast, the colleagues in whom he had confided his new agricultural plans met and plotted against him. When he returned unexpectedly to Moscow he found that the Praesidium of the Communist Party – including those who were his nominees – had turned against him. He demanded the right to address the full

Central Committee, but when he spoke to it on October 14 he was unable to secure a majority, and resigned.

Khrushchev was succeeded as First Secretary of the Communist Party by Leonid Brezhnev, one of those most eager to see him ousted. The new Chairman of the Council of Ministers – effectively Prime Minister of the Soviet Union – was Aleksei Kosygin. A few days after Khrushchev's fall a forty-page document was circulated to Communist Party organizations listing twenty-nine reasons for his demise. Among the charges were 'nepotism', 'rude personal behaviour', the encouragement of a 'personality cult' – the very charge of which he had earlier accused Stalin – the arbitrary dismissal of officials, 'errors' during the Cuban missile crisis, including the sending of Soviet missiles to Cuba, 'gross errors' in economic planning and the failure to monitor Chinese scientific progress – a failure, if such it was, that was given striking immediacy on October 16 – the day after his public ousting – when the Chinese exploded their first atom bomb.

In sport, the East-West rivalry reached a climax during the Olympic Games in Tokyo, when the United States won thirty-six gold medals and the Soviet Union thirty. For the first time, television pictures of the Games – or of any sporting event – were sent by an experimental relay system by satellite, from Tokyo, via space, to the United States, where they could be transmitted locally. From the United States, one set of film was transferred to Europe by jet plane. But the main importance of the games was the re-emergence of Japan, which since its defeat almost two decades earlier had lived with the shame of its wartime record. The games were opened by the Emperor Hirohito: the man who had agreed to his country's surrender in 1945. Ninety-four nations paraded their athletes before him. This was the first Olympic Games to be held in Asia, fulfilling Japan's desire for Asian paramountcy, not in the political or military spheres, but in the sporting arena. Pride came too as Japan won the third largest number of gold medals – sixteen. In its domestic economy, Japan continued to make impressive strides, with forty per cent of the world's shipping being built in Japanese shipyards.

*   *   *

On Christmas Eve, in Saigon, Vietcong terrorists exploded a bomb in Brinks Hotel, where American advisers were staying. Two Americans were killed and more than fifty injured. Under the Gulf of Tonkin resolution – and with his massive electoral majority – Johnson could have taken retaliatory action. He refrained from doing so, not wanting to 'jar' the American public during the holiday season. The Vietcong had no such inhibitions. They were already carrying out attacks on villages in the South: one of them, attacked in December, was a Catholic village, Binh Gia, forty miles south-east of Saigon: less than an hour's drive from the capital.

On December 28, as a gesture of defiance and assurance, Binh Gia was occupied by the Vietcong for eight hours. Five days later a South Vietnamese army unit was ambushed near the village and destroyed. As the battle for Binh Gia continued, almost 200 South Vietnamese troops were killed, as were five American advisers. There was a limit to how long Johnson could resist the mounting clamour from his generals and advisers for more decisive action. His own mind was not averse to moving the war into a higher gear, though he had repeatedly hesitated, realizing that the American public might not be ready for too dramatic a gesture. When, in the aftermath of the Brinks Hotel bomb and the Binh Gia attacks, the American Ambassador in Saigon, General Taylor, advocated air strikes against the North – a solution favoured by many of Johnson's advisers – it was Johnson who, in his reply to the ambassador, indicated an even greater American entanglement. 'I have never felt that this war will be won from the air,' Johnson wrote, 'and it seems to me that what is much more needed and would be more effective is a larger and stronger use of rangers and special forces and marines, or other appropriate military strength on the ground and on the scene.' Johnson added that this 'might involve the acceptance of larger American casualties', but insisted: 'I myself am ready to substantially increase the number of Americans in Vietnam if it is necessary to provide this kind of fighting force against the Vietcong.' The die was being cast.

The Soviet Union had no such entanglements as were beginning to draw the Americans into a distant land and a military quagmire. Their control over Eastern Europe was complete and unchallenged: it seemed to many Western observers to be unchallengeable. Considerable progress was also being made to establish Soviet influence outside Europe. In April, after President Ben Bella of Algeria visited Moscow, a Soviet-Algerian pact for economic and technological co-operation was signed. Indonesia and India both signed agreements that year for arms supplies from the Soviet Union. From Cuba, President Castro visited Moscow and signed a new Soviet-Cuban trade agreement. President Nasser of Egypt was made a Hero of the Soviet Union; the Soviets, as well as making a substantial loan to Egypt, offered support with regard to the Arab-Israel conflict 'in conformity with the legitimate rights of the Arabs'. Soviet arms and military equipment began to flow to Egypt, at first slowly but then with increasing momentum, creating alarm inside Israel that a time would soon come when Egypt would be tempted to invade.

In Poland, censorship was tightened and stricter rules applied to the allocation of paper needed by magazines that might criticize the Communist regime. In Czechoslovakia there were clashes in the streets of Prague between young people and the security forces; arrests and imprisonments followed. There was Communist Party criticism of what was called the 'alarming lack of interest' in Communism among university graduates intending to become teachers. Inside the Soviet Union, discrimination against Jews affected school, university and commercial life, but emigration was virtually impossible.

On the morning of 16 October 1964 the Chinese Government exploded a nuclear device in the atmosphere. Under the previous year's Test Ban Treaty, such tests had been banned by the Soviet Union, the United States and Britain. The fallout of the Chinese test reached western Canada on the morning of October 19 and spread during the following three days to the Great Lakes, the Mississippi valley, Florida, the Atlantic seaboard of the United States and the St Lawrence river.

The United States responded with an underground nuclear test, permitted under the treaty. It was carried out in Mississippi, one of the areas affected by the Chinese fallout.

In 1964 the United States Surgeon General issued a report that confirmed the link between smoking and lung cancer and disease.

On the positive side, drugs were being developed to facilitate organ grafting. That year's Nobel Prize for Chemistry went to Dorothy Hodgkin of Oxford University, who had determined the structure of cholesterol.

Two musicals that were to give pleasure for years to come had their premieres in New York in 1964: *Hello, Dolly!* and *Fiddler on the Roof.* That year the Beatles made their first tour of the United States, as did their fellow British group the Rolling Stones. For millions of people, popular culture eclipsed the turmoil of a world in conflict.

On 4 January 1965, President Johnson announced his aim: the creation of a Great Society. There would be medical care for the poor (Medicaid) and for the elderly (Medicare), and Federal financial support for elementary and secondary education, supplementary educational, and nutritional and health care for disadvantaged children before they enrolled in school (Head Start). Legislation included a scheme for national teachers' training, which enabled the Federal government to recruit teachers for local communities that could not afford them, and provide extra money for college classrooms and libraries. Measures were passed for air and water pollution control, and for the most ambitious Federal housing programme yet undertaken in the United States.

A centrepiece of Johnson's legislative efforts was civil rights, where the Southern States were obstructing black voter registration, despite the 1964 Act. In Selma, Alabama, there were demonstrations against the failure of the Alabama legislature to allow blacks to register, and to uphold the voting rights secured in 1964. Almost 3,000 demonstrators were arrested. On February 4 Johnson appealed to the whole country to exert 'moral pressure' on behalf of black would-be voters.

On March 9 Martin Luther King went to Selma to protest against the force used by the highway patrolmen against voting rights demonstrators. On the following day 500 marchers, among them many clergymen, were stopped by troops at the entrance to the town. The marchers knelt, prayed, and dispersed. That night three of the clergymen were attacked by white vigilantes, and one of the clergymen was killed. On March 15 Johnson insisted that blacks must be allowed to register as voters without further hindrance or delay. Using the emotive words of the civil rights movement's protest song *We Shall Overcome*, he told the legislators in Washington: 'What happened in Selma is part of a larger movement which reaches into every section and State of America. It is the effort of American Negroes to secure for themselves the full blessings of American life. Their cause must be our cause too. It is not just Negroes, but all of us. And we shall overcome.'

A new Voting Rights Bill was submitted to Congress. On March 25 a white woman, Viola Liuzzo, who had been taking civil rights workers in her car to a civil rights demonstration, was shot dead. Her killers were members of the racist Ku Klux Klan. In a defiant speech, Johnson said he would no more be intimidated by Klan terrorists than by 'terrorists' in North Vietnam.

On August 11, after a highway patrolman arrested a black driver on suspicion that he was drunk, riots broke out in Watts, a largely black suburb of Los Angeles, and more than a thousand fires were started. Thirty-four rioters were killed. A commission of enquiry found that resentment at unemployment was a major cause, as were the slum conditions in which many of the black community lived. On August 15, as the fires in Watts were still burning, the new Voting Rights Bill came into law, guaranteeing all American citizens the right to vote, whatever their colour, race or religion.

On the night of 6–7 February 1965 the Vietcong attacked an American air base in the central highlands of South Vietnam. Eight Americans were killed and ten American warplanes destroyed on the ground. Johnson retaliated at once, ordering American bombers to strike at strategic targets in North Vietnam. He did so, not by means of a declaration of war, but by virtue of the Gulf of Tonkin resolution which Congress had passed six months earlier. The first target was a North Vietnamese army camp sixty miles north of the 17th parallel that divided North and South Vietnam. Ironically, because of bad weather, this first attack was ineffective. Ten days later the first Soviet surface-to-air missiles reached the North Vietnamese port of Haiphong.

The bombing operation, devised as a one-off retaliatory strike, was replaced on Johnson's orders by a bombing programme envisaged as a continuous eight-week series of unbroken attacks. When it ended three years later the number of bombs dropped had exceeded that of all the bombs dropped in the Second World War in both Europe and Asia. The first of the new bombing attacks was carried out on March 2. Six days later the first American combat troops went ashore. Their assignment was defensive: to protect a United States air base. They were not intended to be a combat force attacking the Vietcong. But the American commander, General Westmoreland, made it clear that 'a good offence is the best defence', and began to plan accordingly, persuading Johnson that troops should patrol the countryside beyond the bases they were there to protect. It was a short step from going on patrol outside a base to opening fire on Vietcong, or suspected Vietcong.

On April 7 Johnson declared that the United States 'will not be defeated', nor would she withdraw from Vietnam either openly 'or under the cloak of a meaningless agreement'. He did, however, put forward proposals to end the conflict: including a massive aid programme for all South-East Asia, including North Vietnam, and 'unconditional discussions' on the Vietnamese conflict. The Secretary General of the United Nations, U Thant, called Johnson's proposals 'positive, forward looking, and generous'. On the following day the North Vietnamese produced proposals of their own: the United States must withdraw all its troops, arms and bases in South Vietnam. The political future of South Vietnam must be settled by the South Vietnamese people themselves, without any foreign interference, 'in accordance' with the programme of the National Front for the Liberation of South Vietnam. Vietnam must then be reunified.

Johnson could not accept what was in effect a complete surrender to North Vietnam. Eight days after the Vietnamese response he informed the American Ambassador in Saigon, General Taylor, that in addition to the continuing bombing offensive against the north, American troops would be sent out to work, not as advisers, but as an integral part of South Vietnamese army units, entering combat with them. As the American bombing continued, on May 11 the Vietcong launched a military offensive in South Vietnam. As the

South Vietnamese army reached near panic in places, American advisers took command of units that had been left without officers. General Westmoreland called for yet more American troops, telling Johnson that the South Vietnamese armed forces could not stand up to Vietcong pressure 'without substantial US combat support on the ground'. In July, Johnson announced he would multiply the number of American troops already in Vietnam tenfold.

On August 5 more than a thousand Pakistani troops crossed into Indian Kashmir. In response India sent troops into the area controlled by Pakistan. A Pakistani tank attack in the last week of August was repulsed. On September 6, Indian troops and tanks crossed into Pakistan. As fighting spread, Indian aircraft bombed Pakistani airfields and Pakistani ships shelled Indian shore bases. It was not until September 22 that the United Nations was able to secure a cease-fire. More than 3,000 Indian soldiers and at least 2,000 Pakistani soldiers had been killed. Emerging as a mediator, the Soviet Union sponsored peace talks in the Soviet Central Asian city of Tashkent. India and Pakistan withdrew their troops to the pre-war borders.

In other areas that had been under British rule the post-colonial era was turbulent. On 29 January 1965 an attempt in Malaysia by the Pan-Malayan Islamic Party to overthrow the central government was crushed. The attempted coup had been encouraged by Indonesia, which sent troops across the Malaysian border in Borneo, Sabah and Sarawak. Indonesian saboteurs tried to blow up shipping in Singapore harbour. An attempt by the Japanese Government to bring the Malaysian and Indonesian leaders together for talks in Tokyo was rebuffed by Indonesia.

Internal tensions destroyed the unity of Malaysia — itself only a recent creation. A climax came when the central government awarded Singapore an unacceptably small proportion of the textile quotas for the exports of textiles to Britain. There was anger in Singapore when it emerged that some of these quotas had been awarded for factories elsewhere in Malaysia that had not yet been built. On August 9 Singapore broke away from Malaysia to become a small, independent and eventually prosperous State. She was made a member of the United Nations 'by acclamation' on September 21.

In the former British African colony of Ghana, where the collapse of world cocoa prices, as a result of global over-production, undermined the economy, foreign loans were harder and harder to secure. Government was conducted by a single political Party, headed by Kwame Nkrumah, with no other Parties allowed to stand at elections. Economic necessity forced him to accept the intervention of the World Monetary Fund to restructure the Ghanaian economy on the basis of a drastic reduction in government spending, and a cut in the inflated price paid to cocoa farmers.

The conflict of previous years between Christians and Muslims in black Africa continued. In southern Sudan government troops launched punitive expeditions against Christian communities and several thousand black Christians were killed: many of them hacked to death. Hundreds were murdered inside the Anglican Cathedral at Juba. Similar slaughter took place in the Congo, where many Christian missionaries and members of their African congregations were killed, and others were tortured.

On February 18, Gambia, a country with a population of only 320,000, achieved independence from Britain. But the prospect of independence in Southern Rhodesia, whose white minority refused to cede power to the black majority, led on November 11 to a Unilateral Declaration of Independence (UDI) by the white political leaders under the Prime Minister, Ian Smith. The British Government under Harold Wilson struggled to persuade Smith – a Second World War fighter pilot – to withdraw from this provocative stance. But for fifteen years Smith defied all pressures – including a British oil embargo – to allow majority rule.

The fabric of Communist control in the Soviet Union and throughout Eastern Europe seemed unbreakable. A group of Communist Party dissidents in Bulgaria, with some support from the army, tried to overthrow the regime, but was crushed. In the Soviet Union Alexander Solzhenitsyn was among a number of writers attacked in the newspaper *Izvestya* for 'negativism'. The editor of *Pravda*, who came to the writer's defence, was dismissed from his post. A month later two Soviet writers, Andrei Sinyavsky and Yuly Daniel, were arrested for having smuggled their own writings out of the country for publication in the West.

While the arts remained under scrutiny and restraint, Soviet sporting and scientific endeavour were given the strongest support. On March 18 a Soviet astronaut, Lieutenant-Colonel Aleksei Leonov, became the first person to 'walk in space', emerging from his capsule for a few minutes while it was in orbit. As the space race continued an American, Major Edward White, repeated this feat within three months, leaving his space capsule and drifting alongside it, weightless in space, for twenty minutes, attached to the spacecraft by a lifeline, and able to propel himself about by means of a small hand-held jet.

Determined to put the first men on the moon, the Americans were accelerating their space launches with growing success. On March 23 a manned spacecraft was sent into orbit: the first of five to be launched in the United States that year. Its two astronauts, Virgil Grissom and John Young, were the first to manoeuvre a space ship while outside the earth's gravitational pull. On April 6 the world's first commercial communications satellite was put into orbit, 35,000 kilometres above the surface of the Earth. It could transmit both telephone calls – up to 240 simultaneous two-way conversations – and television pictures.

Chinese weapons were being sent to North Vietnam, and Chinese military engineers were employed repairing the rail links between southern China and North Vietnam that had been damaged – on the North Vietnamese side of the border – in American bombing raids. As a signal to China that a wider war could not be ruled out, the United States Secretary of State, Dean Rusk, warned that the 'idea of sanctuary is dead': that if China became involved in the conflict, United States retaliation was certain.

A second Chinese atom bomb was exploded on May 14, more powerful than the first – its strength and nature were analysed by Western scientists from the fallout, which did not respect national borders. Japan and India both protested at the test. Their protests were ignored. The Soviet Union also protested, pointing out that the test was in violation of the 1963 Test Ban Treaty on bombs exploded in the atmosphere. Its protest was likewise ignored.

Inside China, the existing system whereby all school and university students spent two months a year doing physical labour was replaced by a revised scheme, under which the time spent in fields and factories was increased to six months. The idea, the party explained, was to create a new generation of 'worker-intellectuals'. Art and literature were brought more closely under what was described in the Chinese newspapers as 'the brilliant red banner of Mao Tse-tung's thinking'.

Religion in China continued to be repressed. In September all the Buddhist monks at a monastery in Shansi Province were expelled. In October a British missionary of Jehovah's Witnesses, Stanley Jones, released after seven years in prison in Shanghai, spoke of how his treatment had been so much better than that of the Chinese Christian prisoners incarcerated with him. Not a single Catholic or Protestant newspaper or magazine was allowed – for an estimated thirty to forty million Christian Chinese.

In November two young American anti-Vietnam War protesters committed suicide by setting themselves on fire: one in front of the Pentagon in Washington and the other at the United Nations in New York. Opinion polls, which were increasingly being used to monitor shifts and changes in the public mood, and which Johnson studied avidly, showed more than three quarters of all Americans favouring a cease-fire. Johnson told his inner circle: 'The weakest link in our armour is American public opinion. Our people won't stand firm in the face of heavy losses, and they can bring down the government.' The North Vietnamese could take encouragement from the growth of the anti-war movement inside the United States, starting with the first 'teach-in' against the war at the University of Michigan.

On December 17 it was announced from Washington that there were 165,000 American troops in South Vietnam. That day Johnson ordered a bombing halt of thirty-seven days, to start on Christmas morning. On the ground, however, the American military commanders sanctioned only a one-day cease-fire, after which they ordered the renewal of American ground attacks on Vietcong positions and villages believed to be harbouring and helping the Vietcong – there were hundreds of such villages, and the attacks were mounted with considerable force.

On 12 January 1966 President Johnson told Congress: 'The days may become months and the months may become years, but we will stay as long as aggression commands us to battle.' He was challenged by Senator Fulbright, a leading fellow-Democrat, who warned that by its deeper and deeper involvement in Vietnam the United States was 'in danger of losing its perspective of what exactly is within the realm of its power and what is beyond it'. Fulbright concluded starkly: 'We are not living up to our capacity and promise as a civilized example to the world.'

The social reform to which Johnson was committed was not eclipsed by the Vietnam War. On January 17 he appointed Robert C. Weaver as the first ever black American to a position in the Cabinet. Weaver became head of the Department of Housing and Urban Development, at the centre of the urgent task of the renewal and replacement of millions of substandard dwellings, many of them in the black ghettos of northern cities, including New York and Chicago. On April 28 Johnson initiated further civil rights legislation to end discrimination in jury service. On October 11 he signed an Act whereby impoverished school children received food funded by the Federal government. On November 3 he signed another Act providing $1 billion for the rebuilding of more than sixty inner cities across the United States.

The impact of Vietnam on the ability to maintain effective social programmes was emphasized, however, when severe cutbacks had to be introduced in the Federal War on Poverty programme. Of the $680 million intended that year to help more than nine million Americans, only $200 million was made available, and fewer than three million people were to be its beneficiaries. When Johnson told Congress that $335 million was the 'irreducible minimum' required by the programme, Congress had nevertheless cut $135 million from it. The Vietnam War was beginning to take its toll on the Great Society.

The needs of that society were many and immediate. When the Senate rejected a Civil Rights Bill intended to bring to an end discrimination in housing, there was anger in many black communities, but there were those in Washington who argued that the public at large was not yet ready to accept integration in residential areas. The weather that summer was unseasonably hot; on July 14, after the thermometer had soared to 100°F, there were riots in Chicago and three blacks were killed. On July 22 there were riots in Brooklyn; an eleven-year-old black boy was killed by a sniper's bullet. Violence spread to Atlanta, Georgia, to Omaha, Nebraska and to San Francisco. To the alarm of those in Washington who wished to push ahead with anti-discriminatory legislation, in a Gallup Poll late in the year, fifty-two per cent of those whites questioned said that they thought the government was moving too fast in the direction of civil rights. But the process of change seemed irreversible. The first black American to sit in the United States Senate was elected on November 8: Edward Brooke, a Republican from – and for – Massachusetts.

In South Africa, the triumph of the Nationalist Party and of apartheid was complete. On 18 March 1966 the government banned as an unlawful organization the autonomous Defence and Aid Fund, under which legal aid was provided for political prisoners, and financial and moral support given to their families. On March 23 a leading barrister, Abram Fischer, was sentenced to life imprisonment for his support of the banned African National Congress and for his membership of the banned Communist Party. During his trial he denounced racial prejudice as a 'wholly irrational phenomenon'. As a Jew he knew what terrifying results racial prejudice could have.

In the elections held one week after Fischer's sentence, on March 30, the racial policy of apartheid was strengthened yet further when the Nationalists won their highest ever representation in the 170-seat parliament: 126 seats. At the same time, the opposition United Party declined from 49 to 39 seats, while the multi-racial Progressive Party obtained only one seat, that of Helen Suzman, an outspoken opponent of apartheid.

The new government was vigilant in banning any public opposition. A visit by Senator Robert Kennedy, who was as opposed to apartheid in South Africa as to racial discrimination in the United States – against which his assassinated brother had fought – was accompanied by a ban on all non-South African journalists entering the country, so that Kennedy's visit could not be reported impartially.

In a speech at the University of Cape Town, Kennedy told a crowd of 15,000 people, many of them students: 'The essential humanity of man can be protected and preserved only where Government must answer not just to those of a particular religion or a particular race, but to all its people.' And in a powerful voice of encouragement for human rights activity everywhere, Kennedy declared: 'Each time a man stands up for an ideal, or acts to improve the lot of others, or strikes out against injustice, he sends forth a tiny ripple of hope. And crossing each other from a million different centers of energy and daring, those ripples build a current which can sweep down the mightiest walls of oppression.'

Colonial and European rule in Africa was virtually at an end. Other than Southern Rhodesia, which stubbornly clung to its white-dominated independence, the only colonial power with extensive rule remaining in Africa was Portugal. France had promised an imminent referendum on independence to French Somaliland. Britain had granted both Bechuanaland (Botswana) and Basutoland (Lesotho) independence that year and promised it for Swaziland three years hence. But the troubles in the independent States of sub-Saharan Africa were legion. In Nigeria – which had achieved independence six years earlier – the first of two military rebellions that year took place on January 15, when the Prime Minister and the Finance Minister were among the government leaders killed, as were two of the regional Prime Ministers. The ensuing civil war led to as many as 40,000 deaths. In addition to the tragedies of killing on such a scale, one of Nigeria's most overpopulated regions had also to find shelter for more than a million internal refugees. By the end of the year, the country was effectively divided into two States.

In Ghana the one-Party rule of Kwame Nkrumah was ended by a military coup, carried out while Nkrumah was on an official visit to China. Civilian government was restored, Nkrumah's close links to China and the Soviet Union were denounced, the Chinese and Russian advisers whom he had brought in were sent home, and Ghana re-established relations with Britain. The independent judiciary which Nkrumah had undermined was restored. The hut where he had been born fifty-seven years earlier – which he had turned into a place of devoted national pilgrimage – was bulldozed to the ground.

For the next six years he lived in exile, dying in a sanitarium in Roumania.

In the former French colonies in Africa, Chad was combating a Muslim rebellion stimulated by neighbouring Sudan. In the Islamic Republic of Mauritania there was distress among the African population when Arabic was made compulsory in all secondary schools. In the Central African Republic, the Chief of Staff, Colonel Bokassa, seized power, declaring himself to be 'emperor'. Diplomatic relations with China, which the previous government had cultivated, were broken. France, welcomed back, undertook to build the airstrips and roads, and bring in the heavy equipment, needed to develop the country's uranium deposits. In Senegal, there was a breakthrough in the creation of African cultural sensitivity when the first World Festival of Negro Arts was held in Dakar. A total of 2,226 delegates assembled from thirty-seven countries.

In China, an era of internal destruction had begun. The declared enemy was the 'four olds' – old customs, old habits, old culture and old thinking. Ancient buildings, art objects and temples were destroyed by the Red Guard vigilantes of Mao Tse-tung's directives. The reading aloud of Mao Tse-tung's writings, sometimes in vast public gatherings, became a daily feature of Chinese life. The Great Proletarian Cultural Revolution had begun. At the age of seventy-three, Mao Tse-tung was determined to give the Chinese revolution a new impetus, a vigour that he felt it had begun to lose, and a renewed central place for himself.

Violent verbal and physical attacks were made on those who were accused of 'taking the capitalist road' or putting into the Chinese cultural garden 'anti-Socialist poisonous weeds'. Throughout China, encouraged by the authorities, the denunciation of those who were accused of deviating from the true path of Communism intensified. School children and university students were issued with armbands by the leaders of the Cultural Revolution, who declared the students to be 'Red Guards', through whom the renewed revolutionary path would be secured. In Peking, all the Christian churches were shut down, and red flags flew on the Roman Catholic Cathedral – which in 1900 had been the object of a ferocious attack by the Boxer nationalists.

On August 18 tens of thousands of Red Guards, most of them students, led four days of anti-Western demonstrations in Peking. They were applauded by Mao Tse-tung, who appeared on the Tiananmen Gate as the youngsters paraded in front of him, each one holding up in his hand a copy of the 'little red book' in which Mao Tse-tung's thoughts had been printed. In referring to him, speakers were encouraged to use the words: 'our great teacher, great leader, great supreme commander and great helmsman'. As well as destroying old buildings, temples, and museum pieces that were the pride of ancient Chinese culture, Red Guards attacked their school teachers, school administrators, local party officials, and even their parents. Many thousands of individuals died under the blows of these attacks. Hundreds of leading intellectuals were beaten to death, or committed suicide. Among those who killed themselves was Lao She; his novel *Cat Country*, published in 1932, had been a powerful denunciation of Chinese who turned on each other during the civil war, at a time when danger threatened from Japan. One passage of the novel read: 'The only result of revolution is to increase the number of soldiers in arms and the number of corrupt officials preying on the common people. In this kind of situation the common people will go hungry whether they like it or not.'

Mao Tse-tung was calling on the power and anger of these very 'common people' to turn against Chinese sensitivities and sensibilities that were at the centre both of ancient Chinese culture and his own earlier revolutionary structures.

In the Soviet Union, as a prelude to the trial of the writers Andrei Sinyavsky and Yuly Daniel, there were attacks on the two men in the Soviet newspapers. In the West forty-nine leading writers signed an appeal for their release. Foreign journalists were refused admission to the court. The writers were accused of smuggling their work to the West and publishing it there: work that was 'being actively used in the ideological struggle against the Soviet Union'. After a four-day trial, during which they pleaded not guilty, Sinyavsky was sentenced to seven years and Daniel to five years of 'strict regime in a corrective labour camp': a sentence normally handed out to hardened and dangerous criminals. Not only Western writers and intellectuals, but almost all the Communist Parties of western Europe, protested against the sentences. A protest by sixty-two Soviet writers was neither published in the Soviet press, nor effective in securing even a reduction of the sentences.

It was not only intellectual independence of thought that was stimulating the anger of the Soviet authorities. An upsurge in drunkenness and 'hooliganism' was leading to far heavier prison sentences than hitherto. For acts of hooliganism involving the use of an 'offensive weapon', up to seven years' imprisonment could be imposed. Swearing in public was among the minor offences for which a ten- to fifteen-day prison sentence could be imposed: for a second such sentence the penalty was at least six months in prison.

In East Germany the Ministry of Culture was criticized by the Party for not keeping a 'tighter rein' on intellectual dissent, and the minister was dismissed. In Poland, amid celebrations of 1,000 years of Polish statehood, Cardinal Wyszynski was criticized by the Communist regime for having wanted to put the 1,000-year achievements of Poland before the achievements of Communism since 1945. Foreign bishops who had been invited to the Church ceremonies were not allowed to enter Poland, and Wyszynski was forbidden to go abroad. Four church seminaries were closed down.

Gomulka meanwhile strengthened Poland's links with the Soviet Union, doubling the supply of raw material from the Soviet Union, and agreeing that Polish purchases of wheat – hitherto mainly from Canada – would come henceforth principally from the Soviet Union. Polish writers, in a collective protest, called for clemency on behalf of the imprisoned Soviet writers, Daniel and Sinyavsky, and a young Polish intellectual, Professor Kolakowski – a Marxist philosopher at Warsaw university – declared publicly that without greater intellectual and cultural freedom in Poland there could be no 'genuine democratic freedom'. He was promptly expelled from the Communist Party.

In Czechoslovakia, which unlike Poland had a common border with western Europe, the main problem confronting the authorities was the number of Czech citizens seeking to cross the border. In July seventy-eight Czechs were arrested trying to cross into West Germany. Others succeeded in getting across. In Prague, student disaffection was manifest in May, when during the annual student festivities placards were waved with the message: 'Long live the Soviet Union – but on its own resources.' In response, Antonin Novotny, who was both President of Czechoslovakia and First Secretary of the Czechoslovak Communist Party, declared that the Party could not accept such a 'destructive' attitude. Journalists were also under attack, a Party magazine accusing those who had begun to write about Western art and culture – which between the wars had been an integral part of Czech intellectual life – of 'lacking clear Marxist conceptions of culture, attempting to place art beyond the influence of the Party, and paying too little attention to the socialist culture of the socialist countries'.

The voices of change did not come only from outside Party circles. At the Czechoslovak Party Congress in June the leader of the Slovak Communist Party, Alexander Dubček, told the delegates: 'The concept that nationalism is the antithesis of internationalism is a persistent relic of the past.' This was not the orthodoxy that Novotny in Prague, or Brezhnev in Moscow, liked to hear. But as a gesture to the growing criticisms of rigid Party orthodoxy, the anniversary of Czechoslovakia's declaration of independence on 28 October 1918 was restored as National Day. Since the imposition of Communism in 1948, the celebration of National Day had been denounced as a throwback to bourgeois nationalistic tendencies which the Party deplored.

In Hungary, a decade since the harsh repression of 1956, a number of Roman Catholics who had been released after a decade in prison were rearrested on charges of conspiracy. Priests who had been at liberty since 1956 were accused of 'acting under instructions from their Western contacts'.

In August, as American bombing raids in Vietnam continued, averaging 800 tons of bombs dropped each day, General Westmoreland admitted secretly that he found 'no indication that the resolve in the leadership in Hanoi has been reduced'. It was to reduce, and break, that North Vietnamese resolve that the bombing had been launched almost a year and a half earlier. In October, Johnson visited Vietnam. Speaking to a group of soldiers he told them to 'nail the coonskin to the wall'.

On December 13, in a bombing raid in a suburb of Hanoi, more than a hundred North Vietnamese civilians were killed. Eleven days later, on Christmas Eve, Cardinal Spellman, Archbishop of New York, speaking at an American base near Saigon, declared that the war in Vietnam was a war for 'civilization' and that anything less than an American victory was 'inconceivable'. When the British Prime Minister, Harold Wilson, proposed on December 30 that the United States, South Vietnam and North Vietnam should meet – on British territory – to arrange a cease-fire, his offer reflected the fear of escalation. Its rejection showed how, despite the bombing truce, the struggle had become implacable, and, for the Americans, inextricable.

In China the Cultural Revolution continued on its destructive path. Red Guards, mostly students, and the older 'Red Rebels' who worked alongside them, attacked any individual or institution that was said to have 'taken the Capitalist road'. Almost all their victims were hitherto loyal and hard-working Communist functionaries. Red Guard activity in the factories brought disruption in coal mines, steel works and oilfields. The Chinese army alone had the power to curb the anarchy. On 11 February 1967 it placed Peking under military rule and took over the Ministry of Public Security. In Szechwan, soldiers, attempting to restore some semblance of order, killed thousands of 'radicals'. In Wuhan, after the army arrested 500 Red Guard leaders, there was a massive strike in the factories, and protest demonstrations in the streets. The army moved in and a thousand protesters were killed.

In August units of the Red Guard occupied the Foreign Ministry in Peking, disrupted all official business, and appointed their own 'radical' diplomats as ambassadors worldwide. They also attacked the British Embassy and set it on fire. By September, Mao Tse-tung realized the Cultural Revolution, far from 'purifying' the revolution as he had initially declared, was destroying it. The army was ordered in, and thousands more Red Guards were killed in the fighting. On one occasion five workers whom Mao Tse-tung himself sent to the campus of Peking University to try to arm student Red Guard zeal, were shot dead on the campus by the students themselves.

Slowly, the Red Guard were brought under control. 'Workers' Mao-Thought Propaganda' teams, drawn from the army and the 'revolutionary masses', obtained confessions of wrongdoing, and those who confessed returned to the fold of calm and obedience.

The year 1967 marked the fiftieth anniversary of the triumph of Communism in Russia. But a new KGB chief, Yury Andropov, appointed on May 18, made it clear there could be no lessening of vigilance. A decree was issued on November 14 – at the height of the jubilee celebrations – whereby heavier penalties, including prison and labour camp sentences, would be imposed on all those in factories, trade organizations, planning institutes and railways that fell below the norms that had been set them.

That year, the annual congress of Soviet writers refused to invite Alexander Solzhenitsyn. He responded by sending 300 of the delegates a strong attack on the Soviet censorship of literature. This denunciation was then published in Paris, in *Le Monde*, on May 31. Four months later Solzhenitsyn, and Andrei Voznesensky – a fellow-writer outspoken in his criticism of the regime – were condemned by the Soviet Writers' Union for providing the West 'with anti-Soviet propaganda'.

In Poland a campaign against the Catholic Church was launched, its 'hierarchy' being accused of being 'the bastion of internal forces hostile to socialism'. Cardinal Wyszynski, always an outspoken defender of the right of worship, was refused a passport to go to the Vatican, and criticized in the main Communist Party newspaper for his 'unfriendly and disloyal attitude towards the Polish State'. In Czechoslovakia, Jan Beneš, a short-story and film writer who had organized a public protest against the Soviet trial and imprisonment of Daniel and Sinyavsky the previous year, was himself arrested and held in prison for almost two years before being brought to trial and sentenced to five years in prison. More than a hundred Czech writers signed a manifesto, published in the West on September 3, asking for help 'to rescue the spiritual freedom and fundamental rights of every independent artist threatened by the terror of State powers'. The Czech authorities reacted with a law that further curbed freedom of expression. Student demonstrations at the end of October were broken up by force.

*   *   *

Canada had emerged as a strong critic of United States action in Vietnam. In October the External Affairs Ministry called publicly for a halt to the American bombing, without prior conditions, as an essential first step to peace talks. During the summer of 1967 the opposition Australian Labour Party made it clear that if it were to come to power it would demand a halt to the American bombing of the North, or else withdraw the Australian troops. Britain refused to send any troops. Within the United States, opposition to the war was causing Johnson considerable problems. There were half a million American troops in Vietnam, and with conscription notices going out to hundreds of thousands more, Johnson continued to speak of the war as essential and winnable. But his words were less confident than in the previous year. On January 10 he warned that the United States faced 'more cost, more loss, and more agony. For the end is not yet. I cannot promise you that it will come this year – or the next.'

As American and South Vietnamese troops carried out search and destroy missions to find and kill the Vietcong, the civilian death toll mounted. On March 2 an accidental American bombing raid on the South Vietnamese village of Lang Vei killed eighty civilians. In Washington, anti-war demonstrators, many of them chanting 'Hey, hey, LBJ, how many kids did you kill today?' surrounded the Defense Department. Young men who received their draft notices tore them up or burned them in public. Others crossed the border into Canada to avoid serving.

In March, Johnson flew to the Pacific island of Guam for three days of talks with the South Vietnamese Prime Minister, Air Vice-Marshal Ky, who said the Vietcong were 'on the run' and the North Vietnamese supply lines to the South 'near paralysis'. On May 19 the demilitarized zone between South and North Vietnam, which both sides had hitherto respected, was occupied by American and South Vietnamese forces. That day, American bombers attacked targets in the centre of Hanoi. In June, American bombers struck at oil storage tanks, but much of the oil had already been hidden underground, or in well-camouflaged fuel storage dumps, elsewhere. Destroyed bridges – and hundreds of North Vietnamese road bridges had been destroyed – were quickly repaired.

Only ground forces seemed capable of keeping the Vietcong in check. On August 4 Johnson authorized an increase in the number of American troops in Vietnam to over the half million mark, by an additional 45,000. The arrival of these new troops coincided with the publication of the number of Americans killed in action in Vietnam that year: 9,000, bringing the total over the previous two years to 15,000. That statistic caused many Americans who had hitherto supported the war to think again.

In September the American bombing switched from North Vietnam to Vietcong strongholds in the South. These were essentially rural and village targets, against which the bombers could send massive destruction but little careful targeting. Chemical warfare units used herbicides to complete the defoliation. A further 40,000 Vietcong soldiers were killed. 'The enemy's hopes are bankrupt,' General Westmoreland declared during a visit to Washington, but he was wrong. A Vietcong attack on the American base at Khe Sanh lasted five weeks, despite massive bombing of Vietcong positions. After 10,000 Vietcong had been killed, many by napalm, they called off their attack. The Americans had lost 500 marines. The war went on.

In the summer of 1967 a new area of conflict came into prospect on May 16, when President Nasser of Egypt instructed the United Nations to remove its forces from Sinai. Since 1948 the Sinai Desert, which was Egyptian sovereign territory, and the Gaza Strip, which had been occupied by Egypt since 1948, had been the buffer zone between Israel and Egypt. Both areas were patrolled by a United Nations Emergency Force (UNEF) set up after the Israeli-Egyptian war of 1956, when Israeli troops had occupied Sinai but then withdrawn. When Nasser demanded that the United Nations forces withdraw, they did so without protest, not wishing to be in the firing line. By May 19 almost all 3,400 of them had gone. The United Nations had not even asked Nasser for a week or month's delay. Israel was suddenly vulnerable to Egyptian attack. At the same time, Syrian forces along Israel's north-eastern border were put on high alert.

On May 22, three days after the last United Nations troops had left Sinai, Nasser stated that Egypt would no longer allow Israeli shipping bound for the southern Israeli port of Eilat to proceed through the Straits of Tiran. In announcing the blockade, which he did in a speech at an Egyptian air base in Sinai, a hundred miles from Israel's border, Nasser told his pilots: 'We are ready for war.' Freedom of passage for Israeli ships through the Straits of Tiran had been guaranteed by the United States, Britain and France after the Suez War eleven years earlier. 'Our basic objective', Nasser announced on May 26, 'will be to destroy Israel. I probably could not have said such things five or even three years ago. Today I say such things because I am confident.'

Anxious to avoid drawing the nuclear powers into a Middle Eastern war, the American President Lyndon Johnson and the Soviet Prime Minister, Alexei Kosygin made use, for the first time, of the Washington–Moscow telephone 'hot line'. Both men agreed that there would be no direct military intervention by either the United States or the Soviet Union. On May 30, King Hussein of Jordan committed himself to join in the attack on Israel. With a war on three fronts in prospect, its leaders decided to take pre-emptive action, and did so with dramatic swiftness in the early hours of June 5, when, to forestall Egyptian air strikes on military and civilian targets, the Israeli air force struck without warning at more than twenty Egyptian air bases. One third of Egypt's warplanes were destroyed on the ground. Israel appealed to King Hussein not to join in the conflict, but he was persuaded by Nasser – over the telephone – that Egypt, not Israel, had struck the decisive blow, and ordered Jordanian troops to attack. At the same time, Syrian, Iraqi and Jordanian aircraft attacked military targets inside Israel.

On the ground and in the air the attacking forces were driven off. On June 7 Israeli troops occupied the Old City of Jerusalem, which had been under Jordanian rule since 1948. In six days, the Egyptians were driven out of Sinai, the Jordanians were driven off the West Bank, and the Syrians were driven from the Golan Heights. Israel's victory was complete. By June 10 the war was over. Israel found itself in occupation of territory three times its own size, and of a million Arabs on the West Bank and Gaza Strip, who began to call increasingly, not for their return to Egyptian and Jordanian rule, but for autonomy and independence. Israel became an occupying power. During the fighting, 777 Israeli soldiers had been killed. The Arab dead were in excess of 5,000.

Israel's victory put its troops on the eastern bank of the Suez Canal. Israeli warships patrolled within sight of Port Said. One of them was sunk by Egyptian missiles on October 21 – only four months after Israel's military victory – while outside Egyptian territorial waters. Forty-seven Israeli sailors were killed. In retaliation, Israel began an artillery barrage along the whole length of the Suez Canal. The oil refineries of Suez City were set on fire, and tens of thousands of Egyptian civilians were evacuated from both Suez City and Ismailia.

The East-West confrontation had been avoided in Vietnam, but was acute in the sphere of the development of nuclear weapons delivery systems and the counter-measures needed to defend against them. The cost of this nuclear arms race was formidable. On September 18 Robert McNamara announced that the United States was spending $5,000 million to create an anti-ballistic missile (ABM) defence system. The Soviet Union was already putting such a system into place. On November 3 McNamara gave details both of a new Soviet nuclear bomb, which could be delivered through a low-orbiting space rocket (the Fractional Orbital Bombardment System – FOBS), and of the American ability to shoot down this bomb at any point during its first orbit. When several members of Congress asked whether the nuclear arms race was not getting out of hand, and expressed their concern that the Soviet Union might be developing weapons, such as the new space bomb, that could prove superior to the American bombs and defence systems, they were assured by the Pentagon, in a statement on November 8, that the United States was still 'in the lead'.

The United States possessed 1,710 intercontinental ballistic missiles (ICBMs), of which 656 were Polaris missiles in submarines. All these missiles could be fired at targets inside the Soviet Union. The Soviet Union, by contrast, could place no more than 500 ICBMs in the United States. If the Russians were to carry out a first strike without warning, the Pentagon estimated that nine-tenths of the

American missiles that were based on land would survive, and could be used against the Soviet Union in a matter of hours.

A further Pentagon announcement on December 14 gave details of a space vehicle being developed in the United States that had the capacity to carry nuclear bombs. The new delivery system was known as the Multiple Independent Re-entry Vehicle (MIRV).

ABM, ICBM, FOBS, MIRV: these were the shorthand notations of weapons of mass destruction. How far they could serve as a deterrent to any destruction at all was a matter of theory. Fourteen years earlier, Churchill had told the House of Commons: 'These fearful scientific discoveries cast their shadow on every thoughtful mind, but nevertheless I believe that we are justified in feeling that there has been a diminution of tension and that the probabilities of another world war have diminished, or at least have become more remote. I say this in spite of the continual growth of weapons of destruction such as have never fallen before into the hands of human beings. Indeed, I have sometimes the odd thought that the annihilating character of these agencies may bring an utterly unforeseeable security to mankind.'

In medicine, the use of laser beams for surgery was entering into common practice. The laser beam had the power to destroy diseased tissue. An operating theatre equipped for laser surgery had opened in the United States, at Cincinnati, Ohio, where the repairing of torn retinas by laser surgery was a routine operation. A wide range of other medical uses for laser beams included bone and other surgery where the use of a knife was impossible or dangerous.

Another milestone in medicine was reached on December 3, when a South African surgeon, Dr Christiaan Barnard, carried out the first heart transplant operation. His patient, Louis Washkansky, survived for eighteen days. In Cleveland, Ohio, an American surgeon, René Favaloro, was developing the coronary bypass operation. That same year, a new technique, X-ray mammography, was introduced for the detection of breast cancer.

In space, the successes of previous years were overshadowed by the first accidental deaths. On 27 January 1967 three American astronauts were killed in their Apollo space capsule while it was still on the ground. Within three months, on April 24, a Soviet astronaut, Colonel Vladimir Komarov, who had been successfully launched into space, was killed when the parachute on his spacecraft failed, and he was hurled to Earth. But the race to put a man on the Moon continued. On April 19 an unmanned American lunar probe made a soft landing on the Moon, sent back photographs of the Moon's surface, and dug a trench with a mechanical shovel to obtain small rock and dust samples: an essential prerequisite for a manned lunar landing.

The next American experiment was the firing of by far the most powerful rocket ever launched, *Saturn V*, which at more than 3,000 tons weighed as much as a navy destroyer, and on top of which sat the first, unmanned, Apollo space capsule to be sent into orbit. The space capsule re-entered the Earth's atmosphere at 25,000 miles an hour and then came down safely on a parachute into the Pacific.

In New York, starting on December 5, there were daily marches against the Vietnam War as part of the 'Stop the Draft Week'. Outside the United Nations building in New York, twenty-year-old Kenneth d'Elia burnt himself to death, the fourth person to do so within two years. Speaking in the Senate on December 8, Senator Fulbright called the war 'an immoral and unnecessary war' which had 'isolated the United States from its friends abroad, disrupting our domestic affairs and dividing the American people as no other issue of the twentieth century has divided them'. Fulbright added that the United States was 'using its B52s, its napalm, and all those other ingenious weapons of counter-insurgency to turn a small country into a charnel house'.

As the daily protests continued, Senator Eugene McCarthy of Minnesota announced that he would stand as an anti-war candidate in the next year's presidential elections. In his second speech in the Senate in one week, Senator Fulbright spoke angrily on December 13 of America's thirty-two million 'dispossessed children . . . sacrificed to the requirements of the war on Asian Communism'.

CHAPTER TEN

Challenges of Modernity
1968—79

IN VIETNAM, AT THE BEGINNING OF 1968, the government of Hanoi proclaimed a truce for the seven-day period of the Tet holiday. The truce was a skilful act of deception. On the night of January 30–31, three days into the holiday, 70,000 Vietcong troops attacked American and South Vietnamese forces throughout South Vietnam. In Saigon, 4,000 Vietcong struck the centre of the city, penetrating the American Embassy. For six and a half hours the battle for the embassy was seen on television screens throughout the United States, watched by fifty million Americans.

Within twenty-four hours American military authority was restored in Saigon, and almost all the Vietcong attackers were killed. Then an incident took place that was to disturb millions of Americans. On February 1 an Associated Press photographer, Eddie Adams, and a Vietnamese cameraman, Vo Suu, working for the American National Broadcasting Company, saw a patrol of South Vietnamese troops with a prisoner, who was taken up to General Nguyen Ngoc Loan, chief of the South Vietnam police. The general then drew his revolver and shot the prisoner in the head. Adams took a photograph of the execution, and Vo Suu filmed it. The next morning the photograph was in every American newspaper. In the evening NBC broadcast the film. It was edited slightly, explained the journalist and Vietnam war historian Stanley Karnow, 'to spare television viewers the spout of blood bursting from the prisoner's head'. But it made a shocking impression, casting a dark shadow on how the American public regarded the South Vietnamese authorities, their allies.

When the Vietcong overran the important coastal city of Hué they murdered as many as 3,000 supporters of the South Vietnamese authorities. No cameraman or filmmaker with instant access to American television screens was present. After the Vietcong were driven out of Hué, South Vietnamese soldiers carried out reprisals of their own. The bodies of many of those whom they killed were thrown into the same mass graves as those killed by the Vietcong.

In March, as the fighting continued, 50,000 Vietcong were killed. In one instance, in the village of My Lai, American troops massacred a hundred South Vietnamese peasants, women and children among them. American policy in Vietnam was leading to growing protests inside the United States. Senator Albert Gore, father of a future Vice-President, Al Gore, told a student audience in Idaho: 'We are destroying the country we profess to be saving.' At a White House luncheon the singer Eartha Kitt told Johnson's wife: 'You send the best of this country off to be shot and maimed. No wonder the kids rebel and take pot.' On March 12 Senator Eugene McCarthy challenged Johnson for the Democratic nomination, standing in the New Hampshire primary on an anti-Vietnam War ticket. He won forty-two per cent of the vote. Three days later Senator Robert Kennedy declared his candidature. He had offered not to put his name forward for the Presidency if Johnson offered to 're-evaluate' America's role in Vietnam. Johnson declined to do so, declaring on March 17: 'We are going to win.'

As Robert Kennedy began his campaign for the Democratic nomination, Johnson announced he would not run for another Presidential term. He made his announcement at the end of a television broadcast in which he first announced a partial suspension of the bombing of North Vietnam. American bombing would take place only below the twentieth parallel, the area of North Vietnam nearest the South Vietnam border. Ninety per cent of North Vietnamese territory would be excluded from attack. In secret, Johnson authorized negotiations with the North Vietnamese.

Johnson's decision to leave the presidency was not primarily because of Vietnam. He had contemplated resigning at the beginning of the year, before the setbacks of the Tet offensive, and before the McCarthy-Kennedy challenge. His worry, having suffered a severe heart attack in 1955, was that he would die in office. Senators McCarthy and Kennedy competed for the Democratic nomination. In California, where polling took place on June 4, Kennedy won by 46 per cent to 42. Confident of securing the Democratic nomination, and through it the presidency – which fifty-four months earlier had been held by his assassinated brother – he told an enthusiastic crowd of his supporters at a celebratory gathering in the Ambassador Hotel, Los Angeles, on June 5, that he was confident the divisions in the country, whether over race or Vietnam, could be ended. Then, making his way to a room where a press conference was to be held, and taking a short cut through the hotel kitchens to avoid the crowds, he was shot in the head and neck, and on the following day he died. He was forty-two years old, four years younger than his brother had been at the time of the Dallas assassination. Robert Kennedy's assassin, a deranged young man, was arrested, tried and imprisoned for life.

The first face-to-face talks between the Americans and the North Vietnamese began in Paris on May 10. The American negotiators were confident of reaching agreement within months. But the North Vietnamese had no intention of abandoning their aim of control of the whole country, and negotiations dragged on inconclusively. The war also continued. On June 10 it was announced that the total of American combat deaths was more than 25,000.

On November 5 the voters of the United States elected the Republican challenger, Richard Nixon, as President. In his first public speech he declared: 'I will not be the first President of the United States to lose a war.'

In Eastern Europe, the Communist world was in varying degrees of turmoil. In Poland an upsurge in anti-Semitism bewildered the 25,000 Polish Jews, remnant of the pre-war Jewish community of three million. There was much Polish resentment at the part played by individual Jews in the imposition of Communism in Poland after the war. There was also State-sponsored anti-Jewish feeling after Israel's victory a year earlier: the Polish Government had been emphatically on the Arab side. The Jews as a group – some of them having been extremely heartened at Israel's victory – were accused of 'narrow-minded nationalism'. Thousands were forced to leave their jobs in government, the universities and industry. Many Jewish institutions were closed down. More than 14,000 left the country, allowed to do so by hostile administrators glad to see the back of them. Most went to Israel.

In Czechoslovakia, an apparently peaceful revolution was under way. In January the First Secretary of the Czech Communist Party, who had held office for more than fourteen years, was voted out by the Party. His successor was Alexander Dubček. A new President was also elected by the Party, General Svoboda, who in 1945 had led the Czechoslovak Army Corps – a fighting element of the Soviet army – when it entered Brno and Prague.

In what Dubček called 'Socialism with a human face' greater freedom of speech was allowed on radio and television than existed anywhere else in the Soviet bloc. The writer Jan Beneš, sentenced the previous year to five years in prison, was set free, and the rehabilitation of 50,000 Czech victims of Stalinism began. During March the Soviet newspapers began attacking those in Czechoslovakia who placed 'nationalist above internationalist interests'. Among the events that angered the Soviet leadership was the formation in Prague of the Club of Committed Non-Party People. On April 5 the Czech Communist Party gave further offence to the Soviets by announcing that newspaper censorship would be abolished, freedom of assembly assured and the right guaranteed to travel outside Czechoslovakia – to the Communist East or to the capitalist West.

In early May, Dubček was summoned to Moscow. At the same time 25,000 Soviet troops, ostensibly on Warsaw Pact manoeuvres, took up positions in southern Poland along the Czech border. On May 24 it was announced from Moscow that 'joint command staff exercises' in which Soviet troops would take part would be held in June on Czech and Polish soil. They did so, but when the manoeuvres were over the Soviet Union refused to withdraw them from Czechoslovakia. On July 11 *Pravda* declared that the 'counter-revolutionary forces' in Czechoslovakia were more 'treacherous' than those of the Hungarian anti-Communists in 1956. But Dubček and his colleagues were not trying to create a Hungarian-style situation, whereby

Hungary had turned its back on the Warsaw Pact and effectively pulled itself out of the Soviet system. The Czech aim was to find a less coercive form of Communism. This was anathema to Moscow. On July 29 the Soviet leaders summoned the whole Czech Praesidium to a meeting at Cierna-nad-Tisou, a Slovak village on Czechoslovakia's eastern frontier with the Soviet Union. After four days of talks the Soviets agreed to allow the Czechs their own 'road to Socialism'. For their part the Czechs gave the Soviet Union assurances of 'Socialist solidarity'. But Czech newspapers became more and more outspoken in their demand for a more liberal form of Communism, and on the night of August 20–21, Soviet troops crossed the Soviet-Czech border, while airborne troops were landed at the principal Warsaw Pact air bases inside Czechoslovakia.

Also crossing the border into Czechoslovakia were troops from three of its Communist neighbours, Poland, Hungary and East Germany, as well as from distant Bulgaria: in all, half a million men. The principal Czech cities were quickly occupied by predominantly Soviet forces. The Czech Government confined its own troops to their barracks and forbade armed resistance. On August 21, Soviet troops arrested Dubček and most of the Czechoslovak Communist Party leadership. There were clashes in the streets between civilian demonstrators and Soviet troops, in which eighty Czechs were killed. On the following day the Soviets demanded the formation of a government from which all Dubček's supporters would be excluded, or military rule would be imposed. On August 23 there was a one-hour general strike in Prague against the Soviet demand. That day, the Czechoslovak President, General Svoboda, was flown to Moscow. As he began negotiations with the Soviet leaders, Dubček and the other Czech Communist leaders arrested with him two days earlier were brought into the meeting.

There were half a million foreign troops on Czech soil and 500 Soviet tanks in the streets of Prague, which was under curfew. When the Moscow talks were over, Dubček and his colleagues, having given in to the Soviet demands, returned to Prague exhausted and humiliated. The Club of Committed Non-Party People was closed down. Anti-Soviet slogans were removed from all buildings. Press and book censorship was reimposed, and the Czech Government signed a treaty permitting the 'temporary' stationing of Warsaw Pact troops, including Soviet troops, on Czechoslovak soil.

In Moscow a small demonstration against the Soviet invasion of Czechoslovakia had taken place in Red Square on August 25. The leaders of the demonstration, Pavel Litvinov – a nephew of Stalin's Foreign Minister, Maxim Litvinov – and Larisa Daniel, both of whom had protested earlier in the year on behalf of several imprisoned Soviet writers, were charged with slandering the Soviet State. No Western correspondents were allowed in the courtroom. Litvinov was sentenced to five years' internal exile and Larisa Daniel to four. A petition for leniency signed by ninety-five intellectuals from around the world, including many Communists, was ignored.

In the United States, Martin Luther King was planning a nationwide protest that summer to draw attention to the continuing racial inequalities and discrimination. On April 3 he was in Memphis, Tennessee. 'I want you to know tonight,' he told a large crowd of wellwishers and supporters, 'that we as a people will get to the promised land.' On the following day, while standing on the balcony of his hotel, he was shot dead by a white assassin. Riots, accompanied by looting and arson, broke out throughout the United States. In Washington, despite an evening curfew, black rioters surged through the streets setting fire to buildings only a few blocks from the White House. Troops were called in to prevent the rioters reaching the White House itself. The highest number of deaths were in Chicago, with eleven dead, and Washington with ten.

It was only after King's funeral on April 9 that calm was restored. On the following day a law was signed prohibiting discrimination in the sale or letting of houses, and in a move to counter job discrimination he announced a programme of 'affirmative action' whereby all government contractors were obliged to give preference when hiring to blacks and other minority groups. On November 5, Shirley Chisholm became the first black American woman to be elected to the United States Congress. But success in one area of race equality was not matched by success elsewhere. Hispanics, mostly immigrants from Mexico, were expressing their dissatisfaction. Led by César Chávez, head of the United Farm Workers Union, the predominantly

Hispanic farm labourers in California boycotted the grape harvest in protest against low wages and poor conditions.

Sixty-one nations signed a Treaty on the Non-Proliferation of Nuclear Weapons on 1 July 1968. It was a landmark in the attempt to prevent the spread of this destructive power. It had taken ten years of negotiation to reach this goal. Three powers that did possess nuclear weapons, the United States, the Soviet Union and Britain, each signed. A fourth nuclear power, China, not being a member of the United Nations, was not asked to do so. Several of the countries who later signed it subsequently acquired their own nuclear capacity, among them India, Pakistan and Israel. The world's fifth nuclear power, France, abstained from voting on the treaty. Eight weeks later, on August 25, she exploded a Hydrogen bomb in the South Pacific.

On 16 January 1969, in Wenceslas Square in Prague, a Czech student, Jan Palach, set fire to himself in public to protest against the continuing presence of Soviet occupation troops in Czechoslovakia. In his farewell letter he demanded an end to press censorship and the resignation of those politicians put in place since the Soviet occupation 'who do not enjoy the people's confidence'. After his death more than 200,000 people marched in silence through the streets of Prague, factories stopped work for five minutes, and Czech Radio observed a minute's silence, telling its listeners: 'The deepest pain is marked by the deepest silence.'

On March 28 there were mass anti-Soviet demonstrations in the streets of Prague and other Czech cities. Two senior Soviet officials flew to Prague and warned the government that unless anti-Soviet demonstrations ceased the Soviet Union would intervene militarily without first seeking permission. The Czech Government bowed to the threat of force. Press censorship was tightened and the police force strengthened. But the spirit of defiance was strong; in June the playwright Vaclav Havel spoke to trade unionists at the ironworks at Ostrava, although the authorities had declared the meeting illegal. A Soviet delegation visiting a factory in Prague was stoned before it could enter the factory and had to turn away.

On August 21, the first anniversary of the Soviet invasion, the citizens of Prague stayed at home: trams, buses, trains, shops, restaurants, cinemas and theatres were empty. During a protest demonstration four days later, in which 50,000 people took part, two demonstrators were killed by police. The Soviet Union acted with decision: it had already replaced Alexander Dubček by Gustav Husak and a Praesidium more amenable to Soviet wishes. Summoned to the Crimea, Husak agreed to joint Soviet-Czechoslovak manoeuvres on Czech soil within a matter of weeks.

In Poland, eighteen university lecturers and students were imprisoned for 'anti-State and anti-Socialist' activities during 1968. Leading writers who opposed the Communist Party's cultural ideology were refused admission to the annual Writers' Union Congress. At the same time, compulsory manual work was introduced for all students during the university holidays, and a newly established Ideological Commission of the Communist Party supervised school and university teaching and text books.

In Washington, Richard Nixon was sworn in as President on 20 January 1969. When he presented his first domestic programme to Congress on April 14 he told the legislators that promulgating the much-needed social reforms would 'depend in large measure on the prospects for an early end to the war in Vietnam'. Travelling to the Pacific, Nixon issued the 'Declaration of Guam', stressing that the United States must never again be drawn into a Vietnam-type conflict on the Asian mainland. American troops, he said, would not be used to put down insurrections, even insurrections that were Communist-led.

Throughout the first six months of the Nixon presidency, American Moon-landing preparations gripped the public mind and held the attention of millions of television viewers. The Moon landing took place on July 20. A new era of exploration had begun. But the prospect of exploring space could not lessen the widespread sense of 'empty lives, wanting fulfillment' of which Nixon had spoken in his inaugural address. Two weeks of student violence at the University of California at Berkeley in February led the Governor of California, Ronald Reagan, to declare 'a state of extreme emergency'. At the University of Wisconsin, the refusal of the administration to establish a Black Studies programme led to protest demonstrations by white and black students marching arm in arm, and the calling out of the police and National Guard to curb their protest. Anti-war feeling at Harvard led hundreds of students to protest against the university's Reserve Officers' Training Programme.

The war in Vietnam had become the longest ever fought by the United States: longer than either the First or Second World War. Nixon's imperative was to try to end it, and on May 14 he announced a series of decisions aimed at ending the war within a year. The basis was a mutual withdrawal of both American and North Vietnamese troops from South Vietnam, followed by elections. Under Nixon's scheme, the Communist National Liberation Front would be able to put up candidates. This was not acceptable to the South Vietnamese, and Nixon had an uncomfortable meeting on Midway Island, in the Pacific, with President Thieu of South Vietnam, who had no desire to share power with the Communists.

Unable to persuade the South Vietnamese to allow the National Liberation Front to share in the electoral contest, Nixon took unilateral action towards reducing America's commitment, announcing on June 8 the imminent withdrawal of 25,000 American combat troops: one in twenty of those fighting in South Vietnam. On September 16 he announced that a further 35,000 troops would be withdrawn by mid-December. Inside the United States, the scale of anti-war protests grew with every month that the war continued. In November, when the full details of the My Lai massacre of the previous year became public, the White House issued a statement, with Nixon's approval, that the incident was in 'direct violation' of American military policy, and 'abhorrent to the conscience of all American people'.

On December 15, Nixon announced that a further 50,000 troops would leave within the next four months. More than a fifth of the American force was on its way home. At the end of the year it was announced that the number of American dead in Vietnam exceeded 40,000.

Inside the Soviet Union, a new method of dissent had begun to emerge, the clandestine publication and distribution of banned material. Manuscripts that the Communist Party refused to allow to be published were circulated, often in poorly cyclostyled sheets, and eagerly read by those who faced arrest and imprisonment for possession or distribution of these pieces of work, which were known as *samizdat*: privately published. Early in the year a young dissident, Irina Belgorodskaya, was sentenced to one year in a labour camp for having many such clandestine publications in her apartment in Moscow. Her trial, on February 19, lasted only a few hours. On the day of the trial the Party newspaper *Izvestiya* made it clear that 'Marxism-Leninism does not recognize classless freedom of speech'.

In May another dissident was sentenced to three years in prison for giving out copies, produced clandestinely, of works by the imprisoned writers Daniel and Sinyavsky. Other dissidents were not sent to prison, but to mental hospitals, where they were held in secure wards as political prisoners. One such prisoner was a former collective farm chairman. Another was a senior army officer. Both had spoken out on behalf of dissidents. On November 12, the Soviet Writers' Union expelled Alexander Solzhenitsyn. A number of his fellow-writers protested at the expulsion, but the Party would not allow their protests to be published. What was published, and given powerful support in all Soviet newspapers and magazines, was a novel by Vsevolod Kochetov in which he made a strong plea for the isolation of Soviet youth and culture from the outside world.

In China, the anarchic destruction of the Cultural Revolution was coming to an end. The place for the Red Guards, declared the official China News Agency on the anniversary of the first dramatic Red Guard parade in Peking, was 'the countryside, border regions, and stock-breeding areas'. The rigid control of the Communist Party was being restored.

On July 12 there were riots in Northern Ireland between Roman Catholics and Protestants in Londonderry. Since 1966 the Catholic minority in this British province had been alarmed by the provocative acts of Protestants who were afraid of being eclipsed by the growing Catholic population. On August 12 there were clashes between Protestants and Catholics in Belfast, when hundreds of houses were destroyed by fire, and several thousand people – four-fifths of them

Roman Catholic – were made homeless. Ten people were killed and more than a thousand injured. Two days later, John Gallagher, a Roman Catholic, was shot through the heart while running for the sanctuary of St Patrick's Cathedral, Armagh. He was the eleventh victim of the renewed violence that was to claim 3,000 victims in Northern Ireland and on the British mainland by 1992.

As fighting between Catholic and Protestant extremists spread, Harold Wilson ordered British troops to the province. Catholic women served tea and biscuits to the soldiers, who were protecting Catholic areas from Protestant attack. The Protestant Loyalists felt betrayed by Britain, regarding keeping the peace by its very nature a concession to the Irish Republican Army (the IRA). Both sides built up their weaponry, and their grievances.

On October 7 the United States and the Soviet Union agreed to keep the sea-bed free of nuclear weapons. The Soviet Union also agreed to proceed with comprehensive Strategic Arms Limitation Talks (SALT). On November 24, in ceremonies held simultaneously in Washington and Moscow, the nuclear non-proliferation treaty was ratified. On the following day Nixon renounced, on behalf of the United States, all methods of biological warfare, and ordered the destruction of all biological warfare stocks. In future, he said, biological research would be confined to defensive measures, not attack.

The needs of the environment were gradually being understood, and addressed. In the United States, the National Environmental Policy Act made it mandatory for each government decision to be accompanied by a detailed statement regarding its environmental impact. A conference on pollution held in Rome was attended by thirty-nine nations. The destructive effects of the residue of pesticides, in particular DDT, were revealed in both water and soil: Canada imposing a total ban on DDT for more than 90 per cent of the operations using it.

In the United States the first 'jumbo jet' airliner had its maiden flight in 1969 while in France the Anglo-French supersonic airliner Concorde took to the air. Also, almost unnoticed at the time but of inestimable importance for the future, the United States Department of Defence established the Internet – intended as a means of secure communication which could remain fully operational even after the destruction of telephone lines, telegraph poles and radio transmission centres in a nuclear attack. Thirty years later the Internet was becoming the predominant means of communication, and of access to information, for hundreds of millions of people worldwide.

In the Soviet Union, all information was filtered through the rigours of strict censorship, but this was always under attack. On 8 October 1970 the Nobel Prize for Literature was awarded to Alexander Solzhenitsyn, Russia's most outspoken dissident writer. The citation noted the 'ethical force' with which he pursued the traditions of Russian literature. A day later the Soviet Writers' Union called the award and the citation 'unseemly'. In support of Solzhenitsyn, the Russian cellist Mstislav Rostropovich wrote a letter to *Pravda* and three other newspapers defending the award. None of them would publish the letter. It circulated unofficially, part of the growing dissident literature.

In Vietnam the United States continued to try to disengage as many of its troops as possible, and to negotiate an agreement with the North. On 21 February 1970, in a Paris suburb, Henry Kissinger, Nixon's National Security Adviser, held his first secret meeting with a North Vietnamese interlocutor, Le Duc Tho, who had spent much of the recent period in the South in hiding, co-ordinating anti-American activity. Kissinger sought a formula whereby the North Vietnamese would pull their troops out of South Vietnam without any public announcement, leaving the Vietcong as the sole Communist forces in the South. This was unacceptable to the North Vietnamese, who felt that the Vietcong, left to their own devices, without North Vietnamese support, were not strong enough to achieve the Communist objective, the overthrow of the South Vietnamese Government.

On April 20 Nixon announced that another 150,000 American troops would be withdrawn from South Vietnam within a year, leaving fewer than 350,000 there. 'We finally have in sight the just peace we are seeking,' he said. Two days later, as the Cambodian capital, Phnom Penh, was being threatened by local Communist attack, Nixon discussed with his advisers how to help the Cambodian regime, both against North Vietnamese incursions and the

Cambodian Communists. General Creighton Abrams, General West-moreland's successor as commander of the American forces in South Vietnam, argued for the elimination of Communist bases in Cambodia, warning Nixon that unless this was done those bases could serve, at the very moment so many American troops were being withdrawn from South Vietnam, as staging posts for attacks on those who remained. Nixon took the same view, believing that an attack on Communist bases inside Cambodia would show the North Vietnamese leaders 'we were still serious about our commitment in Vietnam', and encouraging them to take the secret Paris negotiations with Kissinger more seriously. Nixon then gave orders for a full-scale American attack into Cambodia: 20,000 American troops, supported by American warplanes, advanced across the border on April 30.

In explaining this widening of the war, Nixon told the American people: 'If, when the chips are down, the world's most powerful nation, the United States of America, acts like a pitiful helpless giant, the forces of totalitarianism and anarchy will threaten free nations and free institutions throughout the world.' The American hopes of capturing both the North Vietnamese and Vietcong headquarters in Cambodia were quickly dashed. They overran the locations, but the personnel had gone. For the anti-war protesters in the United States, to whom Nixon's withdrawals of American troops from Vietnam had been a positive sign, the military entry into Cambodia was a disastrous escalation of the war. Anti-war efforts were renewed and stepped up.

The war also intensified. On May 2 the Americans carried out their first bombing raid over North Vietnam since November 1968. More than 200 State Department officials publicly expressed their opposition. Student demonstrations took place across the country. At Kent State University, in Ohio, students attacked the building used for Reserve Officers training. National Guardsmen fired into the crowd and four students were killed.

The Kent State killings, which an FBI report later described as 'not necessary and not in order', provoked an upsurge of protest. Students and teachers alike went on strike, more than 400 campuses were closed, and 100,000 marchers converged on Washington. Surrounding the White House, they demanded an end to the intervention in Cambodia and to the war in Vietnam. Night after night protesters held vigils in the centre of Washington. The largest took place on the night of May 9–10, filling the whole area around the Lincoln Memorial and in front of the White House. At five in the morning, Nixon himself emerged from the White House, and accompanied only by his valet and a few security men, walked to the Lincoln Memorial and talked to the protesters. A few days earlier he had characterized them as 'campus bums'. He now sought – pugnacious and pathetic in turn – to assure them that what he was doing in Vietnam and Cambodia was right.

In Congress, by majority vote, American ground troops were barred from entering either Cambodia or Laos. The Ho Chi Minh Trail, where it traversed Laos, would have to be attacked by South Vietnamese troops only, although the United States still bombed the trail on Laotian territory.

In Southern Rhodesia, Britain's four-year struggle to persuade the white separatist regime to return to constitutional rule, and eventual black majority rule, finally failed. On March 2 Ian Smith's government declared Rhodesia to be an independent republic. The British Government urged the United Nations Security Council to condemn 'the illegal acts of the racist minority regime'. The United States, which Ian Smith had hoped would recognize his republic and thus lead other nations to do likewise, announced on May 9 that it was closing its consulate in the Rhodesian capital. Only Portugal and South Africa recognized the pariah republic, and continued to supply it with the fuel oil and the basic necessities needed to survive without international support. At the same time, small but determined guerrilla forces entered the country and began to attack government buildings.

In November, as a gesture of defiance to the international community, Ian Smith brought in legislation to enable the government to declare any residential area to be an 'exclusive area', to be lived in by people of one race only.

In South Africa, under the Bantu Laws Amendment Bill, the government forbade the employment of black Africans in a wide range of trades. That parliamentary session was the last to be attended by the three white members who had hitherto the responsibility of representing Coloured voters – those of Indian or mixed race. That representation was henceforth withdrawn. Elsewhere in Africa, different violations of human rights were taking place. In Uganda and Kenya pressure was being imposed on the Indian community to leave. These Kenyan and Ugandan Asians, as they were known, had come from India fifty years earlier, many brought as workers by the British, some as traders. They had become an integral, prosperous and productive element in Ugandan and Kenyan society, but they were not black Africans, and the tide of prejudice had turned against them. They were prevented from trading and physically harassed. During the year, 5,000 left. Within three years 20,000 had followed them. Most, as Commonwealth citizens holding British passports, went to Britain, where they formed the vanguard of one of the most hardworking, and ultimately most successful immigrant groups.

Three years after Israel's defeat of Syria, Jordan and Egypt, the Arab-Israeli conflict continued to flare up. On February 3, Egyptian frogmen sank an Israeli supply ship off the Israeli port of Eilat, in the Gulf of Akaba. In retaliation, Israeli warplanes sank a number of Egyptian minesweepers in the Gulf of Suez. On February 12, in a further Israeli reprisal, seventy Egyptian civilians were killed during an air raid on arms and munitions factories near Cairo. During another Israeli air raid on Egyptian military targets in the Nile Delta, bombs falling off their target killed thirty children on April 8.

What became known as the War of Attrition continued: 593 Israeli soldiers and 127 civilians were killed in Egyptian artillery bombardments, and almost twice the number of Egyptian soldiers were killed by Israeli artillery and air attacks. The Egyptian civilian deaths were also high. On August 7 both sides, exhausted by the conflict, agreed to a cease-fire. Israel remained in occupation of Sinai, an area larger than Israel itself, giving Israelis a sense of near-invulnerability with regard to Egypt. But a more volatile, less controllable adversary had emerged: the Palestinian Liberation Organization (PLO), headed by Yasser Arafat, a force whose terror attacks took place far beyond the confines of the Middle East. On February 13, Palestinian terrorists claimed responsibility for the crash of a Swiss airliner near Zurich that killed forty-seven passengers. Seventeen were Israelis. That same day, seven elderly Jews were killed in an old people's home in Munich. Again the PLO claimed responsibility.

By the beginning of 1970 there were more than 20,000 PLO activists in Jordan, some of whom infiltrated Israel to carry out acts of terror inside the country. On May 22 eight Israeli children between the ages of six and nine were killed when a terrorist shell struck their bus. On November 6 two Israelis were killed when a terrorist bomb went off in the main bus station in Tel Aviv. The pattern of such killings was relentless. Within four years of the end of the 1967 war, 120 Israeli civilians and 183 soldiers had been killed in terrorist attacks. During the same period Israeli troops killed 1,873 infiltrators, many before they could carry out their acts of terror.

Inside Jordan, King Hussein governed a population in which Palestinians were almost as numerous as his own Bedouins. He also had more than 100,000 Palestinian refugees in his kingdom, their refugee camps a fertile breeding ground of hatred against both Israel and Jordan. Every PLO raid mounted from Jordan against Israel confronted Hussein with the possibility of Israeli reprisals. On September 6 the King, himself a pilot, was outraged when PLO hijackers seized four international civil aeroplanes and flew three of them at gunpoint to Dawson's Field, a desert airstrip in northern Jordan, an area effectively beyond Jordanian jurisdiction. There, the PLO held many of the passengers hostage until Britain, West Germany and Switzerland agreed to release convicted Palestinian terrorists being held in their respective jails. The PLO then blew up the planes.

Hussein had been made to look powerless. It was not beyond the bounds of possibility that the PLO might try to seize power in Jordan. Hussein decided on drastic military action. Starting on September 15 his army turned against the PLO. During the fighting, 2,000 PLO fighters, and several thousand Palestinian civilians, were killed. The PLO withdrew from Jordan. Most of them fled to Syria and Lebanon. Arafat took up residence in Lebanon, from where he regrouped his forces.

Natural disasters could drive even the most intense military or political crisis off the front page of the world's newspapers. On May 31 an earthquake in Peru killed more than 50,000 people, making it one of the worst earthquakes of the century. On November 12 an even higher death toll followed a cyclone and tidal wave in East Pakistan (later Bangladesh), when 150,000 people died. Nature could be as destructive as any human killing agency.

Man continued to search for processes to preserve and prolong life. In West Germany the first successful nerve transplant took place in 1970. Considerable progress was made in the treatment of infertility, artificial hip joints and heart surgery. All heart transplants having been temporarily halted throughout the world because of the problems of rejection, work was proceeding on the use of artificial elements, such as plastic pumps and nuclear-powered pacemakers, which could last ten years without replacement.

Environmental problems were becoming a growing part of the international agenda. Factories belching smoke and chemicals, hitherto seen as a sign of a healthy economy, were being recognized as a danger to the quality of life of the communities around them, and indeed a danger to life itself. The motor car also caused mortal injury. In the single year of 1970 a total of 54,633 Americans, of whom almost 2,000 were under the age of five, were killed on the roads. Many others died from motor-car pollution. In 1970 the United States announced new standards for controlling motor vehicle exhaust, with Congress insisting on the manufacture of a virtually 'pollution-free' car within six years.

On 13 June 1971 there was a spur to the American anti-Vietnam War movement when the *New York Times* published hitherto secret 'Pentagon Papers', with details of American policy planning and deception in the prosecution of the war. The government tried to prevent publication, insisting that such secret material was not usually made public for at least fifty years, but the Supreme Court upheld the newspaper's right to publish.

Within the Soviet Union a small Human Rights Committee had been formed in 1970 in Moscow by a group of Soviet writers and intellectuals. They felt confident that publicity could lead to an end to human rights abuses. Encouraged by this, on January 28 the Russian writer and philosopher Vladimir Bukovsky issued a public appeal to Western psychiatrists to protest against the Soviet practice of locking up dissidents in psychiatric hospitals. His appeal included 200 pages of detailed testimony about individuals who were incarcerated. In mid-March he was arrested and held in a mental hospital.

The Human Rights Committee appealed to the delegates of the forthcoming World Psychiatric Association conference, being held in Mexico, to demand the release of Bukovsky from his confinement: his mother had been told by the KGB her son was likely to be declared insane. The protest was successful, and Bukovsky was declared 'normal'. But the committee's call for an end to the misuse of psychiatry for political purposes, although supported by the Mexico conference, was ignored by the Soviet authorities.

Trials against Soviet Jewish activists continued. A Jewish librarian, Raisa Palatnik, was sentenced to two years in labour camp for demanding the right to emigrate. She was thirty-five years old. Taking up her case, a group of British women, calling themselves the '35s', began a campaign that drew public attention to the plight of hundreds of prisoners of conscience, Jews and non-Jews. The Israeli Prime Minister, Golda Meir, appealed to the Soviet Union to allow any Jew who wished to emigrate to Israel to do so. On a visit to Canada, when confronted by Canadian government concern on this issue, the Soviet leader Alexei Kosygin announced that the number of Jews allowed to leave would be substantially increased: it rose from 1,044 in 1970 to more than 13,000 during the course of 1971.

The repercussions of the war in Vietnam were tormenting the United States. On April 24 an estimated 200,000 Americans demonstrated in Washington against the war. Addressing the vast crowd, Senator Vance Hartke of Indiana declared: 'We have bled too much, committed too many horrors, and the time to get out is now. The only way to bring our prisoners of war home is to get out now; the only way we can renew our commitment to mankind is to get out now.'

On November 12 Nixon proclaimed an end to America's 'offensive' role in Vietnam, and announced the withdrawal of another 45,000 troops. Only 182,000 remained. American bombers continued to attack Communist supply lines running along the Ho Chi Minh Trail, through Laos, but even the American air component, which had wreaked such havoc two and three years earlier, was being reduced. In Paris, American negotiations with the North Vietnamese continued.

On the Indian subcontinent, West and East Pakistan had begun to break apart. In East Pakistan, a separatist leader, Sheikh Mujib ur-Rahman, won a massive majority in the elections there and demanded independence. On February 15 the Pakistani Prime Minister, Zulfikar Ali Bhutto, warned Sheikh Mujib to work for a federal rather than a separatist solution. His warning was ignored. There were strikes and riots throughout the East Pakistani province of East Bengal, including the capital, Dacca.

Pakistani troops were flown in to maintain order. On March 23 Sheikh Mujib called again for the transfer of power in East Bengal to the 'elected representatives of the people': in the elections 75 per cent of the voters had voted for separation. As a gesture of defiance the flag of a new nation – Bangladesh – was raised on public buildings in Dacca, while armed 'Bangladeshi' troops marched through the city. On March 25 Sheikh Mujib was arrested by the Pakistani authorities and flown to West Pakistan, where he was held captive. Fighting then broke out between the Pakistani authorities and the East Bengal separatists.

The Indian Government stayed aloof, not wanting to become embroiled in the quarrel of its Muslim neighbour at the two extremities of its land mass, but it could not stay aloof for long. Hindus living in East Bengal were killed by Pakistani troops, and Hindu refugees began to seek sanctuary across the Indian border. By the end of the year the number of refugees was two million.

Both the United States and China were supplying arms to Pakistan to help it retain the unity of the two sections of the country. India, and the imprisoned Sheikh Mujib, saw the arms as enabling Pakistan to maintain its dominance over East Bengal. By the end of October India was training the East Bengali freedom fighters, the Mukti Bahini, on Indian soil, and providing them with arms and ammunition. On December 6 India recognized the independence of East Pakistan, under the name of the 'Democratic Republic of Bangladesh', and within a week, in suport of the Bangladeshi struggle, Indian troops advanced towards Dacca. On December 16 the Pakistani forces in East Bengal surrendered to India. In fighting in Punjab, Jammu and Kashmir, India captured and annexed 1,000 square miles of disputed territory. More than a thousand soldiers had been killed on both sides. Bangladesh became an independent State.

In Northern Ireland, the violence that had broken out between Catholic and Protestant militants in 1969 neither abated nor seemed capable of a political solution. Roman Catholics felt aggrieved at fifty years of British 'misrule' during which their minority rights had been neglected and rebuffed. Protestants felt that the British Government was neglecting their majority interests, which had hitherto secured them a clear predominance in the provincial administration.

On 5 February 1971, Gunner Robert Curtis became the first British soldier to die on active service in Northern Ireland. Television brought in to millions of British homes the sight of British troops being attacked by angry stone-throwing crowds, and having to pull back. As killings and murder increased, every variety of violence seemed to be perpetrated. On March 10 three unarmed Scots soldiers, young men in their late teens, who were off duty – two of them were brothers – were lured to a remote country road and murdered in cold blood. The murderers escaped across the border to the Irish Republic.

Confronted by IRA violence on an increasing scale, on August 9 the British Government introduced internment. This deprived those in detention of the basic rights of judicial procedures, starting with an arrest warrant and including trial by jury. With the arrest that day of 300 IRA men there were shootings, riots and widespread fires in several towns as troops and the IRA fought pitched battles in the streets. In eleven days, forty-four people were killed. An explosion in a Catholic bar killed fifteen people, including the publican's wife and child. On December 7 a number of IRA gunmen entered the home of a Protestant member of the Ulster Defence Regiment and shot him dead. On the following day a Roman Catholic UDR man was shot dead in front of his children. In one year, 173 people had been killed in Northern Ireland, forty-three of them British soldiers.

In March the United States ended restrictions on American citizens visiting China. In April, the Chinese invited an American table-tennis team to tour China. These two events, unique in the annals of Red Chinese-American relations, heralded a turning point in their dialogue. On April 14 Nixon announced that American trade with China would resume. The United States also ended the ban on the transfer of dollars to China, so that Chinese-Americans could send financial support to their relatives for the first time since 1949. American-owned ships, if sailing under foreign flags, were allowed to trade in Chinese ports for the first time since the Korean War.

A further turning point came on July 9, when Nixon's National Security Adviser, Henry Kissinger, went to Peking. His visit lasted for three days, after which the Chinese invited Nixon to China. From Britain, China bought heavy generating equipment and six commercial jet aircraft. A trade agreement with Canada secured China a fivefold increase in the purchase of Canadian grain. On the night of October 25–26 the United Nations in New York voted for the admission of Communist China. Red Chinese exclusion from the world forum was over.

1971 saw the introduction in the United States of the microprocessor, a minute device on a single 'chip' for processing information within a computer. That same year, surgeons developed a fibreoptic endoscope, for looking inside the human body, enabling probings and diagnoses, and eventually surgery, to be conducted without the need for incisions. Neurosurgeons and brain surgeons were using instruments based on new technology, including forceps made of titanium alloy, a strong metal less dense and less tarnishable than steel. In May, Nixon called for an 'all-out war' on cancer, putting the full authority of the President of the United States, and his budgetary influence, behind that war. The search would not fail, Nixon said, because of shortage of money for research. 'If a hundred million dollars this year is not enough, we will provide more money; to the extent that money is needed, it will be provided.'

In London, the British Royal College of Physicians published a report in 1971 showing that smoking was a main cause of lung cancer. Doctors pointed out to smokers that cigarette smoking was as serious a cause of disease in the 1970s as the 'great epidemic diseases' of typhoid, cholera and tuberculosis had been for earlier generations. The United Nations World Health Organization was also active in the anti-smoking campaign. Its method was to encourage tobacco-producing countries to grow other crops.

In the search for a less polluted environment, the Friends of the Earth organization was founded in Britain, with an emphasis on the need for recycling. Its first public action, on May 9, was to dump thousands of Schweppes' non-returnable bottles on the doorstep of the firm's headquarters, as part of its call for recyclable bottles. It was announced in 1971 that 250,000 tons of lead were discharged from car exhausts every year in the United States. Lead poisoning, discovered first among the animals in Staten Island Zoo, was then discovered among humans in New York City. Those living closest to busy roads seemed most at risk. Experiments were begun to produce a commercially viable lead-free petrol. Within five years lead-free petrol was to become compulsory in some States of the United States, and in due course in all of them.

On Sunday 30 January 1972, in Northern Ireland, there was a Roman Catholic protest march in Londonderry against the British Government's policy of internment without trial. As the march was ending, and most of the 10,000 marchers dispersing, stones were thrown at the troops – members of the Parachute Regiment – who responded by chasing after the stone throwers. As they did so, shots were fired, allegedly by IRA snipers. The troops returned fire, killing thirteen people. A British Government inquiry, while insisting that the IRA had opened fire first, admitted that the troops had returned the fire 'very recklessly'.

'Bloody Sunday' became a hated symbol of British repression and the denial of Catholic rights. In Northern Ireland, on average two British soldiers were killed every week. 'No-go' areas, in which the IRA ruled and British troops did not enter, came into being in Belfast and Londonderry. On April 15 the leader of the official

IRA, Joseph McCann, was shot dead by British troops in the centre of Belfast. There were widespread riots and considerable destruction of property. A Protestant militia, the Ulster Defence Association (UDA) was formed, to protect Protestant areas from the IRA. Fighting between the two groups took a regular toll of lives. The total number of deaths in 1972 was 467, including a hundred soldiers.

On February 21 Nixon arrived in China, the first American President to set foot on Chinese soil. During fifteen hours of negotiations in Peking he agreed to allow China to purchase considerable quantities of American goods, including train engines, building equipment, industrial chemicals, trucks and motor-car engines.

Just over a month later, on March 30, the North Vietnamese launched a three-front offensive as ferocious as that of the Tet offensive four years earlier. As many as 120,000 North Vietnamese and Vietcong troops took part, advancing through the Demilitarized Zone, making effective use of first-class Soviet artillery, rockets and tanks. One division of South Vietnamese troops, many of whom had never been in combat, panicked and fled. As the North Vietnamese advanced tens of thousands of Vietnamese civilians fled southward on Highway One. An estimated 20,000 were killed, many by North Vietnamese artillery searching for South Vietnamese units, others by American aircraft trying to bomb North Vietnamese troops, still others by American warships in the South China Sea that, with their powerful naval guns, were seeking out North Vietnamese targets up to ten miles inland – Highway One ran five to six miles inland.

By the time of the North Vietnamese offensive, 400,000 American troops had been withdrawn. Of the 60,000 still in Vietnam, only 6,000 were combat troops. The full weight of the North Vietnamese attack fell on the South Vietnamese who, although outnumbering their adversaries by about five to one, were pushed back by the sheer ferocity of the attack. 'The real problem', Nixon wrote privately, 'is that the enemy is willing to sacrifice in order to win, while the South Vietnamese simply aren't willing to pay that much of a price in order to avoid losing.' All the air power in the world, Nixon wrote, even the renewed heavy bombing of Hanoi and Haiphong, would not be able to prevent a Communist victory 'if the South Vietnamese aren't able to hold on the ground'.

On May 22 Nixon flew to Moscow. As with his visit to China, he was the first American President to make that journey. The Soviet leaders, aware of their country's military weakness with regard to the United States, and of their vulnerability to nuclear attack, were eager to conclude an arms limitation agreement between the two Super Powers. The treaty, signed on May 29, concluding the first round of Strategic Arms Limitation Talks (SALT 1), marked a turning point in the Cold War. The United States and the Soviet Union agreed to limit the number of defensive nuclear missiles to 200 each. The number of offensive nuclear weapons and nuclear-armed submarines was also given an upper limit. The figures for intercontinental ballistic missiles would be fixed at their existing level: 1,618 Soviet and 1,054 American. To indicate his seriousness, Nixon ordered an immediate halt to work being done at three American anti-ballistic missile sites. Then, before leaving Moscow, he signed a Soviet-American charter pledging to prevent nuclear war.

Internally, the Soviet Union was flexing the muscles of control and repression. In the former Baltic States of Lithuania and Latvia – Soviet republics since 1945 – nationalist demonstrations were broken up and their leaders arrested. In Lithuania two priests who had given religious instruction to minors were sent to prison. Two bishops were refused permission to preach and exiled from their bishoprics. The restoration of churches was prohibited, and the teaching of atheism made compulsory in schools. But the courage of those who wished to practise their religion was evident in March, when 17,000 Lithuanian Roman Catholics sent a petition to the United Nations and to Moscow, demanding the right of open worship. In May, a Roman Catholic worker, Roman Kalantas, burnt himself to death in a park in the Lithuanian city of Kaunas in protest against religious repression. As a gesture of solidarity, students demonstrated in the streets. They were dispersed by the police.

Freedom of expression inside the Soviet Union continued to draw stern condemnation. In January, Vladimir Bukovsky was sentenced to seven years' hard labour, to be followed by five years' internal exile in a Soviet city far from Moscow. The charge against him was 'anti-Soviet agitation'. Human rights activists were arrested in Leningrad, Kiev and Vilnius. The main privately printed and clandestinely distributed dissenting magazine, *Chronicle of Current Events*, which listed violations of human rights throughout the Soviet Union, was seized and destroyed. Nationalist groups in the Ukraine were harassed. The poet Iosif Brodsky was expelled from the Soviet Union.

In the Buryat Mongol Republic of the Soviet Union, in the heart of Siberia, the Communist authorities had for many years sought to suppress the Buddhist beliefs of many of the region's inhabitants. A leading Buddhist scholar in the republic, Bidya Dandaron, had first been imprisoned for his beliefs in 1937 at the height of the Stalinist repression, and had spent eighteen years since then in labour camp. In October 1972, a free man but unwilling to be silent, he was arrested and charged with carrying out 'religious propaganda'. He was sentenced to a further five years in labour camp.

In Czechoslovakia, as 100,000 Soviet, Polish, Hungarian and East German troops joined in military manoeuvres on Czech soil, a renewed collectivization campaign was launched and private farming was curtailed. Forty-six dissidents, advocates of a more democratic form of socialism, were sent to prison. Newspapers conducted 'anti-religious' campaigns. The number of theological students was reduced. The reopening of religious orders and monasteries that had earlier been closed down was refused. Nuns were told they did not need nunneries or special places of worship, but could undertake 'useful work in hospitals and other social institutions'.

On June 28, Nixon announced that no more draftees would be sent to Vietnam. The anti-war movement had obtained one of its main objectives. On October 8, after more than a year and a half of negotiation, Le Duc Tho gave Kissinger the terms of an agreement that Kissinger found acceptable. A cease-fire would be arranged by North Vietnam and the United States without South Vietnamese participation. Once the cease-fire was in place, Americans troops would withdraw and all prisoners-of-war would be exchanged. The future political alignment of South Vietnam would be left to the Vietnamese themselves. North Vietnamese troops would remain in South Vietnam. Kissinger made as a condition of their remaining that they would not be resupplied. It was, he later explained, pointless to insist on a North Vietnamese withdrawal. It had been 'unobtainable through ten years of war. We could not make it a condition for a final settlement. We had long passed that threshold.'

On October 21 Kissinger flew to Saigon to obtain General Thieu's acceptance of the agreement. Thieu saw in it nothing but the destruction of South Vietnam and of his government. Nixon was so angered by Thieu's reluctance to accept the agreement that he contemplated threatening Thieu that if he did not agree to the terms that had been worked out in Paris the United States would sign a separate treaty with the North Vietnamese. Inside the White House there was even talk of organizing a coup to overthrow Thieu and put in his place someone less hostile to the proposed treaty. Then, on October 24, Thieu publicly denounced the proposed treaty and insisted that the Communist presence in the south 'must be wiped out quickly and mercilessly'. Kissinger sought desperately to revive the treaty and see it brought into effect. In his first White House press conference, on October 26, he said with confidence that all would be well, telling millions of American viewers: 'We believe that peace is at hand. We believe that an agreement is in sight.'

On November 7 Nixon was re-elected President with an increased majority, winning forty-nine States: he lost only Massachusetts and the District of Columbia. Vietnam remained the dominant focus of his thought and actions. General Thieu was no longer an obstacle to be rebuked or even removed, but an opponent of Communism to be supported.

Thieu had submitted to the United States sixty-nine amendments to the proposed treaty. Nixon instructed Kissinger to take these amendments, which Kissinger regarded as 'preposterous', to Le Duc Tho. On December 13 Le Duc Tho suspended the negotiations and returned to Hanoi for consultations. On the following day, December 14, Nixon warned the North Vietnamese that they had seventy-two hours to begin talking again, and to do so 'seriously' or there would be grave consequences. For four days the North Vietnamese declined to return to the negotiating table. Then, on December 18, the consequences of which Nixon had warned – without spelling them out – were put into operation: a massive American bomber offensive against North Vietnam. For eleven days a total of 3,000 sorties were flown, the main targets being within the heavily populated sixty-mile long corridor between Hanoi and Haiphong. There was only one day on which the bombing was suspended: Christmas Day.

The *New York Times* denounced Nixon for having reverted to 'Stone Age barbarism'. The *Washington Post* called the bombing 'savage and senseless'. The North Vietnamese launched more than 1,200 surface-to-air missiles against the attacking aircraft, of which twenty-six were shot down, and sixty-two American airmen killed. On December 26, after an American request for negotiations to begin again in Paris, the North Vietnamese replied they would be willing to talk again as soon as the bombing offensive stopped. On December 30 Nixon ordered a halt. Within a few days Kissinger and Le Duc Tho arranged to meet again in Paris. They did so on 8 January 1973, and began serious negotiations on the following day. Agreement was reached after five days. The United States could withdraw from its most long-drawn-out, controversial and divisive war.

On 15 January 1973 the United States suspended all military action against North Vietnam. Twelve days later, in Paris, a cease-fire agreement was signed. The United States had given up any attempt to maintain the independence and territorial integrity of South Vietnam. The agreement enabled the Americans to begin to pull out their remaining forces, and end their effective state of war with North Vietnam. Since the United States had become involved in the war seven years earlier almost a million North Vietnamese civilians, soldiers and Vietcong had been killed. The South Vietnamese armed forces lost 181,483 men and 50,000 South Vietnamese civilians were killed. The United States war deaths were 55,337. In those same seven years almost eight times times that number of Americans – 414,774 – had been killed on the roads in the United States.

On February 12 the first of almost 600 United States prisoners of war to be set free under the cease-fire agreement were released. Many had been tortured, particularly those who refused repeated demands to make public anti-war statements. Nixon still retained the option to return the United States to an active military role in Vietnam if the North Vietnamese were to violate the cease-fire terms, but on June 4 the Senate voted to block all funding for American military activity in Vietnam, Laos or Cambodia. At that very moment, Nixon's presidential authority was under attack. His own Special Counsel, John Dean, had accused him publicly of a 'cover-up' with regard to a break-in at the Democratic Party headquarters in the Watergate building in Washington before the 1972 presidential election. It was alleged that Nixon himself had authorized the break-in. The attention of the American public became riveted on a sequence of events each of which appeared to show the President in an ever-worsening light. 'This office is a sacred trust,' Nixon told tens of millions of American television viewers in June, 'and I am determined to be worthy of that trust.' In the end, all trust dissolved, and the House of Representatives asked its Judiciary Committee to establish whether there was sufficient evidence to impeach the President.

On June 16 a United Nations conference on the environment, meeting in Stockholm, agreed to a Declaration on the Human Environment which its authors believed could transform the quality of life on the planet. While recognizing the 'sovereign' right of all States to exploit their own natural resources, the declaration established the legal responsibility to ensure that activities within national jurisdiction or control 'did not cause damage to the environment of other States or areas beyond the limits of national jurisdiction'. On July 23 the Americans launched the first satellite that could survey the earth's resources from space, and monitor their depletion.

At a conference in London to set rules for the dumping of waste products into the sea, ninety-one nations agreed that certain products could not be dumped at sea at any time or in any quantity, however small. These were radioactive substances, fuel oil, mercury and its compounds, and organo-halogen compounds. The enforcement of these rules was to be the responsibility of the signatories. China, a major dumper of pollutants, neither attended the conference nor signed the declaration.

*   *   *

The left-wing government of Salvador Allende in Chile had caused repeated waves of alarm in right-wing and Republican circles in the United States. Allende, a Marxist, had won the Chilean presidential election in September 1970. For three years he had sought to move Chile along the road to socialism. His most striking decision was to nationalize Chile's copper mines, previously partly owned by United States companies. He also defied the United States by ending Chile's trading boycott of Cuba, a boycott followed at Washington's request by all Latin American countries.

On September 11 a military junta, headed by General Augusto Pinochet, seized power in Chile. In two days' fighting in the capital, Santiago, more than 2,500 people were killed. Allende was reported to have committed suicide. Pinochet ordered more than twenty of Allende's senior advisers, as well as his driver and his doctor, to be taken from the presidential palace, where they were sheltering, to an army barracks, where they were tortured and then shot. In the months ahead, 2,528 Chileans were seized and killed, including parliamentarians, university professors, students and trade union leaders. When two leading Chilean churchmen, the Lutheran bishop Helmut Frenz and his Catholic colleague Fernando Ariztia, protested to Pinochet, he told them: 'You are priests with the luxury of mercy. I am a soldier and President of the Chilean nation, under attack from the disease of Communism, which must be eradicated. Marxists and Communists must be tortured, otherwise they will not sing.' For seventeen years Pinochet ruled Chile with an iron hand, with torture as an ever-present threat against his political opponents.

In 1973 the Day of Atonement, the holiest day in the Jewish religious calendar, fell on October 6, a day of fasting and prayer. When, at noon, the sirens sounded and mobilization orders were broadcast over the radio – normally silent on the Day of Atonement – thousands of Israeli soldiers went straight from synagogue to their army camps. At two in the afternoon Egypt and Syria launched a co-ordinated military offensive. The plan had been so well guarded that ninety-five per cent of the Egyptian officers taking part in the attack across the Suez Canal did not know until that morning that the manouevres on which they had been engaged were in fact a prelude to war.

Egyptian troops crossed the Suez Canal and pushed into Sinai. The Syrians swept forward on the Golan Heights. After forty-eight hours, however, Israeli troops and tank reinforcements halted the armies advancing against them, and made plans to counter-attack. Slowly the Israelis pushed back their adversaries. On October 11, having pushed the Syrian troops back to the 1967 cease-fire line on the Golan Heights, Israeli forces advanced into Syria. On October 16 they crossed the Suez Canal and entered Egypt.

Both Egypt and Syria appealed to the Soviet Union for military intervention. The Soviet Union had no intention, however, of becoming embroiled militarily in the Middle East, or of risking a conflict there – directly or by proxy – with the United States, which, as the war was being fought, allocated $2,000 million of military aid to Israel. On October 21 Henry Kissinger, who had become Secretary of State six weeks earlier, was in Moscow for talks with the Soviet leader, Leonid Brezhnev. They agreed to try to bring the war to an end. Kissinger then flew from Moscow to Tel Aviv where he obtained the agreement of the Israeli Prime Minister, Golda Meir, to a cease-fire. But in an attempt to secure a larger foothold on the Egyptian side of the Suez Canal, Israel continued fighting for another day. The cease-fire finally came into effect on October 24. During the course of eighteen days of war, 2,522 Israeli soldiers had been killed. The Egyptian and Syrian losses, although kept secret at the time, were even higher: 3,500 Syrian soldiers were killed on the Golan Heights.

In the aftermath of the war, Henry Kissinger's mediation enabled the Egyptian forces trapped by Israel on the Sinai side of the Suez Canal to return to Egypt. He also negotiated the separation of Israeli and Syrian forces on the Golan Heights. On November 11, following another agreement brokered by Kissinger, Egypt and Israel accepted international monitoring of the cease-fire and a full exchange of prisoners of war. A disengagement agreement between Israel and Syria, with Kissinger's supervision, established a ten-kilometre zone of limited armaments and forces on the Golan Heights, where during the fighting Syria had lost 1,150 tanks.

The apartheid regime in South Africa could not curb the growing unrest in the non-white communities. In the first three months of

1973 there were strikes by African workers in the iron, steel, textile and engineering industries. At the height of the strikes the port of Durban, South Africa's third largest city and main seaport, was brought to a standstill. On September 11, eleven black miners demonstrating in support of their demand for higher pay were shot dead by police. It was thirteen years since the massacre at Sharpeville had shocked liberal opinion throughout the world. In the aftermath of the recent shootings the Prime Minister, John Vorster, praised the police for their 'restraint'. This further incensed those who had been horrified by the way in which the police had used first tear gas, then a baton charge, and finally Sten guns to break up the protest. There was further indignation when it was revealed that, while the mine owners paid out £56 million in wages in 1992, their profits that year had been £322 million.

The National Union of South African Students was at the forefront of the call for greater liberalization. On February 27, eight of its leaders were banned for five years from holding or participating in any meetings, of however small a group, and denied the right to publish or broadcast their views in any form. On March 8 a similar banning order was placed on eight leaders of the Black South African Student Organization. In all sixty people were banned in this manner that year, the banning being ordered by the government without trial or right of appeal.

Elsewhere in Africa the horrors of famine had struck most cruelly in Ethiopia, where, following three successive years of drought, at least 100,000 Ethiopians died. Death on a similar scale – an estimated 80,000 dead – had come to Uganda, not as a result of nature's ravages but of deliberate human cruelty. A new President, Idi Amin, was asserting his power by brutal means. On February 18 the Ugandan judiciary protested that members of his security forces were committing 'widespread interference with the course of justice'. Amin ordered the Minister of Justice to take thirty days leave 'in order to rest'. He was never recalled to his post. Senior army officers who showed unease at the dictatorship were also sent on leave, and never called back.

Amin, who for many years had been the Ugandan army heavyweight boxing champion, was portrayed in the West as a buffoon, and behaved as if he intended to live up to his reputation. On October 28 he turned up uninvited at a meeting of African Heads of State. He expelled almost all the remaining Asians living in Uganda, and proclaimed himself the champion both of Africa and the Arab cause – he was himself a Muslim. The Soviet Union saw its chance to secure a point of influence. He was fêted by Moscow, and accepted a large quantity of Russian arms.

Inside the Soviet Union a leading critic of human rights violations, Andrei Sakharov, the nuclear scientist who had once been among the most privileged of Soviet citizens, was warned by the authorities that he was 'not immune' from Soviet law. Ignoring this, he called a news conference for foreign journalists at which he accused Soviet psychiatrists of 'complicity' in committing political dissidents to mental institutions. Sakharov's courage in matters of human rights, and his continued opposition to nuclear testing – the French had recently exploded a nuclear device in the atmosphere – led Solzhenitsyn to issue a statement recommending him for the Nobel Peace Prize. Solzhenitsyn was himself in trouble, following the publication of his book *The Gulag Archipelago* in the West. The book was based on eyewitness accounts of people who had experienced the Soviet labour camp system. The KGB had searched for the manuscript of the book for some time. A Leningrad woman, Yelizaveta Voronyanskaya, who knew its whereabouts, had been tortured without a break for five days to force her to reveal them. She did so, and then hanged herself.

Solzhenistsyn was expelled from the Soviet Union, and Sakharov was forced to leave Moscow for internal exile in the city of Gorky, 250 miles east of Moscow, where he was forbidden to talk to foreign journalists. For several dissidents the pressures were too great: a Moscow poet, Ilya Gabai, having been subjected to long questioning by the KGB about his connection with the clandestine *Chronicle of Current Events*, killed himself by jumping from an eleventh-floor apartment.

Although the Arab-Israel War of October 1973 had ended in an Israeli victory on the battlefield, it did not end the bloodshed in the Middle East. Palestinian Arab terrorists, based in Lebanon, attacked the Israeli town of Kiryat Shmona on 11 April 1974, killing eighteen men, women and children. A month later, twenty Israeli school-children were killed during a terrorist attack on the town of Ma'alot. The PLO, from its headquarters in Beirut, announced that all foreign tourists in Israel, including Christian pilgrims, would be considered targets. Soon afterwards, on November 13, the PLO leader, Yasser Arafat, addressed the General Assembly of the United Nations. On the following day the General Assembly voted against allowing Israel to speak in the debate on the Middle East.

On December 2 Israel announced that it possessed the means to manufacture nuclear weapons. It was assumed that such weapons had already been produced, or were in the imminent process of manufacture. Within a decade, it was said that Israel had at least 200 nuclear warheads.

In the United States, the scandal that was evolving around the Water-gate break-in and subsequent cover-up reached a climax on July 26, when the Judiciary Committee of the House of Representatives voted, by 27 to 11, to recommend President Nixon's impeachment for having used the powers of his office 'to delay, impede and obstruct the investigation' of the Watergate break-in 'and to conceal the existence and scope of the unlawful covert activities'. On July 29 the committee added a second article of impeachment, that Nixon had abused his executive power by 'violating the constitutional rights of citizens, impairing the due and proper administration of justice and the conduct of lawful inquiries' and by 'contravening the laws governing agencies of the executive branch and the purposes of these agencies'. A third article of impeachment was added on the following day, that Nixon's refusal to honour the congressional subpoenas to surrender the tapes of White House discussions was a 'high misdemeanor'. A fourth item of impeachment, that Nixon had unlawfully concealed from Congress the secret bombing of Cambodia, was rejected. The Vietnam War was not to be part of the indictment.

On August 5 Nixon admitted on television that he had discussed the 'political aspects' of a cover-up of the Watergate burglary within days of the break-in, and had instructed the Federal Bureau of Investigation, whose agents were looking into the burglary, to stop their inquiries. Within twenty-four hours of this admission all ten Republican Congressmen who had voted against impeachment announced they had reversed their decision. Nixon resigned on August 9. It was the first time in United States history that a President had resigned his office.

In July, during the visit by Nixon to Moscow, agreement had been reached to ban smaller underground nuclear tests: those hardest to detect. When Nixon's successor, President Ford, went to Vladivostok that November, for a summit with Brezhnev, a ten-year pact was outlined for the control and limitation of all offensive strategic nuclear weapons and nuclear delivery vehicles. While at Vladivostok, Ford insisted that the Soviet Union's search for closer trade relations with the United States would depend on a more liberal Soviet attitude to Jewish emigration, which had fallen from 34,000 to 20,000 in the two previous years. The Soviet authorities bowed to the pressure and Jewish emigration grew annually, reaching a peak of 50,000 in 1979. Increasingly, the emigrant Jews went to the United States rather than Israel.

Within the Soviet Union, the saga of Solzhenitsyn's courageous dissent was reaching a climax. On February 12, after renewed public criticism of his exposure of Soviet labour camp life in *The Gulag Archipelago*, he was arrested. On the following day he was deprived of Soviet citizenship and flown to West Germany. He was not to return to Russia for almost twenty years, when the Soviet Union itself had ceased to exist. A few months after his enforced exile, his researcher, Gabriel Superfin, was sentenced to five years in a labour camp for 'anti-Soviet agitation'. The official message in Superfin's sentence was clear: not every dissident could expect to be sent out of the country.

In Vietnam, the ability of the South Vietnamese Government to maintain the economic structure of the south was collapsing, but its ability to fight remained formidable. That year 80,000 Vietnamese soldiers and civilians were killed – the highest death toll in any year since the war began.

The scale of United States supplies to South Vietnam was continually being reduced, at the insistence of Congress, while the scale of Soviet and Chinese supplies to North Vietnam was continually growing. The Cambodian capital, Phnom Penh, was under attack by the local Communist Khmer Rouge forces. Although the attack was beaten off, the control of the Phnom Penh government was limited. In addition to the areas of Cambodia controlled by the Khmer Rouge, North Vietnamese Communist forces dominated the eastern and southern parts of the country, using them as a base for their offensive against South Vietnam. The territorial unity of Laos was also affected by the presence of large numbers of North Vietnamese troops, working alongside the local Pathet Lao Communists. But the agreement reached the previous year for the withdrawal of American and Thai troops was honoured: both met the sixty-day deadline that started on April 5.

In China the Communist Party was reasserting its power over the army. Leaders who quoted Mao Tse-tung's declamatory phrase 'Political power grows out of the barrel of a gun' were criticized for not completing the phrase: Mao Tse-tung had gone on to say, 'The Party must control the gun and the gun must never control the Party.' New regional military commanders were appointed, politically loyal to Peking. Party leaders who had been disgraced, humiliated and isolated during the Cultural Revolution were brought back to prominent positions.

The ideological imperatives of Chinese Communism were those of Stalin's Soviet Union of the 1930s. A strong offensive was launched throughout China against Western music. Student newspapers stressed that the 'social content' of music by Bach, Mozart, Beethoven, Schubert and Debussy was limited to unacceptable and harmful 'bourgeois' concepts. 'Some people talk about bourgeois classical music with great relish, are mesmerized by it and prostrate themselves before it, showing their slavish mentality for all things foreign,' the *Peking Review* wrote. Such people 'are nihilists with regard to national art. Their reverence for foreign things is actually reverence for the bourgeoisie.'

The Northern Irish conflict continued to take its toll. In February 1974 an IRA bomb on the British mainland killed twelve people – soldiers and their families – who were on a bus. On April 17 the number killed in the sectarian fighting since 1969 reached a thousand. On May 17 three car-bomb explosions in Dublin killed thirty-two people. A month later eleven people were killed by an IRA bomb which was detonated outside Westminster Hall, London. A further five people were killed when the IRA detonated two bombs in public houses in Guildford.

Terrorism had come from Northern Ireland to the mainland, but successive British Governments – Labour succeeded the Conservatives as the governing Party five days after the Guildford bombs – were equally determined not to give in to the demands for an end to British rule and the unification of Ireland under the Republic. The violence continued: on November 21, IRA bombs were detonated in two public houses in Birmingham, killing twenty-one people. Harold Wilson's new government acted swiftly, passing a Prevention of Terrorism Act through parliament on November 28 in twenty-four hours, giving police the power to hold terrorist suspects for up to five days without charges being laid against them. Suspects could also be banned from the British mainland, or deported from the mainland to Northern Ireland.

In Cyprus, there was turmoil after President Makarios accused the Greek Government in Athens of trying to take control of the island. The Greek junta – the senior army officers who had ruled Greece for the previous seven years – had been pressing its soldiers in Cyprus to assert the authority of Athens. When Makarios asked the Greek military rulers to order their 650 officers on Cyprus to obey the Cyprus Government, they refused. Makarios at once reduced the term of national military service from two years to fourteen months, making 400 of the Greek officers on Cyprus redundant. He then called on Athens to withdraw all its soldiers from the island.

The Greek Government reacted by sending its soldiers into action. On July 15 they attacked the presidential palace with tanks and artillery, and, seizing Cyprus Radio, broadcast mendaciously: 'Makarios is dead.' He had in fact escaped from his palace a few minutes before it was overrun. Fleeing to the west coast of the island he broadcast an appeal to his people to preserve their independence. He was then lifted off by Royal Air Force helicopter to the British sovereign base in the south of the island, from where he was flown to Britain.

The Turkish Government looked with alarm on the Greek action in overthrowing the Government of Cyprus. Under the 1960 Treaty of Guarantee, Turkey, Greece and Britain reserved the right to intervene militarily if no common action could be devised to preserve the Cyprus constitution and the island's independence. On July 17 the Turkish Prime Minister, Bülent Ecevit, flew to London to propose joint Anglo-Turkish intervention. The British Government declined to act. Ecevit returned to Turkey, where on July 19 he and his cabinet colleagues authorized the invasion of Cyprus.

Turkish forces landed in the north – and predominantly Turkish – part of the island on July 20. After two days' fighting a cease-fire was called and the island partitioned along the cease-fire line. In Athens the military regime that had sought Greek control of the island was itself overthrown – without violence – on July 23, to be replaced by a democratic administration. Turkey decided to secure more territory on Cyprus. Between August 14 and August 16, Turkish forces occupied further, largely Turkish-inhabited, territory along the northern coast. Anger at Turkey's war-making led the United States to cut off its substantial military aid to Turkey. A call by the United Nations General Assembly for a Turkish withdrawal from the island was rejected by Turkey. Instead, a United Nations peace-keeping force took up positions along the cease-fire line, and in the divided capital of Nicosia. It was still there when the century came to an end.

Man's impact on the global environment was brought alarmingly to the forefront in 1974, when two American scientists, M. Molina and F.S. Rowland, warned that chlorofluorocarbons (CFCs), as used in domestic fridges and as propellants in domestic aerosols – such as hair sprays and deodorants – were damaging the atmosphere's ozone layer, which filters out ultraviolet radiation from the sun. A quarter of a century later the nations of the world were still struggling to regulate the use of CFCs, and to protect the ozone layer from further damage. But the 'hole' which was identified in the 1970s above Antarctica continued to grow in the following two decades, presenting dangers for generations yet unborn unless stronger international measures could be put into place.

Nature's ravages remained ferocious. Famine in India killed several hundred thousand people: visitors to Bombay were shocked at the sight of the dead and the dying in the gutters and on the pavements of the main streets of such a modern, bustling metropolis. In Bangladesh the scale of the famine was even greater, with as many as one and a half million people dying of starvation. From this horrific disaster came a human act of revitalization: the creation by a young Bangladeshi economist, Muhammad Yunus, of the Grameen ('village') Bank.

Based on the belief that 'every human being, even one barefoot and begging in the street, is a potential entrepreneur', Yunus established the principle of 'micro-credit'. The Grameen Bank lent tiny sums of money to the poorest of the poor, to people without land, education, or even a shelter. More than ninety per cent of the loans went to women, many of whom had never been allowed by their menfolk to handle cash.

Professor Yunus was warned that the poor would never repay, but he argued that, unlike the rich, the poor could not risk not repaying, for these loans were their only chance to escape penury. Using meticulous organization and a repayment system adapted to village needs and income levels, Grameen's recovery record exceeded ninety-eight per cent, far better than high-street lending to small businesses in Britain. A quarter of a century after it came into being Grameen was a £1.43 billion business, lending an average of £21 million a month. Micro-credit banks modelled on it spread to fifty-eight countries, including the United States and Poland.

Twenty-four years after the famine which led to the establishment of the Grameen Bank, the worst floods in Bangladesh's history submerged and destroyed the homes, fields and crops of half of Grameen's two and a half million clients there, forcing the hard, uncertain task of reconstruction to begin again.

In 1974 the population of the world passed four billion: 4,000 million. More than three-quarters of the world's inhabitants were living in poverty, at the edge of starvation, scarcely able to earn enough by their labour or to produce enough food to feed their families. With the world population and global poverty both increasing on an unprecedented scale, the United Nations called for a New International Economic Order, in which the development of the Third World would be a priority, towards which the industrialized nations would take the main responsibility. To emphasize the urgency the United Nations announced that 500 million children, in seventy poor countries, were facing starvation or severe malnutrition.

From the earliest days of 1975 the South Vietnamese Government called on the United States for arms, as North Vietnamese and Vietcong forces overrran the Mekong Delta, pressing ever closer to the capital, Saigon. President Ford ordered a United States naval task force to coastal waters, but limited its efforts to reconnaissance flights over Vietnam and Cambodia to observe what was taking place.

The United States Congress would not contemplate any return of American troops. Time had also run out for a new American intervention. As the Communist forces advanced towards the Cambodian capital, Phnom Penh, Ford had no alternative but to authorize the evacuation of all remaining American diplomatic and military personnel there, five years after America had made its first commitment to help sustain the regime against Communist assault. On April 17 the Khmer Rouge captured Phnom Penh. Thousands of civilians were shot down in the streets in cold blood. Twelve days later all remaining American personnel were evacuated from the South Vietnamese capital, Saigon, which North Vietnamese troops entered later that day. On the following day the South Vietnamese Government surrendered.

Tension remained high. In the second week of May the Cambodian navy seized an American merchant ship, the *Mayaguez*. Its crew of forty was held captive. President Ford reacted immediately, ordering an American aircraft carrier to the Gulf of Thailand. While American bombers struck at the Cambodian air force, destroying seventeen Cambodian warplanes, American marines landed and recaptured the *Mayaguez*. During the struggle fifteen of the landing party were killed. The crew were released.

Following the fall of Saigon and the establishment of a unified Communist government based on Hanoi, thousands of South Vietnamese set off by boat, mostly in hardly seaworthy craft, in search of a place of refuge. Many drowned on the journey. Others were turned away from hostile shores, but 132,000 were given sanctuary in the United States.

On December 3, the Government of Laos fell to the Laotian Communists. The three nations of Indochina – Laos, Cambodia and Vietnam – whose political future had drawn in first France and then the United States, were under the rule of those against whom outside forces had pitted themselves for thirty years. Tens of thousands of lives – many of them the lives of soldiers brought half way round the world – had been lost, in a vain attempt to sustain regimes that finally, amid the violence of civil war, had been swept away.

In the Cold War new weapons were raising new spectres of danger. The Soviet Union had developed a nuclear-armed 'Backfire' bomber that could reach areas of the United States hitherto beyond Soviet bombers. The Soviet Union was also developing intercontinental missiles with multiple warheads: warheads that, from a single missile, could be directed against different targets many miles apart. The Americans were also developing a new weapon, the 'Cruise' missile, which, without a pilot, could be launched from an aeroplane or a submarine. If fired from the White Sea or the Sea of Japan, it too could reach many points in the Soviet Union hitherto beyond range of nuclear assault.

In Northern Ireland, 245 people died during 1975 in terrorist attacks by extremist Catholic and Protestant groups. In June a four-year-old Catholic girl was killed in Belfast by a bomb placed in her father's car, while later that year a six-year-old Protestant girl was killed by gunmen trying to shoot her father. In an attempt at conciliation, on December 5 the British Government ended detention without trial. Forty-six IRA prisoners were released. As they left prison they swore to carry on the struggle.

Detention without trial in Northern Ireland, introduced in 1974 as a reaction to the continuation of terror, had raised protests by human rights groups in Britain. Violations of human rights elsewhere were on a far larger scale. General Pinochet's regime in Chile was condemned by the United Nations General Assembly on December 9 for 'the institutionalized practice of torture'. Its call to Pinochet 'to restore and safeguard essential human rights and fundamental liberties' was ignored.

Worldwide, urban pollution was becoming a major heath hazard. So severe was the air pollution in Madrid in January 1975 that citizens were urged to breathe through their noses not their mouths, to take no outdoor physical exercise, and to talk as little as possible except indoors. In Britain, legislation was introduced giving every worker in factory or shop the right to be told the details of work-related pollution.

The industrialized nations were faced with the dangers of their own economic success and industrial expansion. The Third World countries had no such perspective. Those without raw materials on any significant scale had to turn to the industrialized nations for financial and material aid. The intense poverty in the Third World was even augmented in some countries by despotic rulers stealing the wealth of their own people, sometimes literally sending it out of the country in suitcases to safe banking havens. Henry Kissinger warned: 'The division of the planet between north and south, between rich and poor, could become as grim as the darkest period of the Cold War.'

Enormous deficits were accumulated by countries which had been struggling for many years to build up some minimal global competitiveness. During 1975, as oil prices remained artificially high as a result of the Arab world's punishment of Israel, both Zaire and Zambia lost more than three-quarters of the currency reserves with which they had begun the year. Bangladesh had no reserves at all: it was dependent for its economic survival, and for feeding its population, on Western aid and credit. In February the United Nations Development Programme agreed that ten 'low-income' countries would be the beneficiaries of technical aid in excess of $80 million. Smaller sums were allocated to Burma for agriculture, forestry and fisheries; to Kenya for rural development; to Kuwait for industry; and to Nigeria for agriculture and education. The amount of money involved was very small indeed compared to the scale of poverty and indebtedness.

In India, more than sixty million people were living on the margin of starvation. India's eastern neighbour, Bangladesh, was even more at risk. Severe flooding regularly added to the plight of millions of people, whose homes and meagre possessions were washed away. At the same time, political turmoil made any orderly evolution of improvement impossible. In Bangladesh, in January, Sheikh Mujib ur-Rahman declared a one-Party State and established a virtual dictatorship. In August he was murdered by four army majors. His family was murdered with him. There followed a struggle for power within the army.

In Africa, those countries which had just acquired independence from Portugal were in grave economic difficulties, exacerbated in Angola by civil war between factions that had hitherto focused their struggle against the Portuguese. The victorious group, the Marxist-Leninist Popular Movement for the Liberation of Angola (MPLA) was sent military help from both the Soviet Union – which sent arms and military advisers – and Cuba, which sent 5,000 combat troops. The rival group, the National Union for Total Independence of Angola (UNITA) fought on, but the MPLA's Soviet weaponry was decisive. On November 24 President Ford warned the Soviet Union that the despatch of weapons, and of Soviet military advisers, had introduced the rivalry of Great Powers to Africa for the first time since the collapse of European colonial rule fifteen years earlier.

India, which prided itself on being 'the world's largest democracy', was in constitutional turmoil. The opposition claimed the government was maintaining power only by devious and corrupt methods, and put this to the judgment of the courts. On June 12 a judge of the Allahabad High Court held that the election by which the Prime Minister, Indira Gandhi – Jawaharlal Nehru's daughter – had been elected to parliament was void. He then disqualified her from holding public office for six years, on the grounds of 'corrupt practices' during the election. But she was allowed to remain Prime Minister pending an appeal to the Supreme Court.

Before that appeal could be heard, Mrs Gandhi used her Prime Ministerial powers to order the arrest of more than 600 opposition leaders, impose press censorship and declare a state of emergency. In November, after retrospective changes were made in the election law, the Supreme Court reversed the earlier verdict of 'corrupt practices'. The Press Council of India, set up to protect freedom of the press, was dissolved. A boost in the Indian economy gave Mrs Gandhi a respite: the grain harvest that year was one of the best on record. The previous year's discovery of oil was proving substantial, and a viable source of natural gas was also discovered. But the democratic values for which India had fought, and which Mrs Gandhi's father had embodied, were suborned.

In Portugal, popular pressure, given public expression by the Socialist Party, had led to the collapse of the dictatorship. An army attempt to restore dictatorship had been put down by force, and the Portuguese people went to the polls for the first democratic elections in more than half a century. A Parliamentary government was then set up, headed by the Socialist leader Mario Suares. The Communists had won only 2.5 per cent of the votes, but felt that their time for action had come. Revolutionary Councils were established in Lisbon and elsewhere, and Revolutionary Brigades set up. On November 25, soldiers sympathetic to the Communists seized air force bases around Lisbon, but were defeated by a force of commandos loyal to the government. Communists also seized the radio and television stations, from which they broadcast appeals for an uprising. They were soon driven out, street demonstrations in favour of the revolution were dispersed, and democracy was restored.

Portugal's political unrest had repercussions 10,000 miles away. Indonesia had been created after the Second World War from the former Dutch East Indies, the most easterly island of which, Timor, had been divided in the seventeenth century between the Dutch and the Portuguese. When Indonesia had become independent in 1949, West Timor became Indonesian, but East Timor remained Portuguese. In 1975, while Portugal was mired in conflict, the Indonesian army invaded East Timor. A year later it was annexed. For the following quarter of a century Indonesian security forces fought against East Timor separatists, and more than 200,000 people were killed.

In Spain, where democracy had disappeared almost forty years earlier, 500 civil servants signed a pro-democracy manifesto on February 6.

But Franco continued to rule with an iron hand. Basque and Catalan separatists felt the full rigour of police control. After the killing of several policemen, a law was passed whereby a person accused of murdering a policeman would be tried by summary court martial, with a mandatory death sentence on conviction. On September 18 five Basque separatists were convicted of killing policemen, and were sentenced to death. Pope Paul VI made a public plea that their lives should be spared. Fifteen European governments withdrew their ambassadors in protest, including all those of the European Economic Community. At the United Nations, Mexico called for Spain's expulsion.

Franco ignored the appeals and protests, and the executions were carried out on September 27. There were attacks on Spanish embassies and Spanish Government property in Lisbon, Ankara, Rome and Milan. This, Franco said – in a speech from the balcony of the royal palace on October 1, the thirty-ninth anniversary of his becoming Head of State – was proof of 'an international plot of Masons, Jews and Communists'.

Two weeks after his speech, eighty-three-year-old Franco was taken ill with influenza. On November 20 he died. His death was followed two days later by the restoration of the monarchy – under King Juan Carlos – and the promise of the re-establishment of parliamentary government for the first time since the collapse of the republican regime in 1939. Juan Carlos had been 'trained' by Franco from 1960 onwards, and recognized as the heir to the throne by the Franco government in 1969; but as soon as he came to the throne he showed a democratic independence of spirit which Franco's senior advisers hoped they had stamped out. As his first step towards true liberalization, on November 26 the King ordered the release of 500 of Franco's political prisoners. Six months later the ban on political Parties, which had been in force for more than a quarter of a century, was lifted. Western Europe's longest lasting dictatorship was at an end.

In 1975 the World Health Organization reported the elimination of viral smallpox in all but three of the thirty countries where it had been endemic ten years earlier. In the three countries still affected, it was being rapidly eradicated in India and Bangladesh. Only Ethiopia had yet to be freed from that killer.

The handicapped were beginning to receive recognition as a group that should be encouraged to play its fullest possible part in national life. A lead was taken on 29 November 1975 in the United States with the Education for All Handicapped Children Act, under which every publicly funded school was required to provide 'appropriate education' for all handicapped school-age children, irrespective of disability. The future of education also benefited that year by the marketing of the first 'personal computer'.

The United Nations had more than doubled its size since its establishment thirty years earlier, at the end of the Second World War. At the General Assembly in 1976, more than 140 nations participated in the debates. As a sign of the growing recognition of the importance and the problems of post-colonial Africa, the United Nations Economic and Social Council met for the first time in Africa, at Abidjan in the Ivory Coast. A few months later the fourth session of a United Nations conference on Trade and Development met in the Kenyan capital, Nairobi.

Some areas of conflict were receding. On 19 September 1976 Ian Smith, the Rhodesian Prime Minister, accepted the principle of majority rule. Two months earlier, on July 20, the last American servicemen had been withdrawn from Thailand, where they had been stationed as allies of a country threatened by Communist neighbours. Their presence there had begun twelve years earlier. At the height of the war in Vietnam there had been 50,000 Americans in Thailand.

In the Soviet Union, several dissidents were allowed to emigrate in 1976, among them Andrei Amalrik, who had written a book critical of the Soviet Union, and Vladimir Bukovsky, who had published an account of the treatment of dissidents in mental hospitals. Bukovsky was the beneficiary of an exchange: he was allowed to leave for the West when the military regime in Chile released the Chilean Communist leader, Luis Corvalan, from prison, and allowed him to make his home in the Soviet Union.

The Soviet authorities found a way of issuing a warning to anyone tempted to see the path of dissent as the road to emigration. The Bukovsky-Corvalan exchange took place on December 18. Within three days, Bukovsky's associate, Vladimir Borisov, who had helped him collect material on mental hospital abuses, was himself arrested and confined in a mental institution.

There was a setback to the Soviet presentation of its military prowess when a Soviet pilot, flying a MiG-25 'Foxbat' fighter and interceptor aircraft, landed in Japan and sought asylum. The Foxbat had been believed by the United States – encouraged in this belief by Soviet secrecy and innuendo – to be the world's 'most advanced' fighter aircraft. Its existence had alarmed the United States defence establishment. When the defector's plane was examined, however, it was found to be less effective as a fighter or as an interceptor – and, critically, far heavier and thus less speedily manoeuvrable – than its American counterparts. In the United States, 1976 marked the two hundredth anniversary of independence from Britain. Bicentennial year was also election year. The challenger chosen by the Democrats was the Governor of Georgia, Jimmy Carter, who declared that he was 'twice born' – first at birth and then when he 'committed himself to Jesus'. In answer to the charge that he was an outsider, a provincial unknown, 'Jimmy who?', not well versed in the ways of Washington, he gained public support by distancing himself from those in Washington who were tarred by the stigmas of Vietnam and Watergate. 'The insiders have had their chances, and they have not delivered,' he said. 'Their time has run out.' President Ford lost and Carter became President.

In Northern Ireland the sectarian violence continued. On January 6, after fifteen people had been killed in two days, a Special Air Service (SAS) elite unit was sent from the British mainland to try to restore order. On July 21 the British Ambassador to Dublin was murdered. The intensity of sectarian violence reached a pitch of public revulsion on August 10, when three children who were walking with their mother were killed by an IRA car which crashed into them after its driver had been shot dead by soldiers. The death of the Maguire children created an instant backlash. Later in the week a group of Catholic women, led by Mairead Corrigan, the children's aunt, and

Betty Williams, created a protest movement, the Peace People, which asked women throughout the province to help them bring the killings to an end.

On August 14, after the IRA threatened the leaders of the Peace People with death, 10,000 women, most of them Catholics but including some Protestants, took part in a peace rally. Two weeks later, peace marches were held all over Northern and Southern Ireland. Protestant and Catholic women marched together, embraced, and wept.

From Germany and Norway came words of admiration for the Peace People, and considerable financial support. The IRA, however, denounced the Peace People and, on October 23, attacked a peace march. Sixteen of the marchers had to be taken to hospital. Five days later a leading Republican, Maire Drumm, was shot dead by Protestant gunmen in a Belfast hospital. In November the IRA renewed its attacks against off-duty Ulster Defence Regiment members: fifteen were murdered by the end of the year. On December 13 a spate of IRA bombs brought the centre of Belfast to a halt. As 1976 came to an end the bombing campaign intensified. The Peace People did not give up their work, but they could not compete with the tyranny of extremism.

As extremists on both sides meted out death in Northern Ireland, in California a law permitted those who were terminally ill to authorize the removal of life-support equipment. In Britain, the Race Relations Act made incitement to race hatred an offence, and established a Commission on Race Equality to monitor discrimination and take steps to reduce it.

In South Africa, student demonstrators in the Soweto suburb of Johannesburg began a protest on June 16 against a government proposal for compulsory teaching in Afrikaans. The protest continued for nine days. When police opened fire on the demonstrators, seventy-six students were killed. On July 6 the government dropped its education proposal. But anti-apartheid demonstrations took place throughout the country, and were dispersed by force. By the end of the year, 500 black South Africans had been killed. Many had been shot dead by riot police using automatic rifles.

*   *   *

In the Middle East, civil war had broken out the previous July in Lebanon between the Christian and Muslim communities. The PLO under Yasser Arafat was also based in Lebanon, and Iraq and Libya sent troops to support the Muslims. Beirut was divided, with Christian East Beirut and Muslim West Beirut exchanging frequent shellfire. As street fighting spread in the capital, many civilians were massacred.

In May, 6,000 Syrian troops entered Lebanon. In Beirut, pro-Syrian and anti-Syrian Palestinians fought for control. An Arab Peace Force of 10,000 men was formed by the Arab League, and intervened to try to stop the Palestinian civil war inside Beirut. Like the Syrian troops before it, it failed, and withdrew. On August 12 Tell al-Za'atar, a Muslim enclave in Christian East Beirut, was overrun, and its inhabitants, many of them the families of Palestinian refugees from the 1948 Arab-Israel war, were massacred by the Christian Falangist militia.

The Arab Peace Force, increased to 30,000, was designated a 'deterrent force'. Both sides withdrew from the areas they had overrun. The Lebanese accepted the presence of the PLO in their midst. On November 15 the Arab Peace Force, made up almost entirely of Syrian troops, entered Beirut, establishing its own quasi-military rule. In the course of the fighting, 40,000 people – Lebanese Christians, Lebanese Muslims, and Palestinians – had been killed.

Israel was also caught up in conflict. On June 27 an Air France passenger airliner on its way from Tel Aviv to Paris was hijacked by Arab terrorists shortly after takeoff from Athens. The pilot was ordered to fly to Benghazi in Libya, where the hijackers separated out the Israeli and Jewish passengers, and then released the non-Jews. The Jews – ninety-eight in all – were flown on to Entebbe in Uganda, 2,500 miles from Israel, and held hostage at Entebbe airport.

Inside Israel, amid a sense of terrible impotence, the balance of public opinion was that the freedom of the hostages must be secured by complying with the hijackers' demands. These included the release of Palestinian terrorists of Yasser Arafat's Fatah (victory) movement being held in Israeli prisons. On July 3 the Prime Minister, Yitzhak Rabin, and his Cabinet, decided to free the kidnap victims by an armed intervention of their own.

Four large carrier aircraft took part in the mission, flying from the southernmost point of the Sinai, Sharm el-Sheikh, directly to Entebbe. All the terrorists – Arabs and Germans – were killed during the raid, as were three of the civilian hostages caught in the crossfire. The commander of the rescue mission, Yonatan Netanyahu, was also killed, by a bullet through the heart. Twenty years later his brother Benjamin – who also served as a commando – was to become Prime Minister of Israel. One of the hostages, an elderly woman named Dora Bloch, had been taken to the local hospital before the rescue raid, after some meat caught in her throat and she began to choke. She was murdered after the raid, while still in the hospital.

On January 8, the Chinese Prime Minister, Chou En-lai, died at the age of seventy-eight. He had been ill with cancer for four years. Mao Tse-tung was also seriously ill. In June it was announced that he would receive no more foreign visitors. In July, Marshal Chu Teh, the commander of the Long March in 1934 and 1935, and victor of the Communist-Kuomintang military struggle from 1946 to 1949, died. He was ninety years old. While mourning their military hero, the people of China were being prepared to learn of the demise of their Great Leader. But before they could do so, on July 28, China was hit by an earthquake more severe than any in the history of the world since the sixteenth century. At least a quarter of a million Chinese were killed. With a stubbornness derived from almost thirty years of rigid Communist rule, all outside aid was refused, even from the United Nations.

Mao Tse-tung died in Peking on September 9. He was eighty-three years old. Although 300,000 Chinese filed past his body in the Great Hall of the People, the grief was less spontaneous and less widespread than when Chou En-lai had died eight months earlier. The dictator had been a remote and frightening figure, associated increasingly with frenetic and cataclysmic change. Following his death, Hua Kuo-feng became ruler of China. One of his first acts was to order the arrest – and detention in a secret location – of four of those who had been closest to Mao Tse-tung – the four leaders of the Cultural Revolution – including Mao Tse-tung's widow. They were accused of having served as a 'Gang of Four' acting against the orders of the true leader. That China would change in the aftermath of Mao Tse-tung's death was clear, even in small things: within six months, Beethoven was rehabilitated and the ban on Shakespeare lifted.

While China struggled to adjust to the deaths of Chou En-lai and Mao Tse-tung, India, the world's second most populous country, entered the second year of Indira Gandhi's emergency. On January 8, the right of an individual to seek the protection of the law courts with regard to freedom of expression, assembly, movement or residence, was suspended. Press censorship was maintained, and several newspapers closed down entirely. The independent news agencies were amalgamated into a single government agency, and six foreign correspondents were expelled for defying the censorship. Power was being accrued by Indira Gandhi's son Sanjay, who announced a five-point programme for India that was intended to have wide-reaching social effects, and had echoes of Gandhism in it: family planning, tree planting, a ban on dowries, 'each one, teach one' and the end to caste discrimination.

As the population of India reached 600 million, Sanjay Gandhi also led a campaign, in conjunction with his family planning programme, for massive sterilization, both of men and women: this led to an outcry in the West, particularly when in some States the 'reward' offered in return for a vasectomy was a radio. There were many peasants for whom such an inducement was eagerly acceptable.

With the exception of the Soviet Union, the imperial and colonial era was over. From the Baltic Sea to the Pacific Ocean, and from the Arctic Ocean to the Caspian Sea, the Soviet Union was ruler of many dozens of national groups, each forced to pledge its language, flag, national heroes, even religion – for there were several Muslim republics in Soviet Central Asia – to the greater good, and political will, of Moscow. The United States had relinquished its control over the Philippines. Holland had long seen an end to its possession in the Dutch East Indies. France was almost gone from Africa. Portuguese rule in Africa was ended. Globally, little was left of the British and French Empires. On June 18, Britain conceded independence to the Seychelles, an island group – of 115 islands in all, spread over 400,000 square miles of the Indian Ocean – which it had ceded from France in 1810. The Seychelles became the 145th member of the United Nations. Its population, of little more than 50,000, was a mixture of English expatriates, a French upper class, Chinese and Indian traders, and African and Asian workers. It was also becoming a tourist paradise in the era of package holiday tours. Within two years of independence, a coup took place and the Seychelles became a one-party State: a situation that was to last for more than a decade.

Natural disasters caused far greater loss of life in 1976 than any of the military or civil conflicts that year. In addition to the quarter of a million Chinese killed in the earthquake in central China, 23,000 people died in the Central American republic of Guatemala on February 4, when ten towns were completely destroyed. Considerable financial help was sent by both the United States and Venezuela; but – just as China had refused all United Nations help, so Guatemala refused any help from Britain, because of a territorial dispute with the self-governing British colony of Belize – which had been known until 1973 as British Honduras.

Whether the needs of the world were exceeded by its resources was much debated. From May 31 to June 11 a special United Nations conference on Human Settlements (Habitat) was held in Vancouver. It proposed a series of definite measures, to be undertaken in the main by the wealthier industrialized nations, whereby basic living needs – shelter, clean water and a decent physical environment – could be made available to every inhabitant of the globe. There was no shortage of recipients for aid. More than 400,000 Lebanese had been forced from their homes, or lost their homes altogether during the Lebanese civil war. There had been earthquakes in Guatemala and West Irian, floods in Pakistan, and severe drought and crop failure in Cape Verde. Cambodia, Laos and Vietnam were struggling to recover from the ravages of the Vietnam War: it was the Canadian government that made the first, and largest national contribution for humanitarian assistance there, giving the United Nations a cheque for $250,000. The United States provided $2 million for the last of the campaigns to eliminate smallpox in Ethiopia.

By far the largest national contributions were to the United

Nations Development Programme. In the urgent need to build up agricultural training in the poorest countries, more than $500 million was raised, a fifth of which came from Britain, West Germany and Japan. The irony was not lost on keen-eyed observers that two of the three main donors had been nations which, thirty years earlier, had emerged defeated, devastated and bankrupt from the Second World War.

In 1976, Apple computers was founded in the United States, by Steven Jobs and Stephen Wozniak. They were to be part of a world-wide revolution in easier, swifter and more efficient communication, whereby the world of business, the world of administration and the world of leisure were all enhanced.

The two Super Powers were edging ever closer to agreement with regard to their nuclear armaments. In March 1977 the American Secretary of State, Cyrus Vance, went to Moscow with new proposals for the second Strategic Arms Limitation Talks (SALT II). Two months later, after many difficulties and disagreements, a 'new framework for negotiations' was announced and the talks edged towards agreement. There were no longer flashpoints of potential conflict between the United States and the Soviet Union. In July, observers from NATO were invited to witness Soviet ground/air exercises inside Russia. Details of troop concentrations in both the Warsaw Pact and Russian Baltic Sea manoeuvres were reported to NATO as a matter of course. Both East Germany and Poland were in negoti-ation with West Germany. The future of Berlin – although the Berlin Wall still divided the city – was no longer an issue threatening blockades.

Vietnam pursued its course as a Communist State. Korea remained divided, with neither the United States nor the Soviet Union prepared to become embroiled in the continuing disputes between North and South. The decision by President Carter to with-draw 33,000 American ground troops from South Korea signalled to the South Koreans just how much it would have to become its own protector, despite Carter's assurance that the United States was 'committed' to the defence of South Korea.

Super Power rivalries no longer held their earlier element of danger. But regional and local conflicts continued to lead to heavy loss of life and misery. In Cambodia there were border clashes with Thailand, and in one incident the civilian inhabitants of three Thai villages were massacred. They were accused of sheltering Cambodian resistance groups. To secure his border against infiltration by groups hostile to his dictatorial regime, the Cambodian Prime Minister, Pol Pot, ordered the depopulation of a strip of territory just inside his border. This was done with great cruelty. Pol Pot was also perpetrating terrifying crimes inside his country. The total death toll during five years of Khmer Rouge domination was a million and a half, out of a total population of eight million. In neighbouring Laos, a full-scale military operation was launched, supported by Vietnamese troops, against the Meo tribesmen who were fighting to prevent Communist control of their villages. Dozens of Meo villages were destroyed, and their inhabitants forced out of the hills, to prevent them from supporting the Meo guerrilla groups that fought on.

The main focus of tyranny in Africa was in Uganda. In February there were mass killings of members of the Acholi and Langi tribes. On February 8 the Anglican Archbishop of Uganda, Janani Luwum, met with eighteen Ugandan bishops and drafted a letter to Idi Amin, accusing the security services of torture. 'We have buried many who have died as a result of being shot,' they wrote.

The letter of protest was sent to Amin, and a copy smuggled across the border into Kenya, where many Ugandan exiles had gathered. On February 17 Archbishop Luwum, himself a member of the much-persecuted Acholi tribe, was found dead. The Ugandan government insisted he had been killed in a road accident while trying to escape the country. But eyewitnesses had seen bullet holes in the archbishop's body. Two of Amin's Cabinet Ministers were among those murdered with the archbishop.

Tens of thousands of Ugandans sought asylum outside the country, including Amin's former Ministers of Health, Justice and Information.

In Rhodesia, even as the all-white government of Ian Smith was being pressed strongly by the United States and Britain to honour its pledge of majority rule, a 'war of liberation' was being fought by those who preferred to seize power rather than wait for it to be transferred. It was the thirteenth year of illegal independence, and the two main guerrilla groups, the Zimbabwe African People's Union (ZAPU), under Joshua Nkomo, and the Zimbabwe African National Union (ZANU), under Robert Mugabe, had united to form a single political and fighting force, the Patriotic Front. Rejecting negotiations, it carried out continual attacks on Rhodesian military installations, operating from bases in both Mozambique and Zambia. ZAPU was able to call upon arms and ammunition from the Soviet Union; ZANU from China.

The Smith regime carried out a series of military raids into the countries in which the Rhodesian guerrillas were based. During a Rhodesian army attack into Mozambique in November, 1,200 members of the Patriotic Front were killed. Inside Rhodesia the killings mounted. In February three Jesuit priests and four Dominican nuns were murdered at a mission station forty-three miles east of the capital, Salisbury, bringing the number of murdered missionaries to thirteen in nine months. The death toll during the year was 1,759 ZANU and ZAPU guerrillas killed, a thousand black Rhodesians, 244 members of the Rhodesian security forces, and fifty-six white Rhodesians. In measures designed to cut off the guerrillas from local support, the Smith government resettled more than a quarter of a million Africans in 'protected villages'.

In South Africa, on average a black African was dying each month while being held in detention – and there was outrage in the West after the death in police detention of Steve Biko, founder of the moderate 'Black Consciousness' movement. Several South African newspapers expressed their scepticism at the government's claim that Biko had died after going on hunger strike. Pressure for an inquiry was such that the government gave in: the inquiry revealed that Biko had been kept naked and in shackles while in detention, and had been driven, naked, in the back of a truck all the way from Port Elizabeth to Pretoria while suffering serious brain damage. The cause of death was given as a head injury. The world was shocked at this act of brutality by the white government.

Following Steve Biko's death there was violence in many black townships in South Africa. In an attempt to bring the full weight of the law down on the demonstrators, many of whom were supporters of Biko's Black Consciousness movement, the government banned the organization and detained its leaders. Another civil rights organization, the Christian Institute, which spanned all Christian denominations and all races, was banned at the same time.

Hitherto, the Western nations had hesitated before agreeing to an arms embargo against South Africa. Steve Biko's murder and the subsequent banning orders hardened Western opinion. When the call for a mandatory arms embargo came before the United Nations Security Council, there was no one willing to veto it. Canada, which, as a former Commonwealth partner, had been promoting its trade with South Africa, brought all its promotional activities to a halt.

In the Horn of Africa, war had broken out between Ethiopia and Somalia. Somali forces quickly overran much of south-eastern Ethiopia: the Somali-inhabited Ogaden region was almost entirely under Somali control by the end of July. But Soviet military aid to Ethiopia, some of it sent by air, enabled the Marxist ruler, Colonel Mengistu, to halt the Somali attack. The Somali Government, hitherto much beholden to the Soviet Union for arms and support, expelled several thousand Soviet experts who had been helping create a military and industrial infrastructure for the country, and appealed to the United States, Britain, France and West Germany for arms. They refused to comply until the fighting with Ethiopia ended. Only Saudi Arabia sent arms and munitions. Both West Germany and the United States did agree, at the end of the year, to send agricultural aid and medicines. Somalia was too poor a country to sustain a war and also a subsistence domestic economy. As the fighting continued, the economic plight of most Somalis lapsed from hardship to disaster.

For the Ethiopians, internal rivalries led to a struggle even bloodier than that on the battlefield. Colonel Mengistu murdered his rivals – former colleagues – and instituted a reign of terror in which as many as 2,000 opponents of his regime were killed, several hundred during anti-government riots. By turning for support to the Soviet Union, Mengistu was able to acquire the arms needed to sustain his tyranny. The United States military mission was expelled, and American arms sales were suspended.

In an attack on those suspected of supporting the banned rival Marxist Ethiopian People's Revolutionary Party, a further thousand Ethiopians were killed by government forces. 'It is a historical obligation to clean up vigilantly using the revolutionary sword,' declared Mengistu, in calling for what he called a 'red terror' against opponents of the regime. At the end of November, Amnesty International put the number of those assassinated by the regime in political killings during the previous eight months at more than 100,000.

The scale of the killings in the Ethiopian countryside was unknown. Mengistu frequently exhorted his troops to root out 'bandits', 'feudalists' and 'anarchists', and they were undoubtedly vigilant, and ruthless, in doing so. The main source of revolt was in Eritrea. There, the insurgent forces, themselves Marxist, overran all the main Ethiopian strongholds, until Mengistu could only supply the capital, Asmara, by air.

At the edge of the Ethiopian-Somali war and the Ethiopian-Eritrean conflict, France's last African colony, Djibouti, became independent on June 2, after more than a century of French rule. It was the smallest and poorest of the independent African States. France agreed to maintain French economic aid, and to keep 4,500 French troops in the new republic as protection against external attack.

In Israel, a new government, headed by the right-wing Likud leader Menachem Begin, came to power on June 20. When President Carter asked Begin if he would accept a Palestinian State on the West Bank, he replied that such a State would be a 'mortal danger' to Israel: it would become a Soviet base two and a half hours flying time from Odessa. But he was prepared to offer 'full autonomy' to the Palestinians on the West Bank and in Gaza, and hinted at a possible agreement between Israel and Egypt. Secret Israeli-Egyptian negotiations began in Morocco on September 16. On November 7, in a speech to the Egyptian Parliament in Cairo, Sadat astounded his own parliamentarians, and the Israeli public, by saying he wanted to address the Israeli Parliament – the Knesset – in Jerusalem. 'I am willing to go to the ends of the earth for peace,' he said. Although Jerusalem was only 265 miles from Cairo, in political terms it was indeed the ends of the earth.

On November 19 Sadat landed, in an Egyptian plane, at Israel's Ben Gurion airport. To Begin, waiting on the tarmac with several hundred Israeli dignatories, he said: 'No more war. Let us make peace.' On November 20 he addressed the Israeli parliament, and in front of the incredulous members of the Knesset, and more than a million Israeli television viewers, shook hands with Begin on the podium. It was only four years since their two countries had been locked in war.

One of the four Arab nations at war with Israel since 1948 was breaking ranks and making peace. The public mood in Israel was full of the expectation of an end to conflict. In one year, with the help of the United States, agreement was reached.

A United Nations agency, the World Health Organization, proposed the year 2000 as the time when 'health for all' would have been achieved. To this end, it increased its budget for research into cancer and tropical diseases. Success was reported in the continued elimination of smallpox from India and Bangladesh. But fighting between Ethiopia and Somalia meant the long-cherished aim of eliminating smallpox in Ethiopia that year could not be fulfilled.

The United Nations agencies struggled to meet the urgent needs of many nations. Help was provided for the survivors of earthquakes in Turkey and Roumania – where 1,500 people were killed in March. Massive aid was sent to those affected by drought in Vietnam and Sri Lanka (formerly Ceylon). A tornado in Bangladesh had made hundreds of thousands homeless. A tornado which struck southern India on November 19 killed more than 8,000 people. Refugees from civil strife in Angola, Rhodesia and the Western Sahara required immediate help: basic shelter and food with which to survive at all.

In India, Indira Gandhi, after a two-year emergency rule, called an election, released the opposition leaders whom she had imprisoned, and, when defeated at the polls by the electorate, laid down the premiership. One by one the measures she had taken to curb freedom of expression were removed.

Human rights remained at the forefront of the international agenda, stimulated by an agreement signed in Helsinki in 1975. Yet in many regions of the world the human rights which Helsinki guaranteed were under sustained attack. In the Soviet Union, in anticipation of the signature in Belgrade of what was known as the Helsinki Final Act – linking international trade agreements with the ending of human rights violations – Brezhnev authorized strenuous measures against those human rights activists who, under the legal auspices of the Helsinki Agreement, had established Helsinki monitor groups in several Soviet cities. In February, two members of the twelve-member co-ordinating group of monitors, Dr Yury Orlov and Alexander Ginzburg, were arrested. Another member, Ludmilla Alekseeva, was 'encouraged' to emigrate. Members of local Helsinki monitor groups in the Ukraine, Georgia and Lithuania were arrested. Also arrested was one of the spokesmen of the Moscow group, Anatoly Shcharansky, a Jew who had been refused permission three years earlier to emigrate to Israel. He was sentenced to thirteen years' incarceration.

On November 5 the Soviet Union announced a general amnesty for prisoners. The euphoria among human rights activists throughout the world quickly subsided when it was made clear by the Soviet authorities that the amnesty applied only to criminals, not to political prisoners. Prison was not the only means of striking at dissent. When a Moscow University philosopher, Alexander Zinoviev, wrote a novel satirizing Soviet society, he could not get it published in Russia, so he had it published in Switzerland. As a result, he was dismissed from his job and refused any further academic employment.

In Czechoslovakia, 242 human rights activists signed a petition – Charter 77 – criticizing the violation of human rights by the Czechoslovak Government. Following the example of the Helsinki monitors in the Soviet Union, the Charter 77 signatories set up a nationwide movement to monitor violations of human rights. By the end of the year almost a thousand Czechs had signed the Charter. It was a courageous act of defiance. Many intellectuals in the West, including Communist Party members, expressed public support for the Charter's aims. The Czechoslovak Government took action to deter scrutiny of its human rights record; many Charter signatories were dismissed from their jobs, some were arrested, brought to trial and imprisoned, among them the playwright Vaclav Havel – who twenty years later was to be President of Czechoslovakia.

As a gesture of support to Charter 77, the Dutch Foreign Minister, on an official visit to Prague, insisted on seeing one of the three spokesmen of the movement, the seventy-seven-year-old philosopher Professor Jan Patocka. After the Foreign Minister's return to Holland, Professor Patocka – who was already under official displeasure for refusing to apply political criteria for promotions in the Academy of Sciences, whose educational institute he headed – was interrogated at length by the police. Within days of his interrogation he suffered a brain haemorrhage and died.

Human rights violations were not confined to the Communist bloc. On 17 January 1977 the European Human Rights Commission found Turkey guilty of torture in Cyprus. On February 7, at the European Court of Human Rights – which had been set up under the auspices of the Council of Europe – the British Government admitted 'malpractices' against prisoners in Northern Ireland six years earlier, and promised never again to use the sleep deprivation techniques which had led to the accusation. On February 21 the Argentine Commission for Human Rights gave a figure of 2,300 as the number of Argentinians killed during the eleven-month rule of General Videla. In an additional, deeply disturbing development, 20,000 to 30,000 Argentinians had simply disappeared. They were never seen again. It later emerged that the bodies of many of them, after they been murdered, were flown over the sea and dumped in the Atlantic. In Chile, on March 12, all political Parties were banned and censorship tightened. On May 18 a report by the International Commission of Jurists estimated that during the first two years of Idi Amin's rule in Uganda between 80,000 and 90,000 people had been killed: and the killings were continuing.

In Iran, opposition to the rule of the Shah gained in intensity throughout the year. From Paris, the Muslim religious leader, the Ayatollah Khomeini, an exile for fifteen years, called for uprisings against the secular authority. In the holy city of Qom, the Ayatollah's spiritual base, rioting began on 7 January 1978. Troops loyal to the Shah opened fire and sixty demonstrators were killed. On July 23 there were mass demonstrations in the holy city of Meshed, and several dozen demonstrators were killed. On August 12 military rule was imposed in Isfahan. In retaliation, Islamic fundamentalists set fire to a cinema in Abadan, and 430 people were killed. This escalating political strife was briefly and terribly overshadowed on September 16, when an earthquake in Iran killed 21,000 people. World sympathy was roused, and aid was flown in from many nations to help feed the survivors and provide them with shelter.

The impulse of Islamic fervour continued. In November there were six days of rioting in Teheran. A strike of oilworkers in December paralysed the country's main source of foreign exchange, and Iran's oil production fell so low that it could no longer meet even domestic needs. On December 10 a million people marched through the streets of Teheran, calling for the Ayatollah Khomeini's return and the Shah's abdication.

While the Shah battled to prevent the rise of militant Islam, his eastern neighbour, Afghanistan, was moving to another extreme: Communism. For five years the government of Muhammad Daud had suppressed Islamic groups with severity, moving steadily closer in its international alignments to the United States, and to the Shah's Iran. On April 27, Daud was assassinated, as were many of his closest supporters. The leaders of the predominantly military coup proclaimed a Republican Revolutionary Council, sought immediate support from the Soviet Union – which was forthcoming – and on April 30 proclaimed a democratic republic. It was to be run on Marxist lines.

China was seeking greater contact with the outside world. In February a barter agreement was signed with Japan, under which Chinese oil and coal were exchanged for Japanese steel and advanced technology industrial plants. Also in February the European Economic Community and China signed their first agreement. In December the Chinese signed a trade and technology agreement with the United States.

Domestically, the Chinese Government was turning its back on the rigidity of the past. The Chinese People's Political Consultative

Conference, which had not met since the Cultural Revolution, set new, more realistic targets for economic development. The ban on foreign loans, and on foreign investment in China – bans on which Mao Tse-tung had insisted – were swept away. Joint Chinese-foreign projects, which he had strongly opposed, were welcomed.

The Soviet Union also faced ideological challenges. In April there were riots in the Georgian capital, Tbilisi, where the Georgian language had been refused the status of the official language of the republic. The Party bowed to the public protest. In Estonia, there was growing hostility to the dominance of Moscow. Russian dissidents, who continued to monitor the Soviet Union's fulfilment of the human rights clauses of the Helsinki agreement, were arrested and brought to trial. Six sentences in rapid succession that year were given wide publicity by the Soviet authorities.

In Poland, disaffection with the Communist authorities led to the setting up of a Students' Solidarity Committee, 'Solidarity', which was active in all Poland's university cities. 'Flying academic courses' were organized in private homes, in which lessons were given to challenge the Communist-imposed curricula in the State universities. In January, sixty-five leading Polish intellectuals, scholars and university teachers formed an Educational Courses Society to ensure that the flying courses were as well-taught and as effective as possible. The authorities frowned on the venture, but did not suppress it.

A new era had begun in Poland, where more and more groups tested how far the non-Communist and Catholic impetus of the mass of the Poles could be pushed. Free trade unions were being set up, also with the 'Solidarity' label, in most industrial cities. A Peasants' Self-Defence Committee was set up by the quarter of a million Polish farmers who had been allowed, on a small scale, to own and manage their own farms. These farmers refused to pay their State pension contributions, on the grounds that they were too high, and demanded the right to be consulted when decisions on farming policy came up. The Party leaders bowed to their demands. Another bastion of Polish life, the Polish Writers' Union, issued a strong criticism of the censorship laws, and elected four well-known critics of the regime to its inner council. In response, the Party agreed to set up a system whereby grievances regarding censorship could be heard and remedied.

Throughout this ferment in Poland, the Catholic Church – which also condemned censorship – took the lead in calling for change. The catalyst came on October 16, when Cardinal Wojtyla, of Cracow, was elected Pope, as John Paul II. He was the first non-Italian Pope since 1522, and the first Pole ever to become Pope. For a country with such deep Catholic roots and beliefs, this was an electric moment. The Communist Party, for all its efforts to present itself as nationally and economically responsible, could not compete with this groundswell of enthusiasm, with its potent combination of widespread religious feeling and strong national identity. A Polish Pope seemed to offer the Poles everything their powerful Soviet neighbour could not.

The Pope's installation Mass in the Vatican was transmitted live on Polish television. During the televised ceremony the streets of Poland's cities were virtually deserted. Then, millions of Poles went to churches throughout the country in an unprecedented demonstration, in any Communist country, of religious zeal. During a Mass held in Warsaw a few days later, thousands of worshippers crowded into the church or pressed around the open doors as appeals were made from the pulpit for respect for human rights in Poland, and for an end to the falsification of history: the Party was determined not to allow anti-Soviet facts to be publicized or commemorated. As speaker after speaker called for a new Polish national policy, the worshippers expected the authorities to stop the proceedings. They did not. Power was moving gradually but perceptibly from the Party centres, with all their apparatus of police and undercover control, to the public.

In one other Communist country the flame of dissent burned bright: the members of Charter 77 in Czechoslovakia, their numbers continually increasing, circulated clandestine accounts of violations of human rights. They also held two meetings with dissidents in Poland; a third meeting was prevented by the Czech police. The authorities made persistent efforts to stop the circulation of Charter 77 material, and to arrest those who took part in these activities. So many arrests were made, and so many activists put in prison, that a new opposition group was formed: the Committee for the Defence of Unjustly Persecuted Citizens.

*   *   *

President Sadat's surprise visit to Jerusalem in 1977 had led to high expectations in Israel that an agreement could be reached. Among those in Israel calling for a peace treaty with Egypt after Sadat's visit were a group of army officers, calling themselves 'Peace Now', who wrote to Menachem Begin at the start of 1978 urging him to pursue 'the road to peace'. The United States offered its services as an intermediary.

Encouraged by President Carter, and under his auspices, on 4 September 1978 Begin and Sadat met at the presidential retreat of Camp David, in Maryland. Carter had invited Jordan, Syria, Saudi Arabia and the Palestinians to participate with Sadat on the Arab side, but they declined to do so. Sadat negotiated tenaciously on his own. Without the other Arab States, however, there could be no peace treaty, as Carter had hoped, to resolve the Middle East conflict. What emerged in its place, after almost two weeks of virtually unbroken talks, was a 'Framework for Peace in the Middle East'. The preamble stated that it would be elaborated into specific peace treaties through future negotiations.

The Camp David Accords were signed on September 17. The first accord – which was not to be implemented even in part for two decades, called for the implementation of an autonomy plan for the Palestinians on the West Bank and in the Gaza Strip, to be followed after five years by a 'permanent settlement'. Under this accord, Israel was committed to recognize, for the first time since its foundation thirty years earlier, 'the legitimate rights of the Palestinian people', and what was called 'their just requirements'.

In half the nations of Africa there was turmoil. In Zaire – the former Congo – civil unrest, brutal repression and massacres marked the rule of President Mobutu. On Mobutu's return from a visit to the Middle East and Europe in search of aid, he claimed to have forestalled a coup and sentenced nine officers and four civilians to death. International appeals for clemency were ignored.

Mobutu had put his military support behind the dissident anti-Marxist forces in the Angolan civil war. In retaliation the Marxist-led Angolan Government, with Cuban, East German and Soviet support, encouraged anti-Mobutu Zaireans to capture the copper-mining town of Kolwezi. Mobutu appealed for help to Belgium, to protect Europeans in the region from massacre by the rebels. The Belgians sent several thousand troops. But more than a hundred Europeans were massacred before these troops arrived. When, finally, Zairean government troops entered Kolwezi, hundreds of people accused of supporting the rebels were killed.

In Chad, independent from France since 1960, a civil war was being fought, fuelled by Libyan support for the main rebel group. In Equatorial Guinea (formerly Spanish Guinea), ten of the twelve Cabinet Ministers who had been appointed at independence a decade earlier had been murdered, and two-thirds of the members of the Independence Assembly had disappeared. A quarter of the population of 400,000 had fled across the neighbouring borders. Forced labour and cruel tortures were imposed on those who remained. 'The economy is a shambles,' reported the International Commission of Jurists, 'and the infrastructure, both human and physical, is now devastated.'

In Uganda, the tyranny of Idi Amin continued. Amin's security forces dealt ruthlessly with all whom he perceived as his opponents. In March, Raphael Sebugwawo-Amooti, a leading judge and chairman of the Industrial Court, was shot dead. In July the United States Congress voted to suspend almost all trade with Uganda, a government, the resolution stated, which 'engages in the international crime of genocide'. In October, Amnesty International announced that the civilian death toll over the previous eight years was at least 300,000.

The death of Jomo Kenyatta in Kenya pointed up the problems which dictatorial leadership, based on the national struggle for independence, could create. The search for a successor to Kenyatta was fraught with potential inter-tribal rivalry between leading members of Kenyatta's Kikuyu and the Kalenjin, to which the main contender for the presidency, Daniel arap Moi, belonged. Moi, a former head teacher and Chief Scout of Kenya, won important Kikuyu support however, and was elected President unopposed. Among his first actions was a pledge to root out the smuggling, land-seizures and corruption that had become endemic. As a sign that he intended – in the fifteenth year of Kenya's independence – to follow the path of Western democratic procedures, President Moi released all the political detainees who had been held for opposition activities during the Kenyatta regime. In December he announced the start of a five-year campaign to combat adult illiteracy.

Kenya was not alone among the States of Africa to move away from autocratic rule. In Upper Volta the military regime voluntarily transferred power to civilian rule, elections were held and an all-civilian government appointed. In Niger, advantage was taken of the fourfold increase in uranium prices since the oil crisis five years earlier, providing much increased revenue. For Guinea, in the twentieth year of independence, improved relations with France – the former colonial ruler – offered the chance, as for Kenya, of closer ties with the European Economic Community. But, as with so many African States, the shadow of human rights abuse could not be fully removed. In the words of O.E. Wilton-Marshall, a British writer on African affairs: 'As to the large number of political prisoners in Guinea there was no certainty whether they were alive or dead.'

In Rhodesia, as an earnest of Ian Smith's desire to accept majority rule, white Cabinet Ministers began sharing their portfolios with black Ministers. Political detainees were released. The ban on political activity by the Patriotic Front was revoked. But in September forces loyal to the Zimbabwe African People's Union (ZAPU), headed by Joshua Nkomo, using a Soviet heat-seeking missile, shot down an Air Rhodesia passenger aircraft on a domestic flight. Thirty-eight passengers and crew were killed when the plane was hit. Eighteen people survived. Of them, ten were massacred by guerrillas who found the wreckage. In response – having pledged 'more action, less talk', Ian Smith ordered an air attack on a guerrilla camp, and 300 guerrillas were killed. Guerrilla activity intensified. Ian Smith mobilized all white adult males below the age of fifty. But more and more of the country was coming under guerrilla control: in those areas, no taxes were paid to the government, schools and missions were forced to close, and agricultural production was impeded. On June 23, twelve Britons were brutally murdered at a church mission station. In December, guerrillas blew up a major fuel-storage depot near Salisbury. The prospect for a settlement looked bleak at the end of a year in which 5,500 Rhodesians – black and white – had been killed.

In Namibia (formerly South-West Africa), which South Africa had ruled as a mandatory power since the defeat of Germany in 1918, the United Nations was pressing for a full South African withdrawal. But a new South African Prime Minister, P.W. Botha, was adamant that South Africa should continue to administer the diamond-rich region. Guerrillas from the South-West African People's Organization (SWAPO), based in Zambia and Angola, carried out repeated raids across the border, in one of which ten South African soldiers were killed. South African forces entered Zambia and Angola and sought in vain to destroy the guerrilla bases.

In South Africa itself there was no let-up in apartheid. At least 4,000 black South Africans, including many schoolchildren, were receiving guerrilla training in Angola, Libya and Tanzania. In March, two bombs were exploded in Port Elizabeth, and two people killed. Members of the 'Black Consciousness' movement – of which the murdered Steven Biko had been a leader – continued to be banned from any political activity, or held in detention: seventy-eight of them were incommunicado, in solitary confinement.

There was a growing realization in the United Nations that the overriding issue facing more than a quarter of its members was that of poverty: at a meeting of the Economic and Social Council it was revealed that seventeen African nations were suffering from severe drought and increased desertification, as well as from a plague of locusts that was devastating such crops as had managed to survive the drought. Urgent measures also had to be put in place, not against drought but against flooding, in both India and Sudan: this was done through the United Nations Disaster Relief Office. Another continuing United Nations battle was being fought under the authority of the United Nations High Commissioner for Refugees. Among those to whom it was giving food and shelter were black refugees from South Africa and Rhodesia; Zaireans who had fled their country to avoid the civil war; a quarter of a million refugees from Pol Pot's Cambodian regime of terror who had crossed into Thailand and Vietnam; 200,000 Burmese refugees who had fled to Bangladesh; and tens of thousands of Vietnamese 'boat people': 2,500 boat people, on board a freighter, were refused sanctuary in Malaysia after a terrifying voyage. The Malaysian Government pointed out, in defence of its refusal, that it had already allowed 45,000 Boat People ashore. Canada, France and the United States agreed to take in the 2,500. When the United Nations High Commissioner for Refugees called a conference in December, to try to find countries willing to take in the Boat People, thirty-seven countries agreed to attend. But they would grant only 5,000 extra places between them.

As the year came to an end, a new war was taking place. On Christmas Day, Vietnam invaded Cambodia, intent on overthrowing Pol Pot's Khmer Rouge regime and installing a rival Communist government acceptable to Vietnam in its place.

On 7 January 1979 a combined force of Vietnamese troops and Cambodian rebels captured the Cambodian capital, Phnom Penh, and drove out the Khmer Rouge. An era of tyranny and mass murder was over, although the Khmer Rouge reconstituted themselves as a guerrilla force in both the north-east and south-west of the country. A People's Republic of Kampuchea was set up, Kampuchea being the new name for Cambodia, bringing the whole of former French Indochina under Communist rule.

Not Communism, but Islamic fundamentalism, was struggling to gain power in Iran. Demonstrators in every city demanded that the Shah be deposed and the exiled Ayatollah Khomeini be allowed back. As demands for the Ayatollah's return reached a crescendo, the Shah offered the premiership to a senior politician, Dr Shahpur Bakhtiar, who agreed to take the job only if a political settlement was reached with the Islamic movement and the Shah himself left the country. Recognizing the strength of the Islamic movement's street demonstrations, and realizing he could not order the army to open fire on such vast crowds, the Shah left Iran on January 16 for exile. He was never to return.

On February 1, as street demonstrations for the Ayatollah Khomeini's presence intensified, Bakhtiar invited the Ayatollah back. In Teheran, tens of thousands of demonstrators demanded an Islamic State. Bakhtiar called in United States marines to restore order in Teheran. After two days' heavy fighting the marines were forced to withdraw. Within days, Islamic militants occupied army barracks in and around the capital. On February 12 Bakhtiar resigned and left for exile.

The Ayatollah Khomeini established a government. Those branded enemies of the Islamic revolution were brought to trial and executed. All political Parties and organizations were banned, and all independent and non-Islamic newspapers were closed down. Banks and industries were nationalized. People known to be hostile to the new Islamic order were attacked in the streets and killed or beaten up.

On October 22 the deposed Shah arrived in the United States for medical treatment. On November 4 Iranian students, followers of Khomeini, broke into the American Embassy in Teheran and took sixty-six Americans hostage. They would only be released, said the students, if the Shah was sent back to Iran for trial. President Carter refused to do this, and on November 14 froze all Iranian Government financial assets held in the United States, and forbade American companies from buying Iranian oil.

Five days after the freezing of the Iranian assets, thirteen of the hostages were set free. The Iranian Government announced that the remaining fifty-three would be brought to trial as spies. Carter replied that the United States would seek a peaceful resolution to the crisis, but that there were 'other remedies available' to it. He did not say what these were, but it was pointed out by his spokesman that the United Nations Charter included clauses that would justify, in a case like this, unilateral military action.

The Shah left the United States on December 15, for exile in Panama. But the hostages were still held, despite repeated American appeals for them to be released. On December 21 Carter ordered a nuclear-powered American aircraft-carrier naval force to the Arabian Sea.

At the beginning of the year, hoping to facilitate a peace treaty between Egypt and Israel, Carter flew to the Middle East, visiting Egypt and Israel. His efforts were rewarded. Flying to Washington, Sadat and Begin signed a treaty of peace at the White House, and in a televised ceremony the two former adversaries embraced.

In return for an end to the state of war between Israel and Egypt,

Begin agreed to give up the Sinai peninsula. This was made palatable, strategically, when Carter agreed that the United States would build two military airfields for Israel in the Israeli south, in the Negev Desert, in return for the four airfields that Israel evacuated in Sinai. Carter also secured from Congress the largest-ever American foreign aid package for the two signatories: a total of $5,000 million over a three-year period. On May 27 the borders between Egypt and Israel were opened for the first time since 1949, and regular commercial flights between Cairo and Tel Aviv began. The treaty was the first between Israel and any of its Arab neighbours: Begin and Sadat were both awarded the Nobel Prize for Peace.

The United States continued to monitor the situation within Israel with regard to the Palestinians, and in September formally condemned Begin's government for allowing Israeli Jews to purchase land in the Occupied Territories. This, in the words of the State Department, was 'contrary to the spirit and intention of the peace process'. But land purchases continued, and within a decade more than a hundred Israeli settlements had been built on the West Bank and in the Gaza Strip.

Even as President Carter was putting the final touches to his Middle Eastern diplomacy, the Strategic Arms Limitation Talks with the Soviet Union were proceeding. SALT I had established that agreement could be reached. SALT II had to lay down specific targets. On June 18, these were signed by Carter and Brezhnev in Vienna, setting a ceiling of strategic missiles or bombers on each side. With the signing of SALT II, the Cold War looked as if it was on the wane. But it was not yet dead. Even as the Senate was debating ratifying SALT II, discussion was suspended while the United States protested at the presence of 3,000 Soviet combat troops in Cuba.

The Russians insisted, truthfully, that the troops were there to train Cuban soldiers: they were not part of any intended offensive force. The United States replied that, whatever its current intentions, the force was a combat one. On September 7 Carter told the American people that the United States had the right 'to insist that the Soviet Union respect our interests and our concerns, if the Soviet Union expects us to respect their sensibilities and concerns'. The word 'respect' was carefully chosen: the time of verbal threats and accelerated military confrontation was over. Intelligence air surveillance of Cuba was increased, and a newly created Rapid Deployment Force was sent to carry out manoeuvres at Guantanamo, the sovereign American naval base on Cuba.

As a measure of caution, Carter announced on December 12 that there would be a small increase in defence spending, of five per cent a year for 1981 and up to four and a half per cent a year for the five following years. Congress, always uneasy at any increase in government spending, was initially critical. But the criticism was swept aside a mere fifteen days later when, on December 27, Soviet troops moved into Afghanistan, where there were already at least 1,500 Soviet advisers, most of them military personnel. One result of the Soviet invasion of Afghanistan was that the United States Senate refused to ratify the Strategic Arms Limitation agreement, SALT II, which Carter and Brezhnev had signed in Vienna in June.

For the twelve months before the Soviet invasion, Afghanistan had been in ferment. A pro-Soviet regime, headed by Nur Muhammad Taraki, which had seized power the previous April, had imprisoned many Islamic religious leaders, who were demanding a more religious, Islamic orientation in the government and laws of the State. Islamic fervour in the region was deeply disturbing to the Soviet leaders, whose own Central Asian republics, while firmly under the control of secular, atheistic Moscow, were made up almost entirely – other than by a minority of Russian settlers and officials – of Muslims.

On 14 February 1979 the American Ambassador to Afghanistan, Adolph Dubs, was kidnapped by Afghan Islamic fundamentalists who said they would only release him if the Muslim religious leaders imprisoned by President Taraki were released. The American government began negotiations with the kidnappers, who were holding Dubs captive in a hotel in Kabul. Even while the negotiations were continuing, Taraki, at the suggestion of his senior Soviet advisers, sent Afghan police against the kidnappers. In the resultant gun battle Dubs was killed. The United States protested to the Soviet Union about the role of its advisers in ordering the assault while the Americans were still negotiating with the kidnappers.

On August 12, a group of thirty Russians who were visiting a Muslim shrine at Kandahar were murdered by Afghan fundamentalists. There was indignation in the Soviet Union, and fear among the Soviet advisers in Afghanistan that the power of the central government was waning. On September 16 President Taraki was overthrown by Hafizullah Amin. In the gun battle around the presidential palace, Taraki was killed. More Soviet advisers arrived to prop up the Kabul government. But Hafizullah Amin's promise to restore Kabul's authority throughout the country within thirty days was beyond fulfilment.

The Soviet Union decided to take unilateral action. On December 24, Brezhnev ordered a two-day military airlift of Soviet troops into Kabul. It was the largest Soviet troop movement outside Russia's borders since the invasion of Czechoslovakia eleven years earlier. With the arrival of Soviet troops in force, Hafizullah Amin's government was overthrown, and Amin killed. He was replaced by a Soviet nominee, Babrak Karmal. On December 28, as soon as the scale of the invasion was clear, President Carter denounced the Soviet action as a 'blatant violation' of accepted rules of international behaviour, and 'a threat to peace'.

In Turkey, religious divisions between Sunni and Shi'ite Muslims led to violent clashes and heavy loss of life. At the beginning of 1979 martial law was in place in thirteen of Turkey's sixty-seven provinces, set up by Bülent Ecevit, the Turkish Prime Minister, with the support of his Republican People's Party, a left-of-centre alignment with a commitment to secular and democratic procedures. In April there was unrest in the Kurdish regions, and six more provinces were put under martial law. Left- and right-wing political factions were also in violent conflict. Among those murdered was Abdi Ipeçki, the editor of the influential newspaper *Milliyet*, who supported Ecevit's moderate stance.

In dealing with the inter-religious rioting, and even with the Kurdish uprising, Ecevit insisted that the army must, in the final analysis, be accountable to the civil authority. The higher echelons of the army began to associate themselves more actively with the opposition right-wing Justice Party, headed by Süleyman Demirel. On October 15, having failed to restore public order, and after losing his majority in the Senate to the Justice Party in the elections, Ecevit resigned, and was succeeded by Demirel, at the head of a right-wing coalition.

One of Demirel's first actions was to allow the Palestine Liberation Organization to open an office in the capital, Ankara, and to give it the status of a diplomatic mission. This was after Palestinian terrorists had occupied the Egyptian Embassy in Ankara, killing two Turkish policemen and an Egyptian who tried to escape from the building. The PLO was protesting against the Egyptian-Israeli peace treaty.

Terrorism in Northern Ireland continued throughout the year, but however violent the deaths, and however widespread the destruction of property, neither the Labour government under James Callaghan, nor his Conservative successor as Prime Minister, Margaret Thatcher, were prepared to contemplate political change in the province under the threat of violence. Both insisted that direct rule from London would continue until law and order were fully restored. Nor would they agree to give convicted murderers the 'special category' status that they were demanding. Those in prison claimed that they were political prisoners, not criminal murderers.

On the eve of the general election of May 3 that brought Margaret Thatcher and the Conservatives to power, an IRA gunman shot dead the British Ambassador to Holland, Sir Richard Sykes. Eight days later an outspoken opponent of terrorism, the Conservative Member of Parliament Airey Neave, was killed by a bomb planted by the IRA in the House of Commons car park. Meanwhile, an increasing quantity of money and arms was reaching the IRA from the United States.

IRA violence reached a climax of destructive futility on August 27, when the long-retired Admiral of the Fleet Earl Mountbatten of Burma – who in 1947 had orchestrated the transfer of British power in India – was blown up while on a fishing trip in the Irish Republic. Three people were killed with him, including his grandson. That same day, eighteen British soldiers on patrol in Northern Ireland were killed by landmines detonated from across the border. These deaths brought the total death toll from terrorist violence on both sides of the political divide to 2,000.

After Mountbatten's funeral, Margaret Thatcher met the Irish Prime Minister, Jack Lynch, and prevailed upon him to instruct his army and police forces to co-operate with Britain in cross-border security. This agreement, a courageous one for an Irish Prime Minister to reach, proved his nemesis: it was so widely criticized in the Irish Republic as a craven act of appeasement to Britain that within four months he resigned. But the Republican dream, a united Ireland ruled from Dublin − whether achieved by terror or by diplomacy − was not to prove a realistic item in what remained of the twentieth century.

On September 29 Pope John Paul II arrived in the Republic of Ireland. He was the first Pope to visit that Catholic country. Speaking to a vast crowd, he said: 'I appeal to you in language of passionate pleading. On my knees I beg you to turn away from the paths of violence and return to the paths of peace. Further violence will only drag down to ruin the land you claim to love and the values you claim to cherish.'

In Africa, starting on April 10, the first multi-racial elections were held in Rhodesia. As a result of the voting the white regime's authority came to an end, and was transferred to a black majority government. Rhodesia was renamed Zimbabwe. On April 11, the day after polling began in Rhodesia, Idi Amin's despotic regime was overthrown in Uganda. Amin fled the country which he had ruled with such terror for six years, finding eventual sanctuary, as a Muslim, in Saudi Arabia. Tens of thousands of his supporters also fled, crossing the border into Zaire as refugees.

In Ghana, after a coup led by a former junior air force officer, Flight-Lieutenant Jerry Rawlings, executions aimed at 'house-cleaning and ridding the country of corruption' were immediate and widespread. General Kutu Acheampong, a former Head of State, and Major-General Emmanual Utaka, commander of the border guards, having been accused of corruption while in power, were executed on a firing range in front of a large number of onlookers. Six other senior officers were shot ten days later, among them the former commander of the air force and the former commander of the navy. Elections followed, after a ten-year hiatus, and parliamentary rule was restored. Nigeria also returned to civilian rule. In Chad, 5,000 Muslims were massacred in a single violent episode, one of many. Eleven factions were contending for power, each with an army to back its claims. A truce in August was followed by the establishment of a coalition government, with French troops keeping a watchful but nervous eye over a new Government of National Unity.

In Czechoslovakia the Communist authorities continued their attempts to destroy the influence of the Charter 77 human rights movement. Vaclav Havel and five other leaders were convicted of subversion and sentenced to five years in prison. Clandestine pamphlets denounced human rights abuses, and there was a proliferation of illegal lectures and theatrical performances.

In Poland, workers were demanding the right to strike. Catholic, peasant and student groups each called for an end to Communist rigidity. Fifty leading intellectuals, including several Party members, called for 'a radical change in the politico-social system'. When Pope John Paul paid his first visit to Poland as Pope, thirteen million people turned out to see him. In a speech in Warsaw on June 2, he declared: 'Christ cannot be kept out of the history of man in any part of the globe, certainly not in Poland.' In September a new opposition group, the Confederation of Independent Poland, was formed as a political Party, with a secret membership, pledged to secure 'full freedom and independence' for Poland.

The Soviet Union was confronted by an upsurge in individual defections. When the Bolshoi Ballet company toured the United States, three leading members sought, and were granted, asylum. A later tour of the United States by the Soviet State Orchestra was cancelled on orders from Moscow.

For her work in helping the homeless and the dying in Calcutta, many of whom were refugees from the conflict in Bangladesh a decade earlier, Albanian-born Mother Teresa was awarded the Nobel Peace Prize. She had supervised the setting up of 700 shelters and clinics throughout India. The Roman Catholic order of Missionaries of Charity to which she belonged worked throughout the world. Its 158 branches had almost 2,000 sisters caring for the poor and the dying.

CHAPTER ELEVEN

Renewed Expectations
1980—89

IN AFGHANISTAN, 80,000 Soviet troops were under repeated attack by Islamic guerrilla forces. In retaliation the Soviet army brought in helicopter gunships and napalm bombs. To show its disapproval of the Soviet occupation, on 4 January 1980 the United States suspended sales of high-grade American technology and curtailed Soviet fishing privileges in American waters. There was also an immediate American embargo on the imminent sale of seventeen million tons of grain to the Soviet Union. To compensate the American farmers who were selling the grain, it was bought by the American Government. The other main grain exporting countries, including all the European Economic Community countries, agreed not to make up the shortfall. But Argentina, having joined the boycott, then reopened its grain markets to Soviet purchase within a matter of months.

Forty-five governments, including the United States, Canada, West Germany and Japan, persuaded their Olympic Committees to boycott the Moscow Olympics. But disapproval of the Soviet action in Afghanistan did not lead to total isolation. On June 30 the West German Chancellor, Helmut Schmidt, flew to Moscow and signed a series of Soviet-West German measures for trade and energy co-operation. Within six months a Franco-German consortium took over a large-scale Soviet aluminium project from which an American company had withdrawn because of the embargo. An electric-steel project from which a joint American-Japanese consortium withdrew was taken over by a French group.

One area where the United States reached agreement with the Soviet Union was that neither power should become directly involved in the war which broke out in September between Iran and Iraq. The Iraqis wanted control of the Shatt al-Arab waterway, which gave Iran access to the Tigris and Euphrates rivers, Iraq's waterways. They failed, despite a war lasting eight years and costing tens of thousands of lives on both sides.

A rise in the murder rate in the United States was such that on average one American was murdered every half hour. Among the victims in 1980 was the former Beatle John Lennon, shot dead at the entrance to his apartment block in New York. In the coming decade more than 275,000 Americans were to be murdered in the United States: five times the number of American servicemen killed in Vietnam. In 1980 alone, a further 51,000 Americans were killed on the roads, almost exactly the five-year Vietnam war death toll. In the decade which started in 1980 almost half a million Americans were to be killed on the roads.

Another statistic, yet to impinge on American consciousness, marked the year 1980: the death of forty people from AIDS (Acquired Immune Deficiency Syndrome). By 1992, twenty years after the first reported deaths, 170,000 Americans had died of the disease. In Africa the figure was far higher.

On January 23, during his State of the Union message, President Carter spoke of the fifty-three American citizens still being held hostage in Iran, 'innocent victims of terrorism and anarchy'. If the hostages were harmed, he said, 'a severe price will be paid. We will never rest until every one of the victims is released.'

In March the Iranian students holding the hostages let it be known they would be willing to hand them over to the ruling Revolutionary Council, a move seen as a way forward to eventual release. But Ayatollah Khomeini insisted the students continue to hold the hostages at the American Embassy. The United States broke off diplomatic relations with Iran and banned all trade except small quantities of essential foodstuffs and medicine.

Pressed to do so by the United States, the nine European Economic Community countries agreed on April 22 to introduce sanctions against Iran. They did so hoping that force could be averted. Unknown to them, Carter had already decided to take military action. In strictest secrecy, on April 24 six American transport aircraft, with ninety commandos on board, flew from an air base in Egypt to a remote desert air strip in Iran. There they were to rendezvous with eight American helicopters. These were to fly the 500 miles from their aircraft carrier, refuel at the desert airstrip, and then six of them would fly to the outskirts of Teheran, from where the commandos would make their way to the embassy and bring the hostages out.

At the rendezvous point in the desert, two of the eight helicopters broke down and a third was damaged on landing. As six helicopters were the minimum considered necessary for success, the operation was called off. On April 25, Carter went on television to tell the American people: 'I ordered the rescue mission in order to safeguard American lives, to protect America's national interest, and to reduce the tensions in the world that have been caused. It was my decision to attempt the rescue operation. It was my decision to cancel it.'

Secret negotiations secured the release of the hostages at the beginning of 1981 by an unusual, and subsequently controversial, method. Without Congress being informed, illegal arms sales to the Contra rebels in Nicaragua, who were seeking to overthrow the left-wing government there, were used on the authority of Carter's successor, President Reagan, to pay Iran the money which she had secretly demanded for the release of the hostages.

The political ferment in Poland led, by the middle of August, to half a million shipyard workers in Gdansk and other Polish Baltic ports coming out on strike. They were joined by 200,000 coal miners in Silesia. On August 16 a committee linking all striking factories was set up under the leadership of a shipyard worker, Lech Walesa. The strikers' demands, at first limited to economic improvements, widened to include freedom of speech, an end to censorship, the release of political prisoners and the establishment of free, independent trade unions. Under the banner of Solidarity these unions sprung up despite official opposition. Factories declared themselves for Solidarity and took over the management. Solidarity also demanded that the Catholic Church be given access to the media, and allowed to broadcast Sunday Mass.

After first refusing to do so, the Polish Communist authorities opened negotiations with Walesa in Gdansk and with strike committees elsewhere. Agreement was reached on August 31, when Solidarity was officially recognized as an independent, self-governing trade union, the first time any independent trade union organization had been allowed to function in a Communist country. The release of political prisoners, on which Solidarity had insisted, was conceded. Press censorship laws were relaxed. The broadcast of Catholic Mass on radio and television was not only permitted, but became a regular Sunday feature of television broadcasting.

Soviet newspapers, reflecting the alarm among the Soviet leadership, denounced the Polish Communist leaders for their weakness, and warned of 'anti-Socialist' and 'counter-revolutionary' forces at work inside Poland. The Polish Government understood the warning signs, and held back on implementing its agreement with Solidarity. In response, on October 3, several million workers throughout Poland went on a token strike for one hour, an indication of what they could do if the government did not honour the August 31 agreement in full. Solidarity also added demands: the publication of their own weekly newspaper and access to the media similar to that already conceded to the Catholic Church. In a surprise judgment, the Polish Supreme Court not only upheld Solidarity's right to organize strikes, but allowed it to delete from its constitution the hitherto compulsory clause acknowledging the 'supremacy' of the Communist Party.

East German, Czechoslovak and Soviet newspapers began a sustained attack on Walesa and Solidarity for working 'alongside' anti-Socialist forces to overthrow Communism in Poland. Forty Soviet divisions, more than 50,000 men, were sent to the Ukrainian and East German borders of Poland. Poland responded by bringing its own troops in eastern Poland to eighty per cent readiness for combat.

The United States took action to protect Poland from a possible Soviet attack. On December 3 the State Department warned that Poland 'should be allowed to solve its domestic problems without outside interference'.

No Soviet invasion took place. Poland continued on its course of moving slowly away from Communism and its Soviet mentor. In Czechoslovakia, by contrast, the dissident movement continued to be harassed by the Party, police and secret police. It did not give up, however, announcing with pride at the end of the year that as many as 200 books by banned authors had been published clandestinely.

Inside the Soviet Union, dissent was carefully monitored and restrained. Hundreds of known dissidents were forced to leave Moscow during the Olympic Games to prevent them having any contact with Westerners. One of the most outspoken dissidents, Andrei Sakharov, was banished from Moscow altogether, sent for a second time to 'internal exile' 250 miles to the east, to Gorky, a city out of bounds to foreigners. The day before leaving, he signed a statement together with other Russian monitors of the Helsinki Agreement, denouncing the Soviet invasion of Afghanistan.

Jews, Baptists and Russian Orthodox priests who sought greater freedom of worship were arrested, tried and imprisoned, as were those who criticized the Soviet abuse of psychiatric detention. Among those expelled from the Soviet Union in 1980 was Vladimir Borisov, one of the leaders of the free trade union movement founded two years earlier. The movement itself was crushed. No Lech Walesa was to be allowed to emerge in the Soviet Union.

In China, Christian worship, which had been fiercely repressed during the Cultural Revolution, was again permitted. In June, a Roman Catholic bishop, Deng Yiming, who had been in prison without respite for twenty-two years after refusing to break with the Vatican, was released. The Protestant churches in China were allowed to reopen their theological seminaries and reprint the Bible for the first time in almost a quarter of a century. Buddhist temples, smashed and desecrated during the Cultural Revolution, were repaired at the Communist government's expense, and monks and nuns were allowed to worship there. In Chinese-annexed Tibet, Tibetan Buddhists were allowed to visit their holy shrines.

The religious needs of China's Muslims were also given official support, the government making financial contribution to the reopening of more than 150 mosques. The Koran was reprinted and the Haj, the annual pilgrimage to Mecca, was permitted again. But for the first year it was allowed, because of strong official intimations of dislike, only sixteen Chinese Muslims made the journey, out of a Muslim population variously estimated at between ten and forty million.

In South Africa, the Senate, which had been a focus of independent thought, was abolished, and extra powers were given to the President. A sixty-member presidential advisory council that was set up contained no African members. Bishop Desmond Tutu, a campaigner against apartheid whose voice was becoming increasingly influential abroad, was refused permission to leave South Africa. In June, thirty Africans were killed during clashes with police.

Presidential election year in the United States saw Carter challenged by a former Governor of California, Ronald Reagan – once a Hollywood film star – who at the age of sixty-nine was already beyond the normal retiring age. When the American voters went to the polls on November 4, Reagan won all but six States. Carter's defeat marked the first time since 1932 that an elected President had been denied a second term by the electorate. In the Senate, for the first time in almost thirty years, Republicans gained control, giving Reagan the power to secure whatever legislation he put forward.

On 13 February 1980, a commission chaired by the German Social Democrat Willy Brandt, published its report on 'North–South: a programme for survival'. The report warned of the dangers facing the world in the coming decades: 'There are already 800 million absolute poor and their numbers are rising; shortages of grain and other foods are increasing the prospect of hunger and starvation; fast-growing populations, with another two billion people in the next two decades, will cause much greater strains on the world's food and resources.'

Brandt stressed that 'the industrial capacity of the North is underused, causing unemployment unprecedented in recent years, while the South is in urgent need of goods that the North could produce'. The current features of global economics – 'rapid inflation, erratic exchange rates, and unpredictable interventions by governments' –

were seriously disrupting the trade and investment 'on which an immediate return to world prosperity depends'.

The solutions to this, the report stated, would involve a large-scale transfer of resources to developing countries. It would have to include an international energy strategy and a global food programme with increased emergency food aid and a system for 'long-term food security'. The report concluded: 'It will not be possible for any nation or group of nations to save itself either by dominion over others or by isolation from them. On the contrary, real progress will only be made nationally if it can be assured globally. And this global approach cannot be limited to economic problems: it must also take into consideration the great complexity of human society.'

The more affluent regions of the world continued to find new areas of leisure and improvement. In Japan, the Sony company launched the 'Walkman', a small, portable, personal tape recorder and player. A new American communications satellite was launched into orbit around the Earth, able to relay 12,000 telephone calls and two colour television channels at any one time. A new method of sending facsimile letters and documents through the telephone was inaugurated – the 'fax' – which was to become ubiquitous within a decade, far beyond the Western and industrialized world.

Not wanting to expose its citizens to Western ideas, the Soviet authorities tried to exercise stringent control over those who could have access to fax machines. At the end of each Moscow University day, the office fax machines would be dismantled, to prevent students from using them after hours. But control of communications, an essential adjunct to control of thought, was becoming harder and harder to maintain in the face of increasingly rapid technological developments.

The travails of Africa in no way lessened in 1981, or were to lessen in the remaining years of the century. Poverty was too widespread, national indebtedness too high, tribal division too deep, regional rivalries too strong, and the clash of religions and cultures too intense to enable large areas of the continent to find sufficient calm to cultivate the soil, establish a flourishing urban and industrial base, or maintain – let alone raise – standards of living.

In Ethiopia, civil war, even when confined to two regions, accentuated the daily burden of subsistence: at almost no time during the year were less than four million people in need of emergency relief. In Somalia the problems of civil unrest were compounded by a two-year drought. As many as 650,000 refugees from the drought-stricken areas were receiving help from the United Nations High Commissioner for Refugees, in the form of minimal shelter and basic foodstuffs.

The removal of President Amin had not ended the scourge of violent tribal rivalry in Uganda. Amin's successor, President Milton Obote, lacked the authority to maintain inter-tribal peace. His soldiers were for the most part northerners. The southerners, especially the Baganda tribe, were subjected to fierce persecution by the central government. Torture and murder were a daily occurrence. Thousands of Ugandans fled into neighbouring Zaire, to join the Ugandan refugees of the 1979 war who had remained in Zaire rather than return and risk more bloodshed. By the end of 1981 there were as many as 200,000 Ugandan refugees in Zaire, and a further 80,000 in Sudan: homeless, penniless, without a livelihood.

In Gambia, the President, Sir Dawda Jawara, who had been the country's first Prime Minister after independence, was overthrown while in London attending the wedding of Prince Charles and Lady Diana Spencer. Returning to Gambia he enlisted the help of Senegalese troops to put down the rebellion. As many as a thousand people were killed before his authority was restored. Further south, in Ghana, Flight-Lieutenant Jerry Rawlings was finally overthrown. 'What I regret most is not having a clearer understanding of the system,' he said. 'I thought it was just a question of cleaning it up, getting rid of the rottenness. I did not realize that the return of democracy would permit those same corrupt forces to retain their hold on Ghanaian life. We have not transferred power through the ballot box, we have just transferred administration around members of the same elite.'

In Namibia, negotiations for a timetable for elections and independence were accepted in principal by the two main contending parties, South Africa – which had administered the territory since the Treaty of Versailles more than sixty years earlier – and the South

West Africa People's Organization (SWAPO). But as negotiations continued, South African army units crossed the border to destroy SWAPO bases inside Angola, and 2,500 SWAPO guerrillas were killed.

The South African government was also active against the guerrilla forces of the banned African National Congress, which had set up bases in neighbouring Mozambique. On January 29 a South African commando unit, crossing more than twenty miles of Mozambique territory, reached a suburb of the capital, Maputo, and attacked the houses in which ANC members were living. Twelve ANC members were killed. The government of Mozambique, itself largely staffed by members of a former guerrilla movement, FRELIMO, was also confronted by its own internal guerrilla warfare, conducted by the Mozambique Resistance Front, which attacked main roads and strategic villages. To secure domestic peace, President Samora Machel promised to rid the police and armed forces of those who carried out 'arbitrary arrests, beatings and torture'.

In the Soviet Union, national agitation was growing. In March there were protest demonstrations in the Georgian capital, Tbilisi, against the 'russification' of Georgian culture, and demands for more Georgian history to be taught in the republic's schools. In October there was an incident in Estonia when, after a basketball match, several hundred young Estonians vented their anti-Russian feeling. Despite this growth in protest, dissidents who had been monitoring Soviet abuses of psychiatry were all but crushed: the last well-known member of the group who was still at liberty, Feliks Serebrov, was sentenced to four years' hard labour followed by five years' internal exile.

In Poland, as many as 700,000 students and workers went on strike on January 24 in protest against the privileges granted to Party members, and called for the removal of 'corrupt and inefficient' Party officials. A new Prime Minister, General Jaruzelski, the former Defence Minister, promised to consult with Solidarity about all new laws but warned that 'counter-revolution' would be stopped by force. He was summoned to Moscow, where he promised to act without delay to end 'anarchy and disarray' in Poland. On returning from

Moscow, his call for a three-month moratorium on strikes was agreed to by Solidarity.

Despite Moscow's unease, Jaruzelski continued to make concessions to Solidarity. A new labour code was promulgated, granting the right to strike. Following sit-ins by university students, the government agreed to the establishment of an Independent Association of Polish Students. In March, when militia broke into a borough council meeting in Bydgoszcz and beat up Solidarity members, half a million Polish workers went on strike in protest. A few days later Jaruzelski bowed to demands that the government recognize the private peasants' trade union, Rural Solidarity. *Pravda* accused the Polish Communist leadership of making 'endless concessions to anti-Socialist forces'.

The Soviet Union demonstrated its military strength during March and April by a three-week Warsaw Pact land exercise close to the Polish border, and then in September with Soviet naval manoeuvres in the Baltic, with the practise landing of 25,000 troops on the Baltic coast of Lithuania and Latvia, only 150 miles from the Polish border. It was the largest Soviet landing exercise since the end of the Second World War.

In September the first Solidarity Congress was held in Gdansk. It called for free parliamentary and local elections. Many members spoke angrily about the continued Soviet pressures. At a meeting of its national commission in Gdansk on December 12, Solidarity again demanded free elections. As its demands were being broadcast, the government cut off all radio and telephone links between the commission and the outside world. At midnight, on December 13, Jaruzelski imposed martial law throughout Poland. Three-quarters of the Solidarity leaders were arrested and interned, as were more than 40,000 pro-democracy activists, workers, academics, journalists, intellectuals and clergy. Strikes throughout the country were broken up by the security forces using armoured vehicles and tear gas, and more than 200 demonstrators were killed.

Eighteen years later, in a democratic Poland, students and teachers debated whether Jaruzelski's action had seriously retarded the advent of reform, or whether it prevented a Soviet invasion, with far worse consequences of bloodshed and repression.

*   *   *

More than 100,000 Soviet troops were in Afghanistan. The number of Afghan refugees who had crossed the border into Pakistan was estimated by the United Nations at 2,400,000: the largest number of refugees in any one country. The resources of the United Nations High Commissioner for Refugees could only care – at fullest stretch – for 1,700,000 of them. A call on November 18 by the United Nations General Assembly for the withdrawal of foreign troops from Afghanistan was ignored by the Soviet Union.

President Reagan was taking an even sterner stance towards the Soviet Union than his predecessor. On January 29, at his first press conference, he opposed the ratification of SALT II – which the Senate had refused to pass in the wake of the Soviet invasion of Afghanistan – because it allowed the Soviet Union to continue to increase its nuclear weapons to the accepted level for both countries. He would agree to embark on 'discussions leading to negotiations', he said, only if the negotiations aimed to achieve an actual reduction in the number of nuclear weapons held by both sides. More than twelve per cent of the Soviet gross national product was being spent on arms: 250 intercontinental ballistic missiles had been built in the previous twelve months, and the number of aircraft and tanks built during that period was more than four times the previous year. It was hypocritical of the Soviet Union to talk about disarmament, Reagan said, when it had decided to embark upon an 'arms race' with such a high level of expenditure and increase in arms production. Reagan added that the Soviet Union could not win the arms race. The Russian leaders knew this was true.

Talks on limiting medium- and short-range nuclear weapons opened in Geneva on November 30. The United States offered to remove all 572 of its intermediate-range nuclear missiles from Europe if the Soviet Union dismantled its medium-range nuclear missiles that were targeting Europe. It also proposed that the Strategic Arms Limitation Talks (SALT), which essentially enabled each power to maintain parity with the other even if this meant the weaker power building more, should be started under a new title, the Strategic Arms Reduction Talks (START), and pursue a genuine and substantial reduction of nuclear arms by both sides. As a sign of the seriousness of this proposal, which marked a turning point in the history of

Great Power disarmament, the talks, when they began, were held in private. There was to be no public posturing.

A crisis arose, not over the nature of the disarmament plan, but over Poland. With the imposition of martial law in December, Reagan introduced sanctions against the Soviet Union for what he denounced as its 'heavy and direct' responsibility for the crushing of Solidarity. The twice-weekly Aeroflot flights from the Soviet Union to the United States were suspended. The Soviet purchasing commission office in New York was closed. Licences for American firms to export electronic equipment, computers and high-technology materials to the Soviet Union were withdrawn. Talks on a long-term agreement about American export of grain to the Soviet Union were postponed. Tighter restrictions were imposed on the entry of Soviet merchant ships to United States ports.

Punitive measures were also imposed on Jaruzelski's government. Poland's airline, Lot, was barred from flying to the United States, and the Polish fishing fleet was banned from using American territorial waters.

On June 7, on the orders of its Prime Minister, Menachem Begin, Israel launched an attack on Iraq's nuclear reactor, then under construction near Baghdad. Begin and his expert advisers were convinced that Iraq was about to start manufacturing an atom bomb. The uranium had been supplied, expensively, by France. During the raid the reactor was destroyed. In the election held on June 30, less than four weeks after the raid, Begin's Likud Party won the largest bloc of seats and he remained Prime Minister. On the occupied West Bank, more than eighty Israeli settlements had been built, many of them adjacent to Arab towns and villages, and another forty were planned. Palestinian Arab protests at the continued occupation, and at the expropriation of land on which many of the settlements and the roads leading to them were built, led to a growing number of commercial strikes, student demonstrations, stone throwing and even fire bombs. In the Gaza Strip, the Israeli Governor of Rafah was killed. In retaliation for student participation in the protests, Israel closed down the main West Bank institute of higher education, Bir Zeit University.

On October 6 President Sadat was assassinated in Cairo. His greatest crime in the eyes of his assassins was that he had made peace with Israel.

It was announced by the United Nations in April that half of the world's ten million refugees were in Africa. Of those, eighty per cent were in the continent's poorest regions. At a United Nations conference attended by ninety-nine States, it was agreed to pledge $560 million – exactly 1,000th of the world's arms bill that year – to help them: $56 per refugee. The Soviet Union declined to participate in the conference or to contribute to the relief, arguing that it was not responsible for the 'aftermath of colonialism'. It was, however, a principal salesman of arms to that region.

In the Chinese province of Szechwan, severe flooding made one and a half million people homeless. For the first time since the Chinese Communist revolution, the government of China appealed to the United Nations for help. That help was forthcoming. Also appealing to the United Nations, to the Human Rights Commission, were three African States – Equatorial Guinea, the Central African Republic and Uganda – each of which asked for help in restoring human rights in their own countries.

Another United Nations agency, the World Health Organization, faced a global challenge. In search of profits, several international corporations were actively promoting substitutes for breast milk in the developing countries. Alarm was caused because of the dilution of this substitute milk, and also because of inadequate sterilization. To protect babies, a voluntary code of practice was drawn up, and governments were invited to ask their national corporations to subscribe to it. The aim was to ban all advertising of the substitute products. Only the United States, where the commercial lobby was particularly strong, opposed the code.

The World Health Organization also tried to reduce the enormous sums of money spent on cigarette advertising in the developing world by international companies, and the sale in poor countries of cigarettes with a higher tar content than was acceptable in the West because of the danger to health. The pressure from tobacco manufacturers was almost impossible to counter, however, and as the century came to an end the opening up of the mass market of China, which had only recently been exposed to Western imports on a substantial scale, enabled the tobacco manufacturers to take full advantage of the lack of any adequate anti-smoking campaigns there. By the last year of the twentieth century, more than 2,000 Chinese were dying every day from lung cancer and other smoking-related diseases: an annual death toll of almost three-quarters of a million.

In 1982 the spotlight of conflict turned to the Falkland Islands in the South Atlantic. It was more than 200 years since Britain had acquired the Falklands, and 150 years since they had become a British colony. The Argentine claim to the islands – known to the Argentinians as Las Malvinas – was itself more than a century old. In 1980 Britain had offered the Falkland islanders formal recognition of Argentine sovereignty linked to a long lease-back agreement which meant they would remain administered by Britain. The islanders rejected separation from Britain or loss or diminution of British sovereignty. No serious crisis was anticipated; on 9 February 1982 Margaret Thatcher defended the British Government's plans to scrap the South Atlantic survey ship *Endurance*, Britain's only substantial permanent naval presence in the area.

On April 2, Argentinian forces landed on the islands and quickly overran them. For three hours, a company of Royal Marines who were stationed there fought to defend the capital, Port Stanley, but they were outnumbered and forced to surrender. That afternoon Margaret Thatcher announced that a British naval task force was being assembled to 'redress the situation'. At Britain's request an emergency meeting of the Security Council was called in the hope, as Margaret Thatcher expressed it, that 'even at this late hour Argentina would reconsider its rejection of diplomacy'.

On April 3 the United Nations Security Council called for the withdrawal of the armed forces of both sides. As Britain's armed forces in the islands were prisoners of war, and the Argentinian forces were the invading and occupying power, this was disingenuous, but it did satisfy Britain's call for an Argentinian withdrawal. When Argentina refused to comply, the Ministerial Council of the European Community agreed to follow Britain's lead and to ban all imports from Argentina, as well as suspending all financial help.

The first warships of the British naval task force sailed from Britain on April 4, as did two ocean cruise liners which had been rapidly converted into troopships. That day it was announced that Argentine forces had also landed on the island of South Georgia, far to the east of the Falklands, and raised the Argentine flag.

On April 7 Britain imposed a 200-mile 'exclusion zone' around the Falklands, within which any Argentine naval vessel would be liable to attack. The Argentine leader, General Galtieri, insisted that Argentine sovereignty over the islands was not negotiable and that Argentine troops would remain there 'alive or dead'. Margaret Thatcher insisted that all Argentine forces must withdraw before any negotiations began, and that when negotiations did begin, the wishes of the people of the island must be 'paramount'. On April 24, as Britain's naval task force drew ever closer to the islands, the European Community agreed to the 'indefinite' continuation of sanctions against Argentina, despite the defection of Italy and the Irish Republic from the unanimity. On April 30 the United States agreed to impose limited military and economic sanctions. Behind the scenes, President Reagan ensured that Britain received both military supplies and crucial military and naval intelligence.

On April 22 the British naval task force moved into Falkland Islands waters. Three days later a helicopter-borne detachment of Royal Marines landed on South Georgia, where the Argentine force surrendered without fighting. On May 1, British bombers struck at Port Stanley airfield. Then, on May 2, a British submarine torpedoed the Argentine cruiser *General Belgrano*, and 368 Argentine sailors were killed. The cruiser was thirty miles outside the naval exclusion zone when she was sunk. The British Government defended its action by pointing out that it was approaching the British naval task force and was only four or five hours away from it at their combined speeds. Disturbed that the Argentine warship had been sunk outside the exclusion zone, the West German Government expressed its 'consternation' at the loss of life and called for a cease-fire.

The fighting continued. On May 4 an Argentine warplane launched an air-to-sea missile at the British destroyer *Sheffield*. Twenty men on board were killed. On May 21, British troops landed at San Carlos Bay. The Argentine air force struck at the task force ships involved in the landing, sinking three of them. But Argentine losses were heavy: thirty warplanes in the first four days of the landings.

On May 28, British paratroopers captured Darwin and Goose Green. During the attack, seventeen men were killed, including the commanding officer, Colonel H. Jones. More than a hundred Argentine soldiers were killed and 1,400 were taken prisoner. On June 8, while British troops were preparing for their attack on Port Stanley, other British troops, landing at Bluff Cove in an attempt to shorten the march to Port Stanley, were attacked by Argentinian aircraft before they could set up anti-aircraft defences, and fifty British soldiers were killed. The attack on Port Stanley continued, and on June 14, when most of the high ground around the town was in British hands, the Argentine forces surrendered.

Ten thousand Argentinian soldiers were taken prisoner of war. They were only repatriated when their government, following the resignation of President Galtieri, acknowledged, as he had refused to do, that hostilities had ended. At the service of thanksgiving in London on July 26, at St Paul's Cathedral, prayers were said both for the 255 British and the 652 Argentine dead.

Six days before this solemn service of thanksgiving, the IRA detonated two bombs: one under the horses' feet of a group of ceremonial Horse Guards who were riding from their barracks to Whitehall, the other under a bandstand where an army band was playing. Eleven soldiers were killed in the two explosions. The public outrage at these killings, which Margaret Thatcher described as 'the product of evil and depraved minds', did not bring an end to the IRA atrocities. When, in December, a bomb was detonated in a public house in Northern Ireland, eleven British soldiers and five civilians were killed.

In his sermon at the St Paul's service of thanksgiving after the Argentine war, Archbishop Runcie had spoken of the Middle East, where 'every day seems to bring fresh bad news'. On June 3 the Israeli Ambassador in London had been gravely injured by a Palestinian gunman. That same week, PLO units in southern Lebanon renewed their earlier shelling of towns and villages in northern Israel.

No Israelis were killed, but there was considerable public unease inside Israel at the vulnerability of the northern settlements.

On June 6 the Prime Minister, Menachem Begin, ordered Israeli troops to advance into southern Lebanon and establish a buffer zone twenty-five miles deep. His Minister of Defence, Ariel Sharon – who nineteen years later was himself to become Prime Minister – had a more ambitious plan: the advance of Israeli forces as far as Beirut. Sharon's aim was to drive the PLO out of Lebanon altogether. By June 9 the Israeli forces were only two miles south of Beirut airport. Five days later they linked up with the Christian Falangist forces in the east of Beirut, effectively surrounding the PLO-controlled Muslim areas in the west of the city. On June 15, Peace Now, an Israeli grass-roots movement founded a month earlier by six reserve army officers protesting against the ill-treatment of Palestinians in the occupied West Bank and Gaza Strip, put an advertisement in the Israeli newspapers calling for peace negotiations and the recognition of the rights of the Palestinians in the occupied territories. The advertisement asked: 'What are we getting killed for? What are we killing for? Has there been a national consensus for going into this war? Has there been an immediate threat to Israel's existence? Will it get us out of the cycle of violence, suffering and hatred?'

On June 14, Israel began a sustained air and artillery bombardment of West Beirut. More than 400 Israeli tanks and 1,000 artillery pieces, many of them firing down on the built-up area from the high ground, took part in the bombardment: 500 buildings were reduced to ruins. The war had continued for six weeks. 'These six weeks', declared a former Foreign Minister, Abba Eban, on July 3, 'have been a dark page in the moral history of the Jewish people.'

The Israeli shelling of PLO positions in West Beirut continued. A hospital was among the buildings hit. Offshore Israeli naval units intensified the bombardment. Hundreds of PLO fighters were killed. On August 1, Sharon ordered fourteen hours of non-stop air, naval and land bombardment. Two days later Israeli troops entered Beirut and sought to engage the PLO forces in direct combat. It proved a difficult task, culminating on August 11 in a forty-eight-hour aerial bombardment. On August 12 the PLO agreed to leave the city. A multi-national force, including 1,800 American marines, was assembled to protect it as it was evacuated from Beirut by sea. On August 30 Yasser Arafat left Beirut.

On September 1, as Arafat made his way to Tunis, an exile once again, the 'Reagan Plan' was announced by Washington. It included the principle of self-government for the Palestinians of the West Bank and Gaza 'in association with Jordan'. This new plan was presented by the Americans as the next step in the Camp David peace process. The Begin government was resolved, however, not to relinquish Israeli control of the occupied territories, and rejected the American initiative.

Following the departure of the last PLO troops from Beirut, the Syrian troops in the city also left. All was set for Israel's Lebanese ally, the Christian Falange, to take control. But on September 14 their leader, Bashir Jemayel, was assassinated.

Palestinian Muslims claimed responsibility, and Jemayel's Christian Maronite followers swore revenge. On September 15 Israeli troops occupied West Beirut 'in order', Begin explained, 'to protect the Muslims from the vengeance of the Falangists'.

The main concentration of Palestinian Muslims was in the Sabra and Chatila refugee camps. Israeli forces sealed off the two camps from the outside world: 'hermetically sealed' was how one Israeli general later described it. The Israelis believed that when the Falangist soldiers entered the camps they would seek out and kill the Palestinian fighters, not civilians. To help them in this task, Israeli military searchlights illuminated the camps at night. Falangist forces entered them on September 17 and massacred the inhabitants, fighters and civilians alike: 2,300 Palestinian men, women and children. Several hundred PLO fighters were also been killed.

The massacre at Sabra and Chatila shocked the world, and shocked many in Israel, although no Israeli troops took part in the killings. The Israeli soldiers had expected the Christian Falangists to attack Palestinian fighters. What the Christian soldiers did followed the earlier pattern of the Lebanese civil war, the wreaking of vengeance on the civilian population – vengeance, in this case, in the immediate aftermath of the assassination of Bashir Jemayel.

The cost of the war in Lebanon had been high on all sides, military and civilian alike. More than 6,000 PLO troops and Pales-

37. Yucca Flat, Nevada: on 17 March 1953 more than 2,000 United States marines took part in an atomic test. Having emerged from their foxholes immediately after the explosion, they are seen watching the mushroom cloud.

38. A Soviet tank in East Berlin, following the outbreak of strikes on 17 June 1953.

39. Vietnam. French parachutists dropped over Dien Bien Phu, being watched by parachutists who had landed earlier. This photograph was taken on 26 November 1953.

41. Mao Tse-tung and Nikita Khrushchev in Moscow, 1957.

40. Nelson Mandela shortly before his arrest on 12 June 1964. He was kept in prison for twenty-six years.

42. Chinese soldiers read from the Little Red Book, which contained what Chinese newspapers called 'the brilliant red banner of Mao Tse-tung's thinking'.

43. Martin Luther King addressing marchers in Selma, Alabama, 9 March 1965.

44. Prague: Czech demonstrators face a Soviet tank, 26 August 1968.

45. Neil Armstrong (left) and Edwin Aldrin on the surface of the moon, 21 July 1969.

46. United States troops leave their base at Quang Tri on 19 August 1969, as part of President Nixon's policy of reducing the number of American troops in Vietnam.

47. Super-Power summitry: Leonid Brezhnev and Richard Nixon in Washington, 23 June 1973.

48. The Middle East peace process: Henry Kissinger, Yitzhak Rabin and Shimon Peres sign the Israel/Egypt Interim Agreement in Jerusalem, prior to the signing of the final Agreement in Geneva on 4 September 1975. All three were later recipients of the Nobel Peace Prize.

49. Idi Amin in Uganda, at a press conference following the deaths of the Archbishop and two of his Cabinet Ministers, 24 February 1977.

50. Ayatollah Khomeini at Neuphle-le-Château, near Paris, an exile, awaiting his return to Iran. This photograph was taken on 8 November 1978.

51. Peking, 3 June 1989: tanks and a lone demonstrator in Tiananmen Square.

52. Crowds from the British sector in Berlin look over the Berlin Wall,
while a child is lowered onto the eastern side of the wall,
10 November 1989.

53. A Polish sapper, a member of the United Nations Emergency Force (UNEF) clearing mines near the Suez Canal, in the buffer zone between Israel and Egypt. This photograph was taken on 21 March 1974 by a Bulgarian photographer, Encho Mitov.

54. The Korean War Memorial in Washington: American soldiers advancing. A field of lavender represents the mined and muddy terrain. The memorial was opened and dedicated by President Clinton on 27 July 1995.

55. Diana, Princess of Wales, in Angola with thirteen-year-old Sandra Thijca, who lost a leg from an anti-personnel mine while she was working on the land. This photograph was taken by Joao Silva of the Associated Press on 14 January 1997.

tinian civilians were killed by the Israelis. Also killed in the fighting were 600 Syrian troops, 468 Lebanese civilians and 368 Israeli soldiers. On September 19, Israeli troops began their withdrawal from Beirut. Eventually they fell back to a three- to four-mile-deep zone of occupation in southern Lebanon, which they did not evacuate for eighteen years. In this zone continual battles were fought between Israeli troops and the Iranian-supported Hizbullah – Party of God. Hundreds were killed on both sides.

The end of the Lebanon war did not end Middle Eastern acts of terror. On November 4 an attack carried out by Muslim suicide bombers on Israeli military headquarters in the southern Lebanese port of Sidon killed thirty-six Israelis. On December 6 a bomb exploded in a bus in Jerusalem, killing six Israelis, including two children. The PLO claimed responsibility.

In Syria, Muslim opposition to the secular government of Hafez al-Asad led to rioting and civil war. In February the Islamic Front seized control of the town of Hama. The towns of Homs and Aleppo were likewise seething with Islamic fervour. Asad ordered his troops to attack the Muslim strongholds, using tanks and artillery. War planes were also used against Hama, and the centre of the town was destroyed, including the historic mosque. At least 10,000 of the insurgents were killed before Asad regained control.

The hopes of greater liberalism in Poland had been set back when General Jaruzelski declared martial law at the end of 1981. The year 1982 saw no diminution of repression. On October 9, Solidarity was banned. Two days later, to show its disapproval, the United States imposed trade sanctions on Poland. Inside Poland, massive demonstrations were held on behalf of Solidarity. Twenty demonstrators were killed in clashes with the security forces. More than 10,000 Solidarity supporters were imprisoned, including their leader, Lech Walesa. In mid-October Jaruzelski went to Moscow to report to Brezhnev what he had done. A Polish joke had the ailing Brezhnev telling Jaruzelski that Walesa would be released 'over my dead body'. Brezhnev died on November 10. Walesa was released two days later.

Brezhnev's successor, Yuri Andropov, had been the head of the KGB for the previous fifteen years. Sakharov, Russia's best-known dissident, was forced to remain in internal exile far from Moscow. The number of Jews allowed to emigrate fell to its lowest figure since Stalin's death thirty years earlier. Jewish activists were arrested and imprisoned. In Afghanistan the war against the Muslim guerrillas – the Mujaheddin – intensified.

In the war between Iran and Iraq, tens of thousand of soldiers had been killed on both sides. In July a sustained Iranian attempt to capture the post of Basra was unsuccessful. Ayatollah Khomeini was determined to establish an Islamic republic in as much of Iraq as possible, and to link Iraq with Iran in a Fundamentalist federation. But he also faced unrest inside Iran, fomented by Marxist-oriented guerrillas and by the Kurds living in western Iran. The Marxists were defeated. The Kurds, against whom Khomeini launched two military expeditions, retreated into the mountains and fought on.

In the West, in 1982, despite the ebb and flow of economic indicators – dominated by fluctuations in unemployment and inflation – commercialism and the profit motive flourished, as did the expansion of consumerism. Individual enterprise became more highly prized than communal activity. Millionaires gained great esteem and often political influence as well. With the vaunting of private enterprise and private profit came the rapid expansion of trade and communications. On February 19 the first commercial 'jumbo jet', the Boeing 747, went into regular service. On October 7 the New York Stock Exchange announced a record day's trading: more than 147 million shares had changed hands during the day. That year, as technological advances brought popular culture to larger segments of the world's population than ever before, the first Compact Disc (CD) players went on sale.

On 8 March 1983 President Reagan decribed the Soviet Union as 'the focus of evil in the modern world'. That same day, Max Kampelman, chief United States delegate in Madrid at the European Conference on Security and Co-operation, linking security and human rights, gave details of what he called Soviet 'disdain' for the 1975 Helsinki Final Act. 'Only last week', he said, 'two Soviet human rights activists were given twelve-year sentences for offences that included seeking to organize a non-official trade union, and writing poetry which displeased the Soviet authorities.' In the past year 500 Soviet citizens had been convicted for political and religious reasons.

On the day after Reagan's 'evil empire' speech and Kampelman's listing of human rights abuses, the British Government leased the United States the Indian Ocean island of Diego Garcia as a base via which American bombers carrying nuclear weapons could fly to the borders of Soviet Central Asia, and if necessary beyond.

Reagan saw the future defence of the United States as including laser weaponry in space. Prototype laser weapons had already been tested against both incoming missiles and 'attacking' unmanned air-craft. 'Star Wars', as it was called, gave the Soviet leaders cause to hesitate. With the development of space-laser technology, their expensive, much-vaunted nuclear weaponry would become obsolete and useless. Yet the Soviet Union did not have the technology or economic resources to challenge the United States in this innovative and expensive sphere.

More than any single American initiative, Star Wars – although it would clearly take up to a decade to develop fully – spelt the end of the Soviet-American balance of power, and would tilt it signifi-cantly to the American side. Among those who understood the mean-ing of Star Wars, and the inevitable end to Soviet Super Power equality, was the recently appointed Communist Party Secretary responsible for Agriculture, Mikhail Gorbachev, at fifty-two a rela-tively young political leader who was being spoken of in Moscow as a possible successor to the ailing Andropov. Gorbachev had come to the attention of Western observers in March, when he encouraged small groups of peasants to take a more responsible attitude towards agricultural production by allowing them a direct stake in the profits of their collective labour and so increasing their material self-interest. Not pre-selected, rigidly enforced norms, but production targets profitable to the individual would provide the incentive which col-lectivization, the panacea so long adhered to, had failed to provide.

On September 1 a South Korean civil airliner, a Boeing 747, was shot down by a Soviet military aircraft. It had strayed into Soviet air space above the strategically sensitive Sakhalin Island. All 269 people on board were killed, among them an American Congressman. The plane had been tracked for more than two and a half hours before being shot down by an air-to-air missile. While Andropov remained silent, Reagan demanded a full explanation for 'this appalling and wanton deed'. Margaret Thatcher denounced the shooting as 'an atrocity against humanity'. Other governments were more hesitant in their condemnation, so much so that Margaret Thatcher said she found it 'inexplicable that we could not get a clearer condemnation by Europe and clearer action in the wider NATO sphere'. Direct commercial flights from Britain to Moscow were suspended, and on September 29 Thatcher warned that the Soviet Union was a power 'of great military strength, which has consistently used force against its neighbours, which wields the threat of force as a weapon of policy, and which is bent on subverting and destroying the confidence and stability of the Western world'. But despite the shooting down of the airliner, neither Reagan nor Thatcher was willing to halt the strategic arms reduction talks that had begun in the spring, following an offer by Andropov to try to break the deadlock caused by the Soviet invasion of Afghanistan two years earlier. The talks, which were taking place in Geneva, continued, and a call by some Congressmen that the United States reimpose its earlier ban on the sale of pipeline equipment to the Soviet Union was rejected by the administration. The ban had only been lifted in August.

One cause of American hesitation was the Soviet claim, which the United States soon admitted to be true, that an American spy plane had been in the area earlier. The spy plane had, however, already returned to its base in Alaska when the South Korean airliner was shot down.

On November 14, the first American cruise missiles with nuclear warheads arrived at a United States air base in southern England.

In October 1983 the focus of international attention turned to the Caribbean island of Grenada, a former British colony which since 1974 had been an independent State. Its population was little over 80,000. In 1979 the elected government had been overthrown and a People's Revolutionary Government set up. Internal disagreements between members of the government led, on October 16, to the murder of the Prime Minister and the establishment of a revolutionary Military Council.

Six Caribbean countries, members of the Organization of Eastern Caribbean States (OECS), of which Grenada was a member, appealed to Reagan to intervene. In the early hours of October 25, British Intelligence reported that an American invasion of Grenada was imminent. Margaret Thatcher telephoned Reagan and urged him not to launch an attack. The invasion went ahead nevertheless. Thatcher was unyielding in her opposition to it. 'If you are going to announce a new law,' she said five days later, 'that wherever Communism reigns against the will of the people the United States shall enter, then we are going to have terrible war in the world.'

The main landings were carried out by 1,900 American troops. The 636 Cubans who had been building a new airport, employed by a British construction firm, put up no resistance. Forty-three Cuban soldiers at the airport put up resistance but were quickly overrun. A further seventy Cuban soldiers fought with the Grenadian soldiers in the hills. When the fighting ended on October 27, eighteen American troops had been killed, forty-five Grenadians and twenty-five Cubans.

Congress supported Reagan's action. It also supported his requests to help other Central American governments in their struggle to maintain a semblance of democracy, or at least a robust hostility to Marxist doctrines. El Salvador was given money to help fight left-wing Salvadorian guerrillas, who had murdered 5,000 civilans in 1982. But Reagan had to assure Congress he would not send American soldiers there, or even 'combat advisers'. The expansion of the war in Vietnam just over a decade earlier was still a vivid nightmare for many American legislators.

United States troops did support a Nicaraguan exile army, the Contras, which was using Honduras as the base from which to attack into Nicaragua, although Reagan assured Congress the United States was not seeking the overthrow of Nicaragua's left-wing Sandanista government. America's main interest in Nicaragua, he explained, was to make certain that the Sandanista government did not 'infect' its Central American neighbours through the export of subversion and violence. He did not reveal the extent to which the United States was helping the Contras.

Dissent in Eastern Europe was marked in East Germany by the activities of an unofficial 'peace movement', some sixty people in all, known as the 'Jena Group'. They were welcomed by the authorities when they called for Western disarmament, but when they began to call for Eastern bloc disarmament as well, and also opposed military training in East German schools and factories, and the sale of war toys and war games, they quickly fell foul of officialdom. Twenty of their number were expelled from the country.

In Poland, the second visit by John Paul II since he had become Pope electrified a country whose earlier aspirations had been crushed. At a meeting with General Jaruzelski early in his visit, the Pope was outspoken in expressing his hopes that the August 1980 agreement with Solidarity – 'the social reforms worked out at the price of such pain' as he called them – would be adhered to. As many as fourteen million Poles in all assembled at the various places where the Pope spoke. It was an incredible demonstration of the strength of Roman Catholicism and the indefatigable spirit of the Polish people. At each meeting, the crowds displayed hundreds of 'V for Victory' signs – the Churchillian symbol of defiance and hope that had been such an inspiration during the Second World War. Everywhere he spoke, the Pope stressed that every society had the right to 'maintain its own identity'. On July 21, a month after the Pope's visit, Jaruzelski ended martial law in Poland.

The political crisis in Poland had taken its toll in the economic sphere. As many as a third of all Poles were living below the poverty line. When the government announced price rises of up to seventy per cent, both the Catholic Church and Solidarity protested. The award of the Nobel Peace Prize to Lech Walesa boosted his prestige. In a gesture of contempt for the Polish authorities he donated the prize money to a fund run by the Catholic Church in Poland to help private farmers.

In his acceptance speech for the Nobel Prize, Walesa championed the rights of the independent trade unions, and called for the dialogue between government and Solidarity to be renewed. But neither

Walesa, nor the Church, nor the vast majority of Poles whom he and the Church between them represented, wanted to do anything against the Jaruzelski regime that might provoke Soviet intervention.

In Czechoslovakia the Communist authorities ensured there would be no provocation of the Soviet Union. The dissidents of Charter 77 – after six years of activity calling for the upholding of human rights and greater government accountability – continued to circulate protests and petitions, and to make contact with Western European peace movements, but were liable to detention and arrest if they ventured too close to public activity.

By the end of the year, thirty 'prisoners of conscience' were in prison in Czechoslovakia. In the Soviet Union, twenty-five Russian Jews – 'Prisoners of Zion' – were in prison or labour camp for their part in the continuing pressure for emigration. On October 14 a former Jewish prisoner, Iosif Begun, was sentenced to twelve years 'deprivation of liberty': three years in prison, four years in labour camp and five years of internal exile. One of his 'crimes' was that he gave private Hebrew lessons. As well as attacks on Jews, the Soviet authorities continued to clamp down on dissent elsewhere. The poet Irina Ratushinskaya was sentenced to seven years in Siberian labour camps for 'anti-Soviet agitation and propaganda' – in her poems.

In Lebanon, among the armed groups fighting on Lebanese soil in 1983 were the Maronite Christian militia, the Muslim 'Amal' militia, the Druze (an independent Muslim minority then within the Syrian zone of occupation), the Syrian army, Palestinians who had remained in Lebanon after the evacuation from Beirut to Tunis, anti-Syrian fundamentalist Shi'ite Muslims, a quite separate Iranian Shi'ite force and Israeli troops who were gradually withdrawing during the year to a zone in southern Lebanon.

The fighting between Lebanese Christian and Muslim militias, and between Muslim fundamentalist Shi'ite fighters and the Israeli soldiers on Lebanese soil, repeatedly escalated. The American and French peacekeeping forces were also under attack by Iranian Shi'ite fundamentalists. On April 18 a bomb destroyed the United States embassy in Beirut, killing eighty-seven people. On October 23 two simultaneous suicide attacks led to the deaths of 239 American and

58 French soldiers. On November 4, a suicide bomber at an Israeli military headquarters killed 29 Israelis and 32 Lebanese and Palestinian detainees being held in the headquarters. In reprisals for these attacks, the French bombed the Iranian Shi'ite base in Baalbek, and the Israelis bombed Shi'ite and Palestinian guerrilla concentrations in southern Lebanon.

The international community continued to try to keep the peace. Italian and British troops joined the Americans and French. Both American and Saudi Arabian emissaries tried to persuade the Maronite Christian minority in Lebanon to redistribute power more evenly to the Muslim majority. But the Maronites, their numerical situation worsening year by year, feared that with Muslim political dominance would come their own political and physical demise.

A strong impetus to environmental change came in June 1983, when the United States government changed its view on 'acid rain'. Hitherto, Washington had insisted that sulphur and nitrogen oxide emissions from American power stations were not necessarily the cause of the chemical blight affecting millions or trees and polluting thousands of lakes in Canada, as well as in the north-eastern United States. In June a Federal inquiry described man-made pollutants as 'probably the major contributors' to acid rain. Later that month the President's science office urged 'meaningful reductions' in sulphur emissions. In Europe the West German government likewise changed its mind, after as many as a quarter of West German forest trees had been damaged by acid rain.

The problems of pollution were yet more serious in Eastern Europe. Factories were older and methods of production less carefully monitored than in the West. Throughout East Germany and Czechoslovakia, forests were dying. In the coal mining regions hundreds of thousands of people were suffering from respiratory disorders. The situation in the industrial regions of the Soviet Union, though closed to outside scrutiny, was known to be even worse.

In the Third World the desperate search for subsistence had led over the previous decade to over-grazing, over-cultivation and the deforestation of arid and semi-arid lands on a vast scale. Each of these dramatically increased the danger of drought, and, when rains came, of flooding. According to statistics published by the United Nations in November, 150 million people were at that very moment 'on the brink of starvation'. The most endangered were those in twenty-two nations in Africa. From Ethiopia, a stream of starving and destitute refugees was fleeing into the Sudan – where neither food nor shelter awaited them.

It was not Africa alone that was affected by the impoverishment of the land. Bolivia, Peru and Ecuador each suffered severe flooding, accentuated by mudslides that were in many cases created because of the clearing away of trees for development, and which swept away homes and whole villages. The United Nations warned that deforestation and the 'mismanagement' of watersheds would make even the advent of typhoons and hurricanes more devastating.

On 6 September 1983 the 'Helsinki process' which had begun eight years earlier came to an end. That day in Madrid the long-debated 'Concluding Document' of the European Conference on Security and Co-operation was signed. Thirty-five nations put their signatures to it, most importantly the United States and the Soviet Union. Solemnly secured in the document was an agreement to ensure the freedom of the individual 'to profess and practise religion in line with the dictates of his own conscience'. Another clause ensured the rights of workers freely to establish and join trade unions, and the right of unions 'freely to carry out their activities in compliance with national laws'. Also agreed was the granting of exit permits for emigration on the basis of family ties, marriage and the reunification of families, an agreement not to penalize would-be emigrants with regard to jobs, housing and social benefit; and assured freedom of access for all citizens to foreign embassies. The signatories also undertook 'to work for militarily significant, politically binding and verifiable confidence and security-building measures (CSBMs) to reduce the risk of military confrontation anywhere in Europe'. The signatories of the Concluding Document also pledged to 'pursue the solution of outstanding problems through peaceful means' – yet another stage in the twentieth century's attempts to abolish war.

In his novel *Nineteen Eighty Four*, George Orwell, writing just after the Second World War, had envisaged a single, all-embracing totalitarian world order. The Concluding Document of the Helsinki process was a serious effort by many nations to avert the Orwellian nightmare. But not all nations took part. In Chile, General Pinochet's dictatorship had failed to live up to earlier hopes of a significant relaxation. During 1983 more than a hundred people had been killed in the break up of street demonstrations against the regime. In 1984 those demonstrations grew. After an assassination attempt on the head of the secret police, Pinochet declared a state of emergency, reimposed press censorship, and arrested those he believed were organizing further demonstrations. He would wage 'a war to the death against Communism', he promised. On September 4 a protest demonstration in Santiago was savagely broken up, and one of its leaders, Rodolfo Segual, the head of the metalworkers' union, was beaten on the legs and testicles. In police raids, André Jarlan, a French priest active among the poor, was shot in the head and killed. During a general strike a month later, nine people were killed by the police, and all opposition newspapers were banned.

In the Soviet Union, a change in the leadership always raised hopes for a relaxation of the rigidity of the Communist Party system. The death of Andropov in February was no exception, but his successor, Konstantin Chernenko, was very much a member of the old guard, and at the age of seventy-two hardly a man to introduce radical change. The power of the Communist Party, and of the KGB, was undiminished. The Soviet presence in Afghanistan was in its fifth year, with more than 140,000 Soviet soldiers unable to prevent repeated guerrilla attacks on their convoys and bases, and with an ever-rising death toll. Soviet dissidents and Jews active in the emigration movement continued to be imprisoned and sent to labour camps, despite the human rights and emigration provisos of the Helsinki Final Act, which the Soviet Union had signed. Among those prisoners was Anatoli Shcharansky, thirty-six years old and in his seventh year of incarceration, much of it in solitary confinement. Despite mounting Western pressure, he remained in prison.

In Poland, General Jaruzelski made full use of the secret police to curb what he called 'counter-revolutionary forces', and introduced court procedures whereby demonstrators could be arrested and imprisoned with the minimum of formality and documentation.

Arrests of Solidarity supporters were frequent, but Solidarity continued to find means of pressing its demands and widening its influence: creating shadow organizations in every large factory. Study circles on the workings of democracy were set up with the support of Solidarity in hundreds of workplaces and even schools. In July, hoping to defuse dissent, Jaruzelski granted an amnesty to 652 political prisoners, including the imprisoned Solidarity leaders. In welcoming the amnesty, both Lech Walesa and the Church leaders warned that it was not enough: it was also essential to ensure 'implementation of the social accords signed in August 1980'. This Jaruzelski was not prepared to do. The Soviet Union could not accept a move to free trade unions.

Towards the end of the year an increasing number of Roman Catholic priests spoke in their pulpits in favour of Solidarity, and of Polish national aspirations. The anti-Soviet implications of such patriotism were clear. Among those giving what became known as 'Masses for the Fatherland' was a Warsaw priest, Father Jerzy Popieluszko, who drew large crowds to his sermons. On October 19 he disappeared. Eleven days later his body was found in the River Vistula. He had been tortured before being killed. At his funeral on November 3, a bitterly cold day, 300,000 Poles knelt in the streets around his church, and unfurled banned Solidarity banners that had been brought to Warsaw from all over Poland. During the funeral, Lech Walesa declared: 'Solidarity lives because you, Father Popieluszko, died for it.' One result of the murder was the establishment in Polish intellectual, academic and student circles of a number of human rights groups, which monitored human rights abuses and gave them maximum publicity. At the end of the year four secret policemen were charged with Popieluszko's murder, and imprisoned.

In Czechoslovakia, partly inspired by events in Poland, dissent was growing. There was a demand for religious freedom. A petition signed by thousands of people called on the Pope to visit Czechoslovakia for the 1100th anniversary of Christianity in Czechoslovakia. A Papal visit, however, was something the Czech Communist authorities refused to countenance. From their perspective the impact of the Pope's two visits to Poland held grave dangers for Communist control in any country where Christianity had strong roots, not just in Poland, his country of birth. Czech human rights activists, the concluding document of the Madrid Conference circulating among them, called for greater political freedom. Students resented the continuing Communist control of literature and the arts.

Charter 77, despite continual harassment, managed to issue more than twenty statements during the year. One of these called for the support of the human rights monitoring groups set up in Poland in the aftermath of Father Popieluszko's murder. Most embarrassing for the government was the award of the Nobel Prize for literature to the Czech poet Jaroslav Seifert, the 'grand old man' of Czech literature, who had left the Communist Party many years earlier, and was a signatory of Charter 77.

Dissent was also evident in Communist Yugoslavia, where seven students were arrested in Belgrade for having become involved in a 'Free University' which taught freedom of speech and political assembly. One was found dead in unexplained circumstances shortly after his release from police custody. The remaining six were held in custody. After Amnesty International adopted them as 'prisoners of conscience', they were released. Although denounced officially as 'political terrorists' they were not brought to trial.

There was also a revival of national feelings among the Albanian population of the Yugoslav province of Kosovo. The leaders of the movement, some of whom were demanding autonomy within Yugoslavia, others union with Albania, were brought to trial, and imprisoned for terms of up to fourteen years.

In India the Sikhs were demanding political and religious autonomy. In June, Indira Gandhi ordered the Indian army to remove the Sikh militants who, under their leader, Sant Bhindranwale, had taken over the Sikh holy shrine, the Golden Temple at Amritsar. Similar military operations were launched simultaneously against thirty-seven other Sikh holy places which had been occupied in protest at the rejection of Sikh demands for autonomy. During the assault on the temple at Amritsar the soldiers obeyed orders to try to avoid damaging the shrine itself. But when the assault was over, not only had damage been inflicted, but ninety Indian soldiers and 700 Sikh militants had been killed, including Sant Bhindranwale.

On September 25, in response to a pledge by Indira Gandhi, repair work on the Golden Temple was completed. Four days later, Indian troops ended their occupation of the Temple. Two days after that, on October 1, 300 Sikh militants stormed the building and occupied it, in defiance of the warnings of Sikh officials who, in return for the Indian Government's rapid completion of the repairs, had promised there would be no further occupation. The Indian security forces entered the Temple and forced the militants to leave.

A month later, on October 31, Indira Gandhi was assassinated. Her assassins were two Sikhs, members of her personal bodyguard. In an upsurge of anti-Sikh feeling, 500 Sikhs were killed in Delhi and several hundred elsewhere. Mrs Gandhi was succeeded as Prime Minister by her son Rajiv Gandhi, who won a substantial victory at the election. One of his first problems was the impact of the worst accident in modern industrial history, the death of 2,500 people in the early hours of December 3 – three weeks before the election – when poisonous gas leaked from a pesticide factory just outside the city of Bhopal. The placing of a potentially dangerous chemical factory near a population centre, and the poor safety standards being operated by foreign companies based in India, were two of the questions with which Rajiv Gandhi had to grapple, in the wake of popular revulsion at the heavy death toll, and indignation at its cruel effects.

In Mexico City, 500 people had been killed a month earlier, after an explosion at a natural gas processing plant.

A new area of conflict was impinging on the world consciousness in 1984: the revolt of Tamil extremists in Sri Lanka – formerly Ceylon. The insurgents, the 'Tamil Tigers', were demanding secession from Sri Lanka: they lived mainly in the north of the island, and sought political integration with their fellow-Tamils in southern India.

Attacks by Tamil Tigers and reprisals by Sri Lankan forces intensified throughout the year. In the last two weeks of November there were more than 300 violent deaths. On December 7 a hundred Sri Lankan soldiers travelling in convoy on a main road were ambushed and killed. The killings were to continue for the next quarter of a century.

*   *   *

Human rights abuses in Uganda included the arrest of editors who criticized government policy in their newspapers, and the detention without trial of up to 1,500 Ugandans for political dissent. Over the previous four years, during a fierce civil war, three quarters of a million people had been displaced from their homes, and tens of thousands killed. To bring a minimum of food and shelter to the dispossessed, the international relief agencies were operating twenty-one refugee camps.

A Western human rights organization, the Minority Rights Group, denounced Milton Obote's regime in Uganda for its 'cynical and flagrant flouting of human rights'. In Guinea, by contrast, following the death from heart failure of the brutal Ahmad Sekou Touré, founding father, dictator for life and murderer of his political opponents, power was seized by a Military Committee of National Redress, one-party rule was ended and a thousand political prisoners released.

In Northern Ireland the IRA, determined to force a British withdrawal from the province – which had been an integral part of the United Kingdom for three centuries – continued to kill and maim. During the Conservative Party conference in October an IRA bomb was detonated at the Grand Hotel, Brighton. The target was the Prime Minister, Margaret Thatcher. Four people were killed in the explosion; a fifth died some weeks later in hospital. Mrs Thatcher was unhurt. 'Life must go on,' was her reaction, to which the IRA retorted: 'Today we were unlucky, but remember we have only to be lucky once.' In Northern Ireland, sixty-four people were killed that year, some by the IRA, some by Protestant paramilitary organizations, some by the British security forces.

At a United Nations Population Conference held in Mexico City in August 1984, delegates learned that during the previous ten years the world population had increased by 770 million – to 4,800 million. In Africa, four million people were refugees. In many areas, malaria-bearing mosquitoes were becoming resistant to insecticides and anti-malarial drugs. The World Health Organization revealed that 150 million cases of malaria had been reported in the previous year. Another statistic that year came from the United Nations International Children's Emergency Fund: in the nations of the developing world 40,000 children were dying every day.

Famine increased its devastation in 1984, as Ethiopia suffered another season of drought. A massive international aid effort was mounted, with the United States, Canadian, Western European and Australian Governments making the largest contributions. Much of the aid had to go by sea, but emergency air drops, led by a British Royal Air Force team using giant transport aircraft, were carried out in the heart of the stricken areas. The aid came too late to save an estimated three quarters of a million people. But at least ten million more were its beneficiaries.

War and civil war added to the perils of famine: parts of Ethiopia were controlled by the rebel Tigre People's Liberation Front. Near the coast, 4,000 Ethiopian soldiers were killed by another rebel group, the Eritrean People's Liberation Army.

In Mozambique – where the Marxist FRELIMO regime was being challenged by the Mozambique National Resistance movement, supported by South Africa – famine struck as fighting over large areas made agriculture impossible. Within twelve months, as many as 100,000 Mozambicans died of famine.

In Sharpeville, scene of a widely condemned massacre eighteen years earlier, fourteen South African blacks were killed, not by the authorities, but in inter-communal rioting against alleged quislings. Among the victims was the deputy mayor of the township, who was hacked to death. Others who were accused of 'collaboration' with the authorities were killed by the 'necklace': a car tyre put around their neck and then set alight.

As a sign of disapproval of the apartheid regime in South Africa, and giving encouragement to anti-apartheid campaigners worldwide, the Nobel Prize for Peace for 1984 was awarded to Desmond Tutu, the Anglican Bishop of Lesotho. In his acceptance speech he said: 'I have just got to believe God is around. If He is not, we in South Africa have had it.' Tutu became Bishop of Johannesburg a few days after receiving the award, and was made Archbishop two years later. As Secretary-General of the South African Council of Churches since 1978 he championed non-violent civil disobedience.

Violence in the South African black townships was stimulated by a new constitution which excluded blacks from parliament. On 21 March 1985, during a protest march on the anniversary of the Sharpeville killings of 1966, police with automatic weapons fired into the marchers, who were unarmed, and twenty-one people were killed. In August a peaceful march on the prison where Nelson Mandela was being held was broken up by police with whips. That year there were 136 recorded attacks by blacks on police posts and other installations. On December 23 five whites were killed when a bomb was detonated in a shopping centre at a seaside resort.

On March 10 1985 the Soviet leader Konstantin Chernenko died. He was replaced as General Secretary of the Communist Party by Mikhail Gorbachev. As agriculture supremo for the previous seven years, Gorbachev had adopted a practical, efficient and professional approach to agricultural policies. He was fifty-four years old – the youngest member of the Politburo. On April 23 he told the Central Committee of the Communist Party that he intended to end the inertia which had led to a continual fall in Soviet productivity during the previous decade. Corruption, which had become endemic at the highest levels of Party life, would also be ended. Industrial productivity, which was only fifty-five per cent of Western standards, would be subjected to 'scientific-technical renovation'.

Among Gorbachev's new appointments was a man of his own age, Boris Yeltsin, who was put in charge of construction. When, towards the end of the year, it became clear to Gorbachev that the Moscow Communist Party apparatus was unhappy with his reforming activities, he appointed Yeltsin to undertake the modernization of the governing of the capital.

In foreign policy Gorbachev stressed the Soviet commitment to the Strategic Arms Reduction Talks (START). Having recognized the nuclear superiority of the United States, especially with the imminent advent of a comprehensive, laser-based, anti-missile system – Reagan's Star Wars – he declared a moratorium on the Soviet deployment of medium-range nuclear missiles in Europe, enabling the START talks, which had been suspended amid acrimonious disagreement and mutual suspicion a year earlier, to begin again. Gorbachev saw nuclear disarmament as the key to the modernization of the Soviet Union. If he could transfer to the productive world of industry some of the enormous sums of money and technical and scientific prowess being absorbed by the Soviet defence establishment, his internal changes could be based on economic reality.

Reagan and Gorbachev met for the first time in Geneva in November, and agreed to instruct their representatives to 'speed up negotiations' when the disarmament talks reconvened. They also agreed on joint Soviet-American research on nuclear fusion and air safety. A further indication of real change in Soviet policy came when Gorbachev wrote to Reagan to say he would allow American inspectors to visit Soviet underground nuclear testing sites, and offering to negotiate a treaty banning all underground nuclear tests. Reagan responded positively. As a sign of new-found openness it was agreed that Reagan and Gorbachev would each speak on television to the other's people on New Year's Day.

Within the Soviet Union, a sustained campaign, led by Gorbachev himself, against corruption, bribery and inefficiency at every level of society resulted in the dismissal of hundreds of Communist Party officials, and the execution of those judged seriously to have neglected their responsibilities. The word used to describe these changes was *perestroika*: restructuring. Gorbachev explained that this involved 'restructuring of people's psychology'. Without turning away from Communist Party rule, and while preserving the territorial unity of the multi-national Soviet Union, *perestroika* offered the prospect of unprecedented change.

In Poland the cold hand of repression was still not lifting. Changes to the penal code increased the number of political offences that could be punished. Those brought before summary courts were denied the right to legal representation. A Communist Party pronouncement warned the Polish intelligentsia to 'accept the Party's leadership in all aspects of political, life, and struggle against any form of opposition'. Book censorship was strengthened. Student autonomy was reduced. Trade union activities were more strictly controlled. In February three Solidarity leaders were imprisoned for more than two years for 'participating in activities of an illegal union'. But the instinct of defiance could not be crushed. Several clandestine Solidarity newspapers circulated. More than 600 book titles including historical works detailing past Soviet actions against Poland, were published illegally and widely circulated, passed from hand to hand. In October, Solidarity demanded the gradual creation of an 'independent society' in Poland, in which the Communist Party and the State would no longer have a monopoly on education, publishing or the media. The government reacted by dismissing more than a hundred 'politically unreliable' senior academic administrators and professors from their posts in institutions of higher learning throughout Poland.

Gorbachev's spirit of reform alarmed the Communist Party leaders in Czechoslovakia. The party Secretary, Gustav Husak, made a special journey to Moscow to seek reassurance that the path of economic reform and efficiency did not have to be followed in Prague. Returning from Moscow he was able to tell the Central Committee: 'We will not take any of the roads based on market-oriented concepts.' The Czechoslovak Communist Party had also issued a statement doubting that any positive developments would emerge from the Reagan-Gorbachev summit. Particular emphasis was put by the authorities on denouncing the events of 1968, the 'Prague Spring' of a decade and a half earlier. So angered was Alexander Dubček by these attacks that he emerged from his enforced obscurity as a forestry official to write an open letter to three Czechoslovak newspapers defending what he had done. They refused to publish it.

Muslim fundamentalism was becoming a growing matter of concern to Western Christian countries and to human rights organizations. Anger was caused by the punishments imposed in Islamic countries. In the Sudan cutting off a hand was the punishment for theft. Those convicted of adultery were stoned to death, men being buried up to their waist – if they could struggle free while being stoned they were allowed to live. Women were buried up to their armpits. The stones that were thrown had to be not too large, to kill instantly, or too small to be ineffective. From Colonel Khadaffi's Libya, the government-controlled Radio of Vengeance and Sacred Hate broadcast to other Muslim lands criticizing them for not massacring their Jewish populations. Libya's Jews had long since emigrated to Israel.

Hijacking also became a focus of international attention in 1985. On June 15 two Lebanese Muslim gunmen hijacked a TWA commercial airliner with more than a hundred American citizens on board, and forced it to fly to Beirut. During its subsequent journeying from Beirut to Algiers and then back to Beirut one American was shot dead. The hijackers demanded the release of 766 Muslim prisoners held by Israel, most of whom had been captured in the fighting in Lebanon. Intense behind-the-scenes negotiations began, and after eighteen days, following Israel's release of some of its prisoners, the hostages were also released.

It had been a tense crisis for the United States. Vice-President George Bush articulated this when he said: 'We and our similarly threatened friends must see what actions, militarily and otherwise, can be taken to end this increasingly violent and indiscriminate but purposeful affront to humanity.' Security at airports was strengthened, and task forces set up to act as anti-hijack assault teams.

In the Middle East, by far the largest amount of money spent was being used on arms. In the five-year period from 1984 to 1988 the Soviet Union headed the list of sellers of arms to the Middle East with sales of $33,265 million, a third of the total. The United States came second with sales of $14,785 million, well under half of the Soviet figure. Britain and France competed closely for the third place, Britain's $7,870 million being slightly ahead of France's $7,215 million.

The total worldwide arms trade during the five years up to 1988 involved the sale of weaponry costing $248,370 million. By contrast to this figure, the United Nations Agencies had a combined budget of just under $10,000 million.

Natural disasters continued to take their toll. An earthquake that struck Mexico City in September killed more than 7,000 people. So heavy was the loss of life that the city's baseball stadium had to be used as a morgue. The city's largest maternity ward was among the buildings destroyed by the earthquake, but the fifty-eight new-born babies there at the time were all pulled out alive. A baby's muffled cry had led rescue workers to begin frantically digging, until they came to a cavity in the rubble in which the babies were found.

To help the starving millions in Africa, the singer Bob Geldof organized two Live Aid concerts held simultaneously on July 13, one in Wembley Stadium, London, and the other in JFK Stadium, Philadelphia, at which $75 million was raised. The concerts were watched in 160 countries by more than 1.5 billion people, nearly a third of the world's population. The Soviet Union was the only nation that refused to transmit what it denounced as the 'global jukebox'.

In Ethiopia the government moved half a million families from the famine zone to lowland areas in the south and west. Tens of thousands died on the march, lacking strength to complete the journey, or falling victim to lowland diseases, principally malaria, to which they had not hitherto been exposed. When the French relief agency Médecins sans Frontières, revealed the extent of these deaths, its members were expelled from Ethiopia.

Also leaving Ethiopia, airlifted to Israel, were 25,000 Ethiopian Jews, the black descendants of Jews who had arrived from the Arabian peninsula 2,000 years earlier. Known as Operation Moses, the airlift saved them from the depredations of both famine and civil war. In Israel itself, the government released 1,150 Palestinian prisoners, 160 of whom were serving life sentences for murder, in return for three Israeli soldiers who had been captured in Lebanon three years earlier. But violence continued. After three Israelis had been murdered by Palestinian terrorists in Cyprus in September, Israeli warplanes struck at the PLO headquarters near Tunis. In the course of the attack sixty-five Palestinians and Tunisians were killed. In retaliation the PLO hijacked an Italian cruise liner, the *Achille Lauro*, shot one of its passengers, Leon Klinghoffer, an elderly, wheelchair-bound American Jew, and threw his body overboard.

The cycle of reprisal and counter-reprisal continued. On November 23, an Egyptian aircraft was hijacked, and flown to Malta. There, one of the Israeli passengers was killed. On the following day Egyptian commandos stormed the plane. Sixty people, including many of the passengers and all but one of the hijackers, were killed in the ensuing shoot-out. On December 27, fifteen bystanders, Jews and non-Jews, were murdered at Rome airport when Palestinian terrorists opened fire on the El Al Israeli airline ticket counter.

For the second year running, Sri Lanka saw the Tamil separatist movement gain in audacity. In January, when Tamil Tigers blew up a troop train, thirty-eight soldiers were killed. In April, soldiers attacked a Tamil village and killed seventy-five villagers. In May almost a hundred Sinhalese, including many Buddhist monks, were massacred in the holy Buddhist city of Anuradhapura.

In a personal intervention, the Indian Prime Minister Rajiv Gandhi persuaded the Sri Lankan government and the Tamil leaders to halt the fighting and begin talks. These reached an impasse, however, when Sri Lanka refused to accept even the possibility of Tamil secession. For their part the Tamils rejected any proposal that would involve giving up their claim to be a 'distinct nation' with the right at least of self-determination. On August 16, while talks dragged on, news reached the negotiators of the murder in one town of 200 Tamils. The talks were broken off.

Scientific research on environmental pollution led to international collective action in 1985, when the representatives of thirty-five nations met in Helsinki in July to discuss a thirty per cent reduction, over eight years, in sulphur dioxide emissions that crossed national borders. Not every industrial nation agreed, however, to curbs on its factories, citing the expense of anti-pollution measures, and their possible negative effect on production. Among the countries known as the 'main polluters' who did not sign the protocol were Thatcher's Britain, Reagan's United States and Jaruzelski's Poland.

France alone of the nuclear powers was insisting on continuing atmospheric testing of nuclear weapons. A small but active adversary was the Greenpeace movement, which planned to sail a ship, *Rainbow Warrior*, into the test area. While the ship was in harbour in New Zealand, about to sail for the test area, French government agents placed a bomb on board. The ship was blown up and a crewman killed. The nuclear test went ahead. Later the French Government apologized to Greenpeace for the crewman's death, and to New Zealand for having taken action in an area of New Zealand sovereignty. There was no apology for the test.

On 15 January 1986, soon after Margaret Thatcher announced her support for the American Star Wars defence initiative, Gorbachev put forward a set of proposals aimed at 'complete, worldwide nuclear disarmament' by the end of the century. During his speech, in an unprecedented comment by a Soviet leader on a Soviet military commitment, he described the war in Afghanistan as a 'bleeding wound'. He also promised to deal with 'humanitarian issues' in a new light. To this end the Soviet Jewish activist Anatoli Shcharansky was released from prison in February and allowed to go to Israel – where he later became a government Minister in charge of Trade and Industry.

Gorbachev set himself a fast and extremely public pace of reform. At the Party Congress on February 25 he declared the time had come for the leadership 'to tell the party and the people honestly and frankly about deficiencies in our political and practical activities, the unfavourable tendencies in the economy and the social and moral sphere, and about the reasons for them'. It had become necessary to 'renew', 'reinvigorate' and 'restructure' the economy and society. In addition to perestroika – restructuring – Gorbachev called for 'a determined and relentless war on bureaucratic practices' by means of *glasnost* – openness. The public were henceforth to be informed of what was going on, in order to provide a check on abuses of authority.

Openness was something the Communist Party had never tolerated, much less encouraged. Part of its power lay in secrecy, in the ability of the KGB to operate behind tightly closed doors, and in the restricting of circles of knowledge. To call for openness was to put the whole fabric of totalitarian rule on trial. It was quickly and cruelly to be put to the test. On April 26, two months after Gorbachev's first call for openness, two explosions destroyed a nuclear reactor at Chernobyl, in Ukraine. In the blast of the explosion and the radiation poisoning which it generated, 250 people were killed, including two firemen trying to put out the blaze. Despite 'openness', this figure was withheld from the Soviet people, who were later told that thirty-seven had died. Among the many tons of radioactive material that were propelled into the earth's atmosphere by the force of the blast was the radioactive caesium-137. It has a half-life of thirty years. It is easily absorbed by living tissue.

This was the nuclear accident scientists and environmentalists had long dreaded, but the Soviet authorities were silent throughout April 26, 27 and 28. When, on April 29, Swedish scientists announced their discovery of high radioactivity in the winds, the

Soviet authorities said only that an 'accident' had taken place. To calm growing Soviet and international rumours, on April 30 Soviet television showed children at play, allegedly in the region where the nuclear reactor was located. On May 1, when Gorbachev reviewed the annual May Day parade from the viewing stand in the Kremlin, nothing was said or done to suggest that a momentous, even a catastrophic event had taken place five days earlier.

From the western Soviet Union, a radioactive cloud had been on the move since the explosion, crossing Poland, Czechoslovakia and Austria, northern Italy and western Switzerland, including Lake Geneva where the nuclear disarmament talks were taking place. From there – on the day Gorbachev was taking the May Day parade in Moscow – it moved over eastern France and on to Britain. Making a swoop off the Atlantic coast of Ireland, the radioactivity then crossed Britain again before crossing the North Sea and, on May 8, reaching Norway. Other winds carried the radioactivity as far south as Greece and Sicily, as far west as Spain and Portugal, as far north as Finland, and as far south as Roumania and Turkey.

The main effect of the fall-out was an increase in cancer. Estimates of the number of cancer deaths that would be caused during the coming decades varied from a minimum of 5,000 to a maximum of 40,000. Some scientists predicted the number would be as high as half a million. As to radiation-linked genetic abnormalities, there was no means of predicting what, or on what scale, these would occur. It was a cruel case of 'only time will tell'. What did not require time was the anger inside the Soviet Union that the authorities had kept silent for three whole days. Soviet citizens had been taught since the revolution to trust their leaders and their pronouncements. Even when they had been let down in the past it had not been on a matter touching so closely on life and death.

Governments beyond the Soviet Union were also puzzled as to how to react. The French Government denied for several days that the radioactive cloud had passed over France. Food and livestock were affected wherever the cloud had passed. The West German Government was the first to offer monetary compensation to farmers; Sweden did likewise. For several years to come British sheep farmers slaughtered large numbers of sheep judged unsafe for eating. They too were compensated. But monetary compensation could not make up for the fears the radiation cloud engendered, or for the long-term damage it might have brought with it. The full effects of this single explosion will not be known until well into the twenty-first century.

The first political casualty of Chernobyl was the credibility of the Soviet authorities among their own people. Questioning spread rapidly into the national sphere. In mid-December, after the authorities in Moscow replaced a Kazakh as First Secretary of the Kazakh Republic with a Russian, there were unprecedented riots in Alma Ata, the Kazakh capital. Cars were set on fire, shops broken into and looted, and a policeman was killed. He was the first victim of a process of disintegration that was to end five years later with all fifteen republics of the Soviet Union declaring their independence.

As a result of the initial secrecy surrounding Chernobyl, the call for openness accelerated. For the first time details of disasters were broadcast as they took place: first the sinking of a Soviet cruise liner in the Black Sea with the death of 400 passengers, then the attempted hijacking of a Soviet airliner in Siberia, and then the sinking, following a fire, of a Soviet nuclear submarine in the Atlantic. Even the cleanup operations at Chernobyl were shown on Soviet television, and the extent of the damage was made clear. In the sphere of human rights, Gorbachev also reversed the policy of his predecessors. After thirteen years in internal exile, Andrei Sakharov was allowed to go abroad for medical treatment, and told that on his return he could resume his scientific work: he was told all this in a telephone call from Gorbachev himself, an astonishing departure from years of official contempt towards dissidents. One by one the leading victims of Soviet repression were given their freedom: Yuri Orlov, a founder of the Helsinki human rights monitor groups in the Soviet Union, was allowed to emigrate, and Irina Ratushinskaya, the poet, was released from labour camp in Siberia and also allowed to emigrate.

In Poland no such liberalization was taking place. A plea by Solidarity to have talks with the government was ignored. The Catholic Church continued to warn the government of the dangers of ideological rigidity, and strongly criticized the newly introduced 'religious knowledge' classes taught by Marxist teachers. Anti-Soviet feeling, never far from the surface in Poland, was exacerbated by Chernobyl.

After the radioactive cloud had passed over north-eastern Poland, the Polish Government reported dangerous levels of radioactive contamination. The sale of milk from grass-fed cows was banned.

In Czechoslovakia, as in Poland, the Communist Party remained wary of following Gorbachev's openness. The extent to which the Chernobyl fallout had affected Czechoslovakia was not made public, although radiation levels had risen sharply, especially in the eastern region, the border of which was only 450 miles from the explosion. The Czechoslovak Government made no public comment when, at the end of the year, Soviet scientists gave the figure of 40,000 as their estimate of the number of additional cancer deaths that would follow in Europe as a result of the explosion. The dissidents of Charter 77 circulated strong criticism of the government for not having told the truth about Chernobyl. Ironically, as reforms spread in the Soviet Union, more and more Czechs were watching the once-derided Soviet television and reading the hitherto conformist Soviet newspapers for signs of how far openness could go.

The psychological shock waves from Chernobyl were also felt in Yugoslavia, where there were public demonstrations against nuclear power stations. When the European Economic Community imposed a ban on imported meat from Yugoslavia, and on certain vegetable products, there was a realization of how harmful the explosion had been. Perhaps of even greater long-term danger than Chernobyl was a 'hole' in the ozone layer above Antarctica. It was blamed on chlorofluorocarbons (CFCs) released into the atmosphere by aerosol propellants in refrigeration units, in the manufacture of foam, and as solvents. These innocuous, unspectacular chemical adjuncts to modern life possessed a lethal side effect inconceivable to those who had first developed and used them. Since 1980 the European Economic Community countries had imposed a limit on the production of CFCs, though that limit had come to seem too high. Following new scientific evidence in 1986 the United States suggested a lower limit worldwide, warning that if production of the CFC chemicals were to continue at the existing level the ozone layer would continue to be depleted, and by the year 2025 there would be an extra 142,000 cases of skin cancer every year.

*   *   *

In Afghanistan, the Mujaheddin, despite the weight of Soviet weaponry being used against them, bought weapons on the international arms market that enabled them to shoot down Soviet war-planes that had hitherto attacked them with impunity. The new weapons included American and British anti-aircraft missiles and Swiss Oerlikon anti-aircraft guns, bought through middlemen.

Confronted by an end to their superiority in the air, the Soviet military authorities in Afghanistan ordered attacks on Mujaheddin civilian targets. But they remained reluctant to commit Soviet troops to any direct confrontation, and following Gorbachev's description of the Soviet involvement as a 'bleeding wound', the 8,000 Soviet troops were withdrawn. Although more than 100,000 Soviet troops were still in Afghanistan, Gorbachev had signalled a change of policy.

The war in Afghanistan was entering its eighth year. Five million Afghan refugees, a fifth of the country's entire population, were in vast refugee camps in neighbouring Pakistan and Iran. Those in Pakistan were drawn into the communal violence between the local Pathan tribesmen and a refugee community which had come from India almost forty years earlier.

In Sri Lanka, Tamil separatists were in almost total control of the Jaffna peninsula in the north of the island. Only the Sri Lankan army base at Jaffna Fort was under government control. Tamil terror-ist attacks took place throughout the island, even in the capital, Colombo. When an Air Lanka passenger plane was blown up at Katunayake airport, most of the thirty-one dead were European and Japanese tourists. The Sri Lankan Government contemplated bomb-ing the Tamil strongholds in the north, but the Indian Government, whose own Tamil region looked with considerable sympathy on their fellow-Tamils 'struggling to be free', warned it not to do so.

In the civil war in Nicaragua, the left-wing Sandanista government faced renewed attacks from the Contra rebels. Reagan saw the conflict as a challenge to the spread of Communism in Central America. For him Nicaragua was a 'second Cuba' on America's doorstep. His efforts to secure aid for the Contras were persistent but difficult. On March 20 the House of Representatives voted by the narrowest of margins, 222 to 210, to deny him a $100 million aid packet to the Contras.

He described that vote as 'a dark day for freedom'. The Senate rallied to Reagan's support, however, reversing the House vote, which had to be taken again, and on June 26 the House passed the aid package by 221 to 209. Two days later the International Court of Justice in The Hague ruled that United States' aid to the Contras was in violation of international law, which forbade intervention in the internal affairs of a sovereign State. When called upon by the Security Council to comply with the court's judgment the United States cast its veto.

The United States was also involved in a violent dispute with Colonel Khadaffi of Libya, whose government was financing terrorist activity in many parts of the world, including Northern Ireland. In March, after a Libyan missile attack on American aircraft exercising off the Libyan coast, American aircraft attacked military targets in Libya, and fifty-six Libyans were killed. In April, American bombers, some flying from American airbases in Britain, struck at terrorist training camps inside Libya. A hundred people were killed. Khadaffi's support for international terror continued.

In the continuing exploration of space, the American *Challenger* space shuttle was intended to be another advance in the steady scheme of experiment. It was launched on January 28. Seventy-four seconds after lift-off it exploded, its disintegration seen by hundreds of shocked observers and tourists on the ground at the launch centre, and by hundreds of millions of television viewers. All seven people on board were killed. When, within four months, two unmanned American booster rockets and a European Community rocket all failed, the space exploration programme was suspended.

One technological development in 1986, the cellular telephone, was to have extraordinary global repercussions within a decade. By the end of the year there were 115,000 subscribers in Britain, a rate of expansion more than a hundred times faster than that of the telephone when it first became commercially available. By the end of the century, almost no Briton seemed without one. It had become an almost global necessity.

One worldwide theme in 1986 was civil turmoil. In South Africa, as protests against apartheid gathered momentum in 1986, President

Botha established a state of emergency, creating even greater powers of arrest and detention without trial. In August twenty-one people were killed when police opened fire on demonstrators in the African township of Soweto. In China, that December, after three consecutive days of student demonstrations in Shanghai demanding more democracy, the demonstrators were dispersed by police. When the demonstrations spread to Peking the police again broke them up, after which the government announced tighter controls on public meetings.

In South Yemen, during twelve days of fighting in December 1986 between rival factions of the Marxist government, 13,000 Yemenis were killed. In Angola the civil war was in its tenth year. Financial aid to the rebel UNITA forces came from the United States: Reagan received UNITA's leader, Jonas Savimbi, in Washington in January, but the European Parliament in Strasbourg refused to give him a hearing: his close links with South Africa put him beyond its pale. South African forces were indeed giving Savimbi help against the Marxist MPLA, mounting a missile attack in August in which two Soviet supply ships were badly damaged. The Iran-Iraq war continued to be the most costly war in human terms of any conflict then being fought. In a six-week offensive at the beginning of 1987 there were 50,000 Iranian dead.

In Lebanon, the struggle for control of Beirut saw Muslim pitted against Muslim. On 13 February 1987, Shi'ite militiamen prevented a convoy of United Nations vehicles with food and medicine from entering the Palestinian refugee camps at Chatila and Bourj-el-Barajneh. Only after a five-month siege did it become possible for United Nations food and medical supplies to bring relief to 35,000 captive Palestinians.

The civil war in Sri Lanka, already in its fifth year, escalated. In mid-April, despite Indian protests, the Sri Lankan air force bombed the Tamil-held Jaffna peninsula. Retaliation was swift, with 200 people being killed in Tamil attacks on buses and bus stations. On May 22 the Sri Lankan Government launched a full-scale military offensive against the Jaffna peninsula. Six days later Rajiv Gandhi spoke up against what he called the 'cold-blooded slaughter of thousands of Sri Lankan citizens'. On June 3 thirty Buddhist priests were massacred by Tamil gunmen. On the following day, Sri Lankan naval patrol boats turned back an Indian naval flotilla that was trying to bring food and medicine to the Tamils near Jaffna. A day later the Indian air force dropped humanitarian supplies to Jaffna from the air.

To avoid becoming drawn into the civil war in Sri Lanka as the defender of the Tamils, the Indian Government put itself forward as a mediator. Talks followed, and on July 29 the Indian Government signed an accord, agreeing to supervise a Tamil Tiger cease-fire. The Tamil rebels accepted the Indian intervention and began to hand over their arms. In return Sri Lanka released hundreds of Tamils who had been interned. Tamil activists who had been directing the struggle from India, and recruiting Tamil supporters there, returned to Sri Lanka. But even as the handing over of arms continued, rival Tamil groups began an internecine struggle, and the handing over of arms came to a virtual halt.

As fighting between the Tamil factions intensified, the Indian troops who were meant to be supervising the cease-fire found themselves caught in a military confrontation with those they were ostensibly helping. On October 11 the Indian peacekeeping force, 30,000 men in all, launched an armed attack on the Tamil Tigers. In three days' fighting more than 200 Tamil soldiers were killed. Rajiv Gandhi ordered 3,000 reinforcements to be flown in. By the end of the month 500 Indian soldiers had been killed, but by the end of the year Jaffna was under their control. The Indian army had succeeded where the Sri Lankan army had failed.

Within the Soviet Union, Gorbachev continued to seek the modernization of the Communist Party, confident he could preserve the Communist ideology and structure of the Soviet Union, and retain the unity of all its twelve republics. After a Central Committee meeting on 27 January 1987 he ordered the release of 140 political prisoners from prisons and labour camps throughout the Soviet Union, and promised to review all other cases. Among those released was Dr Iosif Begun, then in the fourth year of a twelve-year sentence for having encouraged emigration to Israel. Within two years all twenty-five Jewish 'Prisoners of Zion' had been freed and had left the Soviet Union, most of them for Israel.

At the session on January 27, the Central Committee listened to reform proposals the like of which no Soviet leader had ever put forward. To 'enhance the Communist character of the Soviet Union', Gorbachev proposed 'the extension of Socialist democracy and popular initiative'. A new law would extend self-management in the workplace. Comparable changes would be made in the organization of collective farms. Even the electoral system would be changed, to ensure greater 'popular involvement' at all stages of the selection of the Communist Party candidates. The Party apparatus itself would be 'democratized'. Party Secretaries, from the local to the republic level, would henceforth be elected by secret ballot open to an 'unlimited number' of Party candidates. Communist Party control 'from above' – to which Gorbachev insisted that he remained committed – would henceforth be combined with openness and accountability 'from below'.

Starting that February the election of local Party Secretaries had to involve at least two candidates. Local Communist Party elections due to take place in June would consist of more candidates than there were seats available. Also in June, the 'national discussion of important questions of State life' was enshrined in law.

There was considerable pressure from 'old-guard' Communists to reverse from these changes. At the end of October those senior Party members opposed to 'openness' forced Gorbachev to remove one of his closest allies, Boris Yeltsin, from leadership of the Moscow Communist Party apparatus: an apparatus particularly in need of the changes Gorbachev wished to bring about. One of the charges against Yeltsin was that he had demanded an even faster pace of reforms than Gorbachev – who had himself begun to criticize those who wanted to speed up the pace of reform. A striking manifestation of reform came on November 14, when the ballet dancer Rudolf Nureyev was allowed to return to the Soviet Union to visit his family, for the first time since his defection twenty-six years earlier.

How far Gorbachev wanted to go, and how far he could go, was much debated in the West. That summer he proposed the abolition of an entire category of nuclear weapons: land-based nuclear missiles of both short and intermediate range. At a summit with Reagan in Washington between December 7 and 10 this abolition was agreed. The weapons themselves constituted only four per cent of the nuclear weapons of the two Super Powers, but it was the first time since the lapsed Anti-Ballistic Missile (ABM) Treaty fifteen years earlier that such a comprehensive agreement to disarm had been reached. Both Reagan and Gorbachev's stated aim for future talks was to reduce their strategic nuclear arms stocks by fifty per cent. With the long-term objective of avoiding a nuclear confrontation, both stated their intention to devise measures which would enable both sides 'to ensure predictability in the development of the US-Soviet strategic relationship under conditions of strategic stability, to reduce the risk of nuclear war'.

Gorbachev took another unprecedented step when, on his return from Washington, he appeared on Soviet television to explain what had been achieved. The treaty, he said, was 'a victory for the new political thinking'. Although only four per cent of all Soviet and American nuclear weapons had been eliminated, 'scientists had calculated that just five per cent was sufficient to destroy the world'.

Soviet self-scrutiny, a feature of the policy of openness, led Gorbachev to announce in July that the Stalinist purges could 'never be forgotten or justified'. Following Gorbachev's remark, a Soviet magazine printed an open letter written to Stalin in 1939 by Fedor Raskolnikov, an 'Old Bolshevik' who had taken part in the 1917 revolution, accusing Stalin of 'wading through the blood of yesterday's friends and comrades'. But even for Gorbachev there were limits to what he felt could be revealed. Stalin's order to murder 15,000 Polish officers in 1940 remained a taboo subject.

Throughout 1987 nationalism led to violence in many lands. The Albanian majority in the Kosovo province of Yugoslavia continued to assert its demand for greater autonomy, and clashes between Serbs and Albanians were frequent. In Tibet three Buddhist monks were among those killed when Chinese troops opened fire on unarmed demonstrators protesting against the continuation of Chinese rule. Seventeen Spaniards were killed in June when Basque separatists carried out a car bomb attack in Barcelona. In July, forty Hindus were killed in India when their bus was attacked by Sikh extremists demanding independence: the total Indian death toll that year at the hands of Sikh militants was more than 500.

In Mecca, the holiest city of Islam, Iranian pilgrims, incited by Ayatollah Khomeini, clashed during the annual pilgrimage with Saudi Arabian security forces, and 400 people were killed, including 275 of the Iranians. In Zimbabwe, which had been ruled for several years by its African majority, guerrillas operating independently of government massacred sixteen whites at a Christian mission.

Western European unity took a further step to fulfilment on July 1, when the twelve member States of the European Economic Community signed the Single European Act. The aim of the act was to 'transform relations as a whole among these States into a European Union'. High standards were set for the members, 'in particular to display the principles of democracy and compliance with the law and with human rights'. At a practical level, members of the European Union were committed to abolish trade and employment barriers across their frontiers, to protect the working environment of their citizens, to use their financial resources to 'reduce disparities between the various regions and the backwardness of the least-favoured regions', and to co-ordinate scientific research, technological development, and public health and safety measures. One aim was the creation of a single currency. Another was the creation of a common foreign policy. A third was the continued extension of the community, of which Spain and Portugal were the most recent members.

With the signing of the Single European Act, the European member States, with Britain as an integral if sometimes hesitant part of their collective ideals and institutions, had the capacity to be a 'major player', in the terminology of the time, on the international economic, political and diplomatic scene.

At sea, on December 21, more than 2,000 people drowned when a ferry capsized in the Philippines. It was a worse peacetime maritime disaster than the *Titanic* seventy-five years earlier, when 1,513 people perished.

In September, delegates from forty nations, meeting in Montreal, adopted an extension to the Vienna Convention for the Protection of the Ozone Layer, signed two years earlier, covering all substances known to destroy the ozone layer, including halons – used in many fire extinguishers – which had not hitherto been covered by international agreement. In October the World Commission on Environment and Development, headed by the Norwegian Prime Minister, Mrs Gro Harlem Brundtland, published a report, *Our Common Future*, calling on all governments and international organizations to improve the management of environmental resources in such a way that future global economic development could continue in a 'sustainable' manner. The report stressed that, while meeting the needs of the current generation, it was important not to 'make it impossible' for future generations to meet their own needs.

More than eleven million refugees were being helped with basic supplies by the United Nations High Commissioner for Refugees in 1987, a year during which an ever-increasing number of people were dying of AIDS – it was responsible for 25 per cent of all hospital deaths in Zaire. But the world population continued to rise almost without restraints. On July 11 it was announced that it had doubled since 1950, bringing the number of people in the world to 5,000 million. In a public relations effort designed to highlight this moment, the Secretary-General of the United Nations, Perez de Cuellar, was photographed in a hospital in the Yugoslav city of Zagreb at the birth of 'the world's 5,000 millionth inhabitant'. This child was one of 220,000 babies born that day. Perez de Cuellar told the mother she was lucky, since 'nine out of ten children were born in developing countries'. In those developing countries 40,000 children were dying each day, still leaving a daily population increase world-wide of 180,000 children.

On 8 February 1988 Gorbachev announced that the Soviet forces in Afghanistan would begin their withdrawal in three months' time. The Soviet public had been shocked at the scale of the casualties, and humiliated at having been defied in such a humiliating manner for ten years.

Soviet Communism was changing at a pace even Gorbachev had not forecast. In the early months of 1988, disturbances began in the remote Nagorno-Karabakh Autonomous Region of the Soviet Republic of Azerbaijan. The population of the Nagorno-Karabakh enclave was almost entirely Armenian Christian. The Republic of Azerbaijan of which it was a part was predominately Muslim. On February 20, in a vote unprecedented in any Soviet Autonomous Region, the Nagorno-Karabakh Regional Soviet called for the region to be transferred from Azerbaijan to Armenia.

In Yerevan, the capital of the Armenian Soviet Socialist Republic, an estimated 100,000 Armenians demonstrated on February 22, supporting the incorporation of Nagorno-Karabakh into Armenia. The demonstrations were repeated every day until February 26, when Gorbachev himself appealed on television for them to be brought to an end, and promised to examine the situation personally. All might then have quietened down, but on February 27 reports reached Azerbaijan that two Azeris had been killed the previous week by Armenians. When these reports reached the Azerbaijan port city of Sumgait, which had an Armenian minority, Armenians were attacked in the streets and Armenian shops were looted and burned. In three days' fighting, twenty-six Armenians and six Azeris were killed.

Both in Azerbaijan and in Armenia demands flared up for complete separation from the Soviet Union. No other republics had dared even to hint at separation. The Soviet national anthem lauded 'the unbreakable union of free Republics'. How could two of them secede? What would happen to the other ten?

On June 15 the Armenian Supreme Soviet voted for Nagorno-Karabakh to be transferred from Azerbaijan to Armenia. Two days later the Azerbaijani Supreme Soviet declared this to be a violation of the Soviet constitution. In a counter-move, members of the Azeri minority inside Nagorno-Karabakh attacked Armenians and demanded greater autonomy. When Soviet troops tried to stop the disturbances their intervention was brushed aside. As fighting spread at least thirty Armenians were killed. In Moscow, the Praesidium of the Supreme Soviet rejected any change in the constitutional status of Nagorno-Karabakh. Realizing that their wish to be a legal part of Armenia would not come to pass, tens of thousands of Armenians fled Nagorno-Karabakh and sought refuge in Armenia.

On 17 March 1988, in Geneva, the United States Defence Secretary, Frank Carlucci, announced that the Soviet Union and the United

States had created a 'military contact body', the aim of which was to prevent the escalation of military incidents. On June 1, in Moscow, Reagan and Gorbachev signed the Intermediate-range Nuclear Forces (INF) Treaty, which their respective legislative bodies, the Senate and the Supreme Soviet, had ratified a few days earlier. With regard to future nuclear testing agreements, Gorbachev accepted the American insistence on 'verification'. Hitherto the open scrutiny implied by this word had been an obstacle to agreement. Two months to the day after the signature of the INF Treaty, 'verification' came into being, as the first Soviet intermediate-range nuclear weapons to be dismantled under the treaty were destroyed. This was done in the presence of American observers, in Soviet Kazakhstan.

On June 3, with Gorbachev's encouragement, Andrei Sakharov gave a news conference at the Soviet Foreign Office, during the course of which he attacked Soviet human rights policies and called for the release of all dissidents still being held in Soviet labour camps. Gorbachev agreed. At the Nineteenth Communist Party Congress, which opened in Moscow on June 28 – the first Party Congress since 1941, when the Eighteenth Congress had been called to strengthen Stalin's wartime leadership – Gorbachev told the delegates that a form of Socialism was needed that would be a 'true and tangible humanism in which man is really the measure of all things'. The purpose of all social development, from the economy to 'spiritual life', would be the satisfaction of popular needs. A broad measure of central planning would be combined with a 'great degree of autonomy' for individual enterprises. The basic needs of all would be provided for, including health, education and housing, but individual talent would also be rewarded, in both moral and material terms. Such a society would have a high degree of culture and morality. It would be managed by a system of 'profound and consistent democracy'.

On July 4, three days after the Nineteenth Party Congress ended, the use of psychiatric detention for dissidents was abolished, sweeping away one of the most glaring elements of Soviet human rights abuse. That month Gorbachev promised that a memorial would be built to the victims of Stalin's purges. At the end of July he visited Warsaw, where he said that the 'blank spots' in the history of Russia's relations with Poland should be filled. This opened the way to Soviet admissions of past crimes against hundreds of thousands of Poles, many of whom had been deported by Stalin to Siberia and had perished there. That August, on Gorbachev's instructions, the secret Nazi-Soviet protocol signed in Moscow in August 1939 under which Estonia, Latvia and Lithuania were forcibly incorporated into the Soviet Union, was published. Far from allowing historic wrongs to be set aside, however, publication of this protocol only served to intensify them. On November 16 the Estonian Parliament, hitherto a docile mouthpiece of Moscow, adopted a constitutional amendment giving it the right of veto over all legislation emanating from Moscow that concerned Estonia's 'national' interest. Ten days later the Supreme Soviet Praesidium in Moscow declared the Estonian decision to have been 'unconstitutional'. But the grievance had been voiced and the battle lines drawn for further defiance.

The Eastern European countries were also making demands. At the end of 1988, as a result of pressure from the government in Budapest, Gorbachev was forced to withdraw all Soviet nuclear weapons from Hungary. In Poland, Lech Walesa, whose political movement was still banned, appeared on Polish television to demand free trade unions, freedom of the press, a 'final reckoning with the Stalinist past' and the legalization of Solidarity. He then travelled to Paris for the fortieth anniversary celebrations of the United Nations Declaration of Human Rights. Although holding no public office, he was received with full honours by President Mitterand.

The changes demanded by Gorbachev in the Soviet Union were still being resisted in the satellites. In Bratislava, in March, Czech troops and police dispersed a peaceful religious demonstration. A gathering in Prague in memory of the crushing of the Prague Spring twenty years earlier was likewise brought to an abrupt halt, as was a commemorative march on the 70th anniversary of Czechoslovak independence. When the year ended the Czech Communist Party announced that the 'political pluralism' demanded by Charter 77 was 'out of the question'.

In Hungary, unlike in Czechoslovakia, several non-Communist groupings had been allowed to voice their concerns openly. One of them, the Hungarian Democratic Forum, had 10,000 members by the end of the year. A smaller group, the Alliance of Free Democrats, also emerged that year as the successor to the pre-war democratic opposition. Neither had a place in government, but both were outspoken in calling for democratic reforms. The one remaining taboo in public discussions was criticism of Hungary's links with the Soviet Union.

As each Eastern European country tried to come to terms with the changes in the Soviet Union, Roumania embarked, under President Ceausescu, on a policy of repression. In March, Ceausescu put forward a plan to resettle large numbers of farmers and peasants in the towns. His aim was to demolish 8,000 of Roumania's 13,000 villages by the year 2000. As well as destroying the villages he proposed pulling down churches and levelling cemeteries. Under his perverse vision Roumania was to become a predominately urban society, with giant 'agro-industrial complexes' to sustain both the food and consumer needs of the country.

In October, during a visit to Moscow, Ceausescu rejected Gorbachev's appeals to allow glasnost and perestroika in Roumania. He was determined that Communist rule in Roumania – his rule – would not be weakened or challenged, whatever the Soviet Union might do. The Bulgarian Communist Party also hesitated to move to Soviet-style changes. The founder members of the Bulgarian Independent Association for the Defence of Human Rights, established in January, had almost all been expelled from the country by August. On November 3 a hundred leading Bulgarian intellectuals founded a Club for the Support of Perestroika and Glasnost. It was forced to close down within a few days.

In Yugoslavia, the federal system was proving inadequate to satisfy the growing and conflicting aspirations of the different regions. Deep ethnic divisions were rising to the surface. In Bosnia forty per cent of the population was Muslim. In the Vojvodina there was a large Magyar-speaking minority with historic links to Hungary. The Kosovo province was eighty-five per cent Albanian Muslim. Croatia was predominantly Roman Catholic; Serbia predominantly Orthodox Christian.

During the summer the head of the Serbian Communist Party,

Slobodan Milosevic, took steps to bring Kosovo more under the control of the Serb republic. As his campaign gained momentum three ethnic Albanians – senior and loyal Communist Party members – were forced to resign from their posts for having defended Kosovo's existing provincial autonomy. Starting on November 17 there were five days of demonstrations throughout Kosovo. Ethnic Albanian miners marched in support of continuing autonomy for their province, their race and their faith.

On December 7 an earthquake struck the Soviet Republic of Armenia. Several towns were destroyed and 25,000 people killed in one of the worst earthquakes of the century. Gorbachev, who was in New York, flew back to Moscow and then on to the Armenian capital, Yerevan. There he was confronted by Armenian demonstrators who, despite the human tragedy around them, used his visit to press their demand for Armenian control of the Nagorno-Karabakh enclave in Azerbaijan. They also protested against the recent arrest of five leaders of the Karabakh committee campaigning for Armenia to administer Nagorno-Karabakh. The police ordered the demonstrators to disperse. When they refused to do so, Soviet troops were called in and opened fire. Gorbachev was furious at the politicization of events, accusing 'extreme nationalists' in both Armenia and Azerbaijan of 'using the earthquake disaster for their own political ends', and who, in order to create political instability inflamed 'nationalist passions' at a time when co-operation was essential.

Amid the political crisis, rescue efforts continued. International aid and specialists in disaster relief were rushed to the scene of the earthquake. The fact that the Armenians were Christian also made its impact. The Archbishop of Canterbury, Dr Robert Runcie, called them 'a courageous Christian people who have a special claim on the support of all Christian organizations'.

The war between Iran and Iraq was in its eighth year. In February the combatants sent bombers and missiles against their respective capitals, despite calls from the United Nations that the killing of civilians stop. In March, Iranian troops bombed Halabja, a Kurdish town, with chemical weapons, and 5,000 Kurdish civilians were killed. By using chemical weapons – outlawed by international agreement – Iraq earned the condemnation of most members of the United Nations. The Iraqi ruler, Saddam Hussein, had no compunction, however, in using chemical weapons against his Kurdish minority which, desperate for a less repressive ruler, had supported Iran.

Iran suffered a setback in April when, having mined and damaged an American warship in the Gulf, it faced immediate American retaliation: the destruction of its offshore radar platforms, and the sinking of its few warships. On April 18, two days after the American action, Iraqi forces pushed the Iranian occupation forces out of the Shatt al-Arab, the waterway at the mouth of the Euphrates which Iran had managed to close. Iraq had achieved the success that had eluded it for eight years. On July 18 Iran accepted the United Nations call for a cease-fire, and a withdrawal to the international boundaries. Inside Iraq, pro-Iranian Kurdish fighters refused to stop fighting. Iraq again used chemical weapons against them.

In India, Sikh extremists continued to infiltrate from across the Pakistan border, which Indian troops sealed on April 2. In the three previous months, 645 people had been killed in Sikh-Hindu violence. On May 1, in Sri Lanka, twenty-six passengers were killed when Tamil extremists exploded a land mine under their bus. On December 21 all 258 passengers were killed when a Pan Am passenger air liner flying from Britain to the United States was blown up over Lockerbie, in Scotland, by a terrorist bomb. Eleven people on the ground were also killed.

As the Soviet Union moved towards greater openness, South Africa rigidly maintained the apartheid system. On July 18 Nelson Mandela celebrated his seventieth birthday. He had been a prisoner for twenty-four years. Throughout the world there were protest marches demanding his release.

Human rights were under attack in many parts of the world. On October 5 Amnesty International gave details of eighty countries, out of 135 it had surveyed, which held political prisoners – 'prisoners of conscience' – and which used torture against them. Natural disasters also led to human suffering on a large scale. At the beginning of August severe flooding made more than a million people homeless in Sudan. At the end of August flood waters killed 3,000 people in Bangladesh and left twenty-five million homeless.

Two United Nations agencies, the World Health Organization and the Environment Programme, announced in 1988 that most of the 1,800 million urban dwellers in the world were breathing air of 'unacceptable' quality. Certain cities, of which Milan, Seoul, Rio de Janeiro and Paris were among the worst, had pollution averages above the World Health Organization limits for safety. Another health hazard was the transportation of toxic waste by sea for incineration elsewhere. Meeting in Washington in October, ninety-one nations agreed to ban the export of toxic waste for incineration. The United States Congress also agreed to ban the ocean dumping of sewage sludge as soon after 1991 as possible.

On 6 January 1989 it was announced from Moscow that all victims of Stalin's purges between 1930 and 1950, numbering in the hundreds of thousands, were to be rehabilitated. On February 14 the last Soviet troops left Afghanistan. On March 8, following persistent public demands for greater 'truthfulness' about the death toll in the immediate aftermath of Chernobyl, the authorities admitted that 250 people had died. Every facet of Communist rule was being challenged. On April 9, in Tbilisi, demonstrators demanded the right of Georgia to secede from the Soviet Union. Soviet troops opened fire and nineteen Georgians were killed. On July 10, strikes broke out in the Soviet coalfields. Within ten days 300,000 miners were on strike. On October 9 the Supreme Soviet granted the right to strike. This right, which had helped bring about revolution seventy-two years earlier, had been zealously withheld throughout the Soviet decades.

In Eastern Europe the political turmoil was also dramatic. On January 11 the Hungarian Parliament passed a law which allowed the formation of political parties, ending the forty-year monopoly of the Communist Party, but in Czechoslovakia the heavy hand of Communist repression remained. On February 21 the playwright and human rights activist Vaclav Havel was sentenced to nine months in prison for 'inciting public disorder'.

In Budapest a mass demonstration on March 15 demanded

democracy and national independence for Hungary. By-elections held in Hungary on March 28, in which candidates other than those of the Communist Party were allowed to stand for the first time since 1945, were the first multi-Party elections within the hitherto monolithic Communist bloc. Everywhere the Communist candidates were defeated. Victory went to those whose political platform highlighted democracy, integration into Europe, opposition to Communism and the 'preservation of Hungarian values'.

In Poland, with new strikes spreading and street demonstrations growing, the Polish Government – no longer led by those who had imposed martial law – signed an agreement with Lech Walesa for political and economic reforms. Solidarity was legalized on April 21. A day earlier the Czechoslovak Government had agreed to multi-Party elections, the first in more than forty years. On May 2 the Hungarian Government began to dismantle the 218-mile security fence that had prevented Hungarians from crossing into Austria. On May 17, in Czechoslovakia, Vaclav Havel was released from prison, having served less than a third of his nine-month sentence. That day, in Poland, the Roman Catholic Church was given back the property confiscated from it in the 1950s. It was also given the right to re-establish Catholic schools. On June 4, elections were held in Poland for a new National Assembly. Of those seats reserved for non-Communist political Parties, Solidarity candidates won ninety-nine per cent. The Communist Party candidates were in a minority.

Each change in Eastern Europe raised the spectre of Soviet intervention. But on June 12, in Bonn, the West German Chancellor Helmut Kohl and Mikhail Gorbachev signed a document 'affirming' the right of European States to 'determine their own political systems'.

Following the Hungarian Government's decision to dismantle its sealed border with Austria, ending the stringent border controls that impeded all East–West movement, discontented East Germans, using their Communist documents, travelled through Czechoslovakia to Hungary – travel within the Communist bloc having been a routine matter for several decades – and then 'escaped' westward, through Austria to West Germany. The Hungarian Government made no attempt to stop them leaving the Communist bloc. Within three months 120,000 East Germans used this route to make their way to West Germany.

Within the Baltic Republics of the Soviet Union, the call was rising for greater autonomy, even independence. On August 23 more than two million Estonians, Latvians and Lithuanians linked hands to form a 'human chain' of protest on the fiftieth anniversary of the Nazi-Soviet Pact, as a result of which they had been incorporated in the Soviet Union. Five days later Gorbachev telephoned the Communist Party leader in Lithuania to warn that such demonstrations must stop.

The Baltic Republics were not alone in their ferment. During the last week of August tens of thousands of demonstrators in Kishinev, the capital of the Moldavian Soviet Republic, demanded greater freedom, including official status for the Moldavian language. When similar sentiments were expressed in Ukraine, Gorbachev travelled to Kiev, where he tried to encourage a reformist Communist Party to combat the growing influence of the Ukrainian national movement – RUKH – founded a month earlier, which was calling for the restoration of Ukrainian linguistic and cultural traditions, and for greater autonomy for Ukraine. Gorbachev was determined to prevent the Communist Party being replaced as the dominant force in any of the Soviet republics.

On September 19, at a meeting with Baltic Communist leaders, Gorbachev conceded 'economic autonomy' but demanded respect for the 'federal character' of the Soviet constitution, and respect for the 'unity' of the Communist Party.

In Warsaw the newly elected National Assembly began its first session on September 12. It was the first government in Eastern Europe since 1945 not under Communist control. Its first public announcements were dramatic: the secret police would no longer monitor the opinions of citizens, and censorship would no longer be used to curb expressions of opinion. Five days later the Solidarity candidate, Tadeusz Mazowiecki, was elected Prime Minister of Poland.

In East Germany, starting on September 18, weekly pro-democracy rallies were held in Leipzig. Each week the numbers in the streets grew larger. On October 7 the East German Government began celebrations for the fortieth anniversary of Communist rule. In a gesture of support, Gorbachev flew from Moscow. His presence, and the celebrations themselves, provoked massive street demonstrations by East Germans calling for democratic institutions. Riot police dispersed the protesters.

On October 7, while Gorbachev was in East Berlin, the principal political instrument of Communist rule in Hungary, the Hungarian Socialist Workers' Party, voted by 1,202 votes to 159 for its own dissolution. It also called for guarantees for private property and ownership, and for the privatization of State industries. On the following morning the Party newspaper appeared for the first time without the Marxist slogan 'Workers of the world unite!' Also on October 8 the Latvian Popular Front abandoned its call for greater Latvian autonomy and demanded full secession from the Soviet Union, and the removal of all Soviet troops from Latvian soil.

Street demonstrations throughout East Germany continued, undeterred by the repeated efforts of the police to disperse them. In the end, the police gave up: the crowds were too large and the will to disperse them too weak. On October 18, only eleven days after the anniversary celebrations, the East German Communist Party leader and head of State, Erich Honecker, resigned. His successor, Egon Krenz, went on television to promise 'openness, dialogue and change' and a 'turning point' in how East Germany was to be governed. Asserting that this was 'too little and too late', demonstrators continued to fill the streets.

On October 23, in Hungary, on the anniversary of the 1956 uprising, the speaker of the parliament, Mátyás Szürös, who had just become acting President, proclaimed the 'Hungarian Republic' in place of the 'People's Republic' – Hungary's designation since 1949. Three days later 100,000 pro-democracy demonstrators gathered in the East German city of Dresden, calling for democracy. On November 4 half a million people took part in a pro-democracy rally in East Berlin. In Bulgaria 10,000 demonstrators marched through the streets of Sofia, calling for democracy. There had been no demonstration of this type or size in the forty-five-year rule of the Bulgarian Communist Party.

On November 6, after three quarters of a million protesters marched through the streets of the six main East German cities, the East German Government resigned. Three days later the Central Committee of the East German Communist Party announced that the Berlin Wall would be dismantled and that the 858-mile border between East and West Germany would be opened on the following morning. East Germans could leave the country without restriction.

Starting on the morning of November 10, East Germans poured over the Berlin Wall, and through the growing number of gaps that were being made during the course of the day. That same day, Bulgaria's Communist leader, Todor Zhivkov, who had been in power for thirty-five years at the head of a rigid Communist dictatorship, resigned. He was the longest-serving leader of any Warsaw Pact country. Within days the penalties for 'anti-Socialist agitation' were ended and the ideological branch of the police was dissolved.

On November 20 a new political grouping in Czechoslovakia, the Civic Forum, called for free elections and a multiplicity of political parties. Four days later there were mass resignations of senior Czech Communist Party officials. A twenty-four-hour general strike throughout Czechoslovakia on November 27 was regarded by the millions who participated in it as a national referendum for an end to Communist rule. Before dawn on December 1 the Czechoslovak Communist Party's Politburo, meeting in emergency session, resolved to make an immediate public admission that the 1968 Soviet-led invasion had been 'unjustified and morally wrong'.

Gorbachev was struggling to maintain the unity of the Soviet Empire. On December 1 he denounced the Lithuanian Communist Party leadership for allowing nationalism and 'social-democratic tendencies' to get out of hand. He also tried to maintain the momentum of Soviet-American reconciliation. After a meeting with President Bush on board ship off Malta on December 3 he announced that the Soviet Union would 'never start a war against the United States'. Returning to Moscow, on December 6 he spoke of the 'advisability of keeping the one-Party system'. On the following day – in an unprecedented act of defiance by a Soviet republic – the Lithuanian Parliament voted by an overwhelming majority to abolish the article in Lithuania's constitution under which the Communist Party 'directs and leads society' and was 'the hub of its political system'. The parliamentarians then voted to add a clause to the constitution enabling non-Communists to stand for election.

In East Berlin on December 6 the first-ever round-table meeting of Communist, opposition and Church groups voted to call for free elections within five months, and to replace the secret police by a civilian service under civilian control, accountable to parliament. On December 10 a non-Communist coalition government was established in Prague: Vaclav Havel told a delirious crowd in Wenceslas Square that they had achieved a 'peaceful revolution'.

That day in Sofia 50,000 Bulgarians demanded an end to the supremacy of the Communist Party. On the following day in the streets of Leipzig, 200,000 East Germans demanded the reunification of Germany. Two days later the first of the 580 watchtowers from which East German guards had controlled the East German border and kept it sealed was dismantled. In Bulgaria, all non-Communist political Parties were legalized on December 14, and demonstrations permitted without restriction. From Moscow there came no lead and no guidance, no protest and no indignation. The Soviet Union, so long used to maintaining a sharp watch on all its 'satellites', was struggling with its own internal demons. Only in Roumania did the Ceausescu regime seek to retain Communist control. In November, at his Party Congress, Ceausescu denounced the changes taking place elsewhere in Eastern Europe. As he spoke, he received 125 carefully stage-managed standing ovations.

In the city of Timisoara a Lutheran pastor, László Tökés, an ethnic Hungarian, refused to stop defending ethnic and religious rights. When ordered to leave Timisoara he refused. On December 16, Roumanian security forces tried to remove him by force. His mostly Hungarian congregation resisted. On the following day an even larger demonstration took place in his support joined by many ethnic Roumanians. Security forces and troops opened fire and a hundred demonstrators were killed. There was indignation throughout Roumania at the killings, but Ceausescu failed to appreciate the extent of the anger, and left for a three-day official visit to Iran. He returned on December 20. On the following day he decided to hold a mass rally in Bucharest to demonstrate his popular support. It was a grave miscalculation. The very crowds from whom he had expected vociferous adulation suddenly turned against him.

Anti-Ceausescu demonstrations sprung up throughout the capital. On his direct orders the security troops opened fire. Forty demonstrators were killed. The population of Bucharest, refusing to be cowed, took to the streets in ever-increasing numbers. Ceausescu called on the Minister of Defence, General Milea, to use the army to restore order. Milea refused to do so. His death shortly after his refusal was widely attributed to Ceausescu. The army was outraged, and within hours was on the streets joining with the demonstrators and calling for Ceausescu's overthrow.

On the morning of December 22 Ceausescu and his wife sought refuge in the Communist Party Central Committee building. As they did so a newly formed National Salvation Front, put together by anti-Ceausescu Communist officials, anti-Communist intellectuals and army officers, announced it had taken over power. A vast crowd in front of the Central Committee building demanded Ceaucescu's arrest. He and his wife managed to escape by helicopter from the roof but were captured two days later. Then, on December 25, they faced a short, abusive 'judicial' confrontation with their captors, at a secret location. Found guilty of charges that included genocide and corruption, they were then shot.

In the final days of the overthrow of Ceausescu the secret police had continued to attack army units and civilians, and several hundred people were killed. It was the only serious bloodletting in Eastern Europe during a year of political turmoil. Elsewhere the year ended with the bloodless triumphs, culminating on December 29 when Vaclav Havel – writer, dissident, prisoner – became President of Czechoslovakia. He was the first non-Communist President for forty-one years.

In Communist China, human rights remained under sustained attack. On June 3, in Beijing, protesters in Tiananmen Square demanding greater democracy were fired on by police and troops. Two hundred of the demonstrators were killed, perhaps more. One young man, photographed standing defiantly in front of a line of tanks, caught the imagination of the free world.

*   *   *

On March 24 an oil tanker struck a reef off the coast of Alaska. More than ten million tons of crude oil were spilled. Thousands of birds and hundreds of sea otters were killed. Environmentalists, spurred by the scale of the disaster, urged international agreements to eliminate pollutants that harmed air, water or earth, and calling on companies whose products were environmentally damaging to change them, to restore the environments they had damaged, and to pay compensation for human injury and ill-health.

The Alaskan oil-spill galvanized environmental concerns. But rain forests in South America continued to be burned over vast areas to make way for agricultural and grazing land, while factories in the industrial nations continued to spew out pollution and create acid rain.

The search for international agreements on a global scale had continued throughout the year. On 11 January 1989 a declaration signed by 149 countries outlawed the use in war of poison gas, and toxic and bacteriological weapons. But it was not deaths in combat that gave the gravest cause for thought. On December 12 the United Nations announced that 7,000 children died every day from dehydration, and 6,000 every day from pneumonia. Measles, tetanus and whooping cough between them killed three million children a year. In the 1990s more than 100 million children would die from illness and malnutrition.

CHAPTER TWELVE

Brave New World

1990—99

On new year's day 1990 the Roumanian secret police, the dreaded Securitate, was abolished. Four days later the Roumanian Government announced an amnesty for everyone sentenced for political offences since 1947. Elsewhere in Europe violence erupted as the fall of Communism upset settled patterns of loyalty and obedience. On January 11 anti-Communist demonstrations in Albania were dispersed by police, while inside the Soviet Union 200 Armenians and Azeris were killed in ethnic clashes in the disputed Nagorno-Karabakh enclave. On January 18, Azerbaijan declared war on Armenia: the first time since the formation of the Soviet Union that two republics had fought each other. On the following day, in the predominantly Azerbaijani city of Baku, sixty Armenians were murdered in an Azeri pogrom: no longer Communist victims of Communists, but Christians murdered by Muslims.

Changes inconceivable a year earlier were taking place. On February 24, in elections in the Soviet Republic of Lithuania, the Communist Party came second to those campaigning against the continuation of Communist and Soviet rule. On February 26 Gorbachev agreed to withdraw all Soviet troops from Czechoslovakia within seventeen months. On March 5 he conceded the right, throughout the Soviet Union, of individuals to run their own small businesses and to employ up to twenty people. While economic change fitted his vision of restructuring, political change had become the main public demand. On March 11 the Communist Party gave up its constitutional 'leading role' in the structure of the State. With Gorbachev's approval the constitution was amended: henceforth the Communist Party would 'share' with other political Parties the task of forming and administering policy.

On March 15 Lithuania declared independence: it was the first Baltic republic to break away from the Soviet Union. The Lithuanian move, declared Gorbachev, was 'illegitimate and invalid'. But it had taken place, and overnight the hammer and sickle disappeared, replaced by the long-banned Lithuanian flag. On March 25 Soviet tanks appeared in the streets of the Lithuanian capital, Vilnius. For several hours they drove around the parliament building, inside which the defiant parliamentarians waited. After several hours the Soviet tanks withdrew.

Despite the loss of Lithuania, Gorbachev believed he could still preserve the unity of the Soviet Union, not by force but by openness. On April 22 he authorized publication of full details about Chernobyl. Whether telling the truth could preserve either the Communist system or the unity of the Soviet Union was unclear. On May 1 the traditional Red Square demonstration in Moscow in support of the Communist Party and its leaders witnessed a counter demonstration supporting Lithuania's declaration of independence. On May 4 the Latvian Parliament declared 'an independent democratic republic'. The Estonian Parliament voted its declaration of independence on May 8. All three Baltic republics had detached themselves from the Soviet Union.

Czechoslovakia had chosen a leading dissident, Vaclav Havel, as President. On May 2 Hungary also chose a former dissident, Arpad Goncz, as President. In the aftermath of the 1956 Hungarian uprising he had been imprisoned for six years. On May 20, Roumania held its first free elections since 1937. Two thirds of the seats were won by the anti-Communist National Salvation Front, whose leader, Ion Iliescu, was elected President. On May 29, in the largest of the Soviet republics, the Russian Federation, Boris Yeltsin was elected President, defeating the Communist Party candidate put up by Gorbachev. Within four months, Yeltsin resigned from the Communist Party, declaring that it was not truly reformist.

From May 31 to June 3 Gorbachev, putting Russia's turmoil

behind him, was in Washington at a summit with President Bush. The two men agreed to ban the production of chemical weapons and destroy all but 5,000 tons of their stockpiles. They also agreed to destroy these 5,000 tons as soon as a worldwide ban on chemical weapons was agreed. For the first time in fifty years, an agreement was signed 'normalizing' trade relations between the two countries: and increasing considerably the long-term American grain sales to the Soviet Union.

On June 8, five days after the Washington summit, the new Hungarian President, Arpad Goncz, withdrew Hungary from the Warsaw Pact.

Gorbachev still hoped that a reformed Communist Party could attract majority support, and at the Twentieth Congress of the Communist Party, held between July 2 and 13, pleaded with the delegates for a Communist Party 'freed of its ideological blinkers'. It must, he said, be a tolerant party and a parliamentary party. One month later, as promised the previous year, he issued a series of decrees 'rehabilitating' those who had been murdered by Stalin or imprisoned during the purges. He also restored citizenship to Solzhenitsyn. Six weeks later, on September 26, he presented the Supreme Soviet with a proposed law allowing freedom of religion. The law was passed by 341 votes to one. Within another three weeks, church services were held in St Basil's Cathedral in the Kremlin for the first time since 1918.

Islam, which four years earlier Gorbachev had condemned as an 'enemy of progress and socialism', was given the same freedoms as Christianity, and new mosques were built throughout the Soviet Central Asian Republics.

The pace of change was rapid. At midnight on October 2 the German Democratic Republic formally ceased to exist, and on the following day the two Germanys announced their unification. The Soviet Union made no protest at what it had long declared to be inconceivable. That same day, October 3, the Soviet Union reached agreement with the United States to limit the size of their respective conventional forces in Europe. Twelve days later, Gorbachev was awarded the Nobel Peace Prize.

*   *   *

On 2 February 1990, after two meetings with the imprisoned Nelson Mandela – still incarcerated, and yet clearly on the verge of being given not only his freedom but a major role in South African political life – the Prime Minister, Willem de Klerk, informed the South African Parliament that the ban on the African National Congress was over. Press censorship was relaxed. The execution of convicted prisoners was stopped. All those imprisoned for their membership of banned organizations were to be released. The government would work for universal franchise and 'respect for human rights'. With a firm voice directed towards the white parliamentarians for whom these changes were anathema, de Klerk announced: 'The season of violence is over. The time for reconciliation and reconstruction has come.'

On February 11, de Klerk released Nelson Mandela from prison. Fifty thousand people gathered in Cape Town to welcome him. Like Gandhi four decades earlier in the Hindu-Muslim conflict in India, Mandela was confronted by inter-communal violence that threatened to destroy his vision of a unified majority-ruled South Africa. Dozens of Africans were killed in the week after his release in the fighting between the United Democratic Front, which supported the African National Congress, and the Zulu-based Inkatha movement. On February 25, at the end of his second week of freedom, Mandela urged the fighting factions to stop the killing and throw their weapons into the sea. His appeal was not heeded. Nor could he stop the inhabitants of the African homelands – the Bantustans – from attacking their own African rulers, whom they accused of supporting the apartheid regime. In Ciskei, shops were looted, factories burned down, and fifty people died.

On May 2, Mandela and de Klerk began a three-day meeting near Cape Town with leaders of the white community and the African National Congress. All political prisoners would be released and all exiles invited back. The ANC promised to work towards an end of violence and intimidation within the black community, and between it and the white community. But the white regime could not easily shake off the habits of two generations. In May, after eleven black protesters were shot dead, Mandela warned de Klerk that there could be no negotiations until the 'massacre of blacks' was ended. New talks began on August 8, when the ANC pledged to end its thirty-year armed struggle against the government. Both sides committed themselves to secure change through negotiation. What neither side could halt was the inter-communal killing. In the black townships of the Transvaal 500 people were killed in the course of a few days. Both the Zulu chief, Mangosuthu Buthelezi, and Mandela, appealed for a halt to the killings, but neither man was heeded.

Elsewhere in Africa, the grim cycle of drought and famine was accompanied by civil war. In Somalia the armed forces under the control of President Mohammed Siyad Barre murdered 5,000 civilians within two years. The opposition Somali National Movement had also carried out atrocities: according to the human rights group Africa Watch no fewer than 50,000 civilians and 60,000 soldiers had been killed on both sides since the start of the civil war in 1988. On one occasion, in a stadium in the capital, hecklers had interrupted a speech by President Barre. Troops opened fire on the hecklers and at least a hundred were killed.

In Sri Lanka, the civil war continued with no diminution in savagery. On June 13, Tamil Tigers captured ninety Sinhalese policemen and executed them. They also attacked moderate Tamil groups who were calling for restraint and compromise. Tamil Tigers also turned on the Muslim minority in Sri Lanka. On August 3 more than a hundred Muslims were massacred in a mosque. Two days later, fifty-eight Muslims were murdered in their villages. Within the areas controlled by the government, vigilante squads killed at Tamils at random. On October 23 the European Union protested at Sri Lanka's descent into unrestrained killing. Indian troops, who had been attempting to keep the peace and restrain the Tamil Tigers could do so no longer, and withdrew. They had lost 1,100 dead during their three-year duty.

A new war was about to break upon the international scene when, on August 2, Saddam Hussein's Iraq invaded Kuwait. That day the United Nations Security Council called for 'immediate and uncon-ditional' Iraqi withdrawal. The United States and the Soviet Union issued a joint statement calling for an international ban on arms sales to Iraq, much of whose armoury had been provided over the previous

decade by the Soviet Union, France and Britain. On August 6 the
United Nations imposed sanctions on Iraq, including oil sanctions,
and made them mandatory for all member States. Iraq could neither
sell its own oil abroad, nor import oil.

In a television broadcast on August 8, President Bush compared
Saddam Hussein to Hitler. 'Appeasement does not work', he said.
'No-one should underestimate our determination to confront aggression.' On the following day Iraq announced the formal annexation
of Kuwait. Six days later, on August 13, American and British
warships began a naval blockade of Iraq to ensure the maintenance
of United Nations sanctions. The Canadian Government sent a naval
flotilla: two destroyers and a supply ship, and a squadron of jet
fighters to provide protection for the three ships.

On August 19 Saddam Hussein detained all foreign nationals
who were in Kuwait at the time of the invasion, and held them
hostage near military installations. This, said Bush, was against 'all
accepted norms of international conduct', and on August 22 he
ordered the call-up of 40,000 American military reservists. At an
emergency summit in Helsinki on September 9, Bush and Gorbachev
called on Iraq to withdraw unconditionally from Kuwait and to free
the hostages. Two days later, in Washington, Bush stressed the
importance of the Kuwaiti oilfields to the United States: 'We cannot
permit a resource so vital to be dominated by one so ruthless.'

Saddam Hussein's troops in Kuwait massed along the Saudi
Arabian border. On September 14 Margaret Thatcher ordered a
British armoured brigade to be sent to Saudi Arabia as a protective
shield for the desert kingdom. The despatch of this brigade – 8,000
men together with their tanks and armoured vehicles – was the
largest movement of British troops and armour overseas since the
Korean War forty years earlier.

Details of Iraqi ill-treatment of Kuwaitis reached the West every
day. On September 22 Bush wrote in his diary: 'I've just read a
horrible intelligence report on the brutal dismembering and dismantling of Kuwait. Shooting citizens when they are stopped in their
cars. Exporting what little food there is. Brutalizing the homes.
Dismantling the records. Indeed, making an oasis into a wasteland.'

Bush also pondered a historical precedent. As he later recalled:

'In the first weeks of the crisis, I happened to be reading a book on World War II by the British historian Martin Gilbert. I saw a direct analogy between what was occurring in Kuwait and what the Nazis had done, especially in Poland.' Bush explained: 'The book recounted how the German Army swept through an area, followed closely by special units which would terrorize the population. I saw a chilling parallel with what the Iraqi occupiers were doing in Kuwait. I caught hell on this comparison of Saddam to Hitler, with critics accusing me of personalizing the crisis, but I still feel it was an appropriate one.'

After foreign pleading, Saddam Hussein released most of the hostages he had taken. But he refused to withdraw from Kuwait. On November 22 Britain announced the despatch of a further 14,000 troops to Saudi Arabia, bringing the total to 22,000. Six days later, following a British political crisis, Margaret Thatcher was forced from office and John Major became Prime Minister. On the following day, November 29, the Security Council authorized the use of force against Iraq if Kuwait had not been evacuated by 15 January 1991. Bush tried to allay American fears of a full-scale war. 'Should military action be required,' he said, 'this will not be another Vietnam. This will not be a protracted drawn-out war.' But any American life lost would be 'paid for in full' by Iraq. On December 6, Saddam Hussein announced the release of all remaining Western hostages in Iraq and Kuwait. On December 24 he stated that Israel would be the 'first target' in the event of war.

On 12 January 1991 both Houses of Congress voted in Washington to authorize American military action in the Gulf, though the vote, 52 for and 47 against, was close. The United States provided the Supreme Commander, a Vietnam War veteran, General Schwarzkopf, and by far the largest contingent: 425,000 military, naval and air personnel. Saudi Arabia provided 45,000 men, Egypt 30,000 and Britain 22,000, some of whom had seen action in the Falklands War nine years earlier. Saddam Hussein commanded the fourth-largest army in the world, a million men, of whom 580,000 were on the Kuwaiti front. Many had battle experience in the war with Iran.

The United Nations Security Council resolution of the previous

November, authorizing force to end the Iraqi occupation of Kuwait, became effective on January 15. An ultimatum sent to Iraq was rejected. On January 16 the war began, codenamed Operation Desert Storm. That night the coalition launched air attacks against Iraqi military installations in Kuwait and Iraq. Within twenty-four hours the Iraqi air defence system had its communications network destroyed. Saddam Hussein was so angered by the failure of his anti-aircraft defences that he ordered the execution of his anti-aircraft commander.

On January 18 the first Iraqi Scud missiles were launched against Israel, causing damage to property but no deaths. More Scuds were launched the following day, but Israel deferred to the coalition and refrained from retaliation. On January 23 Iraq launched a third Scud missile attack on Israel. By then, American Patriot missiles were in place to intercept them, and Israelis were taking shelter in sealed rooms, wearing gas masks.

The first Kuwaiti territory liberated by the coalition was a small offshore island from which the Iraqis were driven on January 24. On the following day, in an act of vandalism, Iraq began pumping crude oil from Kuwaiti storage tanks into the Gulf, creating the world's worst crude oil spillage. It was estimated that more than a million birds would die.

On January 30, Iraqi troops crossed the border from Kuwait into Saudi Arabia. Within forty-eight hours they had been driven out. The bombing of Iraq intensified. For a month Iraqi military installations were pounded. When, on February 21, British troops began their heaviest artillery bombardment in action since the Korean War, on Iraqi targets just north of the Saudi Arabian border, Saddam retaliated with a scorched-earth policy in Kuwait, setting more than 150 oil wells on fire. Vast plumes of black smoke turned day into night over Kuwait City.

On February 22, Bush sent an ultimatum to Iraq: either Iraqi forces evacuate Kuwait by the following evening or they would face a 'ground war'. Saddam took no steps to end his occupation, and at dawn on February 24 the coalition launched a ground attack. By the end of the first day 20,000 Iraqi troops had surrendered. In Kuwait

City, Iraqi defenders set a further 150 oil wells on fire, intensifying the pall of black smoke over the city.

Iraq had not lost the ability to retaliate. On February 25 twenty-eight American soldiers were killed by a Scud missile attack. In Israel, 1,600 families lost their homes as a result of continuing Scud attacks, and one civilian died of a heart attack when a Scud exploded nearby. He was the only Israeli victim.

On February 26 Saddam Hussein announced that Iraqi troops were withdrawing from Kuwait. As they withdrew they took with them as much looted property as they could cram into several hundred cars and trucks. As the convoy made its way towards Iraq, along the Mutla Ridge north of Kuwait, it created a four-mile traffic jam, visible from the air and an easy target. It had no anti-aircraft defences. American aircraft attacked and the convoy was destroyed. A few hours later coalition troops and war correspondents reached the wreckage. Televised images of the destruction were seen around the world.

On February 27, coalition forces entered Kuwait City. The United Nations objective had been secured. Kuwait was declared officially 'liberated'. Iraq agreed to rescind its annexation and pay reparations for the damage done in the city. Inside Iraq, coalition forces surrounded the elite troops of the Iraqi Republican Guard. On the following morning, February 28, while Western television was showing the scenes of carnage at the Mutla Ridge, Bush appeared on television to announce the suspension of hostilities. 'Kuwait is liberated,' he declared. 'Iraq's army is defeated; our military objectives are met.' It was the forty-second day of the war.

The coalition forces lost fewer than 200 combatants. Of these a quarter had been killed accidentally by their own side, in ill-named 'friendly fire'. The largest national death toll was that of the Americans: 145 killed in action and 121 killed in accidents. The British lost twenty-four men, the Egyptians ten, the United Arab Emirates six and the French two. The Iraqi losses on the battlefield exceeded 8,000. A further 5,000 Iraqi civilians had been killed during the Allied bombing raids, particularly on Baghdad.

* * *

On March 1, revolts broke out against Saddam Hussein among the Shi'ites in the south and the Kurds in the north. He took immediate steps to crush both insurrections. In the north his air force bombed the city of Kirkuk, which was being held by Kurds. Then, as American troops withdrew under the cease-fire terms from the south, he turned his army and air force against the Shi'ites. After three weeks of fighting the rebellion was at an end. Saddam Hussein, defeated in war, was still master of his country.

Iraq had been forced to agree to United Nations inspection teams. Their task was to search for weapons of mass destruction, principally nuclear, chemical and biological weapons, which it was believed he possessed or was developing. The coalition hoped that the defeat of Iraq would be followed by internal moves to depose Saddam Hussein. This did not happen. The instruments of repression remained in his hands, even as United Nations sanctions bit into his economic solvency. Ten years later he was still ruler of Iraq.

On 13 January 1991, in a desperate attempt to reverse what many considered to be the inevitable break-up of the Soviet federal structure, on January 13 1991, Gorbachev ordered Soviet troops stationed in Lithuania to take over the radio and television centres in Vilnius. In the ensuing protests, thirteen Lithuanians were killed. It was a futile assault. On the following day, from Moscow, Boris Yeltsin, President of the Russian Republic – the largest of the Soviet republics – denounced the violence against the Lithuanians and gave tacit support to Lithuanian independence. Still Gorbachev refused to accept the inevitable. On January 20, during a pro-independence rally in the Latvian capital, Riga, he ordered Soviet troops to occupy the Ministry of the Interior building. Four Latvians demonstrators were killed. This only served to spur Latvian national aspirations.

On February 9 the people of Lithuania voted in a national referendum called to confirm the previous year's declaration of independence. The Soviet military action a month earlier had been totally counterproductive. There was a further blow to Gorbachev on March 3 when seventy-seven per cent of Estonians voted to remain outside the Soviet Union. It was not only the Baltic republics – Soviet since 1945 – that were seeking independence. In the first week of April the capital of the Byelorussian Republic, Minsk, Soviet since 1918, was brought to a halt by a general strike calling for independence. On April 9 the Georgian Soviet Socialist Republic declared independence. In Moscow, Gorbachev was unable to prevent the demands of the Russian Federation – The Russian Federative Soviet Socialist Republic, the largest of the republics – for its own elected presidency, to which Boris Yeltsin was elected on June 12, the first person in the history of the Soviet Union to be elected by popular vote.

On July 1 Gorbachev authorized the signature of a protocol dissolving the Warsaw Pact. That same day he ordered the start of the denationalization of all State enterprises. In an attempt to preserve the Soviet Union he proposed an All-Union Treaty in which 'equal status' with the hitherto dominant Russian Federation was granted to the remaining eleven Soviet republics. August 20 was set for the treaty's signature. Meanwhile, within the Russian Federation, changes were taking place far beyond those contemplated by Gorbachev as part of glasnost or perestroika, when on July 20 Yeltsin banned the Communist Party from all workplaces and all government establishments.

On August 5 Gorbachev flew to the Crimea to a villa on the Black Sea for a two-week break before returning to Moscow to sign the All-Union Treaty. But on the last day of his holiday, leading hard-line Communists, intent on returning the Soviet Union to Communist rule and restoring the territorial and ideological unity of the Soviet Union, held him incommunicado in his villa and attempted to seize power in Moscow.

From its first hours the coup was opposed by Yeltsin and those in Moscow determined not to lose the wide degree of territorial and political independence secured during the previous months. In a series of telephone calls Yeltsin persuaded the Western European leaders to denounce the coup. John Major, the British Prime Minister, took the lead. The leaders of the coup ordered Soviet naval vessels to blockade the Estonian capital of Tallinn, and to move against the Latvian Parliament building in Riga. On August 21 Soviet 'black beret' police were in action in the Lithuanian capital, Vilnius, and one Lithuanian was killed. That day in Moscow, several hundred thousand of Yeltsin's supporters established a civilian barricade round the parliament building from which Yeltsin and his government continued to direct their resistance. Tanks, sent by the coup leaders, failed to break through the barricade in the fighting – three civilians were killed.

That day Gorbachev returned to Moscow, where he praised Yeltsin for having opposed the coup. But his authority had gone. That day Latvia declared its independence and Lithuania reaffirmed its separation from the Soviet Union. On the following day, August 22, Yeltsin, ruler of a non-Communist Russian Republic – the Russian Federation – ordered the Hammer and Sickle flag to be replaced with the pre-revolutionary white, blue and red. Each day saw Gorbachev's power recede. On August 23 Armenia declared independence, as did, on the following day, Ukraine, the agricultural heartland and industrial powerhouse of the Soviet Union. That day, August 24, Gorbachev resigned as leader of the Communist Party. He remained President of the Soviet Union. His last official act as party leader was to disband the Party's Central Committee, through which the Soviet Union had been ruled since 1917.

The Soviet Union was disintegrating. On August 25 Byelorussia declared independence, taking the name Belarus. Two days later Moldavia declared independence, taking the name Moldova. Even the Russian language had lost its power to command. On August 29 all Communist Party activity was suspended in all the former Soviet republics. A day later Azerbaijan declared independence. On August 31 two of the Central Asian Republics of the Soviet Union, Uzbekistan and Kirgizia, did likewise, followed by Tadzhikistan on September 6. Even the memory of Lenin was to be expunged, as the city of Leningrad was renamed St Petersburg, its name in Tsarist days. The Soviet Union still existed, albeit without the Communist Party as its political centre, and with its territorial unity in disarray. The declarations of independence continued: Turkmenistan raising its national flag on October 27.

On December 1, the people of the Ukraine voted in a referendum for independence: ninety per cent favoured total separation from the Soviet Union. A week later three former Soviet Republics, the Russian Federation, Belarus and Ukraine, established a Commonwealth of

Independent States (CIS) and declared the 'end' of the Soviet Union. One remaining republic, Kazakhstan, had still not broken away from the defunct Soviet Union. On December 16 it too declared independence. Five days later the leaders of eight more former Soviet republics joined the Commonwealth of Independent States. Only Georgia declined to do so. Like the three Baltic States, it wanted independence to be absolute. On December 25 Gorbachev formally resigned as President of the dissolved Soviet Union. On the following day the Supreme Soviet, which had ruled the Soviet Union since 1917, met in Moscow and dissolved itself.

Yugoslavia was disintegrating as the Soviet Union had done. On June 25 two of the Federal Republics of Yugoslavia – Croatia and Slovenia – declared their independence. Yugoslav troops – predominantly Serb – advanced towards the respective breakaway capitals, Zagreb and Ljubljana. Several dozen people were killed. After mediation by the European Union the Serb forces withdrew. The war had lasted ten days.

Slovenia settled down to independence as one of Europe's smallest nations, with a population of under two million. But in August, Serb troops re-entered Croatia and fighting between Serbs and Croats intensified. The eastern Croatian town of Vukovar was overrun by the Serbs after being besieged for eighty-six days. A thousand people had been killed during the siege. On October 15, Bosnia-Herzegovina, another of the republics of Yugoslavia, voted to become an independent State. But its multi-racial character – Croat, Serb and Muslim – made it impossible for any one element to claim full control, and it faced two military invasions by Croats and Serbs.

In India, Sikh militants attacked two trains in the Punjab, killing more than seventy passengers. In Zaire, more than a hundred protesters were killed when troops opened fire on a demonstration against the autocratic regime. In South Africa, despite renewed efforts by Nelson Mandela and Chief Buthelezi to calm tensions between their respective followers, thirty-five mourners were killed when gunmen attacked an ANC funeral wake. During the previous four years, 5,000 Black South Africans had been killed in inter-communal violence.

President de Klerk continued on his anti-apartheid course, repealing almost all the repressive legislation. After a break of thirty years, the International Olympic Committee agreed to readmit South Africa to the Olympic Games.

On 20 February 1991, student protesters in the Albanian capital, Tirana, pulled down the statue of the former Communist leader, Enver Hoxha. In Bulgaria, the former Communist ruler, Todor Zhivkov, was put on trial on charges of fraud and embezzlement.

In Bangladesh, on April 29, at least 150,000 people were killed when a cyclone drove the sea ashore, inundating a vast area, the size of south-east England. As winds reached up to 165 miles an hour, 500 fishing boats and their crews were swept away, and a million tons of rice were lost to the sea.

One victim of the Sri Lankan violence in 1991 was the former Indian Prime Minister, Rajiv Gandhi – who had been ousted from the premiership two years earlier but was on the verge of a return to power. On May 21 he was assassinated at an election rally in southern India. His assassin was a young woman, an extremist Tamil separatist who had strapped an explosive charge to her body and came up to him with a garland to put around his neck. Detonating the explosives, she killed herself, Rajiv Gandhi and fifteen others.

In Somalia, the civil war, intensifying in October 1991, led to the deaths of 20,000 people. Of Somalia's six million inhabitants, as many as five million were estimated by the United Nations to be 'undernourished'. The civil war made it almost impossible to get relief supplies to them.

The civil strife in Yugoslavia seemed to reach a positive turning point on 1 January 1992, when Serbia – as the largest component of the Yugoslav Federation was becoming known – and Croatia agreed to the deployment of United Nations troops. But violence did not cease. On January 7 five European Community monitors were killed when their helicopter was shot down over Croatia. On January 15 the countries of the European Community formally recognized the independence of Slovenia and Croatia – the Yugoslav Federation was at an end.

On March 1 the people of Bosnia-Herzegovina voted for independence. The new State was admitted to the United Nations in May. From the outset of its independence it was beset with internal and external strife. Serbia wished to regain it, and Croatia wished to acquire part of it. Its Muslim population wanted their rights protected. The Bosnian Serbs, not wishing to be separated from Serbia, called for the creation of a Greater Serbia of which they would be part. They had boycotted the referendum for independence.

In the fighting which started in March, the Bosnian Serbs were helped by Serbian troops. Behind the lines, Bosnian Serb soldiers turned against the Muslim population with a savagery that became known as 'ethnic cleansing'. Thousands of homes were destroyed, thousands of men held in detention camps amid brutality and privation, and thousands more people – men, women and children – were massacred. On August 4 the United Nations Security Council condemned the Serbian-controlled detention camps in Bosnia. Ten days later the Security Council adopted resolutions denouncing 'war crimes' and calling for military action in support of humanitarian relief operations. British troops were among the first to participate in this relief protection.

By the end of August the Federal Serb and Bosnian Serb forces were in control of seventy per cent of Bosnia. They then declared the areas under their rule to be the Serbian Republic. The remaining thirty per cent of Bosnia declared itself a Muslim-Croat Federation. As a result of international pressure, Serbian troops withdrew from Bosnia. As they did so they handed over the areas they had secured to the local Bosnian Serbs. Bosnia was divided on largely ethnic lines, varying according to military dispositions. Behind the front lines, mass murder continued.

Every republic of the former Soviet Union despatched ambassadors abroad and began the slow process of establishing a national-based foreign policy. On 13 January 1992 the Government of Lithuania signed an agreement with its neighbour Poland, pledging non-interference in each other's internal affairs. The following day Estonia began negotiations for a treaty of mutual non-interference with Yeltsin's Russia. On January 16 Moldova established diplomatic relations with Hungary. At the end of January Ukraine signed a barter deal with Iran, providing Iran with gas and oil in return for chemicals, concrete and steel piping. On February 1 negotiations were concluded in Moscow between the members of the Commonwealth of Independent States and the three Baltic States for the withdrawal of all former Soviet troops.

Flying to Paris on February 7, Presidents Yeltsin and Mitterand signed the first treaty between Russia and the West. Two days later food shortages in Russia led to street demonstrations. On the following day the United States, Canada and the European Community agreed to airlift food to all the former Soviet republics.

The new republics were beset with internal and inter-communal disputes. On February 25, in the Christian-Armenian enclave of Nagorno-Karabakh, 200 Muslim Azeris were killed during ethnic clashes. A month later there was fighting between Ukrainians and Russians in eastern Ukraine and eighteen people were killed. On May 15 all but Ukraine of the former Soviet republics agreed to recognize each other's borders and pledged a 'common defence' against aggression. All eleven members of the Commonwealth of Independent States agreed that summer to send a 'Unified Team' to the Olympic Games in Barcelona. It was to win the largest number of gold medals – forty-five – as against thirty-seven for the United States. Negotiations between Russia and Ukraine about the Soviet Black Sea fleet, once the pride of the Soviet Union, concluded on August 3 with an agreement for three years' joint control of the warships, followed by the division of the fleet equally between Russia and Ukraine.

In Georgia, the Abkhazians, 160,000 of whom lived on the Black Sea coast in and around the port of Sukhumi, rose in revolt on August 14 and demanded their own independent State. After three days of fighting, in which fifty people were killed, the Georgian Government reimposed its authority.

On December 29 the United States and Russia – Yeltsin taking the lead for the former Soviet republics in matters of nuclear defence – signed the long-delayed Strategic Arms Reduction Treaty (START-II). Former Soviet and American nuclear stockpiles were both to be reduced by two thirds.

*   *   *

On June 28 the body of Ignace Paderewski, Poland's first President, was taken from Arlington Cemetery, Virginia, and flown to Warsaw. At the time of Paderewski's death in 1941 the American Government had promised it would be returned to Poland when Poland was free. With Lech Walesa as President, censorship gone, a substantial increase in private ownership in prospect and a multi-Party government in place in which Solidarity was a part, Poland was as free as she had been since before the Second World War.

On July 17 another former Communist country began to dissolve. That day the regional Parliament of Slovakia issued a 'declaration of sovereignty'. It no longer wished to be part of Czechoslovakia. On December 31 Czechoslovakia formally ceased to exist. In its place were two separate and independent republics: the Czech Republic with its capital in Prague and Slovakia with its capital in Bratislava.

In Israel, Yitzhak Rabin, having become Prime Minister for the second time, explained on July 13 that he wanted the Palestinians under Israeli occupation since 1967 – when he had been Chief of Staff and victor – to become partners, not enemies, with Palestinian national and personal rights restored. At a time when apartheid was ending in South Africa, when there were hopes of negotiations between the adversaries in Northern Ireland, and when a post-Communist world had emerged in Eastern Europe, 'it is our duty to ourselves and to our children,' Rabin said, 'to see the new world as it is now – to discern its dangers, explore its prospects and do everything possible so that the State of Israel will fit into this world whose face is changing.'

With the help of his Foreign Minister, Shimon Peres – like Rabin, a former Prime Minister – Rabin acted to break the mould of confrontation. When the army sought permission to enter the Palestinian university campus at Nablus to search for six armed Palestinians believed to be trying to influence student council elections there, Rabin refused. Within a week of coming to power he ordered a freeze on all new settlement building in the West Bank and Gaza. On August 24, talks between Israel and the Palestinians opened in Washington. Four days later, Israel released 800 of the 7,429 Palestinians it was holding in detention. Hopes rose for a new era.

Ethnic violence elsewhere was widespread: 2,000 Sri Lankans were killed in 1992 as the Tamil revolt continued into its tenth year. Muslims and Tamils were also fighting: in one incident 190 Muslims were massacred, in another, fifty-seven Muslims and fifty-three Tamils were killed. In South Africa, more than 7,000 Africans were killed in inter-communal violence between African National Congress and Inkatha Freedom Party supporters in the twenty-seven months up to March 1992. In India, on December 6, after Hindu extremists attacked and destroyed a historic mosque in the Hindu holy city of Ayodhya, riots throughout northern India led to 400 deaths.

On June 3, delegates from more than a hundred nations met in Rio de Janeiro for the first Earth Summit. There were calls for regulations to be set out for an 'environmentally sound' development of the planet. In India, the motor car – a major and growing source of environmental pollution – killed more than 50,000 people that year, also 40,000 in the United States and more than 4,000 in Britain.

In July, 5,000 people a day were dying of starvation in Somalia. American air and sea support was sent at once, and 228,000 tons of grain reached Somalia within a month. At least half the grain was then looted by warring Somali factions. With the authority of the United Nations, a Pakistani force of 500 men was sent to halt the looting but was unable to do so. The warring factions were well-armed, anarchic, and would often shoot to kill without provocation.

By the end of September 300,000 Somalis had died of famine. Thousands more had been killed in factional rivalry. In October, Amnesty International condemned the Somali warlord, General Aydid, for mass executions. For his part Aydid rejected any further United Nations involvement, claiming it was an 'affront' to Somalia's sovereignty. The United Nations Special Representative warned publicly that hundreds of thousands more Somalis would be killed unless the United Nations took immediate and effective action. Food aid unloaded at Mogadishu docks was unable to reach even the northern part of the city, as rebel forces controlled the suburbs. Western journalists photographed hundreds of bales of aid lying idle at the dockside.

On December 3 the United Nations Security Council authorized direct intervention in Somalia, under the leadership of the United States. A day later President Bush ordered 28,000 American troops to Somalia. The first American marines landed at Mogadishu on December 9, their arrival recorded by the same photographers who had earlier shown the world the food aid that could not be distributed because of civil unrest. Several thousand French troops were brought by sea to Mogadishu from Djibouti. These forces took over physical control of famine areas in the south of the country, with a mandate to make the food aid available to those who were so desperately in need of it.

On December 28 a joint force of 200 United States and forty Canadian soldiers arrived by helicopter at the famine-stricken inland town of Belet Huen. As soon as they secured the airfield, cargo planes brought more soldiers. Within seven days, a force of 800 Canadians was supervising the distribution of food.

For the United States, which had masterminded the landings, the Somalia intervention was a humanitarian commitment on a massive scale, constituting a signal to the world that armed forces could have other uses than combat. In February, American military aircraft had flown fifty-four food missions into the former Soviet Union. That year, American non-military aid reached its highest-ever level: $6,154 million. The two largest beneficiaries were Israel ($1,200 million) and Egypt ($892 million) – Israel also received $1,800 million in military aid from the United States, and Egypt $1,300 million: following the Camp David accords five years earlier the United States pledged to ensure as best it could the economic stability of these former adversaries, and their military strength. The third largest amount of American foreign aid went to India: $815 million. Helping to sustain India's democracy was another American foreign policy goal. The countries of Eastern Europe which had so recently broken free from Communism received a total of $431 million between them.

Almost every country in Africa was in receipt of American economic aid. But the total United States economic aid to Africa, $1,391 million, was only slightly in excess of the aid to Israel alone. Even when added up these large sums amounted to only half of one per cent of the United States national budget outlay for the year. The total sum also constituted slightly less than the amount earned by the United States in that same year from arms sales. By far the largest purchaser of American arms was Saudi Arabia, which paid $1,111 million for modern weaponry with which to defend itself if attacked by Iraq or Iran. Every western European country except Ireland, Switzerland and Austria, also purchased arms from the United States. The largest purchaser was newly democratic Spain – $687 million – followed closely by the recently united Germany – $572 million.

On the last day of 1992 – in the final weeks of George Bush's presidency – the United States Department of Defence awarded a number of six-year contracts to manufacturers to develop the 'Brilliant Eyes' satellite. Each 'Brilliant Eyes' satellite was intended to carry sensors that could monitor both space and Earth. These sensors could pinpoint hostile missiles shortly after they had been launched, follow and track them, and discriminate between real warheads and decoys. The sensors would then activate counter-measures. Enemy missiles that had left the atmosphere could be shot down by a new orbiting firing system, 'Brilliant Pebbles'.

'Brilliant Eyes' and 'Brilliant Pebbles' had been intended as America's ultimate defence during the Cold War, and constituted the high point of the Star Wars defence system inaugurated by President Reagan. Under the proposals contracted for on December 31, as many as forty 'Brilliant Eyes' would be in orbit within six years. This whole programme was cancelled by the new President, Bill Clinton, on 13 May 1993, when, in a final affirmation that the Cold War was over, he announced 'the end of the Star Wars Era'. 'Brilliant Eyes' and 'Brilliant Pebbles' were, however, revived in the second year of the twenty-first century by George Bush's son, George W. Bush, who succeeded Clinton as President.

For those who shared the aspiration of global harmony, a landmark was reached on 15 January 1993 with the signature in Paris of a convention banning chemical weapons. It was signed by 120 nations, including the United States and Russia. It was the last international act of the Bush presidency. Five days later, on January 20, Bill Clinton was sworn in as President. Welcoming America's leading

place among the nations of the world, Clinton spoke in his inauguration address of how 'Today a new generation raised in the shadow
of the Cold War assumes new responsibilities in a world warmed by
the sunshine of freedom but threatened still by ancient hatreds and
new plagues.' Abroad the United States would 'not shrink from the
challenges'. Clinton promised to maintain 'American leadership of a
world we did much to make'. When America's vital interests were
challenged, or the will and conscience of the international community
defied, America would act 'with peaceful diplomacy when possible,
with force when necessary'.

Among Clinton's achievements that year was a North America
Free Trade Agreement (NAFTA), linking the United States, Canada
and Mexico in the world's largest free-trade area.

For Western television viewers the year opened with horrific scenes
of mass starvation in Somalia, where factional lawlessness made the
distribution of vital food aid perilous. On 2 January 1993 a British
famine relief worker was shot and killed, the first Western aid worker
to be killed since United States troops had landed. On January 18
the first American marine was killed. Amid continued clashes and
killing, food aid continued to be distributed, including 2,500 tons
of biscuits from Britain. These had been baked, packaged and stored
during the Second World War as 'strategic food stocks' in the event
of a prolonged war. They were sent to Somalia as part of 200,000
tons of British food aid.

At the beginning of June, Somali militiamen tried to seize power
in Mogadishu. Twenty-two Pakistani soldiers of the peacekeeping
force were killed. In an unsuccessful attempt to capture General
Aydid, the leading Somali warlord, four United Nations soldiers and a
hundred Somalis were killed. In an American air raid on his command
headquarters, Aydid escaped injury, but seventy-three Somalis were
killed. In revenge, four Western journalists in Mogadishu were
attacked by a large crowd and killed. During a mob attack on United
Nations peacekeepers on September 9, American helicopter gunships
opened fire to disperse the attackers, a hundred of whom were killed.
On October 4, twelve American soldiers were killed in a battle
against supporters of General Aydid, who continued to evade capture.

In response, President Clinton announced he would double the number of American troops in Somalia.

In the Persian Gulf, Saddam Hussein challenged the United Nations by placing surface-to-air missiles in the No-fly Zone that had been declared in southern Iraq, in order to protect the Shi'ite population of Iraq from attack by Saddam's air force. On January 6 the coalition partners ordered him to remove the missiles or face renewed attack. For ten days he ignored the ultimatum. Then, on January 16, with the approval of its coalition partners, the United States bombed strategic sites near Baghdad. Three Iraqi civilians were killed when a hotel in the city was hit in error. There were further attacks on Iraqi missile sites in southern Iraq. In June, the United States uncovered an Iraqi plot to assassinate former President Bush. The result was a series of American air attacks on targets in Baghdad.

In Bosnia, as details emerged of atrocities committed during Serb 'ethnic cleansing' operations, the United Nations Security Council established an international war crimes tribunal for the former Yugoslavia. This was the first such tribunal since the International Military Tribunals in Nuremberg and Tokyo after the Second World War.

On March 31 the Security Council passed a resolution ordering the Yugoslav Serbs not to fly over Bosnia or intervene in the conflict from the air. The Serbs ignored the resolution. With United Nations approval, NATO agreed to act. On April 12 fifty of its warplanes began to patrol the airspace over Bosnia, to enforce the No-fly Zone and prevent Serb aircraft attacking Muslim positions. That day Serb forces on the ground began an intense artillery bombardment of the predominantly Muslim city of Srebrenica, which they had besieged. Fifty-six Muslims were killed in the bombardment. Six days later the city surrendered to the Bosnian Serbs. On June 13, Bosnian Serb artillery bombarded the besieged Muslim town of Gorazde. Fifty-two people were killed. On the following day Bosnian Muslim troops began a sustained attack on Bosnian Croat villages in Bosnia, determined to drive the Croats out of the region altogether. Thousands of Croats fled.

The behaviour of the Bosnian Serbs created widespread revulsion in Western Europe and the United States. This was heightened on

July 12 when a Serb mortar shell aimed at the centre of Sarajevo hit a group of people queuing for water, killing twelve of those in the queue. By the end of the year there were 22,000 United Nations troops in the disputed province, the two largest contingents being those of France, 3,000, and Britain, 2,500. The peacekeepers watched as warmaking went on.

Repeatedly challenged by hardline Communists, on September 21 Yeltsin dissolved the Russian Parliament. Control of the country would be in his hands alone. Elections would be called within three months. But although dissolved, the Russian Parliament refused to disband. Its members would not even leave their building, voted to strip Yeltsin of his presidential powers, and appointed a leading hardliner as 'acting President' in his place. On the following day all telephone links, water and electricity supplies to the building were cut off. Two days later, on September 24, troops loyal to Yeltsin surrounded the building. For thirteen days it was besieged, with many parliamentarians and their supporters trapped inside it.

On October 3, pro-Communist demonstrators outside the parliament building tried to break the police and army cordon and release those trapped inside. They were beaten back. The following day Yeltsin ordered commando troops, supported by tanks and armoured vehicles, to break into the building. Tanks opened fire, and more than 140 people in the building were killed. When fire broke out as a result of the bombardment, the defiant parliamentarians emerged with their hands up.

The elections Yeltsin promised were held on December 13. The largest share of the vote was won by an extremist nationalist, Vladimir Zhirinovsky, who championed the reconquest of the lost republics. But even Zhirinovsky's Party won only 23.1 per cent, less than a quarter of the votes cast. The principal reformist party, Russia's Choice, led by Yeltsin's ally Yegor Gaidar, came second, with 14.5 per cent of the vote. The Communist Party of the Russian Federation, headed by Gennadii Zyuganov, came third, with 13.6 per cent. In a separate ballot, the electors approved Yeltsin's proposed new constitution. His own presidency had not been on the ballot paper.

*   *   *

In January 1993, the Algerian Government, with army support, cancelled the country's national elections when it became clear that they were likely to be won by the Islamic Salvation Front. Muslim militants, aggrieved at being cheated of power, attacked soldiers and civilians alike. The army responded with ferocity, killing more than 400 militants. After two French surveyors were kidnapped and killed in September, 6,000 foreign residents left the country. By the end of the year, twenty-five foreign nationals had been killed.

In Egypt, Islamic fundamentalists launched a series of attacks on Coptic Christians, foreign tourists and the police. During the course of the year 245 people were killed. The government responded by attacking mosques where militants were hiding. On March 10 twenty-five Muslim extremists were killed in gun battles with police in Cairo and Aswan. In Israel's occupied territories, the West Bank and the Gaza Strip, Palestinian youths, many of them inspired by Muslim fundamentalism, others by secular Palestinian nationalism, had conducted a five-year campaign of harassment and violence against Israeli soldiers and civilians: the Intifada. In search for negotiation rather than confrontation, in strictest secrecy Rabin authorized talks between Israel and the PLO. Until then, successive Israeli Governments had refused to negotiate with the PLO, denouncing it as a terrorist organization and its leader, Yasser Arafat, as a murderer. The first Israeli-PLO talks took place on January 20 at a secluded villa just outside Oslo.

As the secret talks continued, the Intifada intensified. In the first week of February Israeli troops killed a fourteen-year-old boy in a refugee camp in the Gaza Strip. That day three other Palestinian stone throwers were also shot dead. On February 6, confronted by yet more rock throwers, Israeli troops killed a seventeen-year-old boy in Gaza. Two thirds of the Palestinian deaths occurred, according to the Israeli army's own announcements, during incidents where the lives of soldiers were not in danger. The number of Palestinian children aged sixteen and under who were killed had risen. The urgency of finding a new way forward was underlined in March, when figures were released for the death toll during 1992: that year Palestinians had killed eleven Israeli soldiers and eleven Israeli civilians. Israeli troops had killed a hundred Palestinians. And Palestinians, mostly members of the extremist Hamas and Islamic Jihad had killed more than 200 fellow-Palestinians, supporters of compomise.

The Oslo Accords were initialled on August 20. The PLO, hitherto a pariah in Israel's eyes, became a partner. On August 30 the Israeli Cabinet approved self-rule for the Palestinians in the Gaza Strip and Jericho. The PLO put their signature to the plan on September 9. It would administer these areas, fly its flag, tax its people, govern the municipalities, and continue negotiations to extend self-rule to all Palestinian-inhabited areas of the West Bank. Arafat, hitherto leader of a group that had carried out many spectacular acts of terror, pledged the PLO in writing to 'take part in the steps leading to normalization of life, rejecting violence and terrorism, contributing to peace and stability, and participating actively in shaping reconstruction, economic development and co-operation'.

The signing of the Declaration of Principles on September 13 took place on the White House lawn, witnessed by President Clinton. Israel had recognized the PLO, was talking to it and signing agreements with it. The PLO had recognized Israel, and promised to reject violence and terrorism. During his speech on the White House lawn, Rabin appealed directly to the Palestinians. 'We say to you today in a loud and clear voice: Enough of blood and tears. Enough. We harbour no hatred towards you. We have no desire for revenge. We, like you, are people who want to build a home, plant a tree, love, live side by side with you – in dignity, in empathy, as human beings, as free men. We are today giving peace a chance and saying to you: Enough. Let us pray that a day will come when we all will say: Farewell to arms.'

In March, two young boys were killed by an IRA bomb on the British mainland. Revulsion at the killings stimulated the peace movements throughout Ireland, North and South. In Dublin 200,000 people marched in protest against the claim of the IRA to represent the people of Ireland. But the killings and counter-killings continued. In October ten people were killed in an IRA bomb explosion in a mainly Protestant area of Belfast. A week later seven people died when a revenge shooting was carried out against a Catholic bar in Londonderry.

Behind the scenes both John Major and the Irish Prime Minister, Albert Reynolds, were working to find a long-term solution. On December 15 they issued the Downing Street Declaration, calling for an end to inter-communal violence and a lasting political settlement. In the words of the declaration, it was 'for the people of the island of Ireland alone, by agreement between the two parts respectively, to exercise their right of self-determination on the basis of consent, freely and concurrently given, North and South, to bring about a united Ireland' – if they so wished. But the declaration stressed that 'it would be wrong to attempt to impose a united Ireland in the absence of the freely given consent of a majority of the people of Northern Ireland'.

The declaration gained immediate parliamentary, media and popular approval in the Republic of Ireland, where it was judged to have recognized fully all reasonable nationalist and Catholic aspirations; and to have done so without giving cause for the Protestant Unionists to fear that the existing status of Northern Ireland would be altered against their wish. There was a widespread call in both North and South for an immediate end to violence by the paramilitary groups in both communities. Anxiety grew after Christmas, however, when both the IRA and the Loyalist terrorists embarked once more on their murderous courses. The Downing Street Declaration had been rejected by extremists on both sides. But for a growing majority of the people of Northern Ireland it represented the only possible way forward: negotiation, compromise and conciliation.

In South Africa, the moves towards the ending of apartheid were also accompanied by ethnic and inter-communal violence. On July 25 a number of black gunmen burst into a church, killing twelve of the mainly white congregation. On the day after the church killings the draft of South Africa's first post-apartheid constitution was published. But on July 31 there was another outburst of brutal killing, when a hundred blacks were killed in inter-communal violence. In August an American student, Amy Biehl, who was white, was set upon by an crowd of blacks and killed. Four blacks were later imprisoned for her murder. Politicians continued to seek a political solution. On September 7 agreement was reached by a Negotiating

Council consisting of twenty-three different groups, to establish a Transitional Executive Council through which apartheid would cease to exist. Forty-five years of inequality based on race would come to an end. On the day after this agreement, nineteen Africans were killed when black gunmen opened fire on a taxi queue near Johannesburg.

The continuation of violence did not deter those who were determined to move forward from confrontation to co-operation. On September 23 the South African Parliament passed a Bill setting up the Transitional Executive Council and instructed it to prepare for the country's first multi-racial elections, to be held the following spring. On October 15 both Mandela and President de Klerk were awarded the Nobel Peace Prize. The process of dismantling apartheid was unstoppable. When the all-race Transitional Executive Council met on December 7 it marked the first time that black South Africans had a voice in all executive decisions relating to their, and South Africa's, future. Two weeks later, on December 22, the South African Parliament, still elected under the apartheid franchise, voted nevertheless to adopt an interim constitution that would lead to majority rule after the election in four months' time.

On 25 January 1994 President Clinton called for legislation on a wide range of social issues. Among them were gun control, Federal funds for drug treatment, job training for the unemployed, urban renewal and health care. In a warning to Congress with regard to his health care proposals, which were strongly endorsed by his wife Hillary, he declared: 'If you send me legislation that does not guarantee every American private health insurance that can never be taken away, you will force me to take this pen, veto the legislation, and we'll come right back here and start all over again.'

Republican hostility to Clinton's social reform measures effectively impeded them. Health care as he envisaged it was not to come to pass. In addition, a sustained Republican attack on Clinton's alleged financial and personal misconduct was so intense that it threatened to impede the daily business of government. During the mid-term elections on November 8, Clinton's hopes of pursuing his legislative programme were struck a further blow when Republicans gained control both of the Senate and the House of Representatives.

On January 12, Clinton was in the Ukrainian capital, Kiev, negotiating the dismantling of all nuclear warheads on Ukrainian soil. The last Russian troops left Germany on August 31. A week later the last American, British and French troops likewise departed.

In Israel, Yitzhak Rabin continued to push for agreement with the Palestinians. The Cairo Agreement, later known as Oslo I, established a Palestinian Authority, to be headed by Yasser Arafat, with 'legislative, executive, and judicial powers and responsibilities', including its own armed police force, and full control over internal security, education, health and welfare. Israel would retain control of foreign affairs and defence. Under the agreement, Arafat assumed the title of 'Chairman of the Palestinian Authority'. The word used for chairman in the Arabic text was *rais*, which could equally correctly be translated as president, giving him the aura of a Head of State.

The Cairo Agreement was signed on May 4. A few days later, having flown to South Africa, Arafat spoke in a mosque of how the Palestinians would 'continue their Jihad until they had liberated Jerusalem'. To speak of Jihad – Holy War – so soon after concluding an agreement aimed at peace and co-existence shocked the Israeli public. Rabin warned that 'any continuance of violence and terror' called the entire peace process into question. Arafat explained that by Jihad he had not meant 'Holy War' but 'sacred campaign'.

On May 13, only nine days after the signing of the Cairo agreement, all Israeli troops and administrative personnel were withdrawn from Jericho, and four days later from the Gaza Strip. The Palestinian flag was raised over Jericho and Gaza City. In Gaza, Palestinian self-rule extended to all the 800,000 Arab inhabitants. Excluded from Palestinian control were the sixteen Israeli settlements in Gaza, with a total population of 5,000. On May 19, two days after the Israeli withdrawal from Gaza, Rabin met secretly in London with King Hussein of Jordan to prepare a peace treaty between their two countries.

On July 1 Arafat visited Gaza for the first time in twenty-seven years. The housing, education and social welfare of a million Palestinian Arabs, half of them refugees and the descendants of refugees from the war of 1948, had become his responsibility and that of the

Palestinian Authority. Money for his first projects came from the European Union, Japan and the United States. Four years later it was revealed that more than half of the sums received, hundreds of millions of dollars, never found their way to the projects for which they were designated. Near some of the worst slums of the Middle East, the Gaza refugee camps, substantial villas were built for the authority's leaders, using money intended to rehouse the refugees. When Britain and the European Union urged Arafat to audit the money they were sending him, he refused. Five years later the European Union was to stop sending Arafat money until he agreed to a proper accounting system.

Palestinian Muslim fundamentalists opposed to the autonomy plan, who still spoke of the destruction of Israel, carried out repeated acts of terror, hoping to derail the 'peace process', both between Israel and the Palestinian Authority, and between Israel and Jordan. On July 18 a hundred people, most of them Jews, were killed when Iranian-supported Muslim militants exploded a massive bomb at the Jewish community centre in Buenos Aires. Neither side allowed these acts of terror to derail the peace process. On July 25, in Washington, Rabin and King Hussein signed a declaration ending the state of war between their two countries. One result of that war had been Jordan's loss of East Jerusalem and the West Bank in 1967.

On October 14, Rabin, Peres and Arafat were awarded the Nobel Peace Prize as the 'architects' of the Israeli-Palestinian accords. Five days later, twenty-two Israelis were killed when a Palestinian Muslim suicide bomber blew up a bus near Tel Aviv. Five days afterwards, President Clinton embarked on what he called 'a mission inspired by a dream of peace'. After a visit to Sadat's tomb near Cairo, he held talks in Cairo with the Egyptian leader, Hosni Mubarak, and Arafat, and then flew to Akaba for the signing of the Israel-Jordan Treaty of Peace. Within Gaza, Islamic fundamentalists battled with the new Palestinian police under Arafat's command. In one such clash on November 18, fourteen people were killed.

In Bosnia the Serb struggle for control continued. On 5 February 1994, sixty-eight people were killed when a mortar bomb exploded in the market place in Sarajevo. Four days later NATO issued an ultimatum to the Serbs to withdraw their heavy weapons from around Sarajevo, or face NATO air strikes. On February 11 the Bosnian Serbs handed over a proportion of their heavy guns. Two days later they began to withdraw the rest of their heavy artillery.

On February 28, four Serb warplanes penetrated the limits of a NATO No-fly Zone established to protect the Bosnian Muslims. All four were intercepted and shot down. It was the first offensive action in the forty-five years of NATO's existence.

The United Nations secured an agreement on March 17 whereby Bosnian Muslims and Bosnian Serbs agreed to allow civilians free movement in and out of Sarajevo for the first time in two years. At the same time, Bosnian Muslims and Bosnian Croats were negotiating in Washington to create a Muslim-Croat Federation: this was agreed on March 18. The prospect of a return to normal life was emerging. On March 20 more than 20,000 people watched a football match in Sarajevo stadium, one of the buildings which, until the NATO intervention two months earlier, had been subjected to regular Bosnian Serb mortar fire.

The United Nations had designated the Muslim enclaves in the predominantly Serbian areas of Bosnia as safe havens, and warned the Bosnian Serbs not to attack them. When the safe haven of Gorazde was besieged, and no food or medical aid convoys allowed in, NATO planes attacked the Bosnian Serb forces surrounding the town. On the following day, as the siege continued, there were further air strikes. NATO was acting as the military arm of the United Nations.

On April 17 Bosnian Serb tanks reached the centre of Gorazde. Five days later, NATO issued an ultimatum to the Bosnian Serbs to withdraw from the town. Two days later, as United Nations peacekeepers reached the city, the Bosnian Serbs withdrew. They were not prepared to engage in combat with the United Nations.

On June 22 two parliaments met in Sarajevo and agreed to merge. One was the parliament of the predominantly Muslim Bosnian Republic, and the other the parliament of the Muslim-Croat Federation established the previous month. The Bosnian Serbs felt that they could still overwhelm the Sarajevo administration, and at the beginning of August began once more to deploy heavy weapons around Muslim-held enclaves. NATO took immediate action, attacking the heavy weapon concentrations. Two months later, on November 21, NATO carried out its heaviest bombing raid yet, when thirty-nine warplanes attacked a Bosnian Serb airfield in Croatia which was being used to attack a United Nations 'safe area' of besieged Muslims.

On May 27 Solzhenitsyn returned to Russia after twenty years of enforced exile. He was distressed by what he saw. Poverty in the streets, long lines of citizens holding up a few apples or packets of cigarettes or a few items of clothing for sale, ostentatious wealth, a new class of super-rich, the often bloody clashes of private Mafia-style gangs – each mocked the hopes that had been stirred by the collapse of the Soviet system and Soviet Communism. On October 28 Solzhenytsyn addressed the Russian Parliament. Russia, he said, was ruled by an oligarchy, concealed by a 'sham democracy'. And he denounced privatization, the main economic goal of the Yeltsin administration, as a form of 'privateering' that ought to be punished by the law courts.

The territorial integrity of the Russian Federation – the Russian Republic – was being challenged by one of its Muslim autonomous republics, Chechenya, where the pro-Russian government, headed by Doku Zavgayev, had been overthrown by rebels headed by another Chechen leader, General Dudayev, who proclaimed himself President. On November 29 Yeltsin ordered all 'illegal military formations' inside Chechenya to lay down their arms. Dudayev refused. On December 11, determined to restore the authority of Moscow over a region that was constitutionally an integral part of the Russian Federation and Russian sovereignty, Yeltsin ordered Russian troops into Chechenya. The Chechens resisted, and on December 14 Dudayev announced that his people would 'fight to the death'.

On December 19, Russian warplanes bombed the Chechen capital, Grozny. Many civilians were killed. Three days later a Russian ground offensive was launched against Grozny. A new war had begun. A call by Yeltsin that civilian targets should be avoided was ignored by the Russian commanders on the spot. By the end of the year, fifty Russian soldiers had been killed, and 800 Chechens. Travelling to Grozny, Sergei Kovalyov, the Human Rights Commissioner of the

Russian Federation, a Yeltsin nominee, called for an end to what he described as a 'crazy massacre'. But Yeltsin wanted an end to this exercise in independence within the Russian Federation's borders. The leader of the largest political Party in the Russian Parliament, Vladimir Zhirinovsky, was emphatic that 'Russian territorial integrity' must be preserved whatever the cost. Within Chechenya, Dudayev was able to call forth enormous reserves of national, patriotic and Muslim religious fervour. The Chechens were by tradition fighters, and would fight on. The war continued.

As apartheid was dismantled in South Africa, inter-communal violence did not cease. On March 28 sixty people were killed in Johannesburg when Zulu demonstrators tried to march to the African National Congress headquarters. White extremists were also active: on April 24 they detonated a car bomb near the ANC headquarters, killing nine people.

On April 25, the white parliament met for the last time and voted itself out of existence, ending 342 years of white rule – British and Afrikaner. The following day, voting began in the first multi-racial elections ever to be held in South Africa, and on April 27, while the votes were still being cast, the new constitution came into effect. Multi-racial government was henceforth a constitutional fact. When the election results were announced on May 6, the largest party was the African National Congress, with 62.2 per cent of the vote. Its predominantly white opponent, the National Party, secured 20.4 per cent, and the Zulu Inkatha 10.5 per cent.

On May 10, four days after the election results were announced, Nelson Mandela was sworn in as President. That July a South African cricket team played its first match in England since 1965, watched by the Queen. The next month a South African sports team flew to Canada where it participated in the Commonwealth Games. South Africa was a pariah nation no more. Visiting Washington in October, Mandela secured $700 million in promises of aid from the United States.

In Rwanda, two groups were in conflict: the majority 6,975,000 Hutus, and the minority 697,500 Tutsis, the traditional rulers. Hutu attacks on Tutsis reached a fearsome pitch. Hutu human rights activists who protested against the massacres were killed by their fellow-Hutus. On April 23 the International Committee of the Red Cross announced that 100,000 people had been killed in Rwanda in the previous eighteen days. Five days later the toll had doubled to 200,000.

Some of the worst massacres took place inside churches to which Tutsis had fled for sanctuary. By the end of June, when half a million Tutsis had been killed, a Security Council resolution authorized immediate French 'humanitarian' intervention. The first French troops arrived by air the following day. Then the tide of killing turned. It was the turn of the Hutus to flee. By mid-July, 1,200,000 Hutus had fled into the French-protected zone and a further two million into neighbouring Zaire. On August 2, British troops flew to Rwanda to join the French peacekeeping force.

On November 8 the Security Council set up an International Criminal Tribunal for Rwanda, charged with prosecuting those responsible for genocide. The Tutsi-dominated government, encouraged to do so by the United Nations, embarked on a policy of reconciliation. Moderate Hutus were given both the presidency and the premiership. One of the government's most effective measures was to set up military re-education centres where soldiers of the defeated Hutu army could be encouraged to enrol in the new 'patriotic army' in which Tutsi and Hutu served together.

Even without the genocide the life expectancy in Rwanda was no more than forty-five years for men and forty-seven years for women. A massive task faced any government that hoped to bring into being a subsistence economy and even the smallest measure of normal life.

The Downing Street Declaration had opened the way for talks between the Catholics and Protestants of Northern Ireland. The declaration had called for an end to violence in the streets. Extremists ignored the call. On 18 June 1994, while a crowd of Catholics were watching a televised World Cup match in a bar, Ulster Volunteer Force gunmen burst in, killing six of the viewers. But John Major persevered in trying to obtain an end to the violence, in which 3,168 people had died during the previous twenty-five years. His efforts were successful: on August 31 the IRA announced that a cease-fire would come into effect that midnight, both in Northern Ireland and on the British mainland.

The cease-fire held, and on September 15 Major lifted the ban on broadcasting by Sinn Fein members. He also announced there would be a referendum in Northern Ireland on the province's constitutional future. On October 13 the three main Protestant para-military organizations in Northern Ireland declared a cease-fire. Talks between the British Government and Sinn Fein began in Belfast on December 7.

In both the Middle East and Northern Ireland there were hopes of ending the spiral of violence. Such hopes seemed more remote in Sri Lanka, where, on October 24, fifty-seven people were killed in a bomb attack. Among the dead was the opposition presidential candidate. On November 9 Mrs Kumaratunga was elected President, Sri Lanka's first woman Head of State. She set as her goal the restoration of civic calm, and the resolution of the ethnic conflict that had divided the country and taken tens of thousands of lives. She was no stranger to political violence. Her father, a former Prime Minister, had been assassinated in 1959. Her husband, also a former Prime Minister, had been assassinated in 1988. From the first days of her presidency, she opened negotiations with the Tamils. As in Northern Ireland and the Middle East, the year 1994 ended with hopes that the peace process would produce what was spoken of as a 'peace dividend'.

There was no prospect of peace in Chechenya, where throughout the first week of January 1995, Russian forces subjected Grozny to a daily artillery barrage. At the end of the first week of renewed fighting, Sergei Kovalyov, the Human Rights Commissioner of the Russian Federation, who had just returned from Chechenya, again urged Yeltsin to call off the attacks and stop the war. The President, Kovalyov noted, 'mostly kept quiet, made some isolated remarks, and objected to what I was saying'.

Russian troops were acting with a ferocity that did not always confine itself to the field of battle. In one Chechen town, 250 towns-folk were killed. As his troops overran Grozny, Yeltsin set up a pro-Russian 'Government of National Revival'. Undeterred, 200

Chechen fighters mounted a raid on Budenovsk, a Russian city more than sixty miles from the Chechen border. The raiders captured the town and took 2,000 people hostage. As Russian troops counter-attacked the Chechens retreated with their hostages to the town's hospital. After receiving authorization from Yeltsin, the Russians mounted two attacks on the hospital. Both attacks were beaten off, with the loss of hundreds of lives on both sides. The Russians then agreed that in return for the release of the hostages they would allow the Chechens safe passage back to Chechenya. The Chechen terms included a refrigerated lorry to transport their dead.

On July 30 agreement was reached between Russia and the Chechen rebels; a cease-fire would come into effect that day. Russia would release its 1,325 Chechen captives; the Chechens would release the Russians they were holding; most Russian troops would withdraw from Chechenya; and the Chechens would disarm. The constitutional status of Chechenya was left unresolved: this led the rebel leader, General Dudayev, to denounce the treaty his negotiators had signed. But on December 8 Russia signed an agreement in Moscow with the head of the pro-Russian government of the Chechen Autonomous Republic, Doku Zavgayev, under which Chechenya would receive greater autonomy than that accorded to any of the other twenty-five autonomous republics within the Russian Federation. The Chechen Government would be able to open consulates and trade missions abroad, and Chechen military conscripts would not have to serve outside the Chechen borders. All separatist fighters who agreed to lay down their arms would be amnestied. The fighting came to an end – for the time being.

In Bosnia, fighting intensified at the beginning of April 1995. In the Bihac enclave, Bosnian Serbs tried yet again to overrun the Muslims, while in the mountains near Tuzla, Bosnian Serbs were trying to hold back an advance by Muslim forces. The offensive was only held back because of heavy falls of snow. In Sarajevo, Bosnian Serb snipers fired on Croat Catholic churchgoers. NATO jets struck at Bosnian Serb mortar positions.

In the last week of May the Bosnian Serbs embarked on a tactic of seizing United Nations peacekeepers and unarmed military observers, and using them as 'human shields' for their military convoys. French and Ukrainian troops formed the largest two groups of seized men. Six United Nations observers were taken to locations which the Bosnian Serbs knew might be the targets of NATO jets, including a strategic bridge and the main Bosnian Serb radio station, and chained to the potential NATO targets. After strong United Nations protests, the Bosnian Serb commander announced that the chaining would stop.

In all 372 United Nations personnel were being held hostage by the end of May. John Major responded by sending a further 6,700 British troops to Bosnia to protect the troops already there. 'I sent out troops to Bosnia,' he said on May 30, 'and I intend to do everything in my power to ensure that our soldiers are released unharmed.' On British and French initiative a Rapid Reaction Force was set up, of troops who could be moved wherever they were needed on the Bosnian battlefield. This strong stance was effective. On June 2 the Bosnian Serbs released 126 United Nations hostages and promised to release the others within a matter of days.

On July 11, Bosnian Serb forces launched an attack on Srebrenica, the town with 40,000 Muslim inhabitants that was one of the United Nation's 'safe havens'. American and Dutch NATO bombers launched air strikes on the advancing Bosnian Serb tanks, knocked out two, but failed to halt the assault. A third air attack was called off at the request of the Dutch after the 400 lightly armed Dutch soldiers who constituted the United Nations peacekeeping force in Srebrenica received death threats. As the Bosnian Serb troops entered the town as many as 30,000 Muslims fled, abandoning their homes. On the following day a Bosnian Serb mayor was appointed and the United Nations peacekeepers were told they were no longer needed.

A second Muslim safe haven, Zepa, was attacked by the Bosnian Serbs on July 14. A hundred Ukrainian soldiers were the United Nations defence for 15,000 people. NATO warplanes flew overhead but took no action. The siege of Zepa continued for eight days. On July 24 the town was overrun, looted and set on fire.

From Srebrenica, the Bosnian Serbs had taken away 4,000 Muslim men and boys. A further 6,000 refugees who had fled from Srebrenica were unaccounted for, as were 3,000 from Zepa. The United Nations warned that nothing should be done to harm them and repeated its condemnation of 'ethnic cleansing'. Dutch United Nations peace-keepers, reaching Zagreb from Srebrenica on July 22, reported having seen Bosnian Serbs shooting Muslims dead in the streets.

On July 28 Bosnian Croat forces took the initiative, together with two heavily armed brigades of the Croatian Army – 10,000 men in all – crossing the Croatian border into Bosnia, driving the Bosnian Serbs from several towns inside Bosnia, and capturing eighty-five square miles of territory in the predominantly Serb region of Krajina: 13,000 Bosnian Serbs took to the roads as refugees. At the same time, Bosnian Serb forces were trying to destroy the Muslim enclave of Bihac, in which 20,000 Muslims were surrounded. Bihac held out. It was the Croat military offensive that succeeded. Despite widespread international condemnation, by August 4 more than 100,000 Croat troops were advancing into the Serb-held areas of Croatia. In Knin, hundreds of Serb civilians were killed during the Croat air and artillery bombardment.

There was international sympathy for the Bosnian Serbs inside Knin, and in their flight from Krajina, but this sympathy was eclipsed three days later when details emerged of the murder of 2,700 mostly Muslim men and boys from Srebrenica by the Bosnian Serb forces who had driven them out of their homes. The Security Council condemned the refusal of the Bosnian Serbs to allow the Red Cross unrestricted access to the area. It also warned the Croats to stop the war against the Krajina Serbs, and to allow them to return to their homes.

On August 28, Bosnian Serb mortar fire on Sarajevo killed thirty-seven people in the marketplace. NATO responded both by bombing Bosnian Serb positions around the city, and by an ultimatum that all Bosnian Serb heavy weapons around Sarajevo must be removed. The Bosnian Serbs wanted to defy NATO but were told by President Milosevic of Serbia to comply. He recognized that NATO's mood was such that it would take very little more provocation, or the sight of collaboration between his Serb forces and the Bosnian Serbs, for Belgrade itself to be at risk from NATO air strikes.

The Bosnian Serbs obeyed Milosevic, who was in effect their master, and on September 20 began to remove their heavy weapons.

Elsewhere they were driven back by Croat and Muslim forces. As the fighting intensified the Foreign Ministers of Serbia, Croatia and Bosnia met in Geneva to work out a cease-fire and a territorial settlement. On September 8 they reached agreement 'in principle'. Bosnia would remain a separate sovereign State, divided into two 'democratic, self-governing' entities. Forty-nine per cent of Bosnia would be the predominantly Serb areas and would be known as the Serb Republic. Fifty-one per cent, the predominantly Muslim and Croat areas, would be called the Federation of Bosnia and Herzegovina.

Neither Belgrade nor Zagreb would rule the territory their armies had fought over, or had encouraged their ethnic allies to fight over. Bosnian Serbs would not be able to join Greater Serbia. Bosnian Croats would not be able to join Croatia. The sovereign independence of Bosnia would be maintained. There would be a President for all Bosnia, with his capital in Sarajevo, and a Head of State for each of the two regions. The Presidency would rotate, a 'presidential triumvirate' being elected from the Serb, Muslim and Croat communities. The first President was the Muslim leader Alija Izetbegovic. There would also be a Council of State for the whole of Bosnia, and two governments – each with Prime Ministers, Cabinets and civil servants – for the two regions.

The Geneva agreement of September 8 became the basis for negotiations which took place almost immediately, under American auspices, at Dayton, Ohio, at an Air Force Base. President Clinton acted as mediator when matters came to an impasse. Agreement was reached on November 21, then taken to Paris and signed there – as the Dayton Peace Treaty – on December 14. Four days later the first American troops reached Bosnia as part of a NATO-led peace Implementation Force (IFOR) which on December 20 formally took over from the existing United Nations Protection Force (UNPRO-FOR). During the conflict in Bosnia, at least 200,000 civilians had been killed, and two million people made homeless.

In Africa, more than half a million Tutsis had been murdered by Hutus in 1994. Tutsi revenge was not long in coming. On 18 April 1995, after declaring the five refugee camps in the south a 'hotbed'

for Hutu guerrillas intent on wreaking vengeance for the Tutsi massacres of Hutus the previous year, the Rwandan Government ordered
the camps to be closed. Closure meant killing. A United Nations
soldier witnessed the scene in one of the camps: 'The soldiers were
acting like barbarians, chasing and trapping refugees who had escaped
their cordon.' Many of those caught were bayoneted to death. A
worker with a Western charity who was in Kibeho camp at the
height of the massacre told journalists on the following day: 'We
saw the army shooting into the backs of people fleeing the camp,
old people and women, it was indiscriminate.' The Hutu survivors
of the Kibeho massacre were marched to the stadium in a nearby
town where a year earlier thousands of Tutsi had been massacred
by Hutu. As they reached the stadium, wrote Eve-Ann Prentice,
diplomatic correspondent of *The Times*, they were 'stoned or hacked
with machetes by civilians'.

In the peaceful calm of Geneva, the final phases of nuclear disarmament were under discussion. On April 4 Britain announced that
within three years it would scrap its hundred remaining nuclear
bombs. Two days later Britain gave up its right to carry out those
underground nuclear explosions that were permitted 'in exceptional
circumstances' to check the safety and reliability of weapons systems.
France also agreed to give up the safety tests. On August 11, the
fiftieth anniversary of the dropping of the American atom bomb on
Nagasaki, Clinton announced that the United States would also no
longer carry out nuclear tests, even as provided for as tests of safety
procedures. His decision, he said, would enable the world to pull
back from the 'nuclear precipice'.

On September 24, despite a spate of Islamic fundamentalist suicide
bombs and killings inside Israel, agreement was reached between
Israel and the PLO whereby Palestinian self-rule, already in place
in the Gaza Strip and Jericho, would be extended to most of the
West Bank, including all seven Palestinian towns. The agreement
included the creation of a 12,000-strong Palestinian police force to
supervise the transfer of power. The Israeli troop withdrawal was to
be completed within six months, followed twenty-two days later by

elections throughout the Palestinian Authority area for a Palestinian Council.

On September 28 Rabin returned to Washington and once again signed an agreement with Arafat. Known as Oslo II, it provided a timetable for the extension of Palestinian self-rule in the West Bank, going far beyond the Gaza and Jericho transfers of Oslo I. Inside Israel, the opposition parties reviled Rabin for Oslo II. Once, when his wife Leah pulled into the driveway underneath their Tel Aviv apartment, someone shouted out: 'After the next election, you and your husband will hang from your heels in the town square like Mussolini and his mistress. This is what we are going to do to you. Just you wait.'

The Israeli Parliament debated Oslo II on October 5 and 6. When the vote was taken, it passed with a narrow margin: 61 to 59. After the vote the protests against the extension of Palestinian autonomy continued. At a rally in Jerusalem on October 28, Rabin was denounced by several speakers as a traitor who was abandoning the Land of Israel. Determined to show that Oslo II had its supporters, on November 4, a week after the opposition rally in Jerusalem, Rabin was present at a rally in Tel Aviv in support of the peace process. It was a joyful gathering. Israel – having already left Gaza and Jericho – would soon be leaving the densely populated areas of the West Bank where so much blood had been shed, and so much hardship endured, in twenty-eight years of occupation of Arab towns, and in violent confrontation with Arab youth.

Rabin spoke from the platform with emotion and understanding about the peace process. 'This is a course which is fraught with difficulties and pain,' he said. 'For Israel there is no path without pain. But the path of peace is preferable to the path of war.' As the rally came to an end Rabin, normally a shy man, joined in the singing of *The Song of Peace*, which had been composed during the Arab-Israel war of 1973, with its final refrain: 'Do not whisper a prayer, Better sing a song for peace, With a great shout'. The song over, Rabin left the platform and went to his car. As he did so, an assassin rushed up behind him and shot him in the back.

The man who murdered Rabin was an Israeli and a Jew: a twenty-seven-year-old religious law student implacably opposed to Palestinian self-rule. 'I acted alone on God's orders,' he said after his arrest, 'and I have no regrets.' Rabin was seventy-three years old when he was killed. He was succeeded as Prime Minister by seventy-two-year-old Shimon Peres, who continued the quest for agreement with the Palestinians. The Likud opposition insisted that the agreements with the Palestinians gave away too much without adequate guarantees of security against future terrorist attacks.

Peres was determined to honour the agreements Rabin had signed. On November 12, Israeli forces left the West Bank city of Jenin, which came immediately under the rule of the Palestinian Authority. On December 3 the Israelis began to withdraw their troops from Bethlehem. The seven Palestinian policemen who then entered the town marked the start of the rule of the Palestinian Authority. Christmas 1995 was celebrated under the Palestinian flag.

Human rights abuses continued in many nations. In Nigeria, the military regime of General Sani Abacha – whose theft of vast sums of money from his own exchequer led to him being dubbed 'lootocrat' – executed nine of its most outspoken public critics, including the writer Ken Saro-Wiwa. On August 11, in South Korea, Kim Sun-Myung, the man whom Amnesty International described as the world's longest serving 'prisoner of conscience' was released. He was seventy-one years old. Forty-four years earlier, at the age of twenty-seven, he had been imprisoned by the government of South Korea as a North Korean agent. His release came as part of a mass amnesty to mark the fiftieth anniversary of the liberation of South Korea from Japanese rule.

In South Africa, the Truth and Reconciliation Commission set up to hear from all sections of the population about responsibility for the violence of the apartheid years, heard Chief Mangosuthu Buthelezi, head of the Zulu Inkatha Freedom Party – hitherto an opponent of the commission – come before it at the beginning of September and apologize to the African National Congress. As many as 15,000 Africans had been killed in the fighting between the two rival groups during the previous decade. While denying any personal role in the killings, Buthelezi told the commission – headed by Archbishop Desmond Tutu: 'I know that because we are human beings, and therefore sinners, that we still hurt each other even tomorrow. I therefore apologize for past hurts.'

Past hurts could be apologized for. Present hurts could only exacerbate tensions. In Israel, where Islamic fundamentalists rejected the progress being made towards Palestinian autonomy, suicide bombers killed twenty-five Israelis on 25 February 1996 and a further nineteen on March 3. Pressure on Peres to call a halt to the peace process was immediate. The President, Ezer Weizman – a former commander of the Israeli air force – called for a halt to the talks that were taking place for the next stage of the Israel's withdrawal from the West Bank. 'We are at war,' he said, as the funerals of the bomb victims were relayed on television to a traumatized Israeli society. 'We cannot go on like this.'

On March 4 a third suicide bomb, in Tel Aviv, killed twelve people. When Peres visited the scene, an angry crowd, already chanting 'Death to the Arabs', called out: 'Peres, you are next.' Following the suicide bomb of March 4, Peres announced that Israeli troops would act against the Muslim fundamentalist organizations, Hamas and Islamic Jihad, within the areas that had been transferred to Palestinian self-rule.

Starting on March 31, Hizbullah fundamentalists in southern Lebanon launched a series of rocket attacks on northern Israel, forcing tens of thousands of Israelis to spend their nights in air-raid shelters on the eve of the Passover holiday, celebrating the exodus from Egypt. In a retaliatory attack within the Israeli security zone in southern Lebanon, Israeli artillerymen accidentally killed two Lebanese installing a water tank and injured a three-year-old child. The Government of Israel apologized. On April 10, as Hizbullah shelling continued, Peres ordered retaliatory air strikes across Israel's northern border, including an attack on Hizbullah positions in the suburbs of Beirut. Twenty-one people were killed. As the Israeli bombardment continued a building in which several hundred Lebanese civilians were sheltering from the bombardment in the village of Qana was accidentally hit, and ninety-seven Lebanese civilians were killed. Peres issued a full and immediate apology, and offered compensation.

On April 18, Peres and Arafat agreed to resume talks, broken off after the three suicide bombs, on security co-operation between

Israel and the Palestine Authority in tracking down suicide bombers. A week later the PLO agreed to strike out of its charter all references to the destruction of Israel – 'the most important ideological change of the century' Peres called it. Elated by this fulfilment of a crucial element of the Oslo Accords, on the following day the Israel Labour Party, of which Peres was the leader, withdrew its opposition to the eventual creation of an independent Palestinian State.

A cease-fire between Israel and Hizbullah came into effect on April 27 through the mediation of the United States, but as a result of the continued attacks on its soil, there were calls within Israel for all further Israeli withdrawals on the West Bank to be halted. Peres was determined that the peace process should continue. On May 29, the electorate gave a different, if divided verdict. In the parliamentary elections, the Labour Party obtained the largest single block of seats in the parliament, but in that same day's election for Prime Minister – a new constitutional departure – the premiership was won, though by the narrowest of margins, by the leader of the Likud opposition, Benjamin Netanyahu. The votes cast were 1,501,023 for Netanyahu, and 1,471,566 for Peres (50.4 per cent as against 49.5 per cent).

Under the constitutional changes introduced as part of the direct election for Prime Minister, it fell to Netanyahu to try to form a government, even though his Likud bloc did not have the largest number of seats in parliament. He succeeded in forming a government by piecing together a coalition of right-wing and religious Parties, which followed his lead in delaying the further devolution of power on the West Bank to the Palestinian Authority. On October 1, Arafat and Netanyahu met in Washington, encouraged by President Clinton to try to reach agreement, but they failed to do so.

In Algeria, the anger of the Islamic fundamentalists at having been denied the possibility of electoral victory continued to lead to bloodshed. On May 24 the Armed Islamic Front announced: 'We have slit the throats of seven monks.' These were seven French Trappist monks, aged between fifty and eighty-two, who had been kidnapped from their monastery two months earlier. Candles had been lit for their release in Notre Dame in Paris by Christians, Muslims and Jews. When news of the killings reached Paris the candles were extinguished by the Archbishop of Paris, Cardinal Jean-Marie Lustiger, himself of Jewish parentage. 'The candles represented hope for their lives,' he said. 'I wanted them to burn for ever.'

Pope John Paul II condemned the killings as 'barbaric'. In the previous four years 40,000 people had been killed in the violence in Algeria. Most of them were innocent bystanders of the conflict between the government and the fundamentalists. Many were children.

In Russia, on March 31, President Yeltsin announced the partial withdrawal of Russian troops from Chechenya. This did not prevent him ordering continual air strikes against rebel Chechens still holding out in the mountains. On April 21 the leader of the rebels, General Dudayev, was killed during a Russian air strike south of Grozny.

The first round of presidential elections was held in Russia on June 16. Yeltsin headed the poll with just over a third of the votes. His closest rival, only 3.3 per cent behind him, was the Communist candidate, Gennadi Zyuganov. While the people of Russia awaited the second round of the election, the people in Mongolia, casting their votes on June 30, brought to an end seventy-five years of unbroken Communist rule. The second round of the Russian presidential election, held on July 3, brought outright victory to Yeltsin. Within a few days it was learned that he had suffered a mild stroke on the eve of the poll, partially paralysing his left arm.

On August 9 Yeltsin was sworn in as President of Russia. He continued to assert Russia's authority in Chechenya as a new group of breakaway separatists, led by General Aslan Maskhadov, refused to recognize the earlier Russian-Chechen accord. In the week in which Yeltsin was sworn in as President in Moscow, 200 Russian soldiers were killed in the fighting in Chechenya. A week later Grozny was under Chechen separatist control. The Russians responded with air strikes which set much of the city centre on fire. Thousands of citizens fled. Yeltsin sent his security chief, General Alexander Lebed, a former paratrooper, to Chechenya, to warn that the full weight of Russian power would be brought to bear should the rebellion continue. On August 29, Lebed signed a peace agreement with General Maskhadov. Since the Chechen struggle began, 90,000 people had been killed.

It was agreed to delay the issue of Chechen sovereignty until the year 2001.

In the Republic of Belarus the revolutionary changes of five years earlier were being reversed. On November 24, as a result of a referendum, President Lukashenko was granted dictatorial powers. During the Communist era he had been the director of a collective farm.

In Afghanistan, where a decade earlier Russian troops had been fighting to preserve a besieged Communist government, the rebel Taleban Islamic militia whose aim was the imposition of a strict Islamic regime – tightened their siege of Kabul in June, when, in a single day of rocket attacks, sixty civilians were killed. On September 27 the Taleban overran Kabul. From their first days in power, they imposed strict Islamic rule. One casualty was the education of women, which was strictly forbidden. Men and women convicted of adultery were stoned to death.

In the former Yugoslavia, the United Nations was committed to bringing to trial those Bosnian Serbs who had been identified as war criminals, responsible for the 'ethnic cleansing' of thousands of men, women and children. Fifty-two names were on the initial list submitted to the International War Crimes Tribunal at The Hague. The first to be arrested and indicted was Dusan Tadic, who had been flown from Sarajevo to Holland under NATO guard. On January 30, a Bosnian Serb general and a colonel who had taken a wrong turn while driving and strayed into Bosnian government-controlled territory were arrested. They too were flown to The Hague to await trial.

The United Nations located the site of 187 mass graves. In March a United Nations envoy confirmed that at least 3,000 Muslims had been murdered by the Bosnian Serb army after the fall of Srebrenica in July 1995, while 8,000 more were as yet 'unaccounted for'. The United States ambassador to the United Nations, Madeleine Albright, who was taken in March to see a mass grave near Srebrenica, commented: 'It is the most disgusting and horrifying sight for another human being to see.'

Whether the war crimes trials would be pursued against the senior perpetrators was much debated. John Major, the first Western leader to visit the Bosnian Serb Republic, stressed that the most senior of all the Bosnian Serb leaders during the conflict, including Radovan Karadzic and General Ratko Mladic, should be indicted for war crimes and handed over to the United Nations tribunal in The Hague. 'I wouldn't be content for them to just fade away,' he said. On November 29 the United Nations War Crimes Tribunal at The Hague handed down its first sentence. It was on a twenty-five-year-old-Lance-Corporal, Drazen Erdemovic, a Bosnian Serb soldier who had taken part in the massacres of Muslims at Srebrenica. He confessed to the killing of 'at least' seventy people at an execution site where 1,200 unarmed Muslims had been shot dead by Bosnian Serbs, and was sentenced to ten years in prison. The sentence had been a relatively light one, explained the French judge, Claude Jorda, in view of Erdemovic's remorse, and the evidence he had given about other suspected war criminals.

In Burundi, after an army coup on July 25 in which a Tutsi general seized power, more than 6,000 Hutus were killed in less than three weeks. Of these, 4,000 were unarmed civilians. According to Amnesty International, in a statement issued in London on August 22, 'most of these victims were killed after the army came to their villages, ostensibly to obtain information about movements of rebels. Soldiers then assembled the victims and shot them.'

Inside neighboring Zaire, after fierce fighting between the Zairean army and Zairean Tutsi insurgents, the Tutsis captured two provincial capitals at the end of October. They then proceeded to fight and defeat rebel Hutu militiamen who had been terrorizing 700,000 fellow Rwandan Hutus in refugees camps in eastern Zaire. These Hutu militiamen had their own killing squads. Known as the *Interahamwe* – those who kill together – they had been active inside Zaire for more than a year, terrorizing Tutsis and Zairean civilians alike. While retreating back into Rwanda, in one town in eastern Zaire they hacked to death as many as 500 civilians.

On December 29 the last Russian troops left Chechenya. That same day, on the other side of the world, in a ceremony in Guatemala City, an agreement was reached which ended thirty-six years of civil war in which 150,000 Guatemalans had been killed, 50,000 had 'disappeared' – and were certainly dead – and nearly a million people driven from their homes.

In the struggle against disease, a landmark was reached in 1996 when the United Nations World Health Organization announced that smallpox had been eliminated, as a result of the worldwide vaccination campaign begun two decades earlier. The last known case of smallpox, which disfigures and causes blindness and even death, was recorded in Somalia in 1977.

On September 13, speaking in Beijing, the outgoing director of the United Nations World Food Programme, Robert Hauser, described the problems of North Korea, where, for the second year running, more than ten per cent of all crops had been destroyed in floods. For the previous nine months, twenty-two million North Koreans had been on a daily ration of seven ounces of cereal. 'If you go into the countryside you see only skinny people,' he said. 'Many children have pot-bellies, stick-like arms, visible ribs – symptoms of malnutrition. This year they may just make it, but next year the crisis will be worse.'

Despite this plea for international help the North Korean Communist Government, one of the few remaining Communist regimes in the world, would not allow pictures of starving children – pictures of the sort that in Ethiopia had created a massive worldwide response. According to United Nations estimates, North Korea had been able to produce only 3.5 million tonnes of grain annually in recent years, 'well below the 4.8 million tonnes required to meet minimum nutritional needs'.

In July, a United Nations report revealed that half of the world's wealth was owned by just 385 people. Bill Gates, founder of the American computer software company Microsoft, and the world's wealthiest person, was estimated to be worth $39 billion. King Fahd of Saudi Arabia, the Sultan of Brunei and the other 382 members of the so-called 'super-rich', possessed more assets than the entire Gross Domestic Product of countries which contained almost half of the world's population. In eighty-nine of the world's 200 countries, per capita income was falling. During the previous five years the per capita income in the republics of the former Soviet Union had fallen by an eighth. Nineteen countries, including Rwanda and Sudan, had lower per capita incomes than they had had forty years earlier. The United Nations Development Programme administrator, James Speth, commented: 'If present trends continue, economic disparities between the industrial and developing nations will move from inequitable to inhuman.'

On 1 May 1997, in the British General Election, the Conservative Party was defeated after seventeen years in power. The Labour Party's majority, 177, was the largest for any political party since 1945. John Major was succeeded by Tony Blair, under whose leadership Labour, having made a decisive move away from traditional Labour Socialism before the election, took the name New Labour.

In Northern Ireland, following the breakdown of a series of cease-fires, the killings continued on both sides of the sectarian divide. So too did the search for a settlement. On May 16 Blair sought to put Loyalist minds at rest when he said his agenda was 'not a united Ireland'. On July 19 the IRA announced they would accept a cease-fire from noon the following day, a Sunday. It came into effect, and a day later Sinn Fein were invited to the all-Party talks that had been going on for several months without them. When Blair met the Sinn Fein leader Gerry Adams in Belfast on October 13, it was the British Government's first official contact with Sinn Fein since 1921. Within two months, Adams was invited with a Sinn Fein delegation to Downing Street, where Blair offered him 'a choice of history' – violence and despair, or peace and progress. 'It is important', Blair said, 'that I look you in the eye and hear you say that you remain committed to peaceful means. If we were to slip back, I believe we would slip back to something worse than what came before.' Adams stressed his commitment to the principles of democracy and non-violence, but told Blair: 'All the hurt and grief and division which has come from British involvement in Irish affairs has to end.'

In the Serb province of Kosovo, the majority population – Yugoslav citizens since the First World War – were ethnic Albanians: a Muslim minority in a Serb and Christian country. Serb hostility to the Kosovo

Albanians had led to discrimination and even killing. Kosovo Albanian nationalists saw no chance of a relaxation of Serb hostility. Student demonstrations, starting in October and continuing until the end of the year, demanded autonomy, even independence for the province. The clandestine Liberation Army of Kosovo began to attack Serbian security forces. A new area of conflict began to impinge upon the world's already crowded agenda of violence.

In Israel, under the autonomy plan put in place two years earlier, Yasser Arafat exercised political and administrative control in the territory of the Palestinian Authority, including six of the seven Palestinian cities. The peace process took a further step forward on January 15 when Benjamin Netanyahu agreed to transfer eighty per cent of the seventh city, Hebron, to the Palestinian Authority, leaving twenty per cent under Israeli rule. In that twenty per cent area lived almost a thousand Jewish settlers and several thousand Palestinians. Stringent rules were laid down to try to keep the two groups apart. The other six Palestinian towns were already under full Palestinian control.

Israeli troops withdrew from eighty per cent of Hebron on January 17. Two days later Arafat entered the city to a hero's welcome. It was his first visit there in thirty-two years. But even amid agreements and the fulfilment of aspirations, violence erupted without warning. On July 30, a suicide bomber killed thirteen Israelis when he blew himself up in the main market in western, Jewish, Jerusalem. The perpetrator was a Muslim fundamentalist who opposed any Israeli-Palestinian agreement. In response to the killings Arafat promised to 'confront this terrorist act' with action. 'We are doing our best', he said. Netanyahu's office let it be known that the Israeli Prime Minister had replied: 'You have to do more.'

After victory in the American presidential elections at the end of 1996, President Clinton was inaugurated for a second term, on 20 January 1997 – the first Democrat since Franklin Roosevelt sixty years earlier to be sworn in for a second term. He delivered his fifth State of the Union message on February 4, urging Congress to adopt 'a bipartisan process to preserve social security and reform Medicare for the long run', in order to 'give more families access to affordable, quality health-care'. He wanted legislation to ensure that those who were temporarily unemployed would not lose their health insurance, that would enhance existing anti-drug efforts, and make two years of college education, supported by tax credits and scholarships, universal in twenty-first century America.

A Special Prosecutor, Kenneth Starr, was investigating allegations against Clinton and his wife Hillary of property speculation in Arkansas, where Clinton had been Governor before becoming President. As the inquiry evolved, Starr began to delve into sexual harassment charges being raised against the President. On May 27, the Supreme Court ruled that the President had no immunity in the courts for private acts. Clinton persevered with his domestic agenda. On June 14, he launched a year-long 'campaign against racism'. He also prevailed on the Republicans to agree to a bipartisan programme designed to balance the Federal budget in the next five years. Although this involved cuts in Medicare and Medicaid, it was compensated for by increased funding for education and health insurance for children, and expanded health care cover for the children of parents who could not afford health insurance. The budget would be balanced by the year 2002. 'We have fulfilled the responsibility of our generation to guarantee opportunity to the next generation,' Clinton told Congress.

In foreign policy, Clinton persevered with the defensive elements being put in place following the end of the Cold War. On March 20 he attended a summit in Helsinki with President Yeltsin. One result was the signing two months later of the Russia-NATO Founding Act on Mutual Relations, Co-operation and Security, whereby Russia and its former NATO adversary would become partners, sharing knowledge, weaponry and Intelligence information. The signing took place in Paris. Yeltsin was so enthusiastic that, without prior discussion or warning, he told the NATO signatories that he would, as a gesture of goodwill, remove the warheads from all Russian nuclear weapons that were pointing at their countries.

'In the twilight of the twentieth century,' Clinton told the Paris conference, 'we look forward toward a new century with a new Russia and a new NATO, working together in a new Europe of unlimited

658 · HISTORY OF THE TWENTIETH CENTURY

possibility.' Tony Blair, attending his first summit, described himself as a child of the Cold War era, 'raised amid the constant fear of a conflict with the potential to destroy humanity'. Blair added: 'Whatever other dangers may exist, no such fear exists today. Mine is the first generation able to contemplate the possibility that we may live our entire lives without going to war or sending our children to war. That is a prize beyond value.'

One of Clinton's initiatives was with regard to a scourge from earlier wars and civil wars: the anti-personnel mines which for many years after conflicts ended caused death, mutilation and maiming. In every armed conflict, opposing sides planted anti-personnel mines to keep the other side at bay. These mines, dug into the ground, could kill or maim not only when the fighting was taking place but for many years after it, as civilians trod on unsuspected mines. Even those engaged in clearing the vast minefields left by wars were at risk. Among those killed while clearing mines in Afghanistan in 1992 had been a twenty-three-year-old English volunteer, Tim Goggs, who was posthumously awarded the George Medal for his bravery in trying to rescue a colleague injured in the same explosion. Goggs had worked at mine clearance for eighteen months. Taking a lead in the anti-landmine campaign was Diana, Princess of Wales. Visiting Angola she spoke to a number of landmine victims. In Bosnia she met a volleyball team, all of whose members had been injured by mines, and who could only play by propelling themselves forward on their hands and haunches.

At the beginning of 1997 Clinton had issued a unilateral ban on the export from the United States of anti-personnel landmines. But such were the vagaries of national policy that when an international treaty banning anti-personnel landmines was ready for signature in Ottawa in September, the United States declined to sign it. The American government's position was that the Ottawa Treaty failed to exempt South Korea from its provisions. In South Korea, the Pentagon explained, landmines were regarded, by both South Korea and the United States, as essential to the defence of the country, and of the 37,000 American soldiers stationed there. Defending this argument, Clinton himself said: 'No one should expect our people to expose our armed forces to unacceptable risks'. Clinton did propose an alternative strategy in the battle against landmines, instructing the Pentagon to develop 'alternative weapons' which would make the landmine obsolete by the year 2006.

The death of Diana, Princess of Wales in a car crash in Paris in August, only three weeks after she had been photographed with the landmine victims in Bosnia, created a worldwide surge of emotion. Many of the film tributes stressed her work on behalf of the International Campaign to Ban Landmines. In October the charity was awarded the Nobel Peace Prize. In congratulating Jody Williams, the American co-ordinator of the charity, on the award, Clinton said the United States would still not sign the global moratorium which eighty-nine nations had ratified in Ottawa. A few days later it was made known that 300 civilians were being killed or maimed each month by landmines in Cambodia.

In Russia, Yeltsin's personal health and behaviour gave repeated cause for concern. In November 1996 he had undergone a quintuple heart bypass operation. In January 1997 he cancelled all his official engagements for a week: the official Kremlin doctors' report of 'mild fever and influenza symptoms' was not widely believed. It soon emerged he was suffering from pneumonia. His drinking habits had long been notorious, and he spent more and more time out of the public eye. When he did emerge, it could be with bizarre results. On an official visit to Oslo at the end of the year, he appeared to believe that he was in Helsinki – where he had met Clinton nine months earlier.

Within the Arab and Islamic world, Muslim fundamentalism had become a continuous challenge to secular regimes. In Algeria, 50,000 people had been killed in five years of violence. Most of the victims were civilians, often slaughtered in their beds. In one attack, four young men playing dominoes outside their house were chained together and then killed.

In Egypt, Muslim fundamentalists continued to attack foreign tourists, and to be hunted down and killed by the security forces. In November fifty-eight European holidaymakers were massacred outside a temple in Luxor. In Pakistan, thousands of Christians were driven from their homes by Muslim extremists. The homes were then set on fire and churches destroyed.

At midnight on June 30, Britain left Hong Kong, which was returned to China after a hundred years as part of the British imperial and colonial domain. In Britain, Tony Blair warned the Chinese leaders that Hong Kong would be 'destroyed' if they were to renege on their pledges in the Anglo-Chinese Joint Declaration to allow the existing social system and laws to be 'fundamentally unchanged'.

In South Africa, the Truth and Reconciliation Commission continued to hear apologies from both sides of the racial divide. Four white policemen who had been involved in the killing of Steve Biko twenty years earlier were among those voluntarily confessing to their crimes and applying for an amnesty. Donald Woods, the anti-apartheid newspaper editor who had been forced into exile after Biko's murder, said of the amnesty applications: 'It feels good. I've been wondering for years when they would come out of the woodwork. Too much has been hidden for too long.'

On 10 January 1997 the first trial conducted by the United Nations International Criminal Tribunal for Rwanda took place in a courtroom in Tanzania. The first witness, identified for her own safety only as 'K', spoke of how, on 19 April 1994, she was confronted by the accused, the mayor of the town, Jean-Paul Akayesu, a forty-three-year-old Hutu, and a crowd of men whom he was leading, and saw the murder of Tutsis: 'The killers escorted eight people right to the fence of the communal office where they were told to sit down with their arms and legs well out in front of them. At the moment they were going to be killed they raised their arms to beg for mercy but Akayesu said "Quickly" giving the order to have them killed.'

Some of those murdered, K said, 'were attacked to the point of death and then were put in wheelbarrows and buried alive'. Akayesu was found guilty of the murder of at least 2,000 Tutsis.

In South America, vast acres of Brazilian forests were being cut down to make way for mining activity. In Asia, the forests of Indonesia were being burned to create farm land. The result in 1997 was fires which created a cloud of pollution which affected the whole of South-East Asia. According to the Worldwide Fund for Nature, as many as 1,700,000 acres of forest were ablaze on September 25. In parts of Malaysia people were advised to wear masks if they went outside. Airports had to be closed down, as were schools. Hospitals treated hundreds of thousands of people with respiratory ailments.

In the former Soviet Union, a government ecology committee reported that half the country's factories were polluting lakes and rivers. The Caspian Sea was almost too polluted for the caviar-bearing sturgeon to survive in it. The Aral Sea was drying up. Siberian rivers flowing into the North Polar seas were disgorging high levels of toxic waste and crude oil spillage. In the Russian city of Dzerzhinsk, 300 miles east of Moscow, the concentration of dioxins in ground-water – a mere eighteen miles from the River Volga – was estimated at fifty times above the acceptable international standard.

At the beginning of May the focus of world concern turned to South Asia, when details were made public with regard to per capita income, education, literacy and diet. South Asia had fallen behind sub-Saharan Africa to become 'the poorest, most illiterate and mal-nourished region on Earth'. Its average per capita annual income was $309. That of sub-Saharan Africa was $555. In South Asia two thirds of all children were underweight; in sub-Saharan Africa one third. The only statistic that revealed substantial growth in South Asia was that of arms expenditure. India had built up the fourth largest army in the world, Pakistan the eighth largest. Both powers had spent vast sums of money developing nuclear weapons.

India, which ranked 142nd in the world in terms of per capita income, had the world's highest arms import bill. In its capital, Delhi, an estimated one million children aged fifteen and under were working illegally, in conditions of grave hardship. The year 1997 marked the centenary of the discovery, in India, that malaria was spread by mosquitoes. By 1997 anti-malarial drugs existed in pro-fusion, but the malaria-bearing mosquito persisted in its dangerous peregrinations, killing three million people every year.

Another disease that was believed to be capable of elimination, tuberculosis (TB), also continued to cause death on a wide scale.

During 1997 the World Health Organization announced that, despite the existence and availability of effective drug treatments, TB was still 'the world's leading infectious killer' of young people and adults, also killing three million people every year. But in the pantheon of death, smoking had emerged as the greatest killer of them all, exceeding malaria, TB and AIDS. China was the centre of a smoking epidemic: 20,000 Chinese were dying every day of cancer of the lungs and other diseases directly related to smoking.

The computer age came into its own in 1997. That May, the Russian world chess champion, Garry Kasparov, was defeated by Deep Blue, a 'supercomputer' constructed in the United States. A new avenue of global communications had also come into its own, the World Wide Web (WWW). This linked computer screens and their operators in any country, at any time of day or night, with anywhere else in the world they should choose to contact, in a matter of seconds and fragments of seconds. One aspect of the World Wide Web was e-mail, a virtually simultaneous global correspondence system, eliminating the need for pen, ink, stamps, post offices and, most important of all, the passage of time. Instantaneous communication was the final contribution of the twentieth century to the chitter-chatter of mankind, as well as to its serious purposes in the spheres of commerce, government and health.

On 27 April 1998, in an intensification of the Kosovo conflict, Serbian soldiers of the Yugoslav army crossed into the province to confront the national movement. Hundreds of ethnic Albanians were killed. President Milosevic, summoned to Moscow, agreed on June 16 to stop the Serbian attacks, and to open negotiations with the Kosovo Albanians. When the Serb attacks continued, the United States, Russia and the European Union joined in pressing Milosevic to halt them. He declined to do so. At the end of July, Serb soldiers brought death and destruction to yet more villages. Dozens of civilians were killed, and hundreds forced to flee.

The ethnic Albanians took revenge. Dozens of Serb civilians were taken hostage and then killed. Since the beginning of the year, 173 Serbs had disappeared. It was presumed they had been murdered. A renewed Serb military offensive in the second week of September drove 400,000 ethnic Albanians – a quarter of Kosovo's population – to try to escape the advancing troops. In the second week of September, dozens of Albanian villages were burned to the ground.

At the beginning of October the European Union and NATO demanded that Belgrade halt the offensive in Kosovo. Milosevic at first resisted these demands, but the threat of air strikes by NATO was effective. A cease-fire was agreed on October 12 between the Kosovo Liberation Army and the Serbs. The Yugoslav Government also agreed that a 2,000-strong 'verification force' could take up positions in Kosovo to monitor the cease-fire. The force, drawn from thirty-five States, members of the Organization of Security and Co-operation in Europe, OSCE, began to arrive at the end of November. Its soldiers were unarmed. Their power lay in the threat of NATO airstrikes should the Serbs renew hostilities within their Kosovo region.

In nearby Bosnia the NATO-led Stabilization Force was not only maintaining the peace and patrolling the borders, but searching for war criminals. On December 2 it captured General Radislav Krstic, who was wanted for trial as a war criminal by the Hague Tribunal. It was he who had overseen the fall of Srebrenica in 1995, after which several thousand Muslims had been massacred. Three weeks after his capture, a former Bosnian Croat paramilitary commander, Anto Furundzija, was sentenced to ten years in prison for 'violating the laws or customs of war'. He had stood by while another paramilitary soldier beat and raped a female detainee near Vitez in 1993.

The former Warsaw Pact powers of Eastern Europe, once a bastion of Soviet power, were being drawn into the NATO orbit. On May 1 the United States Senate ratified what was known as NATO 'enlargement', to include Poland, Hungary and the Czech Republic. The expansion of NATO, said Clinton, would reduce the prospect of Americans ever being called again 'to fight in the battlefields of Europe'.

In Northern Ireland, new initiatives by Tony Blair, the direct intervention of President Clinton, and the negotiating skills of George

Mitchell, the former United States Senator, secured the long-awaited settlement. After talks chaired by Mitchell, agreement was reached on Good Friday, April 10. Cross-border links between Northern Ireland and the Irish Republic would be strengthened. Catholic participation in Northern Ireland's constitutional, political and economic development would occur on a basis of equality. But union between Northern Ireland and the Republic would not come about without the consent of Northern Ireland's Unionist majority.

Voting took place in Northern Ireland on May 23, when 71 per cent of voters endorsed the Good Friday Accord: 55 per cent of Protestants and 96 per cent of Catholics had cast their votes in favour. In welcoming the result, Tony Blair said: 'Everybody has now said you can make your argument by word, by debate, by argument, by persuasion. But there is no place for the gun and the bomb or violence in the politics of Northern Ireland or any of the island of Ireland. All that is over and gone.' President Clinton hailed what he called 'a springtime of peace', adding: 'Peace is no longer a dream. It is a reality.'

Within three months of this 'reality', a massive bomb blast in Omagh on August 15 killed twenty-nine people, most of them women and children. Catholics and Protestants were among the dead. The bomb was the work of an IRA splinter group which called itself, provocatively, the 'Real IRA'. It was the worst single atrocity during almost thirty years. But it was not allowed by any of the supporters of the Good Friday agreement to halt the process of talking that had already begun. Outrage at the bomb was expressed by all the political Parties engaged in the talks, including the IRA. Gerry Adams announced: 'I am totally horrified by this action and I condemn it without any equivocation'.

The talks continued: they were the new 'reality' of which Clinton had spoken. In recognition of what had been achieved, the Nobel Peace Prize was awarded that October to the two local politicians, John Hume and David Trimble, who had contributed the most, by their leadership, to Catholic-Protestant reconciliation.

In China, dissent continued to be severely punished. On January 24, four Chinese poets were arrested as they planned to publish a new literary review, putting forward the case for a flourishing of art outside the official ideology. Another dissident, Xu Wenli, who had already spent twelve years in prison for advocating democracy, called publicly – in an echo of Lech Walesa's call in Poland nearly two decades earlier – for free trade unions to represent the Chinese workers.

Cinton was invited to China, and came with a list of individual Chinese who were being subjected to human rights violations. His impending visit stimulated courageous protest. On June 25, a few hours before he arrived, seventy-nine Chinese dissidents signed an open letter announcing the creation of a new political Party, the China Democratic Party. This was against China's one-Party Communist constitution. Five of those who tried to register the new Party were arrested and detained at an unknown prison, without legal represen-tation or contact with their families: a violation of China's own criminal law. Undeterred, and confident, Xu Wenli, one of the foun-ders of the new Party, noted: 'It is not like before, when it was "one soldier swimming alone". Now we go out and do this together.'

On June 29, in a speech to students at Peking University, Clinton electrified his young audience with his assertion that no country could prosper, or find political stability, in the twenty-first century 'without embracing human rights and individual freedom'. After Clinton's return to America, violations of human rights continued. In December the United States protested at the arrest of dozens of human rights activists, including Xu Wenli, and also Wang Youcai, one of the student leaders during Tiananmen Square. On December 5 the Associated Press reported from Shanghai that 'in its crackdown on dissent to cyberspace, China put a computer entrepreneur on trial on charges of giving e-mail addresses to an Internet pro-democracy magazine'. Lin Hai, the owner of a software company in Shanghai, had been put on trial in a closed courtroom on charges of subversion for giving the addresses of 30,000 Chinese computer users to a journal published by Chinese dissidents in the United States. Lin Hai had been held incommunicado for eight months before charges were laid against him. During that time the number of Chinese World Wide Web users had more than doubled, from less than a million to more than two million. A further one-and-a-half million accounts were expected to be opened in 1999.

A year and a half before Lin Hai's trial, the first issue of an electronic magazine, *Tunnel*, had appeared in Chinese e-mail boxes – on 4 June 1997. The date had been deliberately chosen: the eighth anniversary of Tiananmen Square. The magazine was almost entirely written by intellectuals inside China, and then distributed to Chinese e-mail boxes from computers in the United States. *Tunnel* described itself as the first electronic magazine 'dedicated to breaking China's information blockade'.

The Chinese Government acted with devious skill, on what used to be the Soviet pattern. On December 20 it allowed Liu Nianchun, one of the human rights activists for whom President Clinton had intervened, to leave China for the United States, together with his wife and daughter. They flew that day to Detroit. On the following day, December 21, as news of Liu's release was gaining China goodwill in the West, a court in Beijing sentenced Xu Wenli to thirteen years in prison and Wang Youcai to eleven years. On the following day a third dissident, Qin Yongmin, was sentenced to twelve years in prison.

In Burma, Aung San Suu Kyi, the leader of the opposition, who had been awarded a Nobel Peace Prize in 1991, went on hunger strike to protest against a decade's exclusion from political life. Braving official censure, a hundred student members of her National League for Democracy demonstrated, demanding that parliament be called and their Party be allowed to participate in free elections. Riot police broke up the demonstration. Suu Kyi ended her strike. Her long fight to restore democracy in Burma continued.

In Indonesia, twelve people were killed in clashes with the police in the capital, Jakarta, after seven hours' fighting in November. The protesters, mainly students, were demanding the introduction of genuine democracy. After more than fifty years of almost continuous dictatorship, and the fall of President Suharto in May, the new regime promised a new openness. But in answer to the demonstration, President Habibie ordered a military crackdown against those he denounced as 'subversives'.

In Rwanda, the death sentences passed by Rwandan courts for war crimes were carried out publicly. One of the accused had appealed

daily over the radio for the Hutu to 'cleanse' their communities of
Tutsi 'cockroaches'. Some of the defenders had been given notice
of the date of their trial, and access to their dossiers, only a few
days before the trial began. After sentence of death had been passed,
Pope John Paul II appealed for amnesty. But the murder of so
many hundreds of thousands of people in the most barbaric circumstances propelled a deep and swift vengeance. The first public
executions took place on April 24, watched by tens of thousands of
people.

On November 16, in The Hague, three United Nations
judges imposed the first international convictions for atrocities
committed against Bosnian Serbs. A Bosnian Croat and two Muslims were convicted of murdering, torturing and raping Serb prisoners
in 1992. The trial had lasted for twenty months. The sentence on a
detention camp warden, found guilty of overseeing guards who
murdered nine Serbs and tortured six, was the first by an international court on the basis of 'command responsibility' since the
International Military Tribunals at Nuremberg and Tokyo. The warden was sentenced to seven years in prison. A camp guard was sent
to prison for fifteen years for murdering three inmates and torturing
others.

Muslim fundamentalist killings in Algeria showed no abatement. A
thousand people, almost all of them civilians, were being killed
every month. At least 65,000 Algerians had been killed by Muslim
fundamentalists during the previous six years. In Afghanistan, the
Taleban were strengthening their control through edicts based on
their interpretation of Islamic law. Anyone possessing a television
set, satellite dish or video recorder would be punished. Television
sets not handed over to the authorities would be smashed. Other
laws being strictly enforced forbade women to work, girls from going
to school, and men from trimming their beards. Another law called
for painting all downstairs windows black, so that women inside
could not be seen from the street.

In neighbouring Iran the relatively more moderate Islamic regime
of President Khatami was having to face the threat of Taleban incursions into its eastern provinces. It was also confronted within Iran

by Islamic extremists who, denouncing Khatami as too moderate, had begun to execute supporters of free speech.

The emergence of black leaders worldwide redressed the balance of prejudice that had been so powerful in earlier decades. In South Africa, Nelson Mandela was a continuing force for reconciliation. In the United States, Kofi Annan, who had been born in Ghana, was the first black African to lead the United Nations, as its Secretary-General. In a report to the United Nations presented on April 16, he pointed out that too many African States were ready to resort to military force, and proposed that they make a public commitment to 'zero growth' in their defence budgets for the following ten years. What was needed above all, he stressed, was 'good governance'. Every African State should stamp out corruption, and show respect for human rights, democracy and the rule of law.

Annan himself intervened to bring cease-fires to a number of violent conflicts that year. In the eastern region of the recently re-named Democratic Republic of Congo (formerly Zaire), ethnic Tutsis had attacked several towns. Uganda and Rwanda had supported them; on November 29, after negotiations in Paris, both countries agreed to a cease-fire. The Tutsis swore to continue the fight.

In Sierra Leone, a rebel movement dislodged from power early in the year embarked on a reign of savage terror. In the Republic of Congo, a country of less than three million people, of whom a quarter were illiterate, hundreds were being killed in civil unrest. In the Sudan, hundreds of thousands were dying of hunger, the victims of famine, while civil war made the despatch of aid almost impossible. The National Islamic Front government in the Sudan, in power for the previous decade, and dominated by Muslim fundamentalist fer-vour, was also carrying out a policy of mass destruction in the pre-dominantly Christian and animist south of the country. An estimated 70,000 villagers were killed in the first six months of 1998. Others were forcibly converted to Islam. Boys were abducted and sold into slavery.

Fears of nuclear proliferation were unexpectedly intensified on May 11, when the Indian Government conducted three underground nuclear tests. In such a poor country, struggling to maintain some basic quality of life for its population of a thousand million, such a programme seemed to many to be both an expensive and dangerous luxury. The danger was that India's neighbour, Pakistan, with which she had fought three wars since 1947, would conduct nuclear tests of her own. The Indian tests were also, Kofi Annan, pointed out, a breach of the international testing moratorium.

International pressure was put on Pakistan not to test any nuclear devices of its own, but on May 28 Pakistan carried out five underground nuclear tests, then a sixth two days later. India and Pakistan had not only defied the international community, but ignored the risks of radioactive contamination.

An important battle in the environmental war occurred on April 30, when agreement was announced in London and Washington whereby the Government of Brazil, helped by the World Wildlife Fund for Nature (WWF) and the World Bank, would set aside sixty-two million acres of rainforest as an internationally recognized 'protected area'. A further 125 million acres would be added to the protected area by the year 2005. The urgent need for this agreement had been underlined in the three months before it was signed when fires, started deliberately – and illegally – to clear the rainforest for farming and grazing, had destroyed an area of forest cover the size of Belgium. The area to be protected was the size of the United Kingdom.

Ecological dangers were becoming a matter of international alarm. The wild Atlantic salmon was believed to be on the verge of disappearing, defeated by industrial waste, polluted run-off from farms, and the construction of dams that prevented its spawning. In July the World Wildlife Fund for Nature announced that some of the most 'exotic' sea creatures to be found around British coasts could be killed off by thousands of tonnes of industrial chemicals, heavy metals and oil pollution unless drastic steps were taken to curb marine pollution. The World Conservation Union, having worked closely with more than 600 scientists worldwide, concluded that 25 per cent of all mammal and amphibian species were in danger of extinction, as were 31 per cent of all fish species, 20 per cent of reptiles and 11 per cent of all bird species. Tigers and pandas were among the species that were soon likely to exist only in zoos. The cause of the threat was man's destruction of their habitat, including forests, wetlands, grasslands and chaparral. Of the 233 species of primate in Brazil, seventy per cent faced extinction; in Madagascar and South-East Asia, fifty per cent. Thirty per cent of the world's coral reefs were in critical condition from pollution.

Man's behaviour also harmed man directly: anti-personnel mines continued to kill and maim thousands of people every year. In August it was announced from Kuwait that more than 1,700 people had been killed by mines since the Iraqi forces were driven out eight years earlier. In addition, eighty-four mine-clearing experts had been killed, and 200 injured, while trying to do their job. Fifty countries were still manufacturing these mines, among them the United States, France, Spain, Italy and Serbia, despite the recently signed Ottawa Treaty.

As 1999, the last year of the century, began, the veneer of civilization showed itself in places to be very thin. In Algeria, on 2 January 1999, Muslim rebels cut the throats of twenty-two people in a remote village, as part of their struggle against the military regime that had refused to allow elections likely to lead to an Islamic victory. Fourteen Algerian soldiers were also killed that week in a rebel ambush. In Burundi, several hundred Hutu civilians were killed, some by Hutu rebels, others in clashes between rebels and government forces. In India, a father and his two sons were burned to death by Hindus because they were Christians.

In Sierra Leone, anti-government rebels, joined by 300 armed mercenaries from Ukraine, entered the capital, set fire to the power station, post office, town hall and United Nations headquarters, and fought with a peacekeeping force that had been sent by several other West African nations. A thousand people were killed in the fighting. Offshore, a British frigate gave haven to Europeans. Its captain was shocked to see bodies of victims of the fighting floating past. 'There are many cases of mutilations,' he said, 'with arms and hands chopped off those who tried to resist rebel activities. They have not acted with any decorum or principles.'

In Yemen, on January 27, three Roman Catholic nuns who worked for the Missionaries of Charity − of which Mother Teresa had been the guiding light – were killed as they left their clinic. Two of them were from India and one from the Philippines. In one South American country, Colombia, 'death squads' killed more than a hundred villagers. At one village, twenty-seven churchgoers attending a baptismal Mass were massacred.

In the Balkans, British and American monitors in Kosovo were preventing Serb soldiers attacking members of the Kosovo Liberation Army. But the intensity of the ethnic conflict defied the most vigilant monitors. On January 16 the bodies of forty-five ethnic Albanians were discovered just outside the village of Racak. They had been brutally killed, and their bodies mutilated. One man had been decapitated. President Clinton declared: 'This was a deliberate and indiscriminate act of murder designed to sow fear among the people of Kosovo.' American and British warplanes were put on a war alert. NATO sent an American general to Belgrade to urge Milosevic to order a halt to the killings. *The Times* wrote on January 19: 'The countries of Europe must not tolerate massacres in their midst and refugees on their doorstep. At some point it must be conceded that the honourable option of diplomacy has been tried and found wanting. There is nothing to suggest that Mr Milosevic will respond to anything short of the most credible of military threats.' Air strikes may be a last resort, the newspaper wrote, 'but Racak has brought that resort very much closer'.

Within two weeks of the Racak killings, twenty-four ethnic Albanians were murdered by Serb soldiers in the village of Rogovo. On January 30 the British Foreign Secretary, Robin Cook, flew to Belgrade to warn Milosevic that unless the killings stopped, NATO would launch air strikes against Serbian positions. Cook then travelled to the Macedonian capital, Skopje, where he warned representatives of the Kosovo Liberation Army that the KLA must also cease fighting and start negotiating. Six nations – the so-called 'Contact Group' of Britain, the United States, Russia, France, Germany and Italy – supported this initiative. In London, one of the founders of the Kosovo liberation movement, Bardhyl Mahmuti, was urged by the British government to persuade his fellow-fighters to enter negotiations.

*   *   *

In the United States, President Clinton was impeached by the Republican-dominated House of Representatives. His trial took place in the Senate, in his absence. The charges related to his private life, to alleged perjury in civil law suits, and to attempts to subvert the course of justice. On January 19, as the Senate trial was in progress, Clinton delivered his State of the Union message, offering American financial help to Russia and other former Soviet republics to enable them to destroy their chemical and biological weapons. Part of the money America would spend on 'threat reduction' would be used to enable 8,000 Russian scientists hitherto employed by the defence industries to work on civilian research, and to dismantle and store nuclear warheads that had been decommissioned.

Clinton, who was acquitted by the Senate of all impeachment charges on February 12, also set up a National Defense Preparedness Office to train and equip police, fire and ambulance workers who would be the first on the scene of any biological or chemical weapons attack within the United States. It would also make plans to forestall those who might try to use computers for terrorism, such as the sabotage of America's electricity grid.

In Indonesia, President Habibie indicated on 28 January 1999 that he might be prepared to grant independence to East Timor. More than 20,000 Indonesian soldiers had been killed since the Indonesian invasion of the former Portuguese colony in 1975. The apparent offer of independence did not, however, halt the killings of East Timorese by paramilitary groups trained by the Indonesian army. In mid-April fighting broke out in the East Timor capital, Dili, as pro-Indonesian militias called for a 'cleansing' of those in favour of independence from Indonesia. Within a few months more than 200 East Timorese had been killed and thousands of homes burned down. Tens of thousands of East Timorese fled for refuge into West Timor.

A referendum was held on August 30, when, despite enormous pressure and intimidation against them, more than eighty per cent of the voters – 871,000 people – voted for independence. By the end of the year a new State, accepted by Indonesia, had joined the international community. The exiled leaders returned: one had been in exile for twenty-four years. East Timor became the United Nations' 188th member State.

In Israel, Benjamin Netanyahu's government was defeated at the polls and replaced by an administration headed by Ehud Barak, a former Commander in Chief, who supported the withdrawal of Israeli troops from Lebanon, a renewal of the Oslo Peace process with the Palestinians and negotiations with Syria for a peace treaty based on Israel's withdrawal from the Golan Heights. Withdrawing from Lebanon was his one success. Syria, first under President Hafez al-Assad and then under his son, would not accept Barak's generous compromise, and nor would Arafat. When Barak was defeated in a election he had called, in February 2001, the situation in the West Bank and Gaza, part occupied by Israel, part administered by the Palestinian Authority, was perilous.

The spread of the Internet in China gave hope to China's first opposition Party for more than half a century, the China Democracy Party. But on February 26 the Communist authorities arrested the Party's young founder, nineteen-year-old Wang Yingzheng, as he was photocopying an article he had written on corruption within the Communist Party. He was charged with attempting to 'subvert State power'. On June 10 a former civil servant, Fang Jue, who had distributed a pro-democracy manifesto, was sentenced to four years in prison. His 'crime' included giving Western journalists a paper he had written calling for greater democracy in China. In Tibet, China was under the international spotlight for its continuing repression. On March 30 a human rights organization charged that one in thirty-three Tibetan male prisoners, and one in twenty female prisoners, of the many thousands held in Tibet's main prison since 1987, had died of maltreatment.

In Iran, as in China, a repressive regime was confronted with the challenge of the Internet, satellite television and the fax machine. Under President Khatami, conciliation towards the West had begun. In an interview with John Simpson of the BBC, Esmail Khoi, an Iranian poet living in exile in London, pointed to the fax machine through which he sent his poems to Iran, and commented: 'This is how Iran will eventually change.'

In Indonesia more than 160 people were killed during inter-religious riots in which churches and mosques were burned. In the city of Ambon, Indonesian troops fired at Christians and Muslims who were fighting each other with firebombs, machetes and even arrows. By the end of one month of fighting 200 people had been killed, many of them hacked to death.

On the Serbian-Albanian border, Serb military engineers laid tens of thousands of anti-personnel mines during the first two months of 1999. The aim was to prevent arms being smuggled across the Albanian border into Kosovo, for the Kosovo Liberation Army. Although Yugo-slavia was a signatory to the 1997 Ottawa accords banning the manufacture of mines, its government remained one of the largest manufacturers, among the twenty-five nations still making them.

In Kosovo, Serb forces continued to destroy ethnic Albanian villages. NATO, which on March 12 had been enlarged to include Poland, the Czech Republic and Hungary, decided to act. On the evening of March 24 the first air strikes were carried out against military targets throughout Serbia. It was the world's largest military campaign since the Gulf War eight years earlier, and the first NATO attack on a sovereign nation since the alliance had been set up fifty years earlier.

The NATO action was designed, President Clinton explained, to stop the repression of the Kosovar Albanians by the Serbs: Milo-sevic 'must either choose peace, or we will limit his ability to make war'. The NATO warplanes taking part in the assault on the first day, during which forty Serb targets were hit, and ten Serb civilians killed, came from fourteen nations: the United States, Britain, Bel-gium, Canada, Denmark, France, Germany, Italy, Holland, Norway, Portugal, Spain, Greece and Turkey. The aircraft in the first assault included eight American B-52 bombers of Vietnam vintage, which flew from a Royal Air Force base in Britain. Circling Serbia, they launched their missiles from outside Serbian airspace. Two of the American warplanes, B-2 stealth bombers, flew non-stop from their base in Missouri to drop satellite-guided bombs. Most of the other aircraft in action flew from bases in Italy, a NATO member. Missiles were also launched from American warships, and from a British submarine, in the Adriatic Sea. Among the NATO nations taking part in the action against Serbia was Germany, four of whose jets participated in air strikes on and near Belgrade on the first night. This was the first German military action beyond its borders since 1945. It came fifty-eight years after the German bombing of Belgrade in the Second World War.

During the first month of the air war, raids were carried out every night against Serbian military targets. Considerable damage was done, with relatively few civilian casualties: less than a hundred in the first thirty days. A further sixty people were killed when NATO aircraft struck in error at a convoy of Kosovar Albanians being driven out of the province. Each day, Serb forces cleared villages, often separating all adult men from women, children and old people. By the third week of April, as many as a thousand Kosovars had been murdered in cold blood by Serb troops and paramilitary units. Almost a million Kosovars, many of whom had seen their close relatives murdered, or had passed massacre sites on their way, were forced across the borders with Macedonia, Albania and Montenegro, where international aid agencies – assisted at first by British troops – did their utmost to relieve their physical plight. Their mental anguish could not be assuaged.

That Milosevic did not break during the first few weeks of the air onslaught was a blow to the hopes of the NATO leaders. But the British and American Governments in particular repeatedly voiced their determination that the Kosovars would eventually be able to return to their homes, that their villages – systematically looted and burned by the Serbs – would be restored, and that those Serbs perpetrating ethnic cleansing would be punished as war criminals. 'Our campaign will continue shifting the balance of power against him until we succeed', Clinton declared on April 18.

Reports of killings of Kosovar Albanians by Serb forces intensified NATO's determination to persevere with the war. On April 21, the British Prime Minister, Tony Blair, commented that the Allies were fighting 'a just war in a just cause for the values of civilization itself. We should have no hesitation and every resolve to see the thing through to the end.'

*   *   *

Germany took a further step towards integration in July, when the parliament moved from Bonn to Berlin. It was the first time for more than half a century that Berlin was Germany's full and undivided capital. Among the buildings brought into use by the new administration was Hermann Goering's former Aviation Ministry, which became the Finance Ministry.

Russia continued to fight separatism. In August more than 400 Muslim separatists were killed in the autonomous region of Dagestan, on the Caspian Sea. In neighbouring Chechenya, rebel fighters continued to challenge the authority of Russia and the superior fire power of Russian troops. 'There will be tough measures, and we will restore order in Dagestan and in other regions in the North Caucasus,' Yeltsin said on August 16. A month later, the Russian Prime Minister, Vladimir Putin, announced that Russia was prepared to resume 'full-scale war' with Chechenya. Daily bombing missions began on September 23, when oil refineries in Grozny were set on fire, and at least fifty Chechen civilians killed. By the end of November the civilian death toll in Grozny had reached more than 500. In the fighting on the ground, 600 Russian soldiers had been killed. In Moscow the 'Soldiers' Mothers Group' called for an end to the fighting. On December 3, Russian soldiers opened fire on a Chechen refugee column led by a woman carrying a white flag. Forty of the refugees were killed.

By the end of the year Russian troops had crushed the Dagestan revolt. His health failing, Boris Yeltsin resigned. His successor as President, Vladimir Putin, followed in Yeltsin's footsteps by ordering a massive military and air attack on the Chechen rebels still holding out in Grozny and the mountains to the south. Within Russia, as a result of this decisive action, Putin's popularity rose.

The war between NATO and Serbia ended on June 10 when Milosevic, unable to oppose Serb popular discontent at the continuing conflict, and air bombardment of Belgrade, agreed to withdraw his troops from Kosovo. In Serbia, 5,000 Serb soldiers and 2,000 Serb civilians had been killed during seventy-eight days and nights of NATO air attacks.

Within twenty-four hours of entering Kosovo, British and German troops found mass graves of victims of 'ethnic cleansing' at five villages. Shocking scenes of these graves were shown on television. Within a week a further fifty mass murder sites had been located. Even while the war was being fought, the International War Crimes Tribunal at The Hague had indicted Milosevic as a war criminal. Two years later a new government in Belgrade handed him over to the International Court at The Hague for trial.

Milosevic agreed to an international force in Kosovo, the return of the refugees, and an autonomous region within which Belgrade could exert no authority. As 1999 came to an end the NATO-led peacekeeping force, K-For (Kosovo Force), was policing the war-torn province, keeping Serbs and ethnic Albanians apart. The force was headed by a German commander, with British, Russian, Ukrainian, French and Canadian soldiers among the peacekeepers.

In fierce fighting between Ethiopia and Eritrea during 1999, there were frequent artillery and tank battles along the disputed border. Several thousand soldiers were killed in March in a battle where Ethiopian soldiers were forced to advance through a minefield, and hundreds of them were blown to pieces. 'I never believed in Holly-wood films until I saw this battle,' commented a young Eritrean female fighter, Yordanos Habte.

Poverty was as epidemic in the Eritrean-Ethiopian borderlands as war. That June, the connection between poverty and governmental indebtedness was recognized by the leaders of the Group of Seven (G7) industrialized nations, who agreed to write off twenty per cent of the money owed them by the poorest nations. Thirty-six developing countries would be the beneficiaries, including Sudan, Uganda, Bolivia, Mozambique and Guyana.

In August 1999 the population of India reached one billion. The only other nation to have reached that figure by the end of the twentieth century, and to have exceeded it, was China. Also in 1999 the world's six billionth person was born. The United States Census Bureau believed this was a baby born on July 19 at Ostrava, in the Czech Republic. The United Nations, using other statistical methods, chose October 13, and a baby born in Sarajevo. Both babies were among more than 25,000 children born that day.

The twentieth century has been given many attributes, among them the century of war, the century of the common man – because, Churchill said, 'in it the common man has suffered most' – and the century of the refugee. In 1980 the United Nations High Commissioner for Refugees was responsible for the needs and well-being of two and a half million refugees within its auspices. By the end of the century that number had risen to twenty-one million. Amid the problems and opportunities of the overpopulated planet, the plight of the refugees was a stark reminder of how harsh life could be. Most if not all the people reading this book, like the author himself, will never have seen, except on television, the depths of human misery which, with all the marvellous achievements which the twentieth century saw, the opportunities created by wealth and leisure, the challenges of creativity and production, nevertheless scarred every region of the world.

MAPS

MAPS

NORWAY

SWEDEN

Gulf of Bothnia

Scapa Flow

Helsinki
Vyborg
Terijoki
Sveaborg
St. Petersburg

North Sea

Stockholm

ESTONIA

LATVIA

Riga
Libau

LITHUANIA

GREAT BRITAIN

Dogger Bank

HELIGOLAND
TERSCHELLING

Kiel

Danzig

Königsberg
Kovno
Vilna

Bremerhaven

Wilhelmshaven

RUSSIA

EAST PRUSSIA
Marienburg

Konitz

Bialystok

London
Dover
Calais
The Hague

Potsdam

Berlin

Posen

Warsaw

Brest-Litovsk

Spithead
Boulogne
Le Havre
Dieppe

Zeebrugge
Rotterdam

GERMANY

Leipzig

Wreschen
Lodz
Kalish

Essen

Brussels
Louvain
Aachen

Lublin

Rouen
Luxembourg

Frankfurt-on-Main

Dresden

Breslau

Brody

UKRAINE

Paris
Le Bourget
Melun

Darmstadt

Prague

Lemberg
(Lvov)

Fontainebleau
Verdun
Metz

Carlsbad

Konopischt

Cracow

Nancy
Strasbourg

Le Mans

Augsburg

Danube

Munich
Friedrichshaven

Vienna
Wiener Neustadt

Budapest

Jassy

FRANCE

Basle
Bern
Zurich

Lausanne
Geneva

SWITZERLAND

Innsbruck

AUSTRIA-

HUNGARY

Dorohoi

Nantes

Lyon

Chamonix

Monza

CARINTHIA

Laibach

Bacau

TRANSYLVANIA

La Courtine

Milan

Venice

Trieste
Agram
(Zagreb)

Alba Julia

Genoa
Rapallo

Po

ROMAGNA

Pola

Fiume

ROUMANIA

Narbonne
Agde

Cannes
Monaco

Ancona

ITALY

Sarajevo

Belgrade

Bucharest

Constanta

Perpignan
Marseille
Toulon

Rhône

Adriatic Sea

WALLACHIA

Danube

SARDINIA
CORSICA

Rome

MONTE-NEGRO

SERBIA

Nis

BULGARIA

Sofia

Black Sea

Naples

Cattaro

Bari
Brindisi

Durazzo

Skopje

Adrianople

TURKEY

ALBANIA

THRACE

Salonika
Smyrna

CORFU

GREECE

Lamia

Dardanelles
MYTILENE

Messina
Reggio

Palermo

SICILY

Aegean Sea

Athens
Piraeus

KOS

Tunis

RHODES

Mediterranean Sea

MALTA

Cape Matapan

CRETE

Copenhagen
DENMARK
Jutland
Isle of Holland
River Rhine
Isonzo
Danube

Baltic Sea

Niemen

Vistula

Vistula

Bug

0	kilometres	500

0	miles	300

© Martin Gilbert 2001

—··—··— European frontiers in 1914

●●●●● The border of Hungary (within Austria-Hungary)

1   Europe, 1900–1914

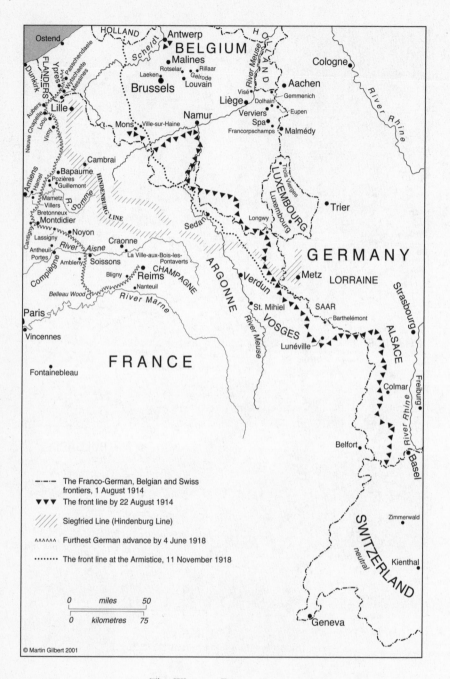

2   The Western Front, 1914–1918

3　From the Aegean Sea to the Black Sea

Frontiers of
1919-1937

B Burgenland
SH Schleswig-Holstein

Narvik
FINLAND
NORWAY
MANNERHEIM
LINE
Helsinki
Leningrad
Gulf of Bothnia
Oslo
SWEDEN
Gulf of Finland
Stockholm
Tallinn
ESTONIA
Scapa Flow
RUSSIA
Baltic Sea
Riga
North
Sea
LATVIA
MEMEL
LITHUANIA
Königsberg
Kovno
DENMARK
DANZIG
Vilna
GREAT BRITAIN
SH
Copenhagen
EAST
PRUSSIA
HOLLAND
The Hague
Rotterdam
Hamburg
Stettin
Oldenburg
Esterwegen
Berlin
Poznan
Warsaw
London
Weimar
POLAND
BELGIUM
GERMANY
Dresden
English Channel
RHINELAND
Cologne
FRANCONIA
Chropaczowa
Dunkirk
Bad Godesburg
HESSE
SUDETENLAND
Lvov
Calais
SAAR
Hersbruck
Prague
Cracow
Dieppe
Nuremberg
CZECHOSLOVAKIA
St. Germain
LIECHTENSTEIN
SUDETENLAND
RUTHENIA
Trianon
Neuilly
BAVARIA
Versailles
Sèvres
Paris
MAGINOT
LINE
LUXEMBOURG
BADEN
Dachau
Munich
Eger
Vienna
Györ
Budapest
Brenner
B
AUSTRIA
HUNGARY
Geneva
SWITZERLAND
Locarno
SOUTH
TYROL
Szent Gotthard
ROUMANIA
FRANCE
Chamonix
Turin
Venice
Zagreb
Belgrade
Bucharest
Milan
Genoa
Rapallo
Nice
Santa Margherita Ligure
Adriatic Sea
YUGOSLAVIA
BULGARIA
SPAIN
ITALY
CORSICA
Civitavecchia
Rome
Foggia
Durazzo
Bari
Skopje
Sofia
ALBANIA
Tirana
Barcelona
MAJORCA
MINORCA
Naples
Brindisi
GREECE
IBIZA
BALEARIC ISLANDS
SARDINIA
Aegean Sea
Mediterranean Sea
Athens
Piraeus
SICILY
0 kilometres 500
Tunis
0 miles 250

© Martin Gilbert 2001

4   Europe, 1919–1939

5   Europe, 1939–1945

Map Scale and Legend

	kilometres		500
0			
0	miles		300

- - - - The armistice line, December 1917

^^^^^ Limit of German occupation, under the Treaty of Brest-Litovsk, March 1918

- · - · - Border of the Soviet Union, 1922 -1939

· · · · · Limit of German advance, 1941-1943

Map Labels

White Sea

Archangel

Gulf of Bothnia

FINLAND

Vasa

Helsinki

Kronstadt

Baltic Sea

Reval (Tallinn)

Narva

St.Petersburg (Petrograd Leningrad)

Vologda

Perm

COURLAND

Riga

LATVIA

Pskov

Bologoe

Nizhni-Novgorod (Gorky)

Dzerzhinsk

Kazan

Ufa

BALTIC STATES

Dvinsk

Tver

Moscow

Novo-Georgievsk

Kovno (Kaunas)

Vilna

Borisov

Smolensk

Katyn

Mogilev

Tula

Orel

Lipetsk

Tambov

Samara

Orenburg

WHITE RUSSIA (BELARUS)

Minsk

Brest-Litovsk

Pinsk

Gomel

Kursk

Voronezh

Saratov

Warsaw

Chernobyl

Zhitomir

Kiev

Kharkov

River Don

River Volga

Tsaritsyn (Stalingrad)

AUSTRIA-HUNGARY

Vinnitsa

Fastov

U K R A I N E

MOLDAVIA

BESSARABIA

Ekaterinoslav

Zaporozhe

DONBASS

Taganrog

Shakhty

Astrakhan

Kishinev

Nikolayev

Odessa

Berdiansk

Kherson

Rostov-on-Don

Budyonnovsk

ROUMANIA

Sea of Azov

KUBAN

Krasnodar

NORTH CAUCASUS

Caspian Sea

Simferopol

Sebastopol

Feodosiya

Novorossisk

Maikop

CHECHENYA

Makhachkala

ABKHAZIA

Sochi

Caucasus

Grozny

DAGESTAN

Derbent

Black Sea

Mount Elbruz

Sukhumi

GEORGIA

Constantinople

Batum

Poti

Tiflis

TRANSCAUCASIA

AZERBAIJAN

Baku

Chanak

Bursa

Trebizond

Rizeh

Kars

ARMENIA

Erivan

NAGORNY-KARABAKH

TURKEY

Erzerum

Mus

Bitlis

PERSIA (IRAN)

ANATOLIA

© Martin Gilbert 2001

6   Western Russia and the Caucasus

7   The Baltic States, Poland and Czechoslovakia

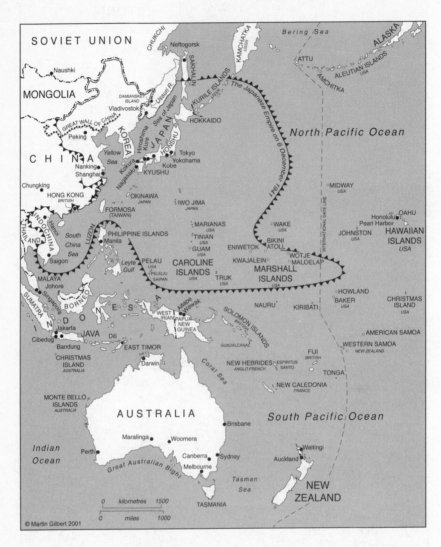

8　The Pacific, Australia and New Zealand

9 Europe, 1945–1999

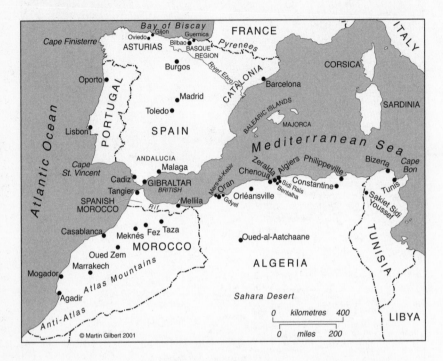

10   The Western Mediterranean

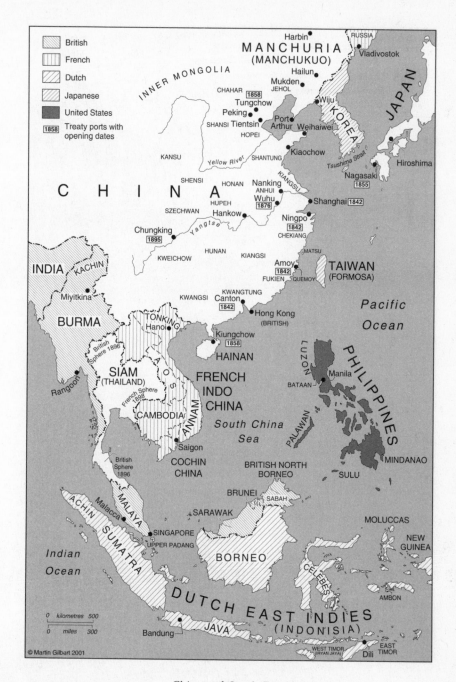

11 China and South-East Asia

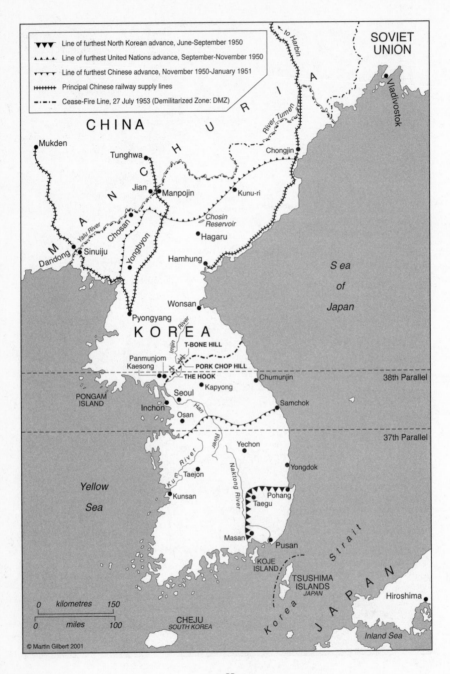

Line of furthest North Korean advance, June–September 1950
Line of furthest United Nations advance, September–November 1950
Line of furthest Chinese advance, November 1950–January 1951
Principal Chinese railway supply lines
Cease-Fire Line, 27 July 1953 (Demilitarized Zone: DMZ)

SOVIET
UNION

to Harbin

Vladivostok

CHINA

MANCHURIA

River Tumen

Mukden

Tunghwa

Chongjin

Jian

Manpojin

Kunu-ri

Chosan

Yalu River

Chosin
Reservoir

Dandong

Sinuiju

Yongbyon

Hagaru

Sea

Hamhung

of

Wonsan

Japan

Pyongyang

KOREA

Imjin River

T-BONE HILL

Panmunjom
Kaesong

PORK CHOP HILL

THE HOOK

Chumunjin

38th Parallel

Seoul

Kapyong

PONGAM
ISLAND

Samchok

Inchon

Osan

Han

37th Parallel

Yechon

Kum River

Yongdok

Yellow

Taejon

Naktong River

Sea

Pohang

Kunsan

Taegu

Masan

Pusan

0   kilometres   150

0   miles   100

KOJE
ISLAND

Korea Strait

J A P A N

TSUSHIMA
ISLANDS
JAPAN

Hiroshima

CHEJU
SOUTH KOREA

Inland Sea

© Martin Gilbert 2001

12   Korea

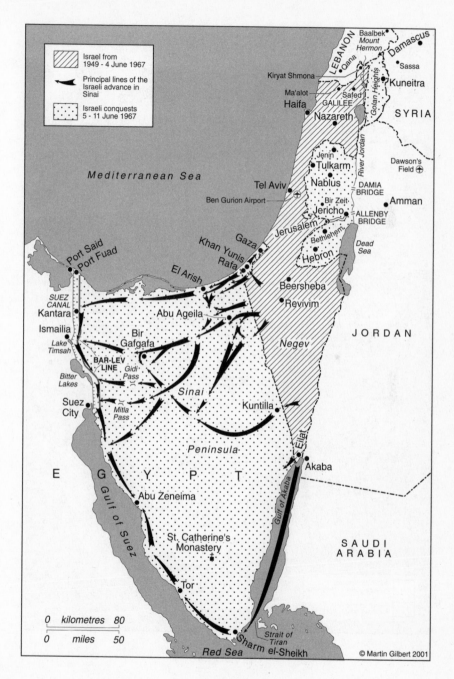

Map labels:

Baalbek
Mount Hermon
Damascus
Qana
Sassa
LEBANON
Kiryat Shmona
Kuneitra
Ma'alot
Safed
Golan Heights
Haifa
GALILEE
SYRIA
Nazareth
Dawson's Field ⊕
Jenin
River Jordan
Tulkarm
Mediterranean Sea
Tel Aviv
Nablus
DAMIA BRIDGE
Amman
Ben Gurion Airport
Bir Zeit
Jericho
Gaza
Jerusalem
ALLENBY BRIDGE
Khan Yunis
Rafa
Bethlehem
Dead Sea
Port Said
Port Fuad
El Arish
Hebron
Beersheba
SUEZ CANAL
Reviyim
Kantara
Abu Ageila
Ismailia
Bir Gafgafa
JORDAN
Lake Timsah
BAR-LEV LINE
Gidi Pass
Negev
Bitter Lakes
Sinai
Suez City
Mitla Pass
Kuntilla
Peninsula
Eilat
E   G   Y   P   T
Akaba
Gulf of Suez
Abu Zeneima
Gulf of Akaba
SAUDI ARABIA
St. Catherine's Monastery
Tor
Strait of Tiran
Sharm el-Sheikh
Red Sea
© Martin Gilbert 2001

Legend:
Israel from 1949 - 4 June 1967
Principal lines of the Israeli advance in Sinai
Israeli conquests 5 - 11 June 1967

0   kilometres   80
0   miles   50

13   Israel and Sinai

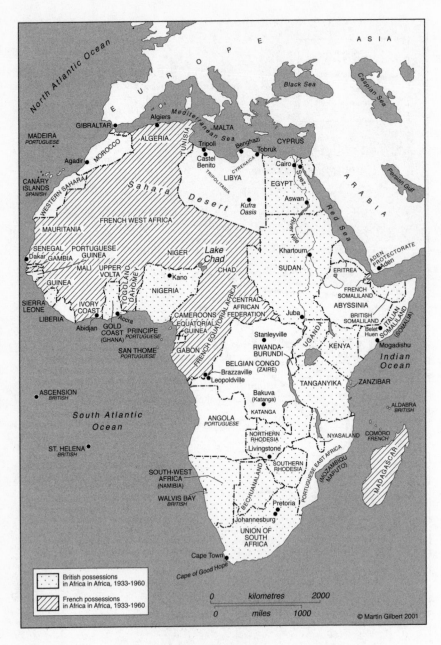

North Atlantic Ocean

ASIA

EUROPE

Black Sea

Caspian Sea

MADEIRA
PORTUGUESE

GIBRALTAR

Algiers

MALTA

CYPRUS

Agadir

ALGERIA

TUNISIA

Tripoli

Castel
Benito

Benghazi

Tobruk

Cairo

ARABIA

Persian Gulf

CANARY
ISLANDS
SPANISH

MOROCCO

Sahara

LIBYA

CYRENAICA

TRIPOLITANIA

EGYPT

Suez

Mediterranean Sea

WESTERN SAHARA

Desert

Kufra
Oasis

Aswan

River Nile

Red Sea

MAURITANIA

FRENCH WEST AFRICA

NIGER

Lake
Chad

Khartoum

ADEN
PROTECTORATE
Aden

SENEGAL
Dakar
GAMBIA

PORTUGUESE
GUINEA

MALI

UPPER
VOLTA

CHAD

SUDAN

ERITREA

FRENCH
SOMALILAND

GUINEA

Kano

NIGERIA

CENTRAL
AFRICAN
FEDERATION

Juba

ABYSSINIA

SIERRA
LEONE

IVORY
COAST

TOGOLAND

DAHOME

CAMEROONS

EQUATORIAL
GUINEA

BRITISH
SOMALILAND

ITALIAN
SOMALILAND
(SOMALIA)

LIBERIA

GOLD
COAST
(GHANA)

Abidjan

Accra

PRINCIPE
PORTUGUESE

FRENCH EQUATORIAL AFRICA

GABON

UGANDA

KENYA

Belet
Huen

Mogadishu

SAN THOME
PORTUGUESE

Stanleyville

RWANDA-
BURUNDI

Indian
Ocean

ASCENSION
BRITISH

BELGIAN CONGO
(ZAIRE)

Brazzaville
Leopoldville

TANGANYIKA

ZANZIBAR

South Atlantic
Ocean

Bakuva
(Katanga)

ALDABRA
BRITISH

KATANGA

ST. HELENA
BRITISH

ANGOLA
PORTUGUESE

NORTHERN
RHODESIA

NYASALAND

COMORO
FRENCH

Livingstone

PORTUGUESE EAST AFRICA
(MOZAMBIQU
MAPUTO)

SOUTH-WEST
AFRICA
(NAMIBIA)

SOUTHERN
RHODESIA

MADAGASCAR

WALVIS BAY
BRITISH

BECHUANALAND

Pretoria

Johannesburg

UNION OF
SOUTH
AFRICA

Cape Town

Cape of Good Hope

British possessions
in Africa in Africa, 1933-1960

French possessions
in Africa in Africa, 1933-1960

0   kilometres   2000

0   miles   1000

© Martin Gilbert 2001

14   Africa

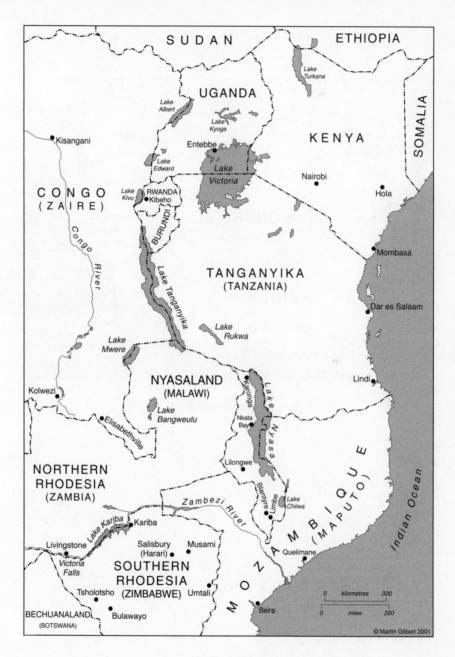

15   East Africa

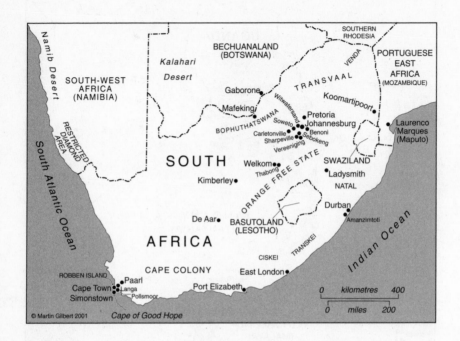

Namib Desert

SOUTH-WEST
AFRICA
(NAMIBIA)

RESTRICTED
DIAMOND
AREA

South Atlantic Ocean

ROBBEN ISLAND

Cape Town
Simonstown

Paarl
Langa
Pollsmoor

© Martin Gilbert 2001

Kalahari
Desert

BECHUANALAND
(BOTSWANA)

SOUTHERN
RHODESIA

VENDA

TRANSVAAL

PORTUGUESE
EAST
AFRICA
(MOZAMBIQUE)

Gaborone

Mafeking

BOPHUTHATSWANA

Koomartipoort

Pretoria
Johannesburg

Soweto
Carletonville
Sharpeville
Vereeniging

Benoni
Sebokeng

Laurenco
Marques
(Maputo)

Witwatersrand

SOUTH

Welkom
Thabong

Kimberley

ORANGE FREE STATE

SWAZILAND

Ladysmith

NATAL

De Aar

BASUTOLAND
(LESOTHO)

Durban

Amanzimtoti

AFRICA

CISKEI

TRANSKEI

Indian Ocean

CAPE COLONY

East London

Port Elizabeth

Cape of Good Hope

0   kilometres   400

0   miles   200

16   Southern Africa

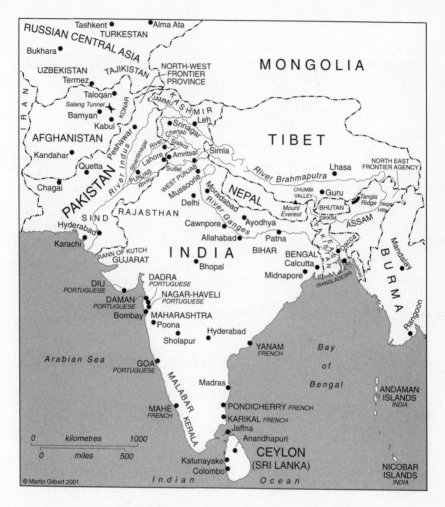

17 The Indian subcontinent and Afghanistan

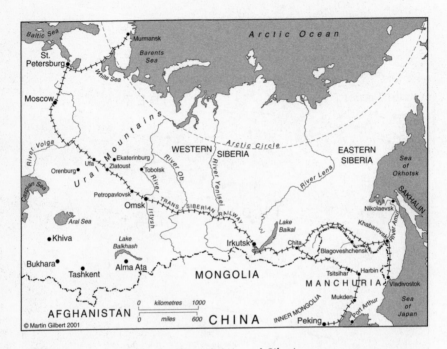

18   Central Asia and Siberia

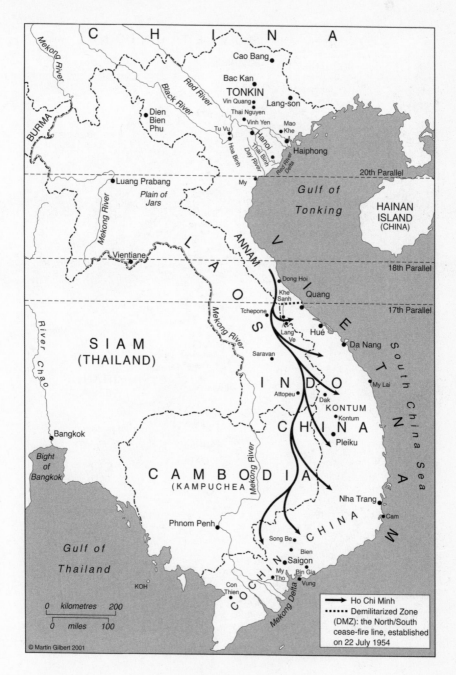

19 Vietnam

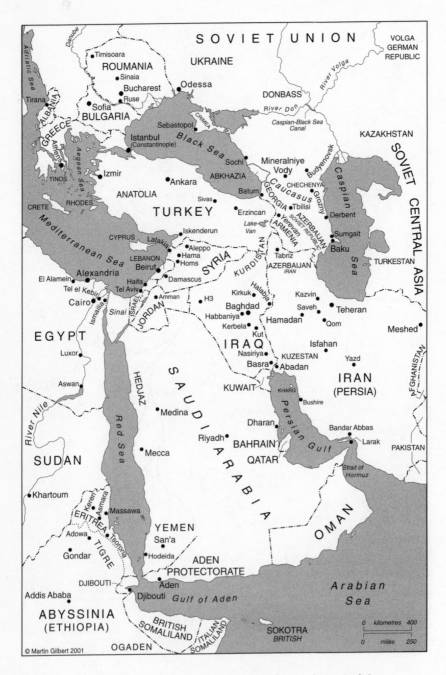

20   The Black Sea region, the Middle East and the Red Sea

21   Yugoslavia

Caribbean Sea

CURACAO
DUTCH

WEST INDIES

BARBADOS *BRITISH*

Atlantic Ocean

PANAMA

Caracas
VENEZUELA
Mount
Roraima
Santa Elena

TRINIDAD *BRITISH*

BRITISH GUIANA (GUYANA)
DUTCH GUIANA
FRENCH GUIANA

Panama
Canal

Bogota

COLOMBIA

Boa
Vista

EQUADOR

Quito

River Amazon

Equator

MARANHAO

A M A Z O N I A

P
E
R
U

Lima

BRAZIL

Pernambuco
(Recife)

Bahia

BOLIVIA

La Paz

Brasilia
Goiania

PARAGUAY

GRAN
CHACO

Rio de Janeiro
Sao Paulo

South
Pacific
Ocean

JUAN
FERNANDEZ
CHILE

Valparaiso

Cordoba

C
H
I
L
E

Santiago
de Chile

ARGENTINA

Buenos Aires

URUGUAY

Punta del Este
Montevideo

Puerto Saavedra

South Atlantic Ocean

PATAGONIA

0   kilometres   1000

0   miles   500

FALKLAND ISLANDS
BRITISH

TIERRA DEL
FUEGO

SOUTH GEORGIA ISLAND
BRITISH

Cape Horn

SOUTH SANDWICH ISLANDS
BRITISH

© Martin Gilbert 2001

22   South America

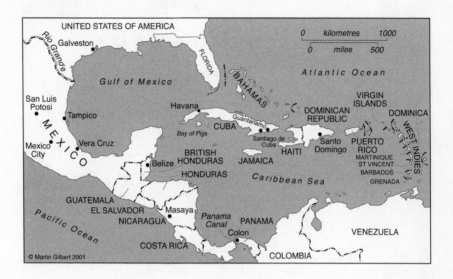

23   Central America

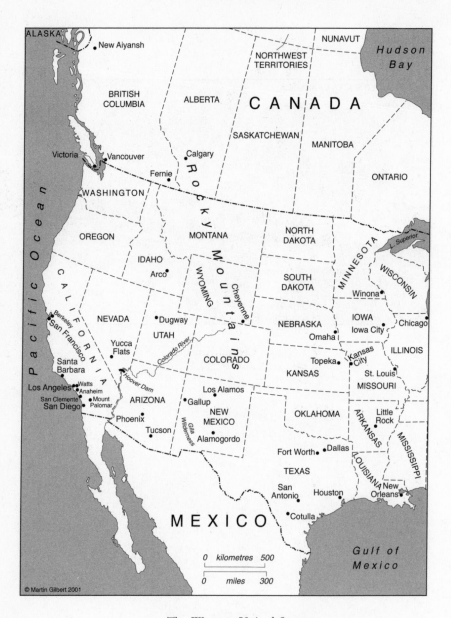

24   The Western United States

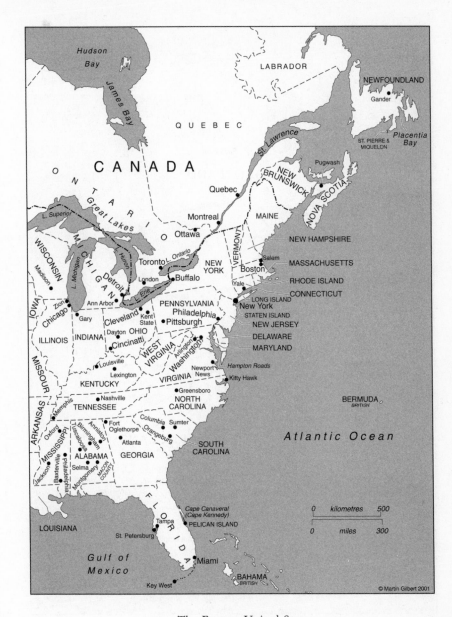

Hudson
Bay

LABRADOR

NEWFOUNDLAND

Gander

James Bay

QUEBEC

ST. PIERRE &
MIQUELON

Placentia
Bay

CANADA

Pugwash

St. Lawrence

NEW
BRUNSWICK

NOVA SCOTIA

Quebec

ONTARIO

L. Superior

Great Lakes

Montreal

Ottawa

MAINE

WISCONSIN

L. Michigan

MICHIGAN

L. Huron

L. Ontario

Toronto

London

Detroit

Buffalo

NEW
YORK

VERMONT

NEW HAMPSHIRE

Salem

MASSACHUSETTS

Boston

Yale

RHODE ISLAND

CONNECTICUT

Madison

IOWA

Zion

Chicago

Ann Arbor

L. Erie

Gary

Cleveland

Kent
State

PENNSYLVANIA

Philadelphia

Pittsburgh

LONG ISLAND

New York

STATEN ISLAND

NEW JERSEY

DELAWARE

MARYLAND

ILLINOIS

INDIANA

Dayton

OHIO

MISSOUR

Louisville

Cincinatti

WEST
VIRGINIA

Arlington

Washington

Lexington

KENTUCKY

VIRGINIA

Newport
News

Hampton Roads

Kitty Hawk

ARKANSAS

Memphis

Nashville

TENNESSEE

Greensboro

NORTH
CAROLINA

BERMUDA
BRITISH

Oxford

Anniston

MISSISSIPPI

Tuscaloosa

Birmingham

Fort
Oglethorpe

Columbia

Sumter

Atlantic Ocean

Baxterville

Philadelphia

ALABAMA

Atlanta

Orangeburg

SOUTH
CAROLINA

Jackson

Selma

MACON
COUNTY

GEORGIA

Montgomery

FLORIDA

LOUISIANA

Cape Canaveral
(Cape Kennedy)

kilometres

500

Tampa

PELICAN ISLAND

St. Petersburg

0

miles

300

Gulf of
Mexico

Miami

BAHAMA
BRITISH

Key West

© Martin Gilbert 2001

25   The Eastern United States

North Atlantic
Ocean

The boundary of the six
counties of Ulster, approved
by both Belfast and Dublin
on 30 March 1922

•Inverness

SCOTLAND

Dundee•

Rosyth•

North

Sea

Glasgow• Edinburgh•

Lockerbie•

•Newcastle

Durham•

Dogger
Bank

Scarborough•

LONDON-
DERRY
Londonderry•
TYRONE
ANTRIM
Omagh•
FERMANAGH
Belfast
ARMAGH
ULSTER
DOWN

YORKSHIRE

Barrow-in-
Furness•
LANCASHIRE
Colne•
York•

Ardee•
Preston•

IRELAND
(IRISH FREE STATE
EIRE
REPUBLIC OF
IRELAND)

Irish Sea

Galway•

Lusk•
Swords•
Dublin•

Holyhead•

Wigan•
Liverpool•
Abram•
Mersey
Barnsley•

Manchester•

Bangor•

Ennis•

W A L E S

Nottingham•

•Limerick

Sheringham•

ENGLAND

Norwich•
Great Yarmouth
Lowestoft•

Fermoy•

Birmingham•
•Coventry

Bletchley•

Cork•

Aldeburgh•

Oxford•
Letchworth•

Ebbw Vale•
Chequers•
Llanelli•
Tredegar•
Cardiff•
Wallingford•
Hendon•
Avonmouth•
Windsor•
London•
Bath•
Aldershot•
Guildford•

Dover•
KENT

CANVEY
ISLAND

0   kilometres   100

0   miles   60

Southampton•
Portsmouth•

Exeter•
Bournemouth•

Portland•
Yarmouth•
Southsea
Spithead
Brighton•
Folkestone

CORNWALL

English Channel

Poldhu•

Dieppe•
FRANCE

© Martin Gilbert 2001

26 Britain

INDEX

compiled by the author

Hottentots: rebel, 18–19, 35, 57

Hötzendorf, Conrad von: and the path to war (1913–14), 70, 71, 74; urges a negotiated peace (1915), 88; renews his call for peace (1916), 89

House, Colonel: and the coming of war in 1914, 73

Houston (Texas): Kennedy in, on way to Dallas, 437

Hoxha, Enver: rules Albania, 325; his statue pulled down, 621

Hsuchow: Chiang Kai-shek advances to, 170; Japanese troops enter a village near, photo 22

Hu Feng: imprisoned, 388

Hua Kuo-feng: succeeds Mao Tse-tung, 516

Hué (South Vietnam): overrun, 469

Hugenberg, Alfred: Hitler joins forces with, 186; demands frontier revision, 193

Hughes, Sarah: swears in a new President, on board an aircraft, 438

Hull, Cordell: Abyssinia, and a wider warning, 230; urges an end to isolationism, 257

Human Rights Committee (Moscow): established, 484; appeals to the West, 485

Hume, John: wins Nobel Prize, 664

Hunan Province (China): Communist activity in, 168, 182–3

Hungarians: in Austria-Hungary, 3; inspire Irish nationalism, 24–5; in New York, 62; in Czechoslovakia, 153; in Hungary, 605

Hungarian Democratic Forum: established (1988), 596–7

Hungary: independent (1918), 110; revolution in (1919), 113; its territory defined (1919), 116; fall of Communism in, 116–17; right-wing ascendancy in, 177–8; banking crisis in, 201; and Hitler's Germany, 218, 295; anti-Semitism in, 221; and Yugoslavia, 226, 597; and the Spanish Civil War, 237; occupies Ruthenia, 259; declares war on Germany, 305; oil fields of, denied to Germany, 309; German population removed from, 315; Communist rule in, 324, 326, 335, 342–3, 346, 354–5; Soviet reparations from, 325; joins Warsaw Pact, 384; protest in, 391; revolution in, 391–2, 392–3, 393, 394–5, 396; 'was, is and will remain a Socialist country', 397–8; a United Nations Committee denied entrance to, 399; Communist rule continues in (1956–), 415–16; and Warsaw Pact manoeuvres, 432, 492; Roman Catholics re-arrested in, 459; and the Czechoslovak revolution (1968), 471–2; and Gorbachev, 596; and the call for democracy, 596–7;

Communism crumbles in, 600, 600–1, 603; East Germans travel through, 601–2; withdraws from Warsaw Pact, 610; signs agreement with Moldova, 622–3; joins NATO, 663, 674

Hupeh Province (China): disastrous floods in, 206–7

Husak, Gustav: replaces Dubček, 475; seeks reassurance in Moscow, 578

Hussein, King (of Jordan): attacks Israel, 464; drives out PLO, 483; makes peace with Israel, 635, 636

Hutus: in Rwanda, 639–40, 645–6, 660, 666–7; in Burundi, 653, 670; in Zaire, 653

Hyderabad: fighting in, 332

Hydrogen bomb: repercussions of, xviii; work begins on, 345; tested by the United States, 361, 376; and 'the risk of making the world uninhabitable', 386–7; Nobel Prize winners protest against, 387; intensification of tests of, 403, 427–8; France tests, 474

Ibarruri, Dolores: at Bolshoi Ballet, 344

Iceland: and NATO, 338

Idaho: a town in, lit by nuclear power, 387; criticism of the Vietnam War voiced in, 469

Iliescu, Ion: an anti-Communist, elected President, 609

Imjjin River: and the Korean War, 358

Immorality Act (1948): and apartheid, 337

Implementation Force (IFOR): for Bosnia, 645

Inchon: an amphibious landing at, 349

Independent Association of Polish Students: established, 552

India: famine in, 5, 505; plague in, 10, 13–14, 19–20, 25, 31, 41–2, 47, 50, 56, 61, 428; earthquakes in, 225, 231; and smallpox, 511–12, 524; tornado in, 524; floods in, 533; nationalist activity in, 25, 45, 118–19, 128–9, 172–3, 189–90, 191–3, 202–4, 207, 222; Indians in administration of, 50; an air mail experiment in, 63; influenza epidemic in, 111; Hindu-Muslim clashes in, 172–3, 203, 231, 322, 328–9, 332, 625; constitutional reforms in, 173–4, 188–90, 225, 231; 'Burma Road' links China with, 258; and the path to independence, and partition, 322–3, 328–9; and Kashmir, 329, 449; and Gandhi's assassination, 331–2; and the Korean War, 354; population growth in, 373, 677; and the Lhasa-India highway, 406; gives asylum to Dalai Lama, 414; and the Soviet Union, 445; Mother Teresa in, 541–2; and China, 451; and the creation of Bangladesh, 486–7; becomes a nuclear power, 474, 661, 668–9; poverty in, 509; constitutional

Papen, Count Franz von: becomes Chancellor, 207; issues Terror Emergency Decree, 208; invites Hitler to join government, 208, 209, 210; resigns, 210

paper cup: introduced, 47

parachute: first use of, 68

Paraguay: a guerrilla incursion into, 410

Paris: and the Olympics, 5; fire in, 19; and the Schlieffen Plan, 48, 78; parliamentary unrest in, 55; rumours of war in, 58; horse-drawn omnibuses in, withdrawn, 68; mobilization orders go out from, 78; Germans fail to reach (1914), 80; Germans seek to reach (1918), 105, 106; Peace Conference at (1919–20), 112, 114–16; the Turkish treaty signed in (1920), 124–5; reparations negotiations in, 137; Locarno Treaty negotiations in, 156; Franco-Spanish frontier of Morocco negotiated in, 157; Surrealism and 'Art Deco' in, 160; first non-stop flight from New York to, 171; and 'enigmatic times', 214; violent clashes in, 223; a secret pact leaked in, 230; Guernica painted in, 246; an assassination in (1938), 255; German troops enter (1940), 269; a bombing raid near (1943), 288; resistance and reprisals in, 292–3; a bombing raid on (1944), 295; uprising in, 301; liberated, 302; Ho Chi Minh negotiates in, 322; Marshall Plan negotiations in, 327; Bao Dai visits, 340; Vietnam proposals in, 352; Tunisian independence talks in, 385; secret French-British-Israeli talks in, 391, 393; talks on Algeria in, 405; a non-stop jet flight to New York from, 408; troops loyal to, in Algiers, 418; a Soviet defector in, 426; a car bomb in, 431; Ayatollah Khomeini in exile in, 434, 526; Solzhenitsyn published in, 461; American-Vietnamese negotiations in, 470, 479, 480, 486, 493, 494; an aircraft on its way to, hijacked, 515; Lech Walesa received with honours in, 596; pollution in, 600; Yeltsin and Mitterand sign treaty in, 623; chemical weapons convention signed in, 627; Dayton Peace Treaty, for Bosnia, signed in, 645; a vigil in, after Algerian killings, 650–1; the Russia-NATO Founding Act signed in, 657; a Democratic Republic of Congo ceasefire in, 668

Paris-Madrid aeroplane race: an accident at start of, 63

Paris Note (1922): and Turkish claims to Eastern Thrace, 140, 141

Paris Peace Conference (1919–20): 112, 114–16, 116

Parks, Rosa: arrested, 386

partisans (in the Second World War): 277, 282, 283, 292, 292–3, 293–4, 294, 301, 311

Passchendaele: battle for (1917), 100–1, 103; ground gained, evacuated (1918), 105; retaken (1918), 108

Passover: rocket attacks during, in Israel, 649

Pasternak, Boris: his novel banned, 403; wins Nobel Prize, 407; 'kinder times will come', 408

Patel, V. P.: and Indian nationalism, 192; imprisoned, 192–3

Pathan tribesmen: in Pakistan, 586

Pathet Lao: challenge the government of Laos, 502; take power, 507

Patocka, Professor Jan: visited, then interrogated, 526

Paton, Alan: an opponent of apartheid, 344–5

Patriot missiles: defend Israel, 615

Patriotic Front (Southern Rhodesia): challenges white rule in Southern Rhodesia, 521

Patton, George S.: in action (1918), 108

Paul VI, Pope: pleads for convicted Basques, 511

Paul, Prince (of Yugoslavia): appointed Regent, 226; bows to German pressure, 274

Paulus, General von: at Stalingrad, 287, 288

Peace Corps: an American initiative, 423

Peace Now: in Israel, 530, 559

Peace Pact (1928): outlaws war, 177; comes into force (1929) as the Kellogg-Briand Pact, 184; and a Nobel Peace Prize, 198

Peace People: urge an end to killings, 514

Peace Resolution (Berlin, 1917): 100

peacekeepers: in Congo, 424; in Lebanon, 568, 588; in Sri Lanka, 589; in Bosnia, 622, 637, 642–5; in Somalia, 625, 626, 628–9, 630; in Rwanda, 640, 646; in Kosovo, 663, 671, 677; in Sierra Leone, 670

Pearl Harbor: attacked, 279; attacking aircraft carriers at, sunk, 285; a nuclear-powered submarine sails from, 405

Peasants' Self-Defence Committee: established, in Poland, 528

Peking: and the Boxer rebellion, 1–3, 9–10; and the Boxer Indemnity, 148–9; a warlord rules, 170; evacuation of (1937), 248; Communists come to power in, 339; Christian churches shut down in, 456; anti-Western demonstrations in, 457; placed under military rule, 460; a Red Guard anniversary in, 477; Kissinger visits, 488; Nixon visits, 490; Mao Tse-tung's death in, 515; pro-democracy demonstrations in, 588; for subsequent index entries see Beijing

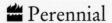 Perennial

Books by Martin Gilbert:

A HISTORY OF THE TWENTIETH CENTURY
The Concise Edition of the Acclaimed World History
ISBN 0-06-050594-X (paperback)

This abridged version of Martin Gilbert's critically acclaimed trilogy on the history of
the twentieth century is a global narrative of the years 1900 to 1999. Beginning in the
age of horse-drawn travel and explorers still charting much of the world, Gilbert moves
forward to the present day. He chronicles war, revolution, political upheaval, disease,
natural and man-made disasters, religious movements, the advancement of science,
medicine, technology, developments in the arts, civil rights, and more.

A HISTORY OF THE TWENTIETH CENTURY — VOLUME ONE: 1900-1933
ISBN 0-380-71393-4 (paperback)

This first volume covers the critical thirty-three years that began the remarkable
twentieth century. From the dawn of aviation through a Great War that left six million
soldiers dead and four vast empires destroyed, to the inauguration of Roosevelt as U.S.
President and Hitler as Chancellor of Germany, and the beginning of Stalin's show
trials in the Soviet Union.

A HISTORY OF THE TWENTIETH CENTURY — VOLUME TWO: 1933-1951
ISBN 0-380-71394-2 (paperback)

This second volume documents the attempts to preserve human values, to maintain
the rule of law, and to uphold the rights and dignity of the individual. It begins as
Roosevelt embarks on the New Deal and ends as Kennedy is elected to the presidency.
In this span Gilbert covers the Depression, the Spanish Civil War, the Japanese
aggression in China, the relentless spread of Nazi power, World War II, the imposition
of the Iron Curtain and the growth of the Cold War, the Berlin Blockade, and the
nuclear confrontation.

A HISTORY OF THE TWENTIETH CENTURY — VOLUME THREE: 1952-1999
ISBN 0-380-71395-0 (paperback)

This final volume has been updated from the hardcover publication to include all of
1999. Careful accounts are made of the wars in Korea, Vietnam, and Bosnia, the
postwar resurrection of Europe, famine in Africa, apartheid, the arms race, the dawn
of the computer age, Neil Armstrong's landing on the moon, and the extraordinary
advances in medical science. Gilbert also addresses Mao's cultural revolution, Martin
Luther King, Jr. and John F. Kennedy's assassinations, and Beijing's Tiananmen Square
incident that shocked the world.

Available wherever books are sold, or call 1-800-331-3761 to order.